Swarm Intelligence and Bio-Inspired Computation

Swarm Intelligence and Bio-Inspired Computation
Theory and Applications

Edited by

Xin-She Yang

Department of Design Engineering and Mathematics,
Middlesex University, UK

Zhihua Cui

Complex System and Computational Intelligence Laboratory,
Taiyuan University of Science and Technology, China

Renbin Xiao

Institute of Systems Engineering,
Huazhong University of Science and Technology, China

Amir Hossein Gandomi

Department of Civil Engineering,
University of Akron, OH, USA

Mehmet Karamanoglu

Department of Design Engineering and Mathematics,
Middlesex University, UK

ELSEVIER

AMSTERDAM • BOSTON • HEIDELBERG • LONDON • NEW YORK • OXFORD
PARIS • SAN DIEGO • SAN FRANCISCO • SINGAPORE • SYDNEY • TOKYO

Elsevier
32 Jamestown Road, London NW1 7BY
225 Wyman Street, Waltham, MA 02451, USA

First edition 2013

British Library Cataloguing-in-Publication Data
A catalogue record for this book is available from the British Library

Library of Congress Cataloging-in-Publication Data
A catalog record for this book is available from the Library of Congress

ISBN: 978-0-12-405163-8

For information on all Elsevier publications
visit our website at store.elsevier.com

This book has been manufactured using Print On Demand technology. Each copy is produced to order
and is limited to black ink. The online version of this book will show color figures where appropriate.

Contents

List of Contributors

János Abonyi Department of Process Engineering, University of Pannonia, Veszprém, Hungary

Rajendra Akerkar Western Norway Research Institute, Sogndal, Norway

Amir Hossein Alavi Department of Civil and Environmental Engineering, Michigan State University, East Lansing, MI, USA

Carlos Arango Ingeniería de Organización, Engineering School of Seville, University of Seville, Camino de los Descubrimientos s/n 41092, Seville, Spain

Ibrahim Aydogdu Civil Engineering Department, Akdeniz University, Antalya, Turkey

Janez Brest Faculty of Electrical Engineering and Computer Science, University of Maribor, Maribor, Slovenia

Xingjuan Cai Complex System and Computational Intelligence Laboratory, Taiyuan University of Science and Technology, Shanxi, China

Jelson Cordeiro Bioinformatics Laboratory, Federal University of Technology Paraná, Curitiba, Brazil

Pablo Cortés Ingeniería de Organización, Engineering School of Seville, University of Seville, Camino de los Descubrimientos s/n 41092, Seville, Spain

Kelton Augusto Pontara Costa Department of Computing, São Paulo State University, Bauru, Brazil

Zhihua Cui Complex System and Computational Intelligence Laboratory, Taiyuan University of Science and Technology, Shanxi, China

E. Doğan Civil Engineering Department, Celal Bayar University, Manisa, Turkey

Alejandro Escudero Ingeniería de Organización, Engineering School of Seville, University of Seville, Camino de los Descubrimientos s/n 41092, Seville, Spain

Iztok Fister Faculty of Electrical Engineering and Computer Science, University of Maribor, Maribor, Slovenia

Iztok Jr. Fister Faculty of Electrical Engineering and Computer Science, University of Maribor, Maribor, Slovenia

Andreas Floros Department of Audio and Visual Arts, Ionian University, Corfu, Greece

Simon Fong Department of Computer and Information Science, University of Macau, Macau SAR, China

Amir Hossein Gandomi Department of Civil Engineering, University of Akron, Akron, OH, USA

Oubay Hassan College of Engineering, Swansea University, Swansea, Wales, UK

Raha Imanirad OMIS Area, Schulich School of Business, York University, Toronto, ON, Canada

Momin Jamil Blekinge Institute of Technology, Karlskrona, Sweden; Harman International, Harman/Becker Automotive Systems GmbH, Karlsbad, Germany

Gilang Kusuma Jati Faculty of Computer Science, Universitas Indonesia, Kampus UI, Depok, Jawa Barat, Indonesia

Maximos A. Kaliakatsos-Papakostas Department of Mathematics, University of Patras, Patras, Greece

Mehmet Karamanoglu Department of Design Engineering and Mathematics, School of Science and Technology, Middlesex University, The Burroughs, London, UK

András Király Department of Process Engineering, University of Pannonia, Veszprém, Hungary

Jonas Krause Bioinformatics Laboratory, Federal University of Technology Paraná, Curitiba, Brazil

Hongbo Liu Department of Computer, Dalian University of Technology, Dalian, China; School of Information Science and Technology, Dalian Maritime University, Dalian, China

Heitor Silvério Lopes Bioinformatics Laboratory, Federal University of Technology Paraná, Curitiba, Brazil

Ruli Manurung Faculty of Informatics, Telkom School of Technology, Jl. Telekomunikasi No. 1, Terusan Buah Batu, Bandung, Jawa Barat, Indonesia

Kenneth Morgan College of Engineering, Swansea University, Swansea, Wales, UK

Rodrigo Yuji Mizobe Nakamura Department of Computing, São Paulo State University, Bauru, Brazil

Luis Onieva Ingeniería de Organización, Engineering School of Seville, University of Seville, Camino de los Descubrimientos s/n 41092, Seville, Spain

Rafael Stubs Parpinelli Applied Cognitive Computing Group, Santa Catarina State University, Joinville, Brazil; Bioinformatics Laboratory, Federal University of Technology Paraná, Curitiba, Brazil

João Paulo Papa Department of Computing, São Paulo State University, Bauru, Brazil

Luís Augusto Martins Pereira Department of Computing, São Paulo State University, Bauru, Brazil

Douglas Rodrigues Department of Computing, São Paulo State University, Bauru, Brazil

M. Rowan Brown College of Engineering, Swansea University, Swansea, Wales, UK

Priti Srinivas Sajja Department of Computer Science, Sardar Patel University, India

M.P. Saka Department of Civil Engineering, University of Bahrain, Isa Town, Bahrain

Shichang Sun Department of Computer, Dalian University of Technology, Dalian, China; School of Computer Science and Engineering, Dalian Nationalities University, Dalian, China

Suyanto Faculty of Informatics, Telkom School of Technology, Jl. Telekomunikasi No. 1, Terusan Buah Batu, Bandung, Jawa Barat, Indonesia

Siamak Talatahari Marand Faculty of Engineering, University of Tabriz, Tabriz, Iran

Tamás Varga Department of Process Engineering, University of Pannonia, Veszprém, Hungary

Michael N. Vrahatis Department of Mathematics, University of Patras, Patras, Greece

Sean Walton College of Engineering, Swansea University, Swansea, Wales, UK

Renbin Xiao Institute of Systems Engineering, Huazhong University of Science and Technology, Wuhan, China

Xin-She Yang Department of Design Engineering and Mathematics, School of Science and Technology, Middlesex University, The Burroughs, London, UK

Julian Scott Yeomans OMIS Area, Schulich School of Business, York University, Toronto, ON, Canada

Hans-Jürgen Zepernick Blekinge Institute of Technology, Karlskrona, Sweden

Preface

Swarm intelligence and bio-inspired computation have become increasingly popular in the last two decades. Bio-inspired algorithms such as ant colony algorithm, bat algorithm (BA), cuckoo search (CS), firefly algorithm (FA), and particle swarm optimization have been applied in almost every area of science and engineering with a dramatic increase in the number of relevant publications. Metaheuristic algorithms form an important part of contemporary global optimization algorithms, computational intelligence, and soft computing.

New researchers often ask "why metaheuristics?", and this indeed is a profound question, which can be linked to many aspects of algorithms and optimization, including what algorithms to choose and why certain algorithms perform better than others for a given problem. It was believed that the word "metaheuristic" was coined by Fred Glover in 1986. Generally, "heuristic" means "to find or to discover by trial and error." Here, "meta-" means "beyond or higher level." Therefore, metaheuristic can be considered as a higher-level strategy that guides and modifies other heuristic procedures to produce solutions or innovations beyond those that are normally achievable in a quest for local optimality. In reality, we are often puzzled and may be even surprised by the excellent efficiency of bio-inspired metehauristic algorithms because these seemingly simple algorithms can sometime work like a "magic," even for highly nonlinear, challenging problems. For example, for multimodal optimization problems, many traditional algorithms usually do not work well, while new algorithms such as differential evolution (DE) and FA can work extremely well in practice, even though we may not fully understand the underlying mechanisms of these algorithms.

The increasing popularity of bio-inspired metaheuristics and swarm intelligence (SI) has attracted a great deal of attention in engineering and industry. There are many reasons for such popularity, and here we discuss three factors: simplicity, flexibility, and ergodicity. Firstly, most bio-inspired algorithms are simple in the sense that they are easy to implement and their algorithm complexity is relatively low. In most programming languages, the core algorithm can be coded within a hundred lines. Second, these algorithms, though simple, are flexible enough to deal with a wide range of optimization problems, including those that are not solvable by conventional algorithms. Third, bio-inspired algorithms such as FA and CS can often have high degrees of ergodicity in the sense that they can search multimodal landscape with sufficient diversity and ability to escape any local optimum. The ergodicity is often due to some exotic randomization techniques, derived from natural systems in terms of crossover and mutation, or based on statistical models such as random walks and Lévy flights.

As most real-world problems are nonlinear and multimodal with uncertainty, such complexity and multimodality may imply that it may not be possible to find the true global optimality with a 100% certainty for a given problem. We often have to balance the solution accuracy and computational cost, leading to a (possibly aggressive) local search method. Consequently, we may have to sacrifice the possibility of finding the true global optimality in exchange of some suboptimal, robust solutions. However, in practice, for the vast majority of cases, many bio-inspired algorithms can achieve the true global optimality in a practically acceptable fixed number of iterations, though there is no guarantee for this to be the case all the time.

The history of bio-inspired computation and SI has spanned over half a century, though the developments have been sped up in the last 20 years. Since the emergence of evolutionary strategies in the 1960s and the development of genetic algorithms (GA) in the 1970s, a golden age with major progress in modern bio-inspired computing is the 1990s. First, in 1992, Marco Dorigo described his innovative work on ant colony optimization (ACO) in his PhD thesis, and in the same year, J.R. Koza published a treatise on genetic programming. Then, in 1995, J. Kennedy and R. Eberhart developed particle swarm optimization (PSO), which essentially opened up a new field, now loosely named as SI. Following this in 1996 and 1997, R. Storn and K. Price published their DE. At the turn of the twenty-first century, Zong Woo Geem et al. developed the harmony search in 2001. Around 2004 to 2005, bee algorithms emerged. S. Nakrani and C. Tovey proposed the honey bee algorithm in 2004, and Xin-She Yang proposed the virtual bee algorithm in 2005. D.T. Pham et al. developed their bee algorithms and D. Karaboga formulated the artificial bee colony all in 2005. In 2008, Xin-She Yang developed the FA for multimodal optimization, and in 2009, Xin-She Yang and Suash Deb developed CS. In 2010, Xin-She Yang first developed the BA, and then Xin-She Yang and S. Deb developed the eagle strategy. More bio-inspired algorithms started to appear in 2012, including krill herd algorithm (KHA) by A.H. Gandomi and A.H. Alavi, flower pollination algorithm by Xin-She Yang, and wolf search algorithm by Rui et al. As we can see, the literature has expanded dramatically in the last decade.

Accompanying the rapid developments in bio-inspired computing, another important question comes naturally: Can an algorithm be intelligent? The answers may depend on the definition of "intelligence" itself, and this is also a debating issue. Unless a true Turing test can be passed without any doubt, truly intelligent algorithms may be still a long way to go. However, if we lower our expectation to define the intelligence as "the ability to mimic some aspects of human intelligence" such as memory, automation, and sharing information, then many algorithms can have low-level intelligence to a certain degree. First, many bio-inspired algorithms use elitism and memory to select the best solution or "survival of the fittest," and then share this information with other agents in a multiple agent system. Algorithms such as artificial neural networks use connectionism, interactions, memory, and learning. Most SI-based algorithms use rule-based updates, and they can adjust their behavior according to the landscape (such as the best values, gradients) in the search space during iterations. To some extent, they can be called "smart" algorithms. Obviously, truly intelligent algorithms are yet to appear in the future. Whatever the forms such intelligent algorithms may take, it would be the holy grail of artificial intelligence and bio-inspired computation.

Despite the above recent advances, there are many challenging issues that remain unresolved. First, there are some significant gaps between theory and practice, concerning bio-inspired computing and optimization. From numerical experiments and applications, we know bio-inspired algorithms often work surprisingly well; however, we do not quite understand why they are so efficient. In fact, it lacks solid theoretical proof of convergence for many bio-inspired algorithms, though the good news is that limited results do start to appear in the literature.

In addition, for most algorithms, we do not know how parameters can exactly control or influence the performance of an algorithm. Consequently, a major challenge is the tuning of algorithm-dependent parameters so as to produce the optimal performance of an algorithm. In essence, parameter tuning itself is an optimization problem. At present, this is mainly carried out by trial and error, and thus very time consuming. In fact, parameter tuning is a very active research area which requires more research emphasis on both theory and extensive simulations.

On the other hand, even though we have seen a vast range of successful applications, however, in most applications, these are still limited to small-scale problems with the number of design variables less than a few dozens or a few hundreds. It is very rare to see larger-scale applications. In reality, many optimization problems may be very large scale, but we are not sure how bio-inspired algorithms can deal with such large-scale problems. As most problems are often nonlinear, scalability may also be a problem, and computational time can be a huge barrier for large-scale problems.

Obviously, there are other challenging issues such as performance measures, uncertainty, and comparison statistics. These challenges also provide golden opportunities for researchers to pursue further research in these exciting areas in the years to come.

This book strives to provide a timely snapshot of the state-of-the-art developments in bio-inspired computation and SI, capturing the fundamentals and applications of algorithms based on SI and other biological systems. In addition to review and document the recent advances, this book analyze and discuss the latest and future trends in research directions so that it can help new researchers to carry out timely research and inspire readers to develop new algorithms.

As the literature is vast and the research area is very broad, it is not possible to include even a good fraction of the current research. However, the contributions by leading experts still contain latest developments in many active areas and applications. Topics include overview and analysis of SI and bio-inspired algorithms, PSO, FA, memetic FA, discrete FA, BA, binary BA, GA, CS and modified CS, KHA, artificial plant optimization, review of commonly used test functions and labor division in ACO. Application topics include traveling salesman problems, feature selection, graph coloring, combinatorial optimization, music composition, mesh generation, semantic web services, optimization alternatives generation, protein folding, berth allocation, data mining, structural optimization, inventory management, and others.

It can be expected that this edited book can serve as a source of inspiration for novel research and new applications. Maybe, in the not very far future, some truly, intelligent, self-evolving algorithm may appear to solve a wide range of tough optimization more efficiently and more accurately.

Last but not the least, we would like to thank our Editors, Dr Erin Hill-Parks, Sarah E. Lay, and Tracey Miller, and the staff at Elsevier for their help and professionalism.

Xin-She Yang, Zhihua Cui, Renbin Xiao,
Amir Hossein Gandomi and Mehmet Karamanoglu
February 2013

Part One

Theoretical Aspects of Swarm Intelligence and Bio-Inspired Computing

1 Swarm Intelligence and Bio-Inspired Computation: An Overview

Xin-She Yang and Mehmet Karamanoglu

Department of Design Engineering and Mathematics, School of Science and Technology, Middlesex University, The Burroughs, London, UK

1.1 Introduction

Swarm intelligence (SI), bio-inspired computation in general, has attracted great interest in the last two decades, and many SI-based optimization algorithms have gained huge popularity. There are many reasons for such popularity and attention, and two main reasons are probably that these SI-based algorithms are flexible and versatile, and that they are very efficient in solving nonlinear design problems with real-world applications. Bio-inspired computation has permeated into almost all areas of sciences, engineering, and industries, from data mining to optimization, from computational intelligence to business planning, and from bioinformatics to industrial applications. In fact, it is perhaps one of the most active and popular research subjects with wide multidisciplinary connections.

Even when considered from a narrow point of view of optimization, this is still a very broad area of research. Optimization is everywhere and is thus an important paradigm by itself with a wide range of applications. In almost all applications in engineering and industry, we are always trying to optimize something—whether to minimize cost and energy consumption, or to maximize profit, output, performance, and efficiency. In reality, resources, time, and money are always limited; consequently, optimization is far more important in practice (Yang, 2010b; Yang and Koziel, 2011). The optimal use of available resources of any sort requires a paradigm shift in scientific thinking; this is because most real-world applications have far more complicated factors and parameters that affect how the system behaves and thus how the optimal design needs are met.

A proper formulation of optimization is an art, which requires detailed knowledge of the problem and extensive experience. Optimization problems can be formulated in many ways. For example, the commonly used method of least squares

Swarm Intelligence and Bio-Inspired Computation. DOI: http://dx.doi.org/10.1016/B978-0-12-405163-8.00001-6

is a special case of maximum-likelihood formulations. By far, the most widely used formulations is to write a nonlinear optimization problem as

$$\text{minimize} \quad f_i(x), \quad (i = 1, 2, \ldots, M) \tag{1.1}$$

subject to the following nonlinear constraints:

$$h_j(x) = 0, \quad (j = 1, 2, \ldots, J) \tag{1.2}$$

$$g_k(x) \leq 0, \quad (k = 1, 2, \ldots, K) \tag{1.3}$$

where f_i, h_j, and g_k are in general nonlinear functions, or even integrals and/or differential equations. Here, the design vector $x = (x_1, x_2, \ldots, x_n)$ can be continuous, discrete, or mixed in d-dimensional space. The functions f_i are called objectives, or cost functions, and when $M > 1$, the optimization is multiobjective or multicriteria (Yang, 2008, 2010b). It is worth pointing out that here we write the problem as a minimization problem; it can also be written as a maximization problem by simply replacing f_i by $-f_i$. When all functions are nonlinear, we are dealing with nonlinear constrained problems. In some special cases when all functions are linear, the problem becomes linear, and we can use the widely used linear programming techniques such as the simplex method. When some design variables can only take discrete values (often integers), while other variables are real continuous, the problem is of mixed type, which is often difficult to solve, especially for large-scale optimization problems. A very special class of optimization is the convex optimization, which has guaranteed global optimality. Any optimal solution to a convex problem is also its global optimum, and most importantly, there are efficient algorithms of polynomial time to solve. These efficient algorithms such as the interior-point methods are widely used and have been implemented in many software packages.

Despite the fact that the above optimization problem looks seemingly simple, it is usually very challenging to solve. There are many challenging issues; two major challenges are the nonlinearity and complex constraints. Nonlinearity in objective functions makes the cost landscape highly multimodal, and potentially nonsmooth, and nonlinearity in constraints complicates the search boundaries and search domains which may be disconnected. Therefore, the evaluations of objectives and the handling of constraints can be time consuming. In addition, not all problems can be written in terms of explicit objective functions. Sometimes, the objectives such as energy efficiency can have a complex, implicit dependence on the design variables. In this case, we may have to deal with optimization problems with black-box type objectives whose evaluations can be by some external, finite-element simulators. Simulations are often the most time-consuming part. In many applications, an optimization process often involves the evaluation of objective functions many times, often thousands and even millions of configurations. Such evaluations often involve the use of extensive computational tools such as a computational fluid dynamics simulator or a finite element solver. Therefore, an efficient optimization algorithm in combination with an efficient solver is extremely important.

Furthermore, even when variables take only integer values such as 0 and 1, such combinatorial optimization problem can still be nondeterministic polynomial-time (NP) hard. Therefore, no efficient algorithm exists for such problems. Specific knowledge about the problem of interest can gain good insights, but in many cases, heuristic approaches have to be used by trial and error. That is probably another reason for the popularity of heuristic and metaheuristic algorithms.

1.2 Current Issues in Bio-Inspired Computing

Despite the popularity and success of SI and bio-inspired computing, there remain many challenging issues. Here we highlight five issues: gaps between theory and practice, classifications, parameter tuning, lack of truly large-scale real-world applications, and choices of algorithms.

1.2.1 Gaps Between Theory and Practice

There is a significant gap between theory and practice in bio-inspired computing. Nature-inspired metaheuristic algorithms work almost magically in practice, but it is not well understood why these algorithms work. For example, except for a few cases such as genetic algorithms, simulated annealing, and particle swarm optimization, there are not many good results concerning the convergence analysis and stability of metaheuristic algorithms. The lack of theoretical understanding may lead to slow progress or even resistance to the wider applications of metaheuristics.

There are three main methods for theoretical analysis of algorithms: complexity theory, dynamical systems, and Markov chains. On the one hand, metaheuristic algorithms tend to have low algorithm complexity, but they can solve highly complex problems. Complexity analysis is an active research area and requires more in-depth analysis (Hopper and Turton, 2000; Yang, 2011c). On the other hand, the convergence analysis typically uses dynamic systems and statistical methods based on Markov chains. For example, particle swarm optimization was analyzed by Clerc and Kennedy (2002) using simple dynamic systems, whereas genetic algorithms were analyzed intensively in a few theoretical studies (Aytug et al., 1996; Greenhalgh and Marshal, 2000; Gutjahr, 2010; Villalobos-Arias et al., 2005). For example, for a given mutation rate (μ), string length (L), and population size (n), the number of iterations in genetic algorithms can be estimated by

$$t \leq \left\lceil \frac{\ln(1-p)}{\ln\{1 - \min[(1-\mu)^{Ln}, \mu^{Ln}]\}} \right\rceil \tag{1.4}$$

where $\lceil u \rceil$ means taking the maximum integer value of u, and p is a function of μ, L, and n (Gutjahr, 2010; Villalobos-Arias et al., 2005).

Theoretical understanding lags behind, and thus there is a strong need for further studies in this area. There is no doubt that any new understanding will provide greater insight into the working mechanism of metaheuristic algorithms.

1.2.2 Classifications and Terminology

There are many ways to classify optimization algorithms; one of the most widely used is based on the number of agents, and another is based on the iteration procedure. The former will lead to two categories: single agent and multiple agents. Simulated annealing is a single-agent algorithm with a zigzag piecewise trajectory, whereas genetic algorithms, particle swarm optimization, and firefly algorithm are population-based algorithms. These algorithms often have multiple agents, interacting in a nonlinear manner, and a subset of which is called SI-based algorithm. For example, particle swarm optimization and firefly algorithm are swarm-based, inspired by swarming behavior of birds, fish, and fireflies or by SI in general.

Another way of classifying algorithms is based on the core procedure of algorithms. If the procedure is fixed without any randomness, an algorithm that starts from a given initial value will reach the same final value, no matter when you run the algorithm. We call this deterministic. For example, the classic Newton—Raphson method is a deterministic algorithm, so is the hill-climbing method. On the other hand, if an algorithm contains some randomness in the algorithm procedure, it is called stochastic, evolutionary, or heuristic or even metaheuristic. For example, genetic algorithms with mutation and crossover components can be called evolutionary algorithms, stochastic algorithms, or metaheuristic algorithms.

These different names for algorithms with stochastic components reflect an issue that there is still some confusion in the terminologies and terms used in the current literature. Algorithms, such as genetic algorithms, developed before the 1980s were called evolutionary algorithms, and now, they can be called both evolutionary-based and metaheuristic. Depending on the sources of inspiration, there are bio-inspired algorithms, nature-inspired algorithms, and metaheuristics in general. However, recent trends call such algorithms "metaheuristic."

Briefly speaking, heuristic means "by trial and error," and metaheuristic can be considered a higher-level method by using certain selection mechanisms and information sharing. It is believed that the word "metaheuristic" was coined by Glover (1986). The multiple names and inconsistency in terminologies in the literature require efforts from research communities to agree on some of the common terminologies and to systematically classify and analyze algorithms. The current dramatic expansion in the literature makes it an even more challenging task.

In this book, we have tried to use metaheuristic, SI, and bio-inspired computation in the right context, with a focus on metaheuristics.

It is worth pointing out that from the mobility point of view, algorithms can be classified as local or global. Local search algorithms typically converge toward a local optimum, not necessarily (often not) the global optimum, and such algorithms are often deterministic and have no ability of escaping local optima. Simple hill-climbing algorithm is an example. On the other hand, we always try to find the global optimum for a given problem, and if this global optimality is robust, it is often the best, though it is not always possible to find such global optimality. For global optimization, local search algorithms are not suitable. We have to use a global search algorithm. In most cases, modern metaheuristic algorithms are intended for global optimization, though they are not always successful or efficient.

1.2.3 Tuning of Algorithm-Dependent Parameters

All metaheuristic algorithms have algorithm-dependent parameters, and the appropriate setting of these parameter values will largely affect the performance of an algorithm. One of the very challenging issues is deciding what values of parameters to use in an algorithm. How can these parameters be tuned so that they can maximize the performance of the algorithm of interest?

Parameter tuning itself is a tough optimization problem. In the literature, there are two main approaches. One approach is to run an algorithm with some trial values of key parameters, and the aim of the test runs is to get good setting of these parameters. These parameters are then fixed for more extensive test runs involving same type of problems or larger problems. The other approach is to use one algorithm (which may be well tested and well established) to tune the parameters of another relatively new algorithm. Then, an important issue arises. If we use algorithm A (or tool A) to tune algorithm B, what tool or algorithm should be used to tune algorithm A? If we use, say, algorithm C to tune algorithm A, then what tool should be used to tune algorithm C? In fact, these key issues are still under active research.

1.2.4 Necessity for Large-Scale and Real-World Applications

SI and bio-inspired computation are very successful in solving many practical problems. However, the size of these problems in terms of number of design variables is relatively small or moderate. In the current literature, studies have focused on design problems with about a dozen of variables or at most about a hundred. It is rare to see studies with several hundred variables. In contrast, in linear programming, it is routine to solve design problems with half a million to several millions of design variables. Therefore, it remains a huge challenge for SI-based algorithms to apply to real-world, large-scale problems.

Accompanying this challenge is the methodology issue. Nobody is sure if we can directly apply the same methods that work well for small, toy problems to large-scale problems. Apart from difference in size, there may be other issues such as memory capacity, computational efficiency, and computing resources needing special care. If we cannot extend existing methods to deal with large-scale problems effectively, often not, then what are the options? After all, real-world problems are typically nonlinear and are often very large-scale. Further and detailed studies are highly needed in this area.

1.2.5   Choice of Algorithms

Even with all the knowledge and all the books written on optimization and algorithms, most readers are still not sure what algorithms to choose. It is similar to visiting a shopping mall to choose a certain product. There are often so many different choices, and to make a right choice is again an optimization problem. In the literature, there is no agreed guideline to choose algorithms, though there are specific instructions on how to use a specific algorithm and what types of problems they can solve. Therefore, the issue of choice still remains: partly experience-based and partly by trial and error.

Sometimes, even with the best possible intention, the availability of an algorithm and the expertise of the decision makers are the ultimate defining factors for choosing an algorithm. Even though some algorithms are better for the given problem at hand, we may not have that algorithm implemented in our system or we do not have access, which limits our choices. For example, Newton's method, hill-climbing, Nelder−Mead downhill simplex, trust-region methods (Conn et al., 2000), and interior-point methods are implemented in many software packages, which may also increase their popularity in applications. In practice, even with the best possible algorithms and well-crafted implementation, we may still not get the desired solutions. This is the nature of nonlinear global optimization, as most of such problems are NP-hard, and no efficient algorithm (in the polynomial-time sense) exists for a given problem. Thus, the challenges of research in computational optimization and applications are to find the right algorithms most suitable for a given problem to obtain good solutions, hopefully also the global best solutions, in a reasonable timescale with a limited amount of resources.

1.3   Search for the Magic Formulas for Optimization

1.3.1   Essence of an Algorithm

Mathematically speaking, an algorithm is a procedure to generate outputs for given inputs. From the optimization point of view, an optimization algorithm generates a new solution x^{t+1} to a given problem from a known solution x^t at iteration or time t. That is,

$$x^{t+1} = A(x^t, p(t)) \qquad (1.5)$$

where A is a nonlinear mapping from a given solution, or d-dimensional vector, x^t to a new solution vector x^{t+1}. The algorithm A has k algorithm-dependent parameters $p(t) = (p_1, \ldots, p_k)$, which can be time dependent and can thus be tuned if necessary.

1.3.2   What Is an Ideal Algorithm?

In an ideal world, we hope to start from any initial guess solution and wish to get the best solution in a single step. That is, to use minimal computational effort.

In other words, this is essentially saying that the algorithm simply has to tell what the best answer is to any given problem in a single step! You may wonder if such an algorithm exists. In fact, the answer is yes for a very specific type of problem— quadratic convex problems.

We know Newton–Raphson method is a root-finding algorithm. It can find the roots of $f(x) = 0$. As the minimum or maximum of a function $f(x)$ has to satisfy the critical condition $f'(x) = 0$, this optimization problem now becomes a problem of finding the roots of $f'(x)$. Newton–Raphson method provides the following iteration formula:

$$x_{i+1} = x_i - \frac{f'(x_i)}{f''(x_i)} \tag{1.6}$$

For a quadratic function, say, $f(x) = x^2$, if we start from a fixed location, say, $x_0 = a$ at $i = 0$, we have $f'(a) = 2a$ and $f''(a) = 2$. Then, we get

$$x_1 = x_0 - \frac{f'(x_0)}{f''(x_0)} = a - \frac{2a}{2} = 0$$

which is exactly the optimal solution $f_{min} = 0$ at $x = 0$, which is also globally optimal. We have found the global optimum in one step. In fact, for quadratic functions that are also convex, Newton–Raphson is an ideal algorithm. However, the world is not convex and certainly not quadratic, real-world problems are often highly nonlinear, there is no ideal algorithm.

For NP-hard problems, there is no known efficient algorithm at all. Such hard problems require a huge amount of research efforts to search for specific techniques, which are still not satisfactory in practice. These challenges can also be a driving force for active research.

1.3.3 Algorithms and Self-Organization

Self-organization exists in many systems, from physical and chemical to biological and artificial systems. Emergent phenomena such as Releigh–Bénard convection, Turing pattern formation, and organisms and thunderstorms can all be called self-organization (Ashby, 1962; Keller, 2009). Although there is no universal theory for self-organizing processes, some aspects of self-organization can partly be understood using theories based on nonlinear dynamical systems, far-from-equilibrium multiple interacting agents, and closed system under unchanging laws (Prigogine and Nicolois, 1967). As pointed out by the cyberneticist and mathematician Ashby (1962), every isolated determinate dynamic system, obeying unchanging laws, will ultimately develop some sort of "organisms" that are adapted to their "environments." For simple systems, going to equilibrium is trivial; however, for a complex system, if its size is so large that its equilibrium states are just a fraction of the vast number of possible states, and if the system is allowed to evolve long enough, some self-organized structures may emerge. The changes in environments can apply pressure on the system to reorganize and adapt to such changes. If the system has sufficient perturbations or noise, often working at the edge of the chaos, some spontaneous formation of structures will emerge as the systems move, far from equilibrium, and select some states, thus reducing the uncertainty or entropy.

The state set S of a complex system such as a machine may change from initial states $S(\psi)$ to other states $S(\phi)$, subject to the change of a parameter set $\alpha(t)$ which can be time dependent. That is,

$$S(\psi) \overset{\alpha(t)}{\to} S(\phi) \tag{1.7}$$

where $\alpha(t)$ must come from external conditions such as the heat flow in Raleigh−Bénard convection, not from the states S themselves. Obviously, $S + \alpha(t)$ can be considered as a larger and a closed system (Ashby, 1962; Keller, 2009). In this sense, self-organization is equivalent to a mapping from some high-entropy states to low-entropy states.

An optimization algorithm can be viewed as a complex, dynamical system. If we can consider the convergence process as a self-organizing process, then there are strong similarities and links between self-organizing systems and optimization algorithms. First, let us discuss the essence of an optimization algorithm.

1.3.4 Links Between Algorithms and Self-Organization

To find the optimal solution x_* to a given optimization problem S with often an infinite number of states is to select some desired states ϕ from all states ψ, according to some predefined criterion D. We have

$$S(\psi) \overset{A(t)}{\to} S(\phi(x_*)) \tag{1.8}$$

where the final converged state ϕ corresponds to an optimal solution x_* to the problem of interest. The selection of the system states in the design space is carried out by running the optimization algorithm A. The behavior of the algorithm is controlled by $p(t)$, the initial solution $x^{t=0}$, and the stopping criterion D. We can view the combined $S + A(t)$ as a complex system with a self-organizing capability.

The change of states or solution to the problem of interest is controlled by the algorithm A. In many classical algorithms such as hill-climbing, gradient information is often used to select states, say, the minimum value of the landscape, and the stopping criterion can be a given tolerance, accuracy, or zero gradient. Alternatively, an algorithm can act like a tool to tune a complex system. If an algorithm does not use any state information of the problem, then the algorithm is more likely to be versatile to deal with many types of problems. However, such black-box approaches can also imply that the algorithm may not be efficient as it could be for a given type of problem. For example, if the optimization problem is convex, the algorithms that use such convexity information will be more efficient than the ones that do not use such information. In order to select states/solutions efficiently, the information from the search process should be used to enhance the search process. In many cases, such information is often fed into the selection mechanism of an algorithm. By far, the most widely used selection mechanism is to select or keep the best solution found so far. That is, some form of "survival of the fittest" is used.

From the schematic representation [see Eq. (1.8)] of an optimization process, we can see that the performance of an algorithm may depend on the type of problem S it solves. Whether the final, global optimality is achievable or not (within a given number of iterations) will also depend on the algorithm used. This may be another way of stating the so-called no-free-lunch theorems.

Optimization algorithms can be very diverse with several dozens of widely used algorithms. The main characteristics of different algorithms will only depend on the actual, often highly nonlinear or implicit, forms of $A(t)$ and their parameters $p(t)$.

1.3.5 The Magic Formulas

The ultimate aim is to find a magic formula or method that works for many problems, such as the Newton–Raphson method for quadratic functions. We wish it could work like a magic to provide the best solution for any problem in a few steps. However, such formulas may never exist.

As optimization algorithms are iterative, an algorithm to solve a given problem P can be written as the following generic formula:

$$x^{t+1} = g(x^t, \alpha, P) \tag{1.9}$$

which forms a piecewise trajectory in the search space. This algorithm depends on a parameter α, starting with an initial guess x_0. The iterative path will depend on the problem (P) or its objective function $f(x)$. However, as algorithms nowadays tend to use multiple agents, Eq. (1.9) can be extended to

$$[x_1, x_2, \ldots, x_n]^{t+1} = g([x_1, \ldots, x_n]^t, [\alpha_1, \ldots, \alpha_k]^t, P) \tag{1.10}$$

which has a population size of n and depends on k different algorithm-dependent parameters. Each iteration will produce n different solutions $[x_1, \ldots, x_n]$. Modern metaheuristic algorithms have stochastic components, which mean some of these k parameters can be drawn from some probability distributions. If we wish to express the randomness more explicitly, we can rewrite Eq. (1.10) as

$$[x_1, x_2, \ldots, x_n]^{t+1} = g([x_1, \ldots, x_n]^t, [\alpha_1, \ldots, \alpha_k]^t, [\varepsilon_1, \ldots, \varepsilon_m]^t, P) \tag{1.11}$$

with m random variables of ε that are often drawn from uniform distributions or Gaussian distributions. In some cases as those in cuckoo search, these random variables can also be drawn from a Lévy distribution (Yang and Deb, 2009).

Although there is no magic formula, each algorithm strives to use fewer iteration t as possible. The only difference among algorithms is the exact form of $g(\cdot)$. In fact, sometimes, the procedure $g(\cdot)$ can be divided into many substeps or procedures with different branches so that these branches can be used in a random manner during iterations. This is the essence of all contemporary SI and bio-inspired metaheuristic algorithms.

1.4 Characteristics of Metaheuristics

1.4.1 Intensification and Diversification

Intensification and diversification are two key components for any metaheuristic algorithm (Blum and Roli, 2003; Yang, 2008). Intensification is also called exploitation, and it uses the local information in the search process so as to generate better solutions. Such local information can be derivative of the objective or the variations of the cost landscape. Diversification is also called exploration, which intends to explore the search space more thoroughly and to help generate diverse solutions. Too much intensification will make the optimization process converge quickly, but it may lead to premature convergence, often to a local optimum, or even a wrong solution. It will also reduce the probability of finding the true global optimum. On the other hand, too much diversification will increase the probability of finding the true optimality globally, but it will often slow down the process with a much lower convergence rate. Therefore, there is a fine balance or trade-off between intensification and diversification, or between exploitation and exploration.

Furthermore, just exploitation and exploration are not enough. During the search, we have to use a proper mechanism or criterion to select the best solutions. The most common criterion is to use the *survival of the fittest*, i.e., to keep updating the current best found so far. In addition, certain elitism is often used, and this is to ensure the best or the fittest solutions are not lost and should be passed on to the next generations (Fogel et al., 1966; Goldberg, 1989; Holland, 1975).

For any algorithm to be efficient, it must somehow provide a mechanism to balance the aforementioned two key components properly. It is worth pointing out that the naïve 50−50 balance is not optimal (Yang, 2011c; Yang and He, 2013). More research in this area is highly needed.

1.4.2 Randomization Techniques

On analyzing bio-inspired algorithms in more detail, we can single out the type of randomness that a particular algorithm is employing. For example, the simplest and yet often very efficient method is to introduce a random starting point for a deterministic algorithm. The well-known hill-climbing with random restart is a good example. This simple strategy is both efficient, in most cases, and easy to implement in practice.

A more elaborate way to introduce randomness to an algorithm is to use randomness inside different components of an algorithm, and various probability distributions such as uniform, Gaussian, and Lévy distributions can be used for randomization (Talbi, 2009; Yang, 2008, 2010b). In essence, randomization is an efficient component for global search algorithms.

Obviously, it still remains an open question that what is the best way to provide sufficient randomness without slowing down the convergence of an algorithm. In fact, metaheuristic algorithms form a hot research topic with new algorithms appearing almost yearly, and new techniques are being explored (Yang, 2008, 2010b).

1.5 Swarm-Intelligence-Based Algorithms

Metaheuristic algorithms are often nature-inspired, and they are now among the most widely used algorithms for optimization. They have many advantages over conventional algorithms, as we can see from many case studies presented in the later chapters of this book. There are a few recent books that are solely dedicated to metaheuristic algorithms (Talbi, 2009; Yang, 2008, 2010a,b). Metaheuristic algorithms are very diverse, including genetic algorithms, simulated annealing, differential evolution, ant and bee algorithms, particle swarm optimization, harmony search, firefly algorithm, and cuckoo search. Here we introduce some of these algorithms briefly, especially those that are based on SI.

1.5.1 Ant Algorithms

Ant algorithms, especially the ant colony optimization (Dorigo and Stütle, 2004), mimic the foraging behavior of social ants. Ants primarily use pheromone as a chemical messenger, and the pheromone concentration can be considered as the indicator of quality solutions to a problem of interest. As the solution is often linked with the pheromone concentrations, the search algorithms often produce routes and paths marked by the higher pheromone concentrations; therefore, ants-based algorithms are particularly suitable for discrete optimization problems.

The movement of an ant is controlled by pheromone, which will evaporate over time. Without such time-dependent evaporation, ant algorithms will lead to premature convergence to the local (often wrong) solutions. With proper pheromone evaporation, they usually behave very well.

There are two important issues here: the probability of choosing a route and the evaporation rate of pheromone. There are a few ways of solving these problems, though it is still an area of active research. For a network routing problem, the probability of ants at a particular node i to choose the route from node i to node j is given by

$$p_{ij} = \frac{\phi_{ij}^{\alpha} d_{ij}^{\beta}}{\sum_{i,j=1}^{n} \phi_{ij}^{\alpha} d_{ij}^{\beta}} \tag{1.12}$$

where $\alpha > 0$ and $\beta > 0$ are the influence parameters, and their typical values are $\alpha \approx \beta \approx 2$. Here, ϕ_{ij} is the pheromone concentration of the route between i and j, and d_{ij} the desirability of the same route. Some *a priori* knowledge about the route such as the distance s_{ij} is often used so that $d_{ij} \propto 1/s_{ij}$, which implies that shorter routes will be selected due to their shorter traveling time, and thus the pheromone concentrations on these routes are higher. This is because the traveling time is shorter, and thus, less amount of pheromone has been evaporated during this period.

1.5.2 Bee Algorithms

Bees-inspired algorithms are more diverse, and some use pheromone and most do not. Almost all bee algorithms are inspired by the foraging behavior of honeybees in nature. Interesting characteristics such as waggle dance, polarization, and nectar maximization are often used to simulate the allocation of the forager bees along flower patches and thus different search regions in the search space. For a more comprehensive review, refer to Yang (2010a) and Parpinelli and Lopes (2011).

Different variants of bee algorithms use slightly different characteristics of the behavior of bees. For example, in the honeybee-based algorithms, forager bees are allocated to different food sources (or flower patches) to maximize the total nectar intake (Karaboga, 2005; Nakrani and Tovey, 2004; Pham et al., 2006; Yang, 2005). In the virtual bee algorithm (VBA), developed by Yang (2005), pheromone concentrations can be linked with the objective functions more directly. On the other hand, the artificial bee colony (ABC) optimization algorithm was first developed by Karaboga (2005). In the ABC algorithm, the bees in a colony are divided into three groups: employed bees (forager bees), onlooker bees (observer bees), and scouts. Unlike the honeybee algorithm, which has two groups of bees (forager bees and observer bees), the bees in ABC are more specialized (Afshar et al., 2007; Karaboga, 2005).

Similar to the ants-based algorithms, bee algorithms are also very flexible in dealing with discrete optimization problems. Combinatorial optimization such as routing and optimal paths has been successfully solved by ant and bee algorithms. In principle, they can solve both continuous optimization and discrete optimization problems; however, they should not be the first choice for continuous problems.

1.5.3 Bat Algorithm

Bat algorithm is a relatively new metaheuristic, developed by Yang (2010c). It was inspired by the echolocation behavior of microbats. Microbats use a type of sonar, called echolocation, to detect prey, avoid obstacles, and locate their roosting crevices in the dark. These bats emit a very loud sound pulse and listen to the echoes that bounce back from the surrounding objects. Depending on the species, their pulse varies in property and can be correlated with their hunting strategies. Most bats use short, frequency-modulated signals to sweep through about an octave, while others more often use constant-frequency signals for echolocation.

Their signal bandwidth varies depending on the species and is often increased by using more harmonics.

The bat algorithm uses three idealized rules: (i) All bats use echolocation to sense distance, and they also "know" the difference between food/prey and background barriers in some magical way. (ii) A bat roams randomly with a velocity v_i at position x_i with a fixed frequency range $[f_{min}, f_{max}]$, varying its emission rate $r \in [0, 1]$ and loudness A_0 to search for prey, depending on the proximity of their target. (iii) Although the loudness can vary in many ways, we assume that the loudness varies from a large (positive) A_0 to a minimum constant value A_{min}. These rules can be translated into the following formulas:

$$f_i = f_{min} + (f_{max} - f_{min})\varepsilon, \quad v_i^{t+1} = v_i^t + (x_i^t - x^*)f_i, \quad x_i^{t+1} = x_i^t + v_i^t \quad (1.13)$$

where ε is a random number drawn from a uniform distribution and x^* is the current best solution found so far during iterations. The loudness and pulse rate can vary with iteration t in the following way:

$$A_i^{t+1} = \alpha A_i^t, \quad r_i^t = r_i^0[1 - \exp(-\beta t)] \quad (1.14)$$

Here α and β are constants. In fact, α is similar to the cooling factor of a cooling schedule in the simulated annealing, which is discussed later. In the simplest case, we can use $\alpha = \beta$, and we have in fact used $\alpha = \beta = 0.9$ in most simulations.

Bat algorithm has been extended to multiobjective bat algorithm (MOBA) by Yang (2011a), and preliminary results suggested that it is very efficient (Yang and Gandomi, 2012). A few other important applications of bat algorithm can be found in the other chapters of this book.

1.5.4 Particle Swarm Optimization

Particle swarm optimization (PSO) was developed by Kennedy and Eberhart (1995) based on the swarm behavior such as fish and bird schooling in nature. Since then, PSO has generated much wider interests and forms an exciting, ever-expanding research subject called swarm intelligence. This algorithm searches the space of an objective function by adjusting the trajectories of individual agents, called particles, as the piecewise paths formed by positional vectors in a quasi-stochastic manner.

The movement of a swarming particle consists of two major components: a stochastic component and a deterministic component. Each particle is attracted toward the position of the current global best g^* and its own best location x_i^* in history, while at the same time it has a tendency to move randomly. Let x_i and v_i be the position vector and velocity of particle i, respectively. The new velocity vector is determined by the following formula:

$$v_i^{t+1} = v_i^t + \alpha \varepsilon_1[g^* - x_i^t] + \beta \varepsilon_2[x_i^* - x_i^t] \quad (1.15)$$

where ε_1 and ε_2 are two random vectors, and each entry takes the values between 0 and 1. The parameters α and β are the learning parameters or acceleration constants, which can typically be taken as, say, $\alpha \approx \beta \approx 2$.

The initial locations of all particles should be distributed relatively uniformly so that they can sample over most regions, which is especially important for multimodal problems. The initial velocity of a particle can be taken as zero, i.e., $v_i^{t=0} = 0$. The new positions can then be updated by

$$x_i^{t+1} = x_i^t + v_i^{t+1} \tag{1.16}$$

Although v_i can be any value, it is usually bounded in some range $[0, v_{max}]$.

There are many variants that extend the standard PSO algorithm (Kennedy et al., 2001; Yang, 2008, 2010b), and the most noticeable improvement is probably to use inertia function $\theta(t)$ so that v_i^t is replaced by $\theta(t) v_i^t$:

$$v_i^{t+1} = \theta v_i^t + \alpha \varepsilon_1 [g^* - x_i^t] + \beta \varepsilon_2 \odot [x_i^* - x_i^t] \tag{1.17}$$

where θ takes the values between 0 and 1. In the simplest case, the inertia function can be taken as a constant, typically $\theta \approx 0.5 \sim 0.9$. This is equivalent to introducing a virtual mass to stabilize the motion of the particles, and thus the algorithm is expected to converge more quickly. Another efficient variant is called accelerated particle swarm optimization (APSO) that proves efficient in solving business optimization problems (Yang et al., 2011).

1.5.5   Firefly Algorithm

Firefly algorithm (FA) was first developed by Yang in 2007 (Yang, 2008, 2009) which was based on the flashing patterns and behavior of fireflies. In essence, FA uses the following three idealized rules:

1. Fireflies are unisexual so that one firefly will be attracted to other fireflies regardless of their sex.
2. The attractiveness is proportional to the brightness and they both decrease as their distance increases. Thus, for any two flashing fireflies, the less brighter one will move toward the more brighter one. If there is no brighter one than a particular firefly, it will move randomly.
3. The brightness of a firefly is determined by the landscape of the objective function.

The movement of a firefly i is attracted to another, more attractive (brighter) firefly j is determined by

$$x_i^{t+1} = x_i^t + \beta_0 \, e^{-\gamma r_{ij}^2}(x_j^t - x_i^t) + \alpha \varepsilon_i^t \tag{1.18}$$

where β_0 is the attractiveness at the distance $r = 0$, and the second term is due to the attraction. The third term is randomization with α being the randomization parameter, and ε_i^t is a vector of random numbers drawn from a Gaussian distribution or uniform distribution at time t. If $\beta_0 = 0$, it becomes a simple random walk. Furthermore, the randomization ε_i^t can easily be extended to other distributions such as Lévy flights.

The Lévy flight essentially provides a random walk whose random step length is drawn from a Lévy distribution

$$L(s, \lambda) = s^{-(1+\lambda)}, \quad (0 < \lambda \leq 2) \tag{1.19}$$

which has an infinite variance with an infinite mean. Here the steps essentially form a random walk process with a power-law step-length distribution with a heavy tail. Some of the new solutions should be generated by Lévy walk around the best solution obtained so far; this will often speed up the local search (Pavlyukevich, 2007).

A demo version of firefly algorithm implementation, without Lévy flights, can be found at Mathworks file exchange web site.[1] Firefly algorithm has attracted much attention (Apostolopoulos and Vlachos, 2011; Gandomi et al., 2011b; Sayadi et al., 2010). A discrete version of FA can efficiently solve NP-hard scheduling problems (Sayadi et al., 2010), while a detailed analysis has demonstrated the efficiency of FA over a wide range of test problems, including multiobjective load dispatch problems (Apostolopoulos and Vlachos, 2011). A chaos-enhanced firefly algorithm with a basic method for automatic parameter tuning is also developed (Yang, 2011b).

1.5.6 Cuckoo Search

Cuckoo search (CS) is one of the latest nature-inspired metaheuristic algorithms, developed by Yang and Deb (2009). CS is based on the brood parasitism of some cuckoo species. In addition, this algorithm is enhanced by the so-called Lévy flights (Pavlyukevich, 2007) rather than by simple isotropic random walks. Recent studies show that CS is potentially far more efficient than PSO and genetic algorithms (Yang and Deb, 2010).

Cuckoos are fascinating birds, not only because of the beautiful sounds they can make but also because of their aggressive reproduction strategy. Some species such as the *Ani* and *Guira* cuckoos lay their eggs in communal nests, though they may remove others' eggs to increase the hatching probability of their own eggs. Quite a number of species engage the obligate brood parasitism by laying their eggs in the nests of other host birds (often other species). For simplicity in describing the standard Cuckoo Search, we now use the following three idealized rules:

1. Each cuckoo lays one egg at a time and dumps it in a randomly chosen nest.
2. The best nests with high-quality eggs will be carried over to the next generations.
3. The number of available host nests is fixed, and the egg laid by a cuckoo is discovered by the host bird with a probability $p_a \in [0, 1]$. In this case, the host bird can either get rid of the egg or simply abandon the nest and build a completely new nest.

[1]http://www.mathworks.com/matlabcentral/fileexchange/29693-firefly-algorithm.

As a further approximation, this last assumption can be approximated by a fraction p_a of the n host nests which are replaced by new nests (with new random solutions). For a maximization problem, the quality or fitness of a solution can simply be proportional to the value of the objective function. Other forms of fitness can be defined in a similar manner to the fitness function in genetic algorithms.

From the implementation point of view, we can use the following simple representations: each egg in a nest represents a solution, and each cuckoo can lay only one egg (thus representing one solution); the aim is to use the new and potentially better solutions (cuckoos) to replace a not-so-good solution in the nests. Obviously, this algorithm can be extended to a more complicated case where each nest has multiple eggs representing a set of solutions. For this present introduction, we use the simplest approach where each nest has only a single egg. In this case, there is no distinction between egg, nest, or cuckoo, as each nest corresponds to one egg which also represents one cuckoo.

This algorithm uses a balanced combination of a local random walk and the global explorative random walk, controlled by a switching parameter p_a. The local random walk can be written as

$$x_i^{t+1} = x_i^t + \alpha s \otimes H(p_a - \varepsilon) \otimes (x_j^t - x_k^t) \tag{1.20}$$

where x_j^t and x_k^t are two different solutions selected randomly by random permutation, $H(u)$ is a Heaviside function, ε is a random number drawn from a uniform distribution, and s is the step size. On the other hand, the global random walk is carried out by using Lévy flights

$$x_i^{t+1} = x_i^t + \alpha L(s, \lambda) \tag{1.21}$$

where

$$L(s, \lambda) = \frac{\lambda \Gamma(\lambda) \sin(\pi \lambda / 2)}{\pi} \frac{1}{s^{1+\lambda}}, \quad (s \gg s_0 > 0) \tag{1.22}$$

Here $\alpha > 0$ is the step-size-scaling factor, which should be related to the scales of the problem of interests. In most cases, we can use $\alpha = O(L/10)$, where L is the characteristic scale of the problem of interest, while in some cases $\alpha = O(L/100)$ can be more effective and can avoid flying too far. Equation (1.22) is essentially the stochastic equation for a random walk. In general, a random walk is a Markov chain whose next status/location only depends on the current location (the first term in Eq. (1.22)) and the transition probability (the second term). However, a substantial fraction of the new solutions should be generated by far field randomization and whose locations should be far enough from the current best solution. This will make sure that the system does not get trapped in a local optimum (Yang and Deb, 2010).

A Matlab implementation is given by the author and can be downloaded.[2] Cuckoo search is very efficient in solving engineering optimization problems (Gandomi et al., 2013; Yang and Deb, 2009).

1.5.7 Flower Pollination Algorithm

Flower pollination algorithm (FPA) was developed by Yang (2012) inspired by the flow pollination process of flowering plants:

1. Biotic and cross-pollination can be considered as a process of global pollination process, and pollen-carrying pollinators move in a way that obeys Lévy flights (Rule 1).
2. For local pollination, abiotic and self-pollination are used (Rule 2).
3. Pollinators such as insects can develop flower constancy, which is equivalent to a reproduction probability that is proportional to the similarity of two flowers involved (Rule 3).
4. The interaction or switching of local pollination and global pollination can be controlled by a switch probability $p \in [0, 1]$, with a slight bias toward local pollination (Rule 4).

In order to formulate updating formulas, we have to convert the aforementioned rules into updating equations. For example, in the global pollination step, flower pollen gametes are carried by pollinators such as insects, and pollen can travel over a long distance because insects can often fly and move in a much longer range. Therefore, Rule 1 and flower constancy can be represented mathematically as

$$x_i^{t+1} = x_i^t + L(\lambda) (x_i^t - g_*)\qquad(1.23)$$

where x_i^t is the pollen i or solution vector x_i^t at iteration t, and g_* is the current best solution found among all solutions at the current generation/iteration. Here $L(\lambda)$ is the parameter that corresponds to the strength of the pollination, which essentially is also a step size. Since insects may move over a long distance with various distance steps, we can use a Lévy flight to mimic this characteristic efficiently. That is, we draw $L > 0$ from a Lévy distribution as described in Eq. (1.22).

For the local pollination, both Rule 2 and Rule 3 can be represented as

$$x_i^{t+1} = x_i^t + \varepsilon(x_j^t - x_k^t)\qquad(1.24)$$

where x_j^t and x_k^t are pollen from different flowers of the same plant species. This essentially mimics the flower constancy in a limited neighborhood. Mathematically, if x_j^t and x_k^t come from the same species or selected from the same population, this equivalently becomes a local random walk if we draw ε from a uniform distribution in [0,1].

In principle, flower pollination activities can occur at all scales, both local and global. But in reality, adjacent flower patches or flowers in the not-so-far-away neighborhood are more likely to be pollinated by local flower pollen than those far away. In order to mimic this feature, we can effectively use a switch probability (Rule 4) or proximity probability p to switch between common global pollination and intensive local pollination. To start with, we can use a naive value of $p = 0.5$ as an initial value. A preliminary parametric showed that $p = 0.8$ may work better for most applications (Yang, 2012).

1.5.8   Other Algorithms

There are many other metaheuristic algorithms, which may be equally popular and powerful, and these include Tabu search (Glover and Laguna, 1997), artificial immune system (Farmer et al., 1986), and others (Koziel and Yang, 2011; Wolpert and Macready, 1997; Yang, 2010a, b). For example, wolf search algorithm (WSA) was developed recently by Rui et al. (2012) based on the wolf pack predating behavior. Preliminary results show that WSA is a very promising algorithm with convincing performance. Other algorithms such as Krill herd algorithm and artificial plant algorithm are described in detail in some relevant chapters of this book.

The efficiency of metaheuristic algorithms can be attributed to the fact that they try to imitate the best features in nature, especially the selection of the fittest in biological systems, which have evolved by natural selection over millions of years.

1.6   Open Problems and Further Research Topics

We have seen that SI and bio-inspired computing have demonstrated a great success in solving various tough optimization problems, and there are still some challenging issues, some of which have been discussed in Section 1.2. In order to inspire further search in this area, we now summarize some of the key open problems:

Theoretical analysis of algorithm convergence: Up to now, only a small fraction of metaheuristic algorithms has some limited mathematical analyses in terms of convergence. More studies are necessary to gain insight into various new algorithms. It is also highly needed to build a framework for theoretical algorithm analysis.

Classification and terminology: There is still some confusion in terms of classifications and terminologies used in the current literature. Further studies should also try to classify all known algorithms by some agreed criteria and ideally also to unify the use of key terminologies. This requires the effort by all researchers in the wider communities to participate and to dedicate their usage in future publications.

Parameter tuning: The efficiency of an algorithm may depend on its algorithm-dependent parameters, and optimal parameter setting of any algorithm itself is an optimization problem. To find the best methods to tune these parameters are still under active research. It can be expected that algorithms with automatic parameter tuning will be a good paradigm shift in the near future.

Large-scale problems: Most current studies in bio-inspired computing have focused on the toy problems and small-scale problems. For large-scale problems, it still remains untested if the same methodology for solving toy problems can be used to get solutions efficiently. For linear programming, it was basically the case; however, nonlinearity often poses greater challenges.

Truly intelligent algorithms: Researchers have strived to develop better and smarter algorithms for many years, but truly intelligent algorithms are yet to emerge. This could be the holy grail of optimization and computational intelligence.

Obviously, challenges also bring opportunities. There is no exaggeration to say that it is a golden time for bio-inspired computing so that researchers can rethink existing methodologies and approaches more deeply and perhaps differently. It is possible that significant progress can be made in the next 10 years. Any progress in theory and in large-scale practice will provide great insight and may ultimately alter the research landscape in metaheuristics. It is can be expected that some truly intelligent, self-evolving algorithms may appear to solve a wide range of tough optimization and classification problems efficiently in the not-so-far future.

References

Afshar, A., Haddad, O.B., Marino, M.A., Adams, B.J., 2007. Honey-bee mating optimization (HBMO) algorithm for optimal reservoir operation. J. Franklin Inst. 344, 452–462.

Apostolopoulos, T., Vlachos, A., 2011. Application of the firefly algorithm for solving the economic emissions load dispatch problem. Int. J. Comb. 2011. (Article ID 523806. <http://www.hindawi.com/journals/ijct/2011/523806.html>).

Ashby, W.R., 1962. Principles of the self-organizing system. In: Von Foerster, H., Zopf Jr., G.W. (Eds.), Principles of Self-Organization: Transactions of the University of Illinois Symposium, 1962. Pergamon Press, London, UK, pp. 255–278.

Aytug, H., Bhattacharrya, S., Koehler, G.J., 1996. A Markov chain analysis of genetic algorithms with power of 2 cardinality alphabets. Eur. J. Oper. Res. 96, 195–201.

Blum, C., Roli, A., 2003. Metaheuristics in combinatorial optimization: overview and conceptual comparison. ACM Comput. Surv. 35, 268–308.

Clerc, M., Kennedy, J., 2002. The particle swarm—explosion, stability, and convergence in a multidimensional complex space. IEEE Trans. Evol. Comput. 6 (1), 58–73.

Conn, A.R., Gould, N.I.M., Toint, P.L., 2000. Trust-region methods, Society for Industrial and Applied Mathematics (SIAM) Press, Philadelphia.

Dorigo, M., Stütle, T., 2004. Ant Colony Optimization. MIT Press, Cambridge, MA.

Farmer, J.D., Packard, N., Perelson, A., 1986. The immune system, adaptation and machine learning. Physica D 2, 187–204.

Fogel, L.J., Owens, A.J., Walsh, M.J., 1966. Artificial Intelligence Through Simulated Evolution. John Wiley & Sons, New York, NY.

Gandomi, A.H., Yang, X.S., Alavi, A.H., 2011. Mixed variable structural optimization using firefly algorithm. Comput. Struct. 89 (23/24), 2325–2336.

Gandomi, A.H., Yang, X.S., Alavi, A.H., 2013. Cuckoo search algorithm: a metaheuristic approach to solve structural optimization problems. Eng. with Comput. 29 (1), 17–35.

Glover, F., 1986. Future paths for integer programming and links to artificial intelligence. Comput. Oper. Res. 13, 533–549.

Glover, F., Laguna, M., 1997. Tabu Search, Kluwer Academic Publishers, Boston.

Goldberg, D.E., 1989. Genetic Algorithms in Search, Optimization and Machine Learning. Addison Wesley, Reading, MA.

Greenhalgh, D., Marshal, S., 2000. Convergence criteria for genetic algorithms. SIAM J. Comput. 30, 269–282.

Gutjahr, W.J., 2010. Convergence analysis of metaheuristics. Ann. Inf. Syst. 10, 159–187.

Holland, J., 1975. Adaptation in Natural and Artificial Systems. University of Michigan Press, Ann Arbor, MI.

Hopper, E., Turton, B.C.H., 2000. An empirical investigation of meta-heuristic and heuristic algorithm for a 2D packing problem. Eur. J. Oper. Res. 128 (1), 34–57.

Karaboga, D., 2005. An Idea Based on Honey Bee Swarm for Numerical Optimization, Technical Report TR06. Erciyes University, Turkey.

Keller, E.F., 2009. Organisms, machines, and thunderstorms: a history of self-organization, part two. Complexity, emergence, and stable attractors. Hist. Stud. Nat. Sci. 39, 1–31.

Kennedy, J., Eberhart, R.C., 1995. Particle swarm optimisation. In: Proceedings of the IEEE International Conference on Neural Networks. Piscataway, NJ, pp. 1942–1948.

Kennedy, J., Eberhart, R.C., Shi, Y., 2001. Swarm Intelligence, Morgan Kaufmann Publishers, San Diego, USA.

Koziel, S., Yang, X.S., 2011. Computational Optimization, Methods and Algorithms. Springer, Germany.

Nakrani, S., Tovey, C., 2004. On honey bees and dynamic server allocation in internet hosting centers. Adapt. Behav. 12 (3–4), 223–240.

Parpinelli, R.S., Lopes, H.S., 2011. New inspirations in swarm intelligence: a survey. Int. J. Bio-Inspired Comput. 3, 1–16.

Pavlyukevich, I., 2007. Lévy flights, non-local search and simulated annealing. J. Comput. Phys. 226, 1830–1844.

Pham, D.T., Ghanbarzadeh, A., Koc, E., Otri, S., Rahim, S., Zaidi, M., 2006. The bees algorithm: a novel tool for complex optimisation problems. In: Proceedings of the IPROMS 2006 Conference, pp. 454–461.

Prigogine, I., Nicolois, G., 1967. On symmetry-breaking instabilities in dissipative systems. J. Chem. Phys. 46, 3542–3550.

Rui, T., Fong, S., Yang, X.S., Deb, S., 2012. Wolf search algorithm with ephemeral memory. In: Fong, S., Pichappan, P., Mohammed, S., Hung, P., Asghar, S. (Eds.), Proceedings of the Seventh International Conference on Digital Information Management (ICDIM2012), (August 22–24), Macau, pp. 165–172.

Sayadi, M.K., Ramezanian, R., Ghaffari-Nasab, N., 2010. A discrete firefly meta-heuristic with local search for makespan minimization in permutation flow shop scheduling problems. Int. J. Ind. Eng. Comput. 1, 1–10.

Talbi, E.G., 2009. Metaheuristics: From Design to Implementation. John Wiley & Sons, New Jersey.

Villalobos-Arias, M., Coello Coello, C.A., Hernández-Lerma, O., 2005. Asymptotic convergence of metaheuristics for multiobjective optimization problems. Soft Comput. 10, 1001–1005.

Wolpert, D.H., Macready, W.G., 1997. No free lunch theorems for optimization. IEEE Trans. Evol. Comput. 1, 67–82.

Yang, X.S., 2005. Engineering optimization via nature-inspired virtual bee algorithms, Artificial Intelligence and Knowledge Engineering Applications: A Bioinspired Approach, Springer, Berlin/Heidelberg, (Lecture Notes in Computer Science, vol. 3562, pp. 317–323).

Yang, X.S., 2008. Nature-Inspired Metaheuristic Algorithms, first ed. Luniver Press, UK.

Yang, X.S., 2009. Firefly algorithms for multimodal optimisation. In: Watanabe, O., Zeugmann, T. (Eds.), Fifth Symposium on Stochastic Algorithms, Foundation and Applications (SAGA 2009), LNCS, vol. 5792, pp. 169–178.

Yang, X.S., 2010a. Nature-Inspired Metaheuristic Algorithms. second ed. Luniver Press, UK.

Yang, X.S., 2010b. Engineering Optimization: An Introduction with Metaheuristic Applications. John Wiley & Sons, New Jersey.

Yang, X.S., 2010c. A new metaheuristic bat-inspired algorithm. In: Cruz, C., Gonzalez, J.R., Pelta, D.A., Terrazas, G., (Eds.), Nature-Inspired Cooperative Strategies for Optimization (NICSO 2010), vol. 284. Springer, SCI, Berlin, pp. 65−74.

Yang, X.S., 2011a. Bat algorithm for multi-objective optimisation. Int. J. Bio-Inspired Comput. 3 (5), 267−274.

Yang, X.S., 2011b. Chaos-enhanced firefly algorithm with automatic parameter tuning. Int. J. Swarm Intell. Res. 2 (4), 1−11.

Yang, X.S., 2011c. Metaheuristic optimization: algorithm analysis and open problems. In: Pardalos, P.M., Rebennack, S. (Eds.), Proceedings of the Tenth International Symposium on Experimental Algorithms (SEA 2011). 5−7 May 2011, Kolimpari, Chania, Greece, Lecture Notes in Computer Sciences, vol. 6630, pp. 21−32.

Yang, X.S., 2012. Flower pollination algorithm for global optimisation. In: Durand-Lose, J., Jonoska, N. (Eds.), Proceedings of the 11th International Conference on Unconventional Computation and Natural Computation (UCNC 2012). 3−7 September 2012, Orléan, France. Springer, Lecture Notes in Computer Science, vol. 7445, pp. 240−249.

Yang, X.S., Deb, S., 2009. Cuckoo search via Lévy flights. Proceedings of the World Congress on Nature & Biologically Inspired Computing (NaBic 2009). IEEE Publications, USA, pp. 210−214.

Yang, X.S., Deb, S., 2010. Engineering optimization by cuckoo search. Int. J. Math. Model. Num. Opt. 1 (4), 330−343.

Yang, X.S., Gandomi, A.H., 2012. Bat algorithm: a novel approach for global engineering optimization. Eng. Comput. 29 (5), 1−18.

Yang, X.S., He, X.S., 2013. Firefly algorithm: recent advances and applications. Int. J. Swarm Intell. 1 (1), 1−14.

Yang, X.S., Koziel, S., 2011. Computational Optimization and Applications in Engineering and Industry. Springer, Germany.

Yang, X.S., Deb, S., Fong, S., 2011. Accelerated particle swarm optimization and support vector machine for business optimization and applications. In: Fong, S., Pichappan, P., (Eds.), Proceedings of the NDT2011, July 2011, Communications in Computer and Information Science, vol. 136, Springer, Heidelberg, pp. 53−66.

2 Analysis of Swarm Intelligence—Based Algorithms for Constrained Optimization

M.P. Saka[1], E. Doğan[2] and Ibrahim Aydogdu[3]

[1]Department of Civil Engineering, University of Bahrain, Isa Town, Bahrain;
[2]Civil Engineering Department, Celal Bayar University, Manisa, Turkey;
[3]Civil Engineering Department, Akdeniz University, Antalya, Turkey

2.1 Introduction

The advancement that took place in stochastic optimization techniques in recent years is beyond anyone's imagination. Stochastic optimization methods are those that generate and use random variables as oppose to mathematical optimization. Several new stochastic optimization techniques are emerged and they are widely applied in obtaining the solution of engineering design optimization problems. These techniques differ from the mathematical programming techniques in the fact that they do not employ gradient descent or quasi-Newton techniques but heuristic search. Heuristic or metaheuristic search algorithm is a trial—error type procedure for solving decision-making problems, which employs a rule of thumb with the expectation of reaching the optimum solution, though there is no guarantee for it. There is always a mix-up between terms heuristics and metaheuristics. A heuristic exploits problem dependent information to find a sufficiently good solution to a specific problem, while metaheuristic is a general-purpose algorithm that can be applied to almost any type of optimization problem. In reality metaheuristic is also heuristic, but a more powerful one that can be viewed as upper-level general method with a guiding strategy in designing underlying heuristic. The rule of thumb selected for exploration of the optimum solution by metaheuristic algorithms may be borrowed from nature, biology, physics, or even social culture (Dreo et al., 2006; Luke, 2010; Yang, 2008, 2011).

Some of the recent metaheuristic techniques are based on swarm intelligence. A swarm is a large number of homogenous, unsophisticated agents that interact locally among themselves and their environment, without any central control or

Swarm Intelligence and Bio-Inspired Computation. DOI: http://dx.doi.org/10.1016/B978-0-12-405163-8.00002-8

management to yield a global behavior to emerge. Biologists are amazed with, for example, what an ant or bee colony achieves. Although single ant or a bee is not a smart individual, their colonies are smart. When it comes to deciding what to do next, most ants or bees do not have any clue. However, as a swarm, they can find the shortest route to the best food source, allocate workers to different tasks, and defend a territory from invaders without having someone in control or as manager. As an individual they are tiny dummies, but they respond quickly and effectively to their environment as colonies. This is what is called swarm intelligence (Kennedy et al., 2001). It is the collective behavior of decentralized and self-organized natural or artificial systems. Metaheuristic optimization techniques based on swarm intelligence are made-up population of simple agents interacting with one another and with their environment as is the case in ant colonies, birds flocking, animal herding, and fish schooling. These techniques imitate the behavior of these colonies in a numerical optimization procedure. They employ what, for example, an ant colony uses to find the shortest route between their nest and food source as a guiding mechanism in order to search design domain to find the optimum solution of an optimization problem. They also utilize some additional strategies, to avoid getting trapped in confined areas of search domain. Latest applications have shown that they are robust, effective, and quite powerful in obtaining near optimum solutions if not optimum in engineering design optimization problems (De Castro and Von Zuben, 2005; Saka, 2012; Yang, 2011).

This chapter intends to review swarm intelligence—based algorithms, summarize their steps, and compare their performance on benchmark optimization problems. The algorithms covered in this chapter are ant colony algorithm, particle swarm optimizer (PSO), artificial bee colony (ABC) algorithm, glowworm swarm algorithm (GSA), firefly algorithm (FFA), cuckoo search algorithm (CSA), bat algorithm (BA), and hunting search (HS) algorithm. Ant colony algorithm is inspired from the way that ant colonies find the shortest route between the food source and their nest (Dorigo et al., 1991). PSO mimics the social behavior of birds flocking (Kennedy and Eberhart, 1995). ABC algorithm imitates the foraging behavior of honeybee colony (Karaboga, 2005). Glowworm swarm optimization algorithm is based on the behavior of glowworms. The behavior pattern of glowworms is the apparent capability of changing the intensity of the luciferin emission and appearing to glow at different intensities (Krishnanand and Ghose, 2005). FFA is similar to glowworm search method and it mimics the idealized behavior of flashing characteristics of fireflies. These insects communicate, search for pray, and find mates using bioluminescence with varying flaying patterns (Gandomi et al., 2011; Yang, 2009). CSA simulates reproduction strategy of cuckoo birds (Yang and Deb, 2010). BA is based on the echolocation behavior of bats with varying pulse rates of emission and loudness (Yang, 2010). HS algorithm is inspired by group hunting of wolves where the wolves hunt in a group. They encircle the prey and gradually tighten the ring of siege until they catch the prey (Oftadeh et al., 2011).

2.2 Optimization Problems

Optimization problems are those in which a set of unknowns $\{x\} = \{x_1 x_2 \cdots x_n\}$ is required to be determined such that an objective function $f(x_i)$, $i = 1, 2, \ldots, n$ is minimized and number of constraint functions is satisfied. These problems have the following mathematical form:

$$\text{Minimize} \quad Z = f(x) \tag{2.1}$$

$$\text{Subject to} \quad h_j(x) = 0, \quad j = 1, \ldots, ne \tag{2.2}$$

$$h_j(x) \leq 0, \quad j = ne + 1, \ldots, m \tag{2.3}$$

$$x_i^\ell \leq x_i \leq x_i^u \tag{2.4}$$

where $x = \{x_1, x_2, \ldots, x_n\}$ is the vector of decision variables in which x_i represents a decision variable (unknown parameter) i which is a quantity that the decision maker controls. n is the total number of decision variables. Decision variables may have continuous or discrete values. The goal of the optimization process is to find the values of decision variables that result in a maximum or minimum of a function called objective function. $f(x_i)$ in Eq. (2.1) represents the objective function which is used as a measure of effectiveness of a decision. The equalities and inequalities in Eqs. (2.2) and (2.3) are called equality and inequality constraints, respectively, which represent the limitations imposed on the decision-making problem that are required to be satisfied. Continuous decision variables have a range of variations shown in Eq. (2.4) and can take any value within that range. Some of the optimization problems do not have any constraints and they only require minimizing or maximizing the objective function. However, most of the optimization problems in practice do have constraints. Swarm intelligence–based algorithms can only handle unconstrained optimization problems. Hence, it becomes necessary to transform the optimization problem with constraints into the one which is unconstrained. This is achieved by either using a penalty function or utilizing fly-back mechanism.

There is several penalty functions method. Very comprehensive review of these techniques is covered by Coello (2002). One of the commonly used penalty function is given in Eq. (2.5):

$$W = Z \left[1 + r \left(\sum_{k=1}^{m} h_k(x_i) \right) \right]^\beta \tag{2.5}$$

where W is the unconstrained objective function, r and β are penalty coefficients that are used to adjust the intensity of penalization. Dynamic and adaptive implementation of penalty coefficients yields more efficient search process (Hasançebi, 2008).

The other way is not to use penalty function to transfer constrained optimization problem into unconstrained one, instead not to allow solution vectors to go out of feasible region. If during the solution process, randomly generated solution vectors flies out of feasible region defined by the problem constraints; this solution vector is forced back to its previous position in the feasible region. By this way, it is guaranteed that solution vectors always remain in the feasible region during iterations which means they satisfy the constraints. This mechanism is enhanced by adaptive error strategy suggested by Doğan and Saka (2012)). In this strategy, optimization problem constraints are evaluated for each solution vector. Those solution vectors that are slightly infeasible are not discarded but kept in the population. They are utilized in the generation of new swarm in the next iteration with the hope of giving feasible solution vectors. In this strategy, initially larger error values are utilized and this value is gradually reduced with each iteration until it reaches to 0.001 or to whatever acceptable error value.

2.3 Swarm Intelligence−Based Optimization Algorithms

Swarm intelligence−based metaheuristic algorithms imitate the social behavior of insect colonies. Commonly accepted definition of swarm intelligence is that it is the property of a system whereby the collective behaviors of unsophisticated agents interacting locally with their environment cause coherent functional global pattern to emerge. These unsophisticated agents communicate with one another directly through physical or visual contact and also indirectly by modifying their surroundings. Unlike in a centralized system where agents receive direct orders on which task to perform, agents in a self-organized system perform tasks based on their situation or surrounding (Herheim, 2005). Swarm intelligence's problem-solving techniques present several advantages over more traditional ones. They are simple, robust, and provide a solution without centralized control or the provision of a global model. Among these algorithms, two successful swarm intelligence methods are the ant colony and particle swarm optimization techniques. These are widely applied to problems ranging from determination of minimal paths in traveling salesman problem to network traffic rerouting in busy telecommunication systems (Del Acebo and De la Rosa, 2008). Swarm intelligence−based algorithms are population-based algorithms where the population consists of unsophisticated agents. Each agent represents potential solution to optimization problem under consideration. During the solution cycles, they change their position and move within the domain with the expectation of improving the solution.

2.3.1 Ant Colony Optimization

Ant colony optimization (ACO) technique is inspired from the way how the ant colonies find the shortest route between the food source and their nest. The biologists studied extensively for a long time how ants manage collectively to solve difficult problems in a natural way that are too complex for a single individual ant. Ants being completely blind, individuals can successfully discover as a colony the shortest path between their nest and the food source. They manage this through their typical characteristic of employing volatile substance called pheromones. They perceive these substances through very sensitive receivers located in their antennas. The ants deposit pheromones on the ground when they travel which is used as a trail by other ants in the colony. When there is choice of selection for an ant between two paths, it selects the one where the concentration of pheromone is more. Since the shorter trail will be reinforced more than the longer one after a while, a great majority of ants in the colony will travel on this route. ACO algorithm is developed by Dorigo et al. (1991), Dorigo (1992), and Dorigo and Stützle (2004) and is used in the solution of traveling salesman. The steps of ACO are as follows:

1. Select the number of ants each of which represents a potential solution to the optimization problem. Define a pool for each decision variable in the optimization problem which consists of possible values that particular variable can take. Assign randomly each ant to each decision variable. Calculate initial pheromone amount (τ_0) as $\tau_0 = 1/Z_{min}$, where Z_{min} is the minimum value of the objective function without penalty violation. The pheromone and visibility values for each decision variable are calculated and defined as given below:

$$\tau_{ij} = \frac{1}{\tau_0}, \quad v_{ij} = \frac{1}{x_{ij}}, \quad i = 1, 2, \ldots, nv \quad j = 1, 2, \ldots, npool \tag{2.6}$$

where x_{ij} is jth value of the design variable i, nv is the total number of design variables in the optimization problem, and $npool$ is the total number of values in the pool from which a value can be selected for decision variable i.

2. Each ant in the colony selects its first design variables. Ants then select values for their decision variables from the value pool. This selection is carried out by a decision process that depends on probability computation given below:

$$P_{ij}(t) = \frac{(\tau_{ij}(t))^{\alpha} \cdot (v_{ij})^{\beta}}{\sum_{j \in allowed}^{ndiv} (\tau_{ij}(t))^{\alpha} \cdot (v_{ij})^{\beta}} \quad i = 1, 2, \ldots, nv \quad j = 1, 2, \ldots, npool \tag{2.7}$$

where $P_{ij}(t)$ is the probability of jth value selected from the pool for decision variable i which is assigned to ant at time t. α and β are parameters which are used to arrange to influence of local trail values and visibility, respectively. This process continues until all ants assign values for their first design variables.

3. Apply local update rule at the end of the each tour. Concentration of pheromone for values selected by ants from the pool is lowered in order to promote exploration in the search. This corresponds to the evaporation of the pheromone substance in the real life. The mathematical expression for this is $\tau_{ij}(t) = \zeta \cdot \tau_{ij}(t)$, where ζ is called local update coefficient whose value changes from 0 to 1. If the value of this parameter is selected close to 1, fast convergence occurs and the algorithm may end up with a local optimum. On the other hand, if the value is chosen close to 0 convergence difficulties arise in the problem.

4. Start assigning a value from the pool for the next decision variable. Continue this assigning procedure until all the ants in the colony has a value for each decision variable.

At the end of the tour, apply local update rule. This procedure continues until all ants assign values for all decision variables. At the end of this process, each ant has a selected value for each decision variable, and all together each ant represents a candidate solution for the optimization problem. If any of the candidate solution does not satisfy constraints, this candidate solution is penalized using the expression $Z_p = Z(1+C)^\varepsilon$, where Z_p is the penalized objective function value of the candidate solution, C is the total constraint violations, and ε is the penalty coefficient.

5. Apply global update scheme using Eq. (2.8):

$$\tau_{ij}(t + n) = \rho \cdot \tau_{ij}(t) + \Delta\tau_{ij}(t) \tag{2.8}$$

where ρ is constant selected between 0 and 1. $(1 - \rho)$ represents the evaporation amount of pheromone between time t and $t + n$ (the amount of time required to complete a cycle). $\Delta\tau_{ij}$ is the change in pheromone amount on the path connecting decision variable i to decision variable j. Value of $\Delta\tau_{ij}$ is represented by the following formula:

$$\Delta\tau_{ij} = \sum_{k=1}^{m} \Delta\tau_{ij}^k \tag{2.9}$$

where k represents any ant from 1 to m (where m is the number of ants) and $\Delta\tau_{ij}^k$ is the change in the pheromone for ant k. Calculation of $\Delta\tau_{ij}^k$ term is described as follows:

$$\Delta\tau_{ij}^k = \frac{1}{Z_k} \tag{2.10}$$

where Z_k is the penalized objective function value for ant k. This is the end of one ant colony algorithm cycle. To start another cycle, all ants are returned to their initial decision variables and above steps are replicated again.

6. Repeat steps 2−5 until the termination criterion is satisfied which is generally taken as the maximum number of iterations.

2.3.2 Particle Swarm Optimizer

The PSO is based on the social behavior of animals such as fish schooling, insect swarming, and birds flocking (Kennedy and Eberhart, 1995). The method considers an artificial swarm which consists of particles (agents). The behavior of each agent in the swarm is simulated according to three rules. The first is *separation* where each agent tries to move away from its neighbors if they are too close. The second is *alignment* where each agent steers toward the average heading of its neighbors. The third is *cohesion* where each agent tries to go toward the average position of its neighbors (Reynolds, 1987). This simulation is extended to have roost by Kennedy et al. (2001). They have amended the above three rules as: each agent is attracted toward the location of the roost; each agent remembers where it was closer to the roost; and each agent shared information with all other agents about its closest location to the roost.

The PSO selects a number of particles to represent a swarm. Each particle in the swarm is a potential solution to the optimization problem under consideration.

A particle explores the search domain by moving around. This move is decided by making use of its own experience and the collective experience of the swarm. Each particle has three main parameters: position, velocity, and fitness. Position represents the decision variables of the optimization problem, velocity determines the rate of change of the position, and fitness is the value of the objective function at the particle's current position. The fitness value is a measure of how good is the solution it represents for the optimization problem. The algorithm starts solving an optimization problem by first initializing each particle. In the initiation phase, each particle is given a random initial position and an initial velocity. The position of a particle represents a solution to the problem and has therefore a value given by the objective function. While moving in the search space, particles memorize the position of the best solution they found. At each iteration of the algorithm, each particle moves with a velocity that is a weighted sum of three components: the old velocity, a velocity component that drives the particle toward the location in the search space where it previously found the best solution so far, and a velocity component that drives the particle toward the location in the search space where the neighbor particles found the best solution so far. There are several variants of particle swarm algorithm. The steps of the algorithm are outlined in the following:

1. Initialize swarm of particles with positions x_0^i and initial velocities v_0^i are randomly distributed throughout the design space. These are obtained from the following expressions:

$$x_0^i = x_{min} + r(x_{max} - x_{min}) \tag{2.11}$$

$$v_0^i = [(x_{min} + r(x_{max} - x_{min}))/\Delta t] \tag{2.12}$$

where the term r represents a random number between 0 and 1, x_{min} and x_{max} represent the design variables of upper and lower bounds, respectively.
2. Evaluate the objective function values $f(x_k^i)$ using the design space positions x_k^i.
3. Update the optimum particle position p_k^i at the current iteration k and the global optimum particle position p_k^g.
4. Update the position of each particle from $x_{k+1}^i = x_k^i + v_{k+1}^i \Delta t$, where x_{k+1}^i is the position of particle i at iteration $k+1$, v_{k+1}^i is the corresponding velocity vector, and Δt is the time-step value.
5. Update the velocity vector of each particle. There are several formulas for this depending on the particular PSO under consideration:

$$v_{k+1}^i = wv_k^i + c_1 r_1 \frac{(p_k^i - x_k^i)}{\Delta t} + c_2 r_2 \frac{(p_k^g - x_k^i)}{\Delta t} \tag{2.13}$$

where r_1 and r_2 are random numbers between 0 and 1, p_k^i is the best position found by particle i so far, and p_k^g is the best position in the swarm at time k. w is the inertia of the particle which controls the exploration properties of the algorithm. c_1 and c_2 are trust parameters that indicate how much confidence the particle has in itself and in the swarm, respectively. Usually they are taken as 2.
6. Repeat steps 2−5 until stopping criteria is met.

In order to control the change of particles' velocities, upper and lower bounds for the velocity change is also limited to a user-specified value of v_{max}. Once the new position of a particle is calculated, using Eq. (2.11), the particle then flies toward it. The main parameters used in the PSO are the population size (number of particles), number of generation cycles, and the maximal change of a particle velocity of v_{max}. One of the latest surveys on the performance comparison of different versions of PSO is given by Liu et al. (2011). A comprehensive review and critical analysis of the existing algorithms in the field of multimodal function optimization is carried out in this study. Furthermore, most of the existing multimodal particle swarm optimization techniques are described and their performances in obtaining the optimum solution of multimodal functions are compared. Their advantages and disadvantages are indicated.

2.3.3 ABC Algorithm

The ABC algorithm mimics the intelligent foraging behavior of a honeybee colony (Karaboga, 2005). In an artificial honeybee algorithm, there are three types of bees which carry out different tasks. The first group of bees are the *employed bees* that locate food source, evaluate its amount of nectar, and keep the location of better sources in their memory. These bees when fly back to hive they share this information to other bees in the dancing area by dancing. The dancing time represents the amount of nectar in the food source. The second group are the *onlooker bees* who observe the dance and may decide to fly to the food source if they find it is worthwhile to visit the food source. Therefore, food sources reach in the amount of nectar attract more onlooker bees. The third group are *scout bees* that explore new food sources in the vicinity of the hive randomly. The employed bee whose food source has been abandoned by the bees becomes a scout bee. Overall, scout bees carry out the exploration, employed and onlooker bees perform the task of exploitation. Each food source is considered as a possible solution for the optimization problem and the nectar amount of a food source represents the quality of the solution which is identified by its fitness value. The ABC algorithm consists of four stages. These stages are initialization phase, employed bees phase, onlooker bees phase, and scout bees phase (Karaboga, 2010).

1. *Initialization phase*: Initialize all the vectors of the population of food sources, x_p, $p = 1, \ldots, np$ by using Eq. (2.11), where np is the population size (total number of artificial bees). Each food source is a solution vector consisting of n variables (x_{pi}, $i = 1, \ldots, n$) and it is a potential solution to the optimization problem under consideration.

$$x_{pi} = x_{li} + rand(0, 1)(x_{ui} - x_{li}) \tag{2.14}$$

where x_{li} and x_{ui} are lower and upper bound on x_i, respectively.

2. *Employed bees phase:* Employed bees search new food sources by using Eq. (2.12):

$$v_{pi} = x_{pi} + \varphi_{pi}(x_{pi} - x_{ki}) \tag{2.15}$$

where $k \neq i$ is a randomly selected food source, φ_{pi} is a random number in range $[-1,1]$. After producing the new food source, its fitness is calculated. If its fitness is better than x_{pi}, the new food source replaces the previous one. The fitness value of the food sources is calculated according to Eq. (2.13):

$$\text{fitness } (x_p) = \begin{cases} \dfrac{1}{1+f(x_p)} & \text{if } f(x_p) \geq 0 \\ 1 + \text{abs}(f(x_p)) & \text{if } f(x_p) < 0 \end{cases} \tag{2.16}$$

3. *Onlooker bees phase*: Unemployed bees consist of two groups. These are onlooker bees and scouts. Employed bees share their food source information with onlooker bees. Onlooker bees choose their food source depending on the probability value P_p which is calculated using the fitness values of each food source in the population as shown in Eq. (2.17):

$$P_p = \frac{\text{fitness}(x_p)}{\sum\limits_{p=1}^{np} \text{fitness}(x_p)} \tag{2.17}$$

After a food source x_{pi} for an onlooker bee is probabilistically chosen, a neighborhood source is determined by using Eq. (2.16) and its fitness value is computed using Eq. (2.17).

4. *Scout bees phase*: The unemloyed bees who choose their food sources randomly are called scouts. Employed bees whose solutions cannot be improved after predetermined number of trials become scouts and their solutions are abondoned. These scouts start to search for new solutions.

5. Phases 2—4 are repeated until termination criteria is satisfied.

A comprehensive survey of the advances with ABC algorithm and its applications is given by Karaboga et al. (2012).

2.3.4 Glowworm Swarm Algorithm

Glowworm swarm optimization algorithm is a swarm intelligence—based algorithm for optimizing multimodal functions which is developed by simulating the behavior of glowworms (Krishnanand and Ghose, 2005, 2009a,b). Glowworms have the capability to change the intensity of the luciferin emission which makes them to glow at different intensities. They interact with each other by glowing. The luciferin-induced glow of a glowworm attracts mates or preys. If a glowworm emits more luciferin, it will glow more brightly and it attracts more of the other glowworms or preys. The brighter the glow, the more is the attraction. The artificial GSA is based on this behavior of glowworms. In the artificial glowworm swarm optimizer, initially n number of glowworms (agents) $(i = 1, \ldots, m)$ is randomly selected to establish an artificial swarm. Each agent represents potential solution to the optimization problem $\{x\} = \{x_1 x_2 \cdots x_n\}$. Each agent in the swarm uses the search domain to select its neighbors and decides its direction of movement by the strength of the signal picked up from them. A glowworm i is attracted to another glowworm j in its neighborhood if the luciferin level of j is higher than that of i. Each glowworm i has the objective function value of $J(x_i(t))$ at its current location $x_i(t)$ into a luciferin value ℓ_i. Each glowworm i regards only those incoming luciferin data by its neighbors; the set of neighbors $N_i(t)$ of glowworm i consist of those glowworms that have a relatively higher luciferin value and that they are located within a dynamic search domain whose range r_d^i is bounded above by a circular range $r_s(0 < r_d^i < r_s)$. Each glowworm i selects a neighbor j with a probability $p_{ij}(t)$ and moves toward it. These movements, that are based only on local information, enable the glowworms to partition into disjoint subgroups, exhibit a simultaneous taxis behavior toward and eventually colocate at the multiple optima of the given objective function.

The steps of the artificial glowworm swarm optimization algorithm are as follows (Krishnanand and Ghose, 2009a,b):

1. Initialize the parameters. It is suggested by Krishnanand and Ghose (2009a,b) to use the following values of algorithmic parameters. $\rho = 0.4$, $\gamma = 0.6$, $\beta = 0.08$, $n_t = 5$, $s = 0.03$, and $\ell_0 = 5$.
2. Distribute swarm of m glowworms randomly in the search space of the optimization problem.
3. Update luciferin of each glowworm i:

$$\ell_i(t) = (1 - \rho)\ell_i(t - 1) + \gamma J(x_i(t)) \qquad (2.18)$$

4. Select the number of glowworms in the neighborhood that has a luciferin value higher than its own within a variable neighborhood range $r_d^i(t)$ $(0 < r_d^i < r_s)$ to obtain the set $N_i(t)$:

$$N_i(t) = \{j: ||x_j(t) - x_i(t)|| < r_d^i(t); \ \ell_i(t) < \ell_j(t)\} \qquad (2.19)$$

   where $||x||$ is the Euclidian norm of x.
5. For each glowworm j in $N_i(t)$, calculate the probability $p_{ij}(t)$:

$$p_{ij}(t) = \frac{\ell_j(t) - \ell_i(t)}{\sum_{k \in N_i(t)} \ell_k(t) - \ell_i(t)} \qquad (2.20)$$

6. Select glowworm j from the neighborhood for glowworm i with the probability $p_{ij}(t)$ and move glowworm i to glowworm j using Eq. (2.21):

$$x_i(t + 1) = x_i(t) + st * \left\{ \frac{x_j(t) - x_i(t)}{||x_j(t) - x_i(t)||} \right\} \qquad (2.21)$$

7. Update the neighborhood range using Eq. (2.19):

$$r_d^i(t + 1) = \min\{r_s, \ \max\{0, \ r_d^i(t) + \beta(n_t - |N_i(t)|)\}\} \qquad (2.22)$$

8. Repeat steps 3−7 until a termination criterion is satisfied.

2.3.5 Firefly Algorithm

The FFA is based on the idealized behavior of flashing characteristics of fireflies (Gandomi et al., 2011; Yang, 2009). These insects communicate, search for pray, and find mates using bioluminescence with varying flaying patterns. The FFA is based on three rules. These are:

1. All fireflies are unisex so they attract one another.
2. Attractiveness is proportional to firefly brightness. For any couple of flashing fireflies, the less bright one will move toward the brighter one. Attractiveness is proportional to the brightness and they both decrease as their distance increases. If there is no brighter one than a particular firefly, it will move randomly.
3. The brightness of a firefly is affected or determined by the landscape of the objective function.

Mathematical interpretation of the above rules is given in the following as explained by Yang (2009).

Attractiveness: In the FFA, attractiveness of a firefly is assumed to be determined by its brightness which is related with the objective function. The brightness i of a firefly at a particular location x can be chosen as $I(x) \propto f(x)$, where $f(x)$ is the objective function. However, if the attractiveness β is relative, it should be judged by the other fireflies. Thus, it will vary with the distance r_{ij} between firefly i and firefly j. In the FFA, the attractiveness function is taken to be proportional to the light intensity by adjacent fireflies and it is defined as

$$\beta(r) = \beta_0 \, e^{-\gamma r^m}, \quad (m \geq 1) \tag{2.23}$$

where β_0 is the attractiveness at $r = 0$.

Distance: The distance between any two fireflies i and j at x_i and x_j is calculated as

$$r_{ij} = \|x_i - x_j\| = \sqrt{\sum_{k=1}^{d} (x_{i,k} - x_{j,k})^2} \tag{2.24}$$

where $x_{i,k}$ is the kth component of the spatial coordinate x_i of the ith firefly.

Movement: The movement of a firefly i which is attracted to another more brighter firefly j is determined by

$$x_i = x_i + \beta_0 \, e^{-\gamma r_{ij}^2}(x_j - x_i) + \alpha\left(\text{rand} - \frac{1}{2}\right) \tag{2.25}$$

where the second term is due to the attraction and the third term is randomization with α being the randomization parameter. "rand" is a random number generator uniformly distributed in [0,1].

The values of parameters in the above equations are generally taken as $\beta_0 = 1$ and $\alpha \in [0, 1]$. Randomization term can be extended to a normal distribution $N(0,1)$ or other distributions. γ characterizes the variation of the attractiveness, and its value determines the speed of convergence and performance of the FFA. In most applications, its value is taken between 0 and 100.

The steps of the FFA are given below (Yang, 2010):

1. Generate initial population of n fireflies $\{x_i\}$, $(i = 1, 2, \ldots, n)$ randomly each of which represents a candidate solution to the optimization problem with objective function of $f(x)$ and decision variables $\{x\} = \{x_1, x_2, \ldots, x_m\}^T$.
2. Compute light intensity using Eq. (2.23) for each firefly $\{\beta\} = \{\beta_1, \beta_2, \ldots, \beta_n\}^T$. The distance between fireflies is computed from Eq. (2.24).
3. Move each firefly i toward other brighter fireflies using Eq. (2.25). If there is other brighter firefly move it randomly.
4. Evaluate new solutions and update light intensity.
5. Rank the fireflies and find the current best solution.
6. Repeat steps 2–5 until termination criterion is satisfied.

2.3.6 Cuckoo Search Algorithm

CSA is originated by Yang and Deb (2010) which simulates reproduction strategy of cuckoo birds. Some species of cuckoo birds lay their eggs in the nests of other birds so that when the eggs are hatched their chicks are fed by the other birds. Sometimes they even remove existing eggs of host nest in order to give more probability of hatching of their own eggs. Some species of cuckoo birds are even specialized to mimic the pattern and color of the eggs of host birds so that host bird could not recognize their eggs which give more possibility of hatching. In spite of all these efforts to conceal their eggs from the attention of host birds, there is a possibility that host bird may discover that the eggs are not its own. In such cases, the host bird either throws these alien eggs away or simply abandons its nest and builds a new nest somewhere else. In CSA, cuckoo egg represents a potential solution to the design problem which has a fitness value. The algorithm uses three idealized rules as given by Yang and Deb (2010). These are: (a) Each cuckoo lays one egg at a time and dumps it in a randomly selected nest. (b) The best nest with high quality eggs will be carried over to the next generation. (c) The number of available host nests is fixed and a host bird can discover an alien egg with a probability of $p_a \in [0, 1]$. In this case, the host bird can either throw the egg away or abandon the nest to build a completely new nest in a new location.

CSA initially requires selection of a population of n eggs each of which represents a potential solution to the design problem under consideration. This means that it is necessary to generate n solution vector of $\{x\} = \{x_1, x_2, \ldots, x_m\}^T$ in a design problem with m decision variables. For each potential solution vector, the value of objective function $f(x)$ is also calculated. The algorithm then generates a new solution $x_i^{\nu+1} = x_i^{\nu} + \beta\lambda$ for cuckoo i, where $x_i^{\nu+1}$ and x_i^{ν} are the previous and new solution vectors. $\beta > 1$ is the step size which is selected according to the design problem under consideration. λ is the length of step size which is determined according to random walk with Levy flights. A random walk is a stochastic process in which particles or waves travel along random trajectories consists of taking successive random steps. The search path of a foraging animal can be modeled as random walk. A Levy flight is a random walk in which the steps are defined in terms of the step lengths which have a certain probability distribution, with the directions of the steps being isotropic and random. Hence Levy flights necessitate selection of a random direction and generation of steps under chosen Levy distribution.

Mantegna (1994) algorithm is one of the fast and accurate algorithm which generates a stochastic variable whose probability density is close to Levy stable distribution characterized by arbitrary chosen control parameter $\alpha(0.3 \leq \alpha \leq 1.99)$. Using the Mantegna algorithm, the step size λ is calculated as:

$$\lambda = \frac{x}{|y|^{1/\alpha}} \qquad (2.26)$$

where x and y are two normal stochastic variables with standard deviation σ_x and σ_y which are given as

$$\sigma_x(\alpha) = \left[\frac{\Gamma(1+\alpha) \sin (\pi\alpha/2)}{\Gamma((1+\alpha)/2)\alpha 2^{(\alpha-1)/2}} \right]^{1/\alpha} \quad \text{and} \quad \sigma_y(\alpha) = 1 \text{ for } \alpha = 1.5 \qquad (2.27)$$

in which the capital Greek letter Γ represents the Gamma function ($\Gamma(z) = \int_0^\infty t^{z-1} e^{-z} dt$) that is the extension of the factorial function with its argument shifted down by 1 to real and complex numbers. If $z = k$ is a positive integer, $\Gamma(k) = (k-1)!$

The steps of the CSA are as follows (Yang and Deb, 2010):

1. Select values for CSA parameters which are the number of nests (eggs) (n), the step size parameter (β), discovering probability (p_a), and maximum number of iterations for termination of the cycles.
2. Generate initial population of n host nests $\{x_i\}, (i = 1, 2, \ldots, n)$ randomly each of which represents a candidate solution to the optimization problem with objective function of $f(x)$ and decision variables $\{x\} = \{x_1, x_2, \ldots, x_m\}^T$.
3. Get a cuckoo randomly by Levy flights using $x_i^{\nu+1} = x_i^\nu + \beta\lambda$ and evaluate its fitness F_i. Here λ is a random walk based on Levy flights which is calculated from Eqs. (2.26) and (2.27).
4. Choose randomly a nest among n (say j) and evaluate its fitness F_j. If $F_j < F_i$, replace j by the new solution.
5. Abandon a fraction of worst nests and built new ones. This is carried out depending on p_a probability parameter. First find out whether each nest keeps its current position (Eq. (2.28)). R matrix stores 0 and 1 values such that any one of them is assigned to each component of ith nest, in which 0 means that current position is kept and 1 implies that the current position is to be updated:

$$\mathbf{R}_i \leftarrow \begin{cases} 1 & \text{if} \quad \text{rand} < p_a \\ 0 & \text{if} \quad \text{rand} \geq p_a \end{cases} \qquad (2.28)$$

New nests are conducted by means of Eq. (2.29):

$$x_i^{t+1} = x_i^t + r \times \mathbf{R}_i \times (\text{Perm}1_i - \text{Perm}2_i) \tag{2.29}$$

where r is a random number between 0 and 1. Perm1 and Perm2 are two row permutations of the corresponding nest. $\mathbf{R}$ defines the probability matrix.

6. Rank solutions and find the current best one.
7. Repeat steps 3–6 until termination criterion is satisfied which is usually taken as the maximum number of iterations.

2.3.7 Bat Algorithm

BA is developed by Yang (2010) which simulates echolocation capability of micro bats. They use sonar called echolocation to detect prey, avoid obstacles, and locate their roosting crevices in the dark. Micro bats emit a very loud sound pulse and listen for the echo that bounces back from the surrounding objects. Their pulses vary in properties and can be correlated with their hunting strategies, depending on the species. They even use the time delay from the emission and detection of the echo, time difference between two ears, and loudness variations of the echoes to build up three-dimensional scenario of the surrounding. They can detect the distance and orientation of the target, type of prey, and even moving speed of the prey such as small insects. The echolocation characteristics of micro bats can be idealized as in the following (Gandomi et al., 2012):

1. All bats use echolocation to sense distance, and they also know the difference between food/prey and background barriers in some magical way.
2. Bats randomly fly with velocity v_i at position x_i with a fixed frequency f_{min}, varying wavelength λ, and loudness A^0 to search prey. They can automatically adjust the wavelength (or frequency) of their emitted pulses and adjust the rate of pulse emission $r \in [0, 1]$ depending on the proximity of their target.
3. Although the loudness can vary in many ways, it is assumed that the loudness varies from a large (positive) A^0 to a minimum A_{min}.

The steps of the algorithm are as follows (Yang, 2010):

1. Initialize the bat population with position x_i and velocity v_i where each bat represents a candidate solution x_i, $i = 1, \ldots, n$ to the optimization problem with m design variables $\{x\} = \{x_1, x_2, \ldots, x_m\}^T$ and an objective function $f(x)$. Initialize pulse rates r_i and the loudness A_i. Define pulse frequency f_i at x_i.
2. Calculate the new solutions x_i^t and velocities v_i^t at time step t as

$$f_i = f_{min} + (f_{max} - f_{min})\beta \tag{2.30}$$

$$v_i^t = v_i^{t-1} + (x_i^{t-1} - x^*)f_i \tag{2.31}$$

$$x_i^t = x_i^{t-1} + v_i^t \tag{2.32}$$

where β is a random vector taken from a uniform distribution in the range [0,1]. x^* is the current global best location (solution) which is located after comparing all the solutions among all the n bats.

3. If a randomly generated number rand $> r_i$, determine a solution among the best solutions.
4. Generate a local solution around the selected best solution by a local random walk.

$$x_{new} = x_{old} + \varepsilon A^t \tag{2.33}$$

where the random number ε is drawn from $[-1,1]$, while A^t is the average loudness of all bats at this time step.

5. If a randomly generated number rand $> A_i$ and $f(x_i) < f(x^*)$ accept new solutions, increase r_i, and reduce A_i:

$$A_i^{t+1} = \alpha A_i^t \quad r_i^{t+1} = r_i^0[1 - \exp(-\gamma t)] \tag{2.34}$$

where α and γ are constants. In fact α is similar to the cooling factor of a cooling schedule in the simulated annealing. For any $\alpha > 0$ and $\gamma < 1$, $A_i^t \to 0$, $r_i^t \to r_i^0$ as $t \to \infty$. In the simplest case, α can be taken equal to γ.

6. Rank the bats and find current best x^*.
7. Repeat steps 2—6 until termination criterion is satisfied which is usually taken as a predetermined maximum number of iterations.

2.3.8 Hunting Search Algorithm

HS algorithm is instigated by Oftadeh et al. (2011). This algorithm is inspired by group hunting of animals such as lions, wolves, and dolphins. The common part in the way of hunting by these animals is that they all hunt in a group. They encircle the prey and gradually tighten the ring of siege until they catch the prey. Each member of the group corrects its position based on its own position and the position of other members during this action. If a prey escapes from the ring, hunters reorganize the group to siege the prey again. The HS algorithm is based on the way as wolves hunt. The steps of the algorithm are given in the following:

1. *Initialize the parameters*: The parameters of HS algorithm are required to be initialized. These are hunting group size (HGS) (number of solution vectors in hunting group), maximum movement toward the leader (MML), and hunting group consideration rate (HGCR) which varies between 0 and 1. The parameters MML and HGCR are used to improvise the hunter position (solution vector).
2. *Initialize the hunting group*: Based on the number of hunters (HGS), the hunting group matrix is filled with feasible randomly generated solution vectors. The values of objective function are computed for each solution vector and the leader is defined depending on these values.
3. New hunters' positions (new solution vectors) $x' = \{x'_1, x'_2, \ldots, x'_n\}$ are generated by moving toward the leader (the hunter that has the best position in the group) as follows:

$$x'_i = x_i + \text{rand} \times \text{MML} \times (x_i^\ell - x_i) \tag{2.35}$$

where MML is the maximum movement toward the leader, rand is a uniform random number [0,1], and x_i' is the position value of the leader for the ith variable.

For each hunter, if the movement toward the leader is successful, the hunter stays in its new position. However, if the movement is not successful (its previous position is better than its new position), it comes back to the previous position. This provides two advantages. First, the hunter is not compared with the worst hunter in the group to allow the weak members to search for other solutions. They may find better solutions. Secondly, for prevention from rapid convergence of the group, the hunter compares its current position with its previous position; therefore, good positions will not be eliminated. The value of MML varies depending on the problem under consideration. The range within $0.05-0.4$ gives good results.

4. *Position correction—cooperation between members*: The cooperation among the hunters is required to be modeled in order to conduct the hunt more efficiently. After moving toward the leader, hunters (based on other hunter positions and some random factors) choose another position to find better solutions. Hunters correct their position either following "*real value correction*" or "*digital value correction*." In real value correction, the new hunter's position $x' = \{x_1', x_2', \ldots, x_n'\}$ is generated from HG, based on hunting group considerations or position corrections. For instance, the value of the first design variable for the jth hunter x_1^j for the new vector can be selected as a real number from the specified $HG(x_i^1, x_i^2, \ldots, x_i^{HGS})$ or corrected using HGCR parameter (chosen between 0 and 1). The variable is updated as follows:

$$x_i^j \leftarrow \begin{cases} x_i^j \in \{x_i^1, x_i^2, \ldots, x_i^{HGS}\} & \text{with probability HGCR} \qquad i = 1, \ldots, n \\ x_i^j = x_i^j \pm Ra & \text{with probability } (1 - HGCR) \quad j = 1, \ldots, HGS \end{cases} \qquad (2.36)$$

The parameter HGCR is the probability of choosing one value from the hunting group stored in the HG. It is reported that selecting values between 0.1 and 0.4 produces better results. Ra is an arbitrary distance radius for the continuous design variable. It can be fixed or reduced during optimization process. Several functions can be selected for reducing Ra. The following is used by Oftadeh et al. (2011).

$$Ra(it) = Ra_{min}(x_i^{max} - x_i^{min}) \, \exp\left(\frac{\ell n(Ra_{max}/Ra_{min}) \times it}{itm}\right) \qquad (2.37)$$

where "it" is the iteration number. x_i^{max} and x_i^{min} are the maximum and minimum possible values for x_i, respectively. Ra_{max} and Ra_{min} are the maximum and minimum of relative search radius of the hunter, respectively, and itm is the maximum number of iterations in the optimization process.

In digital value correction, instead of using real values of each variable, the hunters communicate with each other by the digits of each solution variable. For example, the solution variable with the value of 23.4356 has six meaningful digits. For this solution variable, the hunter chooses a value for the first digit (i.e., 2) based on hunting group considerations or position correction. After the quality of the new hunter position is determined by evaluating the objective function, the hunter moves to this new position; otherwise it keeps its previous position.

5. *Reorganizing the hunting group*: In order to prevent being trapped in a local optimum, they must reorganize themselves to get another opportunity to find the optimum point. The algorithm does this in two independent conditions. If the difference between the values of the objective function for the leader and the worst hunter in the group becomes smaller than a preset constant ε_1 and the termination criterion is not satisfied, then the algorithm

reorganizes the hunting group for each hunter. Alternatively, after a certain number of searches, the hunters reorganize themselves. The reorganization is carried out as follows: the leader keeps its position and the other hunters randomly choose their position in the design space

$$x'_i = x^\ell_i \pm \text{rand} \times (x^{max}_i - x^{min}_i) \times \alpha \times \exp(-\beta \times EN) \tag{2.38}$$

where x^ℓ_i is the position value of the leader for the ith variable. rand is a uniform random number between [0,1]. x^{max}_i and x^{min}_i are the maximum and minimum possible values of variable x_i, respectively. EN counts the number of times that the group has been trapped until this step. As the algorithm goes on, the solution gradually converges to the optimum point. Parameters α and β are positive real values.

6. *Termination*: Steps 3–5 are repeated until maximum number of iterations is satisfied.

2.4 Numerical Examples

Two optimization problems taken from literature (Karaboga and Akay, 2011) are solved by all the algorithms summarized in this chapter and the optimum solutions obtained are compared in order to find out the efficiency of each algorithm. There are 12 decision variables in the first example which is minimization problem and 20 decision variables in the second example which is maximization problem. The values adopted for algorithm parameters in both optimization problems are given in Table 2.1. Maximum number of iterations is taken as 50,000 for all the algorithms to provide equal opportunity to all the algorithms. The optimum solutions are reached at number of iterations much less than this number.

2.4.1 Example 1

This example is a minimization problem. The objective function and the constraints are given below:

$$\text{Minimize} \quad f(x) = 5 \sum_{i=1}^{4} x_i - 5 \sum_{i=1}^{4} x_i^2 - \sum_{i=5}^{13} x_i$$

$$\begin{aligned}
\text{Subject to} \quad g_1(x) &= 2x_1 + 2x_2 + x_{10} + x_{11} - 10 \le 0 \\
g_2(x) &= 2x_1 + 2x_3 + x_{10} + x_{12} - 10 \le 0 \\
g_3(x) &= 2x_2 + 2x_3 + x_{11} + x_{12} - 10 \le 0 \\
g_4(x) &= -8x_1 + x_{10} \le 0 \\
g_5(x) &= -8x_2 + x_{11} \le 0 \\
g_6(x) &= -8x_3 + x_{12} \le 0 \\
g_7(x) &= -2x_4 - x_5 + x_{10} \le 0 \\
g_8(x) &= -2x_6 - x_7 + x_{11} \le 0 \\
g_9(x) &= -2x_8 - x_9 + x_{12} \le 0
\end{aligned}$$

where the bounds are $0 \le x_i \le 1$ ($i = 1, \ldots, 9$), $0 \le x_i \le 100$ ($i = 10, 11, 12$) and $0 \le x_{13} \le 1$.

Table 2.1 Algorithm Parameter Values Used in the Numerical Examples

Ant colony optimizer	Number of ants = 50, $npool$ = 100, α = 1, β = 0.6, ζ = 0.6, ρ = 0.8
PSO	Number of particles = 40, c_1 = 2, c_2 = 2, ω = 0.08, v_{max} = 2
ABC	Total number of bees = 40, limiting value for number of cycles to abandon food source = 400
GSA	Number of glowworms = 80, ρ = 0.4, γ = 0.6, β = 0.08, n_t = 5, s = 0.03, ℓ_0 = 5
FFA	
Example 1	Number of fireflies = 30, α = 0.01, β = 1, β_{min} = 0.2, γ = 1
Example 2	Number of fireflies = 50, α = 0.02, β = 1, β_{min} = 0.2, γ = 1
CSA	Number of nests = 40, p_a = 0.1
BA	Number of bats = 30, f_{max} = 100, f_{min} = 0, α = 0.9, γ = 0.9, A_{min} = 0, r_i^0 = 0.5
HS Algorithm	Number of hunters = 40, MML = 0.005, HGCR = 0.3, Ra_{max} = 0.01, Ra_{min} = 0.0000001, α = 1.2, β = 0.02, maximum number of iterations in one epoch = 25

The global minimum of the optimization problem is at x^* = (1, 1, 1, 1, 1, 1, 1, 1, 1, 3, 3, 3, 1) where six constraints are active (g_1, g_2, g_3, g_4, g_5, g_6, g_7, g_8, g_9) and $f(x^*)$ = −15.

This optimization problem is solved by eight different swarm intelligence−based algorithms and the optimum solutions obtained by each algorithm are listed in Table 2.2. It is interesting to notice that ant colony and ABC algorithms have found the global optimum given above: −15 and −14.9997, respectively. The second best solution is obtained by HS algorithm where the optimum value of the objective function is −14.9627 which is also very close to global optimum of −15. It is not surprising to observe that ant colony algorithm determined the global optimum exactly because the optimum solution of Example 1 is integer solution and ant colony algorithm works very well with integer solutions. The performance of the ABC algorithm is also as efficient as ant colony algorithm in this particular optimization problem. The search histories of the algorithms are shown in Figure 2.1. It is apparent from the figure that ant colony algorithm, ABC algorithm, and HS algorithm have much better convergence rate than other swarm intelligence−based algorithms considered in obtaining the solution of Example 1.

2.4.2 Example 2

This example is a maximization problem. The objective function and the constraints are given below:

$$\text{Maximize } f(x) = \left| \frac{\sum_{i=1}^{n} \cos^4(x_i) - 2\prod_{i=1}^{n} \cos^2(x_i)}{\sqrt{\sum_{i=1}^{n} i x_i^2}} \right|$$

$$\text{Subject to } \quad g_1(x) = 0,75 - \prod_{i=1}^{n} x_i \leq 0$$
$$g_2(x) = \sum_{i=1}^{n} x_i - 7,5 \, n \leq 0$$

where n = 20 and $0 \leq x_i \leq 10$ (i = 1, ... , n).

Table 2.2 Optimum Solutions and Constraint Values of Example 1

	BA	PSO	CSA	HS Algorithm	FFA	ABC	GSA	ACO
x_1	0.99266	0.268957	0.99412	0.997097	0.999749	1	0.999593	1
x_2	0.965705	1	0.99898	0.9999	0.995027	1	0.998283	1
x_3	0.998388	0.998273	0.99651	0.99993	0.996723	1	0.375408	1
x_4	0.979785	1	0.99797	0.999496	0.99828	1	0.999999	1
x_5	0.973136	1	0.99576	0.999201	0.985386	1	0.000312	1
x_6	0.976451	0.996442	0.99822	0.998902	0.995111	1	1	1
x_7	0.94594	0.999964	0.99705	0.99965	0.995311	1	0.999998	1
x_8	0.988192	0.996083	0.98819	0.999425	0.982028	1	1	1
x_9	0.935385	1	0.97699	0.995757	0.99156	1	0.999998	1
x_{10}	1.749514	2.15165	2.87887	2.998194	2.969814	2.9997	1.998898	3
x_{11}	2.225278	2.992848	2.79799	2.997458	2.98175	2.9997	2.99997	3
x_{12}	2.110634	2.992167	2.72006	2.99460	2.954808	3.0003	2.99995	3
x_{13}	0.992474	0.999999	1	0.997209	0.995215	1	0.998658	1
g_1	−2.108479	−2.317583	−0.3369247	−0.0103461	−0.0588777	0	−1.00537	0
g_2	−2.302329	−2.321718	−0.4197872	−0.0131396	−0.0824335	0	−2.251151	0
g_3	−1.880475	−0.0184393	−0.4909381	−0.0082626	−0.0799367	0	−1.252688	0
g_4	−6.191768	9.54×10^{-7}	−5.074092	−4.978586	−5.02818	−5	−5.997844	−5
g_5	−5.50036	−5.007153	−5.193861	−5.001773	−4.978459	−5	−4.986288	−5
g_6	−5.298181	−4.994016	−5.25206	−5.00485	−5.018977	−5	−0.003313065	−5
g_7	−1.183193	−0.8483445	−0.1128445	0	−0.0132269	0	−0.001411844	0
g_8	−0.6702185	$−2.38 \times 10^{-7}$	−0.1955154	0	−0.0037769	0	−0.000019193	0
g_9	−0.8011355	0	−0.2333125	0	−0.0008085	0	−0.000048935	0
f	**−11.58456**	**−13.13744**	**−14.28388**	**−14.9627**	**−14.80281**	**−14.9997**	**−11.8146**	**−15**

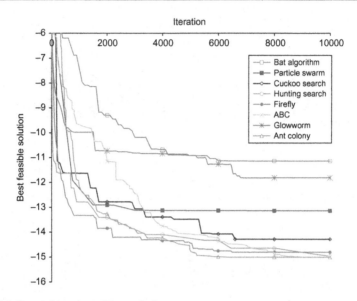

Figure 2.1 Search histories of Example 1.

The known global maximum is at $x_i^* = 1/\sqrt{n}$ $(i = 1, \ldots, n)$, where $f(x_i^*) = 0.803619$, g_1 is close to being active $(g_1 = -10^{-8})$.

Optimum solutions of this maximization problem obtained by eight different swarm intelligence−based algorithm are tabulated in Table 2.3. HS algorithm has attained the optimum solution with the objective function value of 0.7662 which is the closest to global optimum. This is followed by the particle swarm algorithm and CSA where the optimum value of the objective function is determined as 0.7657 and 0.7613, respectively. Search histories of the algorithms are shown in Figure 2.2.

2.5 Summary and Conclusions

In nature, swarm intelligence emerges through the cooperation of large number of unsophisticated agents. This intelligence is decentralized, self-organized, and distributed throughout an environment which is used by a swarm to solve problems of foraging for food, prey evading, or colony relocation. Swarm intelligence algorithms make use of this intelligence to develop a computational tool that can effectively be used to solve complex nonlinear programming problems. In this chapter, eight swarm intelligence−based algorithms emerged in recent years are summarized and they are used to obtain the solution of two constrained optimization problems. It is shown that although they are based on different type of swarm

Table 2.3 Optimum Solutions and Constraint Values of Example 2

	BA	PSO	CSA	HS Algorithm	FFA	ABC	GSA	ACO
x_1	8.746114	3.143878	3.12077	0.31499	3.14922	3.1234	9.459922	3.4281
x_2	7.567183	3.097413	3.08670	0.31216	3.13519	3.0991	0.301951	3.4011
x_3	8.746084	3.09692	3.07581	3.09476	3.11898	3.0927	3.382705	3.0404
x_4	4.15192	3.070699	3.07229	3.06793	3.10603	3.0584	3.740157	2.8847
x_5	1.9262	3.044196	3.04239	3.04124	3.12224	3.0587	3.05096	3.1413
x_6	4.465885	3.02853	3.04059	3.01330	3.11785	3.2849	0.451315	2.503
x_7	4.151972	2.967658	2.94723	2.98601	3.06454	3.0156	2.947624	3.1173
x_8	3.778215	2.96055	2.99808	2.95762	3.09704	3.0358	3.040941	0.4597
x_9	1.926205	1.486292	1.68016	1.41663	3.05696	0.1813	0.116662	2.8746
x_{10}	7.56719	0.359108	0.371808	0.357909	3.06320	0.1331	0.386633	0.6299
x_{11}	4.465941	0.367655	0.432783	0.355152	3.03005	0.1741	0.107381	0.4584
x_{12}	8.746098	2818424	2.821983	2.829171	3.07760	2.9366	3.08424	0.4837
x_{13}	7.567175	0.33906	0.303627	0.350671	3.01152	0.3602	0.42362	0.4717
x_{14}	1.926217	0.340796	0.361948	0.348434	3.01501	0.4544	2.396057	0.4493
x_{15}	8.746104	0.334756	0.308402	0.346316	2.98099	0.441	3.238118	0.4317
x_{16}	3.73873	0.32462	0.313455	0.344786	2.99442	2.9881	0.115588	0.4339
x_{17}	4.107914	0.337194	0.317705	0.342735	1.46608	0.4576	0.274117	0.5426
x_{18}	4.151973	0.352225	0.318799	0.34093	2.97826	0.1918	0.855352	0.4517
x_{19}	4.151949	0.343326	0.31406	0.338807	0.01233	0.3232	3.03368	0.4114
x_{20}	4.151978	0.353239	0.391109	0.337334	2.96903	1.1801	1.044522	0.4069
g_1	-2.180932	5.722×10^{-6}	-7.212×10^{-6}	9.894×10^{-6}	-1×10^7	0	-0.5951577	0
g_2	-118.8393	-117.8406	-117.6653	-117.8587	-93.43337	-115.41	-108.3484	-119.98
f	0.523495	0.7657292	0.7612647	0.766208	0.460955	0.6752	0.505006	0.7553

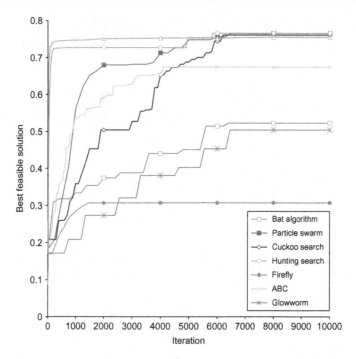

Figure 2.2 Search histories of Example 2.

intelligence, they are all robust and can attain the optimum solutions. However, their performance differs depending on the optimization problem under consideration. Among the eight different swarm intelligence−based algorithms, HS algorithm seemed to be the best one in finding the optimum solutions. In both problems, it has found the optimum solutions which are very close to the global optimum solution compared to those obtained by the other algorithms. However, this algorithm has eight parameters to be initialized which may not be very easy task for a user to decide. One set of parameters that gives good performance for certain type of optimization problem may not be suitable for the other one. ABC algorithm has only one parameter that is the total number of bees to be initialized. With this feature, it is almost parameter free which makes it trouble free for users. CSA is also similar to ABC algorithm regarding the number of parameters. It has only two parameters to be initialized. It should be pointed out that the swarm intelligence−based algorithms used in obtaining the solution of two optimization problems are coded according to their standard forms given by their originators. No enhancements are employed that might improve their performance, some of which are already available in the literature. Furthermore, it is apparent that driving sound conclusions regarding the performance of these algorithms from the results of only two small optimization problems will not be scientifically trustworthy. One needs to consider large number of different types of optimization problems and carry out statistical study before declaring which algorithm is the best. However, from this study, one conclusion can definitely be made. Swarm intelligence offers scientists a tool that can be efficiently used to determine the solution of complex nonlinear programming problems. Its potential has already been discovered. The large number of publications related with swarm intelligence−based algorithms is a clear indication of this fact.

References

Coello, C.A.C., 2002. Theoretical and numerical constraint-handling techniques used with evolutionary algorithms: a survey of the state of the art. Comput. Meth. Appl. Mech. Eng. 191, 1245−1287.

De Castro, L.N., Von Zuben, F.J., 2005. Recent Developments in Biologically Inspired Computing. Idea Group Publishing, Hershey, PA, USA.

Del Acebo, E., De la Rosa, J., 2008. Introducing bar systems: a class of swarm intelligence optimization algorithms. AISB 2008 Convention, Communication, Interaction and Social Intelligence, 1−4 April 2008, University of Aberdeen, UK, vol. 11, pp. 18−23.

Doğan, E., Saka, M.P., 2012. Optimum design of unbraced steel frames to LRFD-AISC code using particle swarm optimization. Adv. Eng. Soft. 44, 150−169.

Dorigo, M., 1992. Optimization, Learning and Natural Algorithms, PhD thesis. Dipartimento Elettronica e Informazione, Politecnico di Milano, Italy.

Dorigo, M., Stützle, M., 2004. Ant Colony Optimization. A Bradford Book, MIT Press, Cambridge, MA.

Dorigo, M., Maniezzo, V., Colorni, A., 1991. Distributed optimization by ant colony. Proceedings of ECAL91-First European Conference on Artificial Life. Elsevier, Paris, France, pp. 134−142.

Dreo, J., Petrowski, A., Siarry, P., Taillard, E., 2006. Meta-Heuristics for Hard Optimization. Springer-Verlag, Berlin.

Hasançebi, O, 2008. Adaptive evolution strategies in structural optimization: enhancing their computational performance with applications to large-scale structures. Comput. Struct. 86 (1-2), 119−132.

Herheim, C-E.J., 2005. Swarm Intelligence and Automatic Development of Algorithms Through Evolution. Ostfold University College, Norway (Mastergrad Oppgave i informatik).

Gandomi, A.H., Yang, X.S., Alavi, A.H., 2011. Mixed variable structural optimization using firefly algorithm. Comput. Struct. 89, 2325−2336.

Gandomi, A.H., Yang, X.S., Alavi, A.H., Talatahari, S., 2012. Bat algorithm for constrained optimization tasks. Neural Comput. Appl. doi:10.1007/s00521-012-1028-9.

Karaboga, D., 2005. An Idea Based on Honey Bee Swarm for Numerical Optimization. Technical Report-TR06, Erciyes University, Engineering Faculty, Computer Engineering Department, Turkey.

Karaboga, D., 2010. Artificial bee colony algorithm. Scholarpedia. 5 (3), 6915.

Karaboga, D., Akay, B., 2011. A modified artificial bee colony (ABC) algorithm for constrained optimization problems. Appl. Soft. Comput. 11, 3021−3031.

Karaboga, D., Gorkemli, B., Ozturk, C., Karaboga, N., 2012. A comprehensive survey: artificial bee colony (ABC) algorithm and applications. Artif. Intell. Rev. doi:10.1007/s10462-012-9328-0.

Kennedy, J., Eberhart, R., 1995. Particle swarm optimization. IEEE International Conference on Neural Networks, vol. 4, IEEE Press, Perth, Australia, pp. 1942–1948.

Kennedy, J, Eberhart, R., Shi, Y., 2001. Swarm Intelligence. Morgan Kaufmann Publishers, Burlington, Massachusetts, USA.

Krishnanand, K.N., Ghose, D., 2005. Detection of multiple source locations using a glowworm metaphor with applications to collective robotics. IEEE Swarm Intelligence Symposium, Pasadena, CA, pp. 84–91.

Krishnanand, K.N., Ghose, D., 2009a. Glowworm swarm optimization: a new method for optimizing multi-modal functions. Int. J. Comput. Intell. Stud. 1 (1), 84–91.

Krishnanand, K.N, Ghose, D., 2009b. Glowworm swarm optimization for simultaneous capture of multiple local optima of multimodal functions. Swarm Intell. 3 (2), 87–124.

Liu, Y., Ling, X., Shi, Z., Lv, M., Fang, J., Zang, L., 2011. A survey on particle swarm optimization algorithm for multimodal function optimization. J. Soft. 6 (12), 2449–2455.

Luke, S., 2010. Essentials of metaheuristics. <http://cs.gmu.edu/ ~ sean/book/metaheuristics/> (accessed 11.12.12).

Mantegna, R.N., 1994. Fast, accurate algorithm for numerical simulation of Levy stable stochastic processes. Phys. Rev. E. 49 (5), 4677–4683.

Oftadeh, R., Mahjoob, M.J., Shariatpanahi, M., 2011. A novel metaheuristic optimization algorithm inspired by group hunting of animals: hunting search. Comput. Math. Appl. 60, 2087–2098.

Reynolds, C.W., 1987. Flocks, herds, and schools: a distributed behavioral model. ACM Comput. Graphics. 21 (4), 25–34.

Saka, M.P., 2012. Recent developments in metaheuristic algorithms: a review. Comput. Technol. Rev. 5, 31–78.

Yang, X.S., 2008. Nature-Inspired Metaheuristic Algorithms. Luniver Press, Frome, UK.

Yang, X.S., 2009. Firefly algorithms for multimodal optimization. In: Watanabe, O., Zeugmann, T. (Eds.), Stochastic Algorithms: Foundations and Applications. Springer-Verlag, Berlin (SAGA 2009, Lecture Notes in Computer Science, 5792, 169-178).

Yang, X.S., 2010. A new metaheuristic bat-inspired algorithm. In: Gonzalez, J.R., et al., (Eds.), Nature Inspired Cooperative Strategies for Optimization (NISCO 2010), vol. 284. Springer, Berlin, pp. 65–74. (Studies in Computational Intelligence).

Yang, X.S., 2011. Metaheuristic optimization. Scholarpedia. 6 (8), 11472.

Yang, X.S., Deb, S., 2010. Engineering optimization by cuckoo search. Int. J. Math. Model. Numer. Optim. 1 (4), 330–343.

3 Lévy Flights and Global Optimization

Momin Jamil[1,2] and Hans-Jürgen Zepernick[1]

[1]Blekinge Institute of Technology, Karlskrona, Sweden; [2]Harman International, Harman/Becker Automotive Systems GmbH, Karlsbad, Germany

3.1 Introduction

Optimization concepts and tools are frequently applied to modern complex engineering, scientific, economic, and quantitative decision problems. The goal in these problems is to find the "best" solution or decision that corresponds to either minimum or maximum of an objective function with or without any constraints. The role of the objective function is to clearly define the problem at hand mathematically and to express the relationship between different parameters of the problem. In case of constrained optimization problems, finding the "best" solution or decision must satisfy a given set of constraints. However, unconstrained optimization problems are independent of any constraints except for the boundary constraints.

These optimization problems could be linear or nonlinear. Nonlinear problems could exhibit multiple local or global solutions. In most cases, the number of solutions is not known *a priori*, and the quality of local and global solutions may differ substantially. Over the years, different approaches have been proposed to handle and solve linear and nonlinear optimization problems. Many of these proposed methods are based on numerical linear and nonlinear programming methods. These methods require substantial gradient information and try to improve the solution in the proximity of an initial guess or a starting point. As a result, the application of these algorithms is rather limited to simple cases. Their performance is also severely hampered if the objective function or constraints have multiple or sharp peaks.

In order to overcome the shortcomings of the gradient-based methods, several approaches have been proposed, most notably the Hooke and Jeeves method (Hooke and Jeeves, 1961), Nelder–Meade simplex method (Nelder and Meade, 1965), the Powell method (Powell, 1964), and the Rosenbrock method (Rosenbrock, 1960). These methods do not require any gradient information and utilize some basic approach of heading downward from an arbitrary starting position. However, they do

Swarm Intelligence and Bio-Inspired Computation. DOI: http://dx.doi.org/10.1016/B978-0-12-405163-8.00003-X

differ in deciding which direction to move and how far to move. The final outcome or solution will somewhat depend on the selection of the initial guess of the starting position. This is not a serious shortcoming of these methods if the parameter space has a single and well-defined minimum. However, if the parameter space is not well behaved, i.e., contains many local minima, it will be difficult to accurately locate a global minimum with these methods. This is due to the fact that the inherent strategies in these methods cannot efficiently explore the search space simultaneously in different directions. Although successive improvements can be made to speed up the downhill movement of the algorithms, this does not lead to an improvement in their ability to find a global minimum and to get trapped in a local minimum.

The remainder of the chapter is organized as follows. In Section 3.2, a brief review of metaheuristic algorithms (MAs) is presented. In Section 3.3, Lévy flights (LFs) in the context of global optimization, the Lévy distribution, a method to generate random numbers within this distribution are discussed. Subsequently, diversification and intensification in global optimization based on LFs are briefly discussed. Section 3.4 discusses MAs using LFs as a search mechanism to solve global optimization problems. Section 3.5 highlights the differences and similarities of different MAs. Finally, conclusions are provided in Section 3.6.

3.2 Metaheuristic Algorithms

The level of complexity in modern real-world problems due to rapid and stochastic changes demanded out-of-the-box thinking approaches to solve such problems. As a result, researchers started adopting ideas from nature and translated them to solve problems in a wide variety of fields. This led to the inception of nature-inspired heuristic or metaheuristic algorithms to solve challenging optimization problems. In the beginning, most of the MAs were presented without any mathematical proof, often inspired by a metaphor drawn from biological systems. After the initial phase, researchers commenced to deepen their knowledge and understanding about these algorithms and to build a theoretical foundation.

MAs have been at the forefront of scientific research since the last few decades. Optimization methods, once dominated by the classical approaches, are constantly encroached by MAs due to their (i) effectiveness, (ii) reasonable computational time, (iii) broad flexibility, (iv) intuitive mathematical formulation, and (v) ability to handle uncertain, stochastic, and dynamic information. MAs are designed and recognized to solve complicated optimization problems where traditional approaches are either ineffective or inefficient. These methods have been proven to be effective in handling problems that were previously thought to be computationally too complex. They aim at defining effective general purpose methods to explore the solution space and to avoid tailoring them to a specific problem. Due to their general purpose nature, they can be applied to a wide range of problems and are an attractive choice from an implementation point of view in general purpose software, such as Matlab, Evolutionary/Classical Solver, Evolver, Generator,

Optworks, SolveXL, GANetXL, and GeneHunter among others. MAs are also referred to as black-box algorithms as they exploit limited knowledge about the problem to be solved. As no gradient or Hessian matrix information is required for their operation, they are also referred to as derivative-free or zero-order algorithms (Brent, 1973). The term zero-order implies that only the function values are used to establish the search vector. Moreover, the function to be optimized does not necessarily have to be continuous or differentiable but may be accompanied by a set of constraints. The choice of method for solving a particular problem depends primarily on the type and characteristics of the problem at hand. It must be stressed that the goal of a particular method used is to find the "best" solution of some sort of a problem compared to finding the optimal solution. In this context, the term "best" refers to an acceptable or satisfactory solution to the problem. This could be the absolute best solution from a set of candidate solutions or may be any of the candidate solutions. The requirements and characteristics of the problem determine if the overall best solution can be found (Engelbrecht, 2005; Venkataraman, 2009).

Many MAs use a pattern matrix (PM), which includes random solutions to problems (Civicioglu and Besdok, 2011). In the context of MAs, PM refers to search agents or population, while each pattern represents an individual agent. For example, in particle swarm optimization (PSO), PM is referred to as swarm, and each pattern corresponds to a particle in a swarm. Similarly, a pattern in cuckoo search (CS) algorithm represents a nest, while in artificial bee colony (ABC) algorithm, a pattern is represented by a nectar. The PM in MAs develops recursively during an iteration process. Therefore, as the number of iterations increases, the population diversity or attribute variety (Civicioglu and Besdok, 2011) decreases resulting in premature convergence of the algorithm. In order to increase the population diversity or PM, new methods to inject new patterns (population members) have also been an active area of research in MAs.

Although a commonly accepted definition of metaheuristics does not exist, there have been several attempts of a formal definition in recent years (see, for example, Osman and Laporte, 1996; Stützle, 1999; Voß et al., 1999). In short, metaheuristics can be summarized as follows:

- MAs employ strategies to effectively perform a search process and to efficiently explore the search space such that near-optimal or optimal solutions are obtained.
- The search mechanisms in MAs range from simple local search procedures to complex learning processes.
- MAs provide approximate solutions and are usually nondeterministic.
- They may incorporate escape mechanisms such as niching and stretching in order to avoid getting trapped in confined areas of the search space.
- Metaheuristics are not problem specific.

Based on the aforementioned discussion, metaheuristics can be considered as a set of algorithmic concepts that can be used to define heuristic methods applicable to a wide range of problems. In other words, they (metaheuristics) are a general purpose algorithmic framework applicable to a wide range of problems with relatively fewer modifications (Dorigo et al., 2006).

Some of the well-known MAs include tabu search (TS) (Glover, 1989, 1990), genetic algorithms (GAs) (Goldberg, 1989), simulated annealing (SA) (Kirkpatrick et al., 1983), ant colony optimization (ACO) (Dorigo and Stützle, 2004), ABC algorithm (Karaboga and Basturk, 2007), bat algorithm (BA) (Yang and Gandomi, 2012), CS (Yang, 2009), PSO (Kennedy and Eberhart, 1995), harmony search (HS) (Lee and Geem, 2005), firefly algorithm (FA) (Yang, 2010), and krill herd algorithm (Gandomi and Alavi, 2012a) among others. MAs can be classified in different ways (Blum and Roli, 2003); however, in this chapter, we will focus on nature-inspired MAs.

3.3   Lévy Flights in Global Optimization

We use the term flight because we are dealing with MAs based on the behavior of birds. However, in literature, LFs or Lévy walks (LWs) have been used interchangeably. Nature does not have a uniform distribution of resources. Foragers, therefore, need a strategy to find these nonuniformly distributed resources in the fastest way for their survival. In general, the search time is a limiting factor which has to be optimized for day-to-day survival of these foragers. The fundamental question for the foragers is: what is the fastest way of finding nonuniformly distributed resources? In order to answer this important question in behavioral ecology, a flurry of experimental and theoretical studies has been triggered (see Bell, 1991; Viswanathan, 2010; Viswanathan et al., 1996 and the references therein). These studies have shown that the search behavior of many foragers is generally sporadic comprising of active search phases and it randomly alternates with phase of fast ballistic motion. The spectrum of search strategies varies from cruise strategy (e.g., for fish) to ambush or sit-and-wait search, where a forager remains stationary for a long period (e.g., rattlesnake) (Bénicho et al., 2005).

A number of theoretical and empirical studies explain and analyze the search strategies of deer, bumble bees (Viswanathan et al., 1999), reindeer (Mårell et al., 2002), microzooplankton (Bartumeus et al., 2003), gray seals (Austin et al., 2004), spider monkeys (Ramos-Frenández et al., 2004), fish (Viswanathan, 2010), and other marine predators (Humphries et al., 2010; Sims, 2010) among many others. These studies have hypothesized LFs or LWs as an optimal search strategy adopted by many foragers. However, it is worth mentioning that foragers adapt their search strategy based on the density of prey, sometimes switching between LFs and Brownian motion (BM). LFs constitute a special class of random walks whose step lengths are drawn from a probability distribution with heavy power-law tails (Shlesinger et al., 1995). They display fractal properties with no typical scale and have applications in diverse biological, chemical, and physical phenomena such as fluid dynamics, dynamic systems, micelles (Shlesinger et al., 1995), economics and finance (Mantegna and Stanley, 2000; Porto and Roman, 2002; Stanley et al., 1999), climate and atmospheric physics (Tsonis et al., 1998, 2003), and soft-mode turbulence (Tamura et al., 2001) to name a few. Even light and spreading depression leading to migraine in humans can be related to LFs (Barthelemy et al., 2008; Grinbergy et al., 2011).

Based on the aforementioned discussion, it is hypothesized that global optimization (GO) is analogous to problems faced by the animal foragers to find food in natural and dynamical environments without *a priori* knowledge about its location. In GO problems, sometimes, there is little or no information about the location of the global optimum (unimodal problems) or optima (multimodal problems). Therefore, stochastic algorithms to solve GO demand search strategies that can effectively and efficiently explore the whole problem search space. The discussion in the preceding paragraphs presents a strong motivation to incorporate LFs based on the Lévy distribution as an underlying search mechanism in these algorithms to solve complicated real-world problems.

3.3.1 The Lévy Probability Distribution

Consider a set of identically distributed random variables $(X_1, X_2, \ldots, X_N)$ each of which having the same probability density function (PDF). A process is called stable if the sum of these random variables has the same probability density distribution as the individual random variables. A Gaussian process is a typical example of a stable process, i.e., a sum of Gaussian random variables also has a Gaussian distribution. It is well known that the Gaussian distribution has a finite second moment. However, there exists a class of probability distribution with infinite second moment, which also yields a stable process. Specifically, the Lévy probability distribution belongs to a special class of symmetric α-stable distributions and is known as α-stable Lévy probability distribution. A symmetric α-stable random variable (r.v.) S is defined by its characteristic function as follows (Gutowski, 2001):

$$\Phi_{\alpha,\sigma} = \mathrm{E}[\exp(izS)] = \exp(-\sigma^\alpha |z|^\alpha) \tag{3.1}$$

where $\mathrm{E}[\cdot]$ denotes the expectation operator, i is a complex number, $z \in \mathbb{R}$, $\sigma \geq 0$, and $\alpha \in (0,2]$ is a scaling factor. The PDF of a symmetric α-stable r.v. is given by the inverse Fourier transform of Eq. (3.1) according to Gutowski (2001) as

$$L_{\alpha,\gamma}(S) = \frac{1}{2\pi} \int_{-\infty}^{\infty} \Phi_{\alpha,\gamma}(z)\exp(izS)dz = \frac{1}{\pi} \int_{0}^{\infty} \exp(-\gamma z^\alpha)\cos(zS)dz \tag{3.2}$$

In this context, α is also called shape parameter and it controls the heaviness of the distribution, i.e., the decay of the tail. It takes values in the interval $0 < \alpha \leq 2$. A small value of α implies that the tails of the distribution contain considerable accumulation of the data, i.e., the random variable values are more likely to be far away from the mean of the distribution. On the other hand, a larger value of α indicates that values of the random variable are at small distances from the mean of the distribution.

The parameter γ controls the scaling of the distribution and can take on any positive value. Without loss of generality, γ can be set to 1 (Gutowski, 2001), and hence, $L_{\alpha,\gamma}(S)$ can be denoted as $L_{\alpha,1}(S)$ or simply by $L_{\alpha}(S)$. A closed-form expression of Eq. (3.2) is not known for general α except for a few special cases. For $\alpha = 1$ and 2, the integral becomes a Cauchy and Gaussian distribution, respectively. Lévy distributions for different values of α are shown in Figure 3.1. It can be seen from Figure 3.1 that for $\alpha < 2$, the shape of the distribution is similar to a Gaussian distribution, but the tail of the distribution falls off much more gently compared to a Gaussian distribution. The difference between non-Gaussian and Gaussian distributions is that the tails of the former are fat or heavy compared to the latter.

3.3.2 Simulation of Lévy Random Numbers

As the analytical form of Eq. (3.2) for general values of α is not known, a method proposed by Mantegna (1994) is normally considered efficient to generate random numbers that follow the Lévy distribution. However, this is not the only method to generate Lévy random numbers (Pantaleo et al., 2009). In Mantegna's algorithm, two stochastic variables X and Y are drawn from normal distribution given as

$$X \sim N(0, \sigma_X^2), \quad Y \sim N(0, \sigma_Y^2) \tag{3.3}$$

where

$$\sigma_X(\alpha) = \left[\frac{\Gamma(1+\alpha)\sin(\pi\alpha/2)}{\Gamma(1+\alpha/2)\alpha 2^{\alpha-1/2}} \right]^{1/\alpha}, \quad \sigma_Y = 1 \tag{3.4}$$

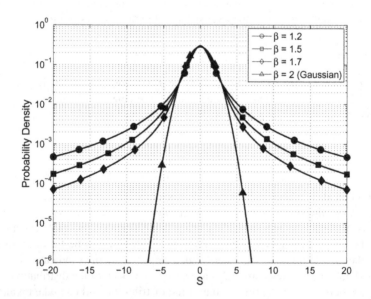

Figure 3.1 Comparison of Lévy probability distributions for different values of α and $\sigma = 1$.

where $\Gamma(\cdot)$ denotes the gamma function. Then, the following nonlinear transformation is applied to generate a random variable V:

$$V = \frac{X}{|Y|^{1/\alpha}} \tag{3.5}$$

This is followed by another nonlinear transformation in order to give an exponential tilt to the distribution of random variable V by defining a new variable W as

$$W = \{[K(\alpha) - 1]e^{-(|V|/C(\alpha))} + 1\}V \tag{3.6}$$

where $K(\alpha)$ is calculated as (Mantegna, 1994)

$$K(\alpha) = \frac{\alpha\Gamma((\alpha+1)/2\alpha)}{\Gamma(1/\alpha)}\left[\frac{\alpha\Gamma((\alpha+1)/2)}{\Gamma(\alpha+1)\sin(\pi\alpha/2)}\right] \tag{3.7}$$

The parameter $C(\alpha)$ is a result of a polynominal fit for the values tabulated by Mantegna (1994). A convergence to a Lévy stable distribution is obtained by generating n independent copies of W given as

$$z = \frac{1}{n^{1/\alpha}}\sum_{k=1}^{N} W_k \tag{3.8}$$

According to Lee and Yao (2001, 2004) and Richer and Blackwell (2006), the Lévy distribution with a scale factor σ other than 1 can be obtained using the following linear transformation:

$$z = \sigma^{1/\alpha}W \tag{3.9}$$

3.3.3 Diversification and Intensification

A random walk is a stochastic process in which humans, animals, or even particles or waves travel along random trajectories. Random walks can be classified as either Brownian random walk or motion or Lévy flights. In BM, the step lengths (S) have a characteristic scale usually defined by the first and the second moment (mean and variance) of the step length density distribution (Viswanathan et al., 2000). On the other hand, an LF is a random walk in which movement displacements or steps (S) are drawn from a Lévy distribution, often in terms of a power-law formula given as (Gutowski, 2001; Yang, 2010)

$$L_\alpha(S) \sim \frac{1}{S^{(\alpha+1)}} \quad |S| \gg 1 \tag{3.10}$$

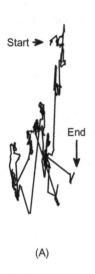

Figure 3.2 Trajectories of an object undergoing: (A) LF ($\alpha = 1.2$, $\sigma = 1$), (B) BM ($\alpha = 2$, $\sigma = 1$) in two dimensions.

(A)   (B)

The second moment of such a power-law distribution is infinite for $0 < \alpha < 2$. More discussions on this topic can be found by Gutowski (2001), Yang (2010), and the references therein. LF describes a search pattern composed of many small clusters of steps and exceptionally long jumps. The term flight means the longest straight line trip between two points that a moving object makes without directional change or pause (Figure 3.2A). Simulated sample trajectories of an object undergoing LF and BM are shown in Figure 3.2A and B, respectively. It can be seen from Figure 3.2A that LF shows a combination of many short and a few long steps compared to BM Figure 3.2B, which shows that the object will return many times to a previously visited location.

The search performed by MAs should be carried out in such a way that it can accomplish the following two goals: (i) intensively explore areas of the search space with high-quality solutions and (ii) move to unexplored areas of the search space when necessary. The concepts for achieving these goals are known as diversification (exploration) and intensification (exploitation) (Glover, 1989, 1990). The diversification and intensification can be achieved in many different ways. The overall efficiency of an optimization algorithm depends on a sound balance between these two components. If the search process operates in favor of diversification compared to intensification, the algorithm will get stuck in a local minimum. This will make it very difficult or even impossible for any algorithm to find a global optimum solution. On the other hand, if the algorithm tends toward intensification compared to diversification, the overall search performance will slow down, making it difficult for an algorithm to converge. Due to the complex nature of many modern optimization problems, simple diversification and intensification mechanisms are not enough to solve these problems.

3.3.3.1   Diversification

The methods based on local search have a severe shortcoming that they tend to spend more time in restricted portions of the search space. This has a negative impact in the sense that large portions of the search space are left unexplored. This means that possible good solutions in these areas are left out from the final solution or the best solution. As the remote areas of the search space are not explored, the opportunities of finding the optimum solution are lost. An algorithmic concept known as diversification can help alleviating this problem by forcing the search mechanism to explore previously unvisited sites in the problem search space.

In MAs, the diversification is achieved by randomization in combination with a deterministic procedure. In this way, the newly generated solutions are distributed as diversely as possible in the problem search space. According to Yang (2011), the simplest and most common way to achieve randomization is given by

$$\mathbf{x}^{t+1} = \mathbf{L}_b + (\mathbf{U}_b - \mathbf{L}_b) \cdot \chi_u \qquad (3.11)$$

where $\mathbf{x}^{t+1}$ is a newly generated solution, $\mathbf{L}_b$ and $\mathbf{U}_b$ denotes the lower and upper bounds of the problem search space, respectively. The random variable $\chi_u \in [0,1]$ is drawn from a uniform distribution. Mutation and crossover operators are other elaborate ways to achieve exploration or diversification in MA. Mutation is an operator that randomly alters the value of a gene from one generation to the next. The mutation ensures that new solutions differ or are far apart from their parents or existing solutions. On the other hand, crossover is a process of taking more than one parent solution and producing a new solution from them. It limits the degree of overdiversification, as new solutions are generated by swapping parts of existing solutions (Yang, 2011).

3.3.3.2   Intensification

The idea behind intensification is that the promising portions of the search space that might contain the best solution should be explored thoroughly. The purpose of introducing intensification is to make sure that these solutions are found within these areas. Random walks are the most common way to achieve intensification. The most common way to achieve it is to generate new solutions around a potential better solution using

$$\mathbf{x}^{t+1} = \mathbf{x}^t + S \cdot \chi_u \qquad (3.12)$$

where $\mathbf{x}^{t+1}$ and $\mathbf{x}^t$ represent new and previous solutions, respectively. The elements of χ_u are drawn from a uniform distribution with zero mean, and S is the step length of the random walk. In general, the step size is chosen in such a way that only the local neighborhood around the local solution is visited. If the step size is too large, the far-off regions in the problem search space have more visitations, thus increasing the diversification but reducing the exploitation. Therefore, a proper step size must be linked to the actual scales of the problem (Yang, 2011).

From this discussion, it can be seen that randomization is usually realized using a uniform or Gaussian distribution. However, this is not the only way to achieve randomization. In recent years, the use of LF based on Lévy distributions has emerged as an alternative to uniform or Gaussian distributions. This can be regarded as an advantage due to (i) reduction in the probability of returning to previously visited sites in the problem search space and (ii) effective and efficient exploration of the far-off regions of the function landscape in GO problems. The second property helps an optimization algorithm to escape local minimum or minima when the function landscape has deep and wide basins. The smaller hill shown in Figure 3.3 for different values of $\alpha < 2$ indicates that random walkers based on the Lévy distribution will spend more time in exploiting a large area of the search space (exploration on a global scale) and less time in searching the small local neighborhood compared to random walkers based on the Gaussian distribution.

Thus, it can be argued that LF has weaker fine-tuning ability than random walkers based on Gaussian distribution for small- to mid-range search regions.

The algorithms based on the Gaussian distribution control the search of the problem search space by altering the mean and the standard deviation of the Gaussian distribution. However, this mechanism of searching the solution space cannot be used due to infinite standard deviation of the Lévy distribution. The scale factor σ, however, can be used to overcome this problem and can be adjusted to alter the Lévy distribution. This adjustment helps to control the search process and also to guarantee the convergence of the algorithm. According to Yang (2008, 2009, 2010),

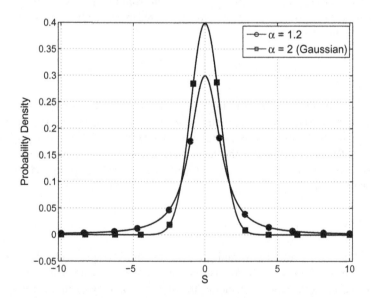

Figure 3.3 Lévy probability distribution for different values of $\alpha = 1.2$ with Gaussian distribution ($\alpha = 2$).

the value of σ is related to the problem domain size, and α can be found with some experimentation. The recommended value of α that performs well on almost all function landscapes is found to be 1.5 (Richer and Blackwell, 2006; Yang, 2008, 2009, 2010). LF is also found to be promising in solving a wide range of multimodal problems without the need to implement function stretching or niching methods. These methods are commonly employed in MAs to help the algorithm find multiple solutions.

3.4 Metaheuristic Algorithms Based on Lévy Probability Distribution: Is It a Good Idea?

3.4.1 Evolutionary Programming Using Mutations Based on the Lévy Probability Distribution

A first study using non-Gaussian-based mutation in evolutionary programming (EP) was carried out by Yao and Liu (1996). The authors proposed fast evolutionary programming (FEP) by replacing Gaussian-based mutation with a Cauchy distribution (Lee and Yao, 1999). FEP was shown to converge to a better solution compared to conventional EP for many multivariate functions used in the study. As the Cauchy distribution is a special case of the Lévy distribution, a generalized version of the FEP algorithm was presented by Lee and Yao (2001, 2004) using nonadaptive and adaptive Lévy mutation (LEP). In LEP, an individual is a pair of real-valued vectors $(\mathbf{x}_i, \eta_i)$, where $\mathbf{x}_i$ is a position vector, while η_i is a standard deviation vector, and the offspring $(\eta_j', \mathbf{x}_j')$ is computed according to Lee and Yao (2004) as

$$\eta_i'(k) = \eta_i(k)\exp\{\tau'N(0, 1) + \tau N_k(0, 1)\} \tag{3.13}$$

$$\mathbf{x}_i'(k) = \mathbf{x}_i(k) + \eta_i'(k)\, \mathrm{L}_\alpha(S) \tag{3.14}$$

The notations $N(0,1)$ and $N_k(0,1)$ in Eq. (3.13) represent random variables drawn from a standard Gaussian distribution fixed for a given value of i and newly generated component k, respectively. The variable $\mathrm{L}_\alpha(S)$ is Lévy distribution random number generated for each i with the parameter α. The parameters τ and τ' are given according to Bäck and Schwefel (1993) as

$$\tau = \frac{1}{\sqrt{2\sqrt{\mu}}} \quad \text{and} \quad \tau' = \frac{1}{\sqrt{2\mu}} \tag{3.15}$$

Due to space constraints, we have presented only the relevant set of equations that highlight the differences between GEP and LEP. For a tutorial overview on evolutionary algorithms, refer to Bäck and Schwefel (1993).

The proposed algorithm given by Lee and Yao (2004) was tested and compared for different values of α on 14 different benchmark functions with three unimodal functions, six multimodal functions with many local minima, and five multimodal functions with relatively fewer local minima. Through a series of experiments carried out by Lee and Yao (2004), it has been shown that both the nonadaptive and adaptive version of LEP is more robust compared to the EP based on Gaussian and Cauchy mutations. The authors have attributed the consistently better results to (i) Lévy mutation that yielded more distinct values than that from mutation based on Gaussian distribution and (ii) efficient exploration of the search area due to large variation, i.e., the fat tail characteristics of the Lévy distribution. For a more detailed discussion on the algorithm, results, and analysis, refer to Lee and Yao (2001, 2004).

3.4.2 Lévy Particle Swarm

In Richer and Blackwell (2006), the possibility of replacing motion of particles in the original particle swarm algorithm with an LF was considered. The aim of this research was to find whether incorporating a Lévy distribution can solve optimization problems more effectively compared to the originally proposed PSO (Kennedy and Eberhart, 1995). The standard version of PSO with the following set of update equations was used as a basis for the Lévy PSO (Kennedy and Eberhart, 1995):

$$\mathbf{v}_i^{t+1} = \chi[w^t \mathbf{v}_i^t + \mathbf{U}(0, \varphi_1) \otimes (\mathbf{p}_i^t - \mathbf{x}_i^t) + \mathbf{U}(0, \varphi_2) \otimes (\mathbf{p}_g^t - \mathbf{x}_i^t)] \qquad (3.16)$$

$$\mathbf{x}_i^{t+1} = \mathbf{x}_i^t + \mathbf{v}_i^{t+1} \qquad (3.17)$$

where $\mathbf{v}$ and $\mathbf{x}$ represent the particle velocity and position, respectively. The subscript i and the superscript t indicate an individual particle in the swarm and the number of iterations, respectively. The vectors $\mathbf{p}_i$ and $\mathbf{p}_g$ refer to the individual memory carried by the particle (the best position it has attained) and the best position found globally by the swarm, respectively. The symbols χ and w^k denote control parameters of the PSO and are known as constriction factor and inertial weight, respectively. The constriction factor χ determines how far a particle can move in a single iteration step and is set to 0.729843788 (Kennedy and Eberhart, 1995) and w is fixed as 1. Further, $\mathbf{U}(0, \varphi_1)$ and $\mathbf{U}(0, \varphi_2)$ are random vectors drawn from a uniform distribution and are generated at each iteration and for each particle. The values of φ_1 and φ_2 can change the behavior of PSO radically. They determine the magnitude of the random forces and control the pull of the particle toward the best position in the memory of the ith particle $\mathbf{p}_i$ and the pull to the best position found globally $\mathbf{p}_g$. The operator $\otimes$ represents element-by-element multiplication.

The heart of the PSO algorithms is a control mechanism that is linked to the effective search area explored by the algorithm. The PSO and its variants control the search by altering mean and standard deviation of the Gaussian distribution where the effective search area is linked to its standard deviation. The particles that are close to $\mathbf{p}_i$ or $\mathbf{p}_g$ will produce small standard deviation such that the regions close to these points will be explored, which in turn leads to convergence. The Lévy PSO presents a simple strategy that would imitate the good convergence properties of the standard PSO but would retain the fat tail property of the Lévy distribution by appropriately setting the Lévy scale parameter σ. In Lévy PSO, the uniform distributions used to determine the attraction of the particles to local and global bests are replaced by a Lévy distribution, i.e., φ_1 and φ_2 are drawn from a Lévy distribution.

In Richer and Blackwell (2006), the performance of Lévy-based PSO with standard PSO and different versions of PSO based on Gaussian distribution, such as Gaussian bare bone PSO (Kennedy, 2003, 2004), Gaussian PSO (Kennedy and Eberhart 1995), Gaussian burst (Kennedy, 2004), and Gaussian pivot (an adaptation of Gaussian bare bone), has been compared. In order to analyze the effectiveness of Lévy-based PSO, Richer and Blackwell (2006) conducted a series of experiments on a selected problem set of nine benchmark functions used by Lee and Yao (2004). The results were analyzed and compared for all the algorithms by using mean fitness value and standard error for each test function. In order to determine if the differences in the mean between the algorithms are significant, the mean values for each problem were compared by using the analysis of variance (ANOVA) with 0.05 as the level of significance. A detailed discussion of this test methodology can be found by Richer and Blackwell (2006). The best performing and most effective algorithm in this study over the problem set turned out to be Lévy-based PSO. The second best algorithm in the study was bare bones PSO based on Lévy distribution, while the other PSO algorithms generally performed less well. Again, not surprisingly, the best performance of Lévy-based PSO algorithms was attributed to the LF based on Lévy distribution with fat tail characteristics.

3.4.3 Cuckoo Search

The CS is a stochastic global search algorithm based on the breeding behavior of certain species of cuckoos (Yang and Deb, 2009). It can be described by the following three idealized rules: (i) each cuckoo lays a single egg which is then dumped in a randomly chosen nest; (ii) the best nests with high quality of solutions will be carried over to the next generation; (iii) the number of host nests is fixed, and there is a probability $p_\alpha \in [0,1]$ that an alien egg is discovered by the host bird. In this case, the host bird can either throw away the alien egg or it may leave the nest. A detailed discussion on the breeding behavior of cuckoos can be found by Payne et al. (2005). Based on such idealization, the basic steps of the CS are presented in the pseudocode shown in Figure 3.4. An important component of the CS is that LFs are used for both local and global search.

A new solution for a cuckoo i is generated by using an LF and is given as (Yang, 2010)

$$\mathbf{x}_i^{t+1} = \mathbf{x}_i^t + \gamma \cdot \mathbf{L}_\alpha(S) \tag{3.18}$$

where $\gamma > 0$ is the step size and relates to the scales of the problem of interest (Yang and Deb, 2009). The LF provides a random walk whose random step length S is drawn from a Lévy distribution with an infinite mean and variance. The subscript α in Eq. (3.18) determines the probability of obtaining Lévy random numbers in the tail of the distribution. The choice of α can have significant impact on the search ability of the CS. The value of $\alpha = 1.5$ has been recommended by Yang and Deb (2009).

In CS, a new egg is generated by performing an LF starting at the position of a randomly selected egg. If the objective function value is found to be better at this randomly selected new position, then the egg is moved to this new position. CS is a relatively simple algorithm with only two adjustable parameters, i.e., p_α and population size n. According to Yang (2009), the convergence rate of the algorithm is not strongly affected by the value of p_α and it is suggested to use $p_\alpha = 0.25$. The comparative study of the CS on a small set of test functions by Yang and Deb (2009) against PSO and GA showed that the convergence behavior of CS in terms of mean and standard deviation of number of function evaluations is superior to

Objective function $f(\mathbf{x})$, $\mathbf{x} = (x_1, x_2, x_3, ..., x_D)^T$, where D is the problem dimension.
Initialize a population of n host nests as $\mathbf{x}_i, (i = 1,2, ..., n)$
For all $\mathbf{x}_i$ do
    Calculate fitness $F_i = f(\mathbf{x}_i)$
end for
while *Number of Objective Evaluation or Generations < Maximum Number of Evaluations or Generations* **do**
    Current position of the population $\mathbf{x}_i$
    Perform Lévy flight from $\mathbf{x}_i$ to generate new egg $\mathbf{x}_k$
    $\mathbf{x}_i \leftarrow \mathbf{x}_k$
    $F_i \leftarrow f(\mathbf{x}_i)$
    Choose a random nest l from all nests
$F_l = f(\mathbf{x}_l)$
    if $(F_i > F_l)$ **do**
    $\mathbf{x}_l \leftarrow \mathbf{x}_i$
    $F_l \leftarrow F_i$
    end if
    Abandon fraction p_a of worse nests and build new nests at new locations (say j) by performing Lévy flight
$F_j = f(\mathbf{x}_j)$
    if $(F_i > F_j)$ **do**
    $\mathbf{x}_j \leftarrow \mathbf{x}_i$
    $F_j \leftarrow F_i$
    end if
Rank the solutions and find the current best
end while

Figure 3.4 Pseudocode of CS via LFs.

both GA and PSO. The use of LF in the CS suggests that it is possible to find all the optima in a problem search space for multimodal functions. Recently, CS has been successfully applied to solve such problems with multiple global minima, both in non-noise and additive white Gaussian noise (AWGN) environments (Jamil and Zepernick, 2013).

3.4.4 Modified Cuckoo Search

Modified cuckoo search (MCS) (Walton et al., 2011) is a modified version of original CS method proposed by Yang and Deb (2009). The MCS addresses the slow convergence of the original CS and incorporates the following two modifications: (i) the calculation of LF step size and (ii) addition of an information exchange mechanism between the eggs (best solutions) that have been determined by the objective function. The pseudocode of the MCS is shown in Figure 3.5.

The first modification is the calculation of LF step size. In CS (Yang and Deb, 2009), the LF step size is constant, while in MCS, the step size decreases with an increase in the number of generations G. Initially, the LF step length is set to $S = 1$, and for each generation, a new LF step size is calculated as $\beta = s/\sqrt{G}$. This leads to a more localized search process and can be regarded similar to the decrease in the inertial constant in PSO. Second, in MCS, a fraction of eggs with the best fitness values is put into a group of top eggs. For each of the top eggs, an egg is picked at random and a new egg is generated on the line connecting these two top eggs. The distance along this line at which a new egg is located is calculated by using inverse golden ratio according to $\varphi = 1 + \sqrt{5}/2$ such that it is closer to the egg with the best fitness value. In some cases, both eggs in the previous step can have the same fitness value. If such a situation is encountered, a new egg is generated at the midpoint. In principle, the golden ratio method can be replaced by a random fraction method, i.e., a new egg is placed at a random distance from the egg with the best fitness value. However, it was found by Walton et al. (2011) that the golden ratio method performs significantly better compared to random fraction. At this point, LF is performed locally from the randomly picked nest position with a step size $s = A/G^2$, which avoids any possibility of picking the same random position twice. These modifications resulted in a rapid convergence to the true global minimum (Walton et al., 2011) even at high numbers of dimensions. The MCS is shown to have better performance compared to the standard CS and has equal or better performance compared to other algorithms used in the comparative study by Walton et al. (2011).

3.4.5 Firefly Algorithm

FA is another stochastic global search algorithm based on the flashing behavior of fireflies and LF (Yang, 2010). FA is based on the following three idealized flashing characteristics of fireflies: (i) all fireflies are unisex so that one firefly will be attracted to other fireflies regardless of their sex; (ii) attractiveness is proportional to their brightness; thus, for any two flashing fireflies, the less brighter one will

```
Define maximum Lévy step size s and Golden ratio φ
Initialize a population of n host nests x_i, (i = 1,2, ..., n)
For all x_i do
        Calculate fitness F_i = f(x_i)
end for
Generation number G = 1
while Number of Objective Evaluation or Generations < Maximum number of Evaluations or
Generations do
G = G + 1
Sort nests by order of fitness
for all nests to be abandoned do
        Current position x_i
        Calculate Lévy flight step size β ← s/√G
        Perform Lévy flight from x_i to generate new egg x_k
        x_i ← x_k
        F_i ← f(x_i)
end for
for all the top nests do
        current position x_i
        Pick another nest from the top nests at random x_j
        If x_i = x_j then
                Calculate Lévy flight step size β ← s/G²
                Perform Lévy flight from x_i to generate new egg x_k
                F_k = f(x_k)
                Choose a random nest l from all nests
                if (F_k > F_l) do
                        x_l ← x_k
                        F_l ← F_k
                end if
        else
                Δx = |x_i − x_j|/φ
                Move distance Δx from the worst nest to the best nest to find x_k
                F_k ← f(x_k)
                Choose a random nest l from all nests
                if (F_k > F_l) then
                        x_l ← x_k
                        F_l ← F_k
                end if
        end if
    end for
end while
```

Figure 3.5 Pseudocode of modified cuckoo search via LFs (Walton, 2011).

move toward the more brighter one. If there is no brighter one, then a particular firefly will move randomly; and (iii) the brightness of a firefly is affected or determined by the landscape of the objective function. The pseudocode of FA to solve unconstrained global optimization problems is shown in Figure 3.6. The three important components of FA are (i) attractivness, (ii) distance, and (iii) movements.

3.4.5.1 *Attractiveness*

Each firefly has its own distinctive attractiveness parameter β which quantifies how strong it can attract other members in the swarm. In FA, the form of

---

Objective function $f(\mathbf{x})$, $\quad \mathbf{x} = (x_1, x_2, x_3, \ldots, x_D)^T$, where D is the problem dimension.

Initialize randomization α, initial attractiveness β_0, light absorption coefficient γ

Generate the initial location of Fireflies as $\mathbf{x}_i$, $(i = 1, 2, \ldots, n)$

For all $\mathbf{x}_i$ do

    Calculate fitness $F_i = f(\mathbf{x}_i)$

    Sort the Fireflies based on their light intensity

end for

while *Number of Objective Evaluation or Generations < Maximum Number of Evaluations or Generations* **do**

    for $i = 1: n$ (loop over all the fireflies)

        for $j = 1: i$ (loop over all the fireflies)

            if $(I_j > I_i)$

            Calculate distance between the fireflies according to (20) or (21)

            Attractiveness β varies with distance r_{ij} via $\exp(-\gamma r_{ij}^2)$

            Generate and evaluate new solutions and update light intensity

        end if

        end for j

    end for i

    Check if the new solutions are within the problem domain size

    Rank the fireflies and find the current best

end while

Figure 3.6 Pseudocode of firefly algorithm via LF for unconstrained global optimization (Yang, 2010).

attractiveness function of a firefly is a monotonically decreasing function of distance between the fireflies and is given as (Yang, 2010)

$$\beta(r) = \beta_0 \exp(-\gamma r_{ij}^2) \tag{3.19}$$

where r is the distance between any two fireflies, β_0 is the initial attractiveness, and γ is an absorption coefficient that controls the decrease of light intensity.

3.4.5.2 Distance

According to Yang (2010), the Cartesian distance between any two fireflies i and j at positions $\mathbf{x}_i$ and $\mathbf{x}_j$ is given as

$$r_{ij} = ||\mathbf{x}_i - \mathbf{x}_j|| = \sqrt{\sum_{k=1}^{D} (x_{i,k} - x_{j,k})^2} \tag{3.20}$$

where D is problem dimension and $x_{i,k}$ represents the kth component of spatial coordinate $\mathbf{x}_i$ of the ith firefly. In case of problems with only two dimensions, Eq. (3.20) becomes

$$r_{ij} = \sqrt{(x_i - x_j)^2 + (y_i - y_j)^2} \tag{3.21}$$

3.4.5.3 Movement

The movement of firefly i to another more brighter firefly j is given as

$$\mathbf{x}_i = \mathbf{x}_i + \beta_0 \exp(-\gamma r_{ij}^2)(\mathbf{x}_j - \mathbf{x}_i) + \phi \cdot \text{sign}[\varepsilon - 0.5] \cdot \mathbf{L}_\alpha(S) \tag{3.22}$$

In Eq. (3.22), the first term represents the current position of a firefly, the second term represents the attraction of less brighter flies toward more brighter flies, and the third term is randomization due to LF. The parameter ϕ is called randomization parameter and is determined by the problem at hand. The notation sign $[\varepsilon - 0.5]$ provides the direction of the movement of the flies, where $\varepsilon \in [0,1]$, while random step length S is drawn from a Lévy distribution. FA is summarized in the pseudocode shown in Figure 3.6.

FA has shown to outperform both GA and PSO in terms of both efficiency and success rate (Yang, 2010). Since its inception, it has attracted a lot of research interest and has also been successfully applied to solve a variety of constrained optimization problems (Apostolopoulos and Vlachos, 2011; Lukasik and Zak, 2009).

3.4.6 Eagle Strategy

Eagle strategy (ES) is a relatively new algorithm based on the foraging behavior of an eagle. It is a two-stage strategy algorithm and attempts to provide a fine balance between exploration and exploitation by using two different algorithms. In the first stage, like an eagle, it scans a whole function landscape to look for possible prey, i.e., a good solution, by performing LF. Once potential prey (solution) has been identified, the eagle changes its strategy from search to chase focusing on capturing the prey (solution) in an efficient manner. From an optimization point of view, this means that a first global search is performed by LF, and then a local optimum can be found by using an efficient local optimizer method. The efficient optimizer may include steepest descent or downhill simplex methods. To avoid being trapped locally, a global search is performed again followed by local search and the process is repeated iteratively. The pseudocode of ES is summarized in Figure 3.7.

In summary, ES uses two different algorithms at different stages and at different times of the iterations. It is worth to mention that ES uses LF for global exploration, which induces enough randomness to explore the function landscape as diversely and effectively as possible. On the other hand, the algorithm used for the

Objective function $f(\mathbf{x})$, $\mathbf{x} = (x_1, x_2, x_3, \ldots, x_D)^T$, where D is the problem dimension.
Parameter initialization for FA
Random initial guess for local optimizer $\mathbf{x}^{t=0}$
while (stop criterion)
    Call FA via LF and do the global exploration of the search space
    Intensive local search around the promising solution found by FA via efficient local optimizer
    If (a better solution is found)
        Update the current best
    end
    Update $t = t + 1$
end while

Figure 3.7 Pseudocode of two-stage ES for unconstrained global optimization problems (Yang, 2010).

intensive local exploitation should be an efficient local optimizer to find local optimum within a minimal number of function evaluations. This stage is fast and efficient compared to the global exploration stage. ES has been tested and compared on a limited set of test functions and has been shown to outperform PSO in terms of efficiency and success (Yang, 2010).

3.5 Discussion

In this section, we highlight the differences and similarities of the aforementioned MAs based on Lévy flight. EP describes the evolution of finite state machines to solve prediction tasks. The state transitions tables of the finite state machines are normally modified using mutations based on uniform distribution. Moreover, like GA, it also utilizes selection and mutation as main operators (Bäck and Schwefel, 1993). However, simple selection and mutation operators are not enough as they might not effectively preserve partial solutions in the intermediate stages of the algorithm. This could hinder the ability of the algorithm to find an optimum solution. By simply replacing a uniformly distributed mutation with Lévy distributed mutations enhances the ability of the algorithm to find an optimum solution to even difficult problems.

The other algorithms such as LF variants of PSO, CS, MCS, FA, and ES all do not use selection and mutation operators. They use LF for global exploration and are able to visit far-off regions in the problem search space. The LF-based versions of CS, MCS, FA, and ES outperform other algorithms such as standard PSO, GA, and ACO for highly nonlinear, global optimization problems. However, standard PSO and Lévy variants of PSO (with the exception of Gaussian bare bones) use a particle velocity to update the position of the particle in the problem search space. As a result, the particles tend to accelerate out of the solution space. Therefore, clamping of the velocity has to be taken into consideration. On the other hand, Lévy bare bones PSO, CS, MCS, FA, and ES rely solely on particle positions to find an optimum solution. However, a proper mechanism has to be introduced in these algorithms to ensure that the particles respect the problem boundary constraints. As a result, these algorithms are rather simpler to implement. Additionally, FA offers two advantages over PSO and other MAs: (i) automatic subgrouping and (ii) ability to deal with multimodal problems. FA can automatically subdivide into subgroups, and each group can potentially swarm around all the optima including local and global minima simultaneously. This is particularly beneficial when dealing with multimodal problems provided that the number of FA is much higher than the number of modes.

3.6 Conclusions

Evidence that many foraging animals use search strategies based on LF or LW governed by power law is accumulating. These search strategies have applications in diverse biological systems, as well as in chemical and physical phenomena, such as the diffusion of fluorescent molecules and cooling behavior. Also, noise could show LF style characteristics under the right conditions (Yang, 2010). Such strategies typically include a long step (fast phase) followed by a phase of diffusion (short steps, slow phase) and can be well modeled by the Lévy distribution. The LF-based strategies can be expected to be useful in environments where no prior knowledge is available, the "targets" are difficult to detect, and the distribution of targets is sparse. Many foragers such as birds, lizards, planktivorous fish, and even pet dogs may spend some time carefully examining a local region and then quickly relocate to a previously unscanned region (Bénicho et al., 2005; Richer and Blackwell, 2006). These tactics have been shown to be superior to random search based on Brownian walk. The extension of these findings into global optimization techniques can be based on the fact that the fat tails of the Lévy distribution will generate candidate solutions that are far from a current optimum and hence promote continued exploration at any stage of the search. This may improve algorithm performance by allowing it to escape from a local optimum.

It can be argued that the essence of these algorithms lies in the efficient and effective search strategies to explore the problem search space (Lee and Yao, 2001, 2004) and communication of information throughout a swarm. This argument seems to be overwhelmingly supported by the findings of Lukasik and Zak (2009), Richer and Blackwell (2006), Walton et al. (2011), Yang (2010), Yang and Deb (2009), and Yang and Gandomi (2012). The applications of these algorithms are diverse and have been successfully applied to a wide range of problems in engineering, data mining, scheduling, and manufacturing processes. For example, CS is found in embedded system design, optimum designing of steel frames, and milling applications. FA has been successfully applied to digital image compression, antenna design, semantic web composition, and clustering among many others.

Most recently, ES coupled with differential evolution has been applied to solve unconstrained and constrained GO (Gandomi et al., 2012b). The LF-based algorithms are shown to produce better or comparable results from their non-LF counterparts (Wikipedia, 2012a, b). Based on the discussion provided in this chapter, it can be argued that LF-based search mechansim in stochastic algorithms to solve global optimization problems is worth pursuing.

References

Apostolopoulos, T., Vlachos, T.A., 2011. Application of the firefly algorithm for solving the economic emissions load dispatch problem. Int. J. Comb. 2011, 1−23.

Austin, D., Bowen, W.D., McMillan, J.I., 2004. Intraspecific variation in movement patterns: modelling individual behaviour in a large marine predator. Oikos. 105, 15−30.

Bäck, T., Schwefel, H.P., 1993. An overview of evolutionary algorithms for parameter optimization. IEEE Evol. Comput. 1, 1−23.

Barthelemy, P., Bertolotti, J., Wiersma, D.S., 2008. A Lévy flight for light. Nature. 453, 495−498.

Bartumeus, F., Peters, F., Pueyo, S., Marrase, C., Catalan, J., 2003. Levy walks: adjusting searching strategies to resource avaliability in microzooplankton. Proc. Natl. Acad. Sci. USA. 100, 12771−12775.

Bell, J.W., 1991. Searching Behaviour: The Behavioural Ecology of Finding Resources. Chapman and Hall, London, New York.

Bénicho, O., Coppey, M., Moreau, M., Suet, P.H., Voituriez, R., 2005. Optimal search strategies for hidden targets. Available online: <http://arxiv.org/abs/cond-mat/0504107> (accessed 8.25.12).

Blum, C., Roli, A., 2003. Metaheuristics in combinatorial optimization: overview and conceptual comparison. ACM Comput. Surv. 35, 268−308.

Brent, R.P., 1973. Algorithms for Minimization Without Derivatives. Prentice Hall, Englewood Cliffs, New Jersey.

Civicioglu, P., Besdok, E., 2011. A conceptual comparison of cuckoo-search, particle swarm optimization, differential evolution and artifical bee algorithms. Artif. Intell. Rev. 39, 315−346.

Dorigo, M., Stützle, T., 2004. Ant Colony Optimization. MIT Press, Cambridge, MA.

Dorigo, M., Birattari, M., Stützle, T., 2006. Ant colony optimization. IEEE Comp. Intell. Mag. 4, 28−39.

Engelbrecht, A.P., 2005. Fundamentals of Computational Swarm Intelligence. John Wiley & Sons, Hoboken, NJ.

Gandomi, A.H., Alavi, A.H., 2012a. Krill Herd: a new bio-inspired optimization algorithm. Comm. Nonlinear Sci. Num. Sim. 17, 4831−4845.

Gandomi, A.H., Yang, X.-S., Talatahari, S., Deb, S., 2012b. Coupled eagle strategy and differential evolution for unconstrained and constrained global optimization. Comput. Math. Appl. 63, 191−200.

Glover, F., 1989. Tabu search—Part I. OSRA J. Comput. 1, 190−206.

Glover, F., 1990. Tabu search—Part II. OSRA J. Comput. 2, 4−32.

Goldberg, D.E., 1989. Genetic Algorithm in Search, Optimization and Machine Learning. Addison-Wesley, Boston, MA.

Grinbergy, Y.Y., Miltzon, J.G., Kraig, R.P., 2011. Spreading depression sends microgila on Lévy flights. PLoS One. 6, e19294.

Gutowski, M., 2001. Lévy flights as an underlying mechanism for global optimization algorithms. Proceedings of the 5th National Conference on Evolutionary Computation and Global Optimization, Jastrzębia Góra, Poland, Warsaw University of Technology Publishing House, pp. 79–86.

Hooke, R.T., Jeeves, A., 1961. Direct search solution of numerical and statistical problems. J. ACM. 8, 212–229.

Humphries, N.E., Querioz, N., Dyer, J.R.M., Pade, N.G., Musyl, M.K., Schaefer, K.M., et al., 2010. Environmental context explains Levy and Brownian movement patterns of marine predators. Nature. 451, 1066–1069.

Jamil, M., Zepernick, H.-J., 2013. Multimodal function optimization with cuckoo search algorithm. Int. J. Bio-Inspired Comput., Inderscience Publishers (in press). <http://www.inderscience.com/info/ingeneral/forthcoming.php?jcode=ijbic>.

Karaboga, D., Basturk, B., 2007. A powerful and efficient algorithm for numerical function optimization: artificial bee colony (ABC). J. Glob. Optim. 39, 459–471.

Kennedy, J.R., 2003. Bare bones particle swarms. IEEE Swarm Intell. Symp.80–87.

Kennedy, J.R., 2004. Probability and dynamics in the particle swarm. Congr. Evol. Comput. 340–347.

Kennedy, J.R., Eberhart, C., 1995. Particle swarm optimization. IEEE Interantional Conference on Neural Networks. Piscataway, NJ, pp. 1942–1948.

Kirkpatrick, S., Gelatt Jr., C.D., Vecchi, M.P., 1983. Optimization by simulated annealing. Science. 220, 671–680.

Lee, C.−Y., Yao, X., 1999. Evolutionary programming made faster. IEEE Trans. Evol. Comput. 3, 82–102.

Lee, C.−Y., Yao, X., 2001. Evolutionary algorithm with adaptive Lévy mutations. Congr. Evol. Comput.568–575.

Lee, C.−Y., Yao, X., 2004. Evolutionary programming using mutations based on Lévy probability distribution. IEEE Trans. Evol. Comput. 8, 1–13.

Lee, K.S., Geem, Z.W., 2005. A meta-heuristic algorithm for continuous engineering optimization: harmony search theory and practice. Comput. Methods Appl. Mech. Eng. 194, 3902–3933.

Lukasik, S., Zak, S., 2009. Computational collective intelligence. Semantic Web, Social Networks and Multiagent Systems. In: Nguyen, N.T., Kowalczyk, R., Chen, S.M. (Eds.), Firefly Algorithm for Continuous Constrained Optimization Tasks. Springer, Berlin, Heidelberg.

Mantegna, R.N., 1994. Fast, accurate algorithm for numerical simulation of levy stable stochastic processes. Phys. Rev. E. 49, 4677–4683.

Mantegna, R.N., Stanley, H.E., 2000. An Introduction to Econophysics. Cambridge University Press, Cambridge, UK.

Mårell, A.J., Ball, P., Hofgraad, A., 2002. A foraging and movement paths of female reinedeer: insights from fractal analysis, correlated random walks and Levy flights. Can. J. Zool. 80, 854–865.

Nelder, J.A., Meade, R., 1965. A simplex method for function minimization. Comput. J. 7, 2051–2056.

Osman, I.H., Laporte, G., 1996. Metaheuristics: a bibliography. Ann. Oper. Res. 63, 513–623.

Pantaleo, E., Facci, P., Pascazio, S., 2009. Simulation of Lévy flights. Phys. Scr. 2009, 1–3.

Payne, R.B., Sorenson, M.D., Klitz, K., 2005. The Cuckoos. Oxford University Press, New York, USA.

Porto, M., Roman, H.E., 2002. Autoregressive processes with exponentially decaying probability distribution functions: application to daily variations of a stock market index. Phys. Rev. E. 65, 046149.

Powell, M.J.D., 1964. An efficient method for finding minimization of a function of several variables without calculating derivatives. Comput. J. 7, 152–162.

Ramos-Frenández, G., Mateos, J.L., Miramontes, O., Cocho, G., Larralde, H., Ayala-Orozco, B., 2004. Levy walk patterns in the foraging movements of spider monkeys (*Ateles geoffroyi*). Behav. Ecol. Sociobiol. 55, 223–230.

Richer, T.J., Blackwell, T.M., 2006. The Lévy particle swarm. IEEE Congress on Evolutionary Computation. Vancouver, Canada, pp. 808–815.

Rosenbrock, H.H., 1960. An automatic method for finding the greatest or least value of a function. Comput. J. 3, 175–184.

Shlesinger, M.F., Zaslavsky, G.M., Frisch, U. (Eds.), 1995. Lévy Flights and Related Topics in Physics. Springer, Heidelberg, Germany.

Sims, D.W., 2010. Tracking and analysis technique for understanding free-ranging shark movements and behaviour. In: Msick, J.A., Carrier, J.C. (Eds.), *Sharks and Their Relatives II—Biodiversity, Adaptive Physiology and Conservation*. CRC Press, Boca Raton, FL, USA, pp. 351–392.

Stanley, H.E., Amaral, L.A.N., Canning, D., Gopikrishnan, P., Lee, Y., Liu, Y., 1999. Econophysics: can physicists contribute to the science of economics? Phys. A. 269, 156–169.

Stützle, T., 1999. Local Search Algorithms for Combinatorial Problems—Analysis, Algorithms and New Application. DISKI-Dissertation zur künstlichen Intelligenz, Sankt Augustin.

Tamura, K., Yusuf, Y., Hidaka, Y., Kai, S.C., 2001. Nonlinear transport and anomalous Brownian motion in soft-mode turbulence. J. Phys. Soc. Jpn. 70, 2805–2808.

Tsonis, A.A., Roebber, P.J., Elsner, J.B., 1998. A characteristics time scale in the global temperature record. Geophys. Res. Lett. 25, 2821–2823.

Tsonis, A.A., Hunt, A.G., Elsner, J.B., 2003. On the relation between ENSO and global climate change. Meterol. Atoms. Phys. 84, 229–242.

Venkataraman, P., 2009. Applied Optimization with Matlab Programming. John Wiley & Sons, Hoboken, NJ, USA.

Viswanathan, G.M., 2010. Fish in Lévy-flight foraging. Nature. 465, 1018–1019.

Viswanathan, G.M., Afanasyev, V., Buldyrev, S.V., Murphy, E.J., Prince, P.A., Stanley, H. E., 1996. Lévy flight search patterns of wandering albatrosses. Nature. 381, 413–415.

Viswanathan, G.M., Buldyrev, S.V., Havlin, S., Da Luz, M.G.E., Raposo, E.P., Stanley, H. E., 1999. Optimizing the sucess of random searches. Nature. 401, 911–914.

Viswanathan, G.M., Afanasyev, V., Buldyrev, S.V., Havlin, S., Da Luz, M.G.E., Raposo, E. P., et al., 2000. Lévy flights in random searches. Phys. A. 282, 1–12.

Voß, S., Martello, S., Osman, I.H., Roucairol, C. (Eds.), 1999. Meta-Heuristics—Advances and Trends in Local and Serach Paradigms for Optimization. Kluwer Academic Publishers, Norwell, MA, USA.

Walton, S., Hassan, O., Morgan, K., Brwon, M.R., 2011. Modified cuckoo search: a new gradient free optimisation algorithm. Chaos, Solitons Fractals. 44, 710–718.

Wikipedia, 2012a. Cuckoo search. [Online] Available from: World Wide Web: <http://en.wikipedia.org/wiki/Cuckoo_search> (accessed 08.08.12).

Wikipedia, 2012b. FireFly algorithm. [Online] Available from: World Wide Web: <http://en.wikipedia.org/wiki/Firefly_algorithm> (accessed 08.08.12).

Yang, X.-S., 2008. Nature-Inspired Metaheuristic Algorithms. Luniver Press.

Yang, X.-S., 2010. Engineering Optimization: An Introduction with Metaheuristic Applications. John Wiley & Sons, United Kingdom.

Yang, X.-S., 2011. Review of metaheuristics and generalized evolutionary walk algorithm. Int. J. Bio-Inspired Comput. 3, 77−84.

Yang, X.-S., Deb, S., 2009. Cuckoo search via Lévy flights. In: World Congress on Nature & Biologically Inspired Computing (NaBIC 2009). Coimbatore, India, pp. 210−214.

Yang, X.-S., Gandomi, A.H., 2012. Bat algorithm: a novel approach for global engineering optimization. Eng. Comput. 29, 464−483.

Yao, X., Liu, Y., 1996. Fast evolutionary programming. Proceedings of the Fifth Annual Conference on Evolutionary Programming, MIT Press, pp. 451−460.

4 Memetic Self-Adaptive Firefly Algorithm

Iztok Fister[1], Xin-She Yang[2], Janez Brest[1] and Iztok Jr. Fister[1]

[1]Faculty of Electrical Engineering and Computer Science, University of Maribor, Maribor, Slovenia; [2]Department of Design Engineering and Mathematics, School of Science and Technology, Middlesex University, The Burroughs, London, UK

4.1 Introduction

Nature has always been a source of inspiration for scientists when searching for solutions to given problems. For example, the collective behavior of social insects like ants, termites, bees, and wasp, as well as other animal societies like flocks of birds or schools of fish, has inspired scientists to design intelligent multiagent systems (Blum and Li, 2008). In the natural world, colonies of social insects consist of a huge number of unsophisticated beings/agents (i.e., individuals) so that a colony as a whole can accomplish complex tasks in cooperation. These tasks are coordinated without any centralized control and are thus self-organized. The fundamentals of collective behavior regarding individuals in colonies have inspired scientists to solve some complex, practical problems. The research field that exploits swarm behavior is referred to as swarm intelligence. Swarm intelligence can be emergent in complex systems, especially, in those systems that are initially demand flexibility and robustness.

The term swarm intelligence was first used by Beni and Wang (1989) in the context of a cellular robotic system. Nowadays, this term also extended to the field of optimization, where the techniques based on swarm intelligence have been applied successfully. Examples of notable swarm intelligence optimization techniques are ant colony optimization (Dorigo and Di Caro, 1999; Korošec et al., 2012), particle swarm optimization (Kennedy and Eberhart, 1999), and artificial bee colony (ABC) (Karaboga and Basturk, 2007). Today, the most promising swarm intelligence optimization techniques include the firefly algorithm (FFA) (Gandomi et al., 2011, 2013; Yang, 2008; Yang et al., 2012; Talatahari et al., 2012), the cuckoo search (Yang and Deb, 2009), and the bat algorithm (Yang, 2010).

Swarm intelligence refers to the collective behavior of social individuals. In nature-inspired metaheuristic algorithms, these individuals are represented as a population of solutions. The population of solutions is maintained, instead of

Swarm Intelligence and Bio-Inspired Computation. DOI: http://dx.doi.org/10.1016/B978-0-12-405163-8.00004-1

searching for a single solution to a problem of interest. Therefore, this type of algorithms is also called population-based. From individuals in a population (also parents), population-based algorithms, such as evolutionary algorithms (EAs), are able to produce new solutions (e.g., offspring) in terms of the operations of mutation and crossover (Eiben and Smit, 2003).

However, population-based algorithms have many advantages over single-point search algorithms, as summarized as the following five points (Prügel-Bennett, 2010):

1. Building blocks are put together from different solutions through crossover.
2. Focusing search again relies on the crossover and means that if both parents share the same value of a variable, then the offspring will also have the same value of this variable.
3. Low-pass filtering ignores distractions within the landscape.
4. Hedging against bad luck in the initial positions or decisions it makes.
5. Parameter tuning is the algorithms' opportunity to learn good parameter values in order to balance exploration against exploitation.

The exploration and exploitation in the FFA need to be defined before taking a closer look at these components for the search process. Exploration and exploitation are the two cornerstones of problem solving by iterative search (Črepinšek et al., 2011). Exploration refers to the moves for discovering the entirely new regions of a search space, while exploitation refers to the moves that focus its search on the vicinity of promising, known solutions found during the search process. Other terminologies for exploration and exploitation used by Blum and Roli (2003) are diversification and intensification that refer to medium- to long-term strategies based on the usage of memory, while exploration and exploitation refer to short-term strategies tied to randomness. In this chapter, the terms exploration and exploitation are used for consistency.

Exploration and exploitation must be balanced in order to make a search move efficiently and effectively. Namely, too much exploration can lead to inefficient search, while too much exploitation can cause the premature convergence of a search algorithm where the search process, usually due to reducing the population diversity, can be trapped into a local optimum (Eiben and Smit, 2003).

How to balance these two components of the search? To date, the balance between exploration and exploitation has been managed indirectly, i.e., by proper control parameter settings. For example, EAs involve various variations (e.g., crossover and mutation) and selection operators that can be controlled via control parameters. A suitable parameter setting depends on the given problem. In fact, a parameter setting suitable for a certain problem can be unsuitable for another. Furthermore, set parameters that are suitable at the beginning of a search process can become unsuitable during the maturing phases of the search. Therefore, a necessity has been arisen for adapting parameters during a search process.

The most complete taxonomy of the parameter setting can be found by Eiben et al. (1999). According to this taxonomy, the authors distinguished between two major forms of parameter setting: parameter tuning and parameter control. In the former case, good values of parameters are set before the run. These values then remain unchanged throughout the run. In the latter case, the parameters start with initial values that are then changed during the run. These values can be changed: deterministic, adaptive, or self-adaptive. Deterministic parameter control occurs when the values of parameters are changed by some deterministic rule. A characteristic of adaptive parameter control is that the direction or magnitude of the change depends on feedback from the search. One example of this control is represented by Rechenberg's 1/5 success rule (Rechenberg, 1973). Finally, the parameters are encoded into representations of individuals and undergo variation operators by self-adaptive parameter control.

The proposed FFA tries to balance the exploration and exploitation more directly during the run of a search process. Directly controlling the balance is difficult (Črepinšek et al., 2011). The first question that must therefore be answered is how to measure exploration and exploitation during a search. Typically, exploration and exploitation are implicitly measured using a diversity of population that plays a crucial role in the success of optimization. Diversity refers to differences among individuals. These differences can arise either at the genotype or phenotype levels. The genotype refers to the structural characteristics of individuals' representation. Phenotype determines the quality of an individual. Population diversity measures how similar individuals are to each other (Neri, 2012). When individuals are distributed over the whole search space, the population has high diversity. On the other hand, when individuals are crowded to a certain region of the search space, it has low diversity.

Unfortunately, diversity is only roughly related to exploration and exploitation (Črepinšek et al., 2011). High diversity is not necessarily a sign that the population consists of fit individuals. It only indicates that individuals are exceedingly dissimilar. On the other hand, low diversity can indicate that the search algorithm has converged to the some optimum. This optimality can either be global or local. In the former case, the algorithm finds the optimal solution, while in the latter case it is trapped into a local optimum, e.g., in case of an EA, premature convergence has arisen.

In place of premature convergence, a phenomenon of stagnation can be typical for swarm intelligence, which can occur when the search algorithm cannot improve the best performance (also fitness) although the diversity is still high. Thus, less-promising regions of the search space are explored.

First of foremost, swarm intelligence is concerned in optimization and robotics. This chapter, however, is devoted to optimization, i.e., how to solve optimization problems using swarm intelligence techniques. One of the latest swarm intelligence techniques is the FFA that is the main subject of this chapter. The main characteristic of fireflies is their flashing light that can be visible, especially, on summer nights in tropical and temperature regions. Such flashing light can be expressed in the form of a physical equation regarding light intensity. This equation can be associated with the objective function of the problem to be optimized. The main advantage of the FFA is to search for more optima simultaneously and thus, it is more suitable for nonlinear, multimodal problems.

In the proposed FFA, a stagnation phenomenon is signaled when the diversity of the population being measured on a phenotype level remains stable, and the best fitness does not improve regarding the prescribed number of generations. If the stagnation condition is detected, the proposed FFA recruits individuals with higher diversity. Thus, the diversity of the entire population is increased and it can therefore be supposed that the search algorithm needs to focus itself on exploring a broader region of the search space.

Three additional features have been applied to the proposed FFA as follows:

1. self-adaptation of control parameters,
2. a new population model,
3. local search heuristics

that will be explained in the remainder of this chapter. A global search algorithm hybridized with a local search is referred to as memetic algorithm by Moscato (1999). In our case, the memetic self-adaptive FFA (MSA-FFA) has been developed and applied to a graph 3-coloring problem (3-GCP). The extensive experiments to be given below show that the results of MSA-FFA are comparable with the results of other tested algorithms.

The rest of this chapter is organized as follows. In Section 4.2, optimization problems and their complexity are discussed. The principles of the MSA-FFA are explained in Section 4.3. Section 4.4 describes a case study in which the MSA-FFA is applied to a graph 3-coloring. Besides a detailed description of this algorithm, the extensive experimental work is illustrated and the obtained results are compared with three other well-known graph coloring algorithms, i.e., Tabucol, HEA, and EA-SAW. Finally, Section 4.5 summarizes the results and a closer look at future work.

4.2   Optimization Problems and Their Complexity

From a system analysis point of view, an optimization problem can be seen as a system consisting of three components: input data, output data, and the model (Eiben and Smit, 2003). The model is treated as a black box that transforms input data into output data. Knowing the model and output data, the optimization problem becomes how to find input data that satisfies the criterion of optimality (Figure 4.1).

Let us suppose, a traveling salesman problem (TSP) is given. Here, an equation (model) is provided that calculates their length (output data) for each arbitrary cycle (input data). The length of the cycle is calculated by an objective function f_{obj}. The task of the optimization system is to find the cycle with the shortest length

Figure 4.1 Optimization problem.

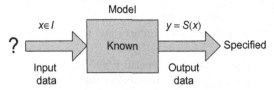

(goal). The shortest cycle represents an optimal solution that can be written as $s^* = S^*(x) = S(x^*)$, while its optimal value can be expressed as $f^*_{obj}(s)$. Note that only one set of input data x can be put on the input. This set of data is referred to as an instance I. Normally the instance $x \in I$ is a vector of elements x_i that are called design or decision variables. In line with this, the optimization problem can be formally defined as a quadrille $P = (I, S, f_{obj}, g)$, where

- I denotes all instances of the input data;
- S is the function that to each instance $x \in I$ assigns a set of feasible solutions $S(x)$;
- f_{obj} is the objective function that to each feasible solution $s \in S(x)$ of instance $x \in I$ assigns the value $f_{obj}(s) \in \mathbb{R}$;
- g denotes the goal that determines when the minimum ($g = \min$) or maximum ($g = \max$) value of objective function is searched for.

Usually, the fitness function f is used in place of the objective function f_{obj}. If we suppose that $\max(f_{obj}(s)) = \min(-f_{obj}(s))$, then the goal $g = \max$ can always be transformed into $g = \min$. In other words, we always search the minimum value of the transformed objective function. As a result, the optimization problem can be reduced to a triple $P = (I, S, f)$. It can arise in three forms, as follows:

1. *Construction form*: The optimal solution s^* and to it the belonging value of the fitness function $f^*(s)$ need to be calculated for the instance $x \in I$.
2. *Nonconstruction form*: The optimal value of the fitness function $f^*(s)$ is needed for the instance $x \in I$.
3. *Decision form*: For the particular instance $x \in I$, it should be discovered whether the optimal value of fitness function $f^*(s)$ is better than a certain prescribed constant K, more formally if $f^*(s) \leq K$.

For example, the shortest cycle (a sequence of cities) and its length need to be found when the TSP problem is given in its construction form. The length of the shortest cycle is demanded when the TSP problem is in nonconstruction form, while in the decision form of TSP, it is necessary to answer the question whether the shortest cycle found is shorter than a certain prescribed length K.

How hard to solve the problem is, depends not on the problem solver, but rather on the features of the fitness function within the search space. The visualization of fitness values' distribution forms a kind of fitness landscape introduced by Wright (1932). Mathematically, the fitness landscape is defined as (S, f, d), where S denotes the search space, f the fitness function that assigns to each solution $s \in S(x)$ with the fitness value $f(s)$, and $d: S \times S \to \mathbb{R}$ is a distance metric that defines the spatial structure of the landscape (Stadler, 1995). The fitness landscape reflects the following characteristics of the problem: multimodality, separability, noise, time dependency, etc.

Optimization problems can be further divided into continuous and discrete. The latter is also referred to as combinatorial. The decision variables for a continuous optimization problem can occupy values within the domain of real values $\mathbb{R}$, while the decision variables for a combinatorial problem have discrete values.

According to the number of objectives involved in the optimization problem, this can be divided into single-objective and multiobjective (also multicriteria).

The task of single-objective optimization is to find the optimal solution according to only one objective function. When the optimization problem involves more than one objective function, the task is to find one or more optimal solutions regarding each objective (Deb, 2001). Here, a solution that is good with respect to one objective can be worse for another, and vice versa. Therefore, the goal of multiobjective optimization is to find a set of solutions that are optimal with respect to all other objectives, and such a set of solutions form a so-called Pareto front. Interestingly, most real-world problems are multiobjective.

Many practical problems have complex constraints. Namely, not all possible combinations of decision variables represent valid solutions. Constraint problems can be divided into two different types: constraint satisfaction problems (CSPs) and constraint optimization problems (COPs). In contrast, if the problem is unconstrained, it is referred to as a free optimization problem (Eiben and Smit, 2003). CSP is defined as a pair $\langle S, \phi \rangle$, where S denotes a search space and ϕ is a Boolean function on S that represents a feasibility condition. In fact, this function divides the search space S into feasible and unfeasible regions. A solution of the CSP is each $\mathbf{s} \in S$ with $\phi(\mathbf{s}) = \text{true}$. On the other hand, COP is defined as a triple $\langle S, f, \phi \rangle$, where S denotes a search space, f is a real-valued fitness function, and ϕ is a Boolean function on S. A solution of this problem is that $\mathbf{s} \in S(\mathbf{x})$ with $\phi(\mathbf{s}) = \text{true}$ and $S(\mathbf{x}) = S(\mathbf{x}^*)$.

In general, algorithms are step-by-step procedures for solving problems (Garey and Johnson, 1979). These procedures can be computer programs, written in specific programming languages. The first programs tried to solve optimization problems by exhaustive search, i.e., by enumerating all possible combinations of decision variables. However, these programs are too time-consuming and impractical for solving most real-world problems. Therefore, more approaches were developed that tried to solve these problems approximately in a reasonable time. Nowadays, there exist optimization algorithms that search for solutions by using gradient-based and heuristic-based search techniques (Deb, 2001). Deterministic and stochastic search principles are applied in these algorithms. While the deterministic principle behaves in a predictably mechanical way, because it always produces the same results, the stochastic principle involves a randomness step within the algorithm. The necessity of widening the applicability of optimization algorithms to various new problem domains has led to robust optimization algorithms inspired by natural and physical principles or characteristics. Essentially, EAs and swarm intelligence belong to this class of algorithms, which also belong to metaheuristic algorithms (Yang, 2008).

If an algorithm successfully solves all instances of some problem P, then we can say that it is capable of solving the problem P. Usually, we are interested in which algorithm solves the problem more efficiently. Normally, the term efficiency is connected with the resources of the computer (time and space) that are occupied by running an algorithm. Generally, the most efficient algorithm is the one that finds the solution to the problem in the fastest way.

In practice, the time complexity of an algorithm is not measured by the effective time necessary for solving the problem on a concrete computer because this measurement suffers from a lack of objectiveness. The same algorithm could be run on different hardware configurations or even on different operating systems. Therefore, the algorithm's complexity is measured in an informal way that determines the complexity with regard to the amount of input data (instance size), necessary for the problem description. In the case of TSP, the complexity of the problem is determined by the number of cities that the traveling salesman must visit.

The time complexity of an algorithm determines the way in which the increase in the instance size influences the time complexity (Garey and Johnson, 1979). This relation can be expressed with the so-called asymptotic time complexity function $O(\hat{f}(n))$ that determines the upper bound of time complexity for problem P. For example, the function $O(n^2)$ denotes that the increase in the instance size n will cause an increase in the time complexity to almost n^2.

When do the problems become hard (Garey and Johnson, 1979)? The algorithmic theory divides problems, with regard to the asymptotic time complexity function, into two classes: P-hard and NP-hard. To the first class belong those problems that have polynomial time complexity $O(n^k)$ and are treated as "easy." In contrast, problems of class NP-hard demonstrate the exponential time complexity $O(2^n)$ and are, therefore, treated as "hard." That is, the exponential time complexity may cause that some increase in the input data can increase solution time of the problem exponentially. In the worst case, we could be waiting for the solution over an infinite period of time.

4.3 Memetic Self-Adaptive Firefly Algorithm

Fireflies can generate flashing light that can be admired on clear summer nights. The flashing light is the result of a process of bioluminescence that comprises a complicated set of chemical reactions. The purpose of firefly flashing may be still debating; however, it can be twofold: to attract possible mating partners (communication) and to warn off potential predators.

The light intensity I_L of a flashing firefly decreases as the distance from source r increases in terms of $I_L \propto 1/r^2$. Additionally, air absorption causes the light to become weaker and weaker as the distance from the source increases. The flashing light represents the inspiration for the development of the FFA by Yang (2008). Here, light intensity is proportional to the fitness function of the problem being optimized (i.e., $I_L(s) \propto f(s)$, where $s = S(x)$ represents a candidate solution).

In order to formulate the FFA, some flashing characteristics of the fireflies are idealized, as follows:

- All fireflies are unisex.
- Their attractiveness is proportional to their light intensity.
- The light intensity of a firefly is affected or determined by the landscape of the fitness function.

Note that light intensity I_L and attractiveness β are in some way synonymous. While the intensity I_L is referred to as an absolute measure of emitted light by the firefly, the attractiveness β is a relative measure of the light that should be seen in the eyes of the beholders and judged by other fireflies (Yang, 2008). The light intensity I_L varied by distance r is expressed by the following equation

$$I_L(r) = I_{L_0} \, e^{-\gamma r^2} \tag{4.1}$$

where I_{L_0} denotes the intensity light at the source and γ is a fixed light absorption coefficient. Similarly, the attractiveness β also depends on the distance r that is calculated according to the following generalized equation

$$\beta(r) = \beta_0 \, e^{-\gamma r^k}, \quad \text{for } k \geq 1 \tag{4.2}$$

The distance between two fireflies i and j is represented as the Euclidian distance:

$$r_{ij} = ||\mathbf{x}_i - \mathbf{x}_j|| = \sqrt{\sum_{k=1}^{n}(x_{ik} - x_{jk})} \tag{4.3}$$

where x_{ik} is the kth element of the ith firefly's position within the search space. Each firefly i moves to another more attractive firefly j as follows:

$$\mathbf{x}_i = \mathbf{x}_i + \beta_0 \, e^{-\gamma r_{ij}^2}(\mathbf{x}_j - \mathbf{x}_i) + \alpha \, N_i(0, 1) \tag{4.4}$$

Equation (4.4) consists of three terms. The first term determines the current position of ith firefly. The second term refers to the attractiveness, while the third term is connected with the randomized movement of ith firefly within the search space. This term consists of the randomization parameter α, and random numbers $N_i(0, 1)$ drawn from a Gaussian distribution. The scheme of FFA is sketched in Algorithm 4.1.

The FFA (Algorithm 4.1) runs on the population of fireflies $P^{(t)}$ that are represented as real-valued vectors $\mathbf{x}_i^{(t)} = (x_{i0}^{(t)}, \ldots, x_{in}^{(t)})$, where $i = 1, \ldots, NP$ and NP denotes the number of fireflies within a population $P^{(t)}$ at generation t. Note that each firefly $\mathbf{x}_i^{(t)}$ is of dimension n. The population of fireflies is initialized randomly (function *InitFFA*) according to the following equation:

$$x_{ij}^{(0)} = (ub - lb) \cdot rand(0, 1) + lb \tag{4.5}$$

where ub and lb denote the upper and lower bounds, respectively. The main loop of the firefly search process that is controlled using the maximum number of generations MAX_GEN consists of the following functions:

- *AlphaNew*: Calculating new values for randomization parameter α. This parameter is modified according to the equation as follows:

$$\Delta = 1 - (10^{-4}/0.9)^{1/\text{MAX\_GEN}}, \quad \alpha^{(t+1)} = (1 - \Delta) \cdot \alpha^{(t)} \tag{4.6}$$

where Δ determines the step size when changing the parameter $\alpha^{(t+1)}$. Note that this parameter decreases with the increasing of generation counter t.

```
01: algorithm Firefly

02: t = 0; x* = ∅; γ =1.0;              // initialize: gen.counter, best solution, attractiveness

03: P⁽ᵗ⁾ = InitializeFFA();            // initialize a population xᵢ⁽⁰⁾ ∈ P⁽⁰⁾

04: while ( t ≤ MAX_GEN ) do            // termination condition

05:    α⁽ᵗ⁾ = AlphaNew();              // determine a new value of α

06:    EvaluateFFA( P⁽ᵗ⁾, f(x) );       // evaluate xᵢ⁽ᵗ⁾ according to f(xᵢ)

07:    OrderFFA( P⁽ᵗ⁾, f(x) );          // sort P⁽ᵗ⁾ according to f(xᵢ)

08:    x* = FindTheBestFFA( P⁽ᵗ⁾, f(x) ); // determine the best solution x*

09:    P⁽ᵗ⁺¹⁾ = MoveFFA( P⁽ᵗ⁾ );        // vary attractiveness according Equation (4)

10:    t = t+1;                         // next generation

11: end while

12: return x*, f(x);                    // postprocess results
```

Algorithm 4.1 Pseudo code of the FFA.

- *EvaluateFFA*: Evaluating the new solution $\mathbf{x}_i^{(t)}$ according to a fitness function $f(\mathbf{s}_i^{(t)})$, where $\mathbf{s}_i^{(t)} = S(\mathbf{x}_i^{(t)})$.
- *OrderFFA*: Ordering solutions $\mathbf{x}_i^{(t)}$ for $i = 1, \ldots, NP$ with respect to the fitness function $f(\mathbf{s}_i^{(t)})$ ascending, where $\mathbf{s}_i^{(t)} = S(\mathbf{x}_i^{(t)})$.
- *FindTheBestFFA*: Determining the best solution within the population $P^{(t)}$. Normally, the best solution becomes $\mathbf{x}^* = \mathbf{x}_0^{(t)}$.
- *MoveFFA*: Moving the fireflies toward the search space according to the attractiveness of their neighbor's solution (Eq. (4.4)).

In order to improve the original FFA, especially in the sense of exploration and exploitation, the following features are incorporated into our new MSA-FFA:

- self-adaptation of control parameters,
- new population scheme,
- more directly controlling the balance between exploration and exploitation during the search process,
- hybridization using local search heuristics.

These features will be discussed in more detail in the remainder of this chapter.

4.3.1 Self-Adaptation of Control Parameters

Population-based algorithms often use the information explored to a certain generation within a population (Bäck, 1998). However, their efficiency depends on the characteristics of the population diversity, i.e. accumulated information about the problem that is written into the genotypes of individuals. The greater the diversity of the population the greater the search power of the population-based algorithm. In summary, how to reach the information accumulated into a population depends primarily on the appropriate setting of the control parameters.

Unfortunately, setting parameters that are appropriate at the beginning of optimization can become inappropriate for later generations. Therefore, the idea of adapting control parameters during optimization arose (Holland, 1992). This idea has overgrown into the self-adaptation of control parameters, where these are encoded into genotypes of individuals and undergo operations of the variation operators (Meyer-Nieberg and Beyer, 2007).

It is worth pointing out that FFA involves three control parameters: the randomization parameter α, the attractiveness β, and the light absorption coefficient γ. All the mentioned parameters are encoded into real-valued vectors in the following form:

$$\mathbf{x}_i^{(t)} = \langle x_{i0}^{(t)}, \ldots, x_{in}^{(t)}; \alpha^{(t)}, \sigma_0^{(t)}; \beta^{(t)}, \sigma_1^{(t)}; \gamma^{(t)}, \sigma_2^{(t)} \rangle, \quad \text{for } i = 1, \ldots, NP \qquad (4.7)$$

where the first part of vector $\mathbf{x}_i^{(t)} = (x_{i0}^{(t)}, \ldots, x_{in}^{(t)})$ represents a position of the ith firefly similar to the original FFA, parameters $\alpha^{(t)}$, $\beta^{(t)}$, and $\gamma^{(t)}$ are the current values of the control parameters, while $\sigma_0^{(t)}$, $\sigma_1^{(t)}$, and $\sigma_2^{(t)}$ refer to their standard deviations (also mutation strengths). Interestingly, the first part is changed according to Eq. (4.4), while the self-adaptive parameters undergo an operation of uncorrelated mutation with three-step sizes (Eiben and Smit, 2003). This mutation is described by the following equations:

$$\sigma_i^{(t+1)} = \sigma_i^{(t)} \cdot e^{(\tau' \cdot N(0,1) + \tau \, N_i(0,1))}, \quad \text{for } i = 1, \ldots, 3 \qquad (4.8)$$

$$\alpha^{(t+1)} = \alpha^{(t)} + \sigma_0^{(t)} \cdot N(0,1)$$

$$\beta^{(t+1)} = \beta^{(t)} + \sigma_1^{(t)} \cdot N(0,1)$$

$$\gamma^{(t+1)} = \gamma^{(t)} + \sigma_2^{(t)} \cdot N(0,1)$$

where $\tau' \propto 1/\sqrt{2n}$ and $\tau \propto 1/\sqrt{2 \cdot \sqrt{n}}$ denote the so-called learning rate. Here, the rule which prevents that the mutation strengths $\sigma_i^{(t)}$ do not fall under a certain minimum value ε_0 is applied:

$$\sigma_i^{(t)} < \varepsilon_0 \Rightarrow \sigma_i^{(t)} < \varepsilon_0, \quad \text{for } i = 1, \ldots, 3 \qquad (4.9)$$

4.3.2 Population Model

The original FFA uses a generational population model, where the entire population is replaced in each generation. Specifically, NP parents produce NP offspring that

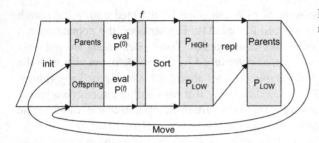

Figure 4.2 Population model.

become parents in the next generation. Here, no selection pressure influences the survival of individuals. In fact, each parent is alive for one generation only. Furthermore, the best solution is not preserved by FFA, i.e., elitism is not used in the original FFA.

Our new population model is presented in Figure 4.2. It can be seen from this figure that the initialized population forms an initial population consisting of two NP individuals, where the first NP individuals represent a subpopulation of parents, while the next NP individuals form a subpopulation of the offspring. Firstly, individuals from the whole population are evaluated (EvalFFA). Second, both the parent and the offspring are placed in ascending order according to their fitness values (OrderFFA). Therefore, the whole population representing a mating pool is divided into high and low subpopulations. The former consists of individuals with the higher fitness, while the latter have the lower fitness values irrespective of whether an individual is either a parent or an offspring. Third, individuals from both subpopulations are replaced by the high subpopulation (ReplaceFFA). Note that the high subpopulation consists of overfit individuals and, therefore, in some way represents an exploitation subpopulation. On the other hand, the low, more explorative subpopulation takes care of diversity. During this phase, the balance between exploration and exploitation can be realized. Fourth, individuals from the high subpopulation represent the parents for the next generation that are reproduced in the sense of Eq. (4.4) (MoveFFA). Finally, the offspring that occupy the low subpopulation enter into the next generation of the search process together with their parents.

Note that this population model is elitist because it ensures that the best individuals are always preserved.

4.3.3 Balancing Between Exploration and Exploitation

The original FFA automatically subdivides the population (swarm) in a problem's search space into subgroups (swarms), where each subgroup explores its own region within this space. As a result, multiple optima can be found simultaneously. Unfortunately, there is no warranty that the global optimum is found by at least one subgroup, unless in the case when the number of fireflies are much higher than the number of modes. Stagnation of FFA can often be detected during the search process if the randomness is reduced too quickly. Furthermore, the population can lose diversity resulting in premature convergence. These phenomena are not only connected with a fitness landscape, as determined by the problem, but also with the nature of the swarm intelligence framework for almost all swarm-based algorithms. Namely, the search process behaves differently if it runs within either evolutionary or swarm intelligence frameworks. That is, a certain conclusion that is valid for the former does not always hold for the latter and vice versa (Neri, 2012).

The proposed MSA-FFA employs a fitness diversity adaptation for preventing the loss of population diversity and balancing the exploration and exploitation. The fitness diversity adaptation methods measure the fitness diversity in order to estimate the population diversity. On the other hand, these measures can also serve for balancing between exploration and exploitation in the search process. Interestingly, the fitness diversity refers to the phenotype level, where these measures can be more efficiently calculated than similar measures on the genotype level.

The fitness diversity metric used in MSA-FFA is defined as follows (Neri et al., 2007):

$$\Psi = 1 - \left| \frac{f_{\text{avg}} - f_{\text{min}}}{f_{\text{max}} - f_{\text{min}}} \right| \tag{4.10}$$

where f_{min}, f_{avg}, and f_{max} are, respectively, the minimum, average, and maximum fitness values within the population. This measure determines where the average fitness is positioned between the minimum and maximum fitness variations in the current population. This metric can occupy any value in the interval $\Psi \in [0, 1]$. That is, when the value of the metric Ψ is close to zero the population diversity is low, while the population diversity is high when this value is close to one. This metric is very sensitive to small variations in the fitness landscapes with plateaus and low-gradient areas (Neri, 2012).

In order to measure population diversity on a genotype level, the concept of moment of inertia is applied to MSA-FFA (Morrison, 2004). The moment of inertia is a measure of how the mass of the individuals is distributed from the center of gravity. In our case, the center of gravity $\bar{\mathbf{x}} = (\bar{\mathbf{x}}_1, \ldots, \bar{\mathbf{x}}_n)$ (also the centroid) is expressed as follows:

$$\bar{x}_i = \frac{1}{NP} \cdot \sum_{j=1}^{NP} x_{ij} \tag{4.12}$$

where $x_{ij} \in \mathbb{R}$, NP is the population size and $\bar{x}_i$ the ith element of the centroid. The moment of the inertia diversity measure is defined as follows:

$$I_C = \sum_{i=1}^{n} \sum_{j=1}^{NP} (x_{ij} - \bar{x}_i)^2 \tag{4.13}$$

where n is a dimensionality of the problem. As a measure of similarity between two individuals at the genotype level, the correlation between individual $\mathbf{x}_i$ and centroid $\bar{\mathbf{x}}$ is introduced as follows:

$$K_i = \frac{1}{n} \cdot \sum_{j=1}^{n} x_{ij} \cdot \bar{x}_j - \bar{\mathbf{x}}_i \cdot \bar{\mathbf{x}} \tag{4.14}$$

where $\bar{\mathbf{x}}_i = \frac{1}{n} \cdot \sum_{j=1}^{n} x_{ij}$, and $\bar{x}_j$ denotes the jth element of the centroid.

At each generation, the fitness diversity Ψ is calculated and then MSA-FFA uses this information to coordinate exploration and exploitation within the search. Let us suppose that the new population model of MSA-FFA divides the population $P^{(t)}$ into two subpopulations: $P_{HIGH}^{(t)}$ and $P_{LOW}^{(t)}$. Individuals in population $P_{HIGH}^{(t)}$ are over-fit and tend to exploit the explored information held into population, as soon as possible. These individuals are ordered according to their fitness ascendency. Usually, this exploitation causes a loss of population diversity that can lead to premature convergence. The subpopulation $P_{LOW}^{(t)}$ consists of underfit individuals but maintains higher population diversity. Individuals within this subpopulation are ordered according to their descending covariance (Eq. (4.14)). The proper selection of individuals from both subpopulations may slow down the fast exploitation process by FFA and direct the search process toward underfit individuals in order to explore new, probably more promising, regions of the search space. Thus, it is expected that population diversity should not decrease too fast so as to maintain a good balance.

Balancing between exploration and exploitation into the MSA-FFA is performed according to the following equation:

$$P_i^{(t+1)} = \begin{cases} (r < (0.5 - \Psi)) \text{ and } (i \neq 0) & \Rightarrow & P_{LOW}^{(t)} \\ \text{otherwise} & \Rightarrow & P_{HIGH}^{(t)} \end{cases}, \text{ for } i = 1 \ldots NP \tag{4.11}$$

where r denotes the randomly generated number from interval $[0,1]$. Note that this equation is implemented into the procedure ReplaceFFA in Algorithm 4.2 and acts as follows: When the metric Ψ is calculated, a selection of those individuals is started that can progress to the next generation. For each individual, a random number $r \in [0,1]$ is generated. If the generated number r is lower than the factor $(0.5 - \Psi)$, the first not-used individual from the population $P_{LOW}^{(t)}$ is taken, otherwise on the same position laid individual from the population $P_{HIGH}^{(t)}$ is preserved. In the former case, the population diversity is being decreased. Therefore, the underfit individuals with the highest covariance are selected for the next generation thus caused an increase in the population diversity. In the latter case, the overfit individuals can progress to the next generation. Here, the value 0.5 represents a threshold that balances the exploration and exploitation components within firefly search. Note that in the worst case when the population diversity is lost, half individuals from both subpopulations contribute as candidates for the new population.

01: **algorithm** MemeticFirefly

02: $t = 0; fe = 0; \mathbf{x}^* = \varnothing;$ // initialize: gen.counter, fun.eval.counter, best solution

03: $P^{(t)} = InitializeFFA();$ // initialize a population $\left\langle \mathbf{x}_i^{(0)}; \alpha^{(0)}, \sigma_0^{(0)}; \beta^{(0)}, \sigma_1^{(0)}; \gamma^{(0)}, \sigma_2^{(0)} \right\rangle \in P^{(0)}$

04: **while** ($fe \leq$ MAX_FE) **do**   // termination condition

05:     $SelfAdaptFFA();$ // self-adapting the control parameters

06:     $fe +=EvalAndImproveFFA(P^{(t)}, f(\mathbf{x}));$ // evaluate and improve $\mathbf{x}_i^{(t)}$ according to $f(\mathbf{x}_i)$

07:     $OrderFFA(P^{(t)}, f(\mathbf{x}));$ // sort $P^{(t)}$ according to $f(\mathbf{x}_i)$

08:     $ReplaceFFA(P_{HIGH}^{(t)}, P_{LOW}^{(t)});$ // replace $P_{HIGH}^{(t)}$ with individuals of $P^{(t)}$

09:     $\mathbf{x}^* = FindTheBestFFA(P_{HIGH}^{(t)}, f(\mathbf{x}));$ // determine the best solution $\mathbf{x}^*$

10:     $P^{(t+1)} = MoveFFA(P_{HIGH}^{(t)});$ // vary attractiveness according Equation (4)

11:     $t = t+1;$ // next generation

12: **end while**

13: **return** $\mathbf{x}^*, f(\mathbf{x});$ // postprocess results

Algorithm 4.2 Pseudo code of the MSA-FFA.

4.3.4   The Local Search

Local search is a kind of improvement heuristics when used properly and effectively. The main characteristic of these heuristics is that the solution is not created anew but by improving the current solution. The local search is defined as an iterative process of exploiting the search region within neighborhood of the current solution. If a better new solution is found, then the current one is replaced by it (Aarts and Lenstra, 1997; Bäck, 1998). The neighborhood of current solution $\mathbf{x}$ is defined as a set of solutions that can be reached by an elementary operator, i.e., $N : S \rightarrow 2^S$. Each solution in their neighborhood N is accessed from the current solution in k-moves. In line with this, these solutions represent the k-neighborhood as well.

The crucial point of the local search algorithm represents a transformation of the current solution through an elementary operator (Hoos and Stützle, 2005). In the case where the number of moves is increased, the operator creates solutions almost randomly. On the other hand, when the number of moves is small, the operator can even return the same solution quite often. Thus, no improvement of the current solution is detected. In a practice, the proper transformation is found somewhere in the middle.

Another crucial step is performed according to the size of the neighborhood. When the neighborhood is small, the solution can be found quickly, but it is possible that the local search algorithm may get stuck in the local minimum. In contrast, when the neighborhood is too large, searching for solutions can take too long.

4.3.5 Scheme of the MSA-FFA

The scheme of the MSA-FFA is presented in Algorithm 4.2.

The MSA-FFA runs on a population of fireflies $P^{(t)}$ that, beside the real-valued problem, variables also encode their control parameters as follows. $x_i^{(t)} = \langle x_{i0}^{(t)}, \ldots, x_{in}^{(t)}; \alpha^{(t)}, \sigma_0^{(t)}; \beta^{(t)}, \sigma_1^{(t)}; \gamma^{(t)}, \sigma_2^{(t)} \rangle$ for $i = 1, \ldots, 2NP$, where NP denotes the number of fireflies in two subpopulations, i.e., subpopulation of parents and subpopulation of offspring. The problem variables $(x_{i0}^{(t)}, \ldots, x_{in}^{(t)})$ are initialized randomly according to Eq. (4.5), while the control parameters $\langle \alpha^{(t)}, \sigma_0^{(t)}; \beta^{(t)}, \sigma_1^{(t)}; \gamma^{(t)}, \sigma_2^{(t)} \rangle$ are set initially to prescribed values.

Note that the setting values of mutation strengths $\sigma_i^{(0)}$ for $i = 1, \ldots, 3$, play especially an important role by a self-adaptive search process. These values determine a region in which the search process can progress. In fact, this search process can progress within the limited interval of these values, also called a progress window. Unfortunately, this region is unknown in advance and usually determined through extensive experimental work, in practice.

The main loop of MSA-FFA incorporates the following functions:

- *SelfAdaptFFA*: Self-adaptation of control parameters according to Eq. (4.8).
- *EvalAndImproveFFA*: Evaluating the new solution $x_i^{(t)}$ for $i = NP, \ldots, 2NP$ with respect to a fitness function f. Note that in the first generation ($t = 0$), the whole population is evaluated, i.e., for $i = 1, \ldots, 2NP$. Each solution is improved in the sense of local search heuristics. However, any implementation of these heuristics depends on the problem to be solved. The number of fitness evaluations depends on the local search heuristic and is unknown in advance. Therefore, this number is obtained as a return value from the procedure.
- *OrderFFA*: Sorting solutions $x_i^{(t)}$ for $i = 1, \ldots, NP$ ascending with regard to the fitness function f and for $i = NP, \ldots, 2NP$ descending with regard to the correlations K_i, thus dividing the population $P^{(t)}$ in $P_{HIGH}^{(t)}$ and $P_{LOW}^{(t)}$
- *ReplaceFFA*: Selecting parents from both subpopulations $P_{HIGH}^{(t)}$ and $P_{LOW}^{(t)}$ and thus balancing between exploration and exploitation. In the sense of elitism, the best solution is preserved in the parents' population.
- *FindTheBestFFA*: Determining the best solution within the population $P^{(t)}$.
- *MoveFFA*: Moving the fireflies toward the search space according to the attractiveness of their neighbor's solution (Eq. (4.4)).

The proposed algorithm terminates when the number of fitness function evaluations exceeds the maximum number of fitness function evaluations MAX_FE.

4.4 Case Study: Graph 3-Coloring

In order to show how the proposed hybridizations of the original FFA influence the results of MSA-FFA, we have carried out a case study by solving the well-known 3-GCP on large-scale graphs (graphs with 1000 vertices). This problem is a well-known, tough combinatorial optimization problem. Note that this kind of optimization problem was seldom solved by swarm intelligence−based algorithms, and this work is among the first attempts.

Graph coloring can informally be defined as follows: How to color an undirected graph $G = (V, E)$, where V represents a set of vertices and E a set of edges (unordered pairs of vertices) with almost k colors so that neither of the two vertices connected with an edge is colored with the same color. If such coloring exists, it is also named as proper k-coloring (Bondy and Murty, 2008). The problem of finding the proper k-coloring is denoted as k-GCP. The minimum number of colors k for which proper coloring exists is also known as the chromatic number χ of graph G. 3-GCP is a special kind of common k-coloring where the number of colors is limited to 3 ($k = 3$). The complexity of the k-GCP is determined as follows: The decision form of this problem is NP-complete, while the construction form is NP-hard (Garey and Johnson, 1979).

To solve this problem exactly, i.e., by enumerating all possible solutions, is only limited to the instances of graphs with less than 100 vertices because of its complexity. Instead, several heuristic methods that approximately solve the problem have emerged in the past. The simplest way of coloring the vertices of graph G is in a greedy fashion. Thus, vertices are ordered in a permutation and colored sequentially one after another. However, the quality of this so-called sequential coloring depends on the permutations of vertices. In order to find a more promising sequence of vertices, many methods for ordering the permutation of vertices have been incorporated into sequential graph coloring algorithms. For example, vertices are ordered randomly by the naive method (Kubale, 2004). Much better ordering can be applied by the DSatur traditional heuristic (Brelaz, 1979), where the vertices are dynamically ordered according to their saturation degrees ρ_v. The saturation degree is defined as the number of distinctly colored vertices adjacent to vertex v (Bondy and Murty, 2008).

Today, some of the most popular algorithms for solving k-GCP are metaheuristics based on local search (Blum and Roli, 2003; Blum et al., 2011). One of the first such metaheuristics was developed by Hertz and de Werra (1987), known under the name Tabucol. At the same time, this was the first application of the Tabu search (Glover, 1986) to graph coloring. Tabucol acts as follows: at first, it generates an initial random k-coloring, which typically contains a large number of conflicting edges. Then, the heuristic iteratively looks for a single vertex that the most decreases the number of conflicting edges when it is recolored with another color, i.e., moved to another color class. A Tabu list prevents the moves from cycling. Proper k-coloring may be obtained after a definite number of iterations. Later, Tabucol was improved by more sophisticated graph coloring algorithms (Dorne and Hao, 1998; Galinier and Hao, 1999).

Other local search heuristics include simulated annealing (Chams et al., 1987; Johnson et al., 1991), iterative local search (Chiarandini and Stützle, 2002; Chiarandini et al., 2007), reactive partial Tabu search (Blöchliger and Zufferey, 2003, 2008; Malaguti et al., 2008), variable neighborhood search (Avanthay et al., 2003), adaptive memory (Galinier et al., 2008), variable search space (Hertz et al., 2008), and population-based methods (Dorne and Hao, 1998; Fleurent and Ferland, 1996; Galinier and Hao, 1999; Lü and Hao, 2010). One of the best population-based algorithms for k-GCP, the hybrid EA (HEA), developed by Galinier and Hao (1999) combines the local search with the partition-based crossover operator. Here, the Tabucol metaheuristic is used as a local search operator. Recently, a distributed graph coloring algorithm that was inspired by the calling behavior of Japanese tree frogs was proposed by Hernández and Blum (2012). For a comprehensive survey of the main methods, see, for example, Galinier and Hertz (2006) and Malaguti and Toth (2009).

This case study was a continuation of work presented by Fister et al. (2012a,b) that introduced the memetic FFA (MFFA) for 3-GCP. This paper was inspired by the hybrid self-adaptive EA of Fister et al. (2013), the hybrid self-adaptive differential evolution of Fister and Brest (2011), and the hybrid ABC of Fister et al. (2012a,b). However, the common characteristic of all these algorithms was solving of the same problem, i.e., the 3-GCP.

MFFA (Fister et al., 2012a,b) exposed excellent results when coloring the medium-scale graphs. This algorithm operates on real-valued vectors whose elements represent weights that determine how hard the vertex is to color. The higher the weight is, the faster it needs to be colored. An initial permutation of vertices is obtained when the vertices are ordered according to the weights. This permutation serves as an input to DSatur traditional heuristic that constructs corresponding 3-coloring. A similar approach was used by Eiben et al. (1998) that developed the EA with a stepwise adaptation of the weights method (EA-SAW), in order to solve the 3-GCP. Instead of DSatur, the greedy algorithm was used for the construction of 3-coloring by the authors of EA-SAW. Two additional features have been applied to MFFA as follows: heuristic swap local search and elitism.

The preliminary results of MFFA for 3-GCP on large-scale graphs were not promising. Over several runs the search process of FFA was detected either as stagnation or as premature convergence. Therefore, the MSA-FFA was proposed, that tries to overcome these drawbacks of MFFA, using the following features:

- self-adaptation of control parameters,
- new population model,
- balancing between exploration and exploitation.

A formal definition of graph 3-coloring is firstly provided in the remainder of this section. Then, the characteristics of MSA-FFA for 3-GCP are described. Next, the experiments and results are illustrated. Finally, the results of the experimental work are summarized and discussed.

4.4.1 Graph 3-Coloring

Graph 3-coloring is formally defined as follows: An undirected graph $G = (V, E)$ is given, where V is a set of vertices $v \in V$ for $i = 1, \ldots, n$ and E denotes a set of edges that associate each edge $e \in E$ for $j = 1, \ldots, m$ to the unordered pair $e = \{v_i, v_j\}$. Then, the vertex 3-coloring is defined as a mapping $c : V \rightarrow S$, where $S = \{1, 2, 3\}$ is a set of three colors and c is a function that assigns one of the three colors to each vertex of G. A coloring s is proper if each of the two vertices connected with an edge is colored with a different color.

Interestingly, 3-GCP belongs to a class of CSPs. Each CSP is represented as a pair $\langle S, \phi \rangle$, where S denotes the search space of feasible solutions $\mathbf{s} \in S$ and ϕ is the feasibility condition on S that divides the search space into feasible and unfeasible regions. To each $e \in E$, the constraint b_e is assigned with $b_e(\langle s_1, \ldots, s_n \rangle) =$ true if and only if $e = \{v_i, v_j\}$ and $s_i \neq s_j$. Suppose that $B^i = \{b_e | e = \{v_i, v_j\} \wedge j = 1, \ldots, m\}$ defines the set of constraints belonging to variable v_i. Then, the feasibility condition ϕ is expressed as a conjunction of all the constraints $\phi(\mathbf{s}) = \wedge_{v \in V} B^v(\mathbf{s})$.

As in evolutionary computation, constraints can be handled indirectly in the sense of a penalty function that punishes the unfeasible solutions. The further the unfeasible solution is from the feasible region, the higher the penalty function. The penalty function is expressed as

$$f(\mathbf{s}) = \min \sum_{i=0}^{n} \psi(\mathbf{s}, B^i) \tag{4.14}$$

where the function $\psi(\mathbf{s}, B^i)$ is defined as

$$\psi(\mathbf{s}, B^i) = \begin{cases} 1 & \text{if } \mathbf{s} \text{ violates at least one } b_e \in B^i \\ 0 & \text{otherwise} \end{cases} \tag{4.15}$$

Note that Eq. (4.1) also represents the objective function. On the other hand, the same equation can be used as a feasibility condition in the sense that $\phi(\mathbf{s}) =$ true if and only if $f(\mathbf{s}) = 0$. The proper graph 3-coloring is found if this condition is satisfied.

4.4.2 MSA-FFA for Graph 3-Coloring

The MSA-FFA consists of the following components and features:

- representation of individuals,
- self-adaptation of control parameters,
- evaluation of fitness function,
- population model,
- balancing between exploration and exploitation,
- moves of individuals,
- initialization procedure,
- termination condition.

Each individual in MSA-FFA is composed of problem variables and control parameters according to Eq. (4.7). Problem variables that determine points in the fitness landscape represent those weights from which an initial permutation of vertices is built by the DSatur traditional heuristic. Control parameters are self-adapted according to Eq. (4.8). In this algorithm, the new population model is implemented as discussed in Section 4.3.2. Additionally, the exploration and exploitation are balanced as proposed in Section 4.3.3, while the individuals are moved through the search space according to Eq. (4.4). The population is initialized according to Eq. (4.5). The search process is terminated, when the proper 3-coloring is found or the maximum number of fitness function evaluations exceeds MAX_FE.

Evaluation of the fitness function is crucial for the results of optimization. This function is problem dependent. On the other hand, an FFA belongs to a kind of general problem solvers, where the good results should be obtained independently of the problem to be solved. Although this algorithm can be applied to several real-world optimization problems, its performance is subject to the No Free Lunch (NFL) theorem (Wolpert and Macready, 1997). According to this theorem, any two algorithms are equivalent in the sense of average performance, when their performance is compared across all possible problems. Fortunately, the NFL theorem can be circumvented for a given problem by hybridization that incorporates the problem-specific knowledge into FFAs.

In the case of MSA-FFA, the problem-specific knowledge can be conducted by the evaluation of the fitness function. In other words, the fitness function is hybridized with the domain-specific knowledge. Two kinds of hybridization are implemented into this, as follows:

1. hybrid genotype−phenotype mapping,
2. heuristic swap local search.

These hybridizations are described in detail in the remainder of this section.

4.4.2.1 Hybrid Genotype−Phenotype Mapping

Many problems are hard to represent within their original problem context. For instance, genetic algorithms (Goldberg, 1989) operate on the population of binary vectors but can also be successfully applied to continuous optimization problems. In that case, a transformation from the binary represented variables to the real-valued solution must be performed. A solution in its problem context is referred to as a phenotype, while the same solution in its encoded form is a genotype. Transformation from a solution in encoded form to a solution in problem context is known as genotype−phenotype mapping.

In MSA-FFA, the genotype is represented as real-valued vector of weights that determine an initial permutation of vertices, while the phenotype determines the graph 3-coloring obtained by DSatur traditional heuristic. The quality of solution is calculated according to Eq. (4.14). The hybrid genotype−phenotype mapping in MSA-FFA transforms the vector of weights into 3-coloring. This mapping consists of two phases:

1. Ordering the vertices $\mathbf{v}_i^{(t)} = (v_{i0}^{(t)}, \ldots, v_{in}^{(t)})$ with regard to weights $\mathbf{x}_i^{(t)} = (x_{i0}^{(t)}, \ldots, x_{in}^{(t)})$ descending and thus determining a permutation of vertices $\Pi(\mathbf{v}_i^{(t)})$.
2. From the permutation of vertices $\Pi(\mathbf{v}_i^{(t)})$ finding the graph 3-coloring $\mathbf{s}_i^{(t)} = (s_{i0}^{(t)}, \ldots, s_{in}^{(t)})$ due to traditional heuristic DSatur and evaluating it according to Eq. (4.14).

Note that the genotype space is much bigger than the phenotype space. The former is determined by the size of the permutation space that can be obtained with

n vertices, i.e., $n!$, while the latter is estimated by the size of the combinatorial space that can be obtained using 3-colors, i.e., 3^n. Unfortunately, inspecting the genotype search space is much easier to implement in an FFA than inspecting the phenotype space because of the many heuristics that are available for exploring the permutation search space.

4.4.2.2 The Heuristic Swap Local Search

When a solution is evaluated by the MFFA, the heuristic swap local search tries to improve it. This heuristic is run until the improvements are detected. The operation of this is illustrated in Figure 4.3, which deals with a solution on G with 9 vertices. This solution is composed of a permutation of vertices **v**, 3-coloring **s**, weights **y**, and saturation degrees ρ. The heuristic swap local search takes the first uncolored vertex in a solution and orders the predecessors according to the descending saturation degree. The uncolored vertex is swapped with the vertex that has the highest saturation degree. In the case of a tie, the operator randomly selects a vertex among the vertices with higher saturation degrees (2-opt neighborhood).

In Figure 4.3, an element of the solution corresponding to the first uncolored vertex 5 is in dark gray and the vertices 0 and 3 with the highest saturation degree are in light gray. From vertices 0 and 3, heuristical swap randomly selects vertex 0 and swaps it with vertex 5 (the right-hand side of Figure 4.3).

4.4.3 Experiments and Results

The goal of the experimental work is to show that MSA-FFA can be successfully applied to 3-GCP on large-scale graphs. As this work continues the experiments as represented in the paper Fister et al. (2012a,b), the same test algorithms were also used in this comparative study, i.e., Chiarandini and Stützle (2012) implementations of HEA and Tabucol and van Hemert (2012) implementation of EA-SAW. In order to help the developers of a new graph coloring algorithms, the authors put these implementations on the Internet to make a comparison with the newly developed algorithms as fairly as possible. Additionally, the basic FFA was also included into comparison in order to obtain suitable conclusions.

The characteristics of MSA-FFA in the experiments were as follows: The population size was fixed at 20. MAX-FE was set at 300,000 by all algorithms to make

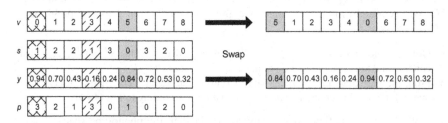

Figure 4.3 Heuristic swap local search.

the fair comparison with the paper of Eiben et al. (1998). Each instance of the graph was executed 25 times. The initial values of the self-adaptive control parameters were set as follows: $\alpha^{(0)} = 0.1$, $\beta^{(0)} = 0.1$, and $\gamma^{(0)} = 0.8$, while the lower and upper bounds of these parameters were self-adapted over the following intervals: $\alpha^{(t)} \in [0.001, 0.2]$, $\beta^{(t)} \in [0.001, 0.2]$, and $\gamma^{(t)} \in [0.1, 1.0]$. Mutation strengths were initially set as $\sigma_0^{(t)} = \sigma_1^{(t)} = \sigma_2^{(t)} = 0.03$, while the minimum value of mutation strengths was limited by $\varepsilon_0 = 0.0001$. The same values of control parameters were also used by the basic FFA. However, these parameters were fixed during the experiments.

The algorithms were compared according to the measures success rate (SR) and average estimations to solution (AES). The former determines how successfully the particular algorithm is by solving the given instance of the graph. It is expressed as a ratio between the number of successfully runs and the number of all runs. The latter determines the efficiency of the particular algorithm and counts the average number of fitness function evaluations needed to find the solution.

Three experiments were conducted during this work in order to show how parameters edge probability and the fitness diversity metric Ψ influence the results of optimization. Additionally, an analysis of the inertia diversity metric is presented during the arbitrary search process.

4.4.3.1 Test Suite

The test suite during the experiments consists of graphs generated using the Culberson random graph generator (Culberson, 2012). The graphs generated by this generator are distinguished according to type, number of vertices n, edge probability p, and the seeds of random number generator q. Three types of graphs were employed during the experiments: uniform (random graphs without variability in sizes of color sets), equipartite, and flat. The edge probability determines when the two vertices v_i and v_j are connected with an edge (v_i, v_j). This parameter was varied in the interval $p \in [0.004, 0.014]$ with a step of 0.0005. Thus, a phase transition phenomenon was captured, where graphs are hard to solve by most of the algorithms. Finally, the seeds were varied in the interval $q \in [1, 10]$ with a step of one. As a result, $3 \times 21 \times 10 = 630$ different graphs were obtained. In summary, each algorithm was executed 15,750 times to complete this experimental setup.

Phase transition is a phenomenon that accompanies almost all NP-hard problems and determines the region where the NP-hard problem passes over the state of "solvability" to a state of "unsolvability," and vice versa (Turner, 1988). Typically, this region is characterized by particular problem parameter. This parameter is the edge probability for 3-GCP. Many authors have determined this region differently. For example, Petford and Welsh (1989) stated that this phenomenon occurs when $2pn/3 \approx 16/3$, Cheeseman et al. (1991) when $2m/n \approx 5.4$, Hayes (2003) when $m/n \approx 2.35$, and Eiben et al. (1998) when $7/n \leq p \leq 8/n$. In the presented case, the phase transition needed to be by $p \approx 0.008$ over Petford and Welsh and over Cheeseman, by $p \approx 0.007$ over Hayes, and $p \in [0.007, 0.008]$ over Eiben et al.

4.4.3.2   Influence of the Edge Probability

The influence of edge probability on the performance of the tested graph coloring algorithms was investigated during this experiment. The tested algorithms solved the test suite of graph, as represented in Section 4.4.3.1. This test suite was selected so that the behavior of the graph coloring algorithms in the phase transition could be observed.

The results of this experiment are illustrated in Figure 4.3 and are divided into six diagrams corresponding to the graphs of different types (uniform, equipartite, and flat). Furthermore, the graphs are compared according to the measures SR and AES. In these diagrams, the average values of the corresponding measures are presented as obtained after 25 runs for each of 10 different seeds.

As shown in Figure 4.4(a), (c), and (e), the performance of MSA-FFA was similar to those of HEA and Tabucol when solving the instances of graphs lower than $p < 0.007$. With increasing the edge probability, performances of this algorithm within the phase transition region $p \in [0.007, 0.010]$ became worse, especially when solving the flat type of graphs. On the other hand, EA-SAW and FFA reported the worse results. When these two algorithms were compared with each other, it can be observed that EA-SAW gets stuck before FFA (e.g., when $p < 0.006$ for uniform and equipartite graphs) and improves the results faster than FFA (e.g., when $p > 0.01$ for the same types of graphs).

According to efficiency (measure AES in Figure 4.4(b), (d), and (f)), the best results were obtained by HEA. The performances of Tabucol were comparable especially when solving the flat graphs. MSA-FFA was competitive with these two algorithms when solving the uniform and equipartite graphs, while EA-SAW and FFA, on average, exposed the worst results for all three types of graphs. Interestingly, Tabucol and HEA also increased AES by $p = 0.013$. This behavior is connected with the phenomenon of second phase transition (Boettcher and Percus, 2004).

4.4.3.3   Influence of the Fitness Diversity Metric

The goal of this experiment was to show how exploration and exploitation are balanced by MSA-FFA. In line with this, the fitness diversity metric Ψ was measured in each generation on the phenotype level. The metric Ψ determines how exploration and exploitation are balanced by firefly search. In order to analyze how this measure behaves over the particular instance of a graph, all 25 runs of MSA-FFA were taken into consideration. Here, the equipartite graph with $p = 0.008$ and $q = 5$ was observed. Note that this instance of a graph is in the phase transition.

The results of this experiment are presented in (Figure 4.5), which is divided in two diagrams: diagram 4.5(a) represents the successfully finished runs (10 runs), while diagram 4.5(b) illustrates the unsuccessful runs (15 runs). In this case, the MSA-FFA reached SR = 0.40 by solving this instance of a graph.

According to Figure 4.5, the fitness diversity measure was stabilized by $\Psi \approx 0.2$. As a result, in each generation, about 30% of the new population was taken from the subpopulation $P_{LOW}^{(t)}$. Note that no significant differences were observed among the runs where the solution was found and runs where the solution was not found.

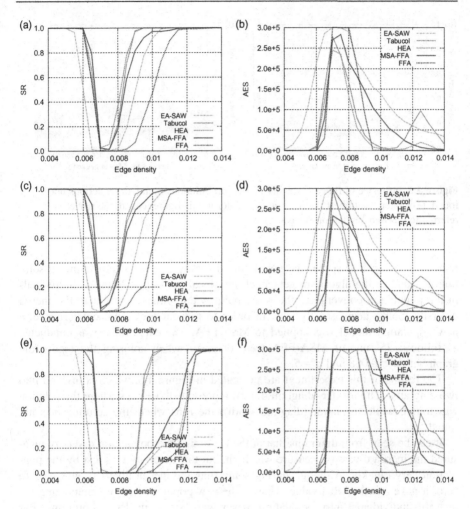

Figure 4.4 Influence of the edge probability on large-scale 3-colored graphs. (a) SR on uniform large-scale graphs. (b) AES on uniform large-scale graphs. (c) SR on equipartite large-scale graphs. (d) AES on equipartite large-scale graphs. (e) SR on flat large-scale graphs. (f) AES on flat large-scale graphs. (For interpretation of the references to color in this figure legend, the reader is referred to the web version of this book.)

4.4.3.4   Influence of the Inertia Diversity Metric

The aim of this experiment was to investigate the behavior of the inertia diversity metric I_C. In contrast to fitness diversity Ψ, it is measured at the genotype level and describes how individuals are dispersed around the centroid (Eq. (4.13)). The theory of EAs for swarm intelligence (Neri, 2012) asserts that population diversity is high at the beginning of the search. As the algorithm progresses toward the better

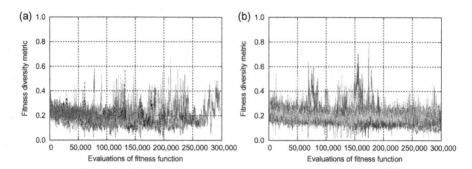

Figure 4.5 Influence of fitness diversity metric. (a) Solutions found. (b) Solutions not found. (For interpretation of the references to color in this figure legend, the reader is referred to the web version of this book.)

regions of the search space, the population diversity decreases until either a solution is found or the algorithm gets stuck into local optimum. When all individuals in the population converge to the same point within fitness landscape, the inertia diversity metric decreases to zero. In order to prevent premature convergence, a new population model was applied to MSA-FFA. The experiment was conducted as follows: 25 runs of MSA-FFA were observed when coloring the equipartite graph with $p = 0.008$ and $q = 5$.

The results of this experiment are presented in Figure 4.6, which is divided into two diagrams. The former (diagram 4.6(a)) represents those runs where the solution was found, while the latter (diagram 4.6(b)) the runs where the solution was not found.

It can be seen from diagrams that at the beginning the population diversity measured the inertia diversity measure was high, but this diversity was lost by the population very quickly. Although during some runs the inertia diversity was near to zero, it never reached this value. That is, the new population model conducting the underfit individuals into population never gets stuck in local optimum. For instance, when using this population model, the SR on the mentioned instance of the graph was increased from $SR = 0.0$ by MFFA to $SR = 0.40$ by MSA-FFA.

4.4.3.5 Convergence Graphs

The convergence of solutions was studied during the last experiments, where the average fitness of the population in certain generation was compared with the best fitness found so far. Thus, two different runs of MSA-FFA were analyzed by solving the equipartite graph with $p = 0.008$ and $q = 5$: in the first, where the solution was found, while in the second, where the solution was not found.

The results of both runs can be seen in Figure 4.7, which is divided into diagrams 4.7(a) (solution found) and 4.7(b) (solution not found).

It can be seen from diagram 4.7(a) that the average fitness consists of a sequence of values that represents hills and valleys. The hills denote an increase of

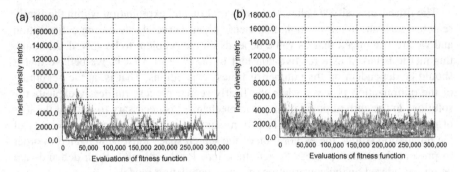

Figure 4.6 Influence of fitness diversity metric. (a) Solutions found. (b) Solutions not found. (For interpretation of the references to color in this figure legend, the reader is referred to the web version of this book.)

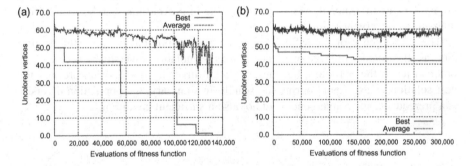

Figure 4.7 Convergence diagrams. (a) Solution found. (b) Solution not found.

the average fitness, while the valleys a decrease of it. However, the average fitness decreased slowly throughout the entire run. This decreasing was more observable at the end of the optimization. On the other hand, the best solution was decreased stepwise. After some big skips, the optimal solution was found.

When the solution was not found (diagram 4.7(b)), the average fitness remained almost constant during the whole run, while the best solution decreased stepwise. Unfortunately, these skips were smaller and usually led the search process to the local optimum.

4.4.3.6 Discussion

The results of these experiments can be summarized as follows: The results of MSA-FFA are comparable with Tabucol and HEA when solving 3-GCP on uniform and equipartite graphs and are slightly worse on flat graphs. However, EA-SAW and FFA gained the unsatisfactory results that are incomparable with the other tested algorithms.

The fitness diversity Ψ balances the exploration and exploitation within the firefly search algorithm. In our opinion, this metric plays a crucial role during optimization and we are convinced that its value depends on the problem to be solved. Although this metric behaved as a relative constant in the case of 3-GCP, we believe that it should be dependent on the number of fitness evaluations. That is, at the beginning of the optimization process, when the firefly search process ruthlessly exploits the solutions in the current population, some mechanism is necessary to prevent the loss of population diversity being too fast. In matured generations, when the diversity of the population is low, the exploration of the search space must be activated in order to prevent the search process to get stuck into local optimum. Both demands are being considered by the construction of a new population model.

The inertia diversity I_C, on the other hand, affirmed the thesis that the population diversity is high at the beginning of the optimization and becomes lower as the population becomes matured. Unfortunately, the population diversity by MSA-FFA is lost in the first 2% of the allowable number of fitness evaluations. Without using the new population model, MSA-FFA is unable to prevent the search process from premature convergence.

The convergence of the MSA-FFA to the global optimum is impossible to predict, as illustrated within convergence graphs. Population diversity is necessary in order to reach the optimum, but the population diversity does not ensure that the best solution is also found during the search. In summary, the population diversity is a prerequisite for convergence, but not also a sufficient condition.

4.5 Conclusions

The FFA is a member of the swarm intelligence algorithms inspired by the collective behavior of social insects and other animal societies when solving diverse optimization problems. Essentially, this algorithm has not extensively been applied to the domain of combinatorial optimization problems. Therefore, this work is among the first of its kind that focused on the behavior of the FFA when solving this class of problems.

In order to prepare the FFA algorithm for solving the combinatorial optimization problems, the following features were proposed:

- new population model,
- explicit control of exploration and exploitation during firefly search,
- self-adaptation of control parameters,
- incorporating local search heuristics.

The new population model introduces selection pressure within the firefly search process. Without this feature, the FFA algorithm is unable to direct deep searching into the promising regions of the search space. Explicit balancing between exploration and exploitation during the firefly search is realized using fitness diversity metric that is calculated in each generation. The control parameters are not set fix during the search process but are self-adapted within the proposed algorithm. Local search heuristics are applied in order to incorporate problem-specific knowledge.

The proposed algorithm is named the MSA-FFA because of the characteristics of the used features. In order to show its quality, the MSA-FFA was applied to graph 3-coloring that is a well-known combinatorial optimization problem. Extensive experiments of MSA-FFA by coloring the large-scale graphs of various types, edge probabilities, and the seeds of a random graph generator were performed and compared with other well-known graph coloring algorithms, like Tabucol, HEA, and EA-SAW. The experiments showed that the results of MSA-FFA are comparable with the results obtained by the other algorithms used in experiments.

In the future, MSA-FFA should also be used for solving other combinatorial optimization problems. How the proposed hybridizations influence on the results of an FFA should be performed as well. Essentially, additional experiments with fitness diversity metric should be conducted in order to obtain more direct control over exploration and exploitation in the FFA, and in fact, in many other swarm-based algorithms as well.

References

Aarts, E., Lenstra, J., 1997. Local Search in Combinatorial Optimization. Princetown University Press, Princetown and Oxford.

Avanthay, C., Hertz, A., Zufferey, N., 2003. A variable neighborhood search for graph coloring. Eur. J. Oper. Res. 151, 379−388.

Bäck, T., 1998. An overview of parameter control methods by self-adaptation in evolutionary algorithms. Fundam. Informaticae. 35, 51−66.

Beni, G., Wang, J., 1989. Swarm intelligence in cellular robotic systems. Proceedings of the NATO Advanced Workshop on Robots and Biological Systems. Tuscany, Italy.

Blöchliger, I., Zufferey, N., 2003. A reactive tabu search using partial solutions for the graph coloring problem. In: Kral, D., Sgall, J. (Eds.), Coloring Graphs from Lists with Bounded Size of Their Union: Result from Dagstuhl Seminar 03391. Department of Applied Mathematics and Institute for Theoretical Computer Science, Prague.

Blöchliger, I., Zufferey, N., 2008. A graph coloring heuristic using partial solutions and a reactive tabu scheme. Comput. Oper. Res. 35 (3), 960−975.

Blum, C., Li, X., 2008. Swarm intelligence in optimization. In: Blum, C., Merkle, D. (Eds.), Swarm Intelligence: Introduction and Applications. Springer-Verlag, Berlin, pp. 43−86.

Blum, C., Roli, A., 2003. Metaheuristics in combinatorial optimization: overview and conceptual comparison. ACM Comput. Surv. 35 (3), 268−308.

Blum, C., Puchinger, J., Raidl, G., Roli, A., 2011. Hybrid metaheuristics in combinatorial optimization: a survey. Appl. Soft Comput. 11 (6), 4135−4151.

Boettcher, S., Percus, A., 2004. Extremal optimization at the phase transition of the three-coloring problem. Phys. Rev. 69 (6), 66−73.

Bondy, J., Murty, U., 2008. Graph Theory. Springer-Verlag, Berlin.

Brelaz, D., 1979. New methods to color vertices of a graph. Commun. ACM. 22, 251−256.

Chams, M., Hertz, A., de Werra, D., 1987. Some experiments with simulated annealing for coloring graphs. Eur. J. Oper. Res. 32, 260−266.

Cheeseman, P., Kanefsky, B., Taylor, W., 1991. Where the really hard problems are. Proceedings of the International Joint Conference on Artificial Intelligence. Morgan Kaufmann, San Francisco, CA, pp. 331–337.

Chiarandini, M., Stützle, T., 2002. An application of iterated local search to graph coloring. In: Johnson, D., Mehrotra, A., Trick, M. (Eds.), Proceedings of the Computational Symposium on Graph Coloring and its Generalizations. Ithaca, New York, NY, pp. 112–125.

Chiarandini, M., Stützle, T., 2012. Online Compendium to the Article: An Analysis of Heuristics for Vertex Colouring. [Online] Available from: <http://www.imada.sdu.dk/~marco/gcp-study/> (accessed 20.09.12.).

Chiarandini, M., Dumitrescu, I., Stützle, T., 2007. Stochastic local search algorithms for the graph colouring problem. In: Gonzalez, T. (Ed.), Handbook of Approximation Algorithms and Metaheuristics, Computer and Information Science Series. Chapman & Hall/CRC, Boca Raton, FL, pp. 63.1–63.17.

Culberson, J., 2012. Graph Coloring Page. [Online] Available from: <http://www.ncbi.nlm.nih.gov/> (accessed 14.09.12.).

Črepinšek, M., Liu, S.-H., Mernik, M., 2011. Analysis of exploration and exploitation in evolutionary algorithms by ancestry trees. Int. J. Inn. Comput. Appl. 3 (1), 11–19.

Deb, K., 2001. Multi-Objective Optimization Using Evolutionary Algorithms. John Wiley & Sons, Chichester, UK.

Dorigo, M., Di Caro, G., 1999. The ant colony optimization meta-heuristic. In: Corne, D., Dorigo, M., Glover, F. (Eds.), New Ideas in Optimization. McGraw Hill, London, UK, pp. 11–32.

Dorne, R., Hao, J., 1998. A new genetic local search algorithm for graph coloring. In: Eiben, A., Bäck, T., Schoenauer, M., Schwefel, H. (Eds.), Parallel Problem Solving from Nature—PPSN, Fifth International Conference, Lecture Notes in Computer Science. Springer-Verlag, Berlin, pp. 745–754.

Eiben, A., Smit, J., 2003. Introduction to Evolutionary Computing. Springer-Verlag, Berlin.

Eiben, A., van Der Hauw, J., van Hemert, J., 1998. Graph coloring with adaptive evolutionary algorithms. J. Heuristics. 4 (1), 25–46.

Eiben, A., Hinterding, R., Michalewicz, Z., 1999. Parameter control in evolutionary algorithms. IEEE Trans. Evol. Comput. 3 (2), 124–141.

Fister, I., Brest, J., 2011. Using differential evolution for the graph coloring. IEEE SSCI2011 Symposium Series on Computational Intelligence: Proceedings. IEEE, Piscataway, NJ, pp. 150–156.

Fister Jr., I., Fister, I., Brest, J., 2012a. A hybrid artificial bee colony algorithm for graph 3-coloring. Lecture Notes in Computer Science. Springer-Verlag, Berlin, pp. 66–74.

Fister Jr., I., Yang, X.-S., Fister, I., Brest, J., 2012b. Memetic firefly algorithm for combinatorial optimization. In: Filipič, B., Šilc, J. (Eds.), Bioinspired Optimization Methods and Their Applications: Proceedings of the Fifth International Conference on Bioinspired Optimization Methods and Their Applications—BIOMA 2012. Jožef Stefan Institute, Ljubljana, pp. 75–86.

Fister, I., Mernik, M., Filipič, B., 2013. Graph 3-coloring with a hybrid self-adaptive evolutionary algorithm. Comput. Optimiz. Appl. 54 (3), 741–770.

Fleurent, C., Ferland, J., 1996. Genetic and hybrid algorithms for graph coloring. Ann. Oper. Res. 63, 437–464.

Galinier, P., Hao, J., 1999. Hybrid evolutionary algorithms for graph coloring. J. Comb. Optimiz. 3 (4), 379–397.

Galinier, P., Hertz, A., 2006. A survey of local search methods for graph coloring. Comput. Oper. Res. 33, 2547−2562.

Galinier, P., Hertz, A., Zufferey, N., 2008. An adaptive memory algorithm for the k-coloring problem. Discrete Appl. Math. 156 (2), 267−279.

Gandomi, A., Yang, X.S., Alavi, A., 2011. Mixed variable structural optimization using firefly algorithm. Comput. Struct. 89 (23), 2325−2336.

Gandomi, A., Yang, X.S., Talatahari, S., Alavi, A., 2013. Firefly algorithm with chaos. Commun. Nonlin. Sci. Numer. Simul. 18 (1), 89−98.

Garey, M., Johnson, D., 1979. Computers and Intractability: A Guide to the Theory of NP-Completeness. W.H. Freeman & Co., New York, NY.

Glover, F., 1986. Future paths for integer programming and links to artificial intelligence. Comput. Oper. Res. 13 (5), 533−549.

Goldberg, D.E., 1989. Genetic Algorithms in Search, Optimization, and Machine Learning. Addison-Wesley, Reading, MA.

Hayes, B., 2003. On the threshold. Am. Sci. 91, 12−17.

Hernández, H., Blum, C., 2012. Distributed graph coloring: an approach based on the calling behavior of Japanese tree frogs. Swarm Intell. 6 (2), 117−150.

Hertz, A., de Werra, D., 1987. Using tabu search techniques for graph coloring. Computing. 39, 345−351.

Hertz, A., Plumettaz, M., Zufferey, N., 2008. Variable space search for graph coloring. Discrete Appl. Math. 156 (13), 2551−2560.

Holland, J., 1992. Adaptation in Natural and Artificial Systems. MIT Press, Cambridge, USA.

Hoos, H., Stützle, T., 2005. Stochastic Local Search. Foundations and Applications. Elsevier, Oxford.

Johnson, D., Aragon, C., McGeoch, L., Schevon, C., 1991. Optimization by simulated annealing: an experimental evaluation, part II; graph coloring and number partitioning. Oper. Res. 39 (3), 378−406.

Karaboga, D., Basturk, B., 2007. A powerful and efficient algorithm for numerical function optimization: artificial bee colony (ABC) algorithm. J. Global Optimiz. 39 (3), 459−471.

Kennedy, J., Eberhart, R., 1999. The particle swarm optimization: social adaptation in information processing. In: Corne, D., Dorigo, M., Glover, F. (Eds.), New Ideas in Optimization. McGraw Hill, London, UK, pp. 379−387.

Korošec, P., Šilc, J., Filipič, B., 2012. The differential ant-stigmergy algorithm. Inf. Sci. 192, 82−97.

Kubale, M., 2004. Graph Colorings. American Mathemetical Society, Rhode Island.

Lü, Z., Hao, J., 2010. A memetic algorithm for graph coloring. Eur. J. Oper. Res. 203, 241−250.

Malaguti, E., Toth, P., 2009. A survey on vertex coloring problems. Int. Trans. Oper. Res.1−34.

Malaguti, E., Monaci, M., Toth, P., 2008. A metaheuristic approach for the vertex coloring problem. INFORMS J. Comput. 20, 302−316.

Meyer-Nieberg, S., Beyer, H.-G., 2007. Self-adaptation in evolutionary algorithms. In: Lobo, F., Lima, C., Michalewicz, Z. (Eds.), Parameter Setting in Evolutionary Algorithms. Springer-Verlag, Berlin, pp. 47−76.

Morrison, R., 2004. Designing Evolutionary Algorithms for Dynamic Environments. Springer-Verlag, Berlin.

Moscato, P., 1999. Memetic algorithms: a short introduction. In: Corne, D., Dorigo, M., Glover, F. (Eds.), New Ideas in Optimization. McGraw Hill, London, UK, pp. 219−234.

Neri, F., 2012. Diversity management in memetic algorithms. In: Neri, F., Cotta, C., Moscato, P. (Eds.), Handbook of Memetic Algorithms, Studies in Computational Inteligence. Springer-Verlag, Berlin, pp. 153−165.

Neri, F., Toivanen, J., Cascella, G., Ong, Y.-S., 2007. An adaptive multimeme algorithm for designing HIV multidrug therapies. IEEE/ACM Trans. Comput. Biol. Bioinform. 4 (2), 264−278.

Petford, A., Welsh, D., 1989. A randomized 3-coloring algorithms. Discrete Math. 74 (1−2), 253−261.

Prügel-Bennett, A., 2010. Benefits of a population: five mechanisms that advantage population-based algorithms. IEEE Trans. Evol. Comput. 14 (4), 500−517.

Rechenberg, I., 1973. Evolutions strategie: Optimierung technischer Systeme nach Prinzipien der biologischen Evolution. Fromman-Holzboog, Stuttgart.

Stadler, P., 1995. Towards a theory of landscapes. In: Lopez-Pena, R., et al., (Eds.), Lecture Notes in Physics: Complex Systems and Binary Networks. Springer-Verlag, Berlin, pp. 77−163.

Talatahari, S., Gandomi, A., Yun, G., 2012. Optimum design of tower structures using firefly algorithm. In: The Structural Design of Tall and Special Buildings. [Online] Available from: <http://dx.doi.org/10.1002/tal.1043/> (accessed 10.03.13).

Turner, J., 1988. Almost all k-colorable graphs are easy to color. J. Algorithms. 9 (1), 63−82.

van Hemert, J., 2012. Jano's Homepage. [Online] Available from: <http://www.vanhemert.co.uk/csp-ea.html/> (accessed 20.09.12.).

Wolpert, D., Macready, W., 1997. No free lunch theorems for optimization. IEEE Trans. Evol. Comput. 1, 67−82.

Wright, S., 1932. The roles of mutation, inbreeding, crossbreeding and selection in evolution. In: Proceedings of the Sixth International Congress of Genetics. 1, 356−366.

Yang, X.S., 2008. Nature-Inspired Metaheuristic Algorithms. Luniver Press, Cambridge.

Yang, X.S., 2010. A new metaheuristic bat-inspired algorithm. In: Gonzalez, J., et al., (Eds.), Nature Inspired Cooperative Strategies for Optimization (NISCO 2010). Studies in Computational Inteligence, Springer-Verlag, Berlin, pp. 65−74.

Yang, X.S., Deb, S., 2009. Cuckoo search via Levy flights. World Congress on Nature and Biologically Inspired Computing (NaBIC 2009). IEEE, Coimbatore, India, pp. 210−214, (s.l.).

Yang, X.S., Hosseini, S., Gandomi, A., 2012. Firefly algorithm for solving non-convex economic dispatch problems with valve loading effect. Appl. Soft Comput. 12 (3), 1180−1186.

5 Modeling and Simulation of Ant Colony's Labor Division: A Problem-Oriented Approach

Renbin Xiao

Institute of Systems Engineering, Huazhong University of Science and Technology, Wuhan, China

5.1 Introduction

Complexity research is a new branch of science in the twenty-first century, and the exploration of complexity is becoming a revolutionary forefront of the contemporary science (Waldrop, 1993). The expression form of complexity is the so-called complex system, and a typical representative of complex systems is the biological system (Gell-Mann, 1994). Therefore, adopting the bionic way to study the system complexity is undoubtedly an important and appropriate choice.

Biological intelligence covers human intelligence and other biological intelligence. There is no doubt that human intelligence greatly surpasses other biological intelligence on the whole. As there are huge difficulties in the complexity research of the human biological system, it is too difficult to directly explore the internal operating mechanisms of the complex systems with the general biological systems, including human intelligence as the object. It is necessary to look for other ways. In accordance with "from specific to general" problem solving thought and progressive principle, conducting research on a certain typical intelligent behavior regularities of other biological systems may be more realistic possibility and better operational implementation in the current stage. Meanwhile, as a transition to guide the complexity research of human biological system, the related results have extensional value. Through such an extension, it can gradually transit to operating mechanism knowledge about general biological system and even general complex systems. So the study of the behavior regularities of biological ant colony and bird flock, which demonstrates emergence of swarm intelligence (Bonabeau et al., 1999) in focus, is getting a great deal of attention and given high priority.

At present, swarm intelligence methods are widely used to solve all kinds of complex problems. From this point, "swarm" can be defined as a group of Agents, which can directly or indirectly communicate with each other by changing the local environment. Such a group of Agents can cooperate with each other to solve distributed problems. Thus swarm intelligence refers to the unpredicted characteristics of global intelligent behavior emerged from the interaction of groups of simple Agents (Xiao and Tao, 2007). Most of the biological systems with social living habits often exhibit similar swarm intelligent behavior. Therefore, the refined artificial system model mainly reflects the behavior characteristics of ant colony (Bonabeau et al., 1999), bird flock (particle swarm) (Kennedy et al., 2011), bee colony (Theraulaz and Bonabeau, 1995), fish school (Kunz and Hemelrijk, 2003), wolves (Nishimura and Ikegami, 1997), bats (Yang, 2011), etc.

In the view of complex system research, the intelligent behavior that group level exhibits belongs to the phenomenon of "emergence" (Holland, 1998). But there exist some differences in the formation mechanism compared with the "emergence" based on the Darwinian evolutionary model. Evolutionary model emphasizes "survival of the fittest," in which individuals with poor fitness will gradually be replaced by better individuals. Swarm intelligence model puts more emphasis on the influence of "learning" on individual behaviors, and the individual adapts to the environment by collecting and processing information. In the swarm intelligence model, it is not substitution among individuals but update of individual "knowledge" in each iteration.

The existing swarm intelligence research mainly refers to swarm intelligence optimization, which with ant colony optimization and particle swarm optimization as a representative. And the relevant research work focuses on the performance improvements of the optimization algorithm, which can be called "method-oriented approach to swarm intelligence." Based on the practical problems, we carried out a series of modeling and simulation approaches to ant colony's labor division aiming at the division and cooperation problems in swarm intelligence. Different from "method-oriented approach to swarm intelligence," the key to the success of such problems is to grasp the features of the problem objects sufficiently, which can be called "problem-oriented approach to swarm intelligence." In the context of three practical problems in the field of production management, according to the problem features, this chapter constructs ant colony's labor division model with multitask for virtual enterprises (Section 5.3), ant colony's labor division model with multistate for pull production systems (Section 5.4), and ant colony's labor division model with multiconstraint for resilient supply chains (Section 5.5), respectively. Then relevant simulation work is carried out based on these models to demonstrate how to implement the "problem-oriented approach to swarm intelligence."

Section 5.2 firstly introduces the labor division behavior of ant colonies, then describes the ant colony's labor division model and briefly provides analysis of the follow-up study. Sections 5.3–5.5 take three practical problems as the background and carry out modeling and simulation approaches to ant colony's labor division with multitask, multistate, and multiconstraint, respectively. Section 5.6 refines and forms the implementation points of "problem-oriented approach to swarm intelligence," mainly including: (i) similarity analysis based on bionic metaphorical;

(ii) feature extraction based on problem objects; and (iii) advanced simulation based on agent technology, where the second is the core of the three points.

5.2   Ant Colony's Labor Division Behavior and its Modeling Description

5.2.1   Ant Colony's Labor Division

In view of biology, self-organized labor division is an important feature of ant colony and other social insects (Xiao, 2006), and there exists the phenomenon of labor division in many insect colonies. In ant colony society, labor division can be divided into several levels. The first level generally consists of individuals engaged in reproduction and individuals engaged in daily work, the next level can be got from the individuals engaged in daily work, such as ants looking for food and ants building nests. An obvious feature of ant colony's labor division is group plasticity, which is caused by the flexibility of individual behaviors, i.e., the proportion of ants implementing different tasks can be changed under the inside pressure of reproduction and external influence of aggressive challenges. Surprisingly, without the whole information about the need of ant colony, ants can automatically achieve individual labor division in the group and make the colony tasks in a relatively balanced state.

An interesting experiment in biology confirmed this fact. A grasshopper was cut into three pieces, the second one was twice larger than the first one, and the third one was twice larger than the second one approximately, and then placed them near the ant nest. It was found that the numbers of ants around each piece were 28, 44, and 89, respectively, after a period of time, almost increased by double amount (Xiao and Tao, 2007).

5.2.2   Ant Colony's Labor Division Model

5.2.2.1   Group Dynamics Model

Nicolis and Pringogine (1977) studied ant colony's labor division to analyze the formation of collaborative group. Their analyses are based on the following universal evolution equation:

$$\frac{dX_i}{dt} = k_i X_i \left[N_i - \sum_j \beta_{ij} X_j \right] - d_i X_i + F_C(\{X_i\}) + F_R(\{X_i\}) + F_M(\{X_i\}, \{X_i^e\})$$

$$(5.1)$$

where k_i is breeding rate, d_i is death rate, nonlinear functions F_C and F_R describe competitive rate and adjustable rate, respectively, F_M represents migration, movement and so on, which depends on internal X_i and external X_i^e.

Suppose that there are two ant groups X_1 and X_2. X_2 has developed the ability to implement labor division, the corresponding species changed from one to two: worker ants Y responsible for the growth of the group and soldier ants Z whose task is only to attack group X_1 (expressed by X later). It is also assumed that this group has developed a mechanism to adjust the individual number of Y and Z.

Now we discuss under what conditions labor division will appear in ecological system. This problem can be seen as the competition between groups X and $(Y + Z)$, or the evolution of groups X and Y influenced by a small structure fluctuation Z. Then we get the following three equations:

$$\frac{dX}{dt} = kX(N - X - Y - Z) - dX - \rho XZ \tag{5.2}$$

$$\frac{dY}{dt} = kY(N - X - Y - Z) - dY - F(Y, Z) \tag{5.3}$$

$$\frac{dZ}{dt} = F(Y, Z) - dZ \tag{5.4}$$

The conclusion obtained from solving and analyzing the equations is that the bigger the value N is, the more favorable the propagation of structure fluctuation responsible for labor division is, which means the development environment needs to be fertile. Observations from some biologists confirmed the conclusion, especially the conclusion related to population size: ant species polymorphism in temperate region is significantly less than that in tropical region, and in the latter case the average size of population is larger. Similarly, the polymorphic degree of worker bees is highly developed in large colonies, whereas in small colonies there is no significant morphological difference between queen bee and worker bees.

The above model mathematically reveals the labor division phenomenon existing in social creatures, but it is difficult to apply to solve practical problems.

5.2.2.2 Fixed Response Threshold Model

Bonabeau et al. (1996) proposed a fixed response threshold model (FRTM) based on the study of ant colony's labor division behavior. The model can be briefly described as follows: each ant is characterized by a fixed response threshold, which describes the ability to respond to external tasks. Differences in response threshold may reflect either actual differences in behavioral responses or differences in the way task-related stimuli are perceived. There exists a stimulus which corresponds to each task, when the intensity of stimulus exceeds an individual's response threshold, the individual engages in the task. When individuals performing a given task are withdrawn, the associated demand increases and so does the intensity of the stimulus, until it eventually reaches the higher characteristic response threshold of the remaining individuals, who are not initially specialized into that task; the increase of stimulus intensity beyond threshold has the effect of stimulating these individuals into performing the task.

Response threshold θ is an internal variable that determines the tendency of an individual to respond to the stimulus s and engage in the corresponding task. For $s \gg \theta$, the individual engages in task with high probability, and $s \ll \theta$ the individual engages in task with low probability.

Assume that there are two sorts of ants performing the same task, let S_i be the state of caste i ($S_i = 0$ corresponds to inactivity, $S_i = 1$ corresponds to performing the task) and θ_i be the response threshold of sort i ($i = 1, 2$).

An inactive individual of sort i ($i = 1, 2$) starts performing the task with a probability P per unit time:

$$P(S_i = 0 \rightarrow S_i = 1) = \frac{s^n}{s^n + \theta_i^n} \quad (n > 1) \tag{5.5}$$

An active individual gives up task performance and becomes inactive with probability p per unit time:

$$P(S_i = 1 \rightarrow S_i = 0) = p \tag{5.6}$$

Variations in stimulus intensity are caused by task performance which reduces stimulus intensity and the natural increase of demand irrespective of whether or not the task is performed. The stimulus intensity s is calculated as formula (5.7):

$$s(t + 1) = s(t) + \delta - \lambda n_{\text{act}} \tag{5.7}$$

where δ is the increase in stimulus intensity per unit time, n_{act} is the total number of active individuals, λ is a scale factor measuring the reduction of stimulus intensity caused by an active individual, i.e., the efficiency of task performance by individuals. Here λn_{act} is a negative feedback, that is to say the more the number of individuals that perform the task, the lower the stimulus intensity, then the smaller the probability of other individuals to select the task, realizing a dynamic balance of task allocation.

Krieger and Billeter (2000) adopted this model into the self-organized task allocation in robots. Their experimental results showed that FRTM is effective for self-organization problem in simple environment, but it needs to be further verified and improved for complex tasks.

5.2.2.3 Time-Dependent Response Threshold Model

Considering the limitations of FRTM, Theraulaz et al. (1998) made an improvement and proposed time-dependent response threshold model (TRTM) that allows response thresholds vary with time. When a task is executed, the corresponding threshold decreases, otherwise the threshold increases. Bonabeau et al. (1999) verified this model and applied it to adaptive retrieve e-mail examples. The basic idea of TRTM is that ants can respond to task requirements with different stimulus intensity, so that the global demand is as low as possible. Discrete the plane to conduct mesh generation, the probability of individual i in state z_i responding to task j with stimulus intensity s_j is shown as formula (5.8):

$$P_{ij} = \frac{s_j^2}{s_j^2 + \alpha\theta_{ij}^2 + \beta d_{z_ij}^2} \tag{5.8}$$

where θ_{ij} is the response threshold for individual i respond to task j and restricted to an interval $[\theta_{min}, \theta_{max}]$ and it can be updated as follows:

$$\theta_{ij}(t + 1) = \theta_{ij}(t) - \xi_0 \tag{5.9}$$

$$\theta_{il}(t + 1) = \theta_{il}(t) - \xi_1, \quad l \in n_j \tag{5.10}$$

$$\theta_{ik}(t + 1) = \theta_{ik}(t) + \varphi, \quad k \neq j \text{ and } k \notin n_j \tag{5.11}$$

where n_j is the neighborhood of task j, ξ_0 and ξ_1 are learning coefficients corresponding to the movement to new location, φ is the forgetting coefficient for other locations. d_{z_ij} is the distance between z_i and j (e.g., it can describe the ability of whether ant i is able to perform task j or not). TRTM is built on the premise that the plane is discrete, which is appropriate for multirobot cooperative simulation (Kude and Bonabeau, 2000) and similar problems.

5.2.3   Some Analysis

FRTM is built based on the following assumption: ants response threshold are constant during discrete time; there are difference in ants and the role of ants are preassigned. The model does not explain the origins of task allocation and the robustness of ant colony's labor division. As a real ant behavior model, it is effective only when the timescale is small enough that threshold can be seen as constant. TRTM has some better performance than FRTM, such as flexibility and robustness; it remains to be discussed whether it has good performance in practical applications or not, due to the lack of simulation experimental comparison with the classic task allocation algorithms (Xiao and Tao, 2007).

In the subsequent part of this chapter, both FRTM and TRTM are generalized called ant colony's labor division model based on response threshold for the simplicity of presentation. According to the features of actual problems, ant colony's labor division model based on response threshold needs to be improved from the following aspects:

1. Ant colony's labor division model based on response threshold is suitable for labor division problem with the same task properties. While in practical applications, the tasks often have heterogeneity; thus an ant colony's labor division model for self-organized allocation with multitask needs to be designed and developed. This model is constructed

in Section 5.3 and applied to the simulation study of multitask allocation in virtual enterprise, the simulation results related to virtual enterprise with the type of supply chain and virtual organization are provided, and the characteristics of ant colony's labor division model with multitask are discussed.

2. There are only two states of the ants, namely, inactivity and performing the task, in ant colony's labor division model based on response threshold. While in practical applications, there exist some differences among Agents with the state of performing the task, e.g., the agent varying from performing task A to performing task B is a kind of state change, but such state change cannot be reflected in ant colony's labor division model based on response threshold. Thus ant colony's labor division model with multistate is built to imitate state transition characteristics of Agent given in Section 5.4, and then the model is applied to the optimization of Kanban control strategy in production management systems with some good results reached.

3. All tasks are homogeneously parallel without resource constraints and sequence in ant colony's labor division model based on response threshold. While in practical applications, the situation of several tasks sharing common resources or performing a task with certain order often happens. Considering such a situation, Section 5.5 constructs an ant colony's labor division model with multiconstraint to describe the resource constraints relationship among nodes at various levels in resilient supply chain network structure, and then the computer simulation is applied to realize the task allocation of resilient supply chains. The simulation results show the excellent performance of the proposed model.

5.3   Modeling and Simulation of Ant Colony's Labor Division with Multitask

5.3.1   Background Analysis

There are many similarities between ant colony's labor division and the establishment and operation of virtual enterprises which can be listed as follows (Xiao and Tao, 2009): (i) they both construct a team consisting of many individuals to complete the task after the task appears; (ii) ants or enterprises decide whether or not to perform the task based on the task and the individual's ability; (iii) they both are spontaneous to engage in the task or not, without any mandatory; (iv) the characteristics of stimuli varying with time in ant colony's labor division model are similar with the market demand changes in virtual enterprise organization. According to the above analysis, we make an extension to FRTM in order to meet the needs of simulation study on virtual enterprise behavior.

Due to the simplicity of FRTM, the corresponding properties of task and individuals are single. It is difficult to fully reflect the complexity of market environment and enterprise behavior, if the model is directly applied to model and simulate virtual enterprise organization. Therefore, it needs to improve the model and redesign the modules of the attributes of the ants, the task execution, the learning rule, and the activation environment of ants. By the characteristic analysis of virtual enterprise organization, the expansion is conducted from the following aspects in this section.

1. There is only one sort of task in FRTM, while in actual market, if a market opportunity appears which needs cooperation of many enterprises to complete, the corresponding task is usually complex and cannot be finished alone by any enterprise in general. Therefore, the task is defined as a total task firstly which can be divided into many different sorts of subtasks in the extended labor division model.

2. Because there is only one sort of task in FRTM, there is also one response threshold value for the corresponding individual. In actual market, every enterprise has its own unique core ability, where it does not mean only the enterprise has such ability or the enterprise has no other abilities, i.e., every enterprise may have several core abilities, but the strength of these abilities is different. In the extended model, each enterprise is seen as an Agent, each subtask correspond to a core ability, and each Agent has several response threshold values corresponding to the subtasks.

3. The ant in FRTM has no memory function and its response threshold is a fixed value remaining unchanged through the whole operation process. That is to say, the individuals lack the ability of learning, no matter how many times they perform a task, their corresponding threshold values are fixed, which obviously does not match the actual situation. It needs to be improved in the extended model, where if an individual engages in a task, its threshold value decreases corresponding to this task, at the same time, the remaining threshold values may increase.

Therefore, Section 5.3.2 proposes an extended model, namely, ant colony's labor division model with multitask. Due to the diversity of virtual enterprise organizational structure, we adopt the idea from simple to complex, and the two typical virtual enterprise instances are chosen to do simulation experiments in Sections 5.3.3 and 5.3.4, respectively, in order to verify the validity of the model proposed in Section 5.3.2. Section 5.3.5 analyzes the characteristics of the proposed model.

5.3.2 Design and Implementation of Ant Colony's Labor Division Model with Multitask

5.3.2.1 Design of Ant Colony's Labor Division Model with Multitask

Compared with FRTM, the major improvement in ant colony's labor division model with multitask is the task performed by ant Agents that is extended from one single attribute to various different attributes, and the corresponding variables in FRTM need to be redefined as follows:

$T = \{T_1, T_2, \ldots, T_q\}$: task set needs to be completed.
T_j $(j = 1, 2, \ldots, q)$: subtask after task decomposition.
s_j $(j = 1, 2, \ldots, q)$: stimulus intensity of subtask j.
$K_i = \{k_1, k_2, \ldots, k_q\}$: core ability set of Agent i, $i = 1, 2, \ldots, N$, N is the total number of Agents.
θ_{ij}: response threshold value of Agent i relative to subtask j, which is determined by core ability.
δ_j: the increase in stimulus intensity of subtask j per unit time.
λ_{ij}: a scale factor measuring the reduction of stimulus intensity of subtask j caused by Agent i, i.e., the efficiency of Agent i to perform subtask j.

$S_{ij}(t)$: state of Agent i to perform subtask j at t time, $S_{ij}(t) = 1$ corresponds to performing the task, $S_{ij}(t) = 0$ corresponds to inactivity.

n^j_{act}: number of Agents to perform subtask j.

$P(S_{ij} = 0 \rightarrow S_{ij} = 1)$: probability of Agent i to perform subtask j.

$P(S_{ij} = 1 \rightarrow S_{ij} = 0)$: probability of Agent i to give up subtask j.

ζ_{ij}: Agent's learning coefficient, which describes the phenomenon that once an Agent i accumulated the experience of performing subtask j, due to the changes of external environment (such as increase of production capacity or decline in production costs in virtual enterprise), the response threshold values corresponding to other similar tasks will reduce.

φ_i: Agent's forgetting coefficient for other tasks, once an Agent i mobilizes resource for the implementation of a certain type of task, the response threshold values corresponding to other tasks will increase. The same Agent has identical forgetting coefficient for all other tasks.

The structure of ant colony's labor division model with multitask can be described as follows.

Environmental Stimuli

When a task T appears to be accomplished, divide it into q subtasks in order to model conveniently: $T = \{T_1, T_2, \ldots, T_q\}$. Similar to FRTM, each subtask corresponds to a stimulus which reflects the urgency of the implementation of the subtask; the higher the stimulus is, the more the number of Agents is attracted to perform the corresponding task. Agents decide whether or not to perform the subtask based on the stimuli and its response threshold values. Similar to the changes of stimuli in FRTM, when subtask is not completed, its stimulus will increase a constant δ_j per unit time. Each subtask can be performed to various degrees according to the participation situation of Agents, which depends on the total number n^j_{act} and performance efficiency λ_{ij}.

Analogous to formula (5.7), the change of stimulus s_j relative to subtask j is shown as formula (5.12):

$$s_j(t + 1) = s_j(t) + \delta_j - \sum_{i=1}^{N} \lambda_{ij} S_{ij}(t) \tag{5.12}$$

where

$$n^j_{act} = \sum_{i=1}^{N} S_{ij}(t) \tag{5.13}$$

Agent Attributes

Each Agent has a single or multiple core capability as well as threshold attribute characteristics (such as productions and sales in virtual enterprises), corresponding to different subtasks. The performance capacity of Agent i corresponding to subtask T_j is calculated by core capability, and the function $f(T_j, K_i)$ can be used.

Once deciding to undertake subtask j for Agent i, the corresponding threshold θ_{ij} is updated according to the following rules:

$$\theta_{il}(t+1) = \zeta_{il} \cdot \theta_{il}(t), \quad l \in n_j \tag{5.14}$$

$$\theta_{ik}(t+1) = \varphi_i \cdot \theta_{ik}(t), \quad k \notin n_j \tag{5.15}$$

where n_j is the set of the number of all subtasks whose stimuli are identical to subtask j, ζ_{il} and φ_i are learning and forgetting coefficients, respectively, $\zeta_{il} < 1$, $\varphi_i > 1$.

Probability of Participation and Exit
Following the probability calculation method in FRTM, analogous to formulas (5.5) and (5.6), there are:

$$P(S_{ij} = 0 \rightarrow S_{ij} = 1) = \frac{s_j^n}{s_j^n + \theta_{ij}^n} \tag{5.16}$$

$$P(S_{ij} = 1 \rightarrow S_{ij} = 0) = p \tag{5.17}$$

where p is a value which is set in advance.

Simulation Principle
1. In a discrete period of time, idle Agent decides whether or not to participate in the task according to its attribute characteristics and external task demand; busy Agent determines whether or not to exit from the task according to the degree of task completion and return on its performance.
2. Agent has the ability to learn, and its attribute characteristics, i.e., threshold level, can be adjusted according to the task performance by itself in the past.
3. Once the task is executed, its stimuli decrease and the performance probability chosen by Agent reduces. If a task is in a state of hunger for a long time, its stimuli will increase automatically until the Agent to perform.

5.3.2.2 Implementation of Ant Colony's Labor Division Model with Multitask

Step 1. Set the discrete time variable $t = 0$ and set the N Agents' attribute values as follows: response threshold θ_{ij}, learning and forgetting coefficients ζ_{ij} and φ_i, as well as subtask stimuli $s_j(0)$.

Step 2. Calculate the states of all Agents according to formulas (5.16) and (5.17) and calculate each number of ants executing different tasks by formula (5.13).

Step 3. Update the attributes of Agents according to formulas (5.14) and (5.15).

Step 4. Update $s_j(t+1)$ according to formula (5.12), if $s_j(t+1) > 0$, then go to step 2, else go to step 5.

Step 5. Output the simulation result.

5.3.3   Supply Chain Virtual Enterprise Simulation

Logistics and distribution is a typical supply chain virtual enterprise, whose goal is to complete a number of tasks. The core abilities of the enterprise units (such as transport capacity and warehouse capacity) are determined and keep unchanged in the short term. Similarly, the time span of distribution tasks is small, experiential learning and adaptive adjustment are unnecessary and also difficult to achieve. So the behavior characteristics of this type of virtual enterprise are as follows: multi-task, single threshold, and no learning.

5.3.3.1   Simulation Example and Parameter Settings

A logistics enterprise has two distribution centers (distribution centers or distribution center is abbreviated as DC in the following) in a city, which deliver appliances and electronic products for the major markets of the city and its suburb towns. The logistics enterprise has 10 customers, their distance with the two DC are listed in Table 5.1 (Xiao and Tao, 2009).

The inventories of the two DC are sufficient, but their transport capacities are different, here the transport capacity means the distance traveled by all vehicles in a day (8 h) measured by kilometer. In addition to transport capacity, the distance between DC and customers affects delivery capacity; therefore, the response ability of DC is determined by transport capacity and distance, which is shown in formula (5.18):

$$P(S_{ij} = 0 \to S_{ij} = 1) = \frac{s_j^2}{s_j^2 + \alpha \cdot \theta_{ij}^2 + \beta \cdot d_{ij}^2} (\alpha = 0.7; \quad \beta = 0.3) \tag{5.18}$$

The probability of DC i quitting subtask j is set as $P(S_{ij} = 1 \to S_{ij} = 0) = 0.2$ and the increase in stimulus intensity of subtask j per unit time is set as $\delta_j = 1.0$. Some other parameter settings can be seen in Xiao and Tao (2009).

5.3.3.2   Simulation Results and Analysis

In order to facilitate the analysis of the model performance, the following two indices are defined to evaluate operation situation of the virtual enterprise.

1. Degree of busyness and idleness, DBE:

$$\text{DBE} = \frac{\text{the actual time spent on task by Agent everyday}}{\text{maximum time could be used by Agent everyday}} \tag{5.19}$$

Table 5.1 List of the Distance Between DC and Customers (unit: kilometers)

	1	2	3	4	5	6	7	8	9	10
First DC	50.0	30.0	70.0	110.0	80.0	120.0	140.0	80.0	90.0	100.0
Second DC	40.0	60.0	75.0	90.0	200.0	100.0	120.0	100.0	60.0	110.0

2. Percent of completion, PC:

$$PC(\%) = \frac{\text{completion task by Agent}}{\text{total task}} \times 100 \tag{5.20}$$

The example is simulated in cycle of month (30 days) according to the model proposed in Section 5.3.2. The DBE of DC is shown in Figure 5.1 and the percentage of the task accomplished by each DC is shown in Figure 5.2, where the upper part of the curve corresponds to the first DC and the lower part corresponds to the second DC.

The following observations can be calculated according to the simulation data:
Average order of each task: $\overline{Q_i} = (Q_1 + Q_2 + \cdots + Q_n)/n \approx 5.283$.

Average completion of task accomplished by the first DC: $\overline{Q_{1,i}} = (Q_{1,1} + Q_{1,2} + \cdots + Q_{1,n})/n \approx 4.482$.

Average completion of task accomplished by the second DC: $\overline{Q_{2,i}} = (Q_{2,1} + Q_{2,2} + \cdots + Q_{2,n})/n \approx 0.802$.

From the above observations and Figure 5.2, we can see that the percentage of the first DC completing the total task is 84.83% and the percentage of the second DC completing the total task is 15.17%; the transport capacity of the first DC and the second DC accounts for 83.33% and 16.67% of the total transport capacity, respectively, and then take into account the effect of distance (the sum of the distance from the first DC to all customers is smaller than that of the second DC), which shows that the simulation results match well the actual situation.

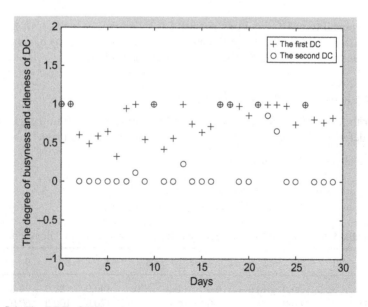

Figure 5.1 The DBE of DC.

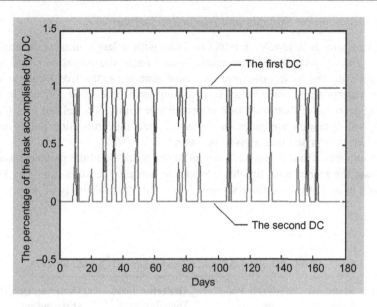

Figure 5.2 The percentage of the task accomplished by each DC.

The order and delivery deadline of customers are randomly generated in the simulation cycle. From Figures 5.1 and 5.2, we can see that the two DC operate in a normal state.

5.3.4 Virtual Organization Enterprise Simulation

As the market competition is increasingly fiercely, the response speed of the product on the market is particularly important. For small and medium enterprises to survive in such situation, an important means is to establish a long-term small and medium enterprise alliance, bring into play their respective advantages and share production tasks. The virtual enterprise organizational form of the simulation example in Section 5.3.3 is a task-oriented temporary organization, and virtual organization enterprise is a long-term cooperation organization based on the organizational structure. The task accomplished by virtual organization enterprise is versatile and changes immediately as the orders change. Since the virtual enterprise has a long life cycle, the core ability of enterprise units may be changed in the forms, such as complete changes, reinforcement, or weakness of the core ability. In order to gain more benefits from cooperation, enterprise units may learn from others and adjust adaptively. So the behavior characteristics of this type of virtual enterprise are as follows: multitask, multithreshold, and learning.

Here we use the example in Li and Xiao (2006) to verify the characteristics of ant colony's labor division model with multitask, which is applied to simulate the construction and operation process of virtual organization enterprise.

5.3.4.1　Simulation Example and Parameter Settings

A city in China is a jewelry production base with a large number of small and medium jewelry processing enterprises. According to the operation situation and combined with the basic principles of virtual enterprise, the five local small and medium enterprises spontaneously form a long-term production alliance to try to solve the problem of their own lack of production ability. The related data for production and operation are given in Table 5.2, and the production ability of five cooperative enterprise units is given in Table 5.3.

Each enterprise unit is seen as a Agent of the model, and the parameters are set as follows: the increase in stimulus intensity of subtask j per unit time $\delta_j = 3.0$, the efficiency of Agent i to perform subtask j $\lambda_{ij} = 1.0$, the probability of Agent to quit

Table 5.2 Related Data for Production and Operation

Product Type	Standard Cost	Standard Time (person-day)	Ordering Time Distribution	Ordering Quantity Distribution
A	350	0.5	Uniform (7, 30)	Uniform (50, 80)
B	1500	3	Uniform (7, 30)	Uniform (50, 80)
C	1300	2.5	Uniform (7, 30)	Uniform (50, 80)
D	850	1.5	Uniform (7, 30)	Uniform (50, 80)
E	680	1	Uniform (7, 30)	Uniform (50, 80)

Table 5.3 Production Ability of Five Cooperative Enterprise Units

Manufacturer	Product List	Production Cost	Production Time (person-day)	Production Capacity (person-day)
M1	A	320	0.5	80
	C	1260	2.2	
	D	815	1	
M2	B	1400	2.6	100
	E	660	0.8	
M3	A	330	0.4	60
	C	1240	2	
M4	D	820	1.4	120
	E	620	1.1	
M5	B	1470	2.4	70
	C	1240	2.1	
	D	840	1.2	

task $p = 0.2$, learning coefficient $\zeta_{il} = 0.9$, and forgetting coefficient $\varphi_i = 1.1$ corresponding to Agent i.

5.3.4.2   Simulation Results and Analysis

The example is simulated in cycle of year (360 days) according to the model proposed in Section 5.3.2. The busyness and idleness of enterprise Agents are calculated according to formula (5.19) and the results are shown in Figure 5.3. The daily total orders of all kinds of products are taken as a total task, and then the total task is divided into subtasks according to the product sorts. Each enterprise unit has its own core ability which is used to choose the subtask as well as its quantity. The percentage of each subtask accomplished by enterprise Agents is calculated according to formula (5.20) and the results are shown in Figure 5.4.

From Figures 5.3 and 5.4, we can obtain the following results:

1. In Figure 5.3, the busyness and idleness of enterprise 1 (corresponding to the top subgraph in Figure 5.3) keep in "1," i.e., enterprise 1 keeps in working at full capacity. And curves corresponding to enterprises 2−5 are in "inverted stalactite" shape, that is, 1 is the baseline with part protruding downward. This shows that the four enterprise units spent most of their time working at full capacity. Thus it can be seen that each of these five enterprise units have basically perform to their best production capacity, neither overload

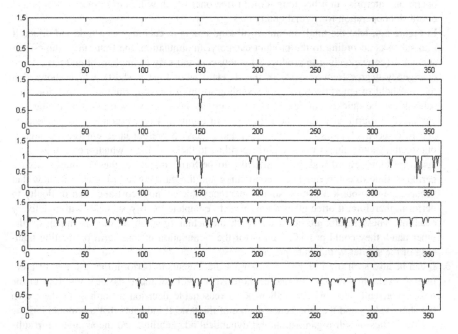

Figure 5.3 Comparison of the busyness and idleness of enterprise Agents.

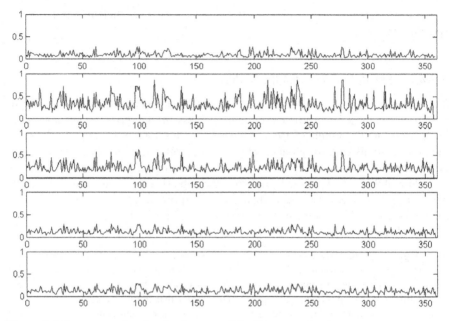

Figure 5.4 Percentage of each subtask accomplished by enterprise Agents.

operation enterprise unit nor long term in free one, which will help to divide profits and establish cooperation for virtual enterprises.

2. In Figure 5.4, take the total amount of all kind orders in each day as a task and divide it into subtasks according to the product category. In simulation, the first curve shows that subtask 1 (corresponding to product A) is low cost and easy to implement and has a large emergency degree (requirements of the standard labor time is short), which shows that the threshold of enterprise unit corresponding to this subtask is minimum; therefore, the subtask can be quickly completed and the corresponding curve is the lowest of the five curves. The fourth curve and the fifth curve in Figure 5.4 (corresponding to products D and E, respectively) show that subtask 4 and subtask 5 present large emergency degree, but the threshold values of Agent corresponding to them are high, which means these subtasks are high reward and large difficulty to perform; therefore, these subtasks need a period of time to complete. The second curve and the third curve in Figure 5.4 show that subtask 2 and subtask 3 exhibit small emergency degree, high cost and high difficulty to perform; therefore, it often takes a long time to complete the two subtasks within delivery deadline. These results are consistent with the actual situation on the one hand; on the other hand, they could provide a basis for the formulation of long-term production planning of the similar virtual enterprises.

3. It can be also seen from Figures 5.3 and 5.4 that Agents to perform the task are different in each cycle, and the quit of one or more Agent will not make the task interrupt in the next cycle, and other Agents will make a reasonable decision according to their own threshold values and the emergence degree of the task. It indicates that the model has the characteristics of self-organization and dynamical adaptability, and the simulation results are often better than other static simulation methods.

5.3.5 Discussion

Through the analysis of the simulation results related to virtual enterprise with the type of supply chain and virtual organization, the intrinsic characteristics of ant colony's labor division model with multitask are summarized as follows:

1. Virtual enterprise is in a complex and volatile market environment, enterprise Agent can adapt to the dynamic changes in simulation environment, and the core capability to accomplish the task can be improved and enhanced through the accumulation and learning in operation process.
2. The enterprise Agent behavior is flexible, whether it participates or not and to what extent depends on synthetic judgment on return, its own ability and external environment, and it can adjust continuously without task assignment by a leader.
3. In the simulation process, some Agents temporarily join or quit the task which does not cause disintegration of virtual enterprise organization, so the model proposed in this section has certain robustness.

Although these characteristics have great significance on the research about modeling and simulation of virtual enterprise, it does not mean the model is applicable to all the virtual enterprise organizational forms. Bao and Jia (2006) believe that the virtual enterprise organizational model is a two layer structure in essence which has core layer and outer layer. The core layer consists of one or more enterprises to establish an Alliance Steering Committee, which is in charge of the work, such as the construction of virtual enterprise, internal coordination, resource integration, and strategic decision. According to the two layer structure of the overall framework, virtual enterprise organizational model can be divided into federation model, star-like model, and parallel model based on the number of members. From the organizational structure and operation mechanism, ant colony's labor division model with multitask is more suitable for parallel model, and it provides an effective tool to explore the complexity and internal mechanism of virtual enterprise organization.

5.4 Modeling and Simulation of Ant Colony's Labor Division with Multistate

5.4.1 Background Analysis

There are only two states of inactivity and performing the task for ants in ant colony's labor division model based on response threshold. However, the states of those Agents performing the tasks may be different in practical applications. It is also a state change for Agents from task A to task B, which is quite difficult to be reflected in the ant colony's labor division model based on response threshold. For example, in production management systems, if the production unit is viewed as Agent and each production unit needs to produce different products, the change from the processing of one product to another is a state change of Agent. An ant colony's labor division model with multistate is established to reflect such a state transition characteristic of Agents in this section.

From a practical point of view, the pull production mode of production management system has a strong similarity to the ant colony's labor division model. Modeling and simulation optimization are implemented for Kanban control strategy in the pull production mode by borrowing ideas from the ant colony's labor division model. Comparing ant colony's labor division model based on response threshold with Kanban control strategy in principle (Dorigo et al., 2000; Krieg, 2005) and through the actual application analysis, the similarity between the two can be summed up in the following several aspects (Xiao et al., 2010).

1. Control mode is a "bottom-up." Swarm intelligence behavior of the ant colony's division labor is the whole emergence phenomenon of the ant individual formed through the internal information transmission, where top-down centralized control mode. Kanban transmission is from the production chain downstream to upstream in the Kanban control strategies.

2. Individual flexibility leads to certain balance in the whole system. In the ant colony's labor division model based on response threshold, the flexibility of individual behaviors produces group plasticity, that is to say the proportion of ants implementing different tasks can be changed under the inside pressure of reproduction and external influence of aggressive challenges, thereby ants can automatically achieve individual labor division in the group and make the colony tasks in a relative balance state. In the Kanban control production system, the production schedule of each execution unit can adjust automatically according to its core capability and external order demands, and making the production system achieve certain balance between production capacity and logistics level.

3. The communication mode between individuals is an indirect transfer mode based on medium within the local range. Ants transfer information simply by the indirect way through the medium of pheromone when they do not know about the global information of the colony needs. As a result, each ant can work busily and orderly according to the overall requirements of the colony. In the Kanban control production system, execution units between the adjacent upstream and downstream are not aware of the global demand information. Moving Kanban is regarded as a media between each other that transfer local demand and supply information, which makes the production system running in good order.

It is difficult to directly apply the ant colony's labor division model based on response threshold proposed in Section 5.2.2 to Kanban control strategy, because the model is too simplified, and its task attribute is single as well as the ability and the state of ants. As a result, there exists no direct correspondence between the control module in the model and Kanban control module in the pull production system. Comparing with the characteristics of the production system using Kanban control strategy, the ant colony's labor division model based on response threshold can be improved from the following several aspects:

1. There are only two kinds of states which are idle and performing the task for ants in ant colony's labor division model based on response threshold. For the Kanban production unit, if Agent's production varieties are k, each production variety represents an activity state of task performance. In addition to consider an idle state without task performed, its

active states are $k + 1$. At the same time, each Agent can adjust the state according to its own ability and the external demand. Therefore, in the ant colony's labor division model with multistate, each Agent needs a state transfer expression to determine that the current state is kept or adjusted.

2. Tasks are single and the only general task is not decomposed into a number of subtasks in the ant colony's labor division model based on response threshold. In actual production systems, flexible level in the workshop is high generally in the production environment of small batch and varieties, where each production could be considered as a task. Therefore, a variety of different tasks are defined firstly in the ant colony's labor division model with multistate based on response threshold. At the same time, the response threshold value of the ant individual is unique due to the only task in the ant colony's labor division model based on fixed threshold. But each production processing unit has its own unique core capability in actual production systems. Therefore, in the ant colony's labor division model with multistate, each ant individual is regarded as an Agent and each task corresponds to an Agent ability so that each Agent possesses multiple response threshold values corresponding to various tasks.

In view of the above, according to the characteristics of Kanban control strategy, Section 5.4.2 redesigns ant activity environment, attribute characteristics, and state transition rules, and puts forward an ant colony's labor division model with multistate. Moreover, the ant colony's labor division model with multistate given in Section 5.4.3 is applied for Kanban control strategy optimization examples in pull production systems.

5.4.2 Design and Implementation of Ant Colony's Labor Division Model with Multistate

5.4.2.1 Design of Ant Colony's Labor Division Model with Multistate

Stimulus Values in Multitask Environment

Agent can implement the total task $T = \{T_1, T_2, \ldots, T_k\}$ including a plurality of different tasks. There exists an environment stimulus value corresponding to each task, which increases accordingly with the increase of time, recorded as δ_j. Agent involves in the execution of the tasks and completes a part of various tasks to different extent, which is determined by the total number n_{act}^j of Agent to complete the tasks and the corresponding accomplishment efficiency φ_j. Hence the stimulus evolutionary equation is shown as formula (5.21), which is similar to formula (5.12):

$$s_j(t + 1) = s_j(t) + \delta_j - n_{act}^j \cdot \varphi_j \tag{5.21}$$

Relative Environment Stimulus Value $s_{\alpha\beta}$ and Relative Threshold $\theta_{\alpha\beta}$

In the ant colony's labor division model with multistate, Agent i can implement task $T = \{T_1, T_2, \ldots, T_k\}$, which consists of a number of different tasks. Thus, Agent i has not only two states of the participation in and out ($S_i = 0$ or $S_i = 1$), but also $k + 1$ states, that is to say, the state set is $S_i = \{0, 1, 2, \ldots, k\}$, where 0 indicates the idle state. Here, there exists the corresponding relationship between k elements in the task set and $k + 1$ elements in the state set. In order to enable them one to one, we assume in particular that there exists a "virtual" task T_0 corresponding to the idle state 0. The "virtual" task T_0 is fulfilled after other tasks are completed. Therefore, its implementation is the most difficult.

Assuming that Agent is implementing task T_α, the state of Agent i is $S_i = \alpha$; if the next task to complete is T_β, the next state of Agent i is $S_i = \beta$. If the Agent execution state is transferred, namely $S_i = \alpha \to \beta$, the two states must be compared. Therefore, it is necessary to calculate the relative environmental stimulus value $\tilde{s}_{\alpha\beta}$ and relative threshold value $\tilde{\theta}_{i\alpha\beta}$ of different tasks, which are shown as formulas (5.22) and (5.23), respectively.

$$\tilde{s}_{\alpha\beta} = \frac{s_\beta}{s_\alpha} \tag{5.22}$$

$$\tilde{\theta}_{i\alpha\beta} = \frac{\theta_{i\beta}}{\theta_{i\alpha}} \tag{5.23}$$

Agent State Transformation

Agents require to be transferred among multiple states when they implement a number of different tasks. Therefore, the state transformation probability is calculated as formula (5.24):

$$P(S_i = \alpha \to S_i = \beta) = \frac{\tilde{s}_{\alpha\beta}^n}{\tilde{s}_{\alpha\beta}^n + \tilde{\theta}_{i\alpha\beta}^n} \tag{5.24}$$

By simplifying the above formula, Agent state transformation expression is obtained finally as formula (5.25):

$$P(S_i = \alpha \to S_i = \beta) = \frac{(s_\beta \cdot \theta_{i\alpha})^n}{(s_\beta \cdot \theta_{i\alpha})^n + (s_\alpha \cdot \theta_{i\beta})^n} \tag{5.25}$$

From formula (5.25), we can see that in the case of other variables unchanged, the smaller value s_α is, the greater value P is; in the situation of other variables unchanged, the larger $\theta_{i\beta}$ is, the smaller value P is. For the idle state, the corresponding "virtual" task is the most difficult to implement. The stimulus value and response threshold of the "virtual" task can be calculated using formulas (5.26) and (5.27), respectively:

$$s_0 = \min\{s_1, s_2, \ldots, s_k\} \tag{5.26}$$

$$\theta_{i0} = \max\{\theta_1, \theta_2, \ldots, \theta_k\} + 1 \tag{5.27}$$

5.4.2.2 Implementation of Ant Colony's Labor Division Model with Multistate

According to the above design idea of the ant colony's labor division model with multistate, the steps of algorithm implementation of the model can be given as follows.

Step 1. Let the discrete time variable $t = 0$ and set the following attribute values of Agents which number is N: response threshold value of ith Agent corresponding to jth state is θ_{ij}, relative environmental stimulus value is $\tilde{s}_{\alpha\beta}$, relative threshold value is $\tilde{\theta}_{i\alpha\beta}$, and the initialization task environment stimulation value is $s_j(0)$.

Step 2. Calculate relative environmental stimulus value $\tilde{s}_{\alpha\beta}$ and relative threshold value $\tilde{\theta}_{i\alpha\beta}$ according to formulas (5.22) and (5.23).

Step 3. Calculate state transformation probability of each individual according to formula (5.25).

Step 4. Update $s_j(t + 1)$ according to formula (5.21), if $s_j(t + 1) > 0$, go to step 2; otherwise, go to step 5.

Step 5. Conduct statistics and output the simulation results.

5.4.3 Simulation Example of Ant Colony's Labor Division Model with Multistate

5.4.3.1 Simulation and Experiment Environment

The simulation example is given as follows: the gear workshop in a production enterprise produces four types of gears at present. In general, gear manufacturing procedures include blank prior heat treatment, rough turning, fine turning, machining keyway, heat treatment (carburizing, quenching, tempering), hole grinding, and gear grinding. Through reasonable simplification, except the inlet and outlet, gear manufacturing in the gear workshop consists of 10 procedures. According to the processing logic and logistics direction, the gear machining procedures are shown in Figure 5.5.

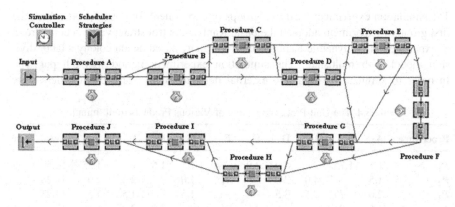

Figure 5.5 Description of gear machining procedures.

The simulation environment is set as follows: operating system Windows XP, CUP at 1.6G, 512M memory. Simulation software is eM-Plant7.5, which is a kind of logistics simulation software developed by American Tecnomatix Company with characteristics of object oriented, graphical, integration, etc., which is mainly applied for modeling and simulation in the production, logistics, and engineering. EM-Plant7.5 is divided into modeling, simulation, bottleneck analysis, optimization, statistics module, etc. In the simulation environment, various performance indicators in production systems can be analyzed, such as the average production efficiency, WIP level, utilization of equipment, workers load balance, and logistics equilibrium condition.

5.4.3.2 Parameters of the Simulation Model

The ant colony's labor division model with multistate is introduced into production systems using Kanban control strategy, essentially as the main information control strategy between processing units to form a scheduling scheme. The process scheduling is adjusted dynamically according to the following ant colony's labor division model with multistate.

For the simulation, in order to adapt to changes of the market and environment characteristics of many varieties and small batch, the gear workshop employs the mixed production system, and dynamically adjusts the type and yield of products in the production system according to the downstream order. The gear workshop includes inlet, outlet, and 10 processing units, where each unit is composed of the machine, entrance cache, and exit cache. For simplicity, we set that the maximum capacity of semifinished products is three pieces in the entrance cache and exit of cache, and the maximum carrying capacity of moving Kanban is one piece each time. The number of product types needs to be processed by the gear workshop is 4, including P_1, P_2, P_3, P_4. According to the processing actual situation, the unit processing time on each procedure of various products can be estimated which is given in Table 5.4.

5.4.3.3 Simulation Results

The simulation experiment used two groups of experiment for comparison, where the first group of experiment adopted the basic Kanban control strategy, the second group of experiment used dynamic Kanban control strategy based on ant colony's labor division model with multistate. The simulation experiment period was 8 h per day. In order to simulate the dynamic external demand, many varieties of orders were

Table 5.4 The Unit Processing Time of Various Products (unit: minutes)

Procedure	A	B	C	D	E	F	G	H	I	J	Total Time
P_1	1.5	1.75	—	4.0	2.0	—	1.5	1.5	—	1.25	13.5
P_2	1.5	—	4.0	2.0	—	1.5	1.0	—	2.25	2.0	14.25
P_3	2.0	1.75	2.5	3.5	—	—	1.5	—	1.5	1.5	14.25
P_4	1.5	2.0	2.5	—	3.0	2.25	—	2.0	2.25	1.5	17

produced in a certain proportion of dynamic random. The ratio of orders for four kinds of products is 5:3:4:2, respectively, but the sum of demand for the first group is identical to that of the second.

The simulation experiment mainly monitored the production efficiency of 10 procedure nodes. Here, the production efficiency η referred to the proportional relationship of processing time t_{pro}, processing preparation time t_{pre}, and variety adjustment time t_{adj}, which is shown as formula (5.28):

$$\eta = \frac{t_{pro}}{t_{pro} + t_{pre} + t_{adj}} \qquad (5.28)$$

Production efficiency reflects the average processing capacity of the processing unit. The higher the production efficiency is, the lower the ratio of the nonmachine processing time in the total production time is. The shorter the product processing cycle is, the lower the production cost is. The maximum production capacity of production system is restricted by the procedure with the highest production efficiency (known as key procedure) in the current control strategy. Production efficiency of procedure nodes in the two simulation experiments is given in Table 5.5.

5.4.3.4 Analysis of Results

The production efficiency for 10 procedures is given in experimental results. On this basis, the average production efficiency can be calculated as formula (5.29):

$$\bar{\eta} = \sum_{i=1}^{n} \eta/n \qquad (5.29)$$

where n is the number of processing units, namely, the number of procedures, in this case, $n = 10$. Average production efficiency can reflect the upgrading space of the production capacity in the production system.

According to the production efficiency of each processing unit, the stability of production and processing in the production system is also further investigated. Here, the balance coefficient ζ is defined to measure this characteristic, and it can be calculated as formula (5.30):

$$\zeta = \frac{\eta_{max} - \eta_{min}}{\bar{\eta}} \qquad (5.30)$$

Table 5.5 Production Efficiency of Procedure Nodes in the Two Simulation Experiments (unit: %)

Procedure	A	B	C	D	E	F	G	H	I	J
Group 1	26.51	27.88	24.63	23.06	29.35	21.70	37.39	23.14	26.01	29.89
Group 2	24.14	28.02	22.78	24.91	27.37	23.49	30.71	25.57	27.03	30.76

Apparently, balance coefficient ζ is the measurement of production efficiency fluctuation of each procedure in the production system, which reflects the production system's stability, that is to say the smaller the coefficient is, the more stable the production system is; the larger the change of the production task is, the more flexible the production system is.

According to Table 5.5, we can obtain average production efficiency $\bar{\eta}_1 = 26.96\%$ and balance coefficient $\zeta_1 = 0.58$ for the first experiment; average production efficiency $\bar{\eta}_2 = 26.48\%$ and balance coefficient $\zeta_2 = 0.30$ for the second experiment.

Based on the first experimental results, we can obtain the following results:

1. The production efficiency for 10 procedures in simulation experiments ranges from 20% to 40%, where the lowest value is 21.70%, the maximum value is only 37.39%, and the average production efficiency is 26.96%. It indicates that the "preparation time" and "adjustment time" of the processing are relatively long, and production adjustment frequency is relatively high; it also means the simulation experimental environment in demand is flexible production mode with small batch and large varieties.
2. According to Table 5.5, the production efficiency of the procedure node G reaches 37.39%, significantly higher than that of other procedure node, which is basically consistent with the intuitive judgment in the actual situation. As seen from Figure 5.5, the upstream inflow end of procedure node G has three lines, and it is the only one that makes three procedures come together, while other procedure nodes have only one or two lines. Both the simulation experiment and the actual situation show that node G becomes the key procedure in the production system using the basic Kanban control strategy. At the same time, the calculated equilibrium coefficient $\zeta_1 = 0.58$, and the value is relatively large, which means the production process is not stable. Once there is a large change in production task, it may be difficult for production system to complete the task.

Comparing the second experimental results with the first one, we can obtain the following results:

1. The average production efficiency in the second experiment is 26.48%, which is almost the same as that of the first experiment. This indicates that the purpose of using dynamic Kanban control strategy based on the ant colony's labor division model with multistate is not to increase the average production efficiency. In general, the average production efficiency is mainly determined by the producing mode. This group of experiment results shows that the simulation experimental environment in need is flexible production mode with small batch and great varieties.
2. According to Table 5.5, in the second experiment, the use of the dynamic Kanban control strategy based on the ant colony's labor division model with multistate makes the production efficiency of the original key procedure node G drop to 30.71%, which indicates that the ant colony's labor division model with multistate can reduce the influence of key procedure G through local information transfer. The highest production efficiency is that of procedure node J (30.76%) and J is the new key procedure, which is substantially equivalent to the production efficiency decreased of the primary key procedure node G. Therefore, the increase of the whole production system capacity would be a little more than the first experiment.
3. In the second simulation experiment, the balance coefficient is $\zeta_2 = 0.30$, which is greatly reduced and about half of the balance coefficient $\zeta_1 = 0.58$ in the first. It indicates that

using dynamic Kanban control strategy based on the ant colony's labor division model with multistate makes the production stability improve obviously, and the production efficiency in each procedure tends to balance, in response to the production of the small batch and many varieties with good flexibility. At the same time, loss and maintenance of equipments can be balanced, which can improve the efficiency of the entire production system and reduce the cost in the long term.

5.5   Modeling and Simulation of Ant Colony's Labor Division with Multiconstraint

5.5.1   Background Analysis

How the intensity and frequency of emergency incidents generate large-scale impact to supply chain operations has became an important issue in supply chain risk management (Wagner and Bode, 2006). Emergency incidents have increased the uncertainty of supply chain environment. In such uncertain circumstances, supply chain systems tend to be more vulnerable and the vulnerability is shown obviously (Tang, 2006a). The main measure to overcome the vulnerability of supply chain is to adopt various effective supply chain risk management strategies, which is embodied primarily in flexible strategy (Tang and Tomlin, 2008) and robust strategy (Tang, 2006b). In the more uncertain environment, supply chain system should have the comprehensive advantages of both flexible and robust strategies. In such circumstances, the concept of supply chain resilience is generated (Ponomarov and Holcomb, 2009). Christopher and Peck (2004) suggests that resilience is the ability to make a supply chain system return to its original or ideal status after an external interruption, and resilient supply chain shows that it has the two abilities on adaptability to environment and recovering ability of the system.

Supply chain resilience shows its ability of self-adaptation and self-coordination of the system, i.e., this supply chain system can adaptively lead the idle source owned by supply chain members and the adjustable resources in supply chain environment to supply chain task allocation. Ant colony is a social inspect group, and its labor division has the obvious features of adaptability and self-coordination (Bonabeau et al., 1996; Theraulaz et al., 1998). As mentioned in Section 5.2.1, an obvious feature of ant colony's labor division is group plasticity, which is caused by the flexibility of individual behaviors, i.e., the proportion of ants implementing different tasks can be changed under the inside pressure of reproduction and external influence of aggressive challenges. Such a characteristic of ant colony's labor division consists with the self-adaptive characteristic of resilient supply chains. As the reason of this consistency between them, we make some research on task allocation in resilient supply chains by utilizing ant colony's labor division model.

Considering the system structure, supply chain has a chain-network structure and some materials flow in this chain network. So the members in different levels of supply chain have special constraints for logistics capacity, which makes supply capacity of suppliers restrict the needs of manufacturers and production capacity of producers limit the sales. Therefore, in the context of supply chain resilience, in order to use ant colony's labor division model to achieve the supply chain task allocation, it should be considered the various supply chain resource constraints entirely. However, current ant colony's labor division models cannot reflect such constraints related to supply chain sufficiently, so some expanded and modified work should be made. Thus in this section, taking the various supply chain resource constraints into account, we propose an ant colony's labor division model with multiconstraint to solve the task allocation problem in resilient supply chains and the main contents of this section are from our previous research work (Xiao et al., 2012).

5.5.2 Design and Implementation of Ant Colony's Labor Division Model with Multiconstraint

5.5.2.1 Design of Ant Colony's Labor Division Model with Multiconstraint

As labor division in the real world, there may be multistate systems or multitask systems, and colonies executing different tasks may have some constraints especially in quantitative. In supply chain systems, there are also many tasks and states related to the roles in supply chain, and the colonies executing tasks in this system also have constraints in quantitative, and the number of colonies, who execute related tasks, is coordinated with the operations of supply chain. Therefore, we theoretically propose an ant colony's labor division model with multiconstraint. It is assumed that there are many tasks, multistate ants, and some quantitative constraints between colonies in this model. Its detailed description is shown as follows.

Suppose in the certain system, there are q tasks to be allocated, the task set $T = \{T_1, T_2, \ldots, T_q\}$. So there are $(q + 1)$ states to be selected for each ant which is regarded as an Agent, the state set $W = \{W_{T1}, W_{T2}, \ldots, W_{Tq}, W_0\}$. W_{Tj} denotes the state of ant in executing task T_j $(0 < j \leq q)$ and W_0 denotes that the ant is in idle state. $S_{ij}(t)$ denotes the state in which ant i executes task T_j and $S_{ij}(t) \in \{0, 1\}$. When it values 1, it means ant i executes task j, while it values 0, it means this ant does not execute the task. Each task T_j corresponds to an environment stimulus value s_j; therefore, environment stimulus value set $s = \{s_1, s_2, \ldots, s_q\}$. The environment stimulus value decreases with the implementation of the task and increases with a fixed value at a unit time, which is shown as formula (5.31):

$$s_j(t + 1) = s_j(t) + \delta - \sum_{i=1}^{N} \chi S_{ij}(t) \tag{5.31}$$

where δ denotes the increasing value of environment stimulus in a unit time, N denotes the total number of ants, χ denotes each ant's execution efficiency, and $j = 1, 2, \ldots, q$.

Core ability set of ant i is denoted as $K_i = \{k_{i1}, k_{i2}, \ldots, k_{iq}\}$, and $k_{i1} + k_{i2} + \cdots + k_{iq} = 1$. k_{ij} shows the core ability of ant i in executing task T_j, and this value of k_{ij} shows the tendency that the ants decide to take some task according to their ability. θ_{ij} denotes the response threshold of ant i relative to task T_j, and this variable shows own ability of ant i to execute the task T_j. A response threshold can be changed with time and the number of times of executing the relative task. When a task is executing, the value of response threshold will decrease; we will use z_1 between 0 and 1 to reduce this value so as to show the increase of ants' learning ability as formula (5.32). When there is no ant to take the task, the relative response threshold will increase by multiplying a number z_2, which is slightly larger than 1 and it indicates that the oblivion effect of ants. It is shown as formula (5.33):

$$\theta_{ij}(t + 1) = z_1 \cdot \theta_{ij}(t) \tag{5.32}$$

$$\theta_{ij}(t + 1) = z_2 \cdot \theta_{ij}(t) \tag{5.33}$$

In many circumstances, there exist some constraints related to the system or its environment, and such constraints may affect the transformation behavior of each ant. In our model, we use vector e to denote the affection, and $e = \{e_1, e_2, \ldots, e_q\}$ $(0 < e_i \le 1)$. The vector e is called constraint vector and e_i is called constraint variable. Its value is related to the constraints of the system or its environment, and different system constraints correspond to different value of e. The probability of ant i to execute task j is related to core capability k_j, response threshold s_j, environment stimulus s_j, and constraint variable e_j, which is shown as follows:

$$p(S_{ij} = 0 \rightarrow S_{ij} = 1) = \frac{e_j k_j s_j^n}{s_j^n + \theta_{ij}^n} \tag{5.34}$$

where $i = 1, 2, \ldots, N; j = 1, 2, \ldots, q$.

The probability of ant i to exit task j is given by formula (5.35):

$$p(S_{ij} = 1 \rightarrow S_{ij} = 0) = u \tag{5.35}$$

where $i = 1, 2, \ldots, N; j = 1, 2, \ldots, q$; u is a fixed small value between 0 and 1.

According to the above generalized ant colony's labor division model with multiconstraint, a specialized ant colony's labor division model with multiconstraint for resilient supply chains is build to solve the task allocation problem of a three-stage supply chain system.

Such a supply chain system is a three-stage system consisting of the supplier, manufacturer, and marketer, and each ant can be in one of the following four kinds of states, i.e., supply state, production state, sales state, and quit state. Therefore, the task aggregation of this supply chain system contains three subtasks, i.e., supply task, production task, and sales task, namely, $T = \{T_1, T_2, T_3\}$, where T_1 denotes supply task, T_2 denotes production task, and T_3 denotes sales task.

Denote the number of ants as N, and $N = N_1 + N_2 + \cdots + N_q + N_0$, among them, $N_i(0 < i \le q)$ denotes the number of ant performing task i, N_0 denotes the number of idle ants. There are sequential constraints in the circumstance of supply chain, and the number of ant executing different tasks denoted as N_i has a certain constraint relation among them. The constraints of q-stage supply chain are $N_1 > N_2 > \cdots > N_q$ in tasks allocation of supply chains. These constraints have the obvious impact on the transformation of ants' states. Such constraints caused by ant number are denoted as the vector $w = \{w_1, w_2, \ldots, w_q\}$. Among them, $w_i = 1$ $(0 < i \leq q)$, and the values of others are determined by formula (5.36):

$$
w_i = \begin{cases} 1 & N_{i-1} > N_i \\ 0 & \text{others} \end{cases} (i > 1) \tag{5.36}
$$

In addition, the percentage of ants performing different tasks also affects the transformation of ant's state. Such constraints caused by the percentage of ant number are denoted as $o = \{o_1, o_2, \ldots, o_q\}$, among them, $0 < o_i < 1$ and o_i denotes the affection of task i. So the constraint variable e_i in the above generalized model can be written as $e_i = w_i o$ and formula (5.34) can be written as formula (5.37):

$$
p(S_{ij} = 0 \rightarrow S_{ij} = 1) = \frac{w_j o_j k_j s_j^n}{s_j^n + \theta_{ij}^n} \tag{5.37}
$$

For the considerations of a three-stage supply chain with the supply chain constraints, the number of supply ants is larger than the number of production ants, and the number of production ants is also larger than the number of sales ants, i.e., $N_1 > N_2 > N_3$. These constraints have an impact on performing tasks, and let constraint vector related to three kinds of tasks be $w = \{w_1, w_2, w_3\}$, where w_i is constraint variable corresponding to T_i. w_i can be value 0 or 1. The value of 1 indicates that the supply chain constraints play the role, and valuing 0 means that no constraints play the role. So w is called constraint indicator vector and w_i is called constraint indicator variable. Obviously, $w_1 = 1$ and it indicates that supply can be increased and it has less restriction in resilient supply chains.

If $N_1 > N_2$, then $w_2 = 1$, else $w_2 = 0$. The value of w_2 indicates that, as production resources are restricted by the capacity of supply, only if capacity of supply is greater than that of production, the production capacity can be increased. If $N_1 > N_2 > N_3$, then $w_3 = 1$, else $w_3 = 0$.

In resilient supply chain system, it should be coordinated the three tasks of supply, production, and marketing among all the ants to reduce resources consumption. It is the effect of the constraints set in supply chain and affects the probability of ants' state transformation. Let $o = \{o_1, o_2, o_3\}$ be for these constraints, where o_i denotes the influence of these constraints to task i. Vector w denotes whether the constraints have the impact on tasks, whereas vector o denotes in which degree these constraints affect the tasks. Both vectors o and w are on the impact of the supply chain constraints. Thus o is called constraint level vector and o_i is called constraint level variable.

Vector o under the three-stage supply chain system can be calculated as follows: when $w_i = 0$, $o_i = 0$ ($i = 1$, 2, 3); when $w_2 = 1$, $o_1 = N_2/N_1$; when $w_2 = 1$ and $w_3 = 0$, $o_2 = N_2/N_1$; when $w_2 = 1$ and $w_3 = 1$, $o_2 = N_3/N_1$, $o_3 = N_3/N_2$.

The probability of ants' state transformation to perform a task is given by formula (5.37), and it is related with core capability, response threshold, environment stimulus, and whether the constraints are satisfied fully.

5.5.2.2 Implementation of Ant Colony's Labor Division Model with Multiconstraint

While the supply chain system is damaged, some participants may withdraw participating in supply chain task allocation and other idle resources should be introduced into task allocation to make supply chain resume to the original or ideal state. In our approach, supply chain system is viewed as ant system. Environment stimuli of supply chain will significantly increase in value due to emergency incidents and these stimuli will change with time and the situation of task allocation. Response thresholds of the ants will be involved with the time and ants' participation times in executing the relative task. Accordingly, emergency incidents can be described as follows. First, we can decrease the number of ants participating in supply task, production task, or sales task to indicate the occurrence of emergency incidents. For example, the fact that the number of supply ants decreases sharply indicates supply ability of supply chain system is damaged by these emergency incidents. Second, once an emergency incident occurs, we can set a large environment stimulus to demonstrate the relative task is urgent.

According to the above impact analysis of emergency incidents on supply chain, the supply chain system simulation scene can be described as follows. There exist three kinds of tasks, namely, supply, production, and sales, in supply chain system, and these tasks are performed by the corresponding ants. Thus the ants can be classified as supply ants, production ants, and sales ants. When the emergency incident occurs, supply chain system is in disruptive damage, which has a significant impact on supply, production, or sales. We assume that the initial stage is with 100 ants in supply, 100 ants in production, 100 ants in sales, and another 100 ants in idle state to indicate the social resources which can be used by supply chain system. The emergency incident affects and damages the supply ability of this supply chain at certain time, such as $t = 5$, which leads to the number of the ants executing supply task decreases and the relative environment stimuli become larger. The task allocation of production and sales is also affected and the number of ants in production and sales will also decrease.

In the default initial state, we assume that there are 100 ants executing supply, production, or sales tasks, respectively, and another 100 ants are regarded as idle resources. According to the different roles of these 400 ants and the above simulation principles, the procedure of simulation algorithm to implementing the proposed model is given and Xiao et al. (2012) describe its contents in detail.

5.5.3 Simulation Results and Analysis

At the beginning of simulation, there exist 400 ants in the supply chain system, and other parameters are set by the default original values. In our simulation experiments, it is supposed that the supply chain system is disrupted by emergency incidents at a certain moment, and we conduct the simulation experiments in the different aspects which cover task allocation status, supply chain coordination, impact of emergency incidents on task allocation, task allocation rate, and task allocation rate with different emergency accidents. The obtained results demonstrate the advantages of the proposed ant colony's labor division model with multiconstraint to solve task allocation in resilient supply chains under emergency incidents.

The detail contents of simulation results and analysis can be seen in Xiao et al. (2012).

5.6 Concluding Remarks

A systematic study on the ant colony's labor division model is carried out to study labor division in swarm intelligence in this chapter. By making a further refinement based on the above work, we construct and propose a new paradigm which is called "problem-oriented approach to swarm intelligence." The proposed paradigm is different from the one of "method-oriented approach to swarm intelligence," which mainly improves the performance of optimization algorithms. The key to the success of such an approach is to grasp the features of problem objects sufficiently (Xiao, 2013).

FRTM is one of the earliest model to describe the behavior of ant colony's labor division. Its individual response threshold is fixed which means that the task performance just affects the intensity of stimuli without changing the threshold, where the response threshold value is an internal variable that decides the tendency of ant individual to respond to external stimuli and perform the corresponding task. On this basis, there are some improved researches on FRTM, such as the introduction of enhanced process to establish the time-varying response threshold model, allowing the response threshold to vary with time. This kind of models is identically named as "ant colony's labor division model based on response threshold." Considering the generality, they provide the theoretical basis for the follow-up research on the ant colony's labor division model.

Sections 5.3−5.5 propose ant colony's labor division model with multitask, multistate, and multiconstraint, respectively. They all have specific application backgrounds and are improved according to characteristics of the problem. The practical application examples show that these improved models have good adaptability and self-organized characteristic. Combined with the application backgrounds, we make further statements on the three improved ant colony's labor division models with problem-oriented feature:

1. Ant colony's labor division model with multitask highlights the diverse nature of virtual enterprise tasks. Considering the individual improving learning ability, it well depicts the

virtual enterprise self-organized behavior characteristics according to the virtual enterprise tasks' dynamic and changeable actual situation. The simulation results show that ant colony's labor division model with multitask owns dynamic adaptability, behavioral flexibility, robustness, etc.

2. Ant colony's labor division model with multistate is also a multitask model and it further highlights the diverse characteristics of product varieties based on the demand of Kanban control in pull production system. Multistate reflects the diversity of varieties and the one-to-one relationship between state and task helps to drive multitask operation. The simulation results show that the dynamic Kanban system based on this model can effectively control production bottlenecks and improve stability of production process.

3. The application background of ant colony's labor division model with multiconstraint is more complex, which is both a multitask model and a multistate model. In order to grasp the key of the problem, its main function is to effectively achieve task allocation in resilient supply chains according to the operational characteristics of resilient supply chains, which mainly consider multiresource-constrained relationship in resilient supply chain system. The simulation results show that this model has excellent performance with fast response and robustness which makes the supply chain more flexible.

The three models mentioned above have logical progressive relationship. The multistate model is also a multitask model. However, between multistate and multitask, it highlights the diverse characteristics of production varieties based on problem features. Multiconstraint model is both a multitask model and a multistate model, which emphasize on multiresource-constrained relationship according to the actual situation of the application background. In a word, summarizing from the dominant factor of the model, multitask model gives priority to task-driven, whereas multistate model gives priority to state-driven and multiconstraint model gives priority to constraint-driven. Their difference is to meet the respective requirements of the virtual enterprise, Kanban control strategy, and resilient supply chain. It shows the customization features of modeling, thus better able to solve practical problems. Therefore, the key to implement problem-oriented approach to swarm intelligence is "feature extraction based on problem objects."

Before feature extraction based on problem objects, there is an important preprocessing link that makes a comparative analysis on characteristics of the ant colony's labor division model and the application background. Only by knowing the similarity between these two, could it be targeted. That is to say, first, we should make arguments and statements about whether the problem is suitable for adopting ant colony's labor division model to solve it. These arguments and statements are generally based on bionic metaphor, e.g., Sections 5.3.1, 5.4.1, and 5.5.1 in this chapter demonstrate the existence of such a similarity by bionic metaphor with a certain length. In view of this, "similarity analysis based on bionic metaphor" is also a key point to implement problem-oriented approach to swarm intelligence.

Seen from the three practical problems in Sections 5.3−5.5, modeling is the description of the problems and revelation of the principles. Due to the complexity of the problem objects, to achieve its solution generally needs simulation and usually adopts advanced simulation technologies, such as Agent-based modeling simulation (Bonabeau, 2002). Therefore, as the follow-up step of feature extraction based on problem objects, "advanced simulation based on agent technology" is the basic technology to implement problem-oriented approach to swarm intelligence.

In summary, the logical structure of the key points to implement "problem-oriented approach to swarm intelligence" is: (i) similarity analysis based on bionic metaphor; (ii) feature extraction based on problem objects; and (iii) advanced simulation based on agent technology, where the second is the core of the three points.

Acknowledgment

This work is supported by the National Natural Science Foundation of China (Grant No. 60974076, 60474077 and 71171089).

References

Bao, G.X., Jia, X.D., 2006. Introduction to Management of Virtual Enterprises. China RenMin University Press, Beijing (in Chinese).

Bonabeau, E., 2002. Agent-based modeling: methods and techniques for simulating human systems. Proc. Natl. Acad. Sci. U.S.A. 99, 7280–7287.

Bonabeau, E., Theraulaz, G., Deneubourg, J.-L., 1996. Quantitative study of the fixed threshold model for the regulation of division of labour in insect societies. Proc. Roy. Soc. Lond. B. 263, 1565–1569.

Bonabeau, E., Dorigo, M., Theraulaz, G., 1999. Swarm Intelligence: From Natural to Artificial Systems. Oxford University Press, New York, NY.

Christopher, M., Peck, H., 2004. Building the resilient supply chain. Int. J. Logistics Manage. 15 (2), 1–13.

Dorigo, M., Bonabeau, E., Theraulaz, G., 2000. Ant algorithms and stigmergy. Future Generation Comput. Syst. 16 (8), 851–871.

Gell-Mann, M., 1994. The Quark and the Jaguar. Freeman, New York, NY.

Holland, J.-H., 1998. Emergence. Addison-Wesley, New York, NY.

Kennedy, J., Eberhart, R.C., Shi, Y.H., 2011. Swarm Intelligence. Morgan Kaufmann Publishers, San Francisco, CA.

Krieg, G., 2005. Kanban-Controlled Manufacturing Systems. Springer, New York, NY.

Krieger, M.J.B., Billeter, J.-B., 2000. The call of duty: self-organized task allocation in a population of up twelve mobile robots. Rob. Auton. Syst. 30 (1), 65–84.

Kude, C.R., Bonabeau, E., 2000. Cooperative transport by ants and robots. Rob. Auton. Syst. 30 (1/2), 85–101.

Kunz, H., Hemelrijk, C.K., 2003. Artificial fish schools: collective effects of school size, body size, and body form. Artif. Life. 9 (3), 237–253.

Li, H.L., Xiao, R.B., 2006. A multi-agent virtual enterprise model and its simulation with swarm. Int. J. Prod. Res. 44 (9), 1719–1737.

Nicolis, G., Pringogine, I., 1977. Self-Organization in Non-Equilibrium Systems. Wiley, New York, NY.

Nishimura, S.-I., Ikegami, T., 1997. Emergence of collective strategies in a prey–predator game model. Artif. Life. 3 (4), 243–261.

Ponomarov, S., Holcomb, M., 2009. Understanding the concept of supply chain resilience. Int. J. Logistics Manage. 20 (1), 124−143.

Tang, C.S., 2006a. Perspectives in supply chain risk management. Int. J. Prod. Econ. 103 (2), 451−488.

Tang, C.S., 2006b. Robust strategies for mitigating supply chain disruptions. Int. J. Logistics Res. Appl. 9 (1), 33−45.

Tang, C., Tomlin, B., 2008. The power of flexibility for mitigating supply chain risks. Int. J. Prod. Econ. 116 (1), 12−27.

Theraulaz, G., Bonabeau, E., 1995. Modeling the collective building of complex architectures in social insects with lattice swarms. J. Theor. Biol. 177 (4), 381−400.

Theraulaz, G., Bonabeau, E., Deneubourg, J.-L., 1998. Response threshold reinforcement and division of labour in insect societies. Proc. Roy. Soc. Lond. B. 265, 327−332.

Wagner, S.M., Bode, C., 2006. An empirical investigation into supply chain vulnerability. J. Purch. Supply Manage. 12 (6), 301−312.

Waldrop, M.-M., 1993. Complexity: The Emerging Science at the Edge of Order and Chaos. Touchstone Books, New York, NY.

Xiao, R.B., 2006. Analysis of characteristics of swarm intelligence and its significance to research of complex systems. Complex Syst. Complexity Sci. 3 (3), 10−19 (in Chinese).

Xiao, R.B., 2013. Swarm Intelligence in Complex Systems. Science Press, Beijing (in Chinese).

Xiao, R.B., Tao, Z.W., 2007. Research progress of swarm intelligence. J. Manage. Sci. China. 10 (3), 80−96 (in Chinese).

Xiao, R.B., Tao, Z.W., 2009. Modeling and simulation of ant colony's labor division for virtual enterprises. J. Manage. Sci. China. 12 (1), 57−69 (in Chinese).

Xiao, R.B., Yi, W.M., Tao, Z.W., Lu, J., 2010. Modeling and simulation of ant colony's labor division for pull production systems. Comput. Integr. Manuf. Syst. 16 (9), 1866−1874 (in Chinese).

Xiao, R.B., Yu, T.Y., Gong, X.G., 2012. Modeling and simulation of ant colony's labor division with constraints for task allocation of resilient supply chains. Int. J. Artif. Intell. Tools. 21 (3), 1−19 (1240014).

Yang, X.-S., 2011. Bat algorithm for multi-objective optimisation. Int. J. Bio-Inspired Comput. 3 (5), 267−274.

6 Particle Swarm Algorithm: Convergence and Applications

Shichang Sun[1,2] and Hongbo Liu[2,3]

[1]School of Computer Science and Engineering, Dalian Nationalities University, Dalian, China; [2]Department of Computer, Dalian University of Technology, Dalian, China; [3]School of Information Science and Technology, Dalian Maritime University, Dalian, China

6.1 Introduction

Particle swarm algorithm is inspired by social behavior patterns of organisms that live and interact within large groups. In particular, it incorporates swarming behaviors observed in flocks of birds, schools of fish, or swarms of bees, and even human social behavior, from which the "swarm intelligence" paradigm has emerged (Clerc, 2006; Fogel, 2006; Gandomi et al., 2013; Kennedy and Eberhart, 2001; Liu et al., 2006; Ozcan and Mohan, 1991; Sun et al., 2007, 2009; Yang, 2010). It could be implemented and applied easily to solve various function optimization problems or the problems that can be transformed to function optimization problems. As an algorithm, its main strength is its fast convergence, which compares favorably with many other global optimization algorithms (Abraham et al., 2006; Boeringer and Werner, 2004; Eberhart and Shi 1998; Liu et al., 2009). In this chapter, we introduce the convergence analysis and applications of particle swarm optimization (PSO) algorithm mainly based on the related previous works.

The classical particle swarm model consists of a swarm of particles, which are initialized with a population of random candidate solutions. They move iteratively through the d-dimension problem space to search the new solutions, where the fitness f can be calculated as the certain qualities measure. Each particle has a position represented by a position vector $\vec{x}_i$ (i is the index of the particle), and a velocity represented by a velocity vector $\vec{v}_i$. Each particle remembers its own best position so far in a vector $\vec{x}_i\#$, and its jth dimensional value is $x_{ij}^{\#}$. The best position vector among the swarm so far is then stored in a vector $\vec{x}^*$ and its jth dimensional value is x_j^*. During the iteration time t, the update of the velocity

Swarm Intelligence and Bio-Inspired Computation. DOI: http://dx.doi.org/10.1016/B978-0-12-405163-8.00006-5

01. Initialize the size of the particle swarm n, and other
02.   parameters; Initialize the positions and the velocities
03.   for all the particles randomly.
04. While (the end criterion is not met) do
05. $t = t + 1$;
06.   Calculate the fitness value of each particle;
07. $\vec{x}^* = argmin_{i=1}^n (f(\vec{x}^*(t-1)), f(\vec{x}_1(t)),$
08. $f(\vec{x}_2(t)), \cdots, f(\vec{x}_i(t)), \cdots, f(\vec{x}_n(t)))$
09.   For $i = 1$ to n
10. $\vec{x}_i^\#(t) = argmin_{i=1}^n (f(\vec{x}_i^\#(t-1)), f(\vec{x}_i(t)))$;
11.   For $j = 1$ to d
12.   Update the j-th dimension value of $\vec{x}_i$ and $\vec{v}_i$
13.   according to Eqs.(1),(3),(2),(4);
14.   Next j
15.   Next i
16. End While.

Algorithm 6.1 Particle swarm algorithm.

from the previous velocity to the new velocity is determined by Eq. (6.1). The new position is then determined by the sum of the previous position and the new velocity by Eq. (6.2):

$$v_{ij}(t+1) = wv_{ij}(t) + c_1 r_1(x_{ij}^\#(t) - x_{ij}(t)) + c_2 r_2(x_j^*(t) - x_{ij}(t)) \qquad (6.1)$$

$$x_{ij}(t+1) = x_{ij}(t) + v_{ij}(t+1) \qquad (6.2)$$

where c_1 is a positive constant, called as coefficient of the self-recognition component, c_2 is a positive constant, called as coefficient of the social component. r_1 and r_2 are the random numbers in the interval [0,1]. The variable w is called as the inertia factor, which value is typically set up to vary linearly from 1 to near 0 during the iterated processing. In the particle swarm model, the particle searches the solutions in the problem space within a range $[-s, s]$ (If the range is not symmetrical, it can be translated to the corresponding symmetrical range.) In order to guide the particles effectively in the search space, the maximum moving distance during one iteration is clamped in between the maximum velocity $[-v_{max}, v_{max}]$ given by Eq. (6.3) and similarly for its moving range given by Eq. (6.4):

$$v_{i,j} = \text{sign}(v_{i,j}) \min (|v_{i,j}|, v_{max}) \qquad (6.3)$$

$$x_{i,j} = \text{sign}(x_{i,j}) \min (|x_{i,j}|, x_{max}) \qquad (6.4)$$

The value of v_{max} is $\rho \times s$, with $0.1 \leq \rho \leq 1.0$ and is usually chosen to be s, i.e., $\rho = 1$. The pseudo-code for PSO algorithm is illustrated in Algorithm 6.1.

6.2 Convergence Analysis

The executing efficiency and effectiveness of the algorithms are ignored in many important works, since it is difficult to evaluate the performance and convergence of considered algorithms. Cristian (2003) discussed the swarm algorithm using standard results from the dynamic system theory. And the exploration–exploitation trade-off is discussed and illustrated. Bergh and Engelbrecht illustrated particle trajectories for general swarms to include the influence of the inertia term. And they also provide a formal proof that each particle converges to a stable point (van den Bergh and Engelbrecht, 2006). Jiang et al. (2007) investigated the swarm algorithm using stochastic process theory. They analyzed the stochastic convergent condition of the particle swarm system and corresponding parameter selection guidelines. It has been shown that the trajectories of the particles oscillate as different sinusoidal waves and converge quickly. Various methods have been used to identify some other particle to influence the individual. Now we analyze the convergence of swarm algorithm through iterative function system and probabilistic theory.

6.2.1 Individual Trajectory

Some previous studies have discussed the trajectory of particles and the convergence of the algorithm (Clerc and Kennedy, 2002; Cristian, 2003; van den Bergh and Engelbrecht, 2006). It has been shown that the trajectories of the particles oscillate as different sinusoidal waves and converge quickly. We represent particle swarm as an iterated function system. The dynamic trajectory of the particle is described based on single individual.

Clerc and Kennedy (2002) have stripped the particle swarm model down to a most simple form . If the self-recognition component c_1 and the coefficient of the social-recognition component c_2 in the particle swarm model are combined into a single term c, i.e., $c = c_1 + c_2$, the best position $\vec{p}_i$ can be redefined as follows:

$$\vec{p}_i \leftarrow \frac{(c_1\vec{p}_i + c_2 p_g)}{(c_1 + c_2)} \tag{6.5}$$

Then, the update of the particle's velocity is defined by

$$\vec{v}_i(t) = \vec{v}_i(t-1) + c(\vec{p}_i - \vec{x}_i(t-1)) \tag{6.6}$$

The system can be simplified even further by using $\vec{y}_i(t-1)$ instead of $\vec{p}_i - \vec{x}_i(t-1)$. Thus, the reduced system is then

$$\begin{cases} \vec{v}(t) = \vec{v}(t-1) + c\vec{y}(t-1) \\ \vec{y}(t) = -\vec{v}(t-1) + (1-c)\vec{y}(t-1) \end{cases}$$

This recurrence relation can be written as a matrix−vector product, so that

$$\begin{bmatrix} \vec{v}(t) \\ \vec{y}(t) \end{bmatrix} = \begin{bmatrix} 1 & c \\ -1 & 1-c \end{bmatrix} \cdot \begin{bmatrix} \vec{v}(t-1) \\ \vec{y}(t-1) \end{bmatrix}$$

Let

$$\vec{P}_t = \begin{bmatrix} \vec{v}_t \\ \vec{y}_t \end{bmatrix}$$

and

$$A = \begin{bmatrix} 1 & c \\ -1 & 1-c \end{bmatrix}$$

we have an iterated function system for the particle swarm model:

$$\vec{P}_t = A \cdot \vec{P}_{t-1} \tag{6.7}$$

For the iterated system determined by Eq. (6.7), the eigenvalues of A are λ_1 and λ_2. We are looking for pair of values (c, k) so that

$$A^k = I \tag{6.8}$$

where I is the identity matrix. We have $\det(A) > 0$ (equal to 1, in fact), so there exists P so that

$$P^{-1}AP = \Lambda \tag{6.9}$$

where

$$\Lambda = \begin{bmatrix} \lambda_1 & 0 \\ 0 & \lambda_2 \end{bmatrix}$$

Equation (6.8) can then be rewritten

$$(P\Lambda P^{-1})^k = \Lambda^k = I \tag{6.10}$$

It means we must have

$$\lambda_1^k = \lambda_2^k = 1 \tag{6.11}$$

But we have

$$
\begin{cases}
\lambda_1 = 1 - \dfrac{c}{2} + \sqrt{\Delta} \\[3mm]
\lambda_2 = 1 - \dfrac{c}{2} - \sqrt{\Delta}
\end{cases}
\tag{6.12}
$$

with c is strictly positive, and

$$
\Delta = \left(1 - \frac{c}{2}\right)^2 - 1
$$

So it is possible for Eq. (6.11) only if the eigenvalues are true complex numbers, i.e., if Δ is strictly negative. It implies that c must be smaller than 4.

It is easy to see that λ_1 and λ_2 are conjugate complex numbers. It means $\lambda_1 = \overline{\lambda}_2$.

So finally we have k solution for $\lambda_1^k = 1$; this solution can be computed by De Moivre's Theorem (Andreescu and Andrica, 2005):

$$
\cos\left(\frac{s2\pi}{k}\right) + i \sin\left(\frac{s2\pi}{k}\right)
$$

where $s = 0, \ldots, K - 1$.

There are an infinity of such cycles but according to Bonabeau et al. (1999) and Clerc (2006), the only possible ones are for cycle sizes $k \in \{3, 4, 5, 6\}$.

For $k = 3$, we have the following root of unity:

$$
1, \ -\frac{1}{2} + \frac{i\sqrt{3}}{2}, \ -\frac{1}{2} - \frac{i\sqrt{3}}{2}
$$

For $k = 4$:

$$
1, \ -1, i, \ -i
$$

For $k = 5$:

$$
1, \frac{\sqrt{5}-1}{4} + i\frac{\sqrt{10+2\sqrt{5}}}{4}, \frac{\sqrt{5}-1}{4} - i\frac{\sqrt{10+2\sqrt{5}}}{4},
$$

$$
\frac{-\sqrt{5}-1}{4} + i\frac{\sqrt{10-2\sqrt{5}}}{4}, \frac{-\sqrt{5}-1}{4} - i\frac{\sqrt{10-2\sqrt{5}}}{4}
$$

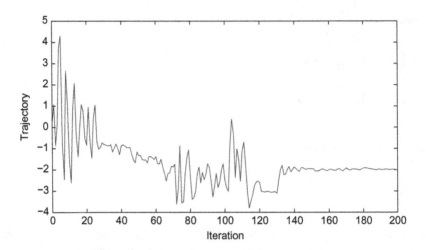

Figure 6.1 Trajectory of a single particle.

For $k = 6$:

$$1, -1, -\frac{1}{2} + \frac{i\sqrt{3}}{2}, -\frac{1}{2} - \frac{i\sqrt{3}}{2},$$

$$\frac{1}{2} + \frac{i\sqrt{3}}{2}, \frac{1}{2} - \frac{i\sqrt{3}}{2}$$

The solution must hold Eq. (6.12) and $0 < c < 4$. It is easy to see that we get only the following solutions:

$$(k, c) = (3, 3), (4, 2), \left(5, \frac{3 - \sqrt{5}}{2}\right), \left[5, \frac{3 + \sqrt{5}}{2}\right] \tag{6.12}$$

The trajectory of a single particle is illustrated in Figure 6.1.

6.2.2 Probabilistic Analysis

For analyzing the convergence of the swarm algorithm, we first introduce the definitions and lemmas (Goldberg, 1989; Guo and Tang, 2001; Halmos, 2005; He et al., 2005; Holland, 1975; Whitley, 1991; Xu et al., 1999).

Consider the problem (P) as

$$(P) = \begin{cases} \min f(\vec{x}) \\ \vec{x} \in \Omega = [-s, s]^n \end{cases} \tag{6.13}$$

where $\vec{x} = (x_1, x_2, \ldots, x_n)^T$. $\vec{x}*$ is the global optimal solution to the problem (P), let $f^* = f(\vec{x}^*)$. Let

$$D_0 = \{ \vec{x} \in \Omega | f(\vec{x}) - f^* < \varepsilon \} \tag{6.14}$$

$$D_1 = \Omega, \quad D_0$$

for every $\varepsilon > 0$.

Since ith dimensional value of the particle's velocity is generated by Eq. (6.1), the variable velocity belongs to the normal distribution. When $v_{max} = s$, $v \sim [-s, s]$. During the iterated procedure from the time t to $t + 1$, let q_{ij} denotes that $\vec{x}(t) \in D_i$ and $\vec{x}(t + 1) \in D_j$. Accordingly, the particles' positions in the swarm could be classified into four states: q_{00}, q_{01}, q_{10}, and q_{01}. Obviously $q_{00} + q_{01} = 1$, $q_{10} + q_{11} = 1$.

Definition 1 (convergence in terms of probability) Let ξ_n be a sequence of random variables and ξ a random variable, and all of them are defined on the same probability space. The sequence ξ_n converges with a probability of ξ if

$$\lim_{n \to \infty} P(|\xi_n - \xi| < \varepsilon) = 1 \tag{6.15}$$

for every $\varepsilon > 0$. The sequence ξ_n converges almost surely or almost everywhere or with probability of 1 or strongly toward ξ if

$$P(\lim_{n \to \infty} \xi_n = \xi) = 1; \tag{6.16}$$

or

$$P\left(\bigcap_{n=1}^{\infty} \bigcup_{k \geq n} [|\xi_n - \xi| \geq \varepsilon] \right) = 0 \tag{6.17}$$

for every $\varepsilon > 0$.

Lemma 1 (Borel−Cantelli Lemma) Let $\{A_k\}_{k=1}^{\infty}$ be a sequence of events occurring with a certain probability distribution, and let A be the event consisting of the occurrences of a finite number of events A_k for $k = 1, 2, \ldots$. Then

$$P\left(\bigcap_{n=1}^{\infty} \bigcup_{k \geq n} A_k \right) = 0 \tag{6.18}$$

if

$$\sum_{n=1}^{\infty} P(A_n) < \infty \tag{6.19}$$

$$P\left(\bigcap_{n=1}^{\infty}\bigcup_{k\geq n}A_k\right)=1 \tag{6.20}$$

if the events are totally independent and

$$\sum_{n=1}^{\infty}P(A_n)=\infty \tag{6.21}$$

Lemma 2 (Particle state transference) $q_{01}=0$, $q_{00}=1$, $q_{11}\leq c\in(0,1)$, and $q_{10}\geq 1-c\in(0,1)$.

Proof: In the swarm algorithm, the best solution is updated and saved during the whole iterated procedure. So $q_{01}=0$ and $q_{00}=1$.

Let $\vec{\hat{x}}$ is the position with the best fitness among the swarm so far as the time t, i.e., $\vec{\hat{x}}=\vec{p}^*$. As the definition by Eq. (6.14), $\exists r>0$, when $\|\vec{x}-\vec{\hat{x}}\|_{\infty}\leq r$, we have $|f(\vec{x})-f^*|<\varepsilon$. Denote $Q_{\hat{x},r}=\{x\in\Omega\|\vec{x}-\vec{\hat{x}}\|_{\infty}\leq r\}$. Accordingly

$$Q_{\hat{x}},r\subset D_0 \tag{6.22}$$

Then,

$$\begin{aligned}
&P\{(\vec{x}+\Delta\vec{x})\in Q_{\hat{x},r}\} \\
&=\prod_{i=1}^{n}P\{|x_i+\Delta x_i-\hat{x}_i|\leq r\} \\
&=\prod_{i=1}^{n}P\{\hat{x}_i-x_i-r\leq\Delta x_i\leq\hat{x}_i-x_i+r\}
\end{aligned} \tag{6.23}$$

where x_i, Δx_i, and $\hat{x}_i$ are the ith dimensional values of $\vec{x}$, $\Delta\vec{x}$, and $\vec{\hat{x}}$, respectively. Moreover, $\hat{v}\sim[-s,s]$, so that

$$P((\vec{x}+\Delta\vec{x})\in Q_{\hat{x},r})=\prod_{i=1}^{n}\int_{\hat{x}_i-x_i-r}^{\hat{x}_i-x_i+r}\frac{\eta}{2\sqrt{2\pi}s}e^{-y^2/2s^2}dy \tag{6.24}$$

Denote $P_1(\vec{x})=P\{(\vec{x}+\Delta\vec{x})\in Q_{\hat{x},r}\}$ and C is the convex closure of level set for the initial particle swarm. According to Eq. (6.24), $0<P_1(\vec{x})<1$ ($\vec{x}\in C$). Again, since C is a bounded closed set, so $\exists\vec{y}\in C$,

$$P_1(\vec{y})=\min_{\vec{x}\in C}P_1(\vec{x}),\quad 0<P_1(\vec{y})<1 \tag{6.25}$$

Considering synthetically Eqs (6.22) and (6.25), so that

$$q_{10}\geq P_1(\vec{x})\geq P_1(\vec{y}) \tag{6.26}$$

Let $c = 1 - P_1(\vec{y})$, thus,

$$q_{11} = 1 - q_{10} \le 1 - P_1(\vec{y}) = c \quad (0 < c < 1) \tag{6.27}$$

and

$$q_{10} \ge 1 - c \in (0, 1) \tag{6.28}$$

Theorem 1 Assume that the swarm algorithm provides position series $\vec{p}_i(t)$ $(i = 1, 2, \ldots, n)$ at time t by the iterated procedure. $\vec{p}^*$ is the best position among the swarm explored so far, i.e.,

$$\vec{p}^*(t) = \arg \min_{1 \le i \le n} (f(\vec{p}^*(t-1)), f(\vec{p}_i(t))) \tag{6.29}$$

Then,

$$P(\lim_{t \to \infty} f(\vec{p}^*(t)) = f^*) = 1(6) \tag{6.30}$$

Proof: For $\forall \varepsilon > 0$, let $p_k = P\{|f(\vec{p}^*(k)) - f^*| \ge \varepsilon\}$, then

$$p_k = \begin{cases} 0 & \text{if } \exists T \in \{1, 2, \ldots, k\}, \vec{p}^*(T) \in D_0 \\ \overline{p}_k & \text{if } \vec{p}^*(t) \notin D_0, t = 1, 2, \ldots, k \end{cases} \tag{6.31}$$

According to Lemma 2,

$$\overline{p}_k = P\{\vec{p}^*(t) \notin D_0, t = 1, 2, \ldots, k\} = q_{11}^k \le c^k \tag{6.32}$$

Hence,

$$\sum_{k=1}^{\infty} p_k \le \sum_{k=1}^{\infty} c^k = \frac{c}{1-c} < \infty \tag{6.33}$$

According to Lemma 1,

$$P\left(\bigcap_{t=1}^{\infty} \bigcup_{k \ge t} |f(\vec{p}^*(k)) - f^*| \ge \varepsilon \right) = 0 \tag{6.34}$$

As defined in Definition 1, the sequence $f(\vec{p}*(t))$ converges almost surely or almost everywhere or with probability 1 or strongly toward f^*, and the theorem is proved.

6.3   Performance Illustration

To illustrate the performance of the algorithms and trace their feasibility and effectiveness, we apply the algorithms to solve the scheduling problem for workflow applications in distributed data-intensive computing environments, the problem of neighbor selection (NS) in peer-to-peer (P2P) topology.

6.3.1   Dataflow Application

With the development of the "high-performance computing", grid, etc., some complex applications are designed by communities of researchers in domains such as high-energy physics, astronomy, biology (Andrieux et al., 2003; Cannataro et al., 2002; Huhlaeva et al., 2003; Venugopal and Buyya, 2006), and human brain planning (Zhong et al., 2005). For implementing and utilizing successfully these applications, one of the most important activities is to find appropriate schedules. The goal is to find an optimal assignment of tasks in the applications with respect to the costs of the available resources. However, the scheduling problem in distributed data-intensive computing environments seems quite different from the one in the traditional situation. Scheduling jobs and resources in these data-intensive applications need to meet the specific requirements, including process flow, data access/transfer, completion cost, flexibility, and availability. All kinds of components in the application can interact with each other directly or indirectly. Scheduling algorithms using traditional computing paradigms barely consider the data transfer problem during mapping computational tasks, and this neglect might be costly in distributed data-intensive applications (Dong and Akl, 2006).

6.3.1.1   Problem Formulation

The scheduling problem in distributed data-intensive computing environments has been an active research topic, and therefore many terminologies have been suggested. Unfortunately, some of the terms are neither clearly stated nor consistently used by different researchers, which frequently makes readers confused. For clarity purposes, some key terminologies are defined as follows:

- Machine (computing unit)
  Machine (computing unit) is a set of computational resources with limited capacities. It may be a simple personal machine, a workstation, a supercomputer, or a cluster of workstations. The computational capacity of the machine depends on its number of CPUs, amount of memory, basic storage space, and other specializations. In other words, each machine has its calculating speed, which can be expressed in number of cycles per unit time (CPUT).
- Data resource
  Data resources are the datasets which effect the scheduling. They are commonly located on various storage repositories or data hosts. Data resources are connected to the computational resources (machines) by links of different bandwidths.
- Job and operation
  A job is considered as a single set of multiple atomic operations/tasks. Each operation will be typically allocated to execute on one single machine without preemption. It has input and output data and processing requirements in order to complete its task. One of

the most important processing requirements is the workflow, which is the ordering of a set of operations for a specific application. These operations can be started only after the completion of the previous operations from this sequence, which is the so-called workflow constraints. The operation has the processing length in number of cycles.

- Workflow application

    A workflow application consists of a collection of interacting components that need to be executed in a certain partial order for solving a certain problem successfully. The components involve a number of dependent or independent jobs, machines, the bandwidth of the network, etc. They have specific control and data dependency between them.

- Schedule and scheduling problem

    A schedule is the mapping of the tasks to specific time intervals of machines. A scheduling problem is specified by a set of machines, a set of jobs/operations, optimality criteria, environmental specifications, and by other constraints. The scheduling problem for workflow applications in distributed data-intensive computing environments is abbreviated to "FDSP".

    To formulate the scheduling problem, suppose a workflow application comprises q jobs $\{J_1, J_2, \ldots, J_q\}$, m machines $\{M_1, M_2, \ldots, M_m\}$, and k data hosts $\{D_1, D_2, \ldots, D_k\}$. In the application, the calculating speed of the machine is $\{P_1, P_2, \ldots, P_m\}$. Each job consists of a set of operations $J_j = \{O_{j,1}, O_{j,2}, \ldots, O_{j,p}\}$. For convenience, we will decompose all the jobs to atomic operations and resort the operations as $\{O_1, O_2, \ldots, O_n\}$. Their processing lengths are $L_1, L_2, \ldots, L_n$, respectively. All the operations are in the specific workflow, and they will be carried out orderly on the machines with data retrieval, data input, and data output. The operations in the workflow can be represented as or be transformed to a directed acyclic graph (DAG), where each node in the DAG represents an operation and the edges denote control/data dependencies.

Definition 2 A workflow graph for data-intensive workflow applications can be represented as $G = (O, E)$, where the set of nodes $O = \{O_1, O_2, \ldots, O_n\}$ corresponds to the set of operations to be executed, and the set of weighted, directed edges E represents both the precedence constraints and the data transfers volume among operations in O. An edge $(O_i, O_j) \in E$ implies that O_j cannot start execution until O_i finishes and sends its result to O_j. We call task O_i predecessor of task O_j and task O_j successor of task O_i. Let $\text{Pred}(O_i)$ denotes the set of all the predecessors of task O_i. Let $\text{Succ}(O_i)$ denotes the set of all the successors of task O_i.

The relation between the operations can be represented by a flow matrix $F = [f_{i,j}]$, in which the element $f_{i,j}$ stores the weight value if the edge $\langle O_i, O_j \rangle$ is in the graph, otherwise it is set to "-1". Figure 6.2 depicts a workflow instance of 7 operations. The recursive loop between O_1 and O_7 can be neglected when the scheduling focused on the stage within the loop. Its flow matrix F is

$$\begin{bmatrix} -1 & 8 & 3 & 9 & -1 & -1 & -1 \\ -1 & -1 & -1 & -1 & 6 & -1 & -1 \\ -1 & -1 & -1 & -1 & 2 & 12 & -1 \\ -1 & -1 & -1 & -1 & -1 & 7 & -1 \\ -1 & -1 & -1 & -1 & -1 & -1 & 4 \\ -1 & -1 & -1 & -1 & -1 & -1 & 8 \\ -1 & -1 & -1 & -1 & -1 & -1 & -1 \end{bmatrix}$$

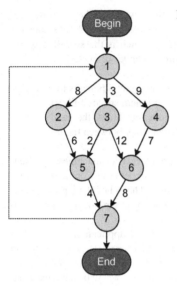

Figure 6.2 An instance with 7 operations.

The data host dependencies of the operations are determined by the retrieval matrix $R = [r_{i,j}]$. The element $r_{i,j}$ is the retrieval time which O_i executes retrieval processing on the data host D_j. There are the other two matrices $A = [a_{i,j}]$ and $B = [b_{i,j}]$, where the element $a_{i,j}$ in the former is the distance between the machines M_i and M_j, and the element $b_{i,j}$ in the latter is the distance between the machine M_i and the data host D_j. For each operation, its completion time is the sum of three components: the input data time, the retrieval data time, and the execution time on the assigned machine. It is to be noted that the input data time can be started to accumulate only after the completion of the previous operations in the workflow.

Given a feasible solution $S = \{S_1, S_2, \ldots, S_n\}$, S_i is the serial number of the machine which the operation O_i is assigned on. Define C_{O_i} ($i \in \{1, 2, \ldots, n\}$) as the completion time that the machine M_{S_i} completes the operation O_i. For the operation O_i, its completion time C_{O_i} can be calculated by Eq. (6.1):

$$C_{O_i} = \sum_{l=1}^{n} f_{l,i} a_{S_l, S_i}$$

$$f_{l,i} \neq -1 \tag{6.35}$$

$$\sum_{h=1}^{k} r_{i,h} b_{S_i, h} + L_i / P_{S_i}$$

To formulate the objective, $\sum C_{M_i}$ represents the time that the machine M_i completes the processing of all the operations assigned on it. Define $C_{max} = \max\{\sum C_{M_i}\}$ as the makespan and $C_{sum} = \sum_{i=1}^{m} (\sum C_{M_i})$ as the flowtime. The scheduling problem is thus to determine both an assignment and a sequence of the operations on all machines that minimize some criteria. Most important optimality criteria are to be minimized:

- the maximum completion time (makespan): C_{max};
- the sum of the completion times (flowtime): C_{sum}.

By minimizing C_{sum}, the average operation is finished quickly, at the expense of the largest operation taking a long time, whereas by minimizing C_{max}, no operation takes too long, at the expense of most operations taking a long time. Minimization of C_{max} would result in maximization of C_{sum}. The weighted aggregation is the most common approach to the problems. According to this approach, the objectives, $F_1 = \min\{C_{max}\}$ and $F_2 = \min\{C_{sum}\}$, are summed to a weighted combination:

$$F = w_1 \min \{F_1\} + w_2 \min \{F_2\} \tag{6.36}$$

where w_1 and w_2 are nonnegative weights and $w_1 + w_2 = 1$. These weights can be either fixed or adapted dynamically during the optimization. The fixed weights, $w_1 = w_2 = 0.5$, are used in this section. Alternatively, the weights can be changed gradually according to Eqs (6.37) and (6.38). The alternate curves ($R = 200$) are showed in Figure 6.3. In fact, the dynamic weighted aggregation (Parsopoulos and Vrahatis, 2002) mainly takes F_1 into account. Because F_2 is commonly much larger than F_1, the final solution would have a large weight ($w_1 \to 1$) on F_1 during minimizing the objective:

$$w_1(t) = |\sin(2\pi t/R)| \tag{6.37}$$

$$w_2(t) = 1 - w_1(t) \tag{6.38}$$

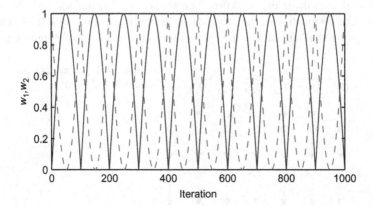

Figure 6.3 The dynamic weight curves.

Definition 3 A scheduling problem for data-intensive workflow applications can be defined as $\Pi = (J(L), M(P), D, G, R, A, B, f)$. If all the jobs are decomposed to atomic operations and the relationship between the operations are transformed to the flow matrix F, the scheduling problem can be represented as $\Pi = (O(L), M(P), D, F, R, A, B, f)$. The key components are operations, machines, and data hosts. For the sake of simplify, the scheduling problem also be represented in triple $T = (O, N, D)$.

Particle Swarm Heuristic for FDSP

For applying particle swarm algorithm successfully for the FDSP problem, one of the key issues is how to map the problem solution to the particle space, which directly affects its feasibility and performance (Salman et al., 2002; Xia and Wu, 2005). We set up a search space of n dimension for an $(n-$Operations, $m-$Machines) FDSP problem. Each dimension is limited to $[1, m + 1)$. For example, consider the $(7-$Operations, $3-$Machines) FDSP, Figure 6.3 illustrates how to map one possible assignment to one particle position coordinates in the particle swarm domain. Each dimension of the particle's position maps one operation, and the value of the position indicates the machine number to which this task/operation is assigned during the course of particle swarm algorithm. So the value of a particle's position should be integer. But after updating the velocity and position of the particles, the particle's position may appear as real values such as 1.4. It is meaningless for the assignment. Therefore, in the algorithm, we usually round off the real optimum value to its nearest integer number. By this way, we convert a continuous optimization algorithm to a scheduling problem. The particle's position is a series of priority levels of assigned machines according to the order of operations. The sequence of the operations will not be changed during the iteration Figure 6.4.

Since the particle's position indicates the potential schedule, the position can be "decoded" to the scheduling solution. It is to be noted that the solution will be unfeasible if it violates the workflow constraints. The operations must be started only after the completion of the previous latest operation in the workflow. The best situation is the starting point of the operation in alignment with the ending point of

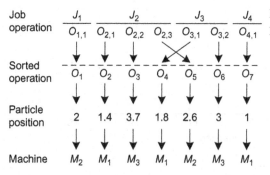

Figure 6.4 The mapping between particle and FDSP.

its previous latest operation. After all the operations have been processed, we get the feasible scheduling solution and then calculate the cost of the solution.

Algorithm Performance Demonstration

To illustrate the effectiveness and performance of the PSO algorithm, we will show an execution trace of the algorithm with the help of the FDSP problem involving an application with 7 operations, 3 machines, and 3 data hosts represented as (O_7, M_3, D_3) problem. The speeds of the 3 machines are 4, 3, 2 CPUT, respectively, i.e., $P = \{4, 3, 2\}$. And the lengths of the 7 operations are 6, 12, 16, 20, 28, 42, 60 cycles, respectively, i.e., $L = \{6, 12, 16, 20, 28, 42, 60\}$. The flow matrix is F, and its other information is given as follows:

$$R = \begin{bmatrix} 6 & 18 & 76 \\ 50 & 4 & 51 \\ 1 & 85 & 15 \\ 19 & 11 & 1 \\ 39 & 12 & 0 \\ 36 & 0 & 74 \\ 61 & 82 & 30 \end{bmatrix}$$

$$A = \begin{bmatrix} 0 & 21 & 95 \\ 21 & 0 & 41 \\ 95 & 41 & 0 \end{bmatrix}$$

$$B = \begin{bmatrix} 0 & 45 & 91 \\ 45 & 0 & 59 \\ 91 & 59 & 0 \end{bmatrix}$$

In our experiments, the algorithms used for comparison were genetic algorithm (GA) and PSO. The algorithms were repeated 20 times with different random seeds. Each trial had a fixed number of 2000 iterations. Other specific parameter settings of the algorithm are described in Table 6.1, as recommended by Clerc and

Table 6.1 Parameter Settings for the Algorithms

Algorithm	Parameter Name	Value
GA	Size of the population	20
	Probability of crossover	0.8
	Probability of mutation	0.09
	Swarm size	20
	Self-coefficient c_1	1.49
PSO	Social coefficient c_2	1.49
	Inertia weight w	$0.9 \rightarrow 0.1$
	Clamping coefficient ρ	0.5

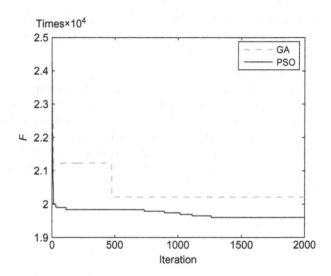

Figure 6.5 Performance for the FDSP (O_7, M_3, D_3).

Kennedy (2002) and Cristian (2003). The fixed weights, $w_1 = w_2 = 0.5$, are used in objective cost function. The average fitness values of the best solutions throughout the optimization run were recorded. The average and the standard deviation were calculated from the 20 different trials. The standard deviation indicates the differences in the results during the 20 different trials.

Figure 6.5 illustrates the performance curve for our algorithm during the search processes for the FDSP problem. The results (F) for all the 20 GA runs were 20212. The best scheduling solution is{3, 1, 2, 3, 1, 3, 1}, in which the makespan is 14983 and the flowtime is 25440. Figure 6.6 illustrates the best scheduling solution offered by GA, in which "W" means the waiting time. The results (F) for 20 PSO runs were {19276, 19276, 19276, 20582, 19276, 19276, 19276, 19276, 20582, 20582, 19276, 19276, 19276, 19276, 19276, 20582, 19276, 19276, 20582}, with an average value of 19602. The standard deviation is 580.2057. The best scheduling solution in the 20 runs is $\{3, 1, 2, 2, 1, 2, 2\}$, in which the makespan is 14578 and the flowtime is 23973. Figure 6.7 shows the PSO best scheduling solution. As shown in Figure 6.5, the operations O_2 and O_3 both have to wait for 1611 unit time before they are processed in the scheduling solution. The operation O_7 is assigned to an effective machine only after all other operations had completed. So the machine M_2 has a longer work time obviously than other machines because of the workflow constraints.

6.3.2 NS Application

P2P computing has attracted great interest and attention of the computing industry and gained popularity among computer users and their networked virtual

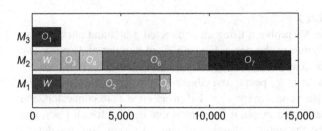

Figure 6.6 A scheduling solution for the FDSP (O_7, M_3, D_3).

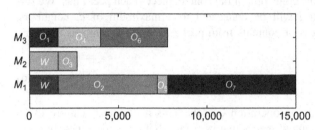

Figure 6.7 A scheduling solution for the FDSP (O_7, M_3, D_3).

communities (Kwok, 2006). It is no longer just used for sharing music files over the Internet. Many P2P systems have already been built for some new purposes and are being used. An increasing number of P2P systems are used in corporate networks or for public welfare (e.g., providing processing power to fight cancer) (Idris and Altmann, 2006). P2P comprises peers and the connections between these peers. These connections may be directed, may have different weights, and are comparable to a graph with nodes and vertices connecting these nodes. Defining how these nodes are connected affects many properties of an architecture that is based on a P2P topology, which significantly influences the performance, search efficiency and functionality, and scalability of a system. A common difficulty in the current P2P systems is caused by the dynamic membership of peer hosts. This results in a constant reorganization of the topology (Duan et al., 2006; Ghosal et al., 2005; Koo et al., 2004; Schollmeier, 2001; Surana et al., 2006).

Kurmanowytsch et al. (2003) developed the P2P middleware systems to provide an abstraction between the P2P topology and the applications that are built on top of it. These middleware systems offer higher-level services such as distributed P2P searches and support for direct communication among peers. The systems often provide a predefined topology that is suitable for a certain task (e.g., for exchanging files). Koulouris et al. (2004) presented a framework and an implementation technique for a flexible management of P2P overlays. The framework provides means for self-organization to yield an enhanced flexibility in instantiating control architectures in dynamic environments, which is regarded as being essential for P2P services to access, routing, topology forming, and application layer resource management. In these P2P applications, a central tracker decides about which peer becomes a neighbor to which other peers. Koo et al. (2006) investigated the NS process in the P2P networks and presented an efficient NS strategy based on GA.

NS Problem in P2P Networks

Koo et al. (2006) model the NS problem using an undirected graph and attempted to determine the connections between the peers. Given a fixed number of N peers, we use a graph $G = (V, E)$ to denote an overlay network, where the set of vertices $V = \{v_1, \ldots, v_N\}$ represents the N peers and the set of edges $E = \{e_{ij} \in \{0, 1\}, i, j = 1, \ldots, N\}$ represents their connectivity: $e_{ij} = 1$ if peers i and j are connected, and $e_{ij} = 0$ otherwise. For an undirected graph, it is required that $e_{ij} = e_{ji}$ for all $i \neq j$, and $e_{ij} = 0$ when $i = j$. Let C be the entire collection of content pieces, and we denote $\{c_i \subseteq C, i = 1, \ldots, N\}$ to be the collection of the content pieces each peer i has. We further assume that each peer i will be connected to a maximum of d_i neighbors, where $d_i < N$. The disjointness of contents from peer i to peer j is denoted by c_i, c_j, which can be calculated as

$$c_i \setminus c_j = c_i - (c_i \cap c_j) \tag{6.39}$$

where $\setminus$ denotes the intersection operation on sets. This disjointness can be interpreted as the collection of content pieces that peer i has but peer j does not. In other words, it denotes the pieces that peer i can upload to peer j. Moreover, the disjointness operation is not commutative, i.e., $c_i \setminus c_j \neq c_j \setminus c_i$. We also denote $|c_i \setminus c_j|$ to be the cardinality of $c_i \setminus c_j$, which is the number of content pieces peer i can contribute to peer j. In order to maximize the disjointness of content, we want to maximize the number of content pieces each peer can contribute to its neighbors by determining the connections e_{ij}'s. Define ε_{ij}'s to be sets such that $\varepsilon_{ij} = C$ if $e_{ij} = 1$ and $\varepsilon_{ij} = \Phi$ (null set) otherwise. Therefore, we have the following optimization problem:

$$\max_{E} \sum_{j=1}^{N} \left| \cup_{i=1}^{N} (c_i \setminus c_j) \cap \varepsilon_{ij} \right| \tag{6.40}$$

subject to

$$\sum_{j=1}^{N} e_{ij} \leq d_i \quad \text{for all } i \tag{6.41}$$

Particle Swarm Heuristic for NS

Given a P2P state $S = (N, C, M, f)$, in which N is the number of peers, C is the entire collection of content pieces, M is the maximum number of the peers which each peer can connect steadily in the session, f is to goal the number of swap pieces, i.e., to maximize Eq. (6.40). To apply the particle swarm algorithm successfully for the NS problem, one of the key issues is the mapping of the problem solution into the particle space, which directly affects its feasibility and performance. Usually, the particle's position is encoded to map each dimension to one directed connection between peers, i.e., the dimension is $N * N$. But the neighbor topology in P2P networks is an undirected graph, i.e., $e_{ij} = e_{ji}$ for all $i \neq j$. We set up a search space of

D dimension as $N * (N - 1)/2$. Accordingly, each particle's position is represented as a binary bit string of length D. Each dimension of the particle's position maps one undirected connection. The domain for each dimension is limited to 0 or 1. For this problem, the discrete particle swarm model (Kennedy and Eberhart, 1997) is introduced. When the particle moves in a state space restricted to zero and one on each dimension, the change of probability with time steps is defined as follows:

$$P(p_{ij}(t) = 1) = f(p_{ij}(t - 1), v_{ij}(t - 1), p_{ij}^{\#}(t - 1), p_j^*(t - 1)) \tag{6.41}$$

where the probability function is

$$\mathrm{sig}(v_{ij}(t)) = \frac{1}{1 + e^{-v_{ij}(t)}} \tag{6.42}$$

At each time step, each particle updates its velocity and moves to a new position according to Eqs (6.6) and (6.7):

$$v_{ij}(t) = wv_{ij}(t - 1) + c_1 r_1(p_{ij}^{\#}(t - 1) - p_{ij}(t - 1)) + c_2 r_2(p_j^*(t - 1) - p_{ij}(t - 1)) \tag{6.43}$$

$$p_{ij}(t) = \begin{cases} 1 & \text{if } \rho < \mathrm{sig}(v_{ij}(t)) \\ 0 & \text{otherwise} \end{cases} \tag{6.44}$$

where ρ is random number in the closed interval $[0,1]$. The particle has a priority levels according to the order of peers. The sequence of the peers will be not changed during the iteration. Each particle's position indicates the potential connection state. The pseudo-code for the particle swarm search method is illustrated in Algorithm 6.2.

$$\begin{bmatrix} 1 & 0 & 0 & 4 & 0 & 6 & 7 & 8 & 0 & 10 & 0 & 12 & 0 & 14 \\ 0 & 0 & 0 & 4 & 5 & 0 & 7 & 0 & 9 & 0 & 11 & 0 & 13 & 0 \\ 0 & 2 & 0 & 0 & 0 & 6 & 0 & 0 & 0 & 0 & 11 & 12 & 0 & 14 \\ 0 & 2 & 3 & 4 & 0 & 6 & 0 & 0 & 0 & 0 & 11 & 0 & 0 & 0 \\ 0 & 2 & 0 & 0 & 0 & 0 & 7 & 8 & 0 & 10 & 0 & 12 & 0 & 14 \\ 1 & 2 & 0 & 0 & 5 & 0 & 0 & 0 & 9 & 10 & 11 & 0 & 13 & 14 \end{bmatrix}$$

The optimal result search by the considered algorithm is 31, and the NS solution is illustrated below:

$$\begin{array}{c c} & \begin{array}{c c c c c c} 1 & 2 & 3 & 4 & 5 & 6 \end{array} \\ \begin{array}{c} 1 \\ 2 \\ 3 \\ 4 \\ 5 \\ 6 \end{array} & \begin{pmatrix} 0 & 0 & 0 & 1 & 1 & 1 \\ 0 & 0 & 0 & 0 & 1 & 1 \\ 0 & 0 & 0 & 1 & 1 & 1 \\ 1 & 0 & 1 & 0 & 0 & 0 \\ 1 & 1 & 1 & 0 & 0 & 0 \\ 1 & 1 & 1 & 0 & 0 & 0 \end{pmatrix} \end{array}$$

01.Initialize the size of the particle swarm n, and other parameters.

02.Initialize the positions and the velocities for all the particles randomly.

03.While (the end criterion is not met) do

04.　　$t = t+1$;

05.　　For s = 1 to n

06.　　　　For i = 1 to N

07.　　　　　　For j = 1 to N

08.　　　　　　　　If $j = i$, $e_{ij} = 0$;

09.　　　　　　　　If $j < i$, $a = j; b = i$;

10.　　　　　　　　If $j > i$, $a = i; b = j$;

11.　　　　　　　　$e_{ij} = p_{[a*N+b-(a+1)*(a+2)/2]}$;

12.　　　　　　　　if $e_{ij} = 1$, calculate c_i, c_j;

13.　　　　　　Next j

14.　　　　　　calculate $f = f + \left| \bigcup_{i=1}^{N} (c_i \setminus c_j) \cap \varepsilon_{ij} \right|$;

15.　　　　Next i

16.　　Next s

17.　　$\vec{p}^* = argmin_{i=1}^{n}(f(\vec{p}^*(t-1)), f(\vec{p}_1(t)),$
　　　　$f(\vec{p}_2(t)), \cdots, f(\vec{p}_i(t)), \cdots, f(\vec{p}_n(t)))$;

18.　　For s = 1 to n

19.　　$\vec{p}_i^{\#}(t) = argmin_{i=1}^{n}(f(\vec{p}_i^{\#}(t-1)), f(\vec{p}_i(t))$;

20.　　　　For d = 1 to D

21.　　　　　　Update the d-th dimension value of $\vec{p}_i$ and $\vec{v}_i$

22.　　　　　　according to Eqs.(43) and (44);

23.　　　　Next d

24.　　Next s

25.End While.

Algorithm 6.2 NS algorithm based on particle swarm algorithm.

We test other three representative instances (problem (25,1400,12), problem (30,1400,15), and problem (35,1400,17)) further. In our experiments, the algorithms used for comparison were GA and PSO. The GA and PSO algorithm share many similarities (Abraham, 2005).

In a GA, a population of candidate solutions (for the optimization task to be solved) is initialized. New solutions are created by applying reproduction operators (mutation and crossover). The fitness (how good the solutions are) of the resulting solutions is evaluated and the suitable selection strategy is then applied to determine which solutions will be maintained into the next generation.

Table 6.2 Parameter Settings for the Algorithms

Algorithm	Parameter Name	Value
GA	Size of the population	int(10 + 2 sqrt(D))
	Probability of crossover	0.8
	Probability of mutation	0.08
	Swarm size	int(10 + 2 sqrt(D))
	Self-coefficient c_1	2
PSO	Social coefficient c_2	2
	Inertia weight w	0.9
	Clamping coefficient ρ	0.5

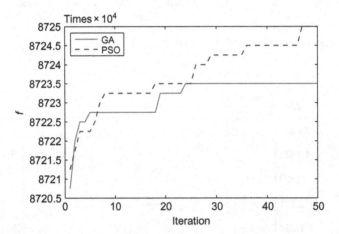

Figure 6.8 Performance for the NS (25, 1400, 12).

The PSO algorithm/GA were repeated four times with different random seeds. Each trial had a fixed number of 50 or 80 iterations. Other specific parameter settings of the algorithms are described in Table 6.2. The average fitness values of the best solutions throughout the optimization run were recorded. The average and the standard deviation were calculated from the four different trials. Figures 6.8–6.10 illustrate the PSO/GA performance during the search processes for the NS problem. As evident, PSO obtained better results much faster than GA, especially for large-scale problems.

6.4 Application in Hidden Markov Models

A hidden Markov model (HMM) is a statistical model in which the system is assumed to be a Markov process with unknown parameters. HMMs have found

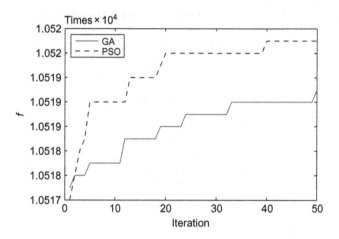

Figure 6.9 Performance for the NS (30, 1400, 15).

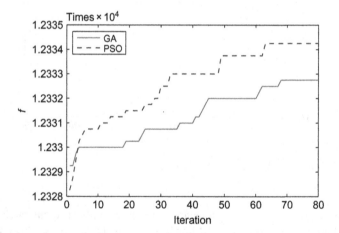

Figure 6.10 Performance for the NS (35, 1400, 17).

applications in many areas including speech recognition and natural language processing (Freitag and McCallum, 2000; Kim et al., 2003; Rabiner, 1989; Seymore et al., 1999; Zhou and Su, 2000). The parameters of HMMs include transition probabilities and emission probabilities. Transition probabilities represent the model state changing probability, and emission probabilities represent the symbols-generating probability while in a particular state. Freitag and McCallum (1999) use shrinkage for smoothing. Self-adaptive design approach (Li et al., 2004) focus on learning the correct states number with a maximum a prior procedure. The design of Zhu et al. (2006) aims to fit the length distribution of sequences. Besides the classical expectation maximization (EM) method for HMMs training, several papers also use evolutionary optimization (Najkar et al., 2010; Meng et al., 2010), and Tabu Search (Chen et al., 2004) instead to achieve better global optima.

Although above methods have made progressive effort to balance the delicacy of structures and the robustness of parameters estimation in many fields, such balanced models still carry uncertainty because in practice the trained model parameters are limited by the sparseness and noisiness of training data. The usage of Viterbi algorithm is limited in its applications because it is traditionally based on certain model parameters. There is room for Viterbi algorithms to perform better by randomizing the learned model parameters. Zeng and Liu (2006) present a hybrid method to allow some degree of uncertainty in HMM's description, but which value to use in the set depends on the task at hand. In the weighting model of Kwon and Un (1996), likelihood is weighted along the state sequence, but the ratio between transition parameters and emission parameters remains constant.

We introduce a hybrid algorithms combining Viterbi and PSO to exploit the randomness of HMMs parameters' training. We make an attempt to demonstrate such exploitation on reoptimizing the HMMs parameters with swarm intelligence. Experiment in part-of-speech (POS) tagging demonstrates the practical application of such a parameters weighting method.

6.4.1 Parameters Weighted HMM

A weighting HMM is represented by $\lambda = (S, V, A, B, \Pi, R)$. $S = \{S_1, \ldots, S_N\}$ is a set of states, N is the number of states in HMM, $V = \{v_1, \ldots, v_M\}$ is a set of output symbols. The state transition matrix $A = a_{ij}$, where $a_{ij} = P[q_{t+1} = S_j | q_t = S_i]$, $1 \leq i, j \leq N$. $B = b_j(k)$ characterizes the observation symbols distribution, $b_j(k) = P[v_k \text{ at } t | q_t = S_j]$, $1 \leq j \leq N$, $1 \leq k \leq M$. The initial states distribution stores in Π. Given an observation sequence, R is the weighting vector. Define $R = R_t$, $0 \leq t < T$, and $C_t < R_t < D_t$, where C and D are constant boundary vectors.

In the sequence recognition problems solved by HMMs, Viterbi algorithm is widely used. It is basically a dynamic programming method to find the optimal state sequence associated with the given observation sequence. The estimation of model parameters provides the "value" functions for this dynamic programming problem.

The recognition algorithm is implemented as PSO−Viterbi, which modifies Viterbi algorithm as follows:

$$\delta_t(j) = \max_{1 \leq i \leq N} [\delta_{t-1}(i) a_{ij}^{R_t}] b_{jo_t}(O_{t+1}) \tag{6.45}$$

where $\delta_t(j)$ is the best score along a single path at time t which accounts for the first t observations and end in state S_j and Eq. (6.2):

$$\delta_t(j) = \max_{q_1, \ldots, q_{t+1}} P[q_1, \ldots, q_t = j, o_1, \ldots, o_t | \lambda] \tag{6.46}$$

From the view of dynamic programming, the value function (6.46) consists of two parts, the vertex value and the node value. However, both the transition probabilities and the emission probabilities carry uncertainty from the sparseness of training data and may not be "optimal" to be used as value function in dynamic programming. The ratio between the vertex value and the node value is adjusted by the weighting vector R in this section.

6.4.2 PSO−Viterbi for Parameters Weighted HMMs

The object function in Eq. (6.46) is hard to use gradient optimization because of the form of recursion in Eq. (6.45). To solve this optimization problem, we turn to a class of method which draws increased attention in the last two decades, namely evolutionary computation (EC). EC is especially fitful because the fitness function is used as a measure of how well one candidate solution solves a problem, sometimes in comparison to the performance of other candidate solutions.

The particle swarm model consists of a swarm of particles, which are initialized with a population of random candidate solutions. They move iteratively through the D-dimension problem space to search the new solutions, where the fitness is maximized.

PSO−Viterbi is to employ swarm intelligence to choose R in defined interval to optimize the original recognition algorithm through the position evolvement of particles. Our algorithm for finding the best state sequence can now be stated in Algorithm 6.3. The parameter r represents the ratio between likelihood and knowledge, and can be used to adjust the confidence for the knowledge used.

6.4.3 POS Tagging Problem and Solution

POS tagging was considered a fundamental part of natural language processing (NLP), which aims to computationally determine a POS tag for a token in text context. POS tagger is a useful preprocessing tool in many NLP applications such as information extraction and information retrieval (Brants, 2000; Chang et al., 2010; Kim et al., 2003; Lin et al., 1999; Salvetti et al., 2004; Zhou and Su, 2000).

POS tagging problem has been modeled with many machine learning techniques, which include HMMs (Kim et al., 2003), maximum entropy models (McCallum et al., 2000), support vector machines, and conditional random fields (Lafferty et al., 2001). Each model can have good performance after careful adjustment such as feature selection, but HMMs have the advantages of small amount of data calculation and simplicity of modeling. In Brants (2000), HMMs combined with good smoothing techniques and with handling of unknown words work better than other models. For such a sequence recognition problem, the classical EM algorithms and Viterbi algorithms for HMMs can be found by Baum and Eagon (1967), Baum and Petrie (1966), Juang and Rabiner (1993), and Rabiner (1989).

The training set in NLP is always sparse and incomplete relative to the numbers of parameters in HMMs, because emission parameters are very high degree when

(1) Get Corpus as training set

(2) Supervised learning to get initial HMM parameters λ

(3) Get observation sequence O

(4) Represent R by PSO's particles

(5) While NOT termination_criteria

(6) Set $best\_f = -\infty$

(7) Initialization: $\psi_1(i) = 0$, $\delta_1(i) = \Pi_i b_i(o_1)$ $1 \leq i \leq N$

(8) For $2 \leq t \leq T$, $1 \leq j \leq N$:

    update $\delta_t(j)$ according to Equ.(1).

    $\psi_t(j) = argmax_{1 \leq i \leq N}[\delta_{t-1}(i)a_{ij}]$

(9) Termination:

    Set $q_t* = argmax_{1 \leq i \leq N}[\delta_T(i)]$

    $MLE = max_{1 \leq i \leq N}[\delta_T(i)]$ - differences

    caused by R in Equ.(1)

    Store state sequence from $t = T-1$ to 1:

    $q_t* = \psi_{t+1}(q_{t+1}*)$

(10)   Caculate *Bonus* using problem-specific knowledge

(11)   Fitness $f = MLE + r * Bonus$

(12)   If $f > best\_f$:

(13) $best\_state\_sequence = q_1...q_T$

(14)   Update positions of particles

(15) End While.

(16) Return $S = best\_state\_sequence$

Algorithm 6.3 PSO−Viterbi for weighting HMMS.

words are used as observations. This leaves uncertainty in HMM parameters. POS tagging is a fundamental part in NLP and is explored with a hybrid PSO−Viterbi algorithms for HMM model.

In order to use knowledge with the sequence recognition solution, the Bonus function is used to give extra score to the path with less unseen samples. This simple Bonus function returns the number of unknown state-observation pairs.

In PSO−Viterbi implementation for POS tagging, log probabilities are used and R is reduced to one dimension. The ratio r can be set to be 3 by experience that reflects high confidence for the knowledge used.

PSO−Viterbi has structural advantages. Back-off tagging is a common way in POS tagging that the later tagger processes the tokens tagged as "unknown" by the former tagger. But back-off tagging can only use one method for a single token. Our approach can use both knowledge including dictionary and morphological forms and statistics including HMM in the fitness function. It is similar to back-off tagging, but knowledge is expressed as a numerical component of the fitness value to cooperate with other method. For further performance improvement, we recommend the usage of fitness function for suffix heuristics.

6.4.4 Experiment

As for POS tagging, different corpus have different number of tags as given in Table 6.3, such as the pioneering Brown Corpus which distinguishes 87 simple tags and has the form of compound tags.

In this experiment, given a sequence set, the Viterbi and the PSO−Viterbi algorithms are launched separately for sequence recognition. Four article categories in Brown Corpus are used for benchmarking. This corpus has POS tagged as 70 states. In each article category, the first 200 sentences are used as test set in 10 groups and the following 700 sentences are employed as training set. To test the effectiveness of PSO−Viterbi in POS tagging, we use raw performance instead of improving techniques such as back-off. PSO parameters are set as given in Table 6.4.

The mean accuracy of two algorithms for each of the four categories is compared in Figure 6.11, and the detailed accuracies are listed in Table 6.5. Figure 6.12 shows the typical convergence plot. As illustrated, PSO−Viterbi usually performs better than Viterbi. The PSO convergence is always fast due to the dimension in this problem.

The validity of HMMs parameters reoptimization through EC is confirmed. Experiments on Brown Corpus show good result on various text categories.

Table 6.3 Corpus Comparison

Corpus Name	Number of Tags	Having Compound Tags
Penn Treebank	36	No
Brown	78	Yes
LOB	135	Yes
UCREL	165	Yes
London-Lund	197	Yes

Table 6.4 Parameter Settings for the Algorithms

Parameter Name	Parameter Value
Inertia	0.5
Cognitive rate	1.0
Social rate	1.0
Population size	10
Maximum evaluations	50

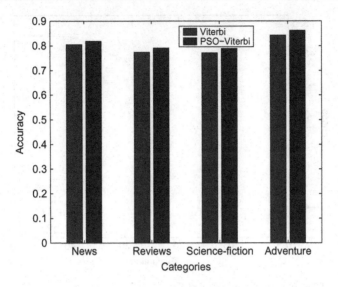

Figure 6.11 Mean accuracy.

Table 6.5 Accuracy Details

Groups	News	Reviews	Science Fiction	Adventure
1	0.8626	0.7748	0.7829	0.8127
2	0.8261	0.7739	0.8086	0.8496
3	0.8602	0.7062	0.7903	0.8663
4	0.8263	0.7306	0.8382	0.8356
5	0.7568	0.8125	0.8467	0.8510
6	0.8304	0.8118	0.7412	0.8816
7	0.8194	0.8366	0.6574	0.8844
8	0.8096	0.7796	0.8144	0.8735
9	0.7467	0.8424	0.7623	0.8653
10	0.8468	0.8320	0.8578	0.8988
Average	0.8185	0.7900	0.7900	0.8619

6.5 Conclusions

PSO is a nature-inspired population-based computational optimization technique. The convergence analysis and some applications of swarm optimization algorithm are presented.

We focused on the convergence of swarm algorithm based on iterative function system and probabilistic theory. Particle swarm was investigated as a case and the swarm model was represented by the iterated function system. The dynamic

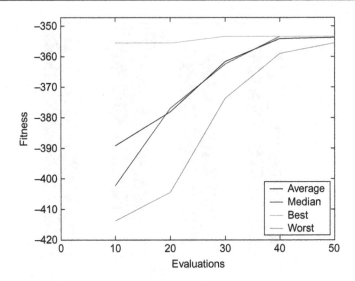

Figure 6.12 Typical convergence rate.

trajectory of the particle was derived. We theoretically proved that the swarm algorithm converges with a probability of 1 toward the global optimal. Algorithm performance curves were illustrated through optimization experiments. The works would be helpful for developing new swarm intelligent swarm models and selecting appropriate parameters (Liu et al., 2007).

We modeled and formulated the scheduling problem for workflow applications in distributed data-intensive computing environments (FDSP). A particle swarm approach was introduced to solve the problem. Empirical results demonstrated that the considered algorithm was feasible and effective. It can be applied in distributed data-intensive applications and meet the specific requirements, including workflow constraints, data retrieval/transfer, job interact, minimum completion cost, flexibility, and availability.

The problem of NS in P2P networks are investigated using a PSO approach. In the considered approach, the particle encodes the upper half matrix of the peer connection through the undirected graph, which reduces the dimension of the search space. We evaluated the performance of the considered PSO algorithm with GA. The results indicate that PSO usually required shorter time to obtain better results than GA, especially for large-scale problems. The swarm algorithm could be an ideal approach for solving the NS problem.

We introduced the swarm algorithm to reoptimize the HMMs. Considering the uncertainty of corpus in training HMMs, a PSO−Viterbi algorithm is derived to show the possibility of HMMs reoptimization through evolutionary computation. The hybrid algorithm iterates in the neighborhood of original HMMs parameters with a fitness function that evaluates the solution of sequence recognition by knowledge as well as by likelihood. Experiment shows good result in POS tagging problem in the field of NLP. Therefore, PSO−Viterbi has its potential advantages to reoptimize HMMs. It also provides a framework for further performance improvement when introducing more knowledge.

These works illustrate the performance of the swarm algorithms and trace their feasibility and effectiveness. With more heuristics approaches, more novel applications are targeted in related fields by swarm algorithms.

References

Abraham, A., 2005. Evolutionary computation. In: Sydenham, P., Thorn, R. (Eds.), Handbook for Measurement Systems Design. John Wiley & Sons Ltd., London, pp. 920−931.

Abraham, A., Guo, H., Liu, H., 2006. Swarm intelligence: foundations, perspectives and applications. In: Nedjah, N., Mourelle, L. (Eds.), Swarm Intelligent Systems, Studies in Computational Intelligence. Springer-Verlag, New York, pp. 3−25.

Andreescu, T., Andrica, D., 2005. Complex Numbers from A to ... Z. Birkhäuser, Boston, MA.

Andrieux, A., Berry, D., Garibaldi, J., Jarvis, S., MacLaren, J., Ouelhadj, D., et al., 2003. Open issues in grid scheduling. UK e-Science Report UKeS-2004-03, April 2004.

Baum, L.E., Eagon, J.A., 1967. An inequality with applications to statistical estimation for probabilistic functions of Markov processes and to a model for ecology. Bull. Am. Math. Soc. 73 (3), 360−363 (kwon 1996 weighting).

Baum, L.E., Petrie, T., 1966. Statistical inference for probabilistic functions of finite state Markov chains. Ann. Math. Stat. 37 (6), 1554−1563.

Boeringer, D.W., Werner, D.H., 2004. Particle swarm optimization versus genetic algorithms for phased array synthesis. IEEE Trans. Antennas Propag. 52 (3), 771−779.

Bonabeau, E., Dorigo, M., Theraulaz, G., 1999. Swarm Intelligence: From Natural to Artificial Systems. Oxford University Press, New York, NY.

Brants, T., 2000. Tnt: a statistical part-of-speech tagger. Proceedings of the Sixth Conference on Applied Natural Language Processing. Association for Computational Linguistics, pp. 224−231.

Cannataro, M., Talia, D., Srimani, P.K., 2002. Parallel data intensive computing in scientific and commercial applications. Parallel Comput. 28, 673−704.

Chang, M.W., Goldwasser, D., Roth, D., Srikumar, V., 2010. Structured output learning with indirect supervision. Proceedings of the International Conference on Machine Learning. IEEE Computer Society, pp. 199−206.

Chen, T.Y., Mei, X.D., Pan, J.S., Sun, S.H., 2004. Optimization of HMM by the tabu search algorithm. J. Inf. Sci. Eng. 20 (5), 949−957.

Clerc, M., 2006. Particle Swarm Optimization. ISTE Publishing Company, London, UK.

Clerc, M., Kennedy, J., 2002. The particle swarm-explosion, stability, and convergence in a multidimensional complex space. IEEE Trans. Evol. Comput. 6, 58−73.

Cristian, T.I., 2003. The particle swarm optimization algorithm: convergence analysis and parameter selection. Inf. Process. Lett. 85 (6), 317−325.

Dong, F., Akl, S.G., 2006. Scheduling algorithms for grid computing: state of the art and open problems. In: Technical Report School of Computing, Queen's University, Canada, January 2006.

Duan, H., Lu, X., Tang, H., Zhou, X., Zhao, Z., 2006. Proximity neighbor selection in structured P2P network. In: Proceedings of Sixth IEEE International Conference on

Computer and Information Technology, IEEE Computer Society Washington, DC, USA (CIT'06), pp. 52.

Eberhart, R.C., Shi, Y., 1998. Comparison between genetic algorithms and particle swarm optimization. In: Proceedings of IEEE International Conference on Evolutionary Computation, pp. 611–616.

Fogel, D.B., 2006. Evolutionary Computation: Toward a New Philosophy of Machine Intelligence, vol. 1. Wiley-IEEE Press.

Freitag, D., McCallum, A., 1999. Information extraction with HMMs and shrinkage. In: Proceedings of the AAAI-99 Workshop on Machine Learning for Information Extraction, Orlando, FL, pp. 31–36.

Freitag, D., McCallum, A., 2000. Information extraction with HMM structures learned by stochastic optimization (1999). Proceedings of the National Conference on Artificial Intelligence. AAAI Press, Menlo Park, CA.

Gandomi, A.H., Yang, X.S., Talatahari, S., Alavi, A.H., 2013. Metaheuristics in modeling and optimization. In: Gandomi, A.H., et al., (Eds.), Metaheuristic Applications in Structures and Infrastructures. Elsevier, Waltham, MA, doi: 10.1016/B978-0-12-398364-0.00001-2 (Chapter 1).

Ghosal, D., Poon, B.K., Kong, K., 2005. P2P contracts: a framework for resource and service exchange. Future Gener. Comput. Syst. 21, 333–347.

Goldberg, D.E., 1989. Genetic Algorithms in Search, Optimization, and Machine Learning. Addison-Wesley Publishing Corporation, Inc.

Guo, C., Tang, H., 2001. Global convergence properties of evolution strategies. IEEE Math. Numer. Sin. 23 (1), 105–110.

Halmos, P., 2005. Measure Theory. Van Nostrand and Co., New York, NY.

He, R., Wang, Y., Wang, Q., Zhou, J., Hu, C., 2005. An improved particle swarm optimization based on self-adaptive escape velocity. Chin. J. Soft. 16 (12), 2036–2044.

Holland, J.H., 1975. Adaptation in Natural and Artificial Systems. University of Michigan Press, Ann Arbor, MI.

Huhlaeva, E., Kalyaevb, V., Kruglovb, N., 2003. Distributed computing environment for data intensive tasks by use of metadispatcher. In: Nuclear Instruments and Methods in Physics Research, A, pp. 415–C417.

Idris, T., Altmann, J., 2006. A market-managed topology formation algorithm for peer-to-peer file sharing networks. Lect. Notes Comput. Sci. 4033, 61–77.

Jiang, M., Luo, Y.P., Yang, S.Y., 2007. Stochastic convergence analysis and parameter selection of the standard particle swarm optimization algorithm. Inf. Process. Lett. 102, 8–16.

Juang, B.H., Rabiner, L.R., 1993. Fundamentals of Speech Recognition. Prentice-Hall, Englewood Cliffs, NJ.

Kennedy, J., Eberhart, R.C., 2001. Swarm Intelligence. Morgan Kaufmann, San Mateo, CA.

Kim, J.D., Rim, H.C., Tsujii, J., 2003. Self-organizing Markov models and their application to part-of-speech tagging. Proceedings of the 41st Annual Meeting on Association for Computational Linguistics—Volume 1. Association for Computational Linguistics, pp. 296–302.

Koo, S.G.M., Kannan, K., Lee, C.S.G., 2004. A genetic-algorithm-based neighbor-selection strategy for hybrid peer-to-peer networks. In: Proceedings of the 13th IEEE International Conference on Computer Communications and Networks, ICCCN04, Chicago, IL, pp. 469–474.

Koo, S.G.M., Kannan, K., Lee, C.S.G., 2006. On neighbor-selection strategy in hybrid peer-to-peer networks. Future Gener. Comput. Syst. 22, 732–741.

Kennedy, J., Eberhart, R., 1997. A discrete binary version of the particle swarm algorithm. In: Proceedings of 1997 IEEE International Conference on Computational Cybernetics and Simulation, pp. 4104–4108.

Koulouris, T., Henjes, R., Tutschku, K., de Meer, H., 2004. Implementation of adaptive control for P2P overlays. Lect. Notes Comput. Sci. 2982, 292–306.

Kurmanowytsch, R., Kirda, E., Kerer, C., Dustdar, S., 2003. Omnix: a topology-independent P2P middleware. In: Proceedings of the 15th Conference on Advanced Information Systems Engineering (CAiSE'03).

Kwok, S., 2006. P2p searching trends: 2002–2004. Inf. Process. Manage. 42, 237–247.

Kwon, O.W., Un, C.K., 1996. Discriminative weighting of HMM state-likelihoods using the GPD method. IEEE Signal Process. Lett. 3 (9), 257–259.

Lafferty, J., McCallum, A., Pereira, F., 2001. Conditional random fields: probabilistic models for segmenting and labeling sequence data. In: Proceedings of the 18th International Conference on Machine Learning, IEEE, pp. 282–289.

Li, J., Wang, J., Zhao, Y., Yang, Z., 2004. Self-adaptive design of hidden Markov models. Pattern Recognit. Lett. 25 (2), 197–210.

Lin, H., Zhan, X., Yao, T., 1999. Example-based Chinese text filtering model. Proceedings of the Fifth International Computer Science Conference. Springer-Verlag, pp. 415–420.

Liu, H., Sun, S., Abraham, A., 2006. Particle swarm approach to scheduling work-flow applications in distributed data-intensive computing environments. Proceedings of the Sixth International Conference on Intelligent Systems Design and Applications. IEEE Computer Society Press, pp. 661–666 (IS-DA'06).

Liu, H., Abraham, A., Clerc, M., 2007. Chaotic dynamic characteristics in swarm intelligence. Appl. Soft. Comput. 7, 1019–1026.

Liu, H., Abraham, A., Snasel, V., 2009. Convergence analysis of swarm algorithm. Proceedings of the 2009 World Congress on Nature & Biologically Inspired Computing. IEEE, pp. 1714–1719.

McCallum, A., Freitag, D., Pereira, F., 2000. Maximum entropy Markov models for information extraction and segmentation. Proceedings of the 17th International Conference on Machine Learning. IEEE, pp. 591–598.

Meng, J., Xu, S., Wang, X., Yi, Y., Liu, H., 2010. Swarm-based HMM training and application in time sequences classification. J. Comput. Inf. Syst. 1, 197–203.

Najkar, N., Razzazi, F, Sameti, H., 2010. A novel approach to HMM-based speech recognition systems using particle swarm optimization. Math. Comput. Model. 52 (11–12), 1910–1920.

Ozcan, E., Mohan, C.K., 1991. Particle swarm optimization: surfing the waves. Intl. Cong. Evol. Comput.1939–1944.

Parsopoulos, K.E., Vrahatis, M.N., 2002. Recent approaches to global optimization problems through particle swarm optimization. Nat. Comput. 1, 235–306.

Rabiner, L.R., 1989. A tutorial on hidden Markov models and selected applications in speech recognition. Proc. IEEE. 77 (2), 257–286.

Salman, A., Ahmad, I., Al-Madani, S., 2002. Particle swarm optimization for task assignment problem. Microproc. Microsys. 26, 363–371.

Salvetti, F., Lewis, S., Reichenbach, C., 2004. Impact of lexical filtering on overall opinion polarity identification. In: Proceedings of the AAAI Spring Symposium on Exploring Attitude and Affect in Text: Theories and Applications, Stanford, CA.

Schollmeier, R., 2001. A definition of peer-to-peer networking for the classification of peer-to-peer architectures and applications. In: Proceedings of the First International August Conference on Peer-to-Peer Computing, P2P 01, Linkoping, Sweden, pp. 101–102.

Seymore, K., McCallum, A., Rosenfeld R., 1999. Learning hidden Markov model structure for information extraction. In: AAAI-99 Workshop on Machine Learning for Information Extraction, pp. 37–42.

Sun, S., Abraham, A., Zhang, G., Liu, H., 2007. A particle swarm optimization algorithm for neighbor selection in peer-to-peer networks. Proceedings of the Sixth Computer Information Systems and Industrial Management Applications. IEEE Computer Society, pp. 166–172.

Sun, S., Liu, H., Lin, H., 2009. A discrete PSO in P2P neighbor selection. J. Zhengzhou University (Natural Science Edition). 41 (1), 86–89.

Surana, S., Godfrey, B., Lakshminarayanan, K., Karp, R., Stoica, I., 2006. Load balancing in dynamic structured peer-to-peer systems. Perform. Eval. 63, 217–240.

van den Bergh, F., Engelbrecht, A.P., 2006. A study of particle swarm optimization particle trajectories. Inf. Sci. 176, 937–971.

Venugopal, S., Buyya, R., 2006. A set coverage-based mapping heuristic for scheduling distributed data-intensive applications on global grids. In: Technical Report. GRIDS-TR-2006-3, Grid Computing and Distributed Systems Laboratory, The University of Melbourne, Australia, March 8, 2006.

Whitley, L.D., 1991. Fundamental principles of deception in genetic search. Foundation of Genetic Algorithms. Morgan Kaufmann Publishers, San Mateo, CA, pp. 221–241.

Xia, W., Wu, Z., 2005. An effective hybrid optimization approach for multi-objective flexible job-shop scheduling problems. Comput. Ind. Eng. 48, 409–425.

Xu, Z., Cheng, G., Liang, Y., 1999. Search capability for an algebraic crossover. J. Xi'an Jiaotong Univ. 33 (10), 88–99.

Yang, X.S., 2010. Nature-Inspired Metaheuristic Algorithms. second ed. Luniver Press, Frome.

Zeng, J., Liu, Z.Q., 2006. Type-2 fuzzy hidden Markov models and their application to speech recognition. IEEE Trans. Fuzzy Syst. 14 (3), 454–467.

Zhong, N., Hu, J., Motomura, S., Wu, J., Liu, C., 2005. Building a data-mining grid for multiple human brain data analysis. Comput. Intell. 21 (2), 177.

Zhou, G.D., Su, J., 2000. Error-driven HMM-based chunk tagger with context-dependent lexicon. Proceedings of the 2000 Joint SIGDAT Conference on Empirical Methods in Natural Language Processing and Very Large Corpora: Held in Conjunction with the 38th Annual Meeting of the Association for Computational Linguistics. Association for Computational Linguistics, pp. 71–79.

Zhu, H., Wang, J., Yang,Z., Song, Y., 2006. A method to design standard HMMs with desired length distribution for biological sequence analysis. .In: Algorithms in Bioinformatics, WABI2006, LNCS, pp. 24–31.

7 A Survey of Swarm Algorithms Applied to Discrete Optimization Problems

Jonas Krause[1], Jelson Cordeiro[1], Rafael Stubs Parpinelli[1,2] and Heitor Silvério Lopes[1]

[1]Bioinformatics Laboratory, Federal University of Technology Paraná, Curitiba, Brazil; [2]Applied Cognitive Computing Group, Santa Catarina State University, Joinville, Brazil

7.1 Introduction

Swarm-based algorithms are inspired by the behavior of some social living beings, such as ants, termites, birds, and fishes. Self-organization and decentralized control are remarkable features of swarm-based systems that, such as in nature, lead to an emergent behavior. Emergent behavior is a property that emerges through local interactions among system components and it is not possible to be achieved by any of the components of the system acting alone (Garnier et al., 2007).

In the beginning, the two mainstreams of the Swarm Intelligence area were ant colony optimization (Dorigo and Stützle, 2004) and particle swarm optimization (PSO) (Kennedy and Eberhart, 2001). In recent years, new swarm intelligence algorithms have appeared, inspired by fish schools (Cai, 2010), gravity and mass interactions (Rashedi et al., 2009), as well as different aspects of the behavior of bees (Abbass, 2001b; Karaboga, 2005; Lucic and Teodorovic, 2002; Pham et al., 2005), bacteria (Passino, 2002), glowworms (Krishnanand and Ghose, 2005), fireflies (Yang, 2008), cockroaches (Havens et al., 2008), bats (Yang, 2009), and cuckoo birds (Yang and Deb, 2009). For a thorough review of recent approaches, see Parpinelli and Lopes (2011). Despite the swarm inspiration common to these approaches, they have their own particular way to exploit and explore the search space of the problem.

Although almost all the above cited algorithms were designed to be applied to continuous optimization, several of them were later adapted to handle discrete domain problems. Unlike the continuous domain, in which the elements have the

Swarm Intelligence and Bio-Inspired Computation. DOI: http://dx.doi.org/10.1016/B978-0-12-405163-8.00007-7

property of varying smoothly, the elements inside a discrete domain—such as integers or binary digits—accept only distinct, separated values. The discrete domain is characterized by dealing with countable sets, either finite or infinite. Binary and combinatorial applications are examples of discrete domain problems.

This work reviews how swarm algorithms, that traditionally deal with continuous domains, can be adapted to discrete problems. In this work, we highlighted their adaptation strategies to handle this class of problems as well as their main features concerning the problem being solved. Note that algorithms created specifically to handle discrete problems are beyond the scope of this work. This is the case, for instance, of the ant colony optimization algorithm (Dorigo and Stützle, 2004), the mosquito host-seeking algorithm (Feng et al., 2009), the calling behavior of Japanese tree frogs algorithm (Hernández and Blum, 2012), the river formation dynamics algorithm (Rabanal et al., 2007), and the intelligent water drops algorithm (Shah-Hosseini, 2007).

Section 7.2 shortly describes the bioinspirations of the main swarm algorithms adapted to discrete problems; Section 7.3 brings the main concerns to handle discrete problems, the discretization methods, and the encoding strategies; Section 7.4 details all the problems and applications addressed by each continuous algorithm; Section 7.5 summarizes and discusses the main issues; and Section 7.6 presents the concluding remarks and points future research directions.

7.2 Swarm Algorithms

For all traditional versions of the algorithms discussed in this survey, in their essence, the candidate solutions are encoded as a set of real variables, which represent a point in a multidimensional space. In this section, we briefly describe the swarm algorithms that are applied or adapted to handle discrete problems.

7.2.1 Particle Swarm Optimization

The PSO metaheuristics was motivated by the coordinate movement of fish schools and bird flocks (Kennedy and Eberhart, 2001). A potential solution to the problem being solved is represented by a particle, and the PSO is a swarm of particles. Particles "flow" through hyperdimensional search space of the problem, and changes to the position of the particles within the search space are based on the sociocognitive tendency of individuals to emulate the success of other individuals. Each individual of a population (in this case, particles) has its own life experience and is able to evaluate the quality of its experience. As social individuals, they also have knowledge about how well their neighbors have behaved. These two kinds of information correspond to the cognitive component (individual learning) and social component (cultural transmission), respectively. Hence, an individual decision is taken considering both the cognitive and social components, thus leading the population (the swarm) to an emergent behavior.

7.2.2   Roach Infestation Optimization

The roach infestation optimization (RIO) was introduced by Havens et al. (2008), who applied to benchmark functions and achieved competitive results, when compared to a standard PSO. Actually, RIO has some elements that resemble the traditional PSO algorithm. In the RIO algorithm, cockroach agents are defined using three simple behaviors:

1. Cockroaches search for the darkest location in the search space and the fitness value is directly proportional to the level of darkness (find darkness phase).
2. Cockroaches socialize with nearby cockroaches (find friend phase).
3. Cockroaches periodically become hungry and leave the friendship to search for food (find food phase).

7.2.3   Cuckoo Search Algorithm

Cuckoo search algorithm (CSA) (Yang and Deb, 2009) is based on the brood parasitism of some cuckoo species. The algorithm uses the Levy flights rather than simple random walk. The CSA uses the following main basic rules:

1. Each cuckoo lays one egg at a time and dumps its egg in a randomly chosen nest.
2. The best nests with high-quality eggs will continue to the next generation.
3. The number of available host nests is fixed, and the egg laid by a cuckoo is discovered by the host bird with a probability $p_a \in [0,1]$. In this case, the host bird can either get rid of the egg or simply abandon the nest and build a new nest.

7.2.4   Firefly Algorithm

The firefly algorithm (FA) was proposed by Yang (2008) and uses three main basic rules:

1. A firefly will be attracted by other fireflies regardless their sex.
2. Attractiveness is proportional to their brightness and decreases as the distance among them increases.
3. The landscape of the objective function determines the brightness of a firefly.

7.2.5   Gravitational Search Algorithm

The gravitational search algorithm (GSA) was created based on the law of gravity and the notion of mass interactions (Rashedi et al., 2009). The GSA uses the theory of Newtonian physics and its searcher agents are the collection of masses. In GSA, there is an isolated system of masses; using the gravitational force, every mass in the system can detect the situation of other masses. The gravitational force is therefore a way of transferring information between different masses. The GSA agents are considered as objects and their performance is measured by their masses. All these objects attract each other by a gravity force, and this force causes a movement of all objects globally toward the objects with heavier masses. The heavy masses correspond to good solutions of the problem. The position of the agent corresponds to a solution of the problem, and its mass is determined using a fitness function.

7.2.6 Bat Algorithm

The bat algorithm (BA) was first presented by Yang (2010). The basic idea behind the BA is that a population of bats (possible solutions) use echolocation to sense distance and fly randomly through a search space updating their positions and velocities. The bats' flight aims at finding food/prey (best solutions). A loudness decay factor acts in a similar role as the cooling schedule in the traditional simulated annealing optimization method, and a pulse increase factor regulates the pulse frequency. As the loudness usually decreases once a bat has found its prey/solution (in order to not to loss the prey), the rate of pulse emission increases in order to raise the attack accuracy.

7.2.7 Glowworm Swarm Optimization Algorithm

The glowworm swarm optimization (GSO) algorithm was first presented by Krishnanand and Ghose (2005) as an application to collective robotics. In this algorithm, each glowworm uses a probabilistic mechanism to select a neighbor that has a luciferin value associated with him and moves toward it. Glowworms are attracted to neighbors that glow brighter (i.e., glowworms that have more luciferin). The movements are based only on local information and selective neighbor interactions. This enables the swarm to divide into disjoint subgroups that can converge to multiple optima of a given multimodal function.

7.2.8 Artificial Fish School Algorithm

In water areas, a fish can always find food at a place where there are plenty of food by following other fishes, hence generally the more the food, the more the fish. Following this rule, artificial fish school algorithm (AFSA) builds some artificial fish (AF), which search an optimal solution in solution space (the environment in which AF live) by imitating fish swarm behavior. Three basic behaviors of AF are defined as follows (Cai, 2010):

1. *Prey*: The fish perceives the concentration of food in water to determine the movement by vision or sense and then chooses the tendency.
2. *Swarm*: The fish will assemble in groups naturally during the moving process, which is a kind of living habits in order to guarantee the existence of the colony and avoid dangers.
3. *Follow*: In the moving process of the fish swarm, when a single fish or several fishes find food, the neighborhood partners will trail and reach the food quickly.

7.2.9   Bacterial Evolutionary Algorithm

The bacterial evolutionary algorithm (BEA) is inspired by bacteria's behavior. Bacteria can transfer DNA to recipient cells through mating and this process is called transduction. By transduction, it is possible to spread the features of a single bacterium to the rest of the population. This genetic recombination mechanism characterizes a microbial evolution process. Male cells directly transfer strands of genes to female cells. After that, those female cells acquire characteristics of male cells and transform themselves into male cells, thus spreading to the entire bacteria population. Genes can be transferred from a single bacterium (host cell) to others (recipient cells) and eventually this would lead to an increase in the evolution speed of the entire population (Nawa and Furuhashi, 1999). The flow of the BEA is described as follows:

1. *Generation of the initial population*: Chromosomes are randomly created and evaluated.
2. *Bacterial mutation*: The bacterial mutation is applied to each chromosome, one by one.
3. *Gene transfer operation*: The gene transfer operation occurs between the chromosomes.

7.2.10   Bee Algorithm

The bee algorithm[1] (BA_1) was first introduced by Pham et al. (2005) and applied to a benchmark of mathematical functions. In this algorithm, a bee is a d-dimensional vector containing the problem variables (a solution). Moreover, a solution represents a visited site (i.e., food source) and has a fitness value assigned to it. The algorithm balances exploration and exploitation by using scout bees that randomly search for new sites and uses recruitment for neighborhood search in sites with higher fitness, respectively. Bees that have the highest fitness are chosen as "selected bees" and sites visited by them (elite sites) are chosen for neighborhood search. The algorithm conducts searches in the neighborhood of the selected sites, assigning more bees to search near to the best sites (recruitment).

7.2.11   Artificial Bee Colony Algorithm

The artificial bee colony (ABC) algorithm was first proposed by Karaboga (2005) for solving multidimensional and multimodal optimization problems. The bees' aim is to discover places of food sources (regions in the search space) with high amount of nectar (good fitness). There are three types of bees: the scout bees that randomly fly in the search space without guidance, the employed bees that exploit the neighborhood of their locations selecting a random solution to be perturbed, and the onlooker bees that use the population fitness to select probabilistically a guiding solution to exploit its neighborhood. If the nectar amount of a new source is higher than the previous one in their memory, they update the new position and forget the previous one (greedy selection). If a solution is not improved by a

---

[1]The subindex 1 is introduced here to differentiate the bee algorithm from the bat algorithm.

predetermined number of trials, then the food source is abandoned by the corresponding employed bee and it becomes a scout bee.

7.2.12   Bee Colony Optimization

The bee colony optimization (BCO) was proposed by Lucic and Teodorovic (2002) and, similarly to ABC, it imitates the bees' behavior in nature when looking for a food, by simulating the foraging behavior. The BCO is based on the constructive concept. It was designed as a method which builds solutions from the scratch within execution steps, unlike the ABC local search which performs iterative improvements of the current best solution. There are two alternating phases of the BCO (forward pass and backward pass) constituting a single step in the BCO algorithm. In each forward pass, every bee agent visits the solution components, creates a partial solution, and after that returns to the hive. Having obtained new partial solutions, the bees meet in the hive and start the backward pass. In the backward pass, all bee agents share information about the quality of their partial solutions. Having all solutions evaluated, each bee decides with a certain probability whether it will stay loyal to its solution or not.

7.2.13   Marriage in Honey-Bees Optimization Algorithm

The marriage in honey-bees optimization (MBO) algorithm was presented by Abbass (2001b). The main idea concerning the algorithm based on bee mating behavior is that the queen is considered the best solution to an optimization problem and, during the mating flight, it selects drones probabilistically for reproduction so as to form the spermatheca. The spermatheca is, then, a pool of selected solutions. New broods are created by crossovering the genotypes of drones and the queen. Natural selection takes place by replacing weaker queens by fitter broods.

7.3   Main Concerns to Handle Discrete Problems

In most swarm intelligence algorithms, the possible solution is encoded as a set of real variables, which represents, for instance, the location of a particle (in PSO) or a source food (in ABC). In these examples, updates in a given vector position (dimension) can be done independently of the remaining ones. The updated values remain within the predefined range for that dimension, the candidate solution is valid (for the sake of simplification, constraints are not considered here). However, for combinatorial problems, such representation is not suitable, provided that a solution is a permutation of integer values. Therefore, updates of a vector that represents a solution for a combinatorial problem must preserve the validity of the permutation. Consequently, to apply the above-mentioned algorithms to discrete optimization problems, it is necessary to adapt the encoding to discrete dimensions.

We characterize the codification of candidate solutions in three encoding schemes. The first encoding uses a binary codification (BC) for candidate solutions. The second encoding uses an integer codification (IC) for candidate solutions. Swarm algorithms that employ BC or IC are adapted to discrete domain since its beginning (i.e., initial swarm). The third encoding deals with real values but uses transformation methods to handle discrete domains. The real solution vector can be transformed into a BC (real-to-binary: RTB) or it can be transformed into an IC (real-to-integer: RTI), where RTI represents a combination of integer values. Swarm algorithms that employ RTB or RTI require these transformations at each iteration loop.

7.3.1 Discretization Methods

In discrete problems, such as combinatorial, binary, and categorical, it is necessary to reduce the number of possible states to feasible solutions. This is done by the discretization of the continuous space by transforming the values into a limited number of possible states. There are several discretization methods, and the main are presented below.

7.3.1.1 Sigmoid Function

The sigmoid function (SF) can be used to transform a continuous space value into a binary one. Such discretization method is very popular (Banati and Bajaj, 2011; Palit et al., 2011), and the transformation is applied to each dimension of the solution vector, as shown in Eq. (7.1), thus forcing each element to be a binary digit:

$$x_{ij} = \begin{cases} 1, & \text{if rand()} \leq \dfrac{1}{1 + \exp(-x_{ij})} \\ 0, & \text{otherwise} \end{cases} \qquad (7.1)$$

with $i = 1, \ldots, N$, $j = 1, \ldots, D$, where N is the population size, D is the dimension size, and rand() is a random number drawn uniformly from [0,1].

7.3.1.2 Random-Key

The random-key (RK) encoding scheme can be used to transform a position from a continuous space into an integer/combinatorial space (Chen et al., 2011; Li et al., 2010). To decode the position, the nodes are visited in ascending order for each dimension. For example, the continuous solution vector $\vec{x}_i = (0.90, 0.35, 0.03, 0.21, 0.17)$ can be decoded as $\vec{x}_i = (5, 4, 1, 3, 2)$.

7.3.1.3 Smallest Position Value

The smallest position value (SPV) method maps the positions of the solution vector by placing the index of the lowest valued component as the first item on a permutated solution, the next lowest as the second, and so on. This method creates an integer vector solution by indexing the position of all the particles (Verma and Kumar, 2012; Yousif et al., 2011).

7.3.1.4 Modified Position Equation

The modified position equation (MPE) method has been used only in the PSO algorithm (Pan et al., 2008; Tasgetiren et al., 2007). As mentioned before, the standard PSO updates the particle position using three choices: follow its own position (X_i^t), go toward its personal best position (P_i^t), or go toward the best particle position of the swarm (G_i^t). After that, the particle position on iteration t can be updated following Eq. (7.2):

$$X_i^t = c_2 \otimes F_3(c_1 \otimes F_2(\omega \otimes F_1(X_i^{t-1}), P_i^{t-1}), G_i^{t-1}) \tag{7.2}$$

where $\lambda_i^t = w \otimes F_1(X_i^{t-1})$ is the velocity of the particle and F_1 is the mutation operator with probability w. A uniform random number r in the range [0,1] is generated and, if it is less than w, then the mutation operator is applied to generate a perturbed permutation of the particle by $\lambda_i^t = F_1(X_i^{t-1})$; otherwise current permutation is kept as $\lambda_i^t = X_i^{t-1}$. In this equation, $\delta_i^t = c_1 \otimes F_2(\lambda_i^t, P_i^{t-1})$ is the cognitive part of the particle; F_2 is the crossover operator with probability c_1. Note that λ_i^t and P_i^{t-1} will be the first and second parents for the crossover operator. It results either in $\delta_i^t = F_2(\lambda_i^t, P_i^{t-1})$ or in $\delta_i^t = \lambda_i^t$ depending on the choice of a uniform random number. The third component of Eq. (7.2), $X_i^t = c_2 \otimes F_3(\delta_i^t, G_i^t)$, is the social part of the particle, where F_3 is the crossover operator with probability c_2. Note that δ_i^t and G_i^{t-1} will be the first and second parents for the crossover operator. It results either in $X_i^t = F_3(\delta_i^t, G_i^{t-1})$ or in $X_i^t = \delta_i^t$ depending on the choice of a uniform random number.

7.3.1.5 Great Value Priority

The great value priority (GVP) method is used to encode a continuous space into a binary one (Congying et al., 2011). First, the position of the solution vector $\vec{x}_i$ with the largest element is selected, where $i = 1, \ldots, N$ and N is the population size. This position is set on the first position of a new vector named as permutation vector $\vec{p}$. Next, the position of the second largest element of $\vec{x}_i$ is selected and placed in the next position of $\vec{p}$. This procedure is repeated successively for all dimensions of $\vec{x}_i$ and, once $\vec{p}$ is fulfilled, Eq. (7.3) is applied to transform it into binary, where $j = 1, \ldots, D$ and D is the dimension size:

$$\vec{x}_{ij} = \begin{cases} 1, & \text{if } \vec{p}_j > \vec{p}_{j+1} \\ 0, & \text{otherwise} \end{cases} \tag{7.3}$$

7.3.1.6 Nearest Integer

In this method, a real value is converted to the nearest integer (NI) by rounding or truncating up or down (Burnwal and Deb, 2012).

7.4 Applications to Discrete Problems

For the algorithms mentioned in Section 7.2, a literature search was done so as to find discrete applications in different domains. Although this search was not exhaustive, it covers the most relevant applications and emphasizes the applicability of those algorithms to discrete problems.

7.4.1 Particle Swarm Optimization

Kennedy and Eberhart (1997) developed the first PSO algorithm for combinatorial optimization problems, where particles were encoded as binary sequences. In the binary version, trajectories are changes in the probability that a coordinate will take a zero or one value. Also, the velocity of the particle may be described by the number of bits changed per iteration or the Hamming distance between the particle at time t and $t + 1$.

Deep and Bansal (2008), Hembecker et al. (2007), Shen et al. (2012), and Wan and Nolle (2009) used the SF method to calculate the trajectory in the binary search space to solve the Knapsack problem (KP). For the same problem, Lopes and Coelho (2005) used a PSO hybridized with a guided local search and some concepts drawn from genetic algorithms (GA). In Li and Li (2009), a binary PSO is proposed to solve the KP using a mutation operator.

A PSO was used to solve the flow shop scheduling problem by Ucar and Tasgetiren (2006). First, a population of particles with continuous values is randomly constructed and then transformed into discrete values by applying the SPV method. The same method was used to solve the single machine total-weighted tardiness problem by Tasgetiren et al. (2004a,b), where the SPV rule is applied to convert the position vector to a job permutation. Verma and Kumar (2012) also used PSO with SPV to solve a combinatorial optimization problem, the DNA sequence assembly. Lin et al. (2010) used a continuous PSO combined with the RK transformation to solve the job shop scheduling problem (JSSP). PSO was hybridized with a local search based on simulated annealing (SA) technique.

Congying et al. (2011) used the PSO in a typical combinatorial optimization problem, the quadratic assignment problem (QAP), and the GVP method was used to transform the continuous space to discrete.

Rosendo and Pozo (2010) presented a hybrid PSO algorithm to solve the traveling salesman problem (TSP). This work maintains the main PSO concept for updating the velocity of the particle using path relinking (Glover and Laguna, 1997) and the Lin–Kernighan (LK) algorithm (Lin and Kernighan, 1973) to improve local search.

Labed et al. (2011) proposed MHPSO, a hybrid PSO to solve the multidimensional KP. As in Lopes and Coelho (2005), it combines PSO with the crossover operator of GA. The crossover operator is applied in both the best position of each particle (*pbest*) and its current position, as well as in the best position obtained by the swarm (*gbest*) and its current position.

To the best of our knowledge, Pan et al. (2008) reported for the first time in the literature a discrete particle swarm optimization (DPSO) algorithm to solve the no-wait flow shop scheduling problem. The particles are represented as discrete job permutations and a new position update method is developed based on the discrete domain that consists of three operators. A new crossover operator was also introduced, and it is able to produce a pair of different permutations even from two identical parents. A block of jobs from the first parent is determined by two-cut points randomly, and this block is moved to the right or left of the solution vector. Then, the offspring permutation is filled out with the remaining jobs from the second parent. The DPSO algorithm is also hybridized with the variable neighborhood (VND) local search by Mladenovic and Hansen (1997) to improve the performance. Tasgetiren et al. (2007) also used DPSO with the MPE method to solve the generalized TSP.

7.4.2 Roach Infestation Optimization

Hendrawan and Murase (2011) proposed a discrete RIO to solve a feature selection problem using a neural network as a predictive tool. A binary encoding vector was used for each roach, and each dimension represents a feature (value 0 or 1). A 0 indicates that the corresponding feature is not selected, while 1 means the opposite. To update the position of the roach, the cockroach velocity is updated with a mutation operator and then the cognition and social parts of the cockroach are updated using a two-point crossover.

7.4.3 Cuckoo Search Algorithm

Burnwal and Deb (2012) demonstrated for the first time a CSA to solve a scheduling problem for a flexible manufacturing system (FMS). They modified the Levy flights from continuous to discrete values using the NI. For the same type of problem, Kumar and Chakarverty (2011) encoded a solution in the CSA in the form of an integer vector.

Gherboudj et al. (2012) proposed a discrete binary CSA to solve the KP. To get binary solutions, the SF was used and Layeb (2011) presented a quantum-inspired cuckoo search algorithm (QICSA) for the same KP but, instead, a binary encoding was used.

7.4.4 Firefly Algorithm

The first FA for combinatorial optimization was put forward by Sayadi et al. (2010) for makespan minimization in a permutation flow shop scheduling problem.

Also, Falcon et al. (2011) used the same ideas for a fault diagnosis problem. In both cases, they used a binary approach: for updating the firefly's position, and SF was applied to each component of the real-valued vector. The SF method was used to transform the values from real to binary by Palit et al. (2011), for the KP, and by Banati and Bajaj (2011), to solve the binary problem of feature selection.

Yousif et al. (2011) introduced a method based on FA for scheduling jobs on grid computing. In this case, the SPV approach was used for updating the positions of the fireflies from continuous position values to discrete permutations.

Fister et al. (2012) used the FA to solve a combinatorial optimization problem, the graph 3-coloring. The RK method was used to convert the real values to discrete.

7.4.5 Bee Algorithm

The BA1 was first applied to continuous optimization functions and later for scheduling jobs (Pham et al., 2007a) and binary data clustering (Pham et al., 2007b). In these papers, the authors used discrete encoding, ensuring that possible solutions would be valid. The BA1 also inspired Bahamish et al. (2008) to create a discrete encoding for the protein tertiary structure prediction (PTSP), a difficult combinatorial optimization problem.

A well-known discrete problem is the generalized assignment problem (GAP), approached by Ozbakir et al. (2010) using a modified BA. In the original BA_1, scout bees continue searching in the solution space until the algorithm is terminated. However, in the modified BA_1, an adaptive penalty coefficient mechanism is employed.

A binary BA_1 (BBA) was proposed by Xu et al. (2010) focusing on a two-level distribution optimization problem (DOP), which expressed the agents (bees) as two binary matrices, representing how to assign each bee to its course or mission.

7.4.6 Artificial Bee Colony

The applicability of the ABC algorithm and the GAP (Baykasoğlu et al., 2007) demonstrates the capability to adapt this algorithm to discrete problems, using the RK method. The ABC was also applied to other discrete problems, such as the JSSP, TSP, and multidimensional KP. For these applications, many variants and hybridisms of the ABC were proposed.

An adaptation of the original ABC method was presented by Banharnsakun et al. (2012) for the JSSP, by changing the behavior of the onlooker bees and using the SF method to transform the continuous values into binary. The proposed new method, called best-so-far ABC, uses all the onlooker bees with the information from all employed bees to make a common decision on a new candidate food source. Because of that, the onlookers can compare information from all candidate sources and they are able to select the best-so-far position. As a result, this modification makes the algorithm converge more quickly since that solution will be biased toward the best solution found so far.

A combinatorial ABC (CABC) with discrete encoding was proposed by Karaboga and Gorkemli (2011) for the TSP. In that work, a new mutation operator from GA was used, and it was adapted to the neighborhood search mechanism of employed and onlooker bees. The hybridism between GA and ABC was also approached by Singh et al. (2011), which used ABC techniques to improve the global search by adding employed and onlooker bees on the search process, and this method was called real genetic bee colony algorithm (RGBCA). A similar hybridism, between ABC and greedy subtour crossover (GSX), was used by Banharnsakun et al. (2010) for the same problem. In this hybrid method, the exploitation process of the ABC algorithm was improved by the GSX, so as to update employed bees' old food sources based on their neighboring food sources, assisting the ABC to generate feasible solutions all the time.

The KP is another classical discrete problem that has been studied using the ABC algorithm. Pulikanti and Singh (2009) used a modified and binary version of ABC for this problem. In the original ABC algorithm, the neighborhood of the best found food sources is searched in order to achieve even better food sources. In the novel ABC algorithm, a hybrid probabilistic mutation scheme was performed for searching the neighborhood of food sources. Here the SF method was used again to convert real values into binary.

Hybrid methods have been used to improve the original ABC algorithm, generally associated to a neighborhood search mechanism to improve global searches. Pacurib et al. (2009) uses this improved search, adding a search iteration operator based on the fixed point theorem of contractive mapping in Banach spaces (discrete vector space) with ABC algorithm to solve Sudoku puzzles.

Another hybrid discrete artificial bee colony (DABC) was proposed by Marinakis et al. (2009), using a two-phase algorithm that combines the DABC and the greedy randomized adaptive search procedure (GRASP). This DABC−GRASP algorithm was created for the solution of clustering problems and the two phases consist of the computation of the activated features by the DABC and the computation of the fitness of each food source by the clustering algorithm.

7.4.7 Bee Colony Optimization

The BCO proposed by Teodorovic and Dell'Orco (2005) was applied to the ride-matching problem and wavelength assignment (RWA) using a discrete encoding. Later, Banerjee et al. (2008) created a hybrid BCO for modeling process and supply chain scheduling; in this case, the SF method was used to transform the continuous space into binary. Davidovic et al. (2012) also used the BCO algorithm for scheduling independent tasks on homogeneous processors; their approach brings a modified BCO which allows the bees a freedom to generate various solutions leading to a diversification of the search process. Wong et al. (2008a) also studied the BCO and applied it to the TSP.

Chong et al. (2006) described a BCO algorithm based on foraging and waggle dance, using the dance duration as determining factor for selecting a new path. This approach was applied to the JSSP with discrete encoding and a neighborhood structure to search for feasible solutions and improve prior solutions (Wong et al., 2008b). A set of priority dispatching rules were used to create the initial solutions.

7.4.8 Marriage in Honey-Bees Optimization Algorithm

The MBO algorithm was applied to the propositional satisfiability problems, known as SAT problems (Abbass, 2001b). MBO was applied to 50 variables of the SAT problems with 215 different constraints, presenting good results for this combinatorial optimization problem with a binary encoding. Later, the algorithm was improved in Abbass (2001a) by using a single queen with multiple workers in the colony and also applied to the 3-SAT problem where each constraint contains exactly three variables.

A conventional annealing approach was used by Teo and Abbass (2001) on the mating flight process to balance search exploration and exploitation, and this modified MBO was applied to SAT problems. This algorithm was also applied in datamining (Benatchba et al., 2005) and scheduling problems (Koudil et al., 2007) with the SF method to convert the continuous space into binary.

The SF method was also used by Marinakis et al. (2008) in an MBO hybridized with GRASP for clustering problems with N objects into K clusters. Yang et al. (2007) combined the MBO with the Nelder–Mead method with the objective of improving its performance and thus creating the Nelder-Mead Marriage in Honey Bees (NMMBO) algorithm to be applied to the TSP.

7.4.9 Other Swarm Intelligence Algorithms

The GSA was applied by Li et al. (2010) with the RK discretization method transforming the continuous solutions into discrete ones. Chen et al. (2011) also applied the GSA to solve the TSP with RK, but integrating the SA technique into the algorithm for accomplishing local search. A binary implementation of GSA was proposed by Papa et al. (2011), together with the SF method, and used for a feature selection problem.

Nakamura et al. (2012) proposed a binary version of the BA to solve the hypercube problem, where each bat is a set of binary coordinates. The equation to update the position of the original BA is replaced by the SF method of discretization.

The GSO was applied by Deng-Xu et al. (2011) to solve the multiconstrained Quality of Service (QoS) multicast routing problem using a discrete vector; this problem is a direct application of the well-known TSP.

Xiangyang et al. (2011) proposed the AFSA to solve KP using the RK method. He et al. (2009) proposed the AFSA mapped into the integer space directly, using a method that ensures that the candidate solution stays in integer space throughout the optimization process.

Balazs et al. (2012) proposed a BEA to solve a permutation flow shop problem with a real-valued vector (arrays). The adaptation of real-valued vectors to permutations is done by using the RK method. Inoue et al. (2000) and Miwa et al. (2002) proposed a binary encoding for the BEA to solve the nurse scheduling problem using mutation and crossover similar to those of GA. Feng and Xiao (2011) applied the same method for a route planning problem.

7.5 Discussion

The algorithms presented in Section 7.2 were originally devised for dealing with continuous search spaces. However, for discrete search spaces, which is the case of binary and combinatorial problems, the key issue is how to adapt the aforementioned algorithms.

In this survey, we selected 64 papers for analysis. Figure 7.1 shows the distribution of the swarm algorithms covered here. It is clearly observed that PSO was the most frequently found algorithm, representing a quarter of all papers analyzed. The ABC algorithm was the second one, representing 13% of the total.

Figure 7.2 summarizes the distribution of the discretization methods (Section 7.3) employed by the algorithms. The most commonly used method is the SF; 62% of the papers used it to transform continuous values into discrete ones. It is worth to mention that SF is also extensively applied in several other areas, such as artificial neural networks, biomathematics, chemistry, and statistics.

The RK method was the second most frequent, found in 18% of the papers. Since this method is exclusive to transform into integer, not binary, when binary values were necessary a combination of the RK method with the GVP was used by Congying et al. (2011). In this combined process, the first stage consisted of transforming the continuous values into discrete using the RK and a second stage using GVP to convert the discrete values in binary ones. The SPV was also used in 10% of the papers to transform continuous into discrete. The MPE method was used in

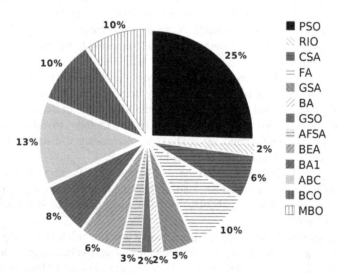

Figure 7.1 Algorithms distribution.

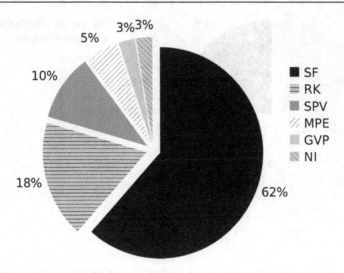

Figure 7.2 Discretization methods.

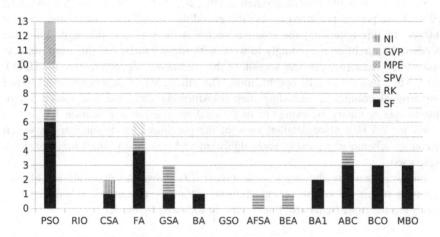

Figure 7.3 Discretization methods used in the algorithms.

5% of the papers. This method was combined with a discrete encoding to handle scheduling and TSP problems. The MPE method was used only in PSO algorithms, but it could be adapted to any other algorithm that uses the same main procedures of PSO, i.e., the update of speed and position. Finally, only 3% of the papers used the NI for this same sort of transformation.

Figure 7.3 summarizes how many times each discretization method was used by each algorithm in the papers surveyed. Note that two of them, RIO and GSO, did not use any discretization method. This is due to the straight encoding schemes

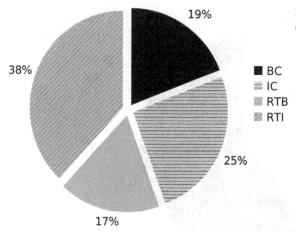

Figure 7.4 Distribution of encoding schemes.

(integer or binary) that do not require further discretization. In two papers, there was no enough information for identifying the discretization method used, so they were not counted in Figure 7.3.

Figure 7.4 lists the encoding schemes (BC, IC, RTB, or RTI—see Section 7.3); 19% of the papers preferred to use the encodings directly as binary and 25% as integer. In this approach, the solution vector is discrete and the algorithm code needs to be modified accordingly to work with these values. For this purpose, several authors created a discrete version of the continuous algorithm, e.g., the DPSO, the CABC, and the DABC optimization. The other 55% of papers preferred to use the original continuous encoding then transforming them the real-valued vector into integer or binary, by using one of the methods presented in Section 7.3.

Figure 7.5 is a more detailed view of the previous plot. It summarizes which encoding scheme was used in each algorithm and how many times these schemes were used.

Finally, regarding the application, Figure 7.6 shows the main classes of problems to which the swarm optimization algorithms were applied. Scheduling problems are the most frequently found, closely followed by the KP.

7.6 Concluding Remarks and Future Research

Real-world discrete and combinatorial problems are usually challenging and require computationally intensive algorithms. Swarm intelligence algorithms have been an interesting alternative for providing satisfactory solutions. The individual characteristics of the continuous swarm algorithms are very useful for these applications. However, to apply them to a discrete problem requires adaptation, hybridization, or modification the original algorithms to handle those sort of problems.

The methods used to achieve this purpose are the most diverse. This survey aims to classify the most common discretization methods and encoding strategies

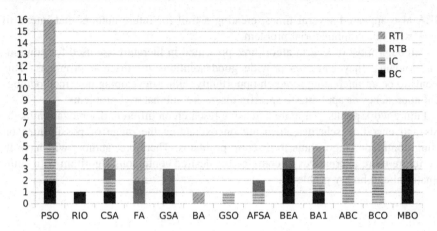

Figure 7.5 Encoding schemes related of swarm algorithms.

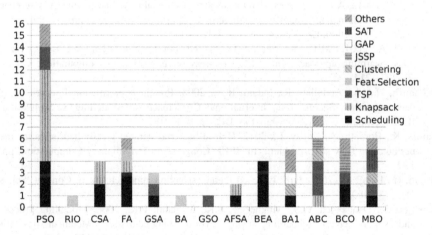

Figure 7.6 Applications of the swarm algorithms.

to guide future authors to select the best method and strategy when working with continuous swarm algorithms for discrete problems. The SF and RK discretization methods appeared most times in the literature review. Both methods seek the transformation of the continuous values handled by the algorithms into discrete ones, requiring an adaptation to deal with possible solutions in a discrete environment.

The results achieved by each paper presented in this survey demonstrate how continuous algorithms can be useful in discrete problems. The large number of papers adapting the PSO for classical combinatorial problems such as Knapsack, Scheduling and TSP support this trend. For the scheduling problem, the FA and

BEA also appeared several times, creating a trail for future authors that intend to work with this combinatorial problem.

Although most of swarm algorithms presented in literature are used for continuous domains, they can also provide good solutions for discrete problems. This seems to be an interesting research opportunity, either developing new methodological approaches or applying to specific discrete/combinatorial problems.

Future work points to a more extensive research on different discretization methods and encoding schemes, focusing on expanding the range of possibilities on using continuous algorithms to discrete problems. Therefore, authors will have in the future more alternatives to combine the desired continuous algorithm with combinatorial and binary problems.

References

Abbass, H., 2001a. A monogenous MBO approach to satisfiability. International Conference on Computational Intelligence for Modelling, Control and Automation. Australia and IEEE ACT Section, Las Vegas, Nevada, July 9–11.

Abbass, H.A., 2001b. MBO: marriage in honey bees optimization a haplometrosis polygynous swarming approach. In: IEEE Congress on Evolutionary Computation, vol. 1, pp. 207–214.

Bahamish, H.A.A., Abdullah, R., Salam, R.A., 2008. Protein conformational search using bees algorithm. Second Asia International Conference on Modelling & Simulation. IEEE Computer Society, Washington, DC, pp. 911–916.

Balazs, K., Horvath, Z., Koczy, L., 2012. Hybrid bacterial iterated greedy heuristics for the permutation flow shop problem. In: IEEE Congress on Evolutionary Computation, pp. 1–8.

Banati, H., Bajaj, M., 2011. Fire fly based feature selection approach. Int. J. Comput. Sci. 8 (4), 473–480.

Banerjee, S., Dangayach, G.S., Mukherjee, S.K., Mohanti, P.K., 2008. Modelling process and supply chain scheduling using hybrid meta-heuristics. Metaheuristics for Scheduling in Industrial and Manufacturing Applications. Vol. 128 of Studies in Computational Intelligence. Springer, Berlin, Germany, pp. 277–300.

Banharnsakun, A., Achalakul, T., Sirinaovakul, B., 2010. ABC-GSX: a hybrid method for solving the traveling salesman problem. In: Second World Congress on Nature and Biologically Inspired Computing, pp. 7–12.

Banharnsakun, A., Sirinaovakul, B., Achalakul, T., 2012. Job shop scheduling with the best-so-far ABC. Eng. Appl. Artif. Intell. 25 (3), 583–593.

Baykasoğlu, A., Ozbakir, L., Tapkan, P., 2007. Artificial bee colony algorithm and its application to generalized assignment problem. In: Chan, F.T.S., Tiwari, M.K. (Eds.), Swarm Intelligence: Focus on Ant and Particle Swarm Optimization. I-tech Education and Publishing, Istanbul, Turkey, pp. 532–564.

Benatchba, K., Admane, L., Koudil, M., 2005. Using bees to solve a data-mining problem expressed as a max-sat one. Artificial Intelligence and Knowledge Engineering Applications: A Bioinspired Approach. Vol. 3562 of Lecture Notes in Computer Science. Springer-Verlag, Heidelberg, pp. 75–86.

Burnwal, S., Deb, S., 2012. Scheduling optimization of flexible manufacturing system using cuckoo search-based approach. Int. J. Adv. Manuf. Technol.1−9.

Cai, Y., 2010. Artificial fish school algorithm applied in a combinatorial optimization problem. Int. J. Intell. Syst. Appl. 1, 37−43.

Chen, H., Li, S., Tang, Z., 2011. Hybrid gravitational search algorithm with random-key encoding scheme combined with simulated annealing. Int. J. Comput. Sci. Net. Secur. 11 (6), 208−217.

Chong, C.S., Sivakumar, A.I., Low, M.Y.H., Gay, K.L., 2006. A bee colony optimization algorithm to job shop scheduling. In: 38th Winter Conference on Simulation, pp. 1954−1961.

Congying, L., Huanping, Z., Xinfeng, Y., 2011. Particle swarm optimization algorithm for quadratic assignment problem. In: International Conference on Computer Science and Network Technology, vol. 3, pp. 1728−1731.

Davidovic, T., Selmic, M., Teodorovic, D., Ramljak, D., 2012. Bee colony optimization for scheduling independent tasks to identical processors. J. Heuristics. 18 (4), 549−569.

Deep, K., Bansal, J.C., 2008. A socio-cognitive particle swarm optimization for multi-dimensional knapsack problem. In: First International Conference on Emerging Trends in Engineering and Technology, pp. 355−360.

Deng-Xu, H., Hua-Zheng, Z., Gui-Qing, L., 2011. Glowworm swarm optimization algorithm for solving multi-constrained QoS multicast routing problem. In: Seventh International Conference on Computational Intelligence and Security, pp. 66−70.

Dorigo, M., Stützle, T., 2004. Ant Colony Optimization. MIT Press, Cambridge, MA.

Falcon, R., Almeida, M., Nayak, A., 2011. Fault identification with binary adaptive fireflies in parallel and distributed systems. In: IEEE Congress on Evolutionary Computation, pp. 1359−1366.

Feng, Q., Xiao, Q., 2011. Bacterial evolutionary route planning for unmanned aerial vehicle. In: Second International Conference on Artificial Intelligence, Management Science and Electronic Commerce, pp. 3808−3811.

Feng, X., Lau, F.C.M., Gao, D., 2009. A new bio-inspired approach to the traveling salesman problem. In: Zhou, J. (Ed.), Complex Sciences. Vol. 5 of Lecture Notes of the Institute of Computer Sciences. Springer, Berlin, Germany, pp. 1310−1321.

Fister, I., Yang, X.-S., Fister, I., Brest, J., 2012. Memetic firefly algorithm for combinatorial optimization. In: Fifth International Conference on Bioinspired Optimization Methods and their Applications, pp. 75−86.

Garnier, S., Gautrais, J., Theraulaz, G., 2007. The biological principles of swarm intelligence. Swarm Intell. 1 (1), 3−31.

Gherboudj, A., Layeb, A., Chikhi, S., 2012. Solving 0−1 knapsack problems by a discrete binary version of cuckoo search algorithm. Int. J. Bio-Inspired Comput. 4 (4), 229−236.

Glover, F., Laguna, M., 1997. Tabu Search. Kluwer Academic, Norwell, MA.

Havens, T.C., Spain, C.J., Salmon, N.G., Keller, J.M., 2008. Roach infestation optimization. IEEE Swarm Intelligence Symposium. IEEE Press, Piscataway, NJ, pp. 1−7.

He, D., Qu, L., Guo, X., 2009. Artificial fish-school algorithm for integer programming. In: International Conference on Information Engineering and Computer Science, pp. 1−4.

Hembecker, F., Lopes, H.S., Godoy Jr., W., 2007. Particle swarm optimization for the multi-dimensional knapsack problem. Proceedings of the Eighth International Conference on Adaptive and Natural Computing Algorithms, Part I. Vol. 4431 of Lecture Notes in Computer Science. Springer-Verlag, Heidelberg, pp. 358−365.

Hendrawan, Y., Murase, H., 2011. Neural-discrete hungry roach infestation optimization to select informative textural features for determining water content of cultured sunagoke moss. Environ. Control Biol. 49 (1), 1−21.

Hernández, H., Blum, C., 2012. Distributed graph coloring: an approach based on the calling behavior of Japanese tree frogs. Swarm Intell. 6 (2), 117−150.

Inoue, T., Furuhashi, T., Maeda, H., Takaba, M., 2000. A study on bacterial evolutionary algorithm engine for interactive nurse scheduling support system. In: 26th Annual Conference of the IEEE Industrial Electronics Society, vol. 1, pp. 651−656.

Karaboga, D., 2005. An Idea Based on Honey Bee Swarm for Numerical Optimization. Technical Report, Erciyes University, Engineering Faculty, Computer Engineering Department.

Karaboga, D., Gorkemli, B., 2011. A combinatorial artificial bee colony algorithm for traveling salesman problem. In: International Symposium on Intelligent Systems and Applications. IEEE Press, Istanbul, Turkey, pp. 50−53.

Kennedy, J., Eberhart, R., 2001. Swarm Intelligence. Morgan Kaufmann, San Francisco, CA.

Kennedy, J., Eberhart, R.C., 1997. A discrete binary version of the particle swarm algorithm. In: IEEE International Conference on Computational Cybernetics and Simulation, vol. 5, pp. 4104−4108.

Koudil, M., Benatchba, K., Tarabet, A., Sahraoui, E.B., 2007. Using artificial bees to solve partitioning and scheduling problems in codesign. Appl. Math. Comput. 186 (2), 1710−1722.

Krishnanand, K.N., Ghose, D., 2005. Detection of multiple source locations using a glowworm metaphor with applications to collective robotics. In: Proceedings of the IEEE Swarm Intelligence Symposium, pp. 84−91.

Kumar, A., Chakarverty, S., 2011. Design optimization for reliable embedded system using cuckoo search. In: Third International Conference on Electronics Computer Technology, vol. 1, pp. 264−268.

Labed, S., Gherboudj, A., Chikhi, S., 2011. A modified hybrid particle swarm optimization algorithm for multidimensional knapsack problem. Int. J. Comput. Appl. 34 (2), 11−16.

Layeb, A., 2011. A novel quantum inspired cuckoo search for knapsack problems. Int. J. Bio-Inspired Comput. 3, 297−305.

Li, X., Wang, J., Zhou, J., Yin, M., 2010. An effective GSA based memetic algorithm for permutation flow shop scheduling. In: IEEE Congress on Evolutionary Computation, pp. 1−6.

Li, Z., Li, N., 2009. A novel multi-mutation binary particle swarm optimization for 0/1 knapsack problem. In: 21st Annual International Conference on Chinese Control and Decision Conference, pp. 3090−3095.

Lin, S., Kernighan, B.W., 1973. An effective heuristic algorithm for the traveling-salesman problem. Oper. Res. 21 (2), 498−516.

Lin, T.-L., Horng, S.-J., Kao, T.-W., Chen, Y.-H., Run, R.-S., Chen, R.-J., et al., 2010. An efficient job-shop scheduling algorithm based on particle swarm optimization. Expert Syst. Appl. 37 (3), 2629−2636.

Lopes, H.S., Coelho, L.S., 2005. Particle swarm optimization with fast local search for the blind traveling salesman problem. International Conference on Hybrid Intelligent Systems, pp. 245−250.

Lucic, P., Teodorovic, D., 2002. Transportation modeling: an artificial life approach. In: 14th IEEE International Conference on Tools with Artificial Intelligence, pp. 216−223.

Marinakis, Y., Marinaki, M., Matsatsinis, N., 2008. A hybrid clustering algorithm based on honey bees mating optimization and greedy randomized adaptive search procedure.

In: Maniezzo, V., Battiti, R., Watson, J.-P. (Eds.), Learning and Intelligent Optimization. Springer-Verlag, Heidelberg, pp. 138–152.

Marinakis, Y., Marinaki, M., Matsatsinis, N.F., 2009. A hybrid discrete artificial bee colony–GRASP algorithm for clustering. In: International Conference on Computers & Industrial Engineering, pp. 548–553.

Miwa, M., Inoue, T., Matsuzaki, M., Furuhasi, T., Okuwa, S., 2002. Nurse scheduling system using bacterial evolutionary algorithm hardware. In: 28th Annual Conference of the IEEE Industrial Electronics Society, vol. 3, pp. 1801–1805.

Mladenovic, N., Hansen, P., 1997. Variable neighborhood search. Comput. Oper. Res. 24, 1097–1100.

Nakamura, R.Y.M., Pereira, L.A.M., Costa, K.A., Rodrigues, D., Papa, J.P., Yang, X.-S., 2012. BBA: a binary bat algorithm for feature selection. Conference on Graphics, Patterns and Images. IEEE Computer Society, Los Alamitos, CA, pp. 291–297.

Nawa, N., Furuhashi, T., 1999. Fuzzy system parameters discovery by bacterial evolutionary algorithm. IEEE Trans. Fuzzy Syst. 7 (5), 608–616.

Ozbakir, L., Baykasoğlu, A., Tapkan, P., 2010. Bees algorithm for generalized assignment problem. Appl. Math. Comput. 215 (11), 3782–3795.

Pacurib, J.A., Seno, G.M.M., Yusiong, J.P.T., 2009. Solving Sudoku puzzles using improved artificial bee colony algorithm. In: Fourth International Conference on Innovative Computing, Information and Control, pp. 885–888.

Palit, S., Sinha, S.N., Molla, M.A., Khanra, A., Kule, M., 2011. A cryptanalytic attack on the knapsack cryptosystem using binary firefly algorithm. In: Second International Conference on Computer and Communication Technology, pp. 428–432.

Pan, Q.-Q., Tasgetiren, M.F., Liang, Y.-C., 2008. A discrete particle swarm optimization algorithm for the no-wait flow shop scheduling problem. Comput. Oper. Res. 35 (9), 2807–2839.

Papa, J.P., Pagnin, A., Schellini, S.A., Spadotto, A., Guido, R.C., Ponti, M., et al., 2011. Feature selection through gravitational search algorithm. In: IEEE International Conference on Acoustics, Speech and Signal Processing, pp. 2052–2055.

Parpinelli, R.S., Lopes, H.S., 2011. New inspirations in swarm intelligence: a survey. Int. J. Bio-Inspired Comput. 3 (1), 1–16.

Passino, K.M., 2002. Biomimicry of bacterial foraging for distributed optimization and control. IEEE Control Syst. Mag. 22 (3), 52–67.

Pham, D., Koc, E., Lee, J., Phrueksanant, J., 2007a. Using the bees algorithm to schedule jobs for a machine. In: Proceedings of Eighth International Conference on Laser Metrology, CMM and Machine Tool Performance, pp. 430–439.

Pham, D.T., Ghanbarzadeh, A., Koc, E., Otri, S., Rahim, S., Zaidi, M., 2005. The Bees Algorithm. Technical Note, Manufacturing Engineering Center, Cardiff University, UK.

Pham, D.T., Otri, S., Afify, A., Mahmuddin, M., Al-Jabbouli, H., 2007b. Data clustering using the bees algorithm. In: 40th CIRP International Seminar on Manufacturing Systems.

Pulikanti, S., Singh, A., 2009. An artificial bee colony algorithm for the quadratic knapsack problem. The 16th International Conference on Neural Information Processing. Vol. 5864 of Lecture Notes in Computer Science. Springer-Verlag, Heidelberg, pp. 196–205.

Rabanal, P., Rodríguez, I., Rubio, F., 2007. Using river formation dynamics to design heuristic algorithms. In: Akl, S.G., Calude, C.S., Dinneen, M.J., Rozenberg, G., Wareham, T. (Eds.), Unconventional Computation. Vol. 4618 of Lecture Notes in Computer Science. Springer, Heidelberg, pp. 163–177.

Rashedi, E., Nezamabadi-Pour, H., Saryazdi, S., 2009. GSA: a gravitational search algorithm. Inf. Sci. 179 (13), 2232–2248.

Rosendo, M., Pozo, A., 2010. Applying a discrete particle swarm optimization algorithm to combinatorial problems. Brazilian Symposium on Neural Networks. IEEE Computer Society, Los Alamitos, CA, pp. 235–240.

Sayadi, M.K., Ramezanian, R., Ghaffari-Nasab, N., 2010. A discrete firefly meta-heuristic with local search for makespan minimization in permutation flow shop scheduling problems. Int. J. Ind. Eng. Comput. 1, 1–10.

Shah-Hosseini, H., 2007. Problem solving by intelligent water drops. In: IEEE Congress on Evolutionary Computation, pp. 3226–3231.

Shen, X., Li, Y., Chen, C., Yang, J., Zhang, D., 2012. Greedy continuous particle swarm optimisation algorithm for the knapsack problems. Int. J. Comput. Appl. Technol. 44 (2), 137–144.

Singh, V., Singh, D., Tiwari, R., Shukla, A., 2011. RGBCA-genetic bee colony algorithm for travelling salesman problem. In: World Congress on Information and Communication Technologies. IEEE Press, Gwalior, India, pp. 1002–1008.

Tasgetiren, M., Liang, Y., Sevkli, M., Gencyilmaz, G., 2004a. Particle swarm optimization algorithm for makespan and maximum lateness minimization in permutation flow shop sequencing problem. In: Fourth International Symposium on Intelligent Manufacturing Systems, pp. 237–250.

Tasgetiren, M., Sevkli, M., Liang, Y.-C., Gencyilmaz, G., 2004b. Particle swarm optimization algorithm for single machine total weighted tardiness problem. In: IEEE Congress on Evolutionary Computation, vol. 2, pp. 1412–1419.

Tasgetiren, M.F., Suganthan, P.N., Pan, Q.-Q., 2007. A discrete particle swarm optimization algorithm for the generalized traveling salesman problem. Ninth Annual Conference on Genetic and Evolutionary Computation. ACM Press, New York, NY, 158–165.

Teo, J., Abbass, H.A., 2001. An annealing approach to the mating-flight trajectories in the marriage in Honey Bees Optimization algorithm. Technical Report CA04/01, School of Computer Science, University of New South Wales at ADFA, Canberra, Australia.

Teodorovic, D., Dell'Orco, M., 2005. Bee colony optimization—a cooperative learning approach to complex transportation problems. In: 16th Mini-Euro Conference on Advanced OR and AI Methods in Transportation, pp. 51–60.

Ucar, H., Tasgetiren, M.F., 2006. A particle swarm optimization algorithm for permutation flow shop sequencing problem with the number of tardy jobs criterion. In: Fifth International Symposium on Intelligent Manufacturing Systems, pp. 237–250.

Verma, R., Kumar, S., 2012. DSAPSO: DNA sequence assembly using continuous particle swarm optimization with smallest position value rule. In: First International Conference on Recent Advances in Information Technology, pp. 410–415.

Wan, N.F., Nolle, L., 2009. Solving a multi-dimensional knapsack problem using hybrid particle swarm optimization algorithm. In: 23rd European Conference on Modelling and Simulation.

Wong, L.-P., Low, M.Y., Chong, C.S., 2008a. A bee colony optimization algorithm for traveling salesman problem. In: Second Asia International Conference on Modelling & Simulation. IEEE Press, Singapore, pp. 818–823.

Wong, L.-P., Puan, C.Y., Low, M.Y.H., Chong, C.S., 2008b. Bee colony optimization algorithm with big valley landscape exploitation for job shop scheduling problems. In: Proceedings of the 40th Winter Simulation Conference, pp. 2050–2058.

Xiangyang, S., Minghao, Z., Yamin, Z., 2011. Improved artificial fish school algorithm to solve knapsack problem. Comput. Eng. Appl. 47 (21), 43.

Xu, S., Ji, Z., Pham, D.T., Yu, F., 2010. Bio-inspired binary bees algorithm for a two-level distribution optimisation problem. J. Bionic Eng. 7, 161–167.

Yang, C., Chen, J., Tu, X., 2007. Algorithm of marriage in honey bees optimization based on the Nelder–Mead method. In: Li, T., Xu, Y., Ruan, D. (Eds.), International Conference on Intelligent Systems and Knowledge Engineering. Advances in Intelligent Systems Research. Atlantis Press, Amsterdam, The Netherlands, pp. 1–7.

Yang, X.S., 2008. Firefly algorithm. Nature-inspired Metaheuristic Algorithms. Luniver Press, Bristol, UK (Chapter 8).

Yang, X.S., 2009. Firefly algorithm, Lévy flights and global optimization. XXVI Research and Development in Intelligent Systems. Springer, London, UK, pp. 209–218.

Yang, X.S., 2010. A new metaheuristic bat-inspired algorithm. Nature Inspired Cooperative Strategies for Optimization. Vol. 284 of Studies in Computational Intelligence. Springer, Berlin, pp. 65–74.

Yang, X.-S., Deb, S., 2009. Cuckoo search via Lévy flights. In: World Congress on Nature and Biologically Inspired Computing, pp. 210–214.

Yousif, A., Abdullah, A.H., Nor, S.M., Abdelaziz, A.A., 2011. Scheduling jobs on grid computing using firefly algorithm. J. Theor. Appl. Inf. Technol. 33 (2), 155–164.

8 Test Functions for Global Optimization: A Comprehensive Survey

Momin Jamil[1,2], Xin-She Yang[3] and Hans-Jürgen Zepernick[1]

[1]Blekinge Institute of Technology, Karlskrona, Sweden; [2]Harman International, Harman/Becker Automotive Systems GmbH, Karlsbad, Germany; [3]Department of Design Engineering and Mathematics, School of Science and Technology, Middlesex University, The Burroughs, London, UK

8.1 Introduction

In the field of evolutionary computation (EC), the reliability, efficiency, and validation of algorithms are frequently done by using common standard benchmark functions from literature. A common practice followed by many researches is to compare different algorithms on a large test set, especially when the test involves function optimization (Gordon and Whitley, 1993; Whitley et al., 1996). However, it must be noted that effectiveness of one algorithm against others simply cannot be measured by the problems that it solves. Therefore, in order to evaluate an algorithm, one must identify the kind of problems where it performs better compared to others. This helps in characterizing the type of problems for which an algorithm is suitable. This is only possible if the test suite is large enough to include a wide variety of problems, such as unimodal, multimodal, regular, irregular, separable, nonseparable, and multidimensional.

Many test functions can be found scattered in different textbooks, in individual research articles or at different web sites, while a single source that contains a comprehensive collection is still missing. Previous attempts to assemble global optimization (GO) test problems can be found by Floudas et al. (1999). Online collections of test problems also exist, such as the GLOBAL library at GAMS World (Gams, 2000), CUTE (Gould et al., 2001), GO test problems collection by Hedar, a collection of test functions (Andrei, 2008; Mishra 2006a,b,c,d,e,f,g; Suganthan et al., 2005; Tang et al., 2008, 2010), a collection of continuous GO test problems (Ali et al., 2005), COCONUT (Neumaier, 2003a), and a subset

Swarm Intelligence and Bio-Inspired Computation. DOI: http://dx.doi.org/10.1016/B978-0-12-405163-8.00008-9

of commonly used test functions (Yang, 2010a,b). Therefore, we present a comprehensive collection of unconstrained optimization test problems that can be used as a benchmark function to validate and compare different optimization algorithms.

In general, unconstrained problems can be classified into two categories namely artificial and real-life problems. The artificial problems can be used to evaluate the behavior of an algorithm sometimes in diverse and difficult situations. Artificial problems may include single global minimum, single or multiple global minima in the presence of many local minima, long narrow valleys, null-space effects, and flat surfaces. These problems can be easily manipulated and modified to test the algorithms in diverse scenarios. On the other hand, real-life problems originate from different fields such as physics, chemistry, engineering, and mathematics. These problems are hard to manipulate and may contain complicated algebraic or differential expressions and may require a significant amount of data to compile. A collection of real-life unstrained optimization problems can be found by Averick et al. (1992).

A function with more than one local optimum is called multimodal. These functions are used to test the ability of an algorithm to escape from local minimum. If the exploration process of an algorithm is poorly designed, then it cannot search the function landscape effectively. This, in turn, leads to an algorithm getting stuck at a local minimum. Multimodal functions with many local minima are among the most difficult class of problems for many algorithms. Functions with flat surfaces pose a difficulty for the algorithms, since the flatness of the function does not give the algorithm any information to direct the search process toward the minima (Stepint, Matyas, PowerSum). Another group of test problems is formulated by separable and nonseparable functions. According to Boyer et al. (2005), the dimensionality of the search space is an important issue with the problem. In some functions, the global minima are very small when compared to the whole search space, such as Easom, Michalewicz ($m = 10$), and Powell. For problems such as Perm, Kowalik, and Schaffer, the global minimum is located very close to the local minima. If the algorithm cannot keep up the direction changes in the functions having a narrow curving valley, in case of functions like Beale, Colville, or cannot explore the search space effectively, in case of function like Pen Holder, Testtube Holder having multiple global minima, it will fail for these kinds of problems. Another problem that algorithms suffer is the scaling problem with a difference of many orders of magnitude between the domain and the function hypersurface, such as Goldstein-Price and Trid.

8.2   A Collection of Test Functions for GO

The goal of GO is to find the best possible elements $\mathbf{x}^*$ from a set of X according to a set of criteria $F = \{f_1, f_2, \ldots, f_n\}$. These criteria are called objective functions expressed in a form of mathematical functions. An objective function is a mathematical function $f:D \subset \Re^n \rightarrow \Re$ subject to optimization. The set D is referred to as the set of feasible points in a search space. In the case of optimizing a single criterion f, an optimum is either its maximum or minimum. GO problems are often defined as minimization problems; however, these problems can be easily converted to maximization problems by negating f. A general GO problem can be defined as follows:

$$\underset{x}{\text{minimize }} f(\mathbf{x}) \tag{8.1}$$

A point $\mathbf{x}^* \in D$ is either a global minimum or maximum. The correct solution of an optimization problem is a set of $\mathbf{x}^*$ of all optimal points in D rather than a single minimum or maximum value. There are normally multiple, often even infinite optimal solutions. The task of the GO algorithm is to find optimal or near-optimal solutions.

The difficulty of a problem generally increases with its dimensionality. If the objective function variables are independent of each other, then an objective function can be decomposed into subobjective functions. Then, each of these subobjectives involves only one decision variable while treating all the others as constant. Such class of problems is called separable problems and can be expressed as

$$f(x_1, x_2, \ldots x_p) = \sum_{i=1}^{p} f_i(x_i) \tag{8.2}$$

The formal definition of separability according to Boyer et al. (2005) is given as

$$\begin{aligned} \arg\, &\underset{x_1,\ldots,x_p}{\text{minimize }} f(x_1, \ldots, x_p) \\ &= \left(\arg\, \underset{x_1}{\text{minimize }} f(x_1, \ldots), \ldots, \arg\, \underset{x_p}{\text{minimize }} f(\ldots, x_p) \right) \end{aligned} \tag{8.3}$$

In other words, a function of p variables is called separable, if it can be written as a sum of p functions of just one variable (Boyer et al., 2005). On the other hand, a function is called nonseparable, if its variables show interrelations among themselves or are not independent. The separability also reflects a measure of difficulty of different benchmark functions. In general, the separable problems are considered relatively easy to solve, while the nonseparable are most difficult problems to optimize due to interrelations among their variables.

In this section, we present a comprehensive collection of unconstrained optimization test problems which can be used to validate the performance of optimization algorithms. For clarity, we have divided the functions based on their modality into two different sections. The dimensions, problem domain size, and optimal solution are denoted by D, $Lb \leq x_i \leq Ub$, and $f(\mathbf{x}^*) = f(x_1, \ldots, x_n)$, respectively. The symbols Lb and Ub represent lower and upper bounds of the variable, respectively. It should be noted that in several cases optimal solution vector and corresponding solutions are known only as a numerical approximation.

8.2.1 Unimodal Test Functions

In this section, we list unimodal test functions that can be used to validate the performance of different optimization algorithms. A function is called unimodal if it contains a single global minimum with no or single local minimum. In the presence of a single local minimum, the task of finding the global minimum becomes a cumbersome task for many optimization algorithms. If an algorithm is not designed properly, algorithms can get stuck in the local minimum. Some of the unimodal functions inherent a certain kind of deceptiveness and are hard to optimize.

The deceptiveness could be that the global minimum is either located on a flat surface or located very close to a global minimum. Sometimes, deceptiveness is due to the fact that the global minimum lie in narrow curving valleys or show fractal properties around global minimum.

If local minimum basin of a function is larger than the global minimum basin, it could also seen as a deceptiveness

1. Aluffi−Pentini's function (nonseparable)

$$f_1(\mathbf{x}) = 0.25x_1^4 - 0.5x_1^2 + 0.1x_1 + 0.5x_2^2$$

subject to $-10 \leq x_i \leq 10$. The global minimum is located at $\mathbf{x}^* = (-1.0465, 0)$, $f(\mathbf{x}^*) \approx -0.3523$.

2. Baluja-1 function (nonseparable)

$$f_2(\mathbf{x}) = \frac{1}{C + \left||y_1| + \sum_{i=2}^{100} |y_i|\right|}$$

where $y_1 = x_1$ and $y_i = x_i + y_{i-1}$, $C = 0.00001$, $-2.56 \leq x_i \leq 2.56$, for $i = 2, \ldots, 100$.

3. Baluja-2 function (nonseparable)

$$f_3(\mathbf{x}) = \frac{1}{C + \left||y_1| + \sum_{i=2}^{100} |y_i|\right|}$$

where $y_1 = x_1$ and $y_i = x_i + \sin(y_{i-1})$, $C = 0.00001$, $-2.56 \leq x_i \leq 2.56$, for $i = 2, \ldots, 100$.

4. Baluja-3 function (nonseparable)

$$f_4(\mathbf{x}) = \frac{1}{C + \sum_{i=1}^{100} |0.0024x_{i-1} - x_i|}$$

where $C = 0.00001$, $-2.56 \leq x_i \leq 2.56$.

5. Beale function (nonseparable)

$$f_5(\mathbf{x}) = (1.5 - x_1 - x_1 x_2)^2 + (2.25 - x_1 - x_1 x_2^2)^2 + (2.625 - x_1 - x_1 x_2^3)^2$$

subject to $-4.5 \leq x_i \leq 4.5$. The global minimum is located at $\mathbf{x}^* = (3, 0.5)$, $f(\mathbf{x}^*) = 0$.

6. Box−Betts quadratic sum function (nonseparable)

$$f_6(\mathbf{x}) = \sum_{i=0}^{D-1} g(x_i)^2$$

where $g(x) = e^{-0.1(i+1)x_1} - e^{-0.1(i+1)x_2} - e^{[-0.1(i+1)-e^{-(i+1)}]x_3}$, subject to $0.9 \le x_1 \le 1.2$, $9 \le x_2 \le 11.2$, $0.9 \le x_3 \le 1.2$. The global minimum is located at $\mathbf{x}^* = (1, 10, 1)$, $f(\mathbf{x}^*) = 0$.

7. Brown function (nonseparable)

$$f_7(\mathbf{x}) = \sum_{i=1}^{D-1} (x_i^2)^{(x_{i+1}^2+1)} + (x_{i+1}^2)^{(x_i^2+1)}$$

subject to $-1 \le x_i \le 4$. The global minimum is located at $\mathbf{x}^* = (0, \ldots, 0), f(\mathbf{x}^*) = 0$.

8. Colville function (nonseparable)

$$f_8(\mathbf{x}) = 100(x_1 - x_2^2)^2 + (1 - x_1)^2 + 90(x_4 - x_3^2)^2 + (1 - x_3)^2$$
$$+ 10.1(x_2 - 1)^2 + (x_4 - 1)^2 + 19.8(x_2 - 1)(x_4 - 1)$$

subject to $-10 \le x_i \le 10$. The global minimum is located at $\mathbf{x}^* = (1, \ldots, 1), f(\mathbf{x}^*) = 0$.

9. Dixon and Price function (nonseparable)

$$f_9(\mathbf{x}) = (x_1 - 1)^2 + \sum_{i=2}^{D} i(2x_i^2 - x_{i-1})^2$$

subject to $-10 \le x_i \le 10$. The global minimum is located at $\mathbf{x}^* = f(2(2i - 2/2i))$, $f(\mathbf{x}^*) = 0$.

10. Easom function (separable)

$$f_{10}(\mathbf{x}) = -\cos(x_1)\cos(x_2)e^{[-(x_1-\pi)^2-(x_2-\pi)^2]}$$

subject to $-100 \le x_i \le 100$. The global minimum is located at $\mathbf{x}^* = (\pi, \pi), f(\mathbf{x}^*) = 0$.

11. Matyas function (nonseparable)

$$f_{11}(\mathbf{x}) = 0.26(x_1^2 + x_2^2) - 0.48x_1 x_2$$

subject to $-10 \le x_i \le 10$. The global minimum is located at $\mathbf{x}^* = (0, 0), f(\mathbf{x}^*) = 0$.

12. Powell function (nonseparable)

$$f_{12}(\mathbf{x}) = \sum_{i=1}^{D/4} (x_{4i-3} + 10x_{4i-2})^2 + 5(x_{4i-1} + x_{4i})^2 + (x_{4i-2} + x_{4i-1})^4 + 10(x_{4i-3} + x_{4i})^4$$

subject to $-4 \le x_i \le 5$. The global minimum is located at $\mathbf{x}^* = (3, -1, 0, 1, \ldots, 3, -1, 0, 1), f(\mathbf{x}^*) = 0$.

13. Quartic function

$$f_{13}(\mathbf{x}) = \sum_{i=1}^{D} i x_i^4 + \text{random}(0, 1)$$

subject to $-1.28 \le x_i \le 1.28$. The global minimum is located at $\mathbf{x}^* = (1, \ldots, 1)$, $f(\mathbf{x}^*) = 0$.

14. Rosenbrock function (nonseparable)

$$f_{14}(\mathbf{x}) = \sum_{i=1}^{D} [100(x_{i+1} - x_i^2)^2 + (x_i - 1)^2]$$

subject to $-30 \le x_i \le 30$. The global minimum is located at $\mathbf{x}^* = (1, \ldots, 1), f(\mathbf{x}^*) = 0$.

15. Modified Rosenbrock function (nonseparable)

$$f_{15}(\mathbf{x}) = 74 + 100(x_2 - x_1^2)^2 + (1 - x)^2 - 400 e^{-(x_1 + 1)^2 + (x_2 + 1)^2 / 0.1}$$

subject to $-2 \le x_i \le 2$. In this function, a Gaussian bump at $(-1, -1)$ is added, which causes a local minimum at $(1, 1)$ and global minimum at $\mathbf{x}^* = (-1, -1), f(\mathbf{x}^*) = 0$. This modification makes it difficult to optimize because the local minimum basin is larger than the global minimum.

16. Schwefel 1.2 function (nonseparable)

$$f_{16}(\mathbf{x}) = \sum_{i=1}^{D} \left(\sum_{j=1}^{i} x_j \right)^2$$

subject to $-100 \le x_i \le 100$. The global minimum is located at $\mathbf{x}^* = (0, \ldots, 0), f(\mathbf{x}^*) = 0$.

17. Schwefel 2.22 function (nonseparable)

$$f_{17}(\mathbf{x}) = -\sum_{i=1}^{D} |x_i| + \prod_{i=1}^{D} |x_i|$$

subject to $-10 \le x_i \le 10$. The global minimum is located at $\mathbf{x}^* = (0, \ldots, 0), f(\mathbf{x}^*) = 0$.

18. Step function (separable)

$$f_{18}(\mathbf{x}) = \sum_{i=1}^{D} (\lfloor x_i \rfloor + 0.5)^2$$

subject to $-100 \le x_i \le 100$. The global minimum is located at $\mathbf{x}^* = (0.5, \ldots, 0.5)$, $f(\mathbf{x}^*) = 0$.

19. Stepint function (separable)

$$f_{18}(\mathbf{x}) = 25 + \sum_{i=1}^{D} \lfloor |x_i| \rfloor$$

subject to $-5.12 \le x_i \le 5.12$. The global minimum is located at $\mathbf{x}^* = (0, \ldots, 0), f(\mathbf{x}^*) = 0$.

20. Sphere function (separable)

$$f_{20}(\mathbf{x}) = \sum_{i=1}^{D} x_i^2$$

subject to $0 \le x_i \le 10$. The global minimum is located at $\mathbf{x}^* = (0,\ldots,0), f(\mathbf{x}^*) = 0$.

21. Sum function (separable)

$$f_{21}(\mathbf{x}) = \sum_{i=1}^{D} ix_i^2$$

subject to $-10 \le x_i \le 10$. The global minimum is located at $\mathbf{x}^* = (0,\ldots,0), f(\mathbf{x}^*) = 0$.

22. Trid 6 function (nonseparable)

$$f_{22}(\mathbf{x}) = \sum_{i=1}^{D} (x_i - 1)^2 - \sum_{i=2}^{D} x_i x_{i-1}$$

subject to $-36 \le x_i \le 36$. The global minimum is located at $f(\mathbf{x}^*) = -50$.

23. Trid 10 function (nonseparable)

$$f_{23}(\mathbf{x}) = \sum_{i=1}^{D} (x_i - 1)^2 - \sum_{i=2}^{D} x_i x_{i-1}$$

subject to $-100 \le x_i \le 100$. The global minimum is located at $f(\mathbf{x}^*) = -200$.

24. Zakharov function (nonseparable)

$$f_{24}(\mathbf{x}) = \sum_{i=1}^{D} x_i^2 + \left(\frac{1}{2} \sum_{i=1}^{D} ix_i \right)^2 + \left(\frac{1}{2} \sum_{i=1}^{D} ix_i \right)^4$$

subject to $-5 \le x_i \le 5$. The global minimum is located at $\mathbf{x}^* = (0,\ldots,0), f(\mathbf{x}^*) = 0$.

8.2.2 Multimodal Function

In this section, we list multimodal test functions with more than one, few or many local minima. Most of these functions are nonseparable making them hard for many optimization algorithms. These functions also have multiple global minima scattered throughout the search space. If an algorithm is not designed properly, it can get stuck in the local minima without ever finding global minima or cannot find all the global minima. Specifically, unimodal test functions can be reported as follows:

1. Ackley function (nonseparable)

$$f_1(\mathbf{x}) = -20\, e^{\left(-0.02\sqrt{D^{-1}\sum_{i=1}^{D} x_i^2}\right)} - e^{\left(D^{-1}\sum_{i=1}^{D} \cos(2\pi x_i)\right)} + 20 + e$$

subject to $-35 \le x_i \le 35$. The global minimum is located at $\mathbf{x}^* = (0,\ldots,0), f(\mathbf{x}^*) = 0$.

2. Alpine function (separable)

$$f_2(\mathbf{x}) = \sum_{i=1}^{D} |x_i \sin(x_i) + 0.1x_i|$$

subject to $-10 \le x_i \le 10$. The global minimum is located at $\mathbf{x}^* = (0, \ldots, 0)$, $f(\mathbf{x}^*) = 0$.

3. Ann-XOR function (nonseparable)

$$a = \frac{x_7}{1 + e^{-x_1 - x_2 - x_5}}$$

$$b = \frac{x_8}{1 + e^{-x_3 - x_4 - x_6}}$$

$$c = \frac{x_7}{1 + e^{-x_5}}$$

$$d = \frac{x_8}{1 + e^{-x_6}}$$

$$e = \frac{x_7}{1 + e^{-x_1 - x_5}}$$

$$f = \frac{x_8}{1 + e^{-x_3 - x_6}}$$

$$g = \frac{x_7}{1 + e^{-x_2 - x_5}}$$

$$h = \frac{x_8}{1 + e^{-x_4 - x_6}}$$

$$f_3(\mathbf{x}) = [1 + e^{-a - b - x_9}]^{-2} + [1 + e^{-c - d - x_9}]^{-2}$$
$$+ [1 - (1 + e^{-e - f - x_9})^{-1}]^2 + [1 - (1 + e^{-g - h - x_9})^{-1}]^2$$

subject to $-35 \le x_i \le 35$. The global minimum is located at $\mathbf{x}^* = (0, \ldots, 0)$, $f(\mathbf{x}^*) = 0$.

4. Becker–Lago function (separable)

$$f_4(\mathbf{x}) = (|x_1| - 5)^2 + (|x_2| - 5)^2$$

subject to $-10 \le x_i \le 10$. The four global minima are located at $\mathbf{x}^* = (\pm 5, \ \pm 5)$, $f(\mathbf{x}^*) = 0$.

5. Bohachevsky 1 function (separable)

$$f_5(\mathbf{x}) = x_1^2 + 2x_2^2 - 0.3 \cos(3\pi x_1) - 0.4 \cos(4\pi x_2) + 0.7$$

subject to $-100 \le x_i \le 100$. The global minimum is located at $\mathbf{x}^* = (0, 0)$, $f(\mathbf{x}^*) = 0$.

6. Bohachevsky 2 function (nonseparable)

$$f_6(\mathbf{x}) = x_1^2 + 2x_2^2 - 0.3 \cos(3\pi x_1)0.4 \cos(4\pi x_2) + 0.3$$

subject to $-100 \le x_i \le 100$. The global minimum is located at $\mathbf{x}^* = (0, 0)$, $f(\mathbf{x}^*) = 0$.

7. Bohachevsky 3 function (nonseparable)

$$f_7(x) = x_1^2 + 2x_2^2 - 0.3 \cos(3\pi x_1 + 4\pi x_2) + 0.3$$

subject to $-100 \le x_i \le 100$. The global minimum is located at $x^* = (0, 0), f(x^*) = 0$.

8. Booth function (nonseparable)

$$f_8(x) = (x_1 + 2x_2 - 7)^2 + (2x_1 + x_2 - 5)^2$$

subject to $-10 \le x_i \le 10$. The global minimum is located at $x^* = (1, 3), f(x^*) = 0$.

9. Branin function (nonseparable)

$$f_9(x) = \left(x_2 - \frac{5.1}{4\pi^2} x_1^2 + \frac{5.1}{\pi} x_1 - 6 \right)^2 + 10 \left(1 - \frac{1}{8\pi} \right) \cos(x_1) + 10$$

subject to $-5 \le x_1 \le 10$, $0 \le x_2 \le 15$. The three global minima are located at $x^* = (\{-3.142, 12.275\}, \{3.142, 2.275\}, \{9.425, 2.425\}), f(x^*) = 0.398$.

10. Branin 2 function (nonseparable)

$$f_{10}(x) = \left(1 - 2x_2 + \frac{\sin(4\pi x_2)}{20} - x_1 \right)^2 + \left(x_2 - \frac{\sin(4\pi x_1)}{2} \right)^2$$

subject to $-10 \le x_i \le 10$. The global minimum is located at $x^* = (0.402357, 0.287408), f(x^*) = 0$.

Bukin functions are almost fractal (with fine seesaw edges) in the surroundings of their minimal points. Due to this property, they are extremely difficult to optimize by any global or local optimization method.

11. Bukin 2 function (nonseparable)

$$f_{11}(x) = 100(x_2 - 0.01x_1^2 + 1) + 0.01(x_1 + 10)^2$$

subject to $-15 \le x_1 \le -5$, $-3 \le x_2 \le 3$. The global minimum is located at $x^* = (-10, 0), f(x^*) = 0$.

12. Bukin 4 function (separable)

$$f_{12}(x) = 100x_2^2 + 0.01||x_1 + 10||$$

subject to $-15 \le x_1 \le -5$, $-3 \le x_2 \le 3$. The global minimum is located at $x^* = (-10, 0), f(x^*) = 0$.

13. Bukin 6 function (nonseparable)

$$f_{13}(x) = 100\sqrt{||x_2 - 0.01x_1^2||} + 0.01||x_1 + 10||$$

subject to $-15 \le x_1 \le -5$, $-3 \le x_2 \le 3$. The global minimum is located at $x^* = (-10, 0), f(x^*) = 0$.

14. Butterfly function (nonseparable)

$$f_{14}(x) = (x_1^2 - x_2^2) \frac{\sin(x_1 + x_2)}{(x_1^2 + x_2^2)}$$

subject to $-D \leq x_i \leq D$. The number of global minima depends on the problem dimensions.

15. Carrom table function (nonseparable)

$$f_{15}(\mathbf{x}) = -\frac{(\cos(x_1)\cos(x_2)e^{|1-[(x_1^2+x_2^2)^{0.5}]/\pi|})^2}{30}$$

subject to $-10 \leq x_i \leq 10$. The four global minima are located at $\mathbf{x}^* = (\pm 9.646157266348881, \pm 9.646134286497169), f(\mathbf{x}^*) = -24.1568155$.

16. Chichinadze function (separable)

$$f_{16}(\mathbf{x}) = x_1^2 - 12x_1 + 11 + 10\cos\left(\frac{\pi x_1}{2}\right) + 8\sin\left(\frac{5\pi x_1}{2}\right) - (1/5)^{0.5} e^{-0.5(x_2-0.5)^2}$$

subject to $-30 \leq x_1 \leq 30$. The global minimum is located at $\mathbf{x}^* = (5.90133, 0.5)$, $f(\mathbf{x}^*) = -42.3159$.

17. Cola Function (nonseparable)

This 17-dimensional function computes indirectly the formula $f(D, u)$ by setting $x_0 = y_0$, $x_1 = u_0$, $x_i = u_{2(i-2)}$, $y_i = u_{2(i-2)+1}$.

$$f_{17}(n, u) = h(x, y) = \sum_{j<i} (r_{i,j} - d_{ij})^2$$

where r_{ij} is given by

$$r_{i,j} = [(x_i - x_j)^2 + (y_i - y_j)^2]^{0.5}$$

subject to $0 \leq x_0 \leq 4$ and $-4 \leq x_i \leq 4 \; \forall i = 1, \ldots, D-1$. It has global minimum $f(\mathbf{x}^*) = 11.7464$. d is a symmetric matrix given by

$$\mathbf{D} = [d_{ij}] \begin{pmatrix} 1.27 \\ 1.69 & 1.43 \\ 2.04 & 2.35 & 2.43 \\ 3.09 & 3.18 & 3.26 & 2.85 \\ 3.20 & 3.22 & 3.27 & 2.88 & 1.55 \\ 2.86 & 2.56 & 2.58 & 2.59 & 3.12 & 3.06 \\ 3.17 & 3.18 & 3.18 & 3.12 & 1.31 & 1.64 & 3.00 \\ 3.21 & 3.18 & 3.18 & 3.17 & 1.70 & 1.36 & 2.95 & 1.32 \\ 2.38 & 2.31 & 2.42 & 1.94 & 2.85 & 2.81 & 2.56 & 2.91 & 2.97 \end{pmatrix}$$

18. Corana function (separable)

$$f_{18}(\mathbf{x}) = \begin{cases} 0.15(z_i - 0.05 \, \text{sgn}(z_i)^2)d_i & \text{if } |v_i| < A \\ d_i x_i^2 & \text{otherwise} \end{cases}$$

where

$$v_i = |x_i - z_i|, \quad A = 0.05$$

$$z_i = 0.2 \left\lfloor \left| \frac{x_i}{0.2} \right| + 0.49999 \right\rfloor \mathrm{sgn}(x_i)$$

$$d_i = (1, \ 1000, \ 10, \ 100)$$

subject to $-500 \le x_i \le 500$. The global minimum is located at $\mathbf{x}^* = (0,0,0,0)$, $f(\mathbf{x}^*) = 0$.

19. Cosine mixture (separable)

$$f_{19}(\mathbf{x}) = -0.1 \sum_{i=1}^{D} \cos(5\pi x_i) - \sum_{i=1}^{D} x_i^2$$

subject to $-1 \le x_i \le 1$. The global minimum is located at $\mathbf{x}^* = (0,0)$, $f(\mathbf{x}^*) = 0.2$ or 0.4, for $n = 2$ and 4, respectively.

20. Cross-in-tray function (nonseparable)

$$f_{20}(\mathbf{x}) = -0.0001(\sin(x_1)\sin(x_2)e^{|100-[(x_1^2+x_2^2)^{0.5}]/\pi|} + 1)^{0.1}$$

subject to $-10 \le x_i \le 10$. The four global minima are located at $\mathbf{x}^* = (\pm 1.349406685353340, \ \pm 1.349406608602084), f(\mathbf{x}^*) = -2.0621218$.

21. Csendes function (separable)

$$f_{21}(\mathbf{x}) = \sum_{i=1}^{D} x_i^6 \left(2 + \sin\frac{1}{x_i} \right)$$

subject to $-1 \le x_i \le 1$. The global minimum is located at $\mathbf{x}^* = (0,\ldots,0), f(\mathbf{x}^*) = 0$.

22. Damavandi function (nonseparable)

$$f_{22}(\mathbf{x}) = \left[1 - \left| \frac{\sin[\pi(x_1-2)]\sin[\pi(x_2-2)]}{\pi^2(x_1-2)(x_2-2)} \right|^5 \right] \times \left[2 + (x_1-7)^2 + 2(x_2-7)^2 \right]$$

subject to $0 \le x_i \le 14$. The global minimum is located at $\mathbf{x}^* = (2,2)$, $f(\mathbf{x}^*) = 0$. The function has global minimum at $(2,2)$ with a very narrow basin of attraction and a very strong local minimum $(7,7)$ with a wide basin of attraction. The function has a value 2 at local minimum.

23. Deb 1 function (separable)

$$f_{23}(\mathbf{x}) = -\frac{1}{D} \sum_{i=1}^{D} \sin^6(5\pi x_i)$$

subject to $-1 \le x_i \le 1$. The function has 5^D evenly spaced local minima.

24. Deb 3 function (separable)

$$f_{24}(\mathbf{x}) = -\frac{1}{D} \sum_{i=1}^{D} \sin^6(5\pi(x_i^{3/4} - 0.05))$$

subject to $-1 \le x_i \le 1$. The function has 5^D unevenly spaced local minima.

25. Deckkers−Aart function (nonseparable)

$$f_{25}(\mathbf{x}) = 10^5 x_1^2 + x_2^2 - (x_1^2 + x_2^2) + 10^{-5}(x_1^2 + x_2^2)^4$$

subject to $-20 \le x_i \le 20$. The two global minima are located at $\mathbf{x}^* = (0, \pm 15)$, $f(\mathbf{x}^*) = -24777$.

26. Egg crate function (separable)

$$f_{26}(\mathbf{x}) = x_1^2 + x_2^2 + 25(\sin^2(x_1) + \sin^2(x_2))$$

subject to $-5 \le x_i \le 5$. The global minimum is located at $\mathbf{x}^* = (0,0), f(\mathbf{x}^*) = 0$.

27. Egg holder function (nonseparable)

$$f_{27}(\mathbf{x}) = \sum_{i=1}^{D-1} \left[-(x_i + 47)\sin\sqrt{\left| x_{i+1} + \frac{x_i}{2} + 47 \right|} - x_i \sin\sqrt{|x_i - (x_{i+1} + 47)|} \right]$$

subject to $-512 \le x_i \le 512$. The global minimum is located at $\mathbf{x}^* = (512, 404.2319)$, $f(\mathbf{x}^*) \approx 959.64$.

28. Exponential function (nonseparable)

$$f_{28}(\mathbf{x}) = - e^{\left(-0.5 \sum_{i=1}^{D} x_i^2 \right)}$$

subject to $-1 \le x_i \le 1$. The global minimum is located at $\mathbf{x}^* = (0, \ldots, 0), f(\mathbf{x}^*) = 0$.

29. Exp-2 function (nonseparable)

$$f_{29}(\mathbf{x}) = \sum_{i=0}^{9} (e^{-i(x_1/10)} - 5e^{-i(x_2/10)} - e^{-i(1/10)} - e^{-i})^2$$

subject to $0 \le x_i \le 20$. The global minimum is located at $\mathbf{x}^* = (1, 10), f(\mathbf{x}^*) = 0$.

30. Freudenstein Roth function (nonseparable)

$$f_{30}(\mathbf{x}) = (x_1 - 13 + ((5 - x_2)x_2 - 2)x_2)^2 + (x_1 - 29 + ((x_2 + 1)x_2 - 14)x_2)^2$$

subject to $-10 \le x_i \le 10$. The global minimum is located at $\mathbf{x}^* = (5,4), f(\mathbf{x}^*) = 0$.

31. Gear function (nonseparable)

$$f_{31}(\mathbf{x}) = \left[\frac{1}{6.931} - \lfloor x_1 \rfloor * \lfloor x_2 \rfloor / (\lfloor x_3 \rfloor * \lfloor x_4 \rfloor) \right]^2$$

subject to $12 \le x_1 \le 60$ and x_1, x_2, x_3, x_4 may be permuted. The global minimum is located at $\mathbf{x}^* = (16, 19, 43, 49), f(\mathbf{x}^*) \approx 2.7e - 12$.

32. Giunta function (separable)

$$f_{32}(\mathbf{x}) = 0.6 + \sum_{i=1}^{2} \left[\sin\left(\frac{16}{15}x_i - 1\right) + \sin^2\left(\frac{16}{15}x_i - 1\right) + \frac{1}{50}\sin\left(\frac{64}{15}x_i - 4\right) \right]$$

subject to $-1 \le x_1 \le 1$. The global minimum is located at $\mathbf{x}^* = (0.45834282,$ $0.45834283)$, $f(\mathbf{x}^*) = 0.060447$.

33. Goldstein−Price function (nonseparable)

$$f_{33}(\mathbf{x}) = [1 + (x_1 + x_2 + 1)^2(19 - 14x_1 + 3x_1^2 - 14x_2 + 6x_1x_2 + 3x_2^2)]$$
$$\times [30 + (2x_1 - 3x_2)^2(18 - 32x_1 + 12x_1^2 + 48x_2 - 36x_1x_2 + 27x_2^2)]$$

subject to $-2 \le x_1 \le 2$. The global minimum is located at $\mathbf{x}^* = (0, -1), f(\mathbf{x}^*) = 3$.

34. Griewank function (nonseparable)

$$f_{34}(\mathbf{x}) = \sum_{i=0}^{D} \frac{x_i^2}{4000} - \prod \cos\left(\frac{x_i}{\sqrt{i}}\right) + 1$$

subject to $-100 \le x_1 \le 100$. The global minimum is located at $\mathbf{x}^* = (0, \ldots, 0)$, $f(\mathbf{x}^*) = 0$.

35. Gulf research problem (nonseparable)

$$f_{35}(\mathbf{x}) = \sum_{i=0}^{99} [e^{-(u_i - x_2)^{x_3}/x_i} - 0.01i]^2$$

where $u_i = 25 + [-50 \ln(0.01i)]^{1/1.5}$, subject to $0.1 \le x_1 \le 100$, $0 \le x_2 \le 25.6$, and $0 \le x_3 \le 5$. The global minimum is located at $\mathbf{x}^* = (50, 25, 1.5), f(\mathbf{x}^*) = 0$.

36. Hansen function (separable)

$$f_{36}(\mathbf{x}) = \sum_{i=0}^{4}(i + 1)\cos(ix_1 + i + 1) \sum_{j=0}^{4}(j + 1)\cos((j + 2)x_2 + j + 1)$$

subject to $-10 \le x_1, x_2 \le 10$. The multiple global minima are located at

$$\mathbf{x}^* = \begin{pmatrix} \{-7.589893, -7.708314\}, \{-7.589893, -1.425128\}, \\ \{-7.589893, 4.858057\}, \{-1.306708, -7.708314\}, \\ \{-1.306708, 4.858057\}, \{4.976478, 4.858057\}, \\ \{4.976478, -1.425128\}, \{4.976478, -7.708314\}, \end{pmatrix}$$

$f(\mathbf{x}^*) = -176.541793$.

37. Hartman 3 function (nonseparable)

$$f_{37}(\mathbf{x}) = -\sum_{i=1}^{4} c_i \, e^{-\sum_{j=1}^{3} a_{ij}(x_j - p_{ij})^2}$$

subject to $0 \le x_j \le 1, j \in \{1, 2, 3\}$ with constants a_{ij}, p_{ij}, and c_j are given as

$$\mathbf{A} = [a_{ij}] = \begin{pmatrix} 3 & 10 & 30 \\ 0.1 & 10 & 35 \\ 3 & 10 & 30 \\ 0.1 & 10 & 35 \end{pmatrix}, \quad \underline{\mathbf{c}} = c_i = \begin{bmatrix} 1 \\ 1.2 \\ 3 \\ 3.2 \end{bmatrix},$$

$$\mathbf{P} = [p_{ij}] = \begin{pmatrix} 0.3689 & 0.1170 & 0.2673 \\ 0.4699 & 0.4837 & 0.7470 \\ 0.1091 & 0.8732 & 0.5547 \\ 0.03815 & 0.5743 & 0.8828 \end{pmatrix}$$

The global minimum is located at $\mathbf{x}^* = (0.1140, 0.556, 0.852), f(\mathbf{x}^*) \approx -3.862782$.

38. Hartman 6 function (nonseparable)

$$f_{38}(\mathbf{x}) = -\sum_{i=1}^{4} c_i \, e^{-\sum_{j=1}^{6} a_{ij}(x_j - p_{ij})^2}$$

subject to $0 \le x_j \le 1, j \in \{1, 2, 3, 4, 5, 6\}$ with constants a_{ij}, p_{ij}, and c_j are given as

$$\mathbf{A} = [a_{ij}] = \begin{pmatrix} 10 & 3 & 17 & 3.5 & 1.7 & 8 \\ 0.05 & 10 & 17 & 0.1 & 8 & 14 \\ 3 & 3.5 & 1.7 & 10 & 17 & 8 \\ 17 & 8 & 0.05 & 10 & 0.1 & 14 \end{pmatrix}, \quad \underline{\mathbf{c}} = c_i = \begin{bmatrix} 1 \\ 1.2 \\ 3 \\ 3.2 \end{bmatrix},$$

$$\mathbf{P} = [p_{ij}] = \begin{pmatrix} 0.1312 & 0.1696 & 0.5569 & 0.0124 & 0.8283 & 0.5586 \\ 0.2329 & 0.4135 & 0.8307 & 0.3736 & 0.1004 & 0.9991 \\ 0.2348 & 0.1451 & 0.3522 & 0.2883 & 0.3047 & 0.6650 \\ 0.4047 & 0.8828 & 0.8732 & 0.5743 & 0.1091 & 0.0381 \end{pmatrix}$$

The global minimum is located at $\mathbf{x}^* = (0.201690, 0.150011, 0.476874, 0.275332, 0.311652, 0.657301), f(\mathbf{x}^*) \approx -3.32236$.

39. Helical valley (nonseparable)

$$f_{39}(\mathbf{x}) = 100 \left[(x_2 - 10\theta)^2 + \left(\sqrt{x_1^2 + x_2^2} - 1 \right) \right] + x_3^2$$

where

$$\theta = \begin{cases} \dfrac{1}{2\pi} \tan^{-1}\left(\dfrac{x_1}{x_2} \right) & \text{if } x_1 \ge 0 \\[3mm] \dfrac{1}{2\pi} \tan^{-1}\left(\dfrac{x_1}{x_2} + 0.5 \right) & \text{if } x_1 \le 0 \end{cases}$$

subject to $-10 \le x_i \le 10$. The global minimum is located at $\mathbf{x}^* = (1, 0, 0), f(\mathbf{x}^*) = 0$.

40. Henrik–Madsen function (separable)

$$f_{40}(\mathbf{x}) = - \sum_{i=1}^{5} \sum_{j=1}^{5} j \sin((j+1)x_i + j)$$

subject to $-10 \le x_i \le 10$. The multiple global minima are located at

$$\mathbf{x}^* = \begin{pmatrix} \{-6.774576, -0.491391\}, \{6.774576, -6.774576\}, \\ \{-6.774576, 5.791794\}, \{-0.491391, -6.774576\}, \\ \{-0.491391, 5.791794\}, \{-0.491391, -0.491391\}, \\ \{5.791794, -6.774576\}, \{5.791794, 5.791794\}, \\ \{5.791794, -0.491391\} \end{pmatrix}$$

$$f(\mathbf{x}^*) = -24.062499$$

41. Himmelblau function (nonseparable)

$$f_{41}(\mathbf{x}) = (x_1^2 + x_2 - 11)^2 + (x_1 + x_2^2 - 7)^2$$

subject to $-5 \le x_i \le 5$. The global minimum is located at $\mathbf{x}^* = (3, 2), f(\mathbf{x}^*) = 0$.

42. Holder Table 1 function (separable)

$$f_{42}(\mathbf{x}) = - |\cos(x_1)\cos(x_2)e^{|1-[(x_1^2+x_2^2)^{0.5}]/\pi|}|$$

subject to $-10 \le x_i \le 10$. The multiple global minima are located at $\mathbf{x}^* = (\pm 9.646168, \pm 9.646168), f(\mathbf{x}^*) = -26.920336$.

43. Holder Table 2 function (separable)

$$f_{43}(\mathbf{x}) = - |\sin(x_1)\sin(x_2)e^{|1-[(x_1^2+x_2^2)^{0.5}]/\pi|}|$$

subject to $-10 \le x_i \le 10$. The multiple global minima are located at $\mathbf{x}^* = (\pm 8.055023472141116, \pm 9.664590028909654), f(\mathbf{x}^*) = -19.20850$.

44. Hosaki function (nonseparable)

$$f_{44}(\mathbf{x}) = \left(1 - 8x_1 + 7x_1^2 - \frac{7}{3}x_1^3 + \frac{1}{4}x_1^4 \right) x_2^2 \, e^{-x_2}$$

subject to $-10 \le x_i \le 10$. The global minimum is located at $\mathbf{x}^* = (4, 2), f(\mathbf{x}^*) \approx -2.3458$.

45. Holzman 2 function (separable)

$$f_{45}(\mathbf{x}) = \sum_{i=0}^{D-1} ix_i^4$$

subject to $-10 \le x_i \le 10$. The global minimum is located at $\mathbf{x}^* = (0, \ldots, 0), f(\mathbf{x}^*) = 0$.

46. Hyper-ellipsoid function

$$f_{46}(\mathbf{x}) = \sum_{i=1}^{D} b^{i-1} x_i^2$$

where b is the base. Commonly used base includes 2 and $10^{6(N-1)}$, subject to $-500 \leq x_1 \leq 500$. The global minimum is located at $\mathbf{x}^* = (0, \ldots, 0)$, $f(\mathbf{x}^*) = 0$.

47. Inverted cosine wave function (nonseparable)

$$f_{47}(\mathbf{x}) = e^{-x_i^2 + x_{i+1}^2 + 0.5 x_i x_{i+1}/8} \cdot \cos\left(4\sqrt{x_i^2 + x_{i+1}^2 + 0.5 x_i x_{i+1}}\right)$$

subject to $-10 \leq x_i \leq 10$. The global minimum is located at $\mathbf{x}^* = (0, \ldots, 0)$, $f(\mathbf{x}^*) = -D + 1$.

48. Jennrich−Sampson function (nonseparable)

$$f_{48}(\mathbf{x}) = \sum_{i=1}^{10} (2 + 2i - (e^{ix_1} + e^{ix_2}))^2$$

subject to $-1 \leq x_i \leq 1$. The global minimum is located at $\mathbf{x}^* = (0.257825, 0.257825)$, $f(\mathbf{x}^*) = 124.3612$.

49. Keane function (nonseparable)

$$f_{49}(\mathbf{x}) = \frac{\sin^2(x_1 - x_2)\sin^2(x_1 + x_2)}{\sqrt{x_1^2 + x_2^2}}$$

subject to $0 \leq x_i \leq 10$. The multiple global minima are located at $\mathbf{x}^* = \{(0, 1.39325), (1.39325, 0)\}$, $f(\mathbf{x}^*) = -0.673688$.

50. Kowalik function (nonseparable)

$$f_{50}(\mathbf{x}) = \sum_{i=1}^{11} \left(a_i - \frac{x_1(1 + x_2 b_i)}{1 + x_3 b_i + x_4 b_i^2}\right)^2$$

where

$a = [0.1957, 0.1947, 0.1735, 0.1600, 0.0844, 0.0627, 0.045, 0.0342, 0.0323, 0.0235, 0.0246]$,

$$b = \left[4, 2, 1, \frac{1}{2}, \frac{1}{4}, \frac{1}{6}, \frac{1}{8}, \frac{1}{10}, \frac{1}{12}, \frac{1}{14}, \frac{1}{16}\right]$$

subject to $-5 \leq x_i \leq 5$ The global minimum is located at $\mathbf{x}^* = (0.192, 0.190, 0.123, 0.135)$, $f(\mathbf{x}^*) \approx 3.0784e - 04$.

51. Langermann 5 function (nonseparable)

$$f_{51}(\mathbf{x}) = \sum_{i=0}^{m} c_i \, e^{-1/\pi \sum_{j=1}^{D} (x_j - A_{ij})^2} \cos\left(\pi \sum_{j=1}^{D} (x_j - A_{ij})^2 \right)$$

subject to $0 \le x_i \le 10$, where $j \in (0, D-1)$ and $m = 5$. It has a global minimum value of $f(\mathbf{x}^*) = -1.4$. The matrix $\mathbf{A}$ and column vector c are given as

$$\mathbf{A} = [a_{ij}] = \begin{bmatrix} 9.681 & 0.667 & 4.783 & 9.095 & 3.517 & 9.325 & 6.544 & 0.211 & 5.122 & 2.020 \\ 9.400 & 2.041 & 3.788 & 7.931 & 2.882 & 2.672 & 3.568 & 1.284 & 7.033 & 7.374 \\ 8.025 & 9.152 & 5.114 & 7.621 & 4.564 & 4.711 & 2.996 & 6.126 & 0.734 & 4.982 \\ 2.196 & 0.415 & 5.649 & 6.979 & 9.510 & 9.166 & 6.304 & 6.054 & 9.377 & 1.426 \\ 8.074 & 8.777 & 3.467 & 1.863 & 6.708 & 6.349 & 4.534 & 0.276 & 7.633 & 1.567 \end{bmatrix}$$

$$\underline{c} = c_i = \begin{bmatrix} 0.806 \\ 0.517 \\ 1.5 \\ 0.908 \\ 0.965 \end{bmatrix}$$

52. Leon function (nonseparable)

$$f_{52}(\mathbf{x}) = 100(x_2 - x_1^2)^2 + (1 - x_1)^2$$

subject to $-1.2 \le x_i \le 1.2$. A global minimum is located at $\mathbf{x}^* = (1, 1), f(\mathbf{x}^*) = 0$.

53. Levy 3 function (separable)

$$f_{53}(\mathbf{x}) = \sum_{i=1}^{5} i \cos((i-1)x_1 + i) \sum_{j=1}^{5} j \, \cos((j+1)x_2 + j)$$

subject to $-10 \le x_i \le 10$. The multiple global minima are located at

$$\mathbf{x}^* = \begin{pmatrix} \{-1.306708, \ -7.708314\}, \{-7.589893, 4.858057\}, \\ \{-1.306708, 4.858057\}, \{4.976478, 4.858057\}, \\ \{-1.306708, \ -1.425128\}, \{4.976478, \ -7.708314\}, \\ \{-7.589893, \ -7.708314\}, \{4.976478, \ -1.425128\}, \\ \{-7.589893, \ -1.425128\} \end{pmatrix}$$

$$f(\mathbf{x}^*) = -176.542$$

54. Levy 5 function (nonseparable)

$$f_{54}(\mathbf{x}) = f_{53}(\mathbf{x}) + (x_1 + 1.42513)^2 + (x_2 + 0.80032)^2$$

subject to $-10 \le x_i \le 10$. The global minimum is located at $\mathbf{x}^* = (-1.3068, -1.4248)$, $f(\mathbf{x}^*) = -176.1375$.

55. Levy 8 function (nonseparable)

$$f_{55}(\mathbf{x}) = \sin^2(\pi y_1) + \sum_{i=0}^{n-2} (y_i - 1)^2(1 + 10\sin^2(3\pi y_i + 1)) + (y_{n-1} - 1)^2(1 + \sin^2(2\pi x_{n-1}))$$

subject to $-10 \le x_i \le 10$. The global minimum is located at $\mathbf{x}^* = (1, \ldots, 1), f(\mathbf{x}^*) = 0$.

56. McCormick function (nonseparable)

$$f_{56}(\mathbf{x}) = \sin(x_1 + x_2) + (x_1 - x_2)^2 - \frac{3}{2}x_1 + \frac{5}{2}x_2 + 1$$

subject to $-1.5 \le x_1 \le 4$, $-3 \le x_2 \le 4$. The global minimum is located at $\mathbf{x}^* = (-0.547, -1.54719)$, $(\mathbf{x}^*) \approx -1.9133$.

57. Mexican hat function (nonseparable)

$$f_{57}(\mathbf{x}) = -20 \frac{\sin\left(0.1 + \sqrt{(x_1 - 4)^2 + (x_2 - 4)^2}\right)}{0.1 + \sqrt{(x_1 - 4)^2 + (x_2 - 4)^2}}$$

subject to $-10 \le x_i \le 10$. The global minimum is located at $\mathbf{x}^* = (4, 4)$, $f(\mathbf{x}^*) = -19.6683$.

58. Michaelewicz 2 function (separable)

$$f_{58}(\mathbf{x}) = -\sum_{i=1}^{D} \sin(x_i)\left(\sin\left(\frac{ix_i^2}{\pi}\right)\right)^{2m}$$

subject to $0 \le x_i \le \pi$, $m = 10$. The global minimum is located at $\mathbf{x}^* = (2.20319, 1.57049)$, $f(\mathbf{x}^*) = -1.8013$ for $n = 2$.

59. Michaelewicz 5 function (separable)

$$f_{59}(\mathbf{x}) = -\sum_{i=1}^{D} \sin(x_i)\left(\sin\left(\frac{ix_i^2}{\pi}\right)\right)^{2m}$$

subject to $0 \le x_i \le \pi$, $m = 10$. The global minimum is located at $\mathbf{x}^* = (2.693, 0.259, 2.074, 1.023, 1.720)$, $f(\mathbf{x}^*) = -4.687$, for $n = 5$.

60. Michaelewicz 10 function (separable)

$$f_{60}(\mathbf{x}) = -\sum_{i=1}^{D} \sin(x_i) \left(\sin\left(\frac{ix_i^2}{\pi}\right) \right)^{2m}$$

subject to $0 \le x_i \le \pi$, $m = 10$. The global minimum is located at $\mathbf{x}^* = (2.693, 0.259, 2.074, 1.023, 2.275, 0.500, 2.138, 0.794, 2.219, 0.533)$, $f(\mathbf{x}^*) = -9.66$ for $n = 10$.

61. Mishra 1 function (nonseparable)

$$f_{61}(\mathbf{x}) = \left| \cos\sqrt{|x_1^2 + x_2^2|} \right|^{0.5} + \frac{x_1 + x_2}{100}$$

subject to $-10 \le x_i \le 10$. The global minimum is located at $\mathbf{x}^* = (-8.4666, -9.9988)$, $f(\mathbf{x}^*) = -0.18466$.

62. Mishra 2 function (nonseparable)

$$f_{62}(\mathbf{x}) = \left| \sin\sqrt{|x_1^2 + x_2^2|} \right|^{0.5} + \frac{x_1 + x_2}{100}$$

subject to $-10 \le x_i \le 10$. The global minimum is located at $\mathbf{x}^* = (-9.94112, -9.99952)$, $f(\mathbf{x}^*) = -0.199441$.

63. Mishra 3 function (nonseparable)

$$f_{63}(\mathbf{x}) = -\ln[\{(\sin(t_1))^2 - (\cos(t_1))^2\} + x_1]^2 + 0.01(x_1 + x_2)$$

subject to $-10 \le x_i \le 10$, where $t_1 = (\cos(x_1) + \cos(x_2))^2 t_2 = (\sin(x_1) + \sin(x_2))^2$. The global minimum is located at $\mathbf{x}^* = (-1.98682, -10)$, $f(\mathbf{x}^*) = -1.01983$.

64. Mishra 4 function (nonseparable)

$$f_{64}(\mathbf{x}) = -\ln\left[\{(\sin(t_1))^2 - (\cos(t_1))^2\} + x_1 \right]^2 + \frac{[(x_1 - 1)^2 + (x_2 - 1)^2]}{10}$$

subject to $-10 \le x_i \le 10$, where $t_1 = (\cos(x_1) + \cos(x_2))^2$ and $t_2 = (\sin(x_1) + \sin(x_2))^2$. The global minimum is located at $\mathbf{x}^* = (2.8863, 1.82326)$, $f(\mathbf{x}^*) = -2.28395$.

65. Modified Ackley function (nonseparable)

$$f_{65}(\mathbf{x}) = \sum_{i=0}^{D} e^{-0.2} \sqrt{x_i^2 + x_{i+1}^2} + 3(\cos(2x_i) + \sin(2x_{i+1}))$$

subject to $-35 \le x_i \le 35$. It is a highly multimodal function with two global minima close to the origin at $\mathbf{x}^* = (\{-1.479252, -0.739807\}, \{1.479252, -0.739807\})$, $f(\mathbf{x}^*) = -3.917275$.

66. Modified Schaffer 1 function (nonseparable)

$$f_{66}(\mathbf{x}) = 0.5 + \frac{\sin^2(x_1^2 + x_2^2)^2 - 0.5}{1 + 0.001(x_1^2 + x_2^2)^2}$$

subject to $-100 \leq x_i \leq 100$. The global minimum is located at $\mathbf{x}^* = (0,0)$, $f(\mathbf{x}^*) = 0$.

67. Meyer−Roth function (nonseparable)

$$f_{67}(\mathbf{x}) = \sum_{i=1}^{5} \left(\frac{x_1 x_3 t_i}{1 + x_1 t_i + x_2 v_i} - y_i \right)^2$$

where

$$t_i = [1.0, 2.0, 1.0, 2.0, 0.1]$$
$$v_i = [1.0, 1.0, 2.0, 2.0, 0.0]$$
$$y_i = [0.126, 0.219, 0.076, 0.126, 0.186]$$

subject to $-20 \leq x_i \leq 20$. The global minimum is located at $\mathbf{x}^* = (3.13, 15.16, 0.78)$, $f(\mathbf{x}^*) \approx 0.4e4$.

68. Miele−Cantrell function (nonseparable)

$$f_{68}(\mathbf{x}) = (e^{-x_1} - x_2)^4 + 100(x_2 - x_3)^6 + (\tan(x_3 - x_4))^4 + x_1^8$$

subject to $-1 \leq x_i \leq 1$. The global minimum is located at $\mathbf{x}^* = (0, 1, 1, 1)$, $f(\mathbf{x}^*) = 0$.

69. Multi-Gaussian function (separable)

$$f_{69}(\mathbf{x}) = -\sum_{i=1}^{5} a_i\, e^{\left(\frac{-(x_1 - b_i)^2 + (x_2 - c_i)^2}{d_i^2} \right)}$$

subject to $-2 \leq x_i \leq 2$. The global minimum is located at $\mathbf{x}^* = (-0.01356, -0.01356)$, $f(\mathbf{x}^*) \approx -1.29695$ (Table 8.1).

Table 8.1 Data for Multi-Gaussian Problem (Ali et al., 2005)

i	a_i	b_i	c_i	d_i
1	0.5	0.0	0.0	0.1
2	1.2	1.0	0.0	0.5
3	1.0	0.0	−0.5	0.5
4	1.0	−0.5	0.0	0.5
5	1.2	0.0	1.0	0.5

70. Normalized Rana function (nonseparable)

$$f_{70}(\mathbf{x}) = \sum_{i=1}^{D} x_i \sin(t_1)\cos(t_2) + (x_j + 1)\cos(t_1)\sin(t_2)$$

subject to $-520 \le x_i \le 520$, where $i = 1,\ldots,D$, $j = (i + 1) \mod D$, $t_1 = \sqrt{|x_{i+1} + x_i + 1|}$, $t_1 = \sqrt{|x_{i+1} - x_i + 1|}$. The global minimum is located near the border of the function landscape $f(\mathbf{x}^*) = -514.041683$.

71. Parsopoulos function (separable)

$$f_{71}(\mathbf{x}) = \cos(x_1)^2 + \sin(x_1)^2$$

subject to $-5 \le x_i \le 5$, where $(x_1, x_2) \in \mathbb{R}^2$. This function has an infinite number of global minima in $\mathbb{R}^2$ at points $(k(\pi/2), \lambda\pi)$, where $k = \pm 1, \pm 3, \ldots$ and $\lambda = 0, \pm 1, \pm 2, \ldots$. For a domain size $-5 \le x_i \le 5$ and $-7 \le x_i \le 7$, the function has 12 and 20 global minima, respectively.

72. Pathological function (nonseparable)

$$f_{72}(\mathbf{x}) = \sum_{i=0}^{D} \left(0.5 + \frac{\sin^2\sqrt{100x_i^2 + x_{i+1}^2} - 0.5}{1 + 0.001(x_i^2 - 2x_i x_{i+1} + x_{i+1}^2)^2} \right)$$

subject to $-100 \le x_i \le 100$. The global minimum is located at $\mathbf{x}^* = (0,\ldots,0)$, $f(\mathbf{x}^*) = 0$.

73. Paviani function (nonseparable)

$$f_{73}(\mathbf{x}) = \sum_{i=0}^{10} [(\ln(x_i - 2))^2 + (\ln(10 - x_i))^2] - \left(\prod_{i=1}^{10} x_i \right)^{0.2}$$

subject to $-2.0001 \le x_i \le 9.9999$. The global minimum is located at $\mathbf{x}^* = (9.351,\ldots,9.351)$, $f(\mathbf{x}^*) \approx -45.778$.

74. Pen holder function (nonseparable)

$$f_{74}(\mathbf{x}) = -\exp\left[-\left| \cos(x_1)\cos(x_2)e^{|1 - (x_1^2 + x_2^2)^{0.5}/\pi|} \right|^{-1} \right]$$

subject to $-11 \le x_i \le 11$. The four global minima are located at $\mathbf{x}^* = (\pm 9.646168, \pm 9.646168)$, $f(\mathbf{x}^*) = -0.96354$.

75. Periodic function (separable)

$$f_{75}(\mathbf{x}) = 1 + \sin^2(x_1) + \sin^2(x_2) - 0.1\, e^{-(x_1^2 + x_2^2)}$$

subject to $-10 \le x_i \le 10$. The global minimum is located at $\mathbf{x}^* = (0,0)$, $f(\mathbf{x}^*) = 0.9$.

76. Perm function (separable)

$$f_{76}(\mathbf{x}) = \sum_{k=1}^{D} \left[\sum_{i=1}^{D} (i^k + \beta)\left(\left(\frac{x_i}{i}\right)^k - 1 \right) \right]^2$$

subject to $-D \leq x_i \leq D$. The global minimum is located at $\mathbf{x}^* = (1, 2, 3, \ldots, D)$, $f(\mathbf{x}^*) = 0$.

77. Pintér function (nonseparable)

$$f_{77}(\mathbf{x}) = \sum_{i=1}^{D} ix_i^2 + \sum_{i=1}^{D} 20.i.\sin^2 A + \sum_{i=1}^{D} i.\log_{10}(1 + i.B^2)$$

where

$$A \quad = x_{i-1}\sin(x_i) + \sin(x_{i+1})$$
$$B \quad = x_{i-1}^2 - 2x_i + 3x_{i+1} - \cos(x_i) + 1$$

and $x_0 = x_D$ and $x_1 = x_{D+1}$, subject to $-10 \leq x_i \leq 10$. The global minimum is located at $\mathbf{x}^* = (0, 0, \ldots, 0), f(\mathbf{x}^*) = 0$.

78. Price 4 function (nonseparable)

$$f_{78}(\mathbf{x}) = (2x_1^3 x_2 - x_2^3)^2 + (6x_1 - x_2^2 + x_2)^2$$

subject to $-10 \leq x_i \leq 10$. The three global minima are located at $\mathbf{x}^* = (\{0, 0\}, \{2, 4\}, \{1.464, -2.506\}), f(\mathbf{x}^*) = 0$.

79. Quadratic function (separable)

$$f_{79}(\mathbf{x}) = -3803.84 - 138.08x_1 - 232.92x_2 + 128.08x_1^2 + 203.64x_2^2 + 182.25x_1x_2$$

subject to $-10 \leq x_i \leq 10$. The global minimum is located at $\mathbf{x}^* = (0.19388, 0.48513)$, $f(\mathbf{x}^*) = -3873.7243$.

80. Quintic function (separable)

$$f_{80}(\mathbf{x}) = \sum_{i=0}^{D} |x_i^5 - 3x_i^4 + 4x_i^3 + 2x_i^2 - 10x_i - 4|$$

subject to $-10 \leq x_i \leq 10$. The global minimum is located at $\mathbf{x}^* = (-1 \text{ or } 2), f(\mathbf{x}^*) = 0$.

81. Ripple 1 function (separable)

$$f_{81}(\mathbf{x}) = \sum_{i=1}^{2} -e^{-2\ln 2\left((x_i - 0.1)/0.8\right)^2} (\sin^6(5\pi x_i) + 0.1 \cos^2(500\pi x_i))$$

subject to $0 \leq x_i \leq 1$. It has 1 global minimum and 252004 local minima. The global form of the function consists of 25 holes, which forms a 5×5 regular grid. Additionally, the whole function landscape is full of small ripples caused by high-frequency cosine function which creates a large number of local minima.

82. Ripple 2 function (separable)

$$f_{82}(\mathbf{x}) = \sum_{i=1}^{2} -e^{-2 \ln 2((x_i - 0.1)/0.8)^2} (\sin^6(5\pi x_i))$$

subject to $0 \leq x_i \leq 1$. Due to the absence of the cosine term, it has no ripples and has one global minimum. The global form of the function is the same as the Ripple 1 function.

83. Root function (nonseparable)

$$f_{83}(\mathbf{x}) = \frac{-1}{1 + |z^6 - 1|}$$

subject to $-1 \le x_i \le 1$, where $z \in \mathbb{C}$, $z = x + jy$. The function has six global minima:

$$\mathbf{x}^* = \begin{pmatrix} \{1,0\}, \{-1,0\}, \\ \{0.5, 0.866025\}, \{0.5, -0.866025\}, \\ \{-0.5, 0.866025\}, \{-0.5, -0.866025\} \end{pmatrix}, f(\mathbf{x}^*) = -1$$

84. Salomon function (nonseparable)

$$f_{84}(\mathbf{x}) = 1 - \cos(2\pi||x||) + 0.1||x||$$

subject to $-100 \le x_i \le 100$, where $||x|| = \sqrt{\sum_{i=1}^{D} x_i^2}$.

85. Schaffer 2 function (nonseparable)

$$f_{85}(\mathbf{x}) = (x_1^2 + x_2^2)^{0.25}[\sin^2(x_1^2 + x_2^2)^{0.1} + 1]$$

subject to $-100 \le x_i \le 100$. The global minimum is located at $\mathbf{x}^* = (0,0), f(\mathbf{x}^*) = 0$.

86. Schwefel function (nonseparable)

$$f_{86}(\mathbf{x}) = 418.9829D - \sum_{i=1}^{D} x_i \sin\left(\sqrt{|x_i|}\right)$$

subject to $-500 \le x_i \le 500$. The global minimum is located at $\mathbf{x}^* = (1, \ldots, 1), f(\mathbf{x}^*) = 0$.

87. Shekel 5 function (nonseparable)

$$f_{87}(\mathbf{x}) = \sum_{i=1}^{5} \frac{1}{\sum_{j=1}^{4} (x_j - a_{ij})^2 + c_i}$$

subject to $0 \le x_j \le 10$, with constants a_{ij} and c_i given in Table 8.2. The global minimum is located at $\mathbf{x}^* = (4, 4, 4, 4), f(\mathbf{x}^*) \approx -10.1499$.

88. Shekel 7 function (nonseparable)

$$f_{88}(\mathbf{x}) = \sum_{i=1}^{7} \frac{1}{\sum_{j=1}^{4} (x_j - a_{ij})^2 + c_i}$$

subject to $0 \le x_j \le 10$, with constants a_{ij} and c_i given in Table 8.2. The global minimum is located at $\mathbf{x}^* = (4, 4, 4, 4), f(\mathbf{x}^*) \approx -10.3999$.

89. Shekel 10 function (nonseparable)

$$f_{89}(\mathbf{x}) = \sum_{i=1}^{10} \frac{1}{\sum_{j=1}^{4} (x_j - a_{ij})^2 + c_i}$$

Table 8.2 Data for Shekel 5, 7, and 10 Problem (Ali et al., 2005)

i		a_{ij}			c_i
	$j = 1$	2	3	4	
S5	1	4	4	4	4	0.1
	2	1	1	1	1	0.2
	3	8	8	8	8	0.2
	4	6	6	6	6	0.4
	5	3	7	3	7	0.4
S7	6	2	9	2	9	0.6
	7	5	5	3	3	0.3
S10	8	8	1	8	1	0.7
	9	6	2	6	2	0.5
	10	7	3.6	7	3.6	0.5

subject to $0 \leq x_j \leq 10$, with constants a_{ij} and c_i given in Table 8.2. The global minimum is located at $\mathbf{x}^* = (4, 4, 4, 4), f(\mathbf{x}^*) \approx -10.5319$.

90. Shubert function (separable)

$$f_{90}(\mathbf{x}) = \prod_{i=1}^{D} \left(\sum_{j=1}^{5} \cos[(j+1)x_j + j] \right)$$

subject to $-10 \leq x_i \leq 10$. The 18 global minima are located at

$$\mathbf{x}^* = \begin{pmatrix} \{-7.0835, 4.8580\}, \ \{-7.0835, -7.7083\}, \\ \{-1.4251, -7.0835\}, \ \{5.4828, 4.8580\}, \\ \{-1.4251, -0.8003\}, \ \{4.8580, 5.4828\}, \\ \{-7.7083, -7.0835\}, \ \{-7.0835, -1.4251\}, \\ \{-7.7083, -0.8003\}, \ \{-7.7083, 5.4828\}, \\ \{-0.8003, -7.7083\}, \ \{-0.8003, -1.4251\}, \\ \{-0.8003, 4.8580\}, \ \{-1.4251, 5.4828\}, \\ \{5.4828, -7.7083\}, \ \{4.8580, -7.0835\}, \\ \{5.4828, -1.4251\}, \ \{.8580, -0.8003\}, \end{pmatrix}$$

$f(\mathbf{x}^*) \approx -186.7309$.

91. Six Hump Camel function (nonseparable)

$$f_{91}(\mathbf{x}) = \left(4 - 2.1x_1^2 + \frac{x_1^4}{3} \right) x_1^2 + x_1 x_2 + (4x_2^3 - 4)x_2^2$$

subject to $-5 \leq x_i \leq 5$. The two global minima are located at $\mathbf{x}^* = \{(-0.0898, 0.7126), \ (0.0898, -0.7126)\}, f(\mathbf{x}^*) = -1.0316$.

92. Styblinski–Tang function (separable)

$$f_{92}(\mathbf{x}) = \frac{1}{2}\sum_{i=1}^{D}(x_i^4 - 16x_i^2 + 5x_i)$$

subject to $-5 \leq x_i \leq 5$. The global minimum is located at $\mathbf{x}^* = \{(-2.903534, -2.903534)\}, f(\mathbf{x}^*) = -78.332$.

93. Testtube holder function (separable)

$$f_{93}(\mathbf{x}) = -4\left[\sin(x_1)\cos(x_2)e^{|(\cos(x_1^2+x_2^2))/200|}\right]$$

subject to $-10 \leq x_i \leq 10$. The two global minima are located at $\mathbf{x}^* = \left\{\left(\pm\frac{\pi}{2}, 0\right)\right\}, f(\mathbf{x}^*) = -10.872300$.

94. Three Hump Camel function (nonseparable)

$$f_{94}(\mathbf{x}) = 2x_1^2 - 1.05x_1^4 + \frac{x_1^6}{6} + x_1 x_2 + x_2^2$$

subject to $-5 \leq x_i \leq 5$. The global minimum is located at $\mathbf{x}^* = (0,0), f(\mathbf{x}^*) = 0$.

95. Trecanni function (separable)

$$f_{95}(\mathbf{x}) = x_1^4 - 4x_1^3 + 4x_1 + x_2^2$$

subject to $-5 \leq x_i \leq 5$. The global minimum is located at $\mathbf{x}^* = \{(0,0), (-2,0)\}, f(\mathbf{x}^*) = 0$.

96. Trefethen function (nonseparable)

$$f_{96}(\mathbf{x}) = e^{\sin(50x_1)} + \sin(60\,e^{x_2}) + \sin(70\,\sin(x_1)) + \sin(\sin(80x_2)) - \sin(10(x_1 + x_2)) + \frac{1}{4}(x_1^2 + x_2^2)$$

subject to $-10 \leq x_i \leq 10$. The global minimum is located at $\mathbf{x}^* = \{(-0.024403, 0.210612)\}, f(\mathbf{x}^*) = -3.30686865$.

97. Trigonometric function (nonseparable)

$$f_{97}(\mathbf{x}) = \sum_{i=0}^{D}\left[D - \sum_{j=1}^{D}\cos(x_j) + i(1 - \cos(x_i) - \sin(x_i))\right]^2$$

subject to $0 \leq x_i \leq \pi$. The global minimum is located at $\mathbf{x}^* = (0, \ldots, 0), f(\mathbf{x}^*) = 0$.

98. Tripod function (nonseparable)

$$f_{98}(\mathbf{x}) = p(x_2)[1 + p(x_1)] + |x_1 + 50p(x_2)[1 - 2p(x_1)]| + |x_2 + 50[1 - 2p(x_2)]|$$

subject to $-100 \leq x_i \leq 100$, where $p(x) = 1$ for $x \geq 0$. The global minimum is located at $\mathbf{x}^* = (0, -50), f(\mathbf{x}^*) = 0$.

99. Ursem 1 function (separable)

$$f_{99}(\mathbf{x}) = -\sin(2x_1 - 0.5\pi) - 3\cos(x_2) - 0.5x_1$$

subject to $-2.5 \leq x_1 \leq 3$ and $-2 \leq x_2 \leq 2$, has a single local and global minimum.

100. Ursem 3 function (nonseparable)

$$f_{100}(\mathbf{x}) = -\sin(2.2\pi x_1 + 0.5\pi).\frac{2 - |x_1|}{2}.\frac{3 - |x_1|}{2}$$

$$-\sin(0.5\pi x_2^2 + 0.5\pi).\frac{2 - |x_2|}{2}.\frac{3 - |x_2|}{2}$$

subject to $-2 \leq x_1 \leq 2$ and $-1.5 \leq x_2 \leq 1.5$. It has a single global minimum and four regularly spaced local minima positioned in a direct line, such that the global minimum is in the middle.

101. Ursem 4 function (nonseparable)

$$f_{101}(\mathbf{x}) = -3\sin(0.5\pi x_1 + 0.5\pi)\frac{2 - \sqrt{x_1^2 + x_2^2}}{4}$$

subject to $-2 \leq x_1 \leq 2$ and $-1.5 \leq x_2 \leq 1.5$. It has a single global minimum positioned in the middle of the search space and four local minima at the corners of the search space.

102. Ursem wave functions (nonseparable)

$$f_{102}(\mathbf{x}) = -0.9x_1^2 + (x_2^2 - 4.5x_2^2)x_1x_2 + 4.7\cos(3x_1 - x_2^2(2 + x_1))\sin(2.5\pi x_1)$$

subject to $-0.9 \leq x_1 \leq 1.2$ and $-1.2 \leq x_2 \leq 1.2$, has a single global minimum and nine irregularly spaced local minima in the search space.

103. Venter Sobiezcczanski function (separable)

$$f_{103}(\mathbf{x}) = x_1^2 - 100\cos(x_1)^2 - 100\cos\left(\frac{x_1^2}{30}\right) + x_2^2 - 100\cos(x_2)^2 - 100\cos\left(\frac{x_2^2}{30}\right)$$

subject to $-50 \leq x_i \leq 50$. The global minimum is located at $\mathbf{x}^* = (0, 0), f(\mathbf{x}^*) = 0$.

104. The W function (separable)

$$f_{104}(\mathbf{x}) = \frac{1}{D}\sum_{i=1}^{D} -\cos(kx_i)e^{-x_i^2/2}$$

subject to $-\pi \leq x_i \leq \pi$. The global minimum is located at $\mathbf{x}^* = (0, 0), f(\mathbf{x}^*) = 0$. The number of local minima is located at kn and $(k + 1)n$ for odd and even k, respectively. For $D = 2$ and $k = 10$, there are 121 local minima.

105. Watson function (nonseparable)

$$f_{105}(\mathbf{x}) = \sum_{i=0}^{29} \left\{ \sum_{j=0}^{4} [(j-1)a_i^j x_{j+1}] - \left[\sum_{j=0}^{5} a_i^j x_{j+1} \right]^2 - 1 \right\}^2 + x_1^2$$

subject to $|x_i| \leq 10$, where the coefficient $a_i = i/29$. The global minimum is located at $\mathbf{x}^* = (-0.0158, 1.012, -0.2329, 1.260, -1.513, 0.9928), f(\mathbf{x}^*) = 0.002288$.

106. Wavy 1 function (nonseparable)

$$f_{106}(\mathbf{x}) = \sum_{i=1}^{D} |2(x_i - 24) + (x_i - 24)\sin(x_i - 24)|$$

subject to $-100 \leq x_i \leq 100$. The global minimum is located at $\mathbf{x}^* = (24, \ldots, 24)$, $f(\mathbf{x}^*) = 0$.

107. Weierstrass function (separable)

$$f_{107}(\mathbf{x}) = \sum_{i=1}^{D} \left[\sum_{k=0}^{kmax} a^k \cos(2\pi b^k(x_i + 0.5)) - Da^k \cos(\pi b^k) \right]$$

subject to $-0.5 \leq x_i \leq 0.5$. The global minimum is located at $\mathbf{x}^* = (0, \ldots, 0), f(\mathbf{x}^*) = 0$.

108. Whitley function (nonseparable)

$$f_{108}(\mathbf{x}) = \sum_{i=1}^{D} \sum_{j=1}^{D} \left[\frac{(100(x_i^2 - x_j)^2 + (1 - x_j)^2)^2}{4000} - \cos(100(x_i^2 - x_j)^2 + (1 - x_j)^2) \right]$$

The global minimum is surrounded by highly multimodal area. The value of global minimum is $f(\mathbf{x}^*) = 1$.

109. Wolfe function (separable)

$$f_{109}(\mathbf{x}) = \frac{4}{3}(x_1^2 + x_2^2 - x_1 x_2)^{0.75} + x_3$$

subject to $-0 \leq x_i \leq 2$. The global minimum is located at $x^* = (0, \ldots, 0), f(\mathbf{x}^*) = 0$.

110. Yang 1 function (nonseparable)

$$f_{110}(\mathbf{x}) = \frac{\sin(x_1^2 + x_2^2)}{\sqrt{x_1^2 + x_2^2}} e^{-\lambda(x_1 - x_2)^2}$$

subject to $-5 \leq x_i \leq 5$, where $\lambda > 0$. The two global minima are located at $\mathbf{x}^* = \{(0.7634, 0.7634), (-0.7634, -0.7634)\}, f(\mathbf{x}^*) = -0.851$.

111. Yang 2 function (separable)

$$f_{111}(\mathbf{x}) = \sum_{i=0}^{D} \epsilon_i |x_i|^i$$

subject to $-5 \leq x_i \leq 5$. The variable ϵ_i $(i = 1, 2, \ldots, D)$ is a random variable uniformly distributed in the interval $[0, 1]$. The global minimum is located at $\mathbf{x}^* = (0, \ldots, 0)$, $f(\mathbf{x}^*) = 0$.

112. Yang 3 function (nonseparable)

$$f_{112}(\mathbf{x}) = \left(\sum_{i=1}^{D} |x_i| \right) e^{-\sum_{i=1}^{D} \sin(x_i^2)}$$

subject to $-2\pi \leq x_i \leq 2\pi$. The global minimum is located at $\mathbf{x}^* = (0, \ldots, 0)$, $f(\mathbf{x}^*) = 0$.

113. Yang 4 function (nonseparable)

$$f_{113}(\mathbf{x}) = \left[e^{-\sum_{i=1}^{D} (x_i/\beta)^{2m}} - 2 e^{-\sum_{i=1}^{D} (x_i)^2} \prod_{i=1}^{D} \cos^2(x_i) \right]$$

subject to $-20 \leq x_i \leq 20$. The global minimum for $m = 5$ and $\beta = 15$ is located at $\mathbf{x}^* = (0, \ldots, 0)$, $f(\mathbf{x}^*) = -1$.

114. Yang 5 function (nonseparable)

$$f_{114}(\mathbf{x}) = \left[e^{-\sum_{i=1}^{D} (x_i/\beta)^{2m}} - 2 e^{-\sum_{i=1}^{D} (x_i-\pi)^2} \prod_{i=1}^{D} \cos^2(x_i) \right]$$

subject to $-20 \leq x_i \leq 20$. The global minimum for $m = 5$ and $\beta = 15$ is located at $\mathbf{x}^* = (\pi, \ldots, \pi)$, $f(\mathbf{x}^*) = -1$.

115. Yang 6 function (nonseparable)

$$f_{115}(\mathbf{x}) = \left[\sum_{i=1}^{D} \sin^2(x_i) - e^{-\sum_{i=1}^{D} x_i^2} \right] e^{\sum_{i=1}^{D} \sin^2 \sqrt{|x_i|}}$$

subject to $-10 \leq x_i \leq 10$. The global minimum for $m = 5$ and $\beta = 15$ is located at $\mathbf{x}^* = (0, \ldots, 0)$, $f(\mathbf{x}^*) = -1$.

116. Zettl function (nonseparable)

$$f_{116}(\mathbf{x}) = (x_1^2 + x_2^2 - 2x_1)^2 + 0.25x_1$$

subject to $-5 \leq x_i \leq 10$. The global minimum is located at $\mathbf{x}^* = (-0.0299, 0)$, $f(\mathbf{x}^*) = -0.003791$.

8.3 Conclusions

A common practice in EC is to test and compare different algorithms on a large set of test functions that offer a diverse set of properties, such as unimodal, multimodal, separable, nonseparable, and multidimensional. Finding such test functions in different textbooks, in individual research articles, or in different web sites is not only a cumbersome but also a time-consuming task. Therefore, we have compiled an extensive list of test functions for GO problems with initial range, formulation, characteristics, dimensions, and *a priori* global minimum or minima. This collection is large enough to cover a set of test functions with a diverse set of properties. Most of these problems are scalable and are easily extendable to higher dimensions.

References

Ali, M.M., Khompatraporn, C., Zabinsky, Z.B., 2005. A numerical evaluation of several stochastic algorithms on selected continuous global optimization test problems. J. Global Optim. 31, 635−672.

Andrei, N., 2008. An unconstrained optimization test functions collection. Adv. Model. Optim. 10 (1), 147−161.

Averick, B.M., Carter, R.G., Moré, J.J., Xue, G.L., 1992. The MINIPACK-2 Test Problem Collection. Mathematics and Computer Science Division, Argonne National Laboratory, IL, USA (Preprint MCS-P153-0692).

Boyer, D.O., Martfnez, C.H., Pedrajas, N.G., 2005. Crossover operator for evolutionary algorithms based on population features. J. Artif. Intell. Res. 24, 1−48.

Flouda, C.A., Pardalos, P.M., Adjiman, C.S., Esposito, W.R., Gümüs, Z.H., Harding, S.T., et al., 1999. Handbook of Test Problems in Local and Global Optimization. Kluwer, Boston, MA.

GAMS WorldGLOBAL Library, 2000. Available online: <http://www.gamsworld.org/global/globallib.html/> (accessed 01.09.2012).

Gordon, V.S., Whitley, D., 1993. Serial and parallel genetic algoritms as function optimizers. In: Forrest, S. (Ed.), Proceedings of the Fifth International Conference on Genetic Algorithms. Morgan Kaufmann, Urbana-Champaign, IL, pp. 177−183.

Gould, N.I.M., Orban, D., Toint, P.L., 2001CUTEr, A Constrained and Un-constrained Testing Environment, Revisited. Available Online: <http://cuter.rl.ac.uk/cuter-www/problems.html/>.

Hedar, A.-R., Global Optimization Test Problems. Available Online: <http://www-optima.amp.i.kyoto-u.ac.jp/member/student/hedar/Hedar_files/TestGO.htm/>.

Mishra, S.K., 2006a. Performance of Differential Evolution and Particle Swarm Methods on Some Relatively Harder Multi-modal Benchmark Functions. Available online: <http://mpra.ub.uni-muenchen.de/1743/>.

Mishra, S.K., 2006b. Performance of the Barter, the Differential Evolution and the Simulated Annealing Methods of Global Optimization on Some New and Some Old Test Functions. Available Online: <http://www.ssrn.com/abstract = 941630/>

Mishra, S.K., 2006c. Repulsive Particle Swarm Method on Some Difficult Test Problems of Global Optimization. Available Online: <http://mpra.ub.uni-muenchen.de/1742/>.

Mishra, S.K., 2006d. Performance of Repulsive Particle Swarm Method in Global Optimization of Some Important Test Functions: A Fortran Program. Available Online: <http://www.ssrn.com/abstract = 924339/>.

Mishra, S.K., 2006e. Global Optimization by Particle Swarm Method: A Fortran Program. Munich Research Papers in Economics. Available Online: <http://mpra.ub.uni-muenchen.de/874/>.

Mishra, S.K., 2006f. Global Optimization by Differential Evolution and Particle Swarm Methods: Evaluation on Some Benchmark Functions. Munich Research Papers in Economics. Available Online: <http://mpra.ub.uni-muenchen.de/1005/>.

Mishra, S.K., 2006g. Some New Test Functions for Global Optimization and Performance of Repulsive Particle Swarm Method. Available Online: <http://mpra.ub.uni-muenchen.-de/2718/>.

Neumaier, A., 2003a. COCONUT Benchmark. Available Online: <http://www.mat.univie. ac.at/ ~ neum/glopt/coconut/benchmark.html/>.

Suganthan, P. N., Hansen, N., Liang, J. J., Deb, K., Chen, Y.-P., Auger, A., et al., 2005. Problem Definitions and Evaluation Criteria for CEC 2005, Special Session on Real-Parameter Optimization. Nanyang Technological University (NTU), Singapore, Technical Report, Available Online: <http://www.lri.fr/ ~ hansen/Tech-Report-May-30-05.pdf/>.

Tang, K., Yao, X., Suganthan, P. N., MacNish, C., Chen, Y.-P., Chen, C.-M., et al., 2008. Benchmark Functions for the CEC'2008 Special Session and Competition on Large Scale Global Optimization, Technical Report, Available Online: <http://nical.ustc.edu. cn/cec08ss.php/>.

Tang, K., Li, X., Suganthan, P.N., Yang, Z., Weise, T., 2010. Benchmark Functions for the CEC'2010 Special Session and Competition on Large-Scale Global Optimization, Technical Report, Available Online: <http://sci2s.ugr.es/eamhco/cec2010_functions. pdf/>.

Whitley, D., Mathias, K., Rana, S., Dzubera, J., 1996. Evaluating evolutionary algorithms. Artif. Intell. 85, 245−276.

Yang, X-S., 2010a. Test Problems in Optimization, Engineering Optimization: An Introduction with Metaheuristic Applications. John Wiley & Sons, Hoboken, NJ. Available Online: <http://arxiv.org/abs/1008.0549/>.

Yang, X-S., 2010b. Firefly algorithm, stochastic test functions and design optimisation. Int. J. Bio-Inspired Comput. 2 (2), 78−84. Available Online: <http://arxiv.org/abs/ 1008.0549/>.

Part Two

Applications and Case Studies

9 Binary Bat Algorithm for Feature Selection

Rodrigo Yuji Mizobe Nakamura[1], Luís Augusto
Martins Pereira[1], Douglas Rodrigues[1], Kelton Augusto
Pontara Costa[1], João Paulo Papa[1] and Xin-She Yang[2]

[1]Department of Computing, São Paulo State University, Bauru, Brazil;
[2]Department of Design Engineering and Mathematics, School of Science and
Technology, Middlesex University, The Burroughs, London, UK

9.1 Introduction

Feature selection attempts to find the most discriminative information aiming to design an accurate learning system. It is often desirable to find features that are simple to extract, invariant to geometric and affine transformations, insensitive to noise, and useful for characterizing patterns in different categories (Duda et al., 2007). The choice of such features is a critical step and strongly depends on the nature of the problem.

Because an exhaustive search to find the optimal set of features in a high-dimensional space may be impractical, the feature selection can be formulated as a combinatorial optimization problem. Thus, a subset of features that leads to the best feature space separability is then employed to map the original dataset to a new one. The objective function can be the accuracy of a given classifier or a different criterion that may consider the best trade-off between the feature extraction computational cost and the effectiveness for pattern discrimination.

Several metaheuristic algorithms derived from the behavior of biological and/or physical systems in the nature have been proposed as powerful methods for global optimizations. Firpi and Goodman (2004) introduced a binary version of the well-known particle swarm optimization in the context of feature selection, and Rashedi et al. (2010) investigated the problem of the curse of dimensionality by means of a binary version of the gravitational search algorithm. Further, Ramos et al. (2011) presented their version of the harmony search for theft detection in power distribution systems. Additionally, several works have addressed the same problem with a wide range of nature-inspired techniques, such as ant colony optimization, genetic

Swarm Intelligence and Bio-Inspired Computation. DOI: http://dx.doi.org/10.1016/B978-0-12-405163-8.00009-0

algorithms, and firefly algorithm (Banati and Bajaj, 2011; Huang et al., 2007; Kanan et al., 2007).

More recently, Yang (2011) proposed a new metaheuristic method for continuous optimization, namely, bat algorithm, which is based on the fascinating capability of microbats to detect their prey, avoid obstacles, and locate their roosting crevices even in complete darkness.

In this work, we present a binary version of the bat algorithm for feature selection purposes, in which the search space is modeled as an n-cube, where n stands for the number of features. In such cases, the optimal (near-optimal) solution is chosen among the 2^n possibilities, and it corresponds to one corner of the hypercube.

The main idea is to associate for each bat a set of binary coordinates that denote whether a feature will belong to the final set of features. The function to be maximized is a classifier's accuracy. More specifically, we need to evaluate each microbat by training a classifier with the selected features encoded by the bat's position and classifying an evaluating set. As the quality of the solution is related with the number of microbats, we need a fast and robust classifier. Therefore, we proposed to use the optimum-path forest classifier (Papa et al., 2009) as the learning algorithm, which has been demonstrated to be efficient for training and effective for classification in several applications.

9.2 Bat Algorithm

Bats are fascinating animals and their advanced capability of echolocation has attracted the attention of researchers from different fields. Echolocation works as a type of sonar, i.e., microbats emit a loud and short pulse of sound, wait until it hits into an object and, after a fraction of time, the echo returns back to their ears (Griffin et al., 1960). According to Metzner (1991), microbats can compute how far they are from an object by variations of the Doppler effect induced by the wing flutter rates of the target insects. In addition, this amazing orientation mechanism makes bats to be able to distinguish the difference between an obstacle and a prey, allowing them to hunt even in complete darkness (Schnitzler and Kalko, 2001).

Yang (2011) developed an interesting optimization technique by means of metaheuristics, known as the bat algorithm, inspired by the behavior of microbats. This technique has been developed to behave as a swarm of microbats tracking prey/foods using their capability of echolocation. In order to model this algorithm, Yang (2011) idealized some rules as follows:

- All bats use echolocation to sense distance, and they also *know* the difference between food/prey and background barriers in some magical way.
- A bat b_i flies randomly with velocity v_i at position x_i with a fixed frequency f_{min}, varying wavelength λ, and loudness A_0 to search for prey. They can automatically adjust the

wavelength (or frequency) of their emitted pulses and adjust the rate of pulse emission r, depending on the proximity of their target.
- Although the loudness can vary in many ways, Yang (2011) assumes that the loudness varies from a large (positive) A_0 to a minimum constant value A_{min}.

Algorithm 9.1 presents the bat algorithm. First, the initial position x_i, velocity v_i, and frequency f_i are initialized for each bat b_i. For each time step t, T being the maximum number of iterations, the movement of the virtual bats is given by updating their velocity and position using the following equations:

$$f_i = f_{min} + (f_{max} - f_{min})\beta \qquad (9.1)$$

$$v_i^j(t) = v_i^j(t-1) + [\hat{x}^j - x_i^j(t-1)]f_i \qquad (9.2)$$

$$x_i^j(t) = x_i^j(t-1) + v_i^j(t) \qquad (9.3)$$

where β denotes a randomly generated number within the interval $[0,1]$. Recall that $x_i^j(t)$ denotes the value of decision variable j for bat i at time step t. The result of f_i (Eq. (9.1)) is used to control the pace and range of the movement of the bats. The variable $\hat{x}^j$ represents the current global best location (solution) for decision variable j which is achieved comparing all the solutions provided by the m bats. Note that bat algorithm works similar to the traditional particle swarm optimization as f_i essentially controls the pace and range of the movement of the bats.

In order to improve the variability of the possible solutions, Yang (2011) proposed to employ random walks. One solution is primarily selected among the current best solutions, and then the random walk is applied in order to generate a new solution for each bat that accepts the condition in *Line 4* of Algorithm 9.1:

$$x_{new} = x_{old} + \varepsilon\overline{A}(t) \qquad (9.4)$$

where $\overline{A}(t)$ stands for the average loudness of all the bats at time t, and $\varepsilon \in [-1, 1]$ attempts to the direction and strength of the random walk. For each iteration of

Objective function $f(x), x = (x^1, ..., x^1)$.
Initialize the bat population x_i, and v_i, $i = 1,2,...,m$.
Define pulse frequency f_i at x_i, $\forall i = 1,2,...,m$.
Initialize pulse rates r_i and the loudness A_i, $i = 1,2,...,m$.

1. While $t < T$
2.   For each bat b_i, do
3.   *Generate new solutions through Equations (1), (2) and (3)*
4.   If $rand > r_i$, then
5.   *Select a solution among the best solutions.*
6.   *Generate a local solution around the best solution*
7.   If $rand < A_i$ and $f(x_i) < f(\hat{x})$, then
8.   *Accept the new solutions.*
9.   *Increase r_i and reduce A_i.*
10. Rank the bats and find the current best $\hat{x}$.

Algorithm 9.1 Bat algorithm.

the algorithm, the loudness A_i and the emission pulse rate r_i are updated as follows:

$$A_i(t + 1) = \alpha A_i(t) \tag{9.5}$$

and

$$r_i(t + 1) = r_i(0) + [1 - e^{-\gamma t}] \tag{9.6}$$

where α and γ are *ad hoc* constants. At the first step of the algorithm, the emission rate $r_i(0)$ and the loudness $A_i(0)$ are often randomly chosen. Generally, $A_i \in [1, 2]$ and $r_i(0) \in [0, 1]$.

9.3   Binary Bat Algorithm

As the reader can observe, each bat moves on the search space toward continuous-valued positions. However, in case of feature selection, the search space is modeled as an n-dimensional Boolean lattice, in which the bat moves across the corners of a hypercube. Since the problem is to select or not to select a given feature, the bat's position is therefore represented by binary vectors.

This work presents a binary version of the bat algorithm restricting the new bat's position to only binary values using a sigmoid function:

$$S(v_i^j) = \frac{1}{(1 + e^{-(v_i^j)})} \tag{9.7}$$

Therefore, Eq. (9.3) can be replaced by

$$x_i^j = \begin{cases} -1, & \text{if } S(v_i^j) > \delta \\ -0, & \text{otherwise} \end{cases} \tag{9.8}$$

where $\delta \sim U(0, 1)$. Consequently, Eq. (9.8) can provide only binary values for each bat's coordinates in the Boolean lattice, which stand for the presence or absence of the features.

9.4   Optimum-Path Forest Classifier

Given a training set, supervised classification algorithms assume some hypothesis to correctly predict the label of each dataset sample, which is represented by a feature vector and a distance function that measures their similarity in the feature space.

The optimum-path forest classifier (Papa et al., 2009) works by modeling the samples as graph nodes, whose arcs are defined by an adjacency relation and weighted by some distance function. Furthermore, a role competition process between some key nodes (prototypes) is carried out in order to partition the graph into optimum-path trees according to some path-cost function. Therefore, in order to design an optimum-path forest-based classifier, one needs to establish three parameters: (i) adjacency relation, (ii) path-cost function, and (iii) methodology to estimate prototypes.

9.4.1 Background Theory

Suppose we have a fully labeled dataset $Z = Z_1 \cup Z_2 \cup Z_3$, where Z_1, Z_2, and Z_3 stand for training, evaluating, and test sets, respectively. Let $S \subset Z_1$ be a set of prototypes of all classes (i.e., key samples that best represent the classes). Let (Z_1, A) be a complete graph whose nodes are the samples $S \in Z_1$, and any pair of samples defines an arc in $A = Z_1 x Z_1$.

Let π_s be a path in the graph that ends in sample $s \in Z_1$, and $\pi_{s'} \cdot (s, t)$ the concatenation between π_s and the arc $(s, t) \in Z_1$. In this work, we employ a path-cost function that returns the maximum arc weight along a path in order to avoid chains and to give the idea of connectivity between samples. This path-cost function is denoted here as ψ and it can be computed as follows:

$$\psi = \begin{cases} 1, & \text{if } s \in S \\ \infty, & \text{otherwise} \end{cases}$$

$$\psi(\pi_s \cdot \langle s, t \rangle) = \max\{(\pi_s), d(s, t)\} \qquad (9.9)$$

Therefore, the idea of optimum-path forest algorithm is to minimize $\psi(\pi_s)$, $\forall t \in Z_1$. An optimal set of prototypes S^* can be found out by exploiting the theoretical relation between minimum spanning tree (MST) (Dijkstra, 1959) and optimum-path tree for ψ (Allène et al., 2007). By computing an MST in the complete graph (Z_1, A) (Figure 9.1A), we obtain a connected acyclic graph whose nodes are all samples of Z_1, and the arcs are undirected and weighted by the distances between adjacent samples. The spanning tree is optimum in the sense that the sum of its arc weights is minimum as compared to any other spanning tree in the complete graph. In the MST, every pair of samples is connected by a single path, which is optimum according to ψ. Thus, the MST contains one optimum-path tree for any selected root node. The optimum prototypes are the closest elements of the MST with different labels in Z_1 (i.e., elements that fall in the frontier of the classes, as we can see in Figure 9.1B).

The optimum-path forest classifier's training phase focuses, essentially, on starting the competition process between prototypes in order to minimize the cost of each training sample. At the final stage of this procedure, we obtain an optimum-path forest, which is a collection of optimum-path trees rooted at each prototype (Figure 9.1C). A sample connected to an optimum-path tree means

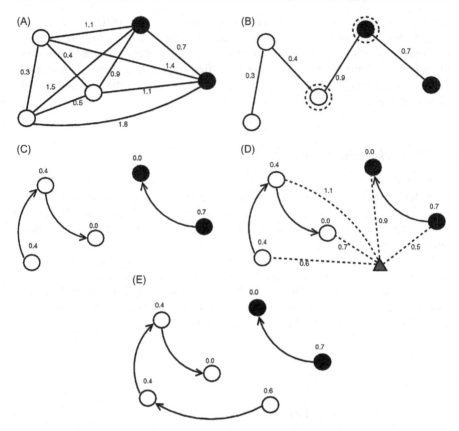

Figure 9.1 (A) Complete graph, (B) MST and the prototypes highlighted, (C) optimum-path forest generated, (D) classification process, and (E) the triangle sample is associated to the white circle class. The values above the nodes are their costs after training, and the values above the edges stand for the distance between their corresponding nodes.

that it is more strongly connected to the root of that tree than to any other root in the forest.

Furthermore, in the classification phase, for any sample $t \in Z_1$, we consider all arcs connecting t with samples $t \in Z_1$ as though t were part of the training graph (Figure 9.1D). Considering all possible paths from S^* to t, we find the optimum path $P^*(t)$ from S^* and label t with the class $\lambda(R(t))$ of its most strongly connected prototype $R(t)$ in S^* (Figure 9.1E). This path can be identified incrementally, by evaluating the optimum cost $C(t)$ as

$$C(t) = \min\{\max\{C(s), \ d(s,t)\}\}, \ \forall s \in Z_1 \qquad (9.10)$$

Let the node s^* in Z_1 be the one that satisfies Eq. (9.10) (i.e., the predecessor $P(t)$ in the optimum path $P^*(t)$). Given that $L(s^*) = \lambda(R(t))$, the classification simply assigns $L(s^*)$ as the class of t. An error occurs when $L(s^*) \neq \lambda(t)$.

9.5 Binary Bat Algorithm

In this section, we present our proposed approach using binary bat algorithm (Section 9.3) together with optimum-path forest classifier (Section 9.4) to find the best combination of features.

Ramos et al. (2011, 2012) have proposed a wrapper approach with harmony search and gravitational search algorithm, respectively, to find a subset of features that maximize the accuracy of the optimum-path forest over a evaluating set. In this case, the classification accuracy of optimum-path forest classifier has been used as the fitness function of the optimization problem.

In this work, we present the binary bat algorithm as an optimization technique to improve the effectiveness of the optimum-path forest. We have that each microbat's position in the search space encodes a string of bits, in which each coordinate denotes the presence or absence of a feature. Furthermore, for each microbat, an optimum-path forest instance is trained using Z_1 and evaluated over Z_2 to assess the fitness value. Note that the training and evaluating sets may be different among the bats because each one of them may encode a different subset of features. Additionally, this methodology is always performed when a microbat updates its position.

The fitness function adopted in this work is an accuracy measure proposed by Papa et al. (2009), which considers the fact that classes may have different concentrations in the dataset. This information avoids a strong estimation bias toward the majority class in high class imbalance datasets.

Let $NZ_2(i), i = [1, c]$, be the number of samples in Z_2 from each class and c the number of classes. We define

$$e_{i,1} = \frac{FP(i)}{|Z_2| - NZ_2(i)} \quad \text{and} \quad e_{i,2} = \frac{FN}{NZ_2(i)}, \quad i \in [1, c] \tag{9.11}$$

where $FP(i)$ and $FN(i)$ are the false positives and false negatives, respectively. That is, $FP(i)$ is the number of samples from other classes that were classified as being from the class $i \in Z_2$, and $FN(i)$ is the number of samples from class i that were incorrectly classified as being from other classes in Z_2. The errors $e_{i,1}$ and $e_{i,2}$ are used to define

$$E(i) = e_{i,1} + e_{i,2} \tag{9.12}$$

where $E(i)$ is the partial sum error of class i. Finally, the accuracy is written as follows:

$$Acc = \frac{2c - \sum_{i=1}^{c} E(i)}{2c} = 1 - \frac{\sum_{i=1}^{c} E(i)}{2c} \tag{9.13}$$

Algorithm 9.2 presents in detail the proposed technique. The first loop in *Lines 1−6* initializes the population of bats. The positions of bats are then

Input: Labeled training Z_1 and evaluating set Z_2, population size m, number of features n, number of iterations T, loudness A, pulse emission rate r, ε, α and θ values.
Output: Subset of features $\hat{x}$ that gives the maximum accuracy over Z_2.
Auxiliary: Fitness vector *fit* of size m, *initial frequency vector* r^0 of size m, global best position vector $\vec{x}$ of size n, and variables acc, $rand$, $maxfit$, $maxindex$, $global\ fit$, β, f_{max} and f_{min}.

  1. For each bat b_i ($\forall i = 1, \ldots, m$), do
  2.   For each j ($\forall j = 1, \ldots, n$), do
  3. $x_i^j \leftarrow Random\{0,1\}$
  4. $v_i^j \leftarrow 0$
  5. $A_i \leftarrow [1,2]$
  6. $r_i \leftarrow [0,1]$
  7. For each iteration t ($t = 1, \ldots, T$), do
  8.   For each bat b_i ($\forall i = 1, \ldots, m$), do
  9.   Create Z_1' and Z_2' from Z_1' and Z_2' respectively, such that both contain only features
            in b_i, in which $x_i^j \neq 0, \forall j = 1, \ldots, n$.
10.   Train classifier over Z_1', evaluate it over Z_2' and store the accuracy in acc.
11. $rand \leftarrow Random[0,1]$
12. $If (rand < A_i$ and $acc > fit_i)$, then
13. $fit_i \leftarrow acc$
14. $A_i \leftarrow \alpha A_i$
15. $r_i \leftarrow r_i^0[1 - e^{-\gamma t}]$
16. $[maxfit, maxindex] \leftarrow \max (fit)$
17. $If (maxfit > globalfit)$, then
18. $globalfit \leftarrow maxfit$
19.   For each j ($\forall j = 1, \ldots, n$), do
20. $\hat{x}^j \leftarrow x_{maxindex}^j$
21.   For each bat b_i ($\forall i = 1, \ldots, m$), do
22. $\beta \leftarrow Random[0,1]$
23. $rand \leftarrow Random[0,1]$
24. $If (rand > r_i)$, then
25.   For each j ($\forall j = 1, \ldots, n$), do
26. $x_i^j \leftarrow x_i^j + \varepsilon \bar{A}$
27. $\sigma \leftarrow Random[0,1]$
28. $If \left(\sigma < 1 \dfrac{1}{1+e^{-x_i^j}} \right), then$
29. $x_i^j \leftarrow 1$
30. $else\ x_i^j \leftarrow 0$
31. $rand \leftarrow Random[0,1]$
32. $If (rand < A_i$ and $fit_i < globalfit)$, then
33.   For each j ($\forall j = 1, \ldots, n$), do
34. $f_i \leftarrow f_{min} + (f_{max} - f_{min})\beta$
35. $v_i^j \leftarrow v_i^j + (\bar{x}^j - x_i^j)f_i$
36. $\sigma \leftarrow Random[0,1]$
37. $If \left(\sigma < 1 \dfrac{1}{1+e^{-v_i^j}} \right), then$
38. $x_i^j \leftarrow 1$
39. $else\ x_i^j \leftarrow 0$
40. Return $\hat{x}$

Algorithm 9.2 Feature selection through BA.

initialized with randomly chosen binary values in *Line 3*, which correspond to whether a feature will be selected or not to compose the new dataset. *Lines 9−10* compose the new training and evaluating sets with the selected features, and *Lines 12−15* evaluate each bat in order to update its fitness value. Furthermore, the loudness A_i and the rate of pulse emission r_i are updated if a new solution has been accepted. While the loudness usually decreases once a bat has found its prey, the rate pulse emission increases (Eqs. (9.5) and (9.6)). In *Line 16*, the function *max* outputs the index and the fitness value of the bat maximizes the fitness function. *Lines 19−20* update the global best position, i.e., $\hat{x}$, with the position of the bat that has achieved the highest fitness function. The loop in *Lines 21−39* is responsible for updating the position and velocity of the bats.

The source code in *Lines 24−30* performs the local search as described in *Lines 4−6* of Algorithm 9.1. The source code in *Lines 32−39* corresponds to the *Lines 7−9* of Algorithm 9.1. At *Line 34*, we update the frequency of each bat as described in Eq. (9.1).

9.6   Experimental Results

In this section, we discuss the experiments conducted to assess the robustness of the binary bat algorithm for feature selection purposes. In order to validate our solution, we have proposed an approach to compare the proposed algorithm with some traditional swarm-based algorithms: firefly algorithm, gravitational search algorithm, harmony search, and particle swarm optimization. The idea is to partition the datasets into k-folds, and for each of them we perform the combinatorial optimization using the metaheuristic algorithms to find the best subset of features. As stated in the previous sections, for each agent, we train an optimum-path forest instance using 70% of the training fold with the features defined by the agent's coordinates and then evaluate with the remaining 30% of the fold to define the agent's fitness value.

After the optimization convergence, we evaluate the solution found out with the remaining $k − 1$ folds. For instance, we define $k = 10$, i.e., we performed 10 rounds of optimization, and for each solution, we evaluate the robustness against the remaining 9-folds. This methodology to evaluate the performance a feature selection algorithm aims to avoid overfitting using a cross-validation independent from the optimization step.

From Figures 9.2 and 9.3, it is clear that for some datasets, the optimization step for finding the best subset of features can indeed improve the accuracy of the optimum-path forest. Note that in the case of breast cancer dataset (Figure 9.2A), the wrapper technique improves utterly the efficiency. However, in others datasets (connect, 9.2B; DNA, 9.2D; letter, 9.3A, and vehicle, 9.3D), the harmony search had a significant loss in accuracy. Furthermore, these experiments with different public datasets confirm the power of exploration of microbats, the results of the

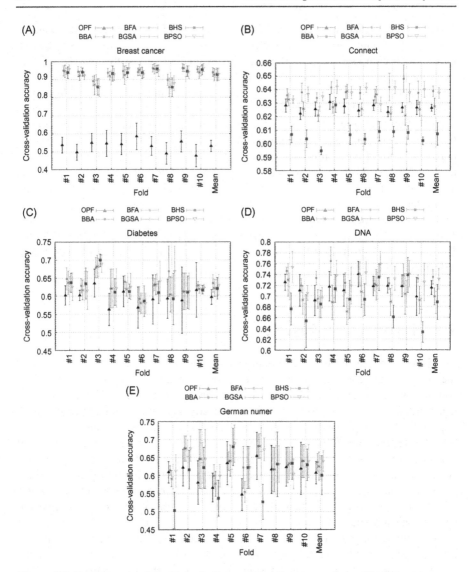

Figure 9.2 Testing accuracies obtained after applying the proposed classification system on (A) breast cancer, (B) connect, (C) diabetes, (D) DNA, and (E) German numer.

binary bat algorithm being at least similar to the traditional particle swarm optimization and Firefly Algorithm.

As shown in Figure 9.4, harmony search achieved the best computational time, due mainly to its structure, in which the position of each agent is updated following certain probability. As we defined its parameter *Harmony Memory Considering Rate*

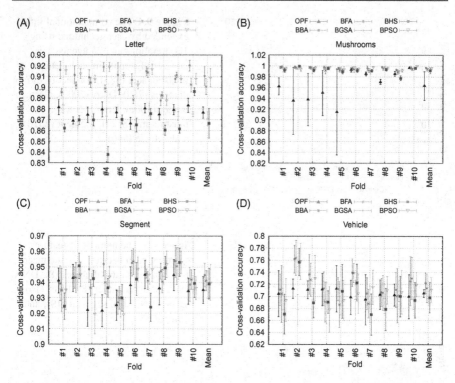

Figure 9.3 Testing accuracies obtained after applying the proposed classification system on (A) letter, (B) mushrooms, (C) segment, and (D) vehicle.

equals to 70%, the new harmony will be composed of musical notes that come from the harmony memory with this probability, and the remaining 30% are given randomly, which simulates the process of music improvisation. Regarding the other algorithms, each agent is updated for each iteration, which requires a training procedure followed by testing using the dataset mapped to a new one considering the string of bits of that agent that becomes quite more computationally costly. In respect to the parameters, we define $\alpha = 0.9$ and $\gamma = 0.9$ for the bat algorithm; $\alpha = 0.1$, $\beta = 1$, and $\gamma = 0.8$ for Firefly Algorithm; $G_0 = 100$ and $\alpha = 20$ for gravitational search algorithm; and $c_1 = 2$, $c_2 = 2$, and $w = 0.9$ for particle swarm optimization.

Finally, referring to Figure 9.5, the binary bat algorithm achieved slightly similar features selected compared to firefly algorithm, harmony search, gravitational search algorithm, and particle swarm optimization. In particular to Connect and DNA datasets, the proposed technique selected more features than the compared algorithms, and has achieved the best overall accuracies together with particle swarm optimization (Figure 9.2B and D).

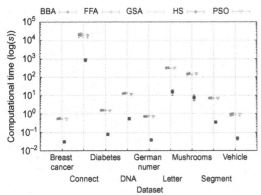

Figure 9.4 The computational time expended by each technique using 100 iterations and 25 agents. The number of sample in each dataset: breast cancer (683), connect (65,577), diabetes (768), DNA (2000), German numer (1000), letter (15,000), mushrooms (8124), segment (2310), and vehicle (846).

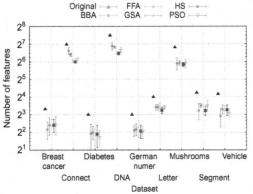

Figure 9.5 The number of features regarding each dataset: breast cancer (10), connect (126), diabetes (8), DNA (180), German numer (8), letter (16), mushrooms (112), segment (19), and vehicle (18).

9.7   Conclusions

In this chapter, we addressed the problem of high dimensionality in object's description by means of finding the most informative features in a search space given by a Boolean hypercube. As the feature selection can be seen as an optimization problem, we have proposed a bat-inspired algorithm for this task. A binary version of the continuous-valued bat algorithm was derived in order to position the bats in binary coordinates along the corners of the search space, which represents a string of bits that encodes whether a feature will be selected or not.

The proposed wrapper approach uses the accuracy of the optimum-path forest to guide a metaheuristic optimization algorithm in order to find the best subset of features. Experiments using a cross-validation methodology and public datasets confirm that the binary bat algorithm can indeed improve the efficiency of the optimum-path forest. Also, it is at least similar to traditional particle swarm optimization and firefly algorithm, and it is more accurate than gravitational search algorithm and harmony search.

References

Allène, C., Audibert, J.-Y., Couprie, M., Cousty, J., Keriven, R., 2007. Some links between min cuts, optimal spanning forests and watersheds. In: Banon, G.J.F., Barrera, J., Braga-Neto, U. de M., Hirata, N.S.T. (Eds.), International Symposium on Mathematical Morphology'07, 8th International Symposium, Proceedings. vol. 2. INPE, pp. 253–264.

Banati, H., Bajaj, M., 2011. Fire fly based feature selection approach. Int. J. Comput. Sci. 8 (4), 473–480.

Dijkstra, E.W, 1959. A note on two problems in connexion with graphs. Numerische Mathematik. 1, 269–271.

Duda, R.O., Hart, P.E., Stork, D.G., 2007. Pattern Classification. Wiley-Interscience, New York, NY.

Firpi, H.A., Goodman, E., 2004. Swarmed feature selection. Proceedings of the Thirty-Third Applied Imagery Pattern Recognition Workshop. IEEE Computer Society, Washington, DC, pp. 112–118.

Huang, J., Cai, Y., Xu, X., 2007. A hybrid genetic algorithm for feature selection wrapper based on mutual information. Pattern Recogn. Lett. 28 (13), 1825–1844.

Griffin, D.R., Webster, F.A, Michael, C.R., 1960. The echolocation of flying insects by bats. Anim. Behav. 8 (3–4), 141–154.

Kanan, H.R., Faez, K., Taheri, S.M., 2007. Feature selection using ant colony optimization (ACO): a new method and comparative study in the application of face recognition system. Proceedings of the Seventh Industrial Conference on Advances in Data Mining: Theoretical Aspects and Applications. Springer-Verlag, Berlin, Heidelberg, pp. 63–76.

Metzner, W., 1991. Echolocation behaviour in bats. Sci. Prog. Edinb. 75 (298), 453–465.

Papa, J.P., Falcão, A.X., Suzuki, C.T.N., 2009. Supervised pattern classification based on optimum-path forest. Int. J. Imag. Syst. Tech. 19 (2), 120–131.

Ramos, C., Souza, A., Chiachia, G., Falcão, A., Papa, J., 2011. A novel algorithm for feature selection using harmony search and its application for non-technical losses detection. Comput. Elect. Eng. 37 (6), 886–894.

Rashedi, E., Nezamabadi-pour, H., Saryazdi, S., 2010. BGSA: binary gravitational search algorithm. Nat. Comput. 9, 727–745.

Ramos, C.C.O., de Souza, A.N., Falcão, A.X., Papa, J.P., 2012. New insights on non-technical losses characterization through evolutionary-based feature selection. IEEE Trans. Power Deliv. 27 (1), 140–146.

Schnitzler, H.U., Kalko, E.K.V., 2001. Echolocation by insect-eating bats. BioScience. 51 (7), 557–569.

Yang, X-S., 2011. Bat algorithm for multi-objective optimisation. Int. J. Bio-Inspired Comput. 3 (5), 267–274.

10 Intelligent Music Composition

Maximos A. Kaliakatsos-Papakostas[1],
Andreas Floros[2] and Michael N. Vrahatis[1]

[1]Department of Mathematics, University of Patras, Patras, Greece;
[2]Department of Audio and Visual Arts, Ionian University, Corfu, Greece

10.1 Introduction

Automatic music composition is an enchanting field of research, inspiring both researchers and musicians. The implementation of systems that perform this task, incorporates an algorithmic part which makes decisions on which notes/sounds will be heard, when they will be heard, for how long and how loud. The intriguing part of automatic composition is the process of formulating such algorithms, in such a manner that the composed music is not too simple or too complex. Referring to the terms "simple" and "complex," someone may find her/himself sort of words when speaking about music. Nevertheless, almost everyone can more easily express an opinion about the complexity of a certain music excerpt. This fact raises the question of how we may be sure that an automatic composition system composes too simple or too complex music. Additionally, how may we be able to compare the compositional capabilities of two such systems? Is there an objective criterion to characterize how "pleasant" is the music produced by such a machine?

These questions among others have led the research community toward a direction to construct systems that have inherited some kind of *intelligence*, which allows them to construct music with a pleasant blend of simplicity and complexity. Specifically, these machines incorporate an intelligent algorithm, which is commonly able to create mathematical objects that may vary from numeric values to abstract string sequences. The underlying intelligence of these algorithms forges the aforementioned objects in a manner that they either produce present rich and complex structure or comply with certain target characteristics defined by humans. These objects could then simply be mapped to the sonic domain and produce subjectively pleasant music, or adjust the parameters of music composition systems and lead the composition process to certain stylistic and aesthetic directions. This chapter presents several theoretic and technical aspects of such systems and proposes their categorization according to their intelligence and the way that this intelligence adheres to music composition. The main motivation for this categorization is the detailed orientation specifications of all the intelligent composition methodologies, which will hopefully facilitate the new-coming researchers and artists interested to enter this field and provide more robust guidelines to the production of new methodologies.

The functionality of the intelligent part of these automatic music composition systems is a parameter that can be used to categorize them into three main categories, depending on the manner that this intelligence is expressed and manipulated. To this end, we propose the following categorization for intelligent music composition (IMC) systems:

1. *Unsupervised intelligent composition*: The algorithmic composition intelligence is expressed through simple rules that produce complex, unpredictable, but yet structured output, a behavior that often resembles natural phenomena.
2. *Supervised intelligent composition*: Intelligent algorithms are utilized to modify the automatic composition system's parameters so that it may be able to compose music that meets some predefined criteria, not necessarily in real time.
3. *Interactive intelligent composition*: The system is acknowledging the human preference in real time and becomes adapted to it, by utilizing intelligent algorithms. Human preference is expressed either by a selection-rating scheme or by performing tasks (such as playing an instrument or adjusting target parameters in real time).

It has to be noted that this chapter focuses on intelligent algorithms that have fostered the creation of numerous automatic composition methodologies. There are some works that are eligible to be included in the IMC methodologies family and have produced interesting results, but their proposed direction has not been extensively used or has been abandoned for the last few years. For example, the utilization of artificial neural networks (ANNs) for music composition (Griffith and Todd, 1999) has not been extensively used in the last decade.[†] Additionally, there is not yet extensive literature concerning composition through models that utilize ant colony optimization as a music composition tool, i.e., in Geis and Middendorf (2008). Several methodologies that this chapter discusses have been implemented to software. Since the aspect of this chapter is purely methodological, the interested reader is referred to the bibliography for these implementations, although several of them are hardly accessible due to outdated web links or platform dependencies. Additionally, the bibliography incorporates many musical examples and links to audio material.

Based on the above considerations, this chapter aims to provide a categorization of IMC techniques in terms of the functionality of each intelligent algorithm employed and the compositional potentialities—limitations that they incorporate. Therefore, this chapter is mainly targeted to the researcher, the musician, and the student of computer science or music informatics. The researcher may find such a categorization interesting and hopefully increase the convenience of literature organization. The musicians, the option to integrate computational intelligence systems

---

[†]This comment refers to the utilization of ANNs as a means to create note sequences, not as automatic fitness raters as discussed later.

in their artistic arsenal, may be informed about the state of the art of IMC and furthermore be facilitated with the extensive amounts of literatures that a nonexpert in informatics has to face in practice. Finally, the student may directly decode the potentialities and limitations of IMC and incrementally obtain the required information to become an expert on the field of IMC or other related fields.

10.2   Unsupervised Intelligent Composition

This class of IMC systems incorporates algorithms inspired by natural phenomena, encompassing simple rules. If these rules are applied recursively, they tend to produce interesting results with rich and complex structure. The fundamental motivation toward using these systems as music composition tools mainly originates from the rich geometric structures that they produce and the corresponding visual representation outcome, which is often observed in nature. Thus the characterization of these systems as "intelligent" is based on the fact that their simple sets of rules trigger complex and sometimes unpredictable behavior, which exposes an underlying endogenous intelligence. The main question that the composing software has to face is the interpretation of this complex output to music objects.

An advantage of these systems is their ability to compose novel and quite intriguing music content. This ability is maintained almost regardless of the interpretation modeling that the composer−programer is applying. This fact, however, creates a vast disadvantage, as it disallows any human involvement in the composition process. The composer is thus unable to have a sense of control over his compositions. Therefore, the integrity, the style, and the aesthetic value of the music produced by such systems are only dependent on the subjective taste of the listener. Since there are no specific target music characteristics, these compositions are rarely submitted to rigorous evaluation and the results mainly revolve around presenting scores of small music excerpts. Thus, for the majority of works in this field, there are no qualitative descriptions of the compositional capabilities of such systems.

10.2.1   Unsupervised Composition with Cellular Automata

Cellular automata (CA) represents a paradigm of systems that encompass simple rules of interaction between a "unit" with its neighboring "units," which are yet able to produce complex behavior. CA can be viewed as simple forms of "discrete" societies, where each individual unit occupies a certain cell on a grid and may have a discrete state. This state is updated in successive time steps in accordance with the state of the unit's neighbors. The dimensionality of the aforementioned grid determines the number of each unit's neighbors (e.g., in a one-dimensional grid, each unit has two neighbors, the unit on its left and right), while the number of states determines the overall system's dynamical behavior. All possible dynamics that may be produced by CA have been classified by Wolfram (2002) in the following categories:

1. Patterns disappear with time or become fixed.
2. Patterns evolve to structures that repeat periodically, cycling through a fixed number of states.
3. Patterns become chaotic and never repeat, forming aperiodic and random states.
4. Patterns grow into complex forms, exhibiting localized structures moving both spatially and temporally.

Music composition has mainly been realized with the utilization of single-dimensional grid worlds with binary states known as "elementary cellular automata" (ECA), two- or three-dimensional worlds with binary states also known as "game of life" (GL), and two- or three-dimensional worlds with p discrete states, often referred to as "crystal growth" (CG) due to the crystal-like form that their visual interpretation exhibits. In the case of the binary states, the state numbers 0 and 1 are assumed, denoting a "dead" or "alive" cell, respectively. The state of each cell is updated in every tick of the clock and is determined by the cell's own state, as well as the state of its neighbors. Similarly, the discrete states of the CG CA is updated with the "domination" of the cells in state $s + 1$ over its neighbors of state s.

Specifically, for the ECA, Wolfram (2002) has documented all possible 256 evolution rules and analyzed the dynamical behavior of these single-dimensional societies. Even though these rules are simple and deterministic, their application results in complex patterns often leading to chaotic behavior, like Rule 30[‡] the evolution of which is depicted in Figure 10.1A.

The evolution of the GL CA abounds in dynamical phenomena, ranging from stable to oscillating and chaotic patterns, which derive from the simple application of the following rules:

1. *Death by underpopulation*: Any alive cell with fewer than two live neighbors dies.
2. *Death by overpopulation*: Any alive cell with more than three alive neighbors dies.
3. *Survival*: Any alive cell with two or three alive neighbors lives on to the next generation.
4. *Birth by reproduction*: Any dead cell with exactly three alive neighbors becomes alive.

The application of these rules is graphically presented in Figure 10.1B, beginning from a random initial population of cells. In a similar fashion, the state of a cell (an integer value ranging from 0 to s) in the CG CA determines the state of its neighbors. If a neighboring cell is in state $s - 1$, then, at the next tick of the clock, it will be converted to s. This rule acts circularly, meaning that the state 0 dominates over the state corresponding to the greatest integer. The application of these rules results in crystal-like oscillating patterns, an example instance of which is depicted in Figure 10.1C. The rules of the GL and CG CA can also be applied on hypercubes of arbitrary dimensions; for music composition though, only two- and three-dimensional versions have been tested (Burraston and Edmonds, 2005; Miranda and Biles, 2007). The dynamics of the emergent social behavior of these discrete societies has attracted

---

[‡]Rule 30 is also used as a random number generator in the mathematical software Mathematica.

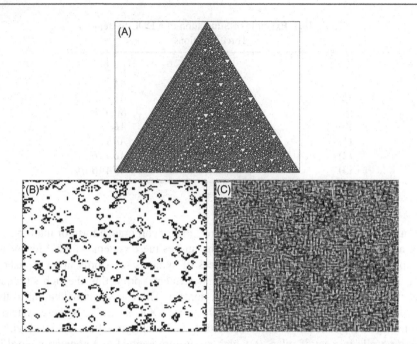

Figure 10.1 Graphical representation of CA. (A) ECA: Evolution of Rule 30 with a single alive cell at the first step. (B) GL: Evolution from a random initial set of alive cells. (C) CG: Evolution of a random initial six-states cell society, the states of which are mapped in a grayscale image.

the attention of composers ever since the epoch of the pioneers of automatic computer composition, like Xenakis (Solomos, 2005). For an extended and thorough review of the methodologies for music production through CA, the reader is referred to Burraston and Edmonds (2005) and Miranda and Biles (2007).

The systems suggested so far for music composition and sound synthesis using CA either utilize the states of the CA to trigger Musical Instrument Digital Interface (MIDI) commands or map these states directly to a sound generator in order to structure a waveform or to perform granular synthesis. In the first case, the graphical representation of the CA is mapped to notes (or groups of notes called chords), onsets, durations, and intensities, with this information assigned to certain instruments. In the latter case, the output of the CA activates specific oscillators with certain frequency—amplitude pairs, or it is projected to certain sound granules and their properties, i.e., sound material of short duration and information regarding their amplitude, length, and repetitiveness.

10.2.2 Unsupervised Composition with L-Systems

The L-systems are parallel generative grammars (Prusinkiewicz and Lindenmayer, 1990) with some variations that allow the production of interesting patterns that

Table 10.1 Example of Simulation of a DOL-System for
Three Iterations

V:	$\{A, B\}$
ω:	AB
P:	$A \rightarrow AB$
	$B \rightarrow A$
(0)	AB
(1)	ABA
(2)	$ABAAB$
(3)	$ABAABABA$

resemble plant-like forms and fractals. Thus, they incorporate a form of intelligence
that assimilates natural creativity, a fact that makes these systems eligible for music
composition. L-systems generate sequences of symbols (or words in an alphabet)
that are then interpreted to music or sound elements, projecting the rich structure
that these strings encompass to the sonic domain. The L-systems belonging to the
simplest form are called *deterministic context-free* (DOL-systems). In these systems,
a set of symbols called alphabet is defined, V, and each symbol is associated with a
rewriting rule in a set of rules, P, which are in turn applied to a nonempty word in
the above-mentioned alphabet, $\omega \in V^+$, creating a new word. A DOL-system can be
described as a triplet $G = \langle V, \omega, P \rangle$. This procedure is applied recursively, creating
new words with new length which may then be transcribed into graphical or music/
sound entities. An example of an L-system with the above form is demonstrated
in Table 10.1.

The consideration of special symbols which are interpreted into special graphical
or musical functionality produces special representations like that illustrated in
Figure 10.2. These symbols are translated into straight lines, turning angles of some
predefined degrees and symbols that are not considered in graphical projection but
function instead as "helping" variables. Among the pioneering works on music production with the L-systems is the work of Prusinkiewicz (1986), who created music
scores by traversing the curves produced by the graphical projection of various
L-systems. Since then, various models have been proposed for the transcription of
the L-systems' rules to music, from note-to-note composition to the creation of
chord progressions based on the neo-Riemannian music space (Gogins, 2010).

Variations of the L-systems have also produced interesting musical results.
For example, the introduction of more variation was achieved by the utilization of
probabilistic grammars (McCormack, 1996), where each symbol is associated to
several rewriting rules according to some probability. Furthermore, musical diversity has also been accomplished with genetic evolution of the rules in Lourenc and
Brand (2009). In this work, no fitness function was provided, thus the production
of music is considered "unsupervised," in contrast to some similar techniques
incorporating evolution of L-systems in Section 10.3.1. For these systems, however, there is lack of a rigorous evaluation and the results revolve around presenting

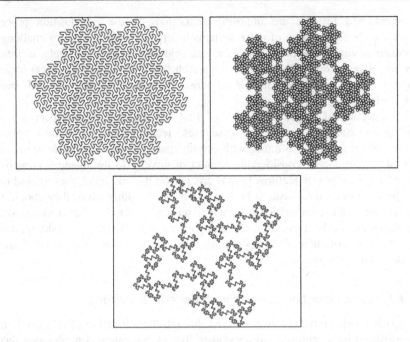

Figure 10.2 Graphical interpretation of the evolution of some well-known L-systems.

isolated music excerpts. In Kaliakatsos-Papakostas et al. (2012c), a study has been presented where some rhythmic attributes of the L-systems indicated extensive randomness in the produced music material. This led to an extension of the L-systems with the finite L-systems (FL-systems), which are able to produce rhythms with a wider spectrum of rhythmic characteristics, i.e., from more stable and predictable to more vague and complex rhythms.

10.3 Supervised Intelligent Composition

In contrast to the methodologies for unsupervised music composition, supervised methodologies aim to produce music that meets some predefined criteria. The systems that pertain to this category utilize intelligent algorithms in order to obtain the ability to compose music under some qualitative guidelines, which are often called "target features" or simply "features." The underlying model that these systems utilize to produce music is either tuned or created from scratch with the utilization of intelligent algorithms toward the directions dictated by the features that the music output has to satisfy. An advantage of the supervised IMC systems is their ability to produce music with certain aesthetic and stylistic orientation (Manaris et al., 2007), in contrast to unsupervised composition systems. This fact, however, may arguably introduce a contraction to the novelty of the composed music, since the aforementioned features are imposing restrictions to the composition process. Therefore, the formulation of these systems incorporates the following challenges: (a) create an *interpretation* of mathematical objects to music, (b) apply an *intelligent algorithm* to optimally traverse the search space of the mathematical objects, and (c) select a *proper set of features* that describe the desired music characteristics.

The selection of proper features is of vital importance for the supervised systems' performance. In an abstract sense, these features should provide landmarks for the system to compose music with certain characteristics, but at the same time allow it to introduce a considerable amount of novelty to the music it composes. The selection of proper features is thus crucial: on the one hand, they should capture the *essence* of the music to be composed; on the other hand, they should not *overdetermine* the compositions. Research on supervised intelligent composition has mainly been driven toward establishing effective intelligent methodologies that tune the composition models, restraining from the formulation of novel features that describe music in a global sense.

10.3.1 Supervised Composition with Genetic Algorithms

Automatic music composition is realized through the utilization of a "model" that is constructed by a composer—programmer. The aforementioned model may incorporate a set of parameters that define its compositional style and capabilities. It is thus crucial that a proper combination of these parameters is defined for the automatic creation of music, so that it may exhibit certain characteristics and aesthetic value of high quality. The utilization of genetic algorithms (GA) provides proper values for these parameters, given a qualitative measure of what the produced music should sound like. Thus, the problems that the composer—programmer faces are related not only to the formulation of a proper parametric model, but also, equally importantly, to the formalization of measurements that accurately describe the target music style.

The GA is a class of algorithms inspired by natural evolution, which iteratively produce better solutions to a problem. These algorithms belong to the wider class of "heuristics," meaning that they initially "guess" a set of random solutions and produce new ones grouped in generations, by utilizing information only from their current generation and their product candidate solutions. Specifically, the candidate solutions within a generation in a GA scheme are evolved using operators resembling natural genetic phenomena (such as crossover and mutation) and a selection procedure that propagates the consecution of generations toward better solutions. A better solution means that the set of the model's parameters that this solution describes gives a more satisfactory result with regard to a qualitative measurement that is called "fitness function." Among the most popular genetic operators are the crossover and mutation. Crossover incorporates the combination of the parameter between two "parent" solutions for the creation of two "children" solutions, while mutation is the random reassignment of certain parameter values of a "parent" solution to produce a new "children solution." The progression from one generation of "parent" solutions to the next is finally accomplished with a selection process that allows the "better" fitted solutions among parents and children to form the new generation.

The key notion in the GA is the *precise* and *informative* description of what a "*better*" solution is. In the case of supervised IMC, *precise* denotes the correct demarcation of the target musical attributes that the automatically composed music should encompass. The term *informative* expresses the necessity to model the target musical attributes in a "continuous" manner as possible, abstaining the hazard to create nonsmooth and discretized error surfaces that abound in local optima.

Among the first works for supervised composition using "objective" musical criteria for the assignment of fitness evaluations was the work of Papadopoulos and Wiggins (1998). In this work, a system was presented which was composing jazz solos over a given chord progression. The solutions to the problem were the melodies themselves, specifically pitch-duration pairs, and after a random initialization, GA with some special genetic operators with "musical meaning" was applied, fostering new generations of possible solutions-melodies. The evaluation process of each candidate solution-melody was based on eight evaluation indicators, borrowed by music theory. The results were reported to be promising; however, a thorough statistical examination of the results was not realized, according also to the authors' opinion in the concluding section of their work. A similar system was introduced by Özcan and Ercal (2008), who also provide a downloadable application called *AMUSE*. In this work, a set of 10 music features were used for fitness evaluation. Furthermore, experimental results of a questionary-based research on a group of 20 participants indicated that these features are linked to human preference at some extent. The utilization of a fitness function based on music theoretic criteria was also utilized for the creation of four-part melodies from scratch (Donnelly and Sheppard, 2011).

On the other hand, features not related to music theory have also been utilized. These features are related to informatics and statistics, measuring aspects of melodic information capacity either through compressibility or through various characteristics of music that can be translated into discrete probabilities. In Alfonseca et al. (2007), the normalized compression distance (NCD) is used to allow a GA composes music pieces that resemble the pieces of a certain style. The sum of NCDs between each possible solution-melody and a set of target pieces in a certain style is computed, and a solution-melody with a better fitness is the one for which a smaller sum of NCDs is obtained. Systems that genetically evolve CA (Lo, 2012) and FL-systems (Kaliakatsos-Papakostas et al., 2012e) for music and rhythm composition have also been presented, where again fitness is calculated with the utilization of probability measures, such as n-Grams (Markov transition tables), Shannon information entropy (SIE), and compression rate.

10.3.2 Supervised Composition Genetic Programming

Genetic programming (GP) works under the same evolutionary principle with the GA that is evolving initially random possible solutions to new ones that are better fitted to the problem at hand. The difference between GP and GA is the problem's formulation. In GA, the optimization process targets at the model's parameters, while the utilization of GP allows the optimization of the model *per se*, since the populations of possible solutions incorporate entire programs that actually form the model. These programs are constituted of short subprogram segments, hierarchically structured in a tree-like representation. The genetic operators are similar to that used by the GA; however, they act on tree branches instead of string-like or numeric chromosomes. The crossover operator, for example, exchanges subtrees of the parents' trees, creating children that comprise combined subprogram parts of their parents. Through a similar selection process as in the GA, new populations of possible solutions-programs are created which are better or equally fitted to the problem at hand.

Although GP offers an entirely new aspect regarding the problem formulation, the fitness evaluation of these programs remains an important issue. In Spector and Alpern (1994), a GP scheme which acted on an *initial* melody-string by performing several musical operations, such as retrograde and transposition, produced novel melodies. The fitness used in this work incorporated measurement on how different certain tonal and rhythmical characteristics are between the initial and the GP-created melodies. In an extension of this work (Spector and Alpern, 1995), an ANN has been presented for the automatic assignment of fitness based on the knowledge that this ANN has been trained on by several target pieces. Some works have also addressed the issue of fitness evaluation by training machine learning tools on features derived by a set of target pieces. For example, in Manaris et al. (2007), ANNs were trained on a set of features that were taken by sets of pieces belonging to a certain style. These features incorporated the fractal dimension (FD) of several music attributes, such as pitch, interval, and duration, and some of their local variability measurements (i.e., higher order derivatives and relative moving averages). The FD can be obtained by any music feature that may be expressed as a discrete probability density function (PDF) and reveals its information capacity by measuring the ratio of the successively ranked probabilities. Among others, self-organizing maps (Phon-Amnuaisuk et al., 2007) have also been trained on specified symbolic music features as automatic fitness raters.

10.4 Interactive Intelligent Composition

Interactive evolution (IE) is a general class of algorithms that transform the problem to formulate a proper fitness function, into the problem to allow the user to assign fitness evaluations based on her/his taste or actions. In this section, we propose the presentation of the IE algorithms in two subcategories: the *subjectively driven* and *performance driven* evolution systems. The *subjectively driven* systems evolve their parameters (or the system *per se*) based on the fitness evaluation provided directly by the user, either in a "select-the-best" fashion or by following a rating procedure. The underlying evolutionary mechanisms remain intact with an exception on the fitness evaluation scheme that is performed by the user. In the *performance driven* systems, on the other hand, the interaction between the user and the system is not limited to the aforementioned rate-and-evolve scheme. Instead, the user feeds the system with her/his actions; the system analyzes these actions and produces a proper musical response. This response in turn, in most cases, affects the human's actions, creating an interactive "dialogue" between the human performer and the system itself.

The subjectively driven IE systems have the advantage to capture the human preference directly, obtaining feedback from the user's responses either in a user-selection fashion or in a user-rating fashion. However, such a fitness assignment scheme demands extensive effort by the user, who would ideally have to rate thousands of musical excerpts in order to drive the evolution to a compositional optimum. Additionally, as the hearing-selecting or rating trials evolve, the compositions "converge" to an optimum, thus obtaining great similarities. Therefore, the user is expected to be hearing and rating irritatingly similar music compositions. This, combined with the fact that a great number of iterative selection or rating turns are necessary, creates an effect that is common to IE called *"user fatigue."* User fatigue restrains the user from focusing on the material under evaluation, forcing her/him to provide inconsistent ratings, a fact that misleads evolution to suboptimal solutions.

The advantage of performance driven interactive systems is that the human and the automatic performer combine their compositional "virtues" in real time, creating music that is both structured and surprising. The human performer does not have direct control over the composition but has the ability to control several aspects of the produced music by transferring feedback to the system through her/his performance. The system on the other side acknowledges this feedback and responds by producing music which encompasses novelty and spontaneity, hopefully inspiring the human performer. Thus, this interactive dialogue integrates the characteristics of the human's structured understanding of music and the IMC's unpredictability. Although the rationale behind the formulation of performance driven systems is solid, their pragmatic realization has to deal with the following question: *how does the system understand the human's performance?* The implementation of such systems therefore faces the same problem as in Section 10.3, which concerns the creation of proper *features* which capture the human's performance without being over- or under-descriptive. Additionally, the responses of these systems have to be prepared in real time, thus the underlying intelligent algorithms have to be as less time-consuming as possible.

It also has to be noted that in several works (Millen (2005), Pestana (2012), among others), the term "interactive" is used to describe the intervention of the human user to the composition process of the underlying system (CA and L-systems, respectively). This term does not meet the specifications that this work utilizes. Nevertheless, we do not argue that this characterization is wrong in any sense; however, it highlights our motivation that interaction is "intelligent" when it incorporates modification of the "intelligent mechanisms" of the system and not the parameter assignment. This fact has also been noted in a previous work

(Blackwell, 2007), by introducing the notion of *"live algorithms"* and describing them as follows: *"The idea that interaction involves state change rather than parameter selection* is an important aspect in the design of live algorithms."

10.4.1 Composing with Swarms

Swarm intelligence (SI) is a branch of computational intelligence that discusses the *collective behavior* emerging within self-organizing societies of *agents*. SI was inspired by the observation of the collective behavior in societies in nature such as the movement of birds and fish. The collective behavior of such ecosystems, and their artificial counterpart of SI, is not encoded within the set of rules that determines the movement of each isolated agent, but it emerges through the interaction of multiple agents. Although several variations have been proposed in the literature, the fundamental set of rules used for music composition is based on the *"boids"* algorithm (Reynolds, 1987). These rules define the movement of each agent by adjusting its acceleration within short time intervals according to some conditions in the environment that it perceives. Specifically, these rules incorporate the following guidelines for the movement of each agent:

1. *Shoaling*: Move toward the center of mass of the agents that you perceive.
2. *Collision avoidance*: Move away from the agents that are too close to you.
3. *Schooling*: Move toward aligning your velocity to the mean velocity of the agents you perceive.

For these rules to be applied, some constants have to be predetermined, such as the radius of agent perception, i.e., at which distance does an agent perceive an object in its environment, and the radius of collision avoidance. These rules define the behavior of each agent, which begins forming organized groups called "swarms," which present collective behavior (combined intelligence as if they were a single organism).

Several parts of the aforementioned social characteristics have been embodied to agents which produce music and sound output, in combination with human interaction. Using the terminology described earlier, these systems are *performance driven*, since the agents receive feedback from the human user which defines some characteristics either of their behavior or of their environment. A thorough review of various methodologies that compose music on the symbolic level can be found by Blackwell (2007). Performance driven interaction in these systems captures the human performance of an instrumentalist or a vocalist, creating "attractors" in the space that the agents move. The agents are gathered around these attractors forming clusters, several spatial characteristics of which are translated into MIDI music information (including pitch, duration, intensity, polyphony, and several motif aspects).

In a similar fashion, computer and human interaction on the sound level has been accomplished with the utilization of swarms (Blackwell, 2008). The human performer's audio input is analyzed and attractors are generated in the space where the swarms move, which attract the swarms. Granulation parameters (pitch, amplitude, duration, gain distance, attack, and decay) are then defined by the position of the agents within this space. An extension of this work with the location of agents determining the spatial localization of sound has been presented by Wilson (2008). An alternative approach, where the human user is not an instrumentalist or a vocalist, was presented by Jones (2008). In the latter work, the user has the ability to create, destroy agents, and deposit food on the agents' space, creating a simplified version of interaction, since the user does not necessarily need to be specialized in music performance.

10.4.2 Interactive Composition with GA and GP

Among the first works for *subjectively driven* IE was a simple rhythm rating scheme using GA evolution according to fitness provided by user ratings (Horowitz, 1994). In a similar fashion (Johanson and Poli, 1998), a system was presented where initially random note sequences were rearranged with the utilization of music function combinations (such as play mirror, play twice, and shift down). Driven by subjective user ratings, the combination of these music functions evolved, providing better combinations. Additionally, an ANN was trained on the positive responses of the user, which was subsequently used as an automatic fitness rater. This allowed some individuals to be discarded before the user had a chance to hear them, thus reducing the effect of user fatigue caused by hearing a great number of successive low-quality melodies. The former work was extended with a combination of GA and GP in the music composition mechanism by Tokui (2000). In this work, short individual melodies were considered as chromosomes and were evolved using GA, while in parallel, functions that determined their temporal arrangement were evolved using GP. Again, user rating was fed into an ANN so that low-rated individuals could be acknowledged and discarded before the user had a chance to hear them. More recent approaches incorporate the evolution of several musical aspects (such as rhythm, tonality, and style) based on separate human ratings for each aspect (Fortier and Van Dyne, 2011; Moroni et al., 2000).

A GP scheme was utilized for subjectively driven evolution of sounds with sound synthesis techniques by Putnam (1994). In this approach, waveforms were directly shaped by functions, which in turn were evolved according to fitness values provided by users. However, using the aforementioned class of functions was mentioned to *"produced little more than irritating noise and evolved (if at all) very slowly"* (Putnam, 1994). In Kaliakatsos-Papakostas et al. (2012b), a GP scheme was used that evolves a class of functions which create waveforms with pleasant and interesting sonic output (Heikkilä, 2011). This subjectively driven scheme successfully evolved sounds-melodies to more preferred ones for each user. This fact allowed to draw some conclusions about possible aesthetic measures for sound, by measuring their difference between unevolved and evolved sounds-melodies. This system has also been utilized to examine the application of depth-adaptive fitness indicators by Kaliakatsos-Papakostas et al. (2012a). This subjectively driven system was observed to converge more quickly to higher rated individuals for the users that utilized a modified version of the standard

GP crossover and mutation operators. This version incorporated a constraint to the depth of the tree representation that these operators acted, according to the fitness assigned by the user (lower fitness allowing action to lower height, thus inflicting greater variability).

The pioneering work of Biles (2002) yielded a hybrid *performance driven* system, called *GenJam*, which utilizes GA to generate musical responses to a human improviser, while being rated for these responses. GenJam receives the music phrases that a human improviser is playing, considers them as chromosomes, and genetically evolves them to generate novel music responses. These responses are then rated by the improviser and subsequently evolved toward better melodies. In an extension of this work, GenJam utilizes an initial database of jazz phrases, a combination of which fosters new generations of phrases after the application of the "crossover" operator (Biles, 2001). In this way, the "fitness bottleneck" is eliminated and the GenJam is allowed to improvise autonomously, without the constant improviser's ratings. In a recent work (Weinberg et al., 2008) (similar to autonomous GenJam), the initial database of phrases was recorded by a jazz piano improviser and then stored to the system's memory. These phrases were blended with the input phrases from the human improviser using GA, forming a music response that included a satisfactory combination of novelty and relativity to the human improviser's phrases. The responses of this system was provided by a two-armed robot device performing on a xylophone, in contrast to most other approaches which use synthetic computer-generated sounds.

Different approaches to population initialization and fitness estimation have recently been suggested for *performance driven* system. In Manaris et al. (2011), Monterey Mirror is presented, which receives human phrases as input and creates music responses from scratch, using GA and a probabilistic population initialization scheme. The initial population is created by utilizing the *Markov transition probability* tables, which derive from the pitch and rhythm information extracted from the phrases provided by the human performer. This population is then evolved using as target, the FD of several features in the human improviser's phrases.

An alternative approach for performance driven interactive composition was followed by Kaliakatsos-Papakostas et al. (2012d), where the user input was analyzed in terms of tonality (chord estimation), Shannon information entropy (SIE) of the pitch class profile (PCP), rhythm characteristics (using some rhythmic features describing note density, syncopation, etc.), and intensity variations. These characteristics were then used as fitness evaluators for three different submodules:

1. The *tone generation submodule* utilizes the differential evolution (DE) algorithm (DE is a continuous variation of the GA with operators that take advantage of possible solution differences) to define the parameters of a chaotic function, so that it may produce responses with similar PCP SIE to the one of the phrases the improviser is playing.
2. The *rhythm submodule* utilizes the genetic evolution of the FL-systems described in Section 10.3.1, based on the rhythm that the improviser is playing within a sliding time window of fixed length.

3. The *intensity submodule* recognizes the mean value and standard deviation of the improviser's intensities and responds with values for intensity drawn by a uniform random number generator with the aforementioned mean and standard deviation.

This system provides responses with multiple "intelligent instrumentalists," which "hear" and "tune-in" to the human improviser's playing style, forming an intelligent band that performs constraint-free improvisation.

10.5 Conclusions

This chapter has presented a short review of a wide range of methodologies that may be considered within the generalized notion of *IMC*. In parallel with a short discussion about what would the term "intelligent" denotes when speaking about automatic music composition, a categorization of IMC methodologies was proposed that grouped methodologies not according to the underlying computational mechanisms, but according to the utilization of the *intelligent part* of the methodologies with regard to the *compositional aims*. The intelligent parts incorporated bioinspired methods, which either produce life-like structures or use notions borrowed by nature (such as evolution and collective behavior) to create human-like compositions. The compositional aims are defined by the composer/ programmer and roughly pinpoint the rate of compositional freedom allowed to the underlying mechanism, in combination with the interactivity of the system's responses.

The intelligent part of the compositional methodologies would be composing music undestructively, without the imposition of restrictions or targets, forming the category of *unsupervised intelligent composition* methods. The imposition of compositional restrictions with the introduction of target features that derive from stylistic directions forms the category of *supervised intelligent composition*. In this category, the intelligent part of the methodologies drives the compositional process toward creating music with specified characteristics, which derive from sets of target pieces or desired music characteristics. Finally the category of *interactive intelligent composition* was presented, which incorporates methodologies that compose music based on the input provided by the human user. This category was further subdivided in the subcategories of *subjectively driven* and *performance driven* methodologies. The former drives the evolution solely according to the user's choices or ratings, whereas the latter decodes the human input into musical information and creates proper music responses.

More methodologies that pertain to the aforementioned categorization can be found within an overwhelming amount of excellent works that were not mentioned in this chapter. The authors hope that the reader was given a representative sample from the state-of-the art systems among the most popular intelligent methodologies. Among the authors' motivations for this chapter is also the establishment of a commonly accepted terminology and categorization of intelligent music methodologies, based on the force that drives their creativity, whether it is nature-like complexity, target-oriented evolution, or human interaction. Such a categorization could be of vital importance to the intelligent music research community and would benefit the researcher, the musician, and the student. The researcher would have immediate access to works that are relative to her/his research. The musician would be facilitated by quickly filtering out the works that are not among her/his artistic scope, without frustratingly going through a great amount of irrelevant material. Finally, the student could constructively understand the motivation behind each intelligent methodology and the mechanisms of the underlying intelligent methods, making the way to expertise less time-consuming and more creative.

References

Alfonseca, M., Cebrian, M., Ortega, A., 2007. A simple genetic algorithm for music generation by means of algorithmic information theory. In: IEEE Congress on Evolutionary Computation, CEC'07, pp. 3035−3042.

Biles, J.A., 2001. Autonomous GenJam: eliminating the fitness bottleneck by eliminating fitness. In: Proceedings of the 2001 Genetic and Evolutionary Computation Conference Workshop Program, GECCO'01, Morgan Kaufmann, San Francisco, CA.

Biles, J.A., 2002. GenJam: evolution of a jazz improviser. In: Bentley, P.J., Corne, D.W. (Eds.), Creative Evolutionary Systems. Morgan Kaufmann Publishers Inc., San Francisco, CA, pp. 165−187.

Blackwell, T., 2008. Swarm granulation. In: Romero, J., Machado, P. (Eds.), The Art of Artificial Evolution, Natural Computing Series. Springer, Berlin/Heidelberg, pp. 103−122.

Blackwell, T.M., 2007. Swarming and music. In: Miranda, E.R., Biles, J.A. (Eds.), Evolutionary Computer Music. Springer, London, pp. 194−217.

Burraston, D., Edmonds, E., 2005. Cellular automata in generative electronic music and sonic art: a historical and technical review. Digit. Creativity. 16 (3), 165−185.

Donnelly, P., Sheppard, J., 2011. Evolving four-part harmony using genetic algorithms. Proceedings of the 2011 International Conference on Applications of Evolutionary Computation—Volume Part II, EvoApplications'11. Springer-Verlag, Berlin/Heidelberg, pp. 273−282.

Fortier, N., Van Dyne, M., 2011. A genetic algorithm approach to improve automated music composition. Int. J. Comput. 5 (4), 525−532.

Geis, M., Middendorf, M., 2008. Creating melodies and baroque harmonies with ant colony optimization. Int. J. Intell. Comput. Cybern. 1 (2), 213−238.

Gogins, M., 2010. Score generating Lindenmayer Systems in the Generalized Contextual Group. Available Online: <http://michaelgogins.com/pdf/Lindenmayer_Systems_Based_on_Riemannian_Transformations.pdf> (accessed 10.15.12).

Griffith, N., Todd, P.M. (Eds.), 1999. Musical Networks: Parallel Distributed Perception and Performance. MIT Press, Cambridge, MA.

Heikkilä, V., 2011. Discovering novel computer music techniques by exploring the space of short computer programs. CoRR abs/1112.1368 (accessed 10.15.12).

Horowitz, D., 1994. Generating rhythms with genetic algorithms. Proceedings of the Twelfth National Conference on Artificial Intelligence (vol. 2), AAAI'94. American Association for Artificial Intelligence, Menlo Park, CA, pp. 1459−1460.

Johanson, B.E., Poli, R., 1998. GP-Music: an interactive genetic programming system for music generation with automated fitness raters. Technical Report CSRP-98-13, University of Birmingham, School of Computer Science.

Jones, D., 2008. AtomSwarm: a framework for swarm improvisation. Proceedings of the 2008 Conference on Applications of Evolutionary Computing, Evo'08. Springer-Verlag, Berlin/Heidelberg, pp. 423−432.

Kaliakatsos-Papakostas, M.A., Epitropakis, M.G., Floros, A., Vrahatis, M.N., 2012a. Controlling interactive evolution of 8-bit melodies with genetic programming. Soft Comput. 16 (2), 1997−2008.

Kaliakatsos-Papakostas, M.A., Epitropakis, M.G., Floros, A., Vrahatis, M.N., 2012b. Interactive evolution of 8-bit melodies with genetic programming towards finding aesthetic measures for sound. In: Proceedings of the First International Conference on Evolutionary and Biologically Inspired Music, Sound, Art and Design, EvoMUSART'12, Malaga, Spain, LNCS, vol. 7247. Springer-Verlag, pp. 140−151.

Kaliakatsos-Papakostas, M.A., Floros, A., Vrahatis, M.N., 2012c. Intelligent generation of rhythmic sequences using finite L-systems. In: Proceedings of the Eighth International Conference on Intelligent Information Hiding and Multimedia Signal Processing, IIHMSP'12, Piraeus, Athens, Greece, pp. 424−427.

Kaliakatsos-Papakostas, M.A., Floros, A., Vrahatis, M.N., 2012d. Intelligent real-time music accompaniment for constraint-free improvisation. In: Proceedings of the 24th IEEE International Conference on Tools with Artificial Intelligence, ICTAI'12, Piraeus, Athens, Greece.

Kaliakatsos-Papakostas, M.A., Floros, A., Vrahatis, M.N., Kanellopoulos, N., 2012e. Genetic evolution of L and FL-systems for the production of rhythmic sequences. In: Proceedings of the Second Workshop in Evolutionary Music Held during the 21st International Conference on Genetic Algorithms and the 17th Annual Genetic Programming Conference (GP), GECCO'12, Philadelphia, PA, pp. 461−468.

Lo, M.Y., 2012. Evolving cellular automata for music composition with trainable fitness functions. Ph.D. Thesis, University of Essex, Essex.

Lourenc, B.F., Brand, C.P., 2009. L-systems, scores, and evolutionary techniques. In: Proceedings of the SMC 2009—Sixth Sound and Music Computing Conference, pp. 113−118.

Manaris, B., Roos, P., Machado, P., Krehbiel, D., Pellicoro, L., Romero, J., 2007. A corpus-based hybrid approach to music analysis and composition. Proceedings of the 22nd National Conference on Artificial Intelligence—Volume 1. AAAI Press, Vancouver, British Columbia, pp. 839−845.

Manaris, B., Hughes, D., Vassilandonakis, Y., 2011. Monterey mirror: combining Markov models, genetic algorithms, and power laws. In: Workshop in Evolutionary Music, IEEE Congress on Evolutionary Computation, CEC'11, New Orleans, LA.

McCormack, J., 1996. Grammar-based music composition. Complexity Int. 3.

Millen, D., 2005. An interactive cellular automata music application in cocoa. In: Proceedings of the 2004 International Computer Music Conference, ICMC'04.

Miranda, E.R., Biles, J.A., 2007. Evolutionary Computer Music. Springer-Verlag New York, Inc., Secaucus, NJ.

Moroni, A., Manzolli, J., Zuben, F.V., Gudwin, R., 2000. Vox populi: an interactive evolutionary system for algorithmic music composition. Leonardo Music J. 10 (1), 49−54.

Özcan, E., Ercal, T., 2008. A genetic algorithm for generating improvised music. In: Monmarché, N., Talbi, E.-G., Collet, P., Schoenauer, M., Lutton, E. (Eds.), Artificial Evolution, Lecture Notes in Computer Science, vol. 4926. Springer, Berlin/Heidelberg, pp. 266−277.

Papadopoulos, G., Wiggins, G., 1998. A genetic algorithm for the generation of jazz melodies. In: Proceedings of the Finnish Conference on Artificial Intelligence (STeP), pp. 7–9.

Pestana, P., 2012. Lindenmayer systems and the harmony of fractals. Chaotic Model. Simul. 1 (1), 91–99.

Phon-Amnuaisuk, S., Law, E., Kuan, H., 2007. Evolving music generation with SOMFitness genetic programming. In: Giacobini, M. (Ed.), Applications of Evolutionary Computing, Lecture Notes in Computer Science, vol. 4448. Springer, Berlin/Heidelberg, pp. 557–566.

Prusinkiewicz, P., 1986. Score generation with L-systems. In: Proceedings of the International Computer Music Conference, ICMA'86, pp. 455–457.

Prusinkiewicz, P., Lindenmayer, A., 1990. The Algorithmic Beauty of Plants. Springer-Verlag New York, Inc., New York, NY.

Putnam, J.B., 1994. Genetic Programming of Music. Available Online: <www0.cs.ucl.ac.uk/staff/ucacbbl/ftp/papers/ep.ps.gz> (accessed 10.15.12).

Reynolds, C.W., 1987. Flocks, herds and schools: a distributed behavioral model. In: Proceedings of the 14th Annual Conference on Computer Graphics and Interactive Techniques, SIGGRAPH'87, pp. 25–34.

Solomos, M., 2005. Cellular automata in Xenakis' music. Theory and practice. In: Proceedings of the International Symposium Iannis Xenakis, pp. 120–137.

Spector, L., Alpern, A., 1994. Criticism, culture, and the automatic generation of artworks. Proceedings of the Twelfth National Conference on Artificial Intelligence (vol. 1), AAAI'94. American Association for Artificial Intelligence, Menlo Park, CA, pp. 3–8.

Spector, L., Alpern, A., 1995. Induction and recapitulation of deep musical structure. In: Proceedings of the IFCAI'95 Workshop on Artificial Intelligence and Music, pp. 41–48.

Tokui, N., 2000. Music composition with interactive evolutionary computation. Communication. 17 (2), 215–226.

Weinberg, G., Godfrey, M., Rae, A., Rhoads, J., 2008. A real-time genetic algorithm in human–robot musical improvisation. Computer Music Modeling and Retrieval Sense of Sounds. Springer-Verlag, Berlin/Heidelberg, pp. 351–359.

Wilson, S., 2008. Spatial swarm granulation. In: Proceedings of the 2008 International Computer Music Conference.

Wolfram, S., 2002. A New Kind of Science. first ed. Wolfram Media, Champaign, IL.

11 A Review of the Development and Applications of the Cuckoo Search Algorithm

Sean Walton, Oubay Hassan, Kenneth Morgan and M. Rowan Brown

College of Engineering, Swansea University, Swansea, Wales, UK

11.1 Introduction

At its most basic level, the goal of optimization is to find a set of inputs which minimizes or maximizes a function. It tends to be the convention that if functions are minimized, a maximization problem can always be formed in terms of a minimization. The function to be minimized is known as the objective function and the space on which its inputs exist is called the solution space. Optimizers search the solution space of the objective function to find the minimum. Traditionally, optimizers have made use of the gradient of the objective function, with respect to the inputs, to decide the direction in which to search. In highly nonlinear problems, the gradient will change throughout the search space and may not point in the direction of the global minimum solution (Diez and Peri, 2010). During the 1950s and 1960s, computer scientists investigated the possibilities of modeling the concepts of evolution as an optimization tool for engineers. The result of this work was the genetic algorithm (Mitchell, 1999), which was one of the first gradient free optimization techniques. Gradient free techniques are heuristic in nature and use large populations of agents to search the solution space. The objective function can be calculated at the position of each agent and a series of rules followed to, hopefully, move the agents toward the global minimum. Examples of such algorithms include particle swarm optimization (Bratton and Kennedy, 2007), differential evolution (Storn and Price, 1997), and cuckoo search (Yang and Deb, 2009). A successful gradient free optimization technique will find a balance between exploring new parts of the search space and refining areas of the search space where current information suggests the minimum might be located. This chapter details the

Swarm Intelligence and Bio-Inspired Computation. DOI: http://dx.doi.org/10.1016/B978-0-12-405163-8.00011-9

development of the cuckoo search algorithm and includes a selection of applications that highlight its versatility.

11.2   Cuckoo Search Algorithm

The cuckoo search algorithm introduced by Yang and Deb (2009) is inspired by the breeding behavior of cuckoos, combined with an efficient random walk behavior that is exhibited by many organisms. In this section, we outline the basics of the original algorithm and detail the implementation and validation performed by the authors.

11.2.1   The Analogy

Before the algorithm itself is detailed, it is worth spending some time discussing the analogy behind cuckoo search. Yang and Deb (2009) were aiming to employ an emulation of cuckoo breeding behavior to drive their optimization algorithm. In the original publication, they specify that an egg in a nest represents a solution and an egg represents a new potential solution. An equivalent representation, which is used throughout this chapter, is to let an egg represent any solution (new or old), with the nests simply being containers for the eggs. Each egg will carry two pieces of information, namely, its coordinates in the solution space and its fitness value. In this way, the nests can be viewed as positions in an array, or computer memory, where this information is stored. Theoretically, a nest may contain one or more eggs, although, in most algorithms, each nest contains only a single egg.

11.2.2   Cuckoo Breeding Behavior

The breeding behavior of cuckoos is particularly aggressive and this motivates its use in an optimization algorithm. Many species of cuckoo lay their eggs in the nests of other birds, which may or may not be of the same species (Yang and Deb, 2010). This behavior is given the term brood parasitism, of which there are three basic types, namely, intraspecific, cooperative, or nest takeover (Payne et al., 2005). If a host bird discovers the cuckoo egg in its nest, it may destroy the egg or abandon the nest altogether. This has lead to the evolution of cuckoo eggs which resemble eggs of locally found birds (Walton et al., 2011b). Yang and Deb (2010) simplified this behavior by introducing three rules:

1. Each cuckoo lays one egg at a time and dumps it into a random nest; the best nests (which contain the highest quality eggs) carry over to the next generation.
2. The number of available host nests is fixed and there is always a probability that the cuckoo egg is discovered by the host.
3. If this happens, the host bird throws the egg away.

The third rule is approximated by discarding a fraction of the eggs and replacing them at each generation. Essentially, these rules provide a selection process for the optimization algorithm, ensuring that the best eggs survive from generation to generation. For a complete algorithm, a method of generating the eggs is required.

11.2.3   Lévy Flights

One of the most powerful features of cuckoo search is the use of Lévy flights to generate new eggs. Every time a step is taken during a Lévy flight, the distance traveled in each search dimension is generated using a probability density function which has a power law tail (Walton et al., 2011a,b). The result is a path made up of many small steps and the occasional large jump. Such a path represents an optimum random search pattern which is frequently found in nature (Viswanathan, 2008). This search pattern has been used in other optimization techniques, and examples may be found by Pavlyukevich (2007) and Yang (2010). One of the defining characteristics of a search pattern resulting from a Lévy flight is that it is scale free (Yang, 2010). The scale free nature means that the search pattern is the same in small-scale searching and in large-scale searching. By searching scale, we are referring to the distance traveled by agents from one generation to the next. Small-scale searching occurs locally in the solution space and large-scale searching occurs globally. This leads to an automatic balance between exploration and refinement. It is this complex random walk strategy that makes cuckoo search stand out when it is compared with other optimization algorithms (Civicioglu and Besdok, 2011). An example of a Lévy flight is shown in Figure 11.1, where Figure 11.1A shows the large-scale search pattern and Figure 11.1B shows the small-scale search pattern. This can be compared with a Gaussian walk, as shown in Figure 11.2, where the random steps are generated using a probability function with a normal distribution. The lack of large jumps in the Gaussian walk means it is less suited to large-scale global searching.

11.2.4   The Algorithm

Using the idealized rules discussed above, the algorithm can be summarized in the following pseudo-code (Yang and Deb, 2009):

1. Generate an initial population of eggs, calculate the fitness of each egg, place each egg in a nest, and rank the nests in order of fitness.
2. Until a stop criterion is met, perform the following steps to find the next generation of eggs:
   a. create an egg using a random Lévy flight from a random egg and evaluate its fitness;
   b. select a random nest and replace the egg in that nest with the newly generated one, if the new egg has a better fitness, else discard the new egg;
   c. remove a fraction of the worst eggs from their nests and generate new eggs to replace them;
   d. rank the nests to find the current best egg.

This simple algorithm has two parameters which can be adjusted. The first is the step size of the Lévy flight, $\alpha > 0$, which controls the scale of the flight by multiplication. The parameter α should be related to the size of the solution space of the objective

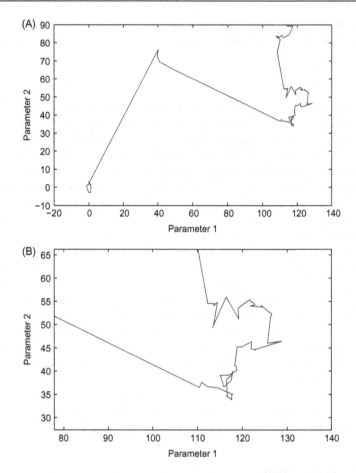

Figure 11.1 The Lévy Flight. (A) An example of a 100-step Lévy flight. Note the small localized searches connected by large jumps. The axis in both these figures represents the first two dimensions in a search space. The Lévy flight step size in this example was set to 1. (B) A zoomed section of the same Lévy flight, which shows the same characteristics as the full flight in (A) highlighting the scale free nature of this process.

function. This parameter could almost be selected automatically if the size of the solution space is known, e.g., it could be set as a percentage of the diagonal of the search space. The second parameter is the fraction, p_a, of eggs to be discarded. Increasing this value will increase the exploration taking place in the algorithm and hence decrease the chance of getting trapped in local minima. Decreasing this value will decrease the exploration increasing the chance of getting trapped in local minima. This represents a small number of user-specified parameters when compared with other optimization algorithms of this type. Yang and Deb (2009) found that the convergence of the algorithm to an optimum solution is largely independent of p_a but that $p_a = 0.25$ yielded best results. This is another strong feature of the cuckoo search algorithm, since many

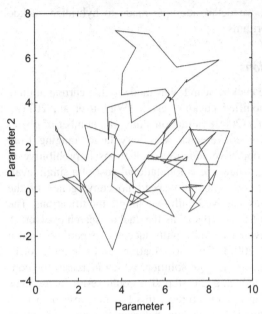

Figure 11.2 Gaussian walk. An example of a 100-step Gaussian walk with a step size of 1. Compared with the Lévy flights, there are no large jumps across the search space.

other optimization algorithms are extremely sensitive to the choice of parameters, which also tend to be problem specific.

11.2.5 Validation

To validate the algorithm, Yang and Deb (2009) compared cuckoo search to particle swarm optimization and genetic algorithm on 10 standard optimization benchmarking functions. Since these algorithms are metaheuristic in nature, the same solution is not guaranteed each time the algorithm is executed. Each algorithm was run 100 times to provide statistical significance to the test. Execution was to stop when the variation of the objective function values was $<10^{-5}$. They provide a percentage success rate at finding the global minima and report the number of function evaluations needed before the stopping criteria was met for each function for each algorithm. For all functions considered, cuckoo search outperformed particle swarm optimization and genetic algorithm in terms of success rate and number of objective function evaluations. Yang and Deb (2009) stated that the reason for this success is both a good balance of local and global searching and a small number of control parameters.

11.3   Modifications and Developments

In this section, we detail some of the modifications and developments that have been made to the cuckoo search algorithm by the wider optimization community. This section is split into two parts. First, a number of modifications to the core algorithm are discussed and, then, we detail attempts made to hybridize cuckoo search with other optimization algorithms.

11.3.1 Algorithmic Modifications

One of the first modifications to the cuckoo search was made by the current authors and lead to the introduction of modified cuckoo search (Walton et al., 2011b). We observed that, in Yang and Deb's (2009) validation study, the number of objective function evaluations needed for convergence was very large, ranging from 3015 to 110,523. This number of objective function evaluations is prohibitive in many real optimization applications, where the computational cost of a single evaluation is large. With this in mind, we sought to speed up convergence of the cuckoo search algorithm and this was achieved with two simple modifications. The first modification was to reduce the Lévy step size as the cuckoo search evolves. A similar modification had previously been made, with success, to particle swarm optimization (Bratton and Kennedy, 2007). This modification results in more localized searching, as the eggs get closer to the final solution, which increases the convergence rate. There is a risk that reducing the step size could result in the eggs getting trapped in subminima but, in our experience, this has not proved to be a problem. Second, we added information exchange between the eggs to model genetic crossover. In the original cuckoo search algorithm, the eggs are essentially searching independently from one another and a certain percentage of the failing searches are restarting each generation. The crossover step is simple and new eggs are generated by randomly linking pairs of the best existing eggs. The best eggs are the ones which are not discarded, i.e., $(1 - p_a)$ times the total number of eggs. A line is constructed between pairs of the top eggs and a new egg generated at a point along the line that lies slightly closer to the better of the two eggs. The inverse of the golden ratio, $\varphi = (1 + 5^{0.5})/2$, is used as the fraction of distance along the line. No additional control parameters are added by these modifications, retaining one of the key strengths of the original cuckoo search. To validate these modifications, we compared the modified cuckoo search to the original algorithm and to two state-of-the-art optimization techniques, namely, a particle swarm algorithm and a differential evolution algorithm. The validation was performed on seven benchmark objective functions, over a range of solution space dimensions. Performance was compared in terms of a convergence rate of distance to the known global minima from the current best egg, with respect to the number of objective function evaluations. In all cases, it was found that the modified cuckoo search outperformed the standard cuckoo search and performed as well as, or better than, particle swarm optimization. Interestingly, as the number of dimensions in the solution space increases, the margin by which the modified cuckoo search outperforms cuckoo search and particle swarm optimization also increases. The modified cuckoo search showed a much faster initial convergence rate than the differential evolution algorithm but, given time, differential evolution would get closer to the minima.

Cuckoo search, like many metaheuristic algorithms, requires that a starting population is specified by the user. Many optimization algorithms show a bias to the starting population (Bratton and Kennedy, 2007), which suggests that this is an aspect of these kinds of algorithms which needs to be considered carefully. In our work on the modified cuckoo search (Walton et al., 2011a,b), we used Latin hyper-cube sampling to pick the initial eggs. Latin hyper-cube sampling is a method which attempts to sample an N-dimensional space with a minimum number of samples. This is achieved by first splitting each dimension into N bins; N samples are then randomly selected such that, when a projection is viewed along any one dimension, there is a sample in each bin (Mifsud et al., 2010). The random nature of this sampling method means a space filling sampling is not guaranteed. Shatnawi and Nasrudin (2011) attempted to address this issue by employing Centroidal Voronoi Tessellation (CVT) as a technique to improve the starting positions of the eggs. If we consider each egg as a Voronoi generator, then each egg is surrounded by a Voronoi cell in the solution space. Each Voronoi cell defines the area of space containing all points closest, in terms of Euclidean distance in this case, to its generator than any of the others. When the centroid of the vertices of a Voronoi cell lies on the same point as the Voronoi generator, then the set of points define a CVT. Figure 11.2 shows an example of a CVT.

Shatnawi and Nasrudin (2011) argued that, if an iterative algorithm (Du and Gunzburger, 1999) is used to move an initial random distribution of eggs close to a CVT, this would result in faster convergence to the global minima, since a CVT is space filling. On the simplest level, a CVT sampling increases the probability of one of the initial eggs being close to the global minima. Their results show a marginal decrease in the number of objective function evaluations required to find the global minima when comparing CVT to a random sampling. However, they note that the additional cost of generating a CVT may outweigh any benefit in function evaluation cost reduction. We would argue that, in real engineering applications, where the objective evaluation cost could be very large, any reduction in the number of objective function evaluations would likely outweigh the added cost of CVT generation.

Another interesting modification to cuckoo search is presented by Lin and Lee (2012). In their paper, they do not directly compare the new algorithm, emotional chaotic cuckoo search, to the unmodified algorithm, so it is hard to gauge the effect of their modifications. However, we feel the modifications may have merit and should be investigated further, so they are included here. The two goals of their modifications were to improve the quality of neighborhood searching, when generating new eggs, and to increase the likelihood of eggs escaping local minima. To address their first goal, they identify an issue with the Lévy flight. The Lévy flight step size α needs to be correctly selected depending on the scale of the problem, which may in some cases be unknown. A Lévy flight with a fixed step size does not display ergodicity, which means there is not an equal chance of an egg traveling through every point in the solution space. Lin and Lee (2012) attempted to address this issue by replacing α with a value taken from a chaotic sequence c_s. Each generation c_s is updated using the equation

$$c_s(t) = 4c_s(t-1)(1 - c_s(t-1))$$

where t is the generation number. This sequence is ergodic and, thus, increases the chance that every possible scale is used during the search, which increases the chance of finding the correct minima. The second goal is addressed by replacing the simple egg replacement scheme of cuckoo search, where an egg replaces another if its fitness is better with an emotional model. The emotional model looks at the difference between the fitnesses, and, based on a logarithmic relationship, only replaces an egg when a certain threshold is breached. This results in an increased probability of moving across hills and valleys in the fitness landscape, thus reducing the chance of getting trapped in subminima.

11.3.2 Hybridization

In the original cuckoo search paper, Yang and Deb (2009) suggested that it may be worth investigating hybridization with existing optimization algorithms. In this section, we detail two such attempts.

Ghodrati and Lotfi (2012) proposed the hybridization of the cuckoo search and particle swarm optimization algorithms. Particle swarm optimization is a common technique used for global optimization (Bratton and Kennedy, 2007). In nature, swarms of animals are found to exhibit complex behavior capable of solving difficult tasks. This is done with only a small number of simple rules governing the behavior of each individual in the swarm (Praveen and Duvigneau, 2009). In particle swarm optimization, this behavior is mimicked by a swarm of individuals exploring the solution space (Diez and Peri, 2010). A particle's velocity, personal memory of the best location found, and global memory of the best position found by the swarm influence its next position. Much as in modified cuckoo search (Walton et al., 2011b), Ghodrati and Lotfi (2012) recognize that the original cuckoo search lacks communication between the individual eggs. They add this communication, using the same equations used in particle swarm optimization, to move the eggs after the Lévy flight step has been performed and before the worst eggs have been discarded. The update rule for a cuckoo's new velocity is

$$v_{t+1} = W_t \cdot v_t + C_1 \cdot \text{rand}() \cdot (\text{pbest} - x_t) + C_2 \cdot \text{rand}() \cdot (\text{gbest} - x_t)$$

where v_t is the cuckoo's velocity at generation t, W_t is an inertia weight, pbest and gbest are the cuckoo's personal best position and the global best position respectively, rand() is a random number between 0 and 1, and the constants C_1 and C_2 are parameters which affect the optimization algorithm. Ghodrati and Lotfi (2012) kept the values of these new parameters constant for their benchmarking, but it needs to be noted that the hybridization with particle swarm optimization has doubled the number of parameters that need to be specified. Over a range of benchmarking functions, they found that the hybrid algorithm outperformed cuckoo search 80% of the time and particle swarm optimization 85% of the time in terms of convergence rate and closeness to the global minima.

When applying optimization techniques to training a neural network, Salimi et al. (2012) proposed a simple hybridization between the modified cuckoo search

(Walton et al., 2011a,b) and a conjugate gradient method. They were training a neural network for classification and pattern recognition purposes. A neural network has a series of weights associated with it, which govern its behavior. Traditionally, a gradient-based method would be used to find the optimum weights. Salimi et al. (2012) found that this technique, which requires an initial guess for the weights, depends greatly on the initial guess, due to the multimodal nature of the problem. They found an increased performance of the trained neural network, if they first used the global optimization properties of the modified cuckoo search to find an initial guess. This was then given to the conjugate gradient solver, which refined the solution. This is a very simple hybridization, which would certainly offer an improvement over just using a cuckoo search in many applications.

11.4 Applications

Since its introduction, there have been a number of real-world applications of the cuckoo search algorithm and its derivatives. In this section, we detail a selection of these applications in two categories: learning and design. Applications in learning deal with problems where a system, usually a neural network, is trained to perform a task. Applications in design deal with more design-based problems.

11.4.1 Applications in Machine Learning

One of the early applications of cuckoo search was presented by Speed (2010). His goal was to evolve an AI to enter the Mario AI competition. The aim of this competition is to produce an AI which can successfully play a level of the Nintendo game Super Mario Brothers. When attempting to produce an AI, the two possible strategies are either to hand code an algorithm or to use optimization to evolve an algorithm. The advantage of evolved algorithms is that they can adapt to new situations, whereas hand-coded AIs need to be recoded. Evolutionary algorithms attempt to evolve a mapping, which uses Mario's in-game state as inputs and gives Mario's actions as outputs. The inputs consist of a 22×22 grid of tiles surrounding Mario, each tile contains information about anything relevant existing inside it, e.g., enemies or power-ups. The outputs are a series of actions which would normally be available to the human player, move left, move right, duck, jump and fireball/move faster. In the case of a Mario AI, the resulting search space for the optimum mapping is extremely large. In addition, the search space is not continuous but made up of a sequence of distinct states. To use a Lévy flight in this context, Speed (2010) devised a mapping which treats a number from the Lévy distribution as a fraction of the total number of states, then changes that number of states. Using this modified version of the cuckoo search, Speed (2010) was able to generate a Mario AI which performed well compared with one generated using a generic genetic algorithm.

Spiking neural models try to replicate the behavior of biological neurons when they are subject to an input current. Such neurons do not generate an output until the total input reaches a specific threshold. A connected network of spiking neurons can be trained, based on a number of parameters associated with each neuron, to perform various tasks. Vazquez (2011) trained such a network to perform pattern recognition tasks. The goal was to input a pattern to the network and have patterns of the same classes result in the same outputs, and different classes result in different outputs. Framing this as an optimization problem, they found cuckoo search was very successful for training this network in a variety of examples. Furthermore, when comparing networks trained using cuckoo search to networks trained using differential evolution, they found that the cuckoo search trained networks gave slightly better results.

Selvi and Purusothaman (2012) applied cuckoo search to the problem of cryptanalysis. The aim is to use heuristic algorithms to break encryption with a view to identifying weaknesses in the system. When comparing many heuristic algorithms, they found cuckoo search worked well at attacking some ciphers, but was not as consistent as other algorithms like particle swarm optimization.

Spam filters are algorithms that detect unsolicited e-mails and prevent them from reaching a user's inbox. Natarajan and Subramanian (2012) applied cuckoo search to this problem by optimizing a bloom filter for spam filtering. A bloom filter is a simple data structure which can check if a string belongs to a particular database of strings. The issue with bloom filters is that there is always the risk of a false positive and, depending on construction of the filter, different strings in the database have different probabilities of producing false positives. Natarajan and Subramanian (2012) constructed an objective function which minimizes the probability of producing false positives on the strings in a spam database which have the highest occurrence in spam mail. A filter constructed in such a way to minimize this objective function would be the optimum spam filter. They found that a filter constructed in this way using cuckoo search outperformed filters not constructed in this fashion.

11.4.2   Applications in Design

Cuckoo search has been benchmarked on a number of structural optimization problems. Gandomi et al. (2011) presented 13 different structural design problems, from the very simple design of an I-beam to more complex gear train designs to optimizing a complete car structure, modeled using finite elements, to withstand a side impact. These types of structural problems are highly nonlinear and have large numbers of design variables with complex constraints. Problems of this type are impossible to solve globally using gradient-based techniques. They compared the ability of cuckoo search to solve these problems to a number of other state-of-the-art optimization algorithms. In most cases, the solutions obtained with cuckoo search were better than when other methods were used. Gandomi et al. (2011) stated that this success is due to the small number of parameters which can be changed in cuckoo search and that the sensitivity of these parameters is small.

Cuckoo search was also applied to the problem of truss optimization problems by Gandomi et al. (2012). As a specific subset of structural problems, truss optimization is a highly nonlinear problem. Truss structures are designed to carry multiple loads under static constraints on the displacement of the structure. Five problems, each with an increased complexity, were presented by Gandomi et al. (2012). They were able to show that cuckoo search outperformed many state-of-the-art optimization algorithms in terms of the quality of the design produced. It should be noted that both Gandomi et al. (2011) and Gandomi et al. (2012) used different numbers of cuckoos for different examples, which suggest they may have had to tune this to each problem. Another example of cuckoo search applied to truss structure optimization is presented by Kaveh et al. (2012). In particular, they looked at the design of steel frame structures. In their examples, the design parameters were made up of the individual beam characteristics. They did not compare the performance of cuckoo search to other algorithms but found good convergence to an improved design, even when applied to designs with 568 trusses.

In machining, the goal is to find a balance between maximizing production rate and quality, while minimizing cost. This balance is found by adjusting manufacturing parameters associated with a particular product. Yildiz (2012) attempted to apply cuckoo search to a case study belonging to this family of problems. The example chosen for investigation was to optimize the cutting parameters in milling operations. In this example, the goal was to maximize the total profit rate by adjusting the cutting speed and feed rate of the milling process. A series of complex constraints were applied to these parameters to ensure feasibility and sufficient product quality. Yildiz (2012) found that not only did cuckoo search find the maximum profit rates, but also it required the smallest number of function evaluations compared to six competing optimization algorithms.

Modified cuckoo search (Walton et al., 2011b) has also been applied to mesh optimization (Walton et al., 2011a, 2012). The goal of this work was to produce suitable unstructured meshes for the use with co-volume solvers, such as the marker and cell algorithm (Harlow and Welch, 1965). These types of methods are computationally efficient, but have mesh requirements that are difficult to impose on complex geometries, namely, a pair of mutually orthogonal meshes are required for the implementation of the solver. A mutually orthogonal mesh can be easily constructed for an existing Delaunay mesh by considering its Voronoi dual. The Voronoi dual is constructed by considering the points defining the Delaunay triangulation as Voronoi generators and the resulting Voronoi vertices then connect to give the dual (e.g., the CVT shown in Figure 11.3). The solver stores unknowns at the vertices of the Voronoi mesh for integration over the Delaunay elements, which introduces the requirement that each Voronoi vertex must lie inside its associated Delaunay element. This is not guaranteed in an unstructured mesh. A Delaunay element which does not contain its Voronoi vertex is considered a bad element. Figure 11.4 shows a section of a two-dimensional mesh containing good and bad elements.

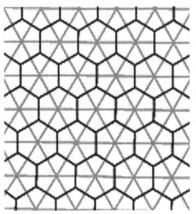

Figure 11.3 Centroidal Voronoi Tessellation. An example of a CVT. The vertices of the equilateral triangles are the Voronoi generators, and the Voronoi vertices connect to form hexagonal Voronoi cells. In this case, the Voronoi generators lie at the center of mass of the Voronoi cells and thus we have a CVT.

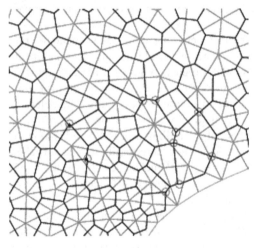

Figure 11.4 Examples of bad elements. A portion of a mesh containing both good and bad elements. The circled Voronoi vertices lie outside their associated elements and indicate the bad elements.

To approach this problem, the possibility of improving an existing mesh, so that it meets these requirements, is considered. An objective function which, when minimized, would produce a near ideal mesh (Walton et al., 2012) is formulated and the modified cuckoo search (Walton et al., 2011b) is applied to the problem. In all the two-dimensional meshes that were tested, modified cuckoo search was able to move every Voronoi vertex inside its associated element. This was unachievable using competing mesh improvement techniques. In the three-dimensional examples presented, modified cuckoo search produced meshes with orders of magnitude less bad elements compared to other techniques. However, the excessive computational cost meant that not all the bad elements were eliminated. Other optimization techniques were also used in place of modified cuckoo search, but it was found that modified cuckoo search outperformed these techniques (Figure 11.4).

11.5 Conclusion

In this review, it has been shown that cuckoo search has been applied successfully to a wide range of problems. Significant numbers of these problems are extremely complex and represent real useful applications. We can identify three main strengths of the cuckoo search which has lead to its success and popularity:

1. It is easy to implement.
2. The Lévy flight.
3. The number of parameters that have to be specified is small.

The importance of ease of implementation of an algorithm should not be underestimated. An engineer or professional, who may not have a background in optimization, is simply more likely to pick a technique which is easier to implement. It also helps that a number of authors have made code available on the Internet which is ready to use and easy to find. The scale free nature of the Lévy flight is clearly an important feature of the cuckoo search. Many of the applications discussed above were problems with very large search spaces. A scale free random walk, like the Lévy flight, is able to efficiently search such spaces. Many authors have given the small number of tuning parameters as one of the most desirable features of the cuckoo search. Most gradient free algorithms, by their nature, have lots of tuning parameters which need to be adjusted for each new problem. If there are less parameters, it will be a lot quicker to tune the optimization algorithm. Cuckoo search also has the advantage, it seems, that these parameters have a small effect on the performance of the algorithm. This means that an "off-the-shelf" cuckoo search implementation is likely to give good results immediately.

A number of modifications have been made to the cuckoo search algorithm. In the most part, these tend to be less concerned with the cuckoo analogy and more with making additions to improve performance. When adding modifications to the cuckoo search algorithm, attempts need to be made to retain both the ease of implementation and the small number of tuning parameters. Currently, most applications of cuckoo search have used the unmodified algorithm. Clearly, there would be some benefit to applying some of the modifications discussed above which have a positive impact on performance to these applications, e.g., the increased convergence rate of modified cuckoo search (Walton et al., 2011b) or finding a better optimum using hybridization with gradient-based methods (Salimi et al., 2012). It would also be good to see a detailed comparison, as the cuckoo search algorithm develops, of performance between the various modifications. It may be the case that a selection of modifications from different cuckoo search algorithms needs to be combined to produce the best performance. Further applications for cuckoo search may include finding optimum parameters in chemical processes like membrane distillation (Alkhudhiri et al., 2012), which may be different for different applications. Other applications may include automatic shape optimization in novel applications such as the BLOODHOUND SSC project to design a land vehicle capable of achieving a speed of 1000 mph (Evans et al., 2011). This could be achieved by coupling cuckoo search with computational fluid dynamic solvers.

References

Alkhudhiri, A., Darwish, N., Hilal, N., 2012. Membrane distillation: a comprehensive review. Desalination. 287, 2–18.

Bratton, D., Kennedy, J., 2007. Defining a standard for particle swarm optimization. In: Proceedings of the 2007 IEEE Swarm Intelligence Symposium.

Civicioglu, P., Besdok, E., 2011. A conceptual comparison of the cuckoo-search, particle swarm optimization, differential evolution and artificial bee colony algorithms. Artif. Intell. Rev.1–32, <http://dx.doi.org/10.1007/s10462-011-9276-0>.

Diez, M., Peri, D., 2010. Robust optimization for ship conceptual design. Ocean Eng. 37, 966–977.

Du, M.F.Q., Gunzburger, M., 1999. Centroidal Voronoi Tessellations: applications and algorithms. SIAM Rev. 41, 637–676.

Evans, B.J., Hassan, O., Jones, J.W., Morgan, K., Remaki, L., 2011. Computational fluid dynamics applied to the aerodynamic design of a land-based supersonic vehicle. Numer. Methods Partial Differ. Equ. 27, 141–159.

Gandomi, A.H., Yang, X.-S., Alavi, A.H., 2011. Cuckoo search algorithm: a metaheuristic approach to solve structural optimization problems. Eng. Comput. 10.1007/s00366-011-0241-y.

Gandomi, A.H., Talatahari, S., Yang, X.-S., Deb, S., 2012. Design optimization of truss structures using cuckoo search algorithm. Struct. Des. Tall Spec. Build. 10.1002/tal.1033.

Ghodrati, A., Lotfi, S., 2012. A hybrid CS/PSO algorithm for global optimization. In: Pan, J.-S., Chen, S.-M. (Eds.), Proceedings of the Fourth Asian Conference on Intelligent Information and Database Systems. Springer, Berlin/Heidelberg.

Harlow, F.H., Welch, J.E., 1965. Numerical calculation of time-dependent viscous incompressible flow of fluid with free surface. Phys. Fluids. 8, 2182–2189.

Kaveh, A., Bakhshpoori, T., Ashoory, M., 2012. An efficient optimization procedure based on cuckoo search algorithm for practical design of steel structures. Int. J. Optim. Civ. Eng. 2, 1–14.

Lin, J.-H., Lee, I.-H., 2012. Emotional chaotic cuckoo search for the reconstruction of chaotic dynamics. In: Mastorakis, N., Mladenov, V., Bojkovic, Z. (Eds.), Latest Advances in Systems Science and Computational Intelligence. WSEAS Press, Wisconsin, USA.

Mifsud, M.J., Shaw, S.T., MacManus, D.G., 2010. A high fidelity low-cost aerodynamic model using proper orthogonal decomposition. Int. J. Numer. Methods Fluids. 63, 468–494.

Mitchell, M., 1999. An introduction to Genetic Algorithms. sixth ed. MIT Press, Cambridge, MA, USA.

Natarajan, A., Subramanian, S., 2012. Bloom filter optimization using cuckoo search. In: Proceedings of the 2012 International Conference on Computer Communication and Informatics, India.

Pavlyukevich, I., 2007. Lévy flights. Non-local search and simulated annealing. J. Comput. Phys. 226, 1830–1844.

Payne, R.B., Sorenson, M.D., Klitz, K., 2005. The Cuckoos. Oxford University Press, Oxford, UK.

Praveen, C., Duvigneau, R., 2009. Low cost PSO using metamodels and inexact pre-evaluation: application to aerodynamic shape design. Comput. Methods Appl. Mech. Eng. 198, 1087–1096.

Salimi, H., Giveki, D., Soltanshahi, M.A., Hatami, J., 2012. Extended mixture of MLP experts by hybrid of conjugate gradient method and modified cuckoo search. Int. J. Artif. Intell. Appl. 3.

Selvi, G., Purusothaman, T., 2012. Cryptanalysis of simple block ciphers using extensive heuristic attacks. Eur. J. Sci. Res. 78, 198−221.

Shatnawi, M., Nasrudin, M.F., 2011. Starting configuration of cuckoo search algorithm using Centroidal Voronoi Tessellations. In: Proceedings of the 11th International Conference on Hybrid Intelligent Systems, Melacca.

Speed, E., 2010. Evolving a Mario agent using cuckoo search and Softmax heuristics. In: Proceedings of the Second International IEEE Consumer Electronics Society's Games Innovations Conference.

Storn, R., Price, K., 1997. Differential evolution—a simple and efficient heuristic for global optimization over continuous spaces. J. Glob. Optim. 11, 341−359.

Vazquez, R.A., 2011. Training spiking neural models using cuckoo search algorithm. In: Proceedings of the 2011 IEEE Congress on Evolutionary Computation.

Viswanathan., G.M., 2008. Levy Flights and superdiusion in the context of biologicalencounters and random searches. Phys. Life Rev. 5, 133−150.

Walton, S., Hassan, O., Morgan, K., 2011a. Using proper orthogonal decomposition to reduce the order of optimization problems. In: Wall, G. (Ed.), Proceedings of the 16th International Conference on Finite Elements in Flow Problems, Munich, p. 173.

Walton, S., Hassan, O., Morgan, K., Brown, M.R., 2011b. Modified cuckoo search: a new gradient free optimisation algorithm. Chaos, Solitons Fractals. 44, 710−718.

Walton, S., Hassan, O., Morgan, K., 2012. Reduced order mesh optimisation using proper orthogonal decomposition and a modified cuckoo search. Int. J. Numer. Methods Eng. 10.1002/nme.4400.

Yang, X.-S., 2010. Firefly algorithm, Lévy flights and global optimisation. In: Bramer, M., Ellis, R., Petridis, M. (Eds.), Research and Development in Intelligent Systems XXVI. Springer, London, pp. 209−218.

Yang, X.-S., Deb, S., 2009. Cuckoo search via Lévy flights. Proceedings of the World Congress on Nature & Biologically Inspired Computing, IEEE Publications, Bangalore, India, pp. 210−214.

Yang, X.-S., Deb, S., 2010. Engineering optimisation by cuckoo search. Int. J. Math. Model. Numer. Optim. 1, 330−343.

Yildiz, A.R., 2012. Cuckoo search algorithm for the selection of optimal machining parameters in milling operations. Int. J. Adv. Manuf. Technol. 10.1007/s00170-012-4013-7.

12 Bio-Inspired Models for Semantic Web

Priti Srinivas Sajja[1] *and Rajendra Akerkar*[2]

[1]Department of Computer Science, Sardar Patel University, India;
[2]Western Norway Research Institute, Sogndal, Norway

12.1 Introduction

Bio-inspired computing is a consortium of loosely knitted subfields that exhibit social behavior and simulates natural processes that exhibit intelligence. It is closely related to the fields such as artificial intelligence and machine learning, biology, and mathematics. This modern approach has sprung from the idea that intelligence emerges as much from cells, bodies, and societies as it does from evolution, development, and learning. Some major aims of bio-inspired models are to propose new unconventional computing architectures and new programming paradigms. Bio-inspired systems possess many desirable properties such as evolution and self-organization that we would like to transfer to our computer systems. The common characteristics of natural systems are as follows:

- They possess large numbers of relatively simple participants/processing entities.
- Processing is decentralized, parallel, and asynchronous.
- Their desired functionality emerges from the interactions of their participants.

These characteristics make natural systems robust to loss of participating entities, parallel in execution, and adaptable to a changing problem domain. By taking inspiration from such natural systems/models, computing models such as artificial neural network (ANN), genetic algorithm (GA), and swarm intelligence (SI) have been proposed.

Bio-inspired models and techniques can be used ubiquitously in a variety of domains. Semantic Web is one of the domains that can utilize the advantages of such systems. Semantic Web allows searching for not only information but also knowledge. Its main purpose is introducing structure and semantic content in the huge amount of unstructured or semi-structured distributed knowledge available on the Web. The prime objective of Semantic Web is to acquire, use, and manage knowledge on distributed environment in automatic way. Semantic Web is stepping

Swarm Intelligence and Bio-Inspired Computation. DOI: http://dx.doi.org/10.1016/B978-0-12-405163-8.00012-0

toward more and more intelligent and human-oriented applications. Demand and expectations from the Web as well as the Semantic Web are ever increasing. As the Web grows and evolves at a fast speed, there is a need for better scalability, efficient knowledge representations, and automated human-like searching and retrieval of the content. On the Web, knowledge comes from different sources, in different formats, and in large volume, which is mainly implicit in nature. Besides these, knowledge has wonderful characteristics of emergence and ability to evolve. The bio-inspired constituents help in knowledge acquisition, utilization, and management to achieve the objectives of making Semantic Web more human-like and knowledge oriented and hence to employ Semantic Web as an instrument for betterment of human lives.

This chapter is focused on presenting a survey of vital bio-inspired techniques that can be used for improving web knowledge source discovery and other applications of the Semantic Web. Section 12.2 introduces some basic idea of the Semantic Web. Section 12.3 discusses three bio-inspired models with applications to the Semantic Web. To demonstrate the use of bio-inspired techniques on the Semantic Web platform, problem of web content filtering is illustrated in Section 12.4. The section describes a generic framework of a neuro-fuzzy system with its different components such as training pages, keyword extraction, fuzzy user profile and its inference, normalization of input values to the base neural network, and fuzzy output. By considering online webpages and fuzzy user profile, the proposed system classifies the webpages into vague categories such as better, good, average, and poor. Section 12.5 presents the conclusions.

12.2 Semantic Web

Semantic Web initiative was set up by the World Wide Web Consortium (W3C) to enable "... an extension of the current Web in which information is given well-defined meaning, better enabling computers and people to work in cooperation" (Berners-Lee et al. 2001). Semantic Web is a continuously evolving system rather than a static entity. This is evident from the following W3C's definition (Berners-Lee et al., 2001):

> Semantic Web is the representation of data on the World Wide Web. It is a collaborative effort led by W3C with participation from a large number of researchers and industrial partners. It is based on the Resource Description Framework (RDF), which integrates a variety of applications using XML for syntax and URIs for naming.

Architecture of the Semantic Web involves a hierarchical assembly (Figure 12.1) of different formats and technologies where each layer exploits the capabilities of the below layer providing a formal description of concepts and relationships within a given domain. The bottom layers in the Semantic Web stack consist of technologies that are widely used in the current web. Semantic Web is

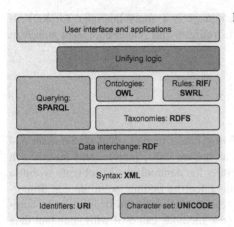

Figure 12.1 Semantic web stack.

created on the basis of these technologies. Further, the middle layer (RDF onward) consists of technologies that have been standardized to support Semantic Web applications.

Unicode is a standard for steady representation of text expressed in the world's several writing systems. The usage of Unicode helps the Semantic Web applications in bridging documents expressed in different human language systems. Uniform resource identifier (URI) is a series of characters used to recognize an abstract or a physical entity. URIs are used in Semantic Web–based systems to describe a resource and its components, enabling interactions over the Web using HTTP. RDF is a data modeling language that provides a framework to describe a resource and its relationship with other resources in a form called triples. A triple consists of a subject, a predicate, and an object, i.e., any statement can be composed into a subject, a predicate, and an object. The framework was extended to that of a full ontology language as described by description logic. This Web Ontology Language is thus more expressive than RDF. Semantic Web paradigm made one small but fundamental change to the architecture of the Web: a resource (i.e., anything that can be identified by a URI) can be about anything. This means that the URIs that were formerly used to denote mostly webpages and other data that have some form of bytecode on the Web can now be about anything from things whose physical existence is outside the Web to abstract concept.

Semantic Web principles are implemented in the layers of web technologies and standards. Unicode and URI layers support use of international character sets and provide means for identifying the objects in Semantic Web. XML layer with name space and schema definitions support in integrating the Semantic Web definitions with other XML-based standards. With RDF and RDF Schema, it is possible to make statements about objects with URIs and define vocabularies that can be referred to by URIs. This is the layer where one can give types to resources and links. Ontology layer supports the evolution of vocabularies as it can define relations between the different concepts.

SPARQL Protocol and RDF Query Language is a query language for RDF. It offers developers and end users a way to retrieve and manipulate data stored in RDF format.

12.3   Constituent Models

Bio-inspired models find their source of inspiration in biological phenomena and social behaviors from live entities such as human cells, insects, and birds. Such algorithms are able to find acceptable results for nontraditional problems within a reasonable amount of time rather than guarantee the optimal solution. The important methods inspired from nature seem to have the ability to deal with the unresolved problems of the Semantic Web. These methods can deal with abundant data and can be used to build high-scalable applications. Most significant bio-inspired methods include genetic algorithms, neural networks, and particle swarm, or ant colony optimization.

12.3.1   Artificial Neural Network

ANN is an information processing paradigm that is inspired by the way biological nervous systems, such as brain, process information. ANN falls under the category of connectionist system in the domain of artificial intelligence (AI) as it stores knowledge implicitly in the connections between the neurons, which are the basic processing units of the network working in a parallel, distributed, and highly asynchronous way. Unlike typical AI-based systems, ANN does not depend on set of intelligent rules or stored knowledge to take decisions, to justify actions taken and to solve problem, but depend on training data or environment provided to it. The basic processing unit mentioned here (neuron) tries to mimic the behavior of biological neuron. Similar to biological neuron, artificial neuron is a function consisting of a mechanism to accept weighted input and process it. If the result of the process is significant enough, the neuron fires the output. Such multiple neurons are connected with each other in different structures/models to achieve human-like behavior. Popular modeling structures are Hopfield model, multilayer perceptron model, and Kohonen model, which are discussed here.

12.3.1.1   Hopfield Network

Hopfield model was proposed by Hopfield (1982) as a theory of memory. Its characteristics include distributed representation and control, fault tolerance, and content-addressable memory. Hopfield proposed a network where all the units are bistate units—either "active" or "inactive." Here, weight of the connections between the neurons has to be set in such a way that the network is stable. Hopfield model consists of a single layer of processing elements where each unit is connected to many other units in the network.

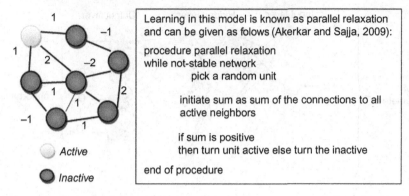

Figure 12.2 Hopfield model and its learning mechanism.

If each unit is connected with every other unit, then the structure is said to be fully connected. All the connections are weighted. It is also a symmetrically weighted network as denoted in Figure 12.2. If the connections are trained with a specific learning method, Hopfield network can perform as a robust content-addressable memory, resistant to connection alterations.

12.3.1.2 Multilayer Perception and Backpropagation Learning

"Perceptrons" is a term coined by Rosenblatt (1958) while studying the basic idea behind the mammalian visual system. A perceptron is an artificial neuron having n input signals with different weights, an activation (processing) function, and a threshold function. A perceptron can efficiently solve the linearly separable problems. However, to solve more realistic problems, there is a need to have complex architecture using multiple neurons. In multilayer preceptron model, such many neurons are arranged in three layers as shown in Figure 12.3. The multilayer perceptron here has n input nodes, h hidden nodes in its (one or more) hidden layers, and m output nodes in its output layer. In Figure 12.3, two hidden layers are shown; however, there may be many depending on the application's nature and complexity. There may be multiple input and output layers if required. W_{ij} is the weight associated with ith node of the input layer to jth node of the next layer. In a similar way, each node of a given layer is connected to every node in its adjacent layer. All connections are in a forward direction only. That is why such a structure is known as fully connected, feed-forward, multilayer network.

The network receives inputs from neurons in the input layer, and the output of the network is given by the neurons in an output layer. In such a network, artificial neurons, which are organized in layers, send their signals "forward" and then the errors are propagated backward. The idea of such backpropagation is to reduce this error until the ANN learns the training data in a supervised manner. While learning, input data from the training set are passed to the input layer of the network. The network calculates and then compares with the actual output from the training set.

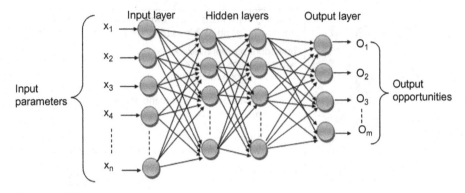

Figure 12.3 Multilayer perceptron.

This phase is known as forward pass. Depending on the distance observed between the calculated output and actual output, weights are adjusted. This phase is known as backward pass. Such many forward and backward passes are experimented on a network to train the network for a set of data. Such multiple sets are used to train the network. At the end, when real input values are fed to the network, it gives the output based on its learning. This algorithm is known as backpropagation learning algorithm in a supervised manner because of two reasons: (i) the error (difference calculated between the correct output and calculated output) is propagated back and the solution (from input to output) is propagated in forward direction and (ii) the training set is a must. The backpropagation algorithm has become the most popular one for training of the multilayer perceptron.

12.3.1.3   Kohonen Self-Organizing Maps

Kohonen self-organizing maps (SOM) (Kohonen, 1990) are feed-forward networks that use an unsupervised learning approach through a process called self-organization. A Kohonen network consists of two layers of processing units called an input layer and an output layer. There are no hidden units. When an input pattern is fed to the network, the units in the output layer compete with each other, and the winning output unit is typically the one whose incoming connection weights are closest to the input pattern (Euclidean distance). Thus, the input is presented, and each output unit computes its closeness or match score to the input pattern. The output that is closest to the input pattern "wins" and earns the right to have its connection weights adjusted. The connection weights are moved in the direction of the input pattern by a factor determined by a learning rate parameter. The Kohonen map creates a topological mapping by not only adjusting the winner's weights but also adjusting the weights of the adjacent output units in proximity to the winner. So not only the winner weights are adjusted but the whole neighborhood of output units is moved closer to the input pattern. Starting from randomized weight values, the output units slowly align themselves such that when an input pattern is presented, a neighborhood of units responds. As training progresses, size of the neighborhood radiating out from the winning unit is decreased. The learning rate will decrease as training progresses, and in some implementations, the learning rate decays with the distance from the winning output unit. A basic Kohonen algorithm can be given as follows (Akerkar and Sajja, 2009):

    randomize weights for all neurons
        for (i = 1 to iteration_number) do
            take one random input pattern
            find the winning neuron and its neighbors
            modify synaptic weights of these neurons
            reduce the η (learning rate) and λ (neighborhood radius)

SOM's descriptive ability is increased by allowing the network to grow, adding a hierarchical dimension and allowing it to start with an initial tree-like structure. These enhancements intuitively allow SOM to fill given space, without the nodes being too distanced from each other, and also to discover eventual hierarchical structures of the search space. Growing hierarchical self-organizing maps (GHSOM) used by Chifu and Letia (2008) consist of a set of SOMs (particularly bidimensional grids) organized as nodes in a hierarchy. GHSOM is initialized with a hierarchy mirroring the one in the taxonomy, and concepts are mapped to some nodes in the corresponding SOM by initializing the node's weights with the vector description of the concept; all other unmapped nodes are initialized randomly. The process continues top-down for all the SOM nodes in the (predefined) initial tree hierarchy. The whole learning process of the GHSOM is terminated when no more nodes are required for further expansion. This learning process does not necessarily lead to a balanced hierarchy (the hierarchy with equal depth in each branch). To summarize, the growth process of the GHSOM is guided by two parameters $\tau 1$ and $\tau 2$. The parameter $\tau 1$ controls the growth process in layer and the parameter $\tau 2$ controls hierarchical growth of GHSOM.

12.3.1.4 Applications of ANN in the Domain of Semantic Web

ANNs are used in classification, optimization, function approximation, compressing of complex data, clustering, diagnosis, advisory, and decision making. In conjunction with the Semantic Web, the ANN can be used in many different ways. This section describes the applications of ANN in the domain of Semantic Web.

Webpage Allocations

To provide qualitative and efficient services, some heavily trafficked web sites use multiple servers. Here ANN can be used to map and store webpage requests to a server. This information is further utilized for improving load balancing among caches of the server. Other alternative is to cache data at client side or router level, which improves efficiency; however, it requires significant amount of cache. Phoha et al. (2002) proposed fast webpage allocation on a server using the self-organizing properties of ANN. Each server is represented as a processing node and competes to serve the object request. Servers closest to the request wins, and if the object is already in the server's cache, relationship between the server and the object request is strengthened using competitive learning.

Clustering and Classification of Web Content

Clustering users based on their web access patterns is an active area of research in web usage mining. Grouping of users can be done in many different ways using approaches such as data mining, concept of mass distribution in Dempster–Shafer's theory, and Markov models. However, these approaches lack the ability to adapt to the change in users' web interests over time. Grouping of users can be done based on ANN. The approach demonstrated by Rangarajan et al. (2004) uses ANN to group hosts, where each host represents an organizationally related group of users, according to their web request patterns. ANN can also be used for web domain clustering (Rangarajan, 2002). Similar work is done by Paliouras et al. (2000) for constructing community models for the users of large web sites. Further, ANN can be used for image and audio classification as shown by Park et al. (2004) and Shao et al. (2003). Lee et al. (2002) have proposed ANN to classify webpages during content filtering focusing on blocking pornographical web content.

Security

With growth of the Web, hackers have found more subtle ways to attack web applications. Injecting invalid SQL, syntactically valid but misleading knowledge in ontology, adware, and so on are popular vulnerabilities of the Web. Consequences of such attacks may damage the client server, steal sensitive information, and bypass authentication. Several techniques have been adopted to identify such vulnerabilities. A firewall called ANNbWAF (Moosa, 2010) is developed to have an eye on such attacks. ANNbWAF uses a trained ANN embedded within the firewall application. During the training phase, a set of normal and malicious data is used to train the ANN. According to the developers, the solution can take care of other types of attacks that take advantage of the lack of input validation such as Cross-site Scripting (XSS). Similar work is done by Becher (2007). ANN can be used to enhance security of distributed environment like the Web because of ability of ANN to offer high encryption capability through the structural hidden layers. ANN can be used to release the constraint on the length of the secret key (used for encryption–decryption) to provide the data integrity and authentication services that can be used for securing wireless web services communication (Woungang et al., 2007).

ANN can be used to detect intrusion. Methods of intrusion detection based on hand-coded rule sets or predicting commands online are laborious to build or not practically feasible. Researchers including Bivens et al. (2002) and Moradi and Zulkernine (2004) used ANN as instrument to employ intrusion detection mechanism.

Searching and Retrieval

Intelligent retrieval of information from tremendous ocean of information on the Web needs dedicated utilities and techniques from modern AI. When it comes to the Semantic Web, not only information but knowledge can also be searched. Caliusco and Stegmayer (2010) discussed an agent that can be used for intelligent web knowledge source discovery. ANN is also useful in improving semantic information retrieval together with synonyms thesaurus (Zhu et al. 2003), or based on text documents (Wermter, 2000).

Backpropagation is a popular approach for information retrieval (Lam and Lee, 1999). However, Chau and Chen (2007) found similarities between nature of Hopfield network and the Web and claimed that asymmetric Hopfield net is suitable to model the Web's structure. According to this approach, any given webpage (say pi) can be defined as a neuron i that represents the page in the network model. A function that calculates a score of the webpage pi based on its content is developed. Further learning, identification, and retrieval of information are done based on this score.

Ontology Management

Several types of ANNs have been used for various tasks in ontology matching such as ontology categorization, classification, or learning matching parameters, such as matching weights, to tune matching systems with respect to a particular matching task (Euzenat and Shvaiko, 2007). Ontology matching is a tedious task and requires human effort. There are different algorithms for implementing the matching process, which can be generally classified along two dimensions, namely, schema based and instance based. For a given schema-level and instance-level information, it is sometimes useful to cluster this input into categories in order to lower the computational complexity of further manipulations with data. ANN can be used to characterize the inputs into different categories as used by Curino et al. (2007). In the GLUE system (Doan et al., 2004), learning techniques are used to semiautomatically create semantic mappings between ontologies and to find correspondences among the taxonomies of two given ontologies.

12.3.2 Genetic Algorithms

GA is aimed to mimic nature's evolutionary approach ("survival of the fittest") in computing. The basic goal is to understand the adaptive processes of natural systems and hence to design artificial systems software that retains the robustness of natural systems. GA is also considered as an adaptive heuristic search algorithm based on the evolutionary ideas of natural selection. GA is useful and efficient when search space is large, complex, or poorly understood; domain knowledge is scarce, or expert knowledge is difficult to encode to narrow the search space; and support from traditional models is not available. Fields such as evolutionary strategy (ES), evolutionary programming (EP), and genetic programming (GP) follow principles of GA. GA employs the natural evolution process by encoding the candidate solutions (individuals) into sequence of genes using alphabet, symbol, and tree of a number. Group of genes (substring) that represent a characteristic in an individual is called genotype. An initial population is formed using multiple encoded individuals. Initial population is evaluated for fitness using a domain-specific fitness function. Poor candidates are removed from the populations and stronger may be repeating themselves. Genes are flipped (mutation) or interchanged with similar

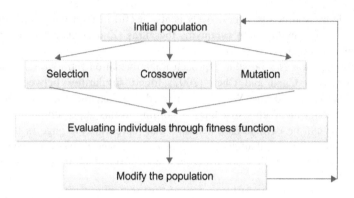

Figure 12.4 Steps of genetic algorithm.

genes from selected mate (crossover) to generate new individuals and refine version of the population. Individuals from the new populations are again tested for their fitness. These steps will be continued till the level of satisfaction is achieved. Figure 12.4 illustrates the procedure.

12.3.2.1 Genetic Algorithm for Semantic Web

Besides to narrow search region, GA can be used to solve problems and can exhibit intelligent behavior in the absence of the traditional model. Such characteristics inspire researchers to employ GA in the domain of Semantic Web. The possibility of querying large amounts of data from distinct as well as heterogeneous sources, in a competent manner, is an open problem. In this perspective, an interesting research area is the determination of query paths—the order in which the parts of a query are evaluated. The order has a major role when it comes to the execution time of the query; therefore, a good algorithm for determining the query path can contribute to intelligent querying. GA has been already tested, with some success, in problems related to this field. Following are some areas in the domain of Semantic Web where GA can be applied.

Information Retrieval and Searching

Searching on the Web has become a challenge due to its dynamic nature. The Web tool called MySpiders (Pant and Menczer, 2002) implements GA managing a population of adaptive crawlers that browse the Web autonomously. Each agent acts as an intelligent client driven by a user query and textual and linkage clues in the crawled pages. Agents autonomously decide links to follow and clues to internalize and focus the search near a relevant source. The tool is available to the public as a threaded Java applet. Similar work is presented by Menczer et al. (2001) called InfoSpider, which is a multiagent system performing dynamic web search. Along with GA, the InfoSpider also uses ANN. InfoSpiders rely on traditional search engines to obtain a set of starting URLs pointing to pages supposedly relevant to the query submitted by the user. An agent is positioned at each of these starting URLs. Each agent checks the current page to find the next link to follow. The analysis includes looking at a small set of words around each hyperlink. Frequencies of query matching terms in such a neighborhood are used as inputs to an ANN that scores each outlink. One link is then picked by the ANN with a probability proportional to its score. After a document has been visited, its similarity to the query is used as a learning signal to update the weights of the neural net.

Yohanes et al. (2011) utilize GA for web crawling to find suitable webpages to be fetched and prove that GA is better than the traditional crawling methods. Chen et al. (1998) also used GA to build a personal search agent. Their results showed that GA could effectively prevent the search agent from being trapped in local optimum, and then it would significantly improve the quality of search results. Multimedia content can also be annotated and retrieved efficiently using GA. Bloehdorn et al. (2005) deal with semantic annotations of multimedia content. Segments extracted from the video content are naturally involved in spatial relationships.

Ontology Management

Ontology is a fundamental building block of Semantic Web content. To create, manage, align, map, and integrate different ontology are the challenging and effort requiring tasks. Ontology alignment is recognized as a fundamental process to achieve an adequate interoperability between people or systems that use different, overlapping ontologies to represent common knowledge. Gil et al. (2008) proposed genetics for ontology alignments (GOAL), a new approach to compute the optimal ontology alignment function for a given ontology input set. The approach is a genetic algorithm which is able to work with multiple goals such as maximizing the alignment precision, maximizing the alignment recall, maximizing the f-measure, or reducing the number of false positives. Ontologies can be presented in the form of hierarchical trees, which make it easy to determine semantic correspondence between any two given ontologies. This situation is shown in Figure 12.5.

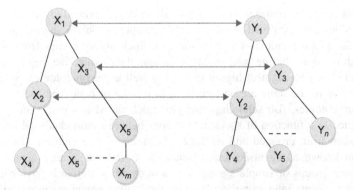

Figure 12.5 Semantic correspondence.

The initial population consists of input ontologies. Mutation and crossover on these trees can be carried out to evolve new ontology. This approach has been utilized by Naya et al. (2010). The authors have presented the detailed genetic algorithm including encoding of ontologies, alignment operations, and population generations.

Panagi et al. (2006) have presented hybrid approach coupling ontologies and a genetic algorithm for realizing knowledge-assisted semantic image analysis. On a given image, first, segmentation is applied to generate partitions. Subsequently, low-level descriptors and fuzzy spatial relations are extracted for the generated image segments. Corresponding domain ontology definitions are obtained from system's knowledge base. GA is applied here to decide the most plausible annotation.

Wang et al. (2006) have presented a novel approach to map ontology using GA. The ontology matching problem is presented as a feature-matching process. The problem of matching is modeled as an optimization problem of a mapping between two compared ontologies. Each ontology has its associated feature sets. According to the work, given a certain mapping as an optimizing object for GA, fitness function is defined as a global similarity measure function between two ontologies based on feature sets. GA is also used by Hogenboom et al. (2008) for determining optimal RDF query path.

Other Applications of GA in the Semantic Web Domain

Generally, GA can be used to control various Semantic Web agents. Automation of web service composition is one of the most important problems in web service research area. A research carried out by Tizzo et al. (2011) describes the use of asynchronous teams (A-Teams) algorithm with agents. The objective of the work is to automatically compose Semantic Web services. There are some dedicated agents that take care of the composition of sequential, parallel, and synchronization control flow patterns. Based on GA, other agents perform the crossover and mutation over these patterns identified by the agents, and the quality of the composition is also evaluated.

12.3.3 Swarm Intelligence

Since its early evolution, the biological systems expressed virtue of self-organizations and exhibited ability to solve complex problem sharing information among the group members for their survival. Such ability comes from their efficient information sharing and communication, their collective behavior toward goal, and ability to engineer highly secured as well as useful colonies. Some popular examples of the same are nest building in termite or honeybee societies, foraging in ant colonies, fish schooling, and bird flocking. SI is a discipline that views intelligence as a function of social interactions between individuals. SI is an inspiration taken from grouped and intelligent behavior of live entities. These entities are often known as agents/swarms. Hence, SI is defined as emergent collective intelligence groups of simple agents. It is a study of collective behavior of (unsophisticated) agents interacting locally with their environment resulting into coherent functional global patterns. As mentioned earlier, the common characteristics of example agents that exhibit SI are to form a group of social agents/insects/live enti-ties, facilitating cooperative transportation between them and division of labor to perform intended tasks such as food, nest, reproduction, and security. Popular mod-els of computing that uses SI are ant colony algorithms and bees algorithm. The following sections describe these models in brief.

12.3.3.1 Ant Colony Optimization Algorithm

More than 30 million ants have been observed working in cooperation in an ant colony to perform tasks such as reproduction, food finding, defense, and nest brooming. Ants can make use of visual as well as chemical landmark and can do compass-based path finding (in some desert ants) and path integration. Ants are one of the best path finders in nature. With an ant colony optimization (ACO), the shortest path in a graph, between two points A and B, is built from a combination of several paths. Various ACOs are based on this concept. Basic steps of algorithms are given as follows:

1. An ant/agent runs randomly around the colony.
2. If it discovers a food source, it returns more or less directly to the nest, leaving a trail of pheromone (a kind of chemical that another ant can identify) in its path.
3. These pheromones attract nearby ants and force them to follow same/similar track.
4. Returning to the colony, these new ants will strengthen the route by adding their own pheromone.
5. If there are two routes to reach the same food source, in a given amount of time, the shorter one will be traveled by more ants than the longer route. By this way, the shorter route will be increasingly enhanced and therefore become more attractive, and the long route will eventually disappear because pheromones are volatile. Eventually, all the ants have determined and therefore "chosen" the shortest route.

Using such intelligent and collective approach, ants can turn up as grand masters in search and exploitation and can solve complex tasks by simple local means. It is to be noted that the cooperative ant productivity is better than the sum of their sin-gle activities. Typical applications of ACO include scheduling and routing problem, graph tree partition problem, assignment problems, classification, information retrieval, data mining and data discovery, and intelligent testing.

12.3.3.2 Bees Algorithm

The way bees hunt for food is complex as their food is distributed unpredictably. Bees need to adjust their flying patterns spatially to the environment and temporally to find the food to avoid risk of being hurt or trapped. The algorithm called bees algorithm is inspired by the food foraging behavior of honey bees and could be regarded as belonging to the category of "intelligent" optimization tools. The typical bees algorithm that can be implemented using computing techniques is as follows:

1. Initialization of agents/utilities called bees.
2. Create an initial population that contains randomly generated candidate which claim for solution and assign this population to bees.

3. Let bees select sites for neighborhood search.
4. Evaluate results provided by bees against desired criteria. This is also called fitness test. One may consider multiple paths/solutions.
5. Select the fittest bee from each path. Meanwhile let other bees search other unexplored area.
6. Continue the process till the desired result is achieved.

Other techniques such as cuckoo search and firefly algorithm are also used for different applications related to the Web (Chifu et al., 2012; Pop et al., 2011).

12.3.3.3 Particle Swarm Optimization

Particle swarm optimization (PSO) is an optimization procedure based on the social behavior of groups of organizations. Flocking of birds or the schooling of fish (Eberhart et al., 2001) are examples. Individual solutions in a population are viewed as "particles" that evolve with time to achieve stronger solution. According to Eberhart et al. (2001), each particle modifies its position in search space according to its own experience and also that of a neighboring particle by remembering the best position visited by itself and its neighbors, thus combining local and global search methods.

When compared with traditional approaches, swarm intelligence offers the potential for tremendous gain in terms of cost, fault tolerance, and overall performance. However, building swarm intelligence may provide robustness, but it makes things quite difficult for both the developer and the human user (Kutsenok and Kutsenok, 2011)). Furthermore, it is necessary to focus on group behavior. To utilize advantages of SI, one may have to face many disadvantages such as lack of reporting and lack of communication to control systems.

To achieve dual advantages, a hybrid approach that uses suitable SI technique embedded with traditional techniques can be used. Small computing agents can be developed that behave as ants or bees to accomplish given task. These agents are both efficient in computing as well as blessed with the characteristics shown by the SI. A multiagent system encompassing such different agents exhibit powerful and integrated solutions to real-world problems.

12.3.4 Application in Different Aspects of Semantic Web

Extensive research has been done in the area of Semantic Web and ant colony. Semantic Web reasoning systems deal with huge distributed and dynamic resources. SI could be used in order to implement an RDF graph traversal algorithm. Key properties of swarms—adaptiveness, robustness, and scalability—correspond to three concepts: no central control, locality, and simplicity. Along these lines, the combination of reasoning and SI can be a practical solution for obtaining reasoning performance by basic means.

The model of a decentralized system uses the traversal of a graph in order to calculate the deductive closure of the graph with respect to the RDF semantics. The role of SI is to reduce the computational cost. In order to calculate the RDF semantic closure over an RDF graph, a set of rules need to be applied repeatedly to the triples in the graph. In metaphor of ants, each insect represents one of these rules, which might be (partially) instantiated. Ants communicate with each other only locally and indirectly. Whenever the condition of a rule matches the node an ant is on, it locally adds the newly derived triple to the graph. Only active reasoning rules are moving in the network and not the data, minimizing network traffic, because schema data is far less numerous than instance data. Having some transition capabilities between graph boundaries, the method converges toward the closure.

Work of Dentler et al. (2009) presents use of SI for RDF graph traversal. Bio-inspired and index-free methodology is realized by self-organizing swarms of autonomous, light-weight entities that traverse RDF graphs by following paths, aiming to instantiate pattern-based inference rules. Rana (2011) described a mechanism to search for resources in unstructured ants-based control using ACO. Madhu et al. (2011) proposed a query interface mechanism to Semantic Web and repository of ontology using ant colony algorithm. Wu and Aberer (2003) used SI to create a model for the dynamic interactions between web servers and users along with relevant feedback by browsing and ranking webpages. Yan et al. (2009) implemented ACO for automatic composition of Semantic Web services by requests by generating a graph of input and output, and then, the composition of web services is transformed into finding a satisfying path in the graph. Further, the ACO is used to identify efficient composition of web services. Holden and Freitas (2004) developed an Ant-Miner that investigates usage of ACO in the field of webpage classification as well as for web content mining. Wang and Xu (2011) presented an improved ACO for ontology matching problem by utilizing different rating functions (base matchers) to evaluate the distance between two ontology entries. The result is stored in the form of distance matrix on which an improved ACO algorithm is applied to extract the best alignment. Hassas (2003) presented an approach to organize web content dynamically using SI. Ratnayake et al. (2008) designed and implemented "Divon," a swarm that emulates a user profile driven approach for Semantic Web information presentation. Work of Bock and Hettenhausen (2010) addressed problem of ontology alignment aiming toward identification of overlaps in heterogeneous knowledge bases. A discrete PSO algorithm is designed in this work in order to solve this optimization problem and compute an alignment of two ontologies.

12.4   Neuro-Fuzzy System for the Web Content Filtering: Application

To demonstrate use of bio-inspired model for Semantic Web, hybridization of fuzzy logic (FL) and ANN technique for content filtering is selected. This section presents a broad framework of the system which can be considered as a problem for research or as a base of commercial system.

Typically, web filtering/Semantic Web mining is carried out in the following manner:

- By providing some set of specifications or metadata in association with the webpage itself. This will be done by the web publisher. Such specification and metadata provide restricted access of the webpage to the audience. A set of specifications for content-rating systems called Platform for Internet Content Selection (PICS) is also offered by many browsers and web filtering systems.
- By blocking some URLs, filtering of content can be made possible. Before presenting the page to the user, the URL is checked with the list of blocked URLs/IP addresses. If the URL is found in the list, content from the URL is not presented. Such lists are popularly known as black lists.
- Web/Semantic Web content filtering can be done using matching keywords or metadata and considering the frequency of such items into the webpage. If the harmful word appears in the page, content will be blocked.

Here we are proposing a neuro-fuzzy approach to filter the web content. ANN is used as a tool to analyze the content in an intelligent manner. FL offers advantage of dealing with user's vague information about choices, preferences, and interest.

The proposed system as demonstrated in Figure 12.6 works as follows.

The system initiates with the process of extracting keywords given by the user from a webpage. User may provide synonym or metadata along with the keyword. From the user's profile, system can identify other synonyms for the bag of words. For every user, a profile needs to be created. This profile consists of personal information such as age, gender, job type, and history. That is, if a male software programmer searches for mirror, generally he wants the set of pages that contains software mirrors and not glass mirrors! Here we propose to store fuzzy values as it is really difficult to store parameters such as personal interest in education or research.

Next step is to calculate the frequency of the synonyms and keywords in the webpage. One may consider importance factor for each variable. For example, appearance of a particular keyword in header section or title of the webpage is more important, and maximum weight can be assigned to this keyword.

Based on frequency of keywords (total n), synonyms (total k) and user's interest and importance factors, $(n + k)$ normalized values are fed to the input layer of ANN. The neural network used here is a multilayer perceptron with a backpropagation learning mechanism. Here the neural network classifies the webpages into five different categories. Using the fuzzy membership functions, categories are presented as poor, below average, acceptable, good, and better webpages. The pages above the acceptable category are presented to the users. However, the user may see other category pages.

Components of Figure 12.6 are described here:

- *Training pages and online pages*: As the proposed system uses supervised learning approach, valid sample training pages need to be provided to the system. This is done during the training phase. While system is executed in real scenario after handsome training, it can use online pages. It is possible to provide choice to determine depth or level

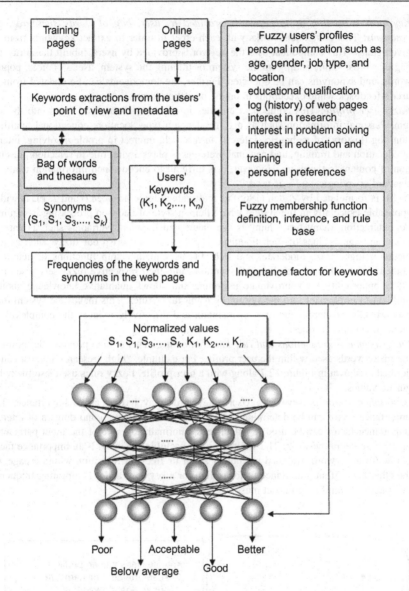

Figure 12.6 Neuro-fuzzy system for web content filtering.

by which the webpage can be explored. This would be useful, as generally a webpage links to many other locations. For example, a university site may have link to its faculty's personal web site or a student's page, which may offer to play online games. In this case, it is advisable to restrict the possible exploration up to a single level, i.e., up to faculty level only.

- *Keywords extraction using keywords provided by user, bag of words, thesaurus, and synonyms*: This component works with each other in order to extract keywords from the given pages. This component uses the keywords provided by users, inbuilt thesaurus, and bag of words. While setting up the system or training the system, user's choices, popular words, and synonyms can be collected. Further, the components can be updated from the user's feedback while executions in online or offline form.
- *Fuzzy user profile*: This component encodes information about valid users into the system. Personal information such as age, gender, job type, location, educational qualification, log (history) of webpages, interests in research, interest in problem solving, interest in education and training, and personal preferences plays a vital role in selection/presentation of content to the users. However, it is difficult to encode such information using the standard crisp logic, so FL is used.

  FL is formulated by Zadeh (1965) as multivalued logic between 0 and 1. FL is widely applicable especially in the system where human style of decision processing is required. For interaction, many times humans use vague and linguistic variables such as amount, price, and age. Values of such linguistic variables are not crisp but fuzzy, such as low, medium, high, poor, moderate, and rich. FL uses membership functions to determine graded membership of such linguistic variables into their respective fuzzy sets. Use of FL offers opportunity for approximate reasoning and allows qualitative knowledge about a problem to implement into the system by using fuzzy rules. This makes the system more user friendly, readable, and easy to maintain and effectively reduces the complexity by reducing number of rules.
- *Fuzzy membership functions and rule-based inference*: This section provides definition of the fuzzy words used within the user profile. For example, "high" research interest can be defined as shown in Figure 12.7 along with a user profile. Fuzzy rules use these fuzzy linguistic values.
- *Importance factor of keywords*: User's keywords may have relative importance. This importance factor can be determined by the nature of application and domain of interest. Importance factor can be used to calculate the normalized value of the input parameters of the base neural network. This information is useful in this way. If an importance factor is low for a keyword, we need not bother about its frequent repetition within a page. On the other hand, if an importance factor is high for a keyword and it is repeating frequently in a page, its significant impact must be considered.

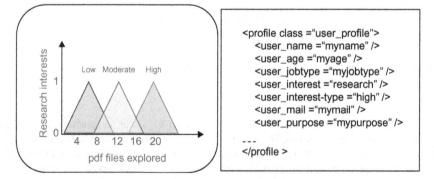

Figure 12.7 An example of membership function and user profile.

- *Normalized values*: Normalized values are calculated using the keywords provided by users, synonyms identified from users information and keywords, and importance factors. These normalized values are provided as input to the base neural network. According to the synonyms and keywords ($n + k$) values, the base neural network structure is designed.
- *Output categories*: Base neural network classifies the webpage into five categories. These categories are poor, below average, acceptable, good, and better. According to the user's cutoff value, standard pages are presented or sorted. Based on this classification, the bag of words can undergo an update.

The framework proposed here is an application of hybrid intelligent technology on web environment. It offers dual advantages of neural network and FL on distributed environment. Furthermore, the aforementioned structure is generic and can be applied to different domains with a minor change. System developed based on this framework can be promoted as commercial product or can be used in conjunction with an independent agent along with search engine/meta search engine for optimizing, ranking, and filtering search result from one or more search engines. This can be considered as a step toward an intelligent search engine.

12.5 Conclusions

Unlike the Web that was initially designed for reading, the Semantic Web aims at a more intelligent web serving machines as well as people. Here, machines can automatically process or "understand" the information if explicit meanings are given to it. In this way, it facilitates sharing and reuse of data across applications, enterprises, and communities. There is a huge amount of knowledge that can be exploited through such automated processing. In this context, bio-inspired algorithms and methods are proving effective to address emerging Semantic Web problems. Bio-inspired models presented in this chapter can be applied to hard and large problems in a variety of areas. For example, the proposed system for web content filtering may be used to block pornographic material or social networking sites, improve page rank of the search engine results, and present filtered pages in a customized way. Many other bio-inspired techniques mentioned in this chapter can be considered as efficient tools that enhance Web/Semantic Web platform in an effective way to exhibit intelligence.

References

Akerkar, R.A., Sajja, P.S., 2009. Knowledge-Based Systems. Jones & Bartlett Publishers, Sudbury, MA.

Berners-Lee, T., Hendler, J., Lassila, O., 2001. The semantic web. Scientific American. 284 (5), 34–43.

Becher, M., 2007. Web Application Firewalls: Applied Web Application Security. VDMVerlag Dr. Mueller e.K, Berlin.

Bivens, A., Palagiri, C., Smith, R., Szymanski, B., Embrechts, M., 2002. Network-based intrusion detection using neural networks. In: Intelligent Engineering Systems through ANN (ANNIE—2002). ASME Press, New York, NY, pp. 579–584.

Bloehdorn, S., Petridis, K., Saathoff, C., Simou, N., Tzouvaras, V., Avrithis, Y., et al., 2005. Semantic annotation of images and videos for multimedia analysis. In: Second European Semantic Web Conference (ESWC). Heraklion, Crete, Greece, pp. 592–607.

Bock, J., Hettenhausen, J., 2010. Discrete particle swarm optimisation for ontology alignment. Inf. Sci.1−22.

Caliusco, M.L., Stegmayer, G., 2010. Semantic web technologies and artificial neural networks for intelligent web knowledge source discovery. In: Badr, Y., Chbeir, R., Abraham, A., Hassanien, A. (Eds.), Emergent Web Intelligence: Advanced Semantic Technologies, Advanced Information and Knowledge Processing. Springer-Verlag London Limited.

Chau, M., Chen, H., 2007. Incorporating web analysis into neural networks: an example in hopfield net searching. IEEE Trans. Syst. Man Cybern. 37 (3), 352−358.

Chen, H., Chung, Y., Ramsey, M., Yang, C., 1998. A smart itsy-bitsy spider for the web. JASIS. 49 (7), 604−618.

Chifu, E.S., Letia, I.A., 2008. Text-based ontology enrichment using hierarchical self-organizing maps. In: Workshop on Nature-Inspired Reasoning for Semantic Web, Germany.

Chifu, V.R., Pop, C.B., Salomie, I, Suia, D.S., Niculici, A.N., 2012. Optimizing the semantic web service composition process using cuckoo search. Stud. Comput. Intell. 382, 93−102.

Curino, C., Orsi, G., Tanca, L., 2007. X-SOM: ontology mapping and inconsistency resolution. In: Fourth European Semantic Web Conference, pp. 3−7.

Dentler, K., Guéret, C., Schlobach, S., 2009. Semantic web reasoning by swarm intelligence. In: Fifth International Workshop on Scalable Semantic Web Knowledge Base Systems, Washington, DC.

Doan, A., Madhavan, J., Domingos, P., Halevy, A., 2004. Ontology matching: a machine learning approach. Handbook on Ontologies in Information Systems. Springer, New York, NY, pp. 385−403.

Eberhart, R., Shi, Y., Kennedy, J., 2001. Swarm Intelligence. Morgan Kaufmann, San Francisco, CA.

Euzenat, J., Shvaiko, P., 2007. Ontology Matching. Springer, London.

Gil, J.M., Alba, E., Montes, J.A., 2008. Optimizing ontology alignments by using genetic algorithms. In: First International Workshop on Nature Inspired Reasoning for the Semantic Web Karlsruhe, Germany.

Hassas, S., 2003. Using swarm intelligence for dynamic web content organization, In: IEEE Swarm Intelligence Symposium, Indianapolis, IN.

Hogenboom, A., Milea, V., Frasincar, F., Kaymak, U., 2008. Genetic algorithms for RDF query path optimization. In: First International Workshop on Nature Inspired Reasoning for the Semantic Web Karlsruhe, Germany.

Holden, N., Freitas, A.A., 2004. Webpage classification with an ant colony algorithm. Eighth International Conference on Parallel Problem Solving from Nature. Springer-Verlag (LNCS 3242), pp. 1092−1102.

Hopfield, J.J., 1982. Neural networks and physical systems with emergent collective computational abilities. Natl. Acad. Sci. USA. 79 (8), 2554−2558.

Kohonen, T., 1990. The self-organizing map. Proc. IEEE. 78 (9), 1464−1480.

Kutsenok, A., Kutsenok, V., 2011. Swarm AI: a general-purpose swarm intelligence technique. Des. Princ. Pract. 5 (1), 7−16.

Lam, S. L. Y. and Lee, D. L. (1999). Feature reduction for neural network based text categorization. In: International Conference on Database Systems for Advanced Applications. Hsinchu, Taiwan, R.O.C.

Lee, P., Hui, S.C., Fong, 2002. Neural networks for web content filtering. IEEE Intell. Syst. 17 (5), 48−57.

Madhu, G., Goverdhan, A., RajiniKanth, T.V., 2011. Intelligent semantic web search engine: a brief survey. Int. J. Web Semant. Technol. 2, 35−42.

Menczer, F., Street, W., Degeratu, M., 2001. Evolving heterogeneous neural agents by local selection. In: Patel, M., Honavar, V., Balakrishnan, K. (Eds.), Advances in the Evolutionary Synthesis of Intelligent Agents. MIT Press.

Moosa, A., 2010. Artificial neural network based web application firewall for SQL injection. World Acad. Sci. Eng. Technol. 64, 12−21.

Moradi, M., and Zulkernine, M. (2004). A neural network based system for intrusion detection and classification of attacks. In: IEEE International Conference on Advances in Intelligent Systems—Theory and Applications. Luxembourg, pp.148−153.

Naya, J.M., Romero, M.M., Loureiro, J.P., Munteanu, C.R., Sierra, A.P., 2010. Improving ontology alignment through genetic algorithms. In: Pose, Marcos Gestal, Cebrián, Daniel Rivero (Eds.), Soft Computing Methods for Practical Environment Solutions: Techniques and Studies. IGI Global, pp. 240−259.

Paliouras, G., Papatheodorou, C., Karkaletsis, V., Spyropoulos, C.D., 2000.Clustering the users of large web sites into communities. In: International Conference on Machine Learning (ICML). Stanford, CA, pp. 719−726.

Panagi, P., Dasiopoulou, S., Papadopoulos, G., Kompatsiaris, I., Strintzis, M.G., 2006. A genetic algorithm approach to ontology-driven semantic, image analysis. In: IEEE International Conference on Visual Information Engineering (VIE). Bangalore, India.

Pant, G., Menczer, F., 2002. MySpiders: evolve your own intelligent web crawlers. Auton. Agent. Multi-Agent Syst. 5, 221−229.

Park, S.B., Lee, J.W., Kim, S.K., 2004. Content-based image classification using a neural network. Pattern Recogn. Lett. 25, 287−300.

Phoha, V.V., Iyengar, S.S., Kannan, R., 2002. Faster webpage allocation with neural networks. IEEE Internet Comput. 6 (6), 18−26.

Pop, C.B., Chifu, V.R., Salomie, I., Baico, R.B., Dinsoreanu, M., Copil, G., 2011.A hybrid firefly-inspired approach for optimal semantic web service composition. In: Second Workshop on Software Services: Cloud Computing and Applications. Timisoara, Romania.

Rana, V., 2011. Blueprint of an ant-based control of semantic web. Int. J. Adv. Technol. 2 (4), 603−612.

Rangarajan, S. K. (2002). Unsupervised Learning Techniques for Web Domain Clustering and its Application for Prefetching, MS Thesis, Louisiana Tech University.

Rangarajan, S.K., Phoha, V.V., Balagani, K., Iyengar, S.S., Selmic, R., 2004. Web user clustering and its application to prefetching using ART neural networks. IEEE Comput. 37 (4), 34−40.

Ratnayake, S., Rupasinghe, R., Ranatunga, A., Adikari, S., de Zoysa, S., Tennakoon, K., et al. 2008. Using swarm intelligence to perceive the semantic web. In: Fourth International Conference on Information and Automation for Sustainability, Colombo, pp. 91−96.

Rosenblatt, F., 1958. The perceptron: a probabilistic model for information storage and organization in the brain. Psychol. Rev. 65 (6), 386–408.

Shao, X., Xu, C., Kankanhalli, M., 2003. Applying neural network on the content-based audio classification. In: Fourth International Conference on Information Communications & Signal Processing, Singapore. Retrieved from: <http://www.comp.nus.edu.sg/~mohan/papers/pcm03-audio.pdf>.

Tizzo, N.P., Coello, J.M.A., Cardozo, E., 2011. Automatic composition of semantic web services using A-Teams with genetic agents. In: IEEE Congress on Evolutionary Computation. New Orleans, LA, pp. 370–377.

Wang, J., Ding, Z., Jiang, C., 2006. GAOM: genetic algorithm based ontology matching. In: IEEE Asia-Pacific Conference on Services Computing, Guangzhou, China.

Wang, X., Xu, Q., 2011. An improved ant colony optimization for ontology matching. In: Third International Conference on Computer Research and Development. Washington, DC, pp. 234–238.

Wermter, S., 2000. Neural network agents for learning semantic text classification. Inf. Retr. 3 (2), 87–103.

Woungang, I., Sadeghian, A., Wu, S., Misra, S., Arvandi, M., 2007. Wireless web security using a neural network-based cipherIn: Radhaman, G., Radha Krishna Rao, G.S.V. (Eds.), IGI Global Publishing, Hershey.

Wu, J., Aberer, K., 2003. Swarm intelligent surfing in the web. In: Third International Conference on Web Engineering. Oviedo, Spain.

Yan, K., Xue, G., Yao, S., 2009. An optimization ant colony algorithm for composition of semantic Web services. In: Asia-Pacific Conference on Computational Intelligence and Industrial Applications. Wuhan, China, pp. 262–265.

Yohanes, B.W., Handoko, Wardana, H.K., 2011. Focused crawler optimization using genetic algorithm. Telkomnika. 9 (3), 403–410.

Zadeh, A.L., 1965. Fuzzy sets. J. Inform. Control. 8, 338–353.

Zhu, X., Huang, S., Yu, Y., 2003.Recognizing the relations between webpages using artificial neural network. In: ACM Symposium on Applied Computing, USA, pp. 1217–1221.

13 Discrete Firefly Algorithm for Traveling Salesman Problem: A New Movement Scheme

Gilang Kusuma Jati[1], Ruli Manurung[1] and Suyanto[2]

[1]Faculty of Computer Science, Universitas Indonesia, Kampus UI, Depok, Jawa Barat, Indonesia; [2]Faculty of Informatics, Telkom School of Technology, Jl. Telekomunikasi No. 1, Terusan Buah Batu, Bandung, Jawa Barat, Indonesia

13.1 Introduction

The traveling salesman problem (TSP) is one of the most studied problems and has received growing attention in artificial intelligence, computational mathematics, and optimization theory in recent years. The traveling salesman problem (TSP) is one of the most studied problems and has received growing attention in artificial intelligence, computational mathematics, and optimization theory since 1930. This problem was defined in the eighteenth century by Sir William Rowan Hamilton, a mathematician from Ireland, and by Thomas Penyngton Kirkman, a British mathematician. A detailed discussion about the work of Hamilton and Kirkman can be found in Biggs et al. (1986). The origins of the TSP are unclear, but it is believed that the general form of the TSP was first studied during the 1930s in Vienna and Harvard, most notably by a mathematician named Karl Menger who defined the problem, considered the obvious brute-force algorithm and observed the nonoptimality of the nearest neighbor heuristic. The problem was later introduced with the name TSP by Hassler Whitney and Merrill at Princeton University. A comprehensive overview about the connection between Menger and Whitney, and the development of the TSP can be found by Schrijver (1960).

The TSP can be described as follows: given a set of cities and known cost of travel (or distance) between each possible pairs, a salesman needs to find the best possible way of visiting all the cities exactly once and return back to the starting point that minimizes the travel cost (or travel distance). An exact solution to this problem involves algorithms that require seeking the possibility of all existing solutions, thus this problem belongs to the class of *nondeterministic polynomial time complete* (NP complete) problems, and it has been proven that there is no scheme or algorithm currently existing that can find the exact solution in polynomial time (Aurora et al.,

Swarm Intelligence and Bio-Inspired Computation. DOI: http://dx.doi.org/10.1016/B978-0-12-405163-8.00013-2

1992). As a result, the execution time complexity of this algorithm will be exponential to the size of the given input. If given n is the number of cities that will be visited, the total number of possible routes covering all cities can be declared as a set of feasible solutions of the TSP and is given as $(n-1)!/2$. A comprehensive overview of this line of research can be found by Gutin and Punnen (2002).

The TSP has several applications even in its purest formulation, such as planning, logistics, and the manufacture of microchips. A direct application of the TSP is drilling problem of printed circuit boards (PCBs) to connect a conductor on one layer with a conductor on another layer, or to position the pins of integrated circuits (Grötschel et al., 1991), overhauling gas turbine engines to guarantee a uniform gas flow through the turbines which have nozzle-guide vane assemblies located at each turbine stage (Plante et al., 1987), analysis of the structure of crystals in X-ray crystallography (Bland and Shallcross, 1989), connecting components on a computer board (Lenstra and Rinnooy Kan, 1975), material handling in a warehouse (Ratliff and Rosenthal, 1983), and vehicle routing problem. Beside the above examples, problems in real life like route distributions of transportation networks, planning of tourist routes, laying of pipelines needed for city planning and engineering construction are interlinked with the problems of finding the shortest route. Thus, it is very important to carry out research on the problem of the shortest route. The process of finding a solution for TSP plays an important role in real life, and it has attracted many scholars to do research on it.

The TSP is used as a benchmark for many optimization methods. Even though the problem is computationally difficult, many methods have been developed to solve TSP such as branch and bound (Land and Doig, 1960), Lin−Kernighan local search (Lin and Kernighan, 1973), heuristic search (Jiang et al., 2005), dynamic programming (Jellouli, 2001), and neural computing network (Abdel-Moetty, 2010). Evolutionary computation, especially metaheuristic algorithms, has shown very promising potential to solve optimization problems like TSP. It has been proven by many published methods to solve TSP, e.g., ant colony optimization by Marco Dorigo and Luca Maria Gambardella that mimic the movements of ants (Dorigo and Gambardella, 1996), genetic algorithm by Lanlan Kang that combined with ant colony optimization (Kang and Cao, 2010), and discrete particle swarm optimization by Matthias Hoffmann that used sequences of transpositions as the difference between tours (Hoffmann et al., 2011). Those researchers proposed methods that are combinations of a metaheuristic algorithm with a local search or other metaheuristic algorithms and focused on small TSP with hundreds of cities (nodes). Generally, accuracies of the methods are very high in that their produced solutions are very close to the known optimum solutions. In Tsai et al. (2004), the researchers focused on large TSP with thousands of cities. The method that they proposed, called HeSEA, is capable of solving a TSP of up to 3038 cities with a deviation of 0% compared to the known optimum solution. It can also solve a TSP of 13,509 cities with a deviation of only 0.74%.

The firefly algorithm (FA) is a nature-inspired metaheuristic optimization algorithm developed by Xin-She Yang that is inspired by the flashing behavior of fireflies (Yang, 2008), originally designed to solve continuous optimization problems

(Lukasik and Żak, 2010; Yang, 2009). However, the FA can be discretized to solve a permutation problem. The discrete firefly algorithm (DFA) has been successfully implemented to solve flow shop scheduling problems. The DFA outperforms existing algorithms such as ant colony algorithm (Sayadi et al., 2010). Recently, the evolutionary discrete firefly algorithm (EDFA) has been developed for solving TSP (Jati and Suyanto, 2011). However, fireflies in EDFA have no direction when moving. Hence, it moves using evolution strategies (ES) concept. So, each firefly will move using inversion mutation. One of the three primary rules in FA states that, for any two flashing fireflies, the less bright one will move toward the brighter one. When the firefly moves to another brighter firefly, the distance between them will decrease. However, the movement scheme for fireflies in EDFA violates these primary rules because the movement scheme does not guarantee that after one firefly moves toward the brighter one, the distance between them will decrease. In this chapter, a new movement scheme is proposed to solve the problem of this movement scheme in EDFA. This new movement scheme guarantees that after one firefly moves toward the brighter one, the distance between them will decrease.

13.2 Evolutionary Discrete Firefly Algorithm

The FA is a metaheuristic algorithm, inspired by the flashing behavior of fireflies. The primary purpose for a firefly's flash is to act as a signal system to attract other fireflies. Now this can idealize some of the flashing characteristics of fireflies so as to consequently develop firefly-inspired algorithms. By idealizing some of the flashing characteristics of fireflies, the firefly algorithm was developed by Yang (2008). FA uses the following three primary rules:

1. All fireflies are unisex which means that they are attracted to other fireflies regardless of their sex.
2. The degree of the attractiveness of a firefly is proportional to its brightness, thus for any two flashing fireflies, the less bright one will move toward the brighter one and their attractiveness will decrease as their distance increases. If there is no brighter one than a particular firefly, it will move randomly.
3. The brightness or light intensity of a firefly is affected or determined by the landscape of the objective function to be optimized.

For a maximization problem, the brightness can simply be proportional to the objective function. Other forms of brightness can be defined in a similar way to the fitness function in genetic algorithms or the bacterial foraging algorithm (Gazi and Passino, 2004).

13.2.1 The Representation of the Firefly

A solution representation for the TSP is a permutation representation as illustrated in Figure 13.1. Here, a firefly represents one solution. We adopt the so-called path representation, which is considered the most natural form of TSP representation for

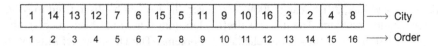

Figure 13.1 The permutation representation of a TSP solution.

chromosomes that represent individuals in genetic algorithms. In this representation, an element of an array represents a city (node) and the index represents the order of a tour. Two adjacent elements thus indicate an edge between two cities that lies along the route, e.g., see Figure 13.1, the edge between nodes 1 and 14 forms part of the route, since they occupy the first two positions in the array. We will use the notation 1 − 14 to denote this edge.

13.2.2 Light Intensity

Light intensity is a value that represents the brightness of a firefly. This value depends on the total path distance of travel routes belonging to a firefly. Since the purpose of the TSP is to find a route with the minimum distance, a firefly which has less distance route will have a higher light intensity (brighter). The light intensity of a firefly x is calculated using Eqs. (13.1) and (13.2),

$$distance\_route = dist(x[1], x[n]) + \sum_{k=1}^{n-1} dist(x[k], x[k+1]) \tag{13.1}$$

$$I = \frac{1}{distance\_route} \tag{13.2}$$

where $dist(i,j)$ is the Euclidean distance from city i to city j with $i, j \in [1,n]$, and n is the number of cities from the TSP problem data. With the above equation, the light intensity of a firefly will increase when the total path distance of travel routes belonging to a firefly decreases. In the FA, light intensity is used as an objective function.

13.2.3 Distance

In continuous optimization problems, the distance between two fireflies is simply calculated using Euclidian distance. For TSP, the distance between firefly i and firefly j can be defined as the number of different edges between them. In Figure 13.2, three edges $12 − 15$, $5 − 7$, and $6 − 11$ in firefly j do not exist in firefly i. Hence, the number of different edges between firefly i and firefly j is 3. Then, the distance between two fireflies is calculated using Eq. (13.3):

$$r = \frac{A}{n} .10 \tag{13.3}$$

Firefly i	1	14	13	12	7	6	15	5	11	9	10	16	3	2	4	8
Firefly j	1	14	13	12	15	5	7	6	11	9	10	16	3	2	4	8

Figure 13.2 The distance between two fireflies i and j is defined as the number of different edges between them.

where r is the distance between any two fireflies, A is the total number of different edges between two fireflies, and n is the number of cities. This equation scales r in the interval $[0,10]^1$ as r will be used for the attractiveness calculation.

13.2.4 Attractiveness

The attractiveness of a firefly is determined by its brightness, which is associated with the encoded objective function. In the original FA, the main form of the attractiveness function $\beta(r)$ can be any monotonic decreasing function:

$$\beta(r) = \beta_0 \, e^{-\gamma r^2} \tag{13.4}$$

where $\beta(r)$ is the attractiveness of a firefly when seen at distance r, r is the distance between two fireflies, β_0 is the brightness of a brighter firefly, and γ is a fixed light absorption coefficient. This scheme is completely adopted by the EDFA.

For any two fireflies, firefly i and another brighter firefly j, we first calculate the distance (r) between firefly i and firefly j by using Eq. (13.3). After that we calculate the attractiveness of firefly j when seen by firefly i at distance r by using Eq. (13.4). If the attractiveness of firefly j is greater than the brightness (light intensity) of firefly i, then firefly i will move toward firefly j, otherwise firefly i will move randomly.

13.2.5 Light Absorption

In essence, the light absorption coefficient γ characterizes the variation of the attractiveness value of a firefly. Its value is very important in determining the speed of convergence and how the FA behaves. In theory, $\gamma \in [0, \infty)$, but in practice γ is determined by the characteristics of the problem to be optimized.

In conditions where $\gamma \to 0$, the attractiveness will be constant and $\beta(r) = \beta_0$. In this case, the attractiveness of a firefly will not decrease when viewed by another. If $\gamma \to \infty$, this means the value of attractiveness of a firefly is close to zero when viewed by another firefly. It is equivalent to cases where the fireflies fly in a very foggy region randomly. No other fireflies can be seen, and each firefly roams in a

---

[1] The role of the constant multiplier here can be accounted for by the light absorption coefficient, γ (Section 13.2.5).

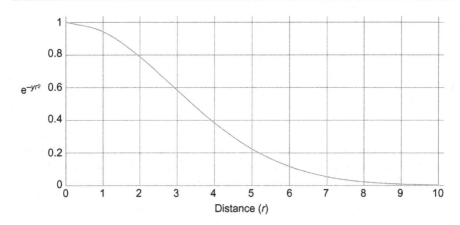

Figure 13.3 The correlation of distances and attractiveness with $\gamma = 0.06$.

completely random way. Therefore, this corresponds to a completely random search method.

The coefficient γ determines how much light intensity changes the attractiveness of a firefly over distances. In the EDFA, γ is in the interval $[0.01, 0.15]$ so that the attractiveness of a firefly viewed by the others will follow the curve shown in Figure 13.3.

This is the correlation between distances and attractiveness. The distance (r) scales in the interval $[1,10]$ to handle the value of $e^{-\gamma r^2}$. If the distance is too high (more than 10), the value of $e^{-\gamma r^2}$ is close to zero, and the attractiveness of a firefly is also close to zero when viewed by another firefly, so the firefly will always move randomly.

13.2.6 Movement

The movement of a firefly i attracted to another brighter (more attractive) firefly j is determined by

$$x_i = \text{rand}(2, A) \tag{13.5}$$

where x_i is the step that must be taken by firefly i to move toward firefly j, and A is the total number of different edges between two fireflies i and j. The length of movement (step) of a firefly will be randomly selected from 2 to A using uniform distribution. When a firefly moves, existing solutions in the firefly are changed. Since the representation of a firefly is a permutation representation, we use inversion mutation to represent the movement.

Actually, a firefly in EDFA has no direction to move. Hence, it moves using ES concept. Each firefly will move using inversion mutation for m times. First, an index on the chromosome will be selected randomly, wherein an inversion mutation is carried out. In other words, each firefly will have m new solutions. After p fireflies move and produce $p \times m$ new solutions, then the p best fireflies will be selected as the new population.

One of the three primary rules in FA states that for any two flashing fireflies, the less bright one will move toward the brighter one. When a firefly moves to another brighter firefly, the distance between them will decrease. This movement scheme violates these primary rules because the movement scheme does not guarantee that after one firefly moves toward the brighter one, the distance between them decreases.

13.2.7 Inversion Mutation

Inversion mutation is used to create new fireflies, i.e., new candidate solutions. First, randomly pick one point from the index of one chromosome (P_1), then select the second point (P_2) by summing the first point (P_1) and the length of movement. With inversion mutation, the path that has been formed can be maintained so the path formed previously is not damaged. Figure 13.4 shows an illustration of inversion mutation.

13.2.8 EDFA Scheme

The scheme of EDFA is illustrated by the following pseudocode. First, each firefly generates an initial solution randomly. For each firefly, find the brightest or the most attractive firefly. If there is a brighter firefly, then the less bright firefly will move toward the brighter one and if there is no brighter one, it will move randomly. When a firefly moves, the existing solution represented by the firefly is changed. Each firefly that moves randomly will generate a new solution using inversion mutation in m different positions on the chromosome. We refer to this constant m as the *updating index*. After p fireflies have moved, there will be $p \times m + 1$ fireflies at the end of an iteration since only the best firefly will be included in the selection process for the next iteration. Then, the p best fireflies will be chosen based on an objective function for the next iteration. This condition will continue until the maximum iteration is reached.

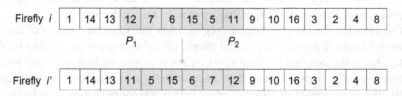

Figure 13.4 Inversion mutation of firefly with length of movement (step) = 5.

Input:
Define objective function $f(x)$, population size p, light absorption coefficient γ, and updating
index m
Begin

```
        List<Firefly> temp = new List<Firefly>
        //initialize population of firefly
        Firefly[] x = new Firefly[p]
        for i = 1 to p do
                x[i] = Generate_Initial_Solution()
        endfor
        repeat
                for i = 1 to p do
                        Firefly f = Get_Most_Attractive_Firefly(x[i])
                        if (f != null) then
                                for j = 1 to m do
                                        Firefly fnew = Move_Firefly(x[i])
                                        temp.Add(fnew)
                                endfor
                        else
                                for j = 1 to m do
                                        Firefly fnew = Move_Random(x[i])
                                        temp.Add(fnew)
                                endfor
                        endif
                endfor
                //select p brightest fireflies from temp
                x = Get_Brightest_Fireflies(temp)
                temp.Clear()
        until stop condition true
        //output best firefly
        Output(x.min)
end
```

13.3   A New DFA for the TSP

Here, we discuss a new movement scheme called edge-based movement to guarantee that after one firefly moves toward the brighter one the distance between them
will decrease. We also discuss the new DFA scheme.

13.3.1   Edge-Based Movement

As described in Section 13.2.6, the movement scheme for fireflies in EDFA violates the primary rules of FA because it does not guarantee that after one firefly
moves toward a brighter one, the distance between them will decrease. Here we
propose a new movement scheme that guarantees such a decrease.

The idea for the new movement begins from the rules that state the distance
between two fireflies must be reduced after a firefly moves toward another brighter
firefly. Since the distance between two fireflies is calculated using the total number
of different edges between them, then when a firefly moves toward another brighter
firefly, the total number of different edges between them must also be reduced. The
total number of different edges between them can be reduced by adding an edge

that exists in the brighter firefly but does not exist in the less bright firefly in such a way that no similar edges between them that existed previously are removed.

The new movement scheme of DFA is illustrated by the following procedure. First, there are two fireflies, firefly i and another brighter firefly j. From all the edges that exist in firefly j but not in firefly i, randomly select one that will be added to firefly i, e.g., edge $x - y$ is the selected edge, where x and y are nodes or cities in the TSP. Find the positions of nodes x and y in firefly i. For each node, we then build a *segment* around it, i.e., a maximally long sequence of edges that contains edges that are also found in firefly j. The procedure to build this segment is simple. Starting from a node, which we consider to be a segment of length 1, we keep extending the segment to the left and right, adding edges that are found in firefly j, until it can no longer be extended. Let us call a segment built starting from node n as S_n, thus the segment built starting from node x is S_x, and the segment built starting from node y is S_y.

Once the two segments have been identified, we must merge them in such a way that nodes x and y appear adjacent to each other in firefly i, thus achieving the objective of adding edge $x - y$ to firefly i. There are four ways to merge these two segments, i.e., inserting S_x before S_y, inserting S_x after S_y, inserting S_y before S_x, and finally inserting S_y after S_x. Note that to ensure that edge $x - y$ appears in firefly i, some inversion of a segment might be required. Executing all four ways of merging these segments will yield four new fireflies (solutions).

Figures 13.5–13.7 illustrate this process through an example. Figure 13.5 shows two fireflies, firefly i and another brighter firefly j. The total number of different edges between them is seven, namely the edges $7 - 12$, $12 - 13$, 14-1, $1 - 8$, $2 - 3$, $10 - 15$, and $5 - 6$ that exist in firefly j but do not exist in firefly i.

Figure 13.6 shows the result of constructing segments in firefly i. The process begins by selecting one of the seven edges above that will be added to firefly i, say $2 - 3$ is the selected edge. We then locate the position of node 2 (marked with x) and node 3 (marked with y) in the chromosome of firefly i. We then construct a segment (edge sequences) for each node. Starting from node 2, we extend the segment to the left to include 4-2 and 8-4, since both these edges are also found in firefly j. However, we stop at node 8 since $7 - 8$ is not found in firefly j. Attempting to extend this segment to the right fails because the edge 2-1 is also not found in firefly j. Likewise for node 3, we extend the segment to the right to include $3 - 16$, 16-11, 11-9, and $9 - 10$, since all of these edges are also found in firefly j. However, we stop at node 10 since $10 - 13$ is not found in firefly j. Attempting to extend this segment to the left fails because the edge 12-3 is also not found in firefly j. In fact, it is guaranteed that each segment can only be extended

Firefly i	6	7	8	4	2	1	5	15	12	3	16	11	9	10	13	14

Firefly j	6	7	12	13	14	1	8	4	2	3	16	11	9	10	15	5

Figure 13.5 Two fireflies with seven different edges.

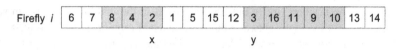

Figure 13.6 Firefly i with the segments of each node in the selected edge.

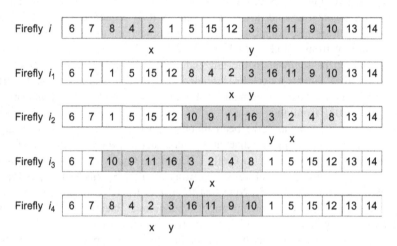

Figure 13.7 Merging process of two segments in firefly.

in one direction, since the aim is to add the edge $x - y$ into firefly i, thus $x - y$ must not previously exist. Thus, S_x is 8-4-2 and S_y is 3-16-11-9-10.

Finally, the merging process of S_x and S_y is illustrated in Figure 13.7. There are four ways to merge these two segments, i.e., inserting S_x before S_y, inserting S_x after S_y, inserting S_y before S_x, and finally inserting S_y after S_x. Fireflies $i_1{}'$, $i_2{}'$, $i_3{}'$, and $i_4{}'$ show the results of applying these four possibilities, yielding four new fireflies (solutions). Note that for fireflies $i_2{}'$ and $i_4{}'$, the segments S_x and S_y had to be inverted to ensure that edge $x - y$ can be added.

Note that in all of these solutions, edge $2 - 3$ has been successfully added to firefly i and has been done in such a way that no other edge belonging to firefly i that also appears in firefly j has been removed as a result. Thus, if distance is measured in terms of the number of different edges between two fireflies, the distance between them has now been decreased.

13.3.2   New DFA Scheme

The scheme of the new DFA, which employs the new edge-based movement described in Section 13.3.1, is illustrated by the following pseudocode. The concept is similar to EDFA, but there are some differences. In the begining, each firefly will generate an initial solution randomly. For each firefly, we find the brightest or the most attractive firefly. If there is a brighter firefly, then the less bright firefly will move toward the brighter one with the new movement scheme and if there is no brighter one, it will move randomly (move with ES concept like in EDFA). When a firefly moves, the existing solution represented by the firefly is changed. Each firefly that moves randomly will generate a new solution using inversion mutation in m different positions, i.e., the updating index, on the chromosome. Each firefly that moves toward a brighter firefly will yield four new solutions, and one solution is chosen randomly. After p fireflies have moved, the total number of fireflies in EDFA will be constant at each generation, but in the new DFA it depends on how many fireflies move randomly and how many move toward the others. For the next iteration, the p best fireflies will be chosen based on an objective function. This condition will continue until the maximum iteration is reached.

Input:
Define objective function $f(x)$, population size p ,light absorption coefficient γ, and updating index m
Begin

    List<Firefly> **temp** = **new** List<Firefly>
    //initialize population of firefly
    Firefly[] **x** = **new** Firefly[p]
    for i = 1 to p do
        x[i] = Generate_Initial_Solution()
    endfor
    repeat
        for i = 1 to p do
            Firefly **f** = Get_Most_Attractive_Firefly(x[i])
            if (f != null) then
                Firefly[] newSolutions = **new** Firefly[4]
                newSolutions = Edge-based_Movement(x[i])
                Firefly fnew = newSolution[Random(1,4)]
                temp.Add(fnew)
            else
                for j = 1 to m do
                    Firefly fnew = Move_Random(x[i])
                    temp.Add(fnew)
                endfor
            endif
        endfor
        //select p brightest fireflies from temp
        x = Get_Brightest_Fireflies(temp)
        temp.Clear()
    until *stop condition true*
    //output best firefly
    Output(x.min)
end

13.4   Result and Discussion

In this chapter, the new DFA is applied to 7 TSP instances obtained from TSPLIB (2011). Table 13.1 lists the problem names, numbers of cities, and the lengths of their known optimal tours. The types of TSP instances in TSPLIB (2011) are based

Table 13.1 Summary of 7 TSPs Taken from TSPLIB: Problem
Names, Number of Cities (nodes), and the Length of the
Optimal Tour

Problem Names	Number of Cities	Length of the Optimal Tour
ulysses16	16	74.109
ulysses22	22	75.665
gr202	202	549.998
tsp225	225	3859
a280	280	2586.769
pcb442	442	50783.547
gr666	666	3952.535

on Euclidian distances, wherein a TSP instance provides some cities with their coordinates. The number in the name of an instance represents the number of provided cities. For example, ulysses16 provides 16 cities with their coordinates. The problem is thus what is the best tour to visit the 16 cities, according to their Euclidian distances, with a condition where each city should be visited only once.

13.4.1 Firefly Population

Population size (p) critically determines the computation time. Here, the new DFA is tested using various population sizes on problem gr202 to investigate its correlation with the number of trials needed by new DFA to obtain the optimum solution. Table 13.2 represents the correlation of the population size with the average trials to reach the optimum solution (with accuracy of 100%). The results reported are averaged after running the experiment 50 times. In new DFA, the average trials decrease when the population size is increased from 2 to 5. But the average trials increase when the population size is 6 or more. Thus, an increasingly large population does not guarantee that FA will reach an optimum solution more quickly. According to Table 13.2, the best population size for new DFA given problem gr202 is 5.

13.4.2 Effect of Light Absorption

The light absorption coefficient (γ) also critically determines the computation time. Various values of light absorption were tested on problem gr202 to evaluate its correlation with the number of trials needed by new DFA to obtain the optimum solution. Table 13.3 illustrates the relationship between the light absorption and the average trials to obtain the optimum solution. The results reported are averaged after running the experiment 50 times. The light absorption coefficient is varied from 0.0001 to 0.21, yielding different average trials. Thus, the light absorption coefficient significantly affects the average trials of new DFA. In new DFA, the average running time decreases when the light absorption coefficient is increased.

Table 13.2 Correlation of the Population Size and the Average Trials Needed by New DFA to Obtain the Optimum Solution

Population Size	Average Trials	Standard Deviation	Average Running Time(s)
2	110,617	51,036	1.651
3	84,110	67,377	1.615
4	59,478	8156	1.426
5	**55,690**	**13,814**	**1.045**
6	58,700	12,755	1.904
7	61,395	22,795	2.593
8	59,761	14,768	2.690
9	71,086	34,471	3.512
10	63,240	14,227	3.583
11	77,126	39,328	4.990
12	58,537	13,095	4.161
13	68,482	36,616	5.203
14	57,359	16,225	4.763
15	59,176	9392	5.328
16	58,489	17,302	5.609
17	68,300	18,489	7.025
18	70,667	14,951	7.390
19	66,508	13,434	8.038
20	61,912	6963	8.455

Note: The bold values represent the best result for all setting parameters. The best result is the minimum value in the column of average trials.

There are two types of firefly movement. The first is where a firefly deliberately moves toward a brighter one (marked as "move toward" in Table 13.3), and the second is a random movement (marked as "move random" in Table 13.3). The number of random moves increases when the light absorption coefficient is increased. This corresponds to the theory that if $\gamma \to \infty$, the value of attractiveness of a firefly is close to zero when viewed by another firefly. It is equivalent to cases where the fireflies fly in a very foggy region randomly. No other fireflies can be seen, and each firefly roams in a completely random way. When $\gamma \geq 0.2$, FA behaves like random search.

13.4.3 Number of Updating Index

The number of updating index (m) also determines the computation time. New DFA is tested using various number of updating index on problem gr202 to investigate its correlation with number of trials needed by new DFA to obtain the optimum solution. Table 13.4 represents the correlation of the number of updating index with the average trials to reach the optimum solution (with accuracy of 100%). The results reported are averaged after running the experiment 50 times.

Table 13.3 Correlation of the Light Absorption Coefficient (γ) and the Average Trials Needed by New DFA to Obtain the Optimum Solution

Light Absorption	Average Move Toward	Average Move Random	Average Trials	Standard Deviation	Average Running Time (s)
0	4566	61,903	66,469	22,776	1.963
0.0001	4382	61,467	65,849	18,438	1.988
0.0002	4349	61,441	65,790	25,685	1.899
0.0003	4366	62,442	66,808	18,993	1.979
0.0004	4152	58,233	62,385	16,805	1.808
0.0005	4258	61,572	65,830	16,309	1.947
0.0006	4350	64,451	68,801	22,867	1.901
0.0007	4115	60,008	64,193	17,321	1.835
0.0008	4276	64,245	68,251	17,397	1.869
0.0009	4046	59,626	63,671	16,139	1.764
0.0010	3961	58,656	62,617	18,608	1.703
0.0020	3704	59,572	63,276	18,214	1.721
0.0030	3379	58,266	61,645	24,869	1.519
0.0040	3325	64,982	68,307	29,716	1.620
0.0050	2757	56,866	59,623	14,037	1.456
0.0060	2728	61,684	64,412	15,617	1.439
0.0070	**2629**	**53,061**	**55,690**	**13,814**	**1.045**
0.0080	2454	67,046	69,500	24,023	1.448
0.0090	2137	62,950	65,807	16,222	1.292
0.0100	1961	63,918	65,879	23,338	1.276
0.0200	886	65,728	66,614	12,555	0.985
0.0300	474	71,377	71,852	15,209	1.024
0.0400	250	75,881	76,131	14,699	0.992
0.0500	129	80,370	80,499	28,774	1.008
0.0600	50	77,086	77,136	13,316	0.989
0.0700	24	83,680	83,705	21,995	1.030
0.0800	9	77,719	77,728	16,071	0.967
0.0900	5	85,464	85,470	27,727	1.060
0.1000	3	79,137	79,140	21,252	1.249
0.1100	3	82,104	82,107	17,631	1.001
0.1200	2	82,545	82,547	17,891	1.004
0.1300	2	83,767	83,769	18,050	1.024
0.1400	1	84,612	84,613	27,421	1.019
0.1500	1	81,360	81,361	19,087	1.006
0.1600	1	84,644	84,645	21,999	0.945
0.1700	1	82,227	82,228	16,755	0.917
0.1800	1	79,272	79,273	22,978	0.903
0.1900	1	82,305	82,305	19,994	0.942
0.2000	0	80,600	80,600	15,834	0.904
0.2100	0	78,786	78,786	14,881	0.884

Note: The bold values represent the best result for all setting parameters. The best result is the minimum value in the column of average trials.

Table 13.4 Correlation of the Number of Updating Index (*m*) and the Average Trials Needed by New DFA to Obtain the Optimum Solution

Number of Updating Index	Average Trials	Standard Deviation	Average Running Time (s)
1	300,514	39,698	5.687
2	67,258	13,404	1.645
3	61,181	20,010	1.679
4	61,854	21,126	1.520
5	63,683	24,264	1.444
6	57,521	13,848	0.699
7	58,128	14,083	0.668
8	60,605	25,405	1.016
9	63,226	37,266	1.190
10	60,629	21,925	0.698
11	**55,690**	**13,814**	**1.045**
12	62,638	18,734	0.532
13	63,533	21,430	1.529
14	69,212	60,871	1.361
15	68,964	63,109	1.568
16	60,572	13,144	0.994

Note: The bold values represent the best result for all setting parameters. The best result is the minimum value in the column of average trials.

In new DFA, the average trials decrease when the number of updating index is increased from 1 to 11. But the average trials become unstable when the number of updating index is 12 or more. A large number of updating index does not guarantee that FA will reach an optimal solution more quickly. According to Table 13.4, the best number of updating index for new DFA for problem gr202 is 11.

13.4.4 Performance of New DFA

New DFA is examined for 7 TSP instances detailed in Table 13.1 to compare its performance with EDFA proposed in Jati and Suyanto (2011). Here, new DFA uses a population size of 5 fireflies and the light absorption coefficient is 0.001. The accuracy is calculated by Eq. (13.6). New DFA is implemented using Visual C#. Net. The results reported are averaged after running the experiment 50 times, the same as for EDFA studied by Jati and Suyanto (2011). The results are summarized in Table 13.5. New DFA obtains the best solution for ulysses16, ulysses22, gr202, and gr666 for all runs. New DFA is not optimal for three other instances: tsp225, a280, and pcb442, but its accuracy is slightly better than that of EDFA. For all seven instances, new DFA runs much faster than EDFA. The average speedup

Table 13.5 The Comparison Between New DFA and EDFA

Problem Names	Best Solution Known	EDFA			New DFA			Speedup Factor
		Average Accuracy	Average Trials	Average Time	Average Accuracy	Average Trials	Average Time	
ulysses16	74.10	100.11	25,160	0.41	100.09	1149	0.01	21.89 ×
ulysses22	75.66	100.20	235,720	6.59	100.18	8987	0.02	26.22 ×
gr202	549.99	100.47	1,443,372	51.16	100.17	55,690	1.04	25.91 ×
tsp225	3859.00	88.33	2,739,000	412.27	88.49	445,398	120.42	6.14 ×
a280	2586.76	88.29	3,592,440	691.88	88.38	548,930	251.76	6.54 ×
pcb442	50,783.54	88.50	8,196,960	3404.21	88.53	1,187,428	167.23	6.90 ×
gr666	3952.53	100.03	1,649,560	393.02	100.08	341,519	51.33	4.83 ×
							Average:	14.06 ×

factor is 14.06 times, where the speedup factor is determined as the ratio between the average trials of the new DFA and EDFA:

$$\text{accuracy} = \frac{\text{best\_solution\_known}}{\text{best\_solution\_found}}.100\% \qquad (13.6)$$

13.5 Conclusion

A new proposed movement scheme, called edge-based movement, works very well in new DFA. Our comparative testing to EDFA shows that the new movement in new DFA produces slightly better accuracy with much faster average time, which in our experiments yielded an average speedup factor of 14.06. Although the new movement guarantees to make an individual closer to brighter one, it does not guarantee to improve the fitness of that individual. Hence, the new DFA should be designed to have an appropriate light absorption so that it has some random movements to make the evolution works well.

Acknowledgment

Many thanks to all colleagues at Universitas Indonesia and Telkom School of Technology for the support given.

References

Abdel-Moetty, S.M., 2010. Traveling salesman problem using neural network techniques. Proceedings of the Seventh International Conference on Informatics and Systems (INFOS). IEEE Computer Society, Washington, DC, pp. 1−6. <http://ieeexplore. ieee.org/xpl/articleDetails.jsp?tp=&arnumber=5461754&pcontentType=Conference + Publications&searchField%3DSearch_All%26queryText%3DTraveling + Salesman + Problem + Using + Neural + Network + Techniques>.

Aurora, S., Lund, C., Motwani, R., Sudan, M., Szegedy, M., 1992. Proof verification and hardness of approximation problems. In: Proceedings of the 33th IEEE Symposium Foundations of Computer Science. IEEE Press, Pittsburgh, PA, pp. 10−22.

Biggs, N.L., Lloyd, E.K., Wilson, R.J., 1986. Graph Theory 1736-1936. Clarendon Press, Oxford (ISBN 978-0-19-853916-2).

Bland, R.E., Shallcross, D.E., 1989. Large traveling salesman problem arising from experiments in X-ray crystallography: a preliminary report on computation. Oper. Res. Lett. 8 (3), 125−128.

Dorigo, M., Gambardella, L.M., 1996. Ant Colonies for the Traveling Salesman Problem. University Libre de Bruxelles, Belgium.

Gazi, K., Passino, K.M., 2004. Stability analysis of social foraging swarms. IEEE Trans. Syst. Man Cybern. Part B—Cybern. 34, 539−555.

Grötschel, M., Jünger, M., Reinelt, G., 1991. Optimal control of plotting and drilling machines: a case study. Math. Methods Oper. Res. 35 (1), 61−84.

Gutin, G., Punnen, A.P., 2002. The traveling salesman problem and its variations, Comb Optim, vol. 12. Springer-Verlag, Berlin, Heidelberg, pp. 1−28.

Hoffmann, M., Mühlenthaler, M., Helwig, S., Wanka, R., 2011. Discrete particle swarm optimization for TSP: theoretical result and experimental evaluations, International Conference on Adaptive and Intelligent System (ICAIS 2011), vol. 6943. Springer-Verlag, Berlin, Heidelberg, Lecture Notes in Artificial Intelligence (LNAI), pp. 416−427.

Jati, G.K., Suyanto, 2011. Evolutionary discrete firefly algorithm for travelling salesman problem, Second International Conference on Adaptive and Intelligent System (ICAIS 2011), vol. 6943. Springer-Verlag, Berlin, Heidelberg, Lecture Notes in Artificial Intelligence (LNAI), pp. 393−403.

Jellouli, O., 2001. Intelligent dynamic programming for the generalized traveling salesman problem. In: Proceedings of the IEEE International Conference on Systems, Man, and Cybernetics, vol. 4. IEEE Computer Society, Washington, DC, pp. 2765-2768.

Jiang, H., Zhou, Z., Zhou, P., Chen, G.L., 2005. Union search: a new metaheuristic algorithm to the traveling salesman problem. J. Univ. Sci. Technol. China. 35, 367−375.

Kang, L., Cao, W., 2010. An improved genetic and ant colony optimization algorithm for travelling salesman problem. Third International Symposium on Information Science and Engineering (ISISE 2010). IEEE Computer Society, Washington, DC, pp. 498−502.

Land, A., Doig, A., 1960. An automatic method of solving discrete programming problems. Econometrica. 28 (3), 497−520.

Lenstra, J.K., Rinnooy Kan, A.H.G., 1975. Some simple applications of the traveling salesman problem. Oper. Res. Q. 26, 717−733.

Lin, S., Kernighan, B., 1973. An effective heuristic algorithm for the traveling-salesman problem. Oper. Res. 21 (2), 498−516.

Lukasik, S., Żak, S., 2010. Firefly algorithm for continuous constrained optimization tasks. Syst. Res. Inst. Pol. Acad. Sci.1−10.

Plante, R.D., Lowe, T.J., Chandrasekaran., R., 1987. The product matrix traveling salesman problem: an application and solution heuristics. Oper. Res. 35, 772−783.

Ratliff, H.D., Rosenthal, A.S., 1983. Order-picking in a rectangular warehouse: a solvable case for the travelling salesman problem. Oper. Res. 31, 507−521.

Sayadi, M.K., Ramezanian, R., Ghaffari-Nasab, N., 2010. A discrete firefly meta-heuristic with local search for makespan minimization in permutation flow shop scheduling problems. Int. J. Ind. Eng. Comput.1−10.

Schrijver, A., 1960. On the history of combinatorial optimization. In: Aardal, K., Nemhauser, G.L., Weismantel, R. (Eds.), Handbook of Discrete Optimization. Elsevier, Amsterdam, pp. 1−68.

Tsai, H.K., Yang, J.M., Tsai, F.Y., Kao, C.Y., 2004. An evolutionary algorithm for large traveling salesman problems. IEEE Transactions on Systems, Man, and Cybernetics, Part B. IEEE Computer Society, Washington, DC, pp. 1718−1729.

TSPLIB95: Ruprecht—Karls—Universitat Heidelberg, 2011. <http://www.iwr.uini-heidelberg.de/groups/comopt/software/TSPLIB95/>. (accessed 09.17.12).

Yang, X.S., 2008. Nature-Inspired Metaheuristic Algorithm. Luniver Press, UK.

Yang, X.S., 2009. Firefly algorithm for multimodal optimization, Proceedings of the Fifth International Conference on Stochastic Algorithms: Foundations and Applications (SAGA'09), vol. 5792. Springer-Verlag, Berlin, Heidelberg, Lecture Notes in Computer Science (LNCS), pp. 169−178.

14 Modeling to Generate Alternatives Using Biologically Inspired Algorithms

Raha Imanirad and Julian Scott Yeomans

OMIS Area, Schulich School of Business, York University, Toronto, ON, Canada

14.1 Introduction

Typical "real-world" decision-making involves complex problems that possess design requirements which are frequently very difficult to incorporate into their supporting mathematical programming formulations and tend to be plagued by numerous unquantifiable components (Brugnach et al., 2007; Janssen et al., 2010; Walker et al., 2003). While mathematically optimal solutions provide the best answers to these modeled formulations, they are generally not the best solutions to the underlying real problems as there are invariably unmodeled aspects not apparent during the model construction phase (Brugnach et al., 2007; Janssen et al., 2010; Loughlin et al., 2001). Hence, it is generally considered desirable to generate a reasonable number of very different alternatives that provide multiple, contrasting perspectives to the specified problem (Matthies et al., 2007; Yeomans and Gunalay, 2011). These alternatives should preferably possess near-optimal objective measures with respect to all of the modeled objective(s), but be as different as possible from each other in terms of the system structures characterized by their decision variables. Several approaches collectively referred to as *modeling-to-generate-alternatives* (MGA) have been developed in response to this multisolution creation requirement (Brill et al., 1982; Loughlin et al., 2001; Yeomans and Gunalay, 2011).

The primary motivation behind MGA is to construct a manageably small set of alternatives that are good with respect to all measured objective(s) yet are fundamentally dissimilar within the prescribed decision space. The resulting set of alternatives should provide diverse approaches that all perform similarly with respect to the known modeled objectives, yet very differently with respect to any unmodeled issues (Walker et al., 2003). Obviously the decision makers must then conduct a subsequent comprehensive comparison of these alternatives to determine which

Swarm Intelligence and Bio-Inspired Computation. DOI: http://dx.doi.org/10.1016/B978-0-12-405163-8.00014-4

options would most closely satisfy their very specific circumstances. Consequently, MGA approaches are necessarily classified as decision support processes rather than the role of explicit solution determination methods assumed, in general, for optimization.

In this chapter, it is shown how to efficiently generate sets of maximally different solution alternatives by implementing a modified version of the nature-inspired firefly algorithm (FA) of Yang (2009, 2010) combined with a concurrent, coevolutionary MGA approach (Imanirad et al., 2012a,b). For calculation and optimization purposes, Yang (2010) has demonstrated that the FA is more computationally efficient than such commonly used metaheuristic procedures as genetic algorithms, simulated annealing, and enhanced particle swarm optimization (PSO) (Cagnina et al., 2008; Gandomi et al., 2011). The MGA procedure extends the earlier approach of Imanirad et al. (2012a,b) by exploiting the concept of coevolution within the FA's solution approach to concurrently generate the desired number of solution alternatives in a single computational run. Hence, this concurrent coevolutionary FA procedure is extremely computationally efficient for MGA purposes. The efficacy of this approach is illustrated using a well-known nonlinear constrained optimization problem (Aragon et al., 2010) and a commonly evaluated benchmark engineering optimization test problem (Cagnina et al., 2008). The procedure is then further extended to incorporate stochastic elements in an FA-based simulation–optimization (SO) MGA approach. This extension is tested on a municipal waste management (MSW) facilities expansion case study taken from Yeomans (2008).

14.2 Modeling to Generate Alternatives

Most mathematical programming methods appearing in the optimization literature have concentrated almost exclusively upon producing single optimal solutions to single-objective problem instances or, equivalently, generating noninferior solution sets to multiobjective formulations (Brill et al., 1982; Janssen et al., 2010; Walker et al., 2003). While such algorithms may efficiently generate solutions to the derived complex mathematical models, whether these outputs actually establish "best" approaches to the underlying real problems is certainly questionable (Brill et al., 1982; Brugnach et al., 2007; Janssen et al., 2010; Loughlin et al., 2001). In most "real-world" decision environments, there are innumerable system objectives and requirements that are never explicitly apparent or included in the decision formulation stage (Brugnach et al., 2007; Walker et al., 2003). Furthermore, it may never be possible to explicitly express all of the subjective components because there are frequently numerous incompatible, competing, design requirements, and, perhaps, adversarial stakeholder groups involved. Therefore, most subjective aspects of a problem necessarily remain unquantified and unmodeled in the resultant decision models. This is a common occurrence in situations where final decisions are constructed based not only upon clearly stated and modeled objectives, but also upon more fundamentally subjective sociopolitical—economic goals and stakeholder preferences (Yeomans and Gunalay, 2011). Numerous "real-world" examples describing these types of incongruent modeling dualities appear in Baugh et al. (1997), Brill et al. (1982), Loughlin et al. (2001), and Zechman and Ranjithan (2004).

When unquantified issues and unmodeled objectives exist, nonconventional approaches are required that not only search the decision space for noninferior sets of solutions but must also explore the decision space for discernibly *inferior* alternatives to the modeled problem. In particular, any search for good alternatives to problems known or suspected to contain unmodeled objectives must focus not only on the noninferior solution set but also necessarily on an explicit exploration of the problem's inferior region.

To illustrate the implications of an unmodeled objective on a decision search, assume that the optimal solution for a quantified, single-objective, maximization decision problem is X^* with corresponding objective value $Z1^*$. Now suppose that there exists a second, unmodeled, maximization objective $Z2$ that subjectively reflects some unquantifiable "political acceptability" component. Let the solution X^a, belonging to the noninferior, two-objective set, represents a potential best compromise solution if both objectives could somehow have been simultaneously evaluated by the decision maker. While X^a might be viewed as the best compromise solution to the real problem, it would appear inferior to the solution X^* in the quantified mathematical model, since it must be the case that $Z1^a \leq Z1^*$. Consequently, when unmodeled objectives are factored into the decision-making process, mathematically inferior solutions for the modeled problem can prove optimal to the underlying real problem. Therefore, when unmodeled objectives and unquantified issues might exist, different solution approaches are needed in order to not only search the decision space for the noninferior set of solutions but also to simultaneously explore the decision space for inferior alternative solutions to the modeled problem. Population-based solution methods like the FA permit concurrent searches throughout a feasible region and thus prove to be particularly adept procedures for searching through a problem's decision space.

The primary motivation behind MGA is to produce a manageably small set of alternatives that are quantifiably good with respect to the known modeled objectives yet are as different as possible from each other in the decision space. In doing this, the resulting alternative solution set is likely to provide truly different choices that all perform somewhat similarly with respect to the modeled objective(s) yet very differently with respect to any unknown unmodeled issues. By generating a set of good-but-different solutions, the decision makers can explore desirable qualities within the alternatives that may prove to satisfactorily address the various unmodeled objectives to varying degrees of stakeholder acceptability.

In order to properly motivate an MGA search procedure, it is necessary to apply a more mathematically formal definition to the goals of the MGA process

(Loughlin et al., 2001; Yeomans and Gunalay, 2011). Suppose the optimal solution to an original mathematical model is X^* with objective value $Z^* = F(X^*)$. The following model can then be solved to generate an alternative solution that is maximally different from X^*:

$$\text{Maximize} \quad \Delta = \sum_i |X_i - X_i^*| \quad [P1]$$
$$\text{subject to} \quad X \in D$$
$$|F(X) - Z^*| \leq T$$

where Δ represents some difference function (for clarity, shown as an absolute difference in this instance) and T is a targeted tolerance value specified relative to the problem's original optimal objective Z^*. T is a user-supplied value that determines how much of the inferior region is to be explored in the search for acceptable alternative solutions.

14.3 FA for Function Optimization

While this section supplies only a relatively brief synopsis of the FA procedure, more detailed explanations can be accessed in Yang (2009, 2010), Gandomi et al. (2011), and Imanirad et al. (2012a,b). The FA is a biologically inspired, population-based metaheuristic. Each firefly in the population represents one potential solution to a problem and the population of fireflies should initially be distributed uniformly and randomly throughout the solution space. The solution approach employs three idealized rules. (i) The brightness of a firefly is determined by the overall landscape of the objective function. Namely, for a maximization problem, the brightness is simply considered to be proportional to the value of the objective function. (ii) The relative attractiveness between any two fireflies is directly proportional to their respective brightness. This implies that for any two flashing fireflies, the less bright firefly will always be inclined to move toward the brighter one. However, attractiveness and brightness both decrease as the relative distance between the fireflies increases. If there is no brighter firefly within its visible neighborhood, then the particular firefly will move about randomly. (iii) All fireflies within the population are considered unisex, so that any one firefly could potentially be attracted to any other firefly irrespective of their sex. Based upon these three rules, the basic operational steps of the FA can be summarized within the pseudocode of Figure 14.1 (Yang, 2010).

In the FA, there are two important issues to resolve: the formulation of attractiveness and the variation of light intensity. For simplicity, it can always be assumed that the attractiveness of a firefly is determined by its brightness which in turn is associated with its encoded objective function value. In the simplest case, the brightness of a firefly at a particular location X would be its calculated objective value $F(X)$. However, the attractiveness, β, between fireflies is relative and will vary with the distance r_{ij} between firefly i and firefly j. In addition, light

Objective Function $F(X)$, $X = (x_1, x_2,... x_d)$
Generate the initial population of n fireflies, X_i, $i = 1, 2,..., n$
Light intensity I_i at X_i is determined by $F(X_i)$
Define the light absorption coefficient γ
while (t < MaxGeneration)
   for $i = 1$: n , all n fireflies
      for $j = 1$: n ,all n fireflies (inner loop)
         if $(I_i < I_j)$, Move firefly i towards j; **end if**
         Vary attractiveness with distance r via $e^{-\gamma r}$
      end for j
   end for i
   Rank the fireflies and find the current global best solution G^*
end while
Postprocess the results

Figure 14.1 Pseudocode of the FA.

intensity decreases with the distance from its source, and light is also absorbed in the media, so the attractiveness needs to vary with the degree of absorption. Consequently, the overall attractiveness of a firefly can be defined as

$$\beta = \beta_0 \exp(-\gamma r^2)$$

where β_0 is the attractiveness at distance $r = 0$ and γ is the fixed light absorption coefficient for the specific medium. If the distance r_{ij} between any two fireflies i and j located at X_i and X_j, respectively, is calculated using the Euclidean norm, then the movement of a firefly i that is attracted to another more attractive (i.e., brighter) firefly j is determined by

$$X_i = X_i + \beta_0 \exp(-\gamma(r_{ij})^2)(X_i - X_j) + a\varepsilon_i$$

In this expression of movement, the second term is due to the relative attraction and the third term is a randomization component. Yang (2010) indicates that α is a randomization parameter normally selected within the range [0,1] and ε_i is a vector of random numbers drawn from either a Gaussian or uniform (generally [−0.5,0.5]) distribution. It should be explicitly noted that this expression represents a random walk biased toward brighter fireflies and if $\beta_0 = 0$, it becomes a simple random walk. The parameter γ characterizes the variation of the attractiveness and its value determines the speed of the algorithm's convergence. For most applications, γ is typically set between 0.1 and 10 (Gandomi et al., 2011; Yang, 2010). In any given optimization problem, for a very large number of fireflies $n \gg k$, where k is the number of local optima, the initial locations of the n fireflies should be distributed relatively uniformly throughout the entire search space. As the FA proceeds, the fireflies begin to converge into all of the local optima (including the global ones). Hence, by comparing the best solutions among all these optima, the global optima can easily be determined. Yang (2010) proves that the FA will approach the global optima when $n \to \infty$ and the number of iterations t is set so that $t \gg 1$. In reality, the FA has been found to converge extremely quickly with n set in the range 20−50 (Gandomi et al., 2011; Yang, 2009).

Two important limiting or asymptotic cases occur when $\gamma \to 0$ and when $\gamma \to \infty$. For $\gamma \to 0$, the attractiveness is constant $\beta = \beta_0$, which is equivalent to having a light intensity that does not decrease. Thus, a firefly would be visible to every other firefly anywhere within the solution domain. Hence, a single (usually global) optima can easily be reached. If the inner loop for j in Figure 14.1 is removed and X_j is replaced by the current global best G^*, then this implies that the FA reverts to a special case of the accelerated PSO algorithm. Subsequently, the computational efficiency of this special FA case is equivalent to that of enhanced PSO. Conversely, when $\gamma \to \infty$, the attractiveness is essentially zero along the sightline of all other fireflies. This is equivalent to the case where the fireflies randomly roam throughout a very thick foggy region with no other fireflies visible and each firefly roams in a completely random fashion. This case corresponds to a completely random search method. As the FA operates between these two asymptotic extremes, it is possible to adjust the parameters α and γ so that the FA can outperform both a random search and the enhanced PSO algorithms (Gandomi et al., 2011).

The computational efficiencies of the FA will be exploited in the subsequent MGA solution approach. As noted, within the two asymptotic extremes, the population in the FA can determine both the global optima and the local optima concurrently. This concurrency of population-based solution procedures holds huge computational and efficiency advantages for MGA purposes (Yeomans and Gunalay, 2011). An additional advantage of the FA for MGA implementation is that the different fireflies essentially work independently of each other, implying that FA procedures are better than genetic algorithms and PSO for MGA because the fireflies will tend to aggregate more closely around each local optimum (Gandomi et al., 2011; Yang, 2010). Consequently, with a judicious selection of parameter settings, the FA will simultaneously converge extremely quickly into both local and global optima (Gandomi et al., 2011; Yang, 2009, 2010).

14.4 FA-Based Concurrent Coevolutionary Computational Algorithm for MGA

The FA-based MGA approach to be introduced is designed to generate a predetermined small number of close-to-optimal, but maximally different alternatives, by essentially adjusting the value of T in [P1] and using the FA to solve the corresponding, maximal difference problem instance. By exploiting the coevolutionary solution structure within the population of the FA, stratified subpopulations within the algorithm's overall population are established as the fireflies collectively evolve toward different local optima within the solution space. In this process, each desired solution alternative undergoes the common search procedure of the FA. However, the survival of solutions depends both upon how well the solutions perform with respect to the modeled objective(s) and by how far away they are from all of the other alternatives generated in the decision space.

A direct process for generating alternatives with the FA would be to iteratively solve the maximum difference model [P1] by incrementally updating the target T whenever a new alternative needs to be produced and then rerunning the algorithm. This iterative approach would parallel the original Hop, Skip, and Jump (HSJ) MGA algorithm of Brill et al. (1982) in which, once an initial problem formulation has been optimized, supplementary alternatives are created one by one through a systematic, incremental adjustment of the target constraint to force the sequential generation of the suboptimal solutions. While this approach is straightforward, it requires a repeated execution of the specific optimization algorithm employed (Imanirad et al., 2012a,b; Yeomans and Gunalay, 2011).

In contrast, the concurrent MGA approach is designed to generate a predetermined number of maximally different alternatives within the entire population in a single run of the FA procedure (i.e., the same number of runs as if FA was used solely for function optimization purposes) and its efficiency is based upon the concept of coevolution (Imanirad et al., 2012a,b). In this coevolutionary approach, prespecified stratified subpopulation ranges within the algorithm's overall population are established that collectively evolve the search toward the creation of the stipulated number of maximally different alternatives. Each desired solution alternative is represented by each respective subpopulation and each subpopulation undergoes the common processing operations of the FA. This approach can be structured upon any standard FA solution procedure containing appropriate encodings and operators that best correspond to the problem. The survival of solutions in each subpopulation depends simultaneously upon how well the solutions perform with respect to the modeled objective(s) and by how far away they are from all of the other alternatives. Consequently, the evolution of solutions in each subpopulation toward local optima is directly influenced by those solutions contained in all of the other subpopulations, which force the concurrent coevolution of each subpopulation toward good but maximally distant regions within the decision space. This coevolutionary concept enables the simultaneous search for, and production of, the set of quantifiably good solutions that are maximally different from each other according to [P1] (Yeomans and Gunalay, 2011).

By employing this coevolutionary concept, it becomes possible to implement an FA-based MGA procedure that concurrently produces alternatives which possess objective function bounds that are somewhat analogous, but inherently superior, to those created by a sequential, iterative HSJ-styled solution generation approach. While each alternative produced by an HSJ procedure is maximally different only from the single, overall optimal solution together with a bound on the objective value which is at least $x\%$ different from the best objective (i.e., $x = 1\%$, 2%, etc.), the concurrent coevolutionary procedure is able to generate alternatives that are no more than $x\%$ different from the overall optimal solution but with each one of these solutions being as maximally different as possible from every other generated alternative that is produced. Coevolution is also much more efficient than the sequential HSJ-styled approach in that it exploits the inherent population-based searches of FA procedures to concurrently generate the entire set of maximally different solutions using only a single population. Namely, while an HSJ-styled approach would need to run n different times in order to generate n different alternatives, the concurrent algorithm is required to run only once to produce its entire set of alternatives irrespective of the value of n. Hence, it is a much more computationally efficient solution generation process.

The steps in the coevolutionary alternative generation algorithm are as follows:

1. Create the initial population stratified into P equally sized subpopulations. P represents the desired number of maximally different alternative solutions within a prescribed target deviation from the optimal to be generated. S_p represents the pth subpopulation set of solutions, $p = 1, \ldots, P$ and there are K solutions contained within each S_p. Note: The value for P must be set *a priori* by the decision maker.

2. Evaluate all solutions in S_p, $p = 1, \ldots, P$, with respect to the modeled objective. Solutions meeting the target constraint and all other problem constraints are designated as *feasible*, while all other solutions are designated as *infeasible*.

3. Apply an appropriate elitism operator to each S_p to preserve the best individual in each subpopulation. In S_p, $p = 1, \ldots, P$, the best solution is the feasible solution most distant in decision space from all of the other subpopulations (the distance measure is defined in Step 6). Note: Because the best solution to date is always placed into each subpopulation, at least one solution in S_p will always be feasible. This step simultaneously selects a set of alternatives that respectively satisfy different values of the target T while being as far apart as possible (i.e., maximally different in the sense of [P1]) from the solutions generated in each of the other subpopulations. By the coevolutionary nature of this algorithm, the alternatives are simultaneously generated in one pass of the procedure rather than the P implementations suggested by the necessary increments to T in problem [P1].

4. Stop the algorithm if the termination criteria (such as maximum number of iterations or some measure of solution convergence) are met. Otherwise, proceed to Step 5.

5. Identify the decision space centroid, C_{ip}, for each of the $K' \leq K$ feasible solutions within $k = 1, \ldots, K$ of S_p, for each of the N decision variables X_{ikp}, $i = 1, \ldots, N$. Each centroid represents the N-dimensional center of mass for the solutions in each of the respective subpopulations, p. As an illustrative example for determining a centroid, calculate $C_{ip} = (1/K')^* \sum_k X_{ikp}$. In this calculation, each dimension of each centroid is computed as the straightforward average value of that decision variable over all of the values for that variable within the feasible solutions of the respective subpopulation. Alternatively, a centroid could be calculated as some fitness-weighted average or by some other appropriately defined measure.

6. For each solution $k = 1, \ldots, K$, in each S_q, calculate D_{kq}, a distance measure between that solution and all other subpopulations. As an illustrative example for determining a distance measure, calculate $D_{kq} = \text{Min}\{\sum_i |X_{ikp} - C_{ip}|; p = 1, \ldots, P, \neq pq\}$. This distance represents the minimum distance between solution k in subpopulation q and the centroids of all other subpopulations. Alternatively, the distance measure could be calculated by some other appropriately defined function.

7. Rank the solutions within each S_p according to the distance measure D_{kq} objective— appropriately adjusted to incorporate any constraint violation penalties. The goal of maximal difference is to force solutions from one subpopulation to be as far apart as possible in the decision space from the solutions of each of the other subpopulations. This step orders the specific solutions in each subpopulation by those solutions which are most distant from the solutions in all of the other subpopulations.

8. In each S_p, apply appropriate FA "change operations" to the solutions and return to Step 2.

14.5 Computational Testing of the FA Used for MGA

As described earlier, "real-world" decision makers generally prefer to be able to select from a set of "near-optimal" alternatives that significantly differ from each other in terms of the system structures characterized by their decision variables. The ability of the coevolutionary FA MGA procedure to concurrently produce such maximally different alternatives will be demonstrated using a widely tested nonlinear constrained optimization problem taken from Aragon et al. (2010) and a benchmark-constrained engineering optimization problem from Cagnina et al. (2008).

The mathematical formulation for the nonlinear optimization test problem is

$$\text{Min } F(X) = (x_1 - 10)^2 + 5(x_2 - 12)^2 + x_3^4 + 3(x_4 - 11)^2$$
$$+ 10x_5^6 + 7x_6^2 + x_7^4 - 4x_6 x_7 - 10x_6 - 8x_7$$

$$\text{subject to} \quad g_1(X) = 2x_1^2 + 3x_2^4 + x_3 + 4x_4^2 + 5x_5 - 127 \leq 0$$
$$g_2(X) = 7x_1 + 3x_2 + 10x_3^2 + x_4 - x_5 - 282 \leq 0$$
$$g_3(X) = 23x_1 + x_2^2 + 6x_6^2 - 8x_7 - 196 \leq 0$$
$$g_4(X) = 4x_1^2 + x_2^2 - 3x_1 x_2 + 2x_3^2 + 5x_6 - 12x_7 \leq 0$$

$$-10 \leq x_i \leq 10, \quad i = 1, 2, 3, 4, 5, 6, 7$$

The optimal solution for the specific design parameters employed within this formulation is $F(X^*) = 680.6300573$ with decision variable values of $X^* = (2.330499, 1.951372, -0.4775414, 4.365726, 0.6244870, 1.038131, 1.594227)$ (Aragon et al., 2010).

As described in the previous section, in order to create the desired alternatives for this problem, it would be possible to place extra target constraints in an incrementally increasing fashion into the original mathematical formulation to force the generation of solutions that were structurally different from the initial optimal solution. Suppose, for example, that 10 additional solution options were to be created through the inclusion of a technical constraint that increased value of the objective in the original model formulation from 1% up to 10% in increments of 1%. By adding these incremental target constraints to the original model and sequentially resolving the problem 10 times, it would be possible to create the prescribed number of maximally different alternatives. However, to improve upon the process of running 10 separate additional instances, the coevolutionary FA MGA method could be run exactly once to concurrently produce all of the desired alternatives. By employing the coevolutionary FA-based MGA algorithm, the optimal solution and the 10 maximally different solutions shown in Tables 14.1 and 14.2 were generated.

Table 14.1 Objective Values and Solutions for the 11 Maximally Different Alternatives

Increment	1% Increment Between Alternatives						
	F(X)	x₁	x₂	x₃	x₄	x₅	x₆	x₇

	$F(X)$	x_1	x_2	x_3	x_4	x_5	x_6	x_7
Optimal	680.630	2.3304	1.9513	−0.4775	4.3657	0.6244	1.0381	1.5942
Alternative 1	683.917	2.3025	1.9353	−0.4881	4.3333	−0.6169	1.0355	1.5889
Alternative 2	687.580	2.2892	1.8985	−0.4605	4.3364	−0.5962	1.0208	1.5782
Alternative 3	696.899	2.2934	1.9096	−0.4397	4.3369	−0.6616	1.0331	1.6176
Alternative 4	705.926	2.3080	1.9171	−0.4724	4.3343	−0.6578	1.053	1.6078
Alternative 5	706.837	2.2913	1.9003	−0.3965	4.3548	−0.6388	1.0796	1.6023
Alternative 6	718.478	2.2904	1.9037	−0.427	4.3637	−0.5871	0.9955	1.6230
Alternative 7	725.652	2.3428	1.9158	−0.4459	4.3929	−0.6672	1.0382	1.6129
Alternative 8	730.091	2.2892	1.8985	−0.4605	4.3364	−0.5962	1.0208	1.5782
Alternative 9	741.897	2.2904	1.9037	−0.427	4.3637	−0.5871	0.9955	1.6230
Alternative 10	747.925	2.3577	1.9121	−0.4395	4.3314	−0.5869	1.0038	1.6148

Table 14.2 Objective Values and Solutions for the 11 Maximally Different Alternatives

Increment	2.5% Increment Between Alternatives						

	$F(X)$	x_1	x_2	x_3	x_4	x_5	x_6	x_7
Optimal	680.630	2.3304	1.9513	−0.4775	4.3657	0.6244	1.0381	1.5942
Alternative 1	687.022	2.3056	1.9076	−0.4245	4.3256	−0.6184	1.0388	1.6067
Alternative 2	711.793	2.3174	1.9111	−0.4084	4.3668	−0.6166	1.0759	1.6116
Alternative 3	730.671	2.2916	1.9496	−0.4442	4.3474	−0.6154	1.0555	1.5864
Alternative 4	744.901	2.3468	1.9118	−0.4087	4.3557	−0.6283	0.9899	1.6024
Alternative 5	756.260	2.2985	1.9019	−0.4452	4.3577	−0.5927	1.0022	1.5770
Alternative 6	779.735	2.3463	1.9397	−0.4338	4.3425	−0.5867	1.0457	1.6301
Alternative 7	796.641	2.3011	1.9128	−0.4282	4.3386	−0.5758	1.0035	1.6227
Alternative 8	811.767	2.3539	1.9579	−0.4543	4.3338	−0.6425	1.0413	1.6155
Alternative 9	832.123	2.3690	1.9208	−0.4181	4.4001	−0.617	1.0411	1.6374
Alternative 10	846.019	2.2967	1.897	−0.4684	4.3467	−0.6374	1.0252	1.5721

The second illustration will apply the MGA procedure to the spring design problem taken from Cagnina et al. (2008). The design of a tension and compression spring has frequently been employed as a standard benchmark test problem for constrained engineering optimization algorithms (Cagnina et al., 2008). The problem involves three design variables: (i) x_1, the wire diameter, (ii) x_2, the coil diameter, and (iii) x_3, the length of the coil. The aim is to essentially minimize the weight subject to constraints on deflection, stress, surge frequency, and geometry. The mathematical formulation for this test problem can be summarized as

Minimize $F(X) = x_1^2 x_2 (2 + x_3)$

subject to $g_1(X) = 1 - \dfrac{x_2^3 x_3}{71,785 x_1^4} \leq 0$

$$g_2(X) = \dfrac{4x_2^2 - x_1 x_2}{12,566(x_1^3 x_2 - x_1^4)} + \dfrac{1}{5108 x_1^2} - 1 \leq 0$$

$$g_3(X) = 1 - \dfrac{140.45 x_1}{x_2^2 x_3} \leq 0$$

$$g_4(X) = \dfrac{x_1 + x_2}{1.5} - 1 \leq 0$$

$0.05 \leq x_1 \leq 2.0 \quad 0.25 \leq x_2 \leq 1.3 \quad 2.0 \leq x_3 \leq 15.0$

The optimal solution for the specific design parameters employed within this formulation is $F(X^*) = 0.0127$ with decision variable values of $X^* = (0.051690, 0.356750, 11.287126)$ (Cagnina et al., 2008). The MGA procedure was used to create the optimal solution and the 10 maximally different solutions as given in Table 14.3.

As described earlier, most "real-world" optimization applications tend to be riddled with incongruent performance requirements that are exceedingly difficult to quantify. Consequently, it is preferable to create a set of quantifiably good alternatives that provide very different perspectives to the potentially unmodeled performance design issues during the policy formulation stage. The unique performance features captured within these dissimilar alternatives can result in very different system performance with respect to the unmodeled issues, hopefully thereby addressing some of the unmodeled issues into the actual solution process.

Table 14.3 Objective Values and Solutions for the 11 Maximally Different Alternatives

Increment	1% Increment Between Alternatives				2.5% Increment Between Alternatives			
	$F(X)$	x_1	x_2	x_3	$F(X)$	x_1	x_2	x_3
Optimal	0.0127	0.05	0.3174	14.0324	0.0127	0.05	0.3174	14.0322
Alternative 1	0.0128	0.05	0.3164	14.1754	0.0128	0.05	0.3165	14.1598
Alternative 2	0.0128	0.0514	0.3472	12.0089	0.0131	0.05	0.3129	14.777
Alternative 3	0.0129	0.0529	0.3862	9.9684	0.0132	0.05	0.3167	14.6402
Alternative 4	0.013	0.0521	0.3656	11.0667	0.0140	0.0557	0.4307	9.5783
Alternative 5	0.0131	0.0527	0.3766	10.5179	0.0143	0.0542	0.4014	11.6481
Alternative 6	0.0134	0.05	0.3157	14.978	0.0146	0.0546	0.4247	10.7556
Alternative 7	0.0135	0.0524	0.3597	11.6966	0.0149	0.0562	0.438	11.1197
Alternative 8	0.0137	0.052	0.3629	12.1615	0.0152	0.0605	0.4836	8.9963
Alternative 9	0.0138	0.0523	0.348	13.3247	0.0156	0.0574	0.3841	14.5182
Alternative 10	0.0140	0.0535	0.3857	14.162	0.0159	0.0553	0.4072	15.0000

The two examples in this section have demonstrated how the coevolutionary MGA modeling perspective can be used to concurrently generate multiple alternatives that satisfy known system performance criteria according to the prespecified bounds and yet remain as maximally different from each other as possible in the decision space. In addition to its alternative generating capabilities, the FA component of the MGA approach simultaneously performs extremely well with respect to its role in function optimization. It should be explicitly noted that the overall best solutions produced by the FA-based MGA procedure for the test problems are indistinguishable from the optimal ones determined by Aragon et al. (2010) and Cagnina et al. (2008).

14.6   An SO Approach for Stochastic MGA

SO is a family of optimization techniques that incorporates stochastic uncertainties expressed as probability distributions directly into its computational procedure (Fu, 2002; Kelly, 2002). While SO holds considerable potential for application to a wide range of stochastic problems, it cannot be considered universally effective due to its accompanying solution time issues (Fu, 2002; Kelly, 2002). Linton et al. (2002) and Yeomans (2008) have shown that SO can be used as a computationally intensive, stochastic MGA technique. Yeomans (2007,2012) examined several approaches to accelerate the search times and solution quality of SO. In this section, it is shown how the FA-based MGA method can be modified to incorporate stochastic uncertainty using SO in order to efficiently generate sets of maximally different solution alternatives.

Suppose the mathematical representation of an optimization problem contains n decision variables, X_i, expressed in vector form as $X = [X_1, X_2, \ldots, X_n]$. If the objective function is represented by F and the problem's feasible region is given by D, then the related mathematical programming problem is to optimize $F(X)$ subject to $X \in D$. In general, it is often exceedingly difficult to find optimal solutions to large stochastic problems when system uncertainties have to be incorporated directly into the solution procedure (Fu, 2002). In modeling stochastic systems, any uncertain elements are represented by stochastic functions. For instance, uncertain parameters within the objective or constraints appear as probability distributions. Additionally, D could contain a set of r constraints of the form $h_j(X) \le 0$, $j = 1, \ldots, r$, that need not *always* be satisfied by every feasible solution instance. Such stochastic conditions in the constraints create solution difficulties because the resulting systems possess only fuzzy feasible region boundaries. Azadivar and Tompkins (1999) considered multiobjective formulations, in which F might consist of a vector-valued function containing q functions F_k, $k = 1, \ldots, q$, whereas Pierreval and Tautou (1997) introduced instances in which D could simultaneously contain decision options from the real, integer, and qualitative domains.

When stochastic conditions exist, values for the constraints and objective can only be efficiently estimated by simulation. Thus, any solution comparison between two distinct decisions $X1$ and $X2$ necessitates the evaluation of some statistic of F modeled with $X1$ to the same statistic modeled with $X2$ (Pierreval and Tautou, 1997). These statistics are calculated by a simulation performed on the solutions, in which each candidate solution provides the decision variable settings in the simulation. While simulation presents a mechanism for comparing results, it does not provide the means for determining optimal solutions to problems. Hence, simulation, by itself, cannot be used as a stochastic optimization procedure.

SO is a broadly defined set of solution approaches that combine simulation with some type of optimization method for stochastic optimization (Fu, 2002). In SO, all unknown objective functions, constraints, and parameters are replaced by one or more discrete event simulation models in which the decision variables provide the settings under which the simulation is performed. Since all measures of system performance are stochastic, every potential solution, X, examined would necessarily need to be evaluated via simulation. As simulation is computationally intensive, an optimization component is employed to guide the solution search through the problem's feasible region using as few simulation runs as possible. Azadivar (1999) identified four broad classes of optimization search strategies that have guided SO searches: (i) gradient-based methods, (ii) stochastic approximation methods, (iii) response surface methods, and (iv) heuristic methods. Because stochastic system problems contain many possible solutions, solution quality can be highly variable unless an extensive search has been performed throughout the problem's entire feasible domain. Population-based heuristic methods like the FA are conducive to these extensive searches because the complete set of candidate solutions maintained in their populations permit searches to be undertaken throughout multiple sections of the feasible region concurrently.

The FA-directed SO approach consists of two alternating computational phases: (i) an "evolutionary phase" directed by the FA module and (ii) a simulation module. As described earlier, the FA maintains a population of candidate solutions throughout its execution. The evolutionary phase considers the entire population of solutions during each generation of the search and evolves from a current population to a subsequent one. Because of the system's stochastic components, all performance measures are necessarily statistics calculated from the responses generated in the simulation module. The quality of each solution in the population is found by having its performance criterion, F, evaluated by simulation. After simulating each candidate solution, the respective fitness values are returned to the FA module to be utilized in the creation of the next generation of candidate solutions.

One primary principle of an FA is that fitter solutions in the current population possess a greater likelihood for survival and progression into the subsequent generation. The FA module evolves the system toward improved solutions in subsequent populations and ensures that the solution search does not become fixated at some local optima. After generating a new candidate solution set in the FA module, the new population is returned to the simulation module for comparative evaluation. This alternating two-phase search process terminates when an appropriately stable system state has been attained.

In order to operationalize the stochastic FA MGA approach, the only requisite modification to the coevolutionary alternative generation algorithm from the previous section is to change Step 2 to now read:

2. Evaluate all solutions in S_p, $p = 1, \ldots, P$, with respect to the modeled objective *using the simulation module*. Solutions meeting the target constraint and all other problem constraints are designated as *feasible*, while all other solutions are designated as *infeasible*.

14.7   Case Study of Stochastic MGA for the Expansion of Waste Management Facilities

The application of the stochastic FA MGA procedure will be illustrated using the MSW facilities expansion case study taken from Yeomans (2008). The region in the facility expansion planning problem consists of three separate municipalities whose MSW disposal needs are collectively met by a landfill and two waste-to-energy (WTE) incinerators.

The notation [a,b] is used to indicate that the value of an uncertain parameter is estimated to lie within the interval between the values of a and b. Furthermore, if variable A represents an uncertain parameter specified by the interval [a,b], then the uncertainty of this variable will be indicated with the notation $\overleftrightarrow{A}$. For consistency, parameters which are constants can be directly represented using the notation, $\overleftrightarrow{A}$, by the interval [a,a]. At the start of the planning period, the landfill possesses an existing capacity of $[0.625,0.775] \times 10^6$ tons and WTE facilities 1 and 2 have processing capacities of [100,125] and [200,250] tons/day, respectively. Both WTE facilities generate waste residues of approximately 30% of the incoming waste streams on a mass basis, and the revenue from the resulting energy resale is approximately [15,25] \$/ton of combusted material.

The planning horizon consists of three separate time periods with each of the periods covering an interval of 5 years. The landfill capacity can be expanded only once over the entire 15-year planning horizon by an increment of $[1.55,1.70] \times 10^6$ tons. Each of the WTE facilities can be expanded by any one of four possible options in each of the three time periods. The maximum possible expansion option in any single time period would increase the processing capacity of a WTE facility by 250 tons/day. These expansion costs escalate over time in order to reflect anticipated future conditions and have been discounted to present value cost terms for use in the objective function. The MSW waste generation rates and the costs for waste transportation and treatment vary both temporally and spatially.

The MSW problem requires the determination of the preferred facility expansion alternatives during the different time periods and the effective allocation of the relevant waste flows in order to minimize the total system costs over the planning horizon. In the mathematical model, the type of waste management facility is identified by subscript i, with $i = 1$ representing the landfill, and $i = 2$ and $i = 3$ corresponding to WTE facilities 1 and 2, respectively. The three municipalities from which the waste originates will be identified using subscript j, $j = 1, 2, 3$. Subscript k, $k = 1, 2, 3$, corresponds to the time period and m, $m = 1, 2, 3, 4$, denotes the expansion option selected for the WTE facilities. The decision variables for the problem will be designated by x_{ijk}, y_k, and z_{imk}, where x_{ijk} represents the proportion of solid waste sent from municipality j to waste processing facility i in period k, y_k corresponds to a binary decision variable for landfill expansion at the start of time period k ($y_k = 1$ if the landfill expands in period k, 0 otherwise), and z_{imk} represents a binary decision variable corresponding to the particular expansion option, m, selected for WTE facility i, $i = 2, 3$, at the start of period k.

The total cost of waste management, in \$/ton, for the waste flowing from municipality j to processing facility i in period k is represented by $\overleftrightarrow{C}_{ijk}$. The per ton cost for transporting waste from municipality j to facility i in period k is $\overleftrightarrow{T}R_{ijk}$, and $\overleftrightarrow{O}P_{ik}$ is the per ton operating cost of processing facility i in period k. The transportation cost per ton of waste from WTE facility i to the landfill in period k is denoted by $\overleftrightarrow{F}T_{ik}$, for $i = 2, 3$. If FE represents the residue flow rate from a WTE facility to the landfill, expressed as a percentage of the incoming mass to the WTE facility, and $\overleftrightarrow{R}E_k$ denotes the per ton revenue from the WTE facilities in period k, then $\overleftrightarrow{C}_{1jk} = \overleftrightarrow{T}R_{1jk} + \overleftrightarrow{O}P_{1k}$ and $\overleftrightarrow{C}_{ijk} = \overleftrightarrow{T}R_{ijk} + \overleftrightarrow{O}P_{ik} + FE\,(\overleftrightarrow{F}T_{ik} + \overleftrightarrow{O}P_{ik}) - \overleftrightarrow{R}E_k$, for $i = 2, 3$, $j = 1, 2, 3$, and $k = 1$, 2, 3. The existing capacity of the landfill, in tons, is $\overleftrightarrow{L}C$ and $\overleftrightarrow{\Delta}LC_k$ represents the additional capacity resulting from the landfill expansion undertaken in period k, $k = 1, 2, 3$; where the cost of this landfill expansion is $\overleftrightarrow{F}LC_k$. The existing capacity, in tons per day, for WTE facility i, $i = 2, 3$ is $\overleftrightarrow{T}C_i$. The amount of incremental capacity expansion, in tons per day, under option m, $m = 1, 2, 3, 4$, for WTE facility i, $i = 2, 3$, at the start of period k, $k = 1, 2, 3$, is provided by $\overleftrightarrow{\Delta}TC_{imk}$; with $\overleftrightarrow{F}TC_{imk}$ corresponding to the capital cost of this expansion. Finally, if the number of days in time period k is L_k and if the number of tons of waste generated daily by municipality j during period k is $\overleftrightarrow{W}G_{jk}$, then the complete mathematical model for MSW management expansion planning is to

$$\text{Minimize:} \quad \text{Cost} = \sum_{k=1}^{3} \overleftrightarrow{F}LC_k y_k + \sum_{i=2}^{3}\sum_{m=1}^{4}\sum_{k=1}^{3} \overleftrightarrow{F}TC_{imk} z_{imk}$$

$$+ \sum_{i=1}^{3}\sum_{j=1}^{3}\sum_{k=1}^{3} L_k \overleftrightarrow{C}_{ijk} \overleftrightarrow{W}G_{jk} x_{ijk} \tag{14.1}$$

$$\text{subject to} \quad \sum_{j=1}^{3}\sum_{k=1}^{k'} L_k \left[\overleftrightarrow{W}G_{jk} x_{1jk} + \sum_{i=2}^{3} \overleftrightarrow{W}G_{jk} x_{ijk} FE \right]$$

$$\leq \sum_{k=1}^{k'} \overleftrightarrow{\Delta}LC_k y_k + \overleftrightarrow{L}C \, k' = 1, 2, 3 \tag{14.2}$$

$$\sum_{j=1}^{3} G_{jk'} x_{ijk'} \leq \sum_{m=1}^{4}\sum_{k=1}^{k'} \overleftrightarrow{\Delta}TC_{imk} z_{imk} + \overleftrightarrow{T}C_i \quad i = 2, 3, \ \ k' = 1, 2, 3 \tag{14.3}$$

$$\sum_{i=1}^{3} \overleftrightarrow{W}G_{jk}x_{ijk} \leq \overleftrightarrow{W}G_{jk} \quad k = 1, 2, 3, \quad j = 1, 2, 3 \tag{14.4}$$

$$\sum_{m=1}^{4} z_{imk} \leq 1 \quad i = 2, 3, \quad k = 1, 2, 3 \tag{14.5}$$

$$\sum_{k=1}^{3} y_k \leq 1 \tag{14.6}$$

$$\sum_{i=1}^{3} x_{ijk} = 1 \quad j = 1, 2, 3, \quad k = 1, 2, 3 \tag{14.7}$$

$$1 \geq x_{ijk} \geq 0 \quad i = 1, 2, 3, \quad j = 1, 2, 3, \quad k = 1, 2, 3 \tag{14.8}$$

$$y_k = 0 \text{ or } 1 \quad k = 1, 2, 3 \tag{14.9}$$

$$z_{imk} = 0 \text{ or } 1 \quad i = 2, 3, \quad k = 1, 2, 3, \quad m = 1, 2, 3, 4 \tag{14.10}$$

The objective function (14.1) contains components relating to the cost/benefit effects resulting from different waste management decisions and the capital costs required for expanding the processing facilities. Constraints (14.2) and (14.3) ensure that the upper limits for waste treatment and disposal in any time period are determined by both the existing facility capacity and any incremental expansion activities occurring in time period k', $k' = 1, 2, 3$, for the landfill and WTE facilities. The dynamic aspects of these constraints result from such considerations as future economic development, population increase, and environmental management activities. Constraint (14.4) establishes the waste disposal quantities generated by each of the three municipalities in each time period. Constraint (14.5) requires that only one option for each WTE facility expansion can be selected in any given time period, and constraint (14.6) stipulates that the landfill could be expanded only once over the entire planning time horizon. Constraint (14.7) ensures the disposal of all waste generated by each municipality in every time period. Finally, constraints (14.8−14.10) provide the technical relationships for the decision variables.

To complete the formulation, Tables 14.4 and 14.5 give the actual values of the various parameters used within the model. Table 14.4 provides the detailed numerical information regarding the various capital costs and expansion options for both the landfill and WTE facilities. It should be duly noted that all of the capital costs are expressed in present value dollars. Table 14.5 gives the details for the waste generation rates for the three municipalities, the operating costs for the three processing facilities, and the transportation costs for waste flows between municipalities and processing facilities over each of the three time periods.

Table 14.4 Capacity Expansion Options and Their Costs for the Landfill and WTE Facilities

	Time Period		
	$k = 1$	$k = 2$	$k = 3$
Capacity expansion option for WTE facility i, $i = 2, 3$ (tons/day)			
$\overset{\leftrightarrow}{\Delta}TC_{i1k}$ (option 1)	100	100	100
$\overset{\leftrightarrow}{\Delta}TC_{i2k}$ (option 2)	150	150	150
$\overset{\leftrightarrow}{\Delta}TC_{i3k}$ (option 3)	200	200	200
$\overset{\leftrightarrow}{\Delta}TC_{i4k}$ (option 4)	250	250	250
Capacity expansion option for the landfill (106 tons)			
$\overset{\leftrightarrow}{\Delta}LC_k$	[1.55,1.70]	[1.55,1.70]	[1.55,1.70]
Capital cost of WTE facility expansion, $i = 2, 3$ ($106 present value)			
$\overset{\leftrightarrow}{F}TC_{i1k}$ (option 1)	10.5	8.3	6.5
$\overset{\leftrightarrow}{F}TC_{i2k}$ (option 2)	15.2	11.9	9.3
$\overset{\leftrightarrow}{F}TC_{i3k}$ (option 3)	19.8	15.5	12.2
$\overset{\leftrightarrow}{F}TC_{i4k}$ (option 4)	24.4	19.1	15.0
Capital cost of landfill expansion ($106 present value)			
$\overset{\leftrightarrow}{F}LC_k$	[13,15]	[13,15]	[13,15]

Using this model, Yeomans (2008) solved this problem using SO strictly as a function optimizer and produced a single best solution to the expansion problem costing $600.2 million. As outlined earlier, planners generally prefer to be able to select from a set of near-optimal alternatives that differ significantly from each other in terms of the system structures characterized by their decision variables. In order to create these alternative planning options, it would be possible to place extra target constraints into the original model as in [P1] which would force the generation of solutions that were different from this newly determined optimal solution. By including such a technical constraint on the objective function, Yeomans (2008) created three alternative expansion options that increased the total system cost of the original, optimized model by target values of 2%, 5%, and 8%, respectively. By adding these specific constraints to the original model, the problem needed to be resolved an additional three times.

However, to improve upon the process of running four separate instances of the SO algorithm to determine these solutions, the stochastic FA-based MGA procedure described in the previous section was run directly producing the four alternatives given in Table 14.6.

This example has demonstrated how the SO MGA modeling approach can be used to efficiently generate multiple, good policy alternatives that satisfy required system performance criteria according to prespecified bounds within highly uncertain environments and yet remain as maximally different from each other as

Table 14.5 Waste Generation, Transportation Costs, and Facility Operating Costs

	Time Period		
	$k = 1$	$k = 2$	$k = 3$
Waste generation (tons/day)			
$\overleftrightarrow{W}G_{1k}$ (Municipality 1)	[200, 250]	[225, 275]	[250, 300]
$\overleftrightarrow{W}G_{2k}$ (Municipality 2)	[375, 425]	[425, 475]	[475, 525]
$\overleftrightarrow{W}G_{3k}$ (Municipality 3)	[300, 350]	[325, 375]	[375, 425]
Cost of waste transportation to the landfill ($/ton)			
$\overleftrightarrow{T}R_{11k}$ (Municipality 1)	[12.1, 16.1]	[13.3, 17.7]	[14.6, 19.5]
$\overleftrightarrow{T}R_{12k}$ (Municipality 2)	[10.5, 14.0]	[11.6, 15.4]	[12.8, 16.9]
$\overleftrightarrow{T}R_{13k}$ (Municipality 3)	[12.7, 17.0]	[14.0, 18.7]	[15.4, 20.6]
Cost of waste transportation to WTE facility 1 ($/ton)			
$\overleftrightarrow{T}R_{21k}$ (Municipality 1)	[9.6, 12.8]	[10.6, 14.1]	[11.7, 15.5]
$\overleftrightarrow{T}R_{22k}$ (Municipality 2)	[10.1, 13.4]	[11.1, 14.7]	[12.2, 16.2]
$\overleftrightarrow{T}R_{23k}$ (Municipality 3)	[8.8, 11.7]	[9.7, 12.8]	[10.6, 14.0]
Cost of waste transportation to WTE facility 2 ($/ton)			
$\overleftrightarrow{T}R_{31k}$ (Municipality 1)	[12.1, 16.1]	[13.3, 17.7]	[14.6, 19.5]
$\overleftrightarrow{T}R_{32k}$ (Municipality 2)	[12.8, 17.1]	[14.1, 18.8]	[15.5, 20.7]
$\overleftrightarrow{T}R_{33k}$ (Municipality 3)	[4.2, 5.6]	[4.6, 6.2]	[5.1, 6.8]
Cost of residue transportation from the WTE facilities to the landfill ($/ton)			
$\overleftrightarrow{F}T_{2k}$ (WTE facility 1)	[4.7, 6.3]	[5.2, 6.9]	[5.7, 7.6]
$\overleftrightarrow{F}T_{3k}$ (WTE facility 2)	[13.4, 17.9]	[14.7, 19.7]	[16.2, 21.7]
Operational cost ($/ton)			
$\overleftrightarrow{O}P_{1k}$ (Landfill)	[30, 45]	[40, 60]	[50, 80]
$\overleftrightarrow{O}P_{2k}$ (WTE facility 1)	[55, 75]	[60, 85]	[65, 95]
$\overleftrightarrow{O}P_{3k}$ (WTE facility 2)	[50, 70]	[60, 80]	[65, 85]

Table 14.6 System Expansion Costs ($ Millions) for the Four Alternatives

	Overall "Optimal" Solution	Best 2% Solution	Best 5% Solution	Best 8% Solution
System Expansion Costs	600.21	602.78	612.54	616.38

possible in the decision space. Given the performance bounds established for the objective in each problem instance, decision makers would be able to feel reassured by the stated performance bounds for each of these options while also being aware that the perspectives provided by the set of dissimilar decision variable structures are as maximally different from each other as is feasibly possible. Hence, if there are stakeholders with incompatible standpoints holding diametrically opposing viewpoints, the policy makers can perform an assessment of these different options without being myopically constrained by a single overriding perspective based solely upon the objective value.

14.8 Conclusions

"Real-world" decision-making problems generally possess multidimensional performance specifications that are compounded by incompatible performance objectives and unquantifiable modeling features. These problems usually contain incongruent design requirements which are very difficult—if not impossible—to capture at the time that supporting decision models are formulated. Consequently, there are invariably unmodeled problem facets, not apparent during the model construction, that can greatly impact the acceptability of the model's solutions. These uncertain and competing dimensions force decision makers to integrate many conflicting sources into their decision process prior to final solution construction. Facing with such incongruencies, it is unlikely that any single solution could ever be constructed that simultaneously satisfies all of the ambiguous system requirements without some significant counterbalancing involving numerous trade-offs. Therefore, any ancillary modeling techniques used to support decision formulation have to somehow simultaneously account for all of these features while being flexible enough to encapsulate the impacts from the inherent planning uncertainties. In this chapter, a coevolutionary MGA approach was introduced that demonstrated how the structures of the computationally efficient, population-based FA could be exploited to concurrently generate multiple, maximally different, near-best alternatives via its coevolutionary solution technique. In this MGA capacity, the coevolutionary approach produces numerous solutions possessing the requisite problem characteristics, with each generated alternative guaranteeing a very different perspective.

The computational examples underscored several important findings with respect to the concurrent coevolutionary FA-based MGA method: (i) the coevolutionary capabilities within the FA can be exploited to generate more good alternatives than planners would be able to create using other MGA approaches because of the evolving nature of its population-based solution searches; (ii) by the design of the MGA algorithm, the alternatives generated are good for planning purposes since all of their structures will be as mutually and maximally different from each other as possible (i.e., these differences are not just simply different from the overall optimal solution as in the HSJ-style approach to MGA); (iv) the approach is very computationally efficient since it need only be run once to generate its entire set of multiple, good solution alternatives (i.e., to generate n solution alternatives, the MGA algorithm needs to run exactly the same number of times that the FA would need to be run for function optimization purposes alone—namely once— irrespective of the value of n); and (v) the best overall solutions produced by the MGA procedure will be very similar, if not identical, to the best overall solutions that would be produced by the FA for function optimization alone. Since FA techniques can be adapted to solve a wide variety of problem types, the practicality of the concurrent coevolutionary MGA approach can clearly be extended into numerous disparate "real-world" applications. These extensions will become the focus of future research.

References

Aragon, V.S., Esquivel, S.C., Coello, C.C.A., 2010. A modified version of a T-cell algorithm for constrained optimization problems. Inter. J. Numer. Methods Eng. 84, 51−378.

Azadivar, F., 1999. Simulation optimization methodologies. In: Proceedings of the 1999 Winter Simulation Conference, December 5−8, Phoenix, AZ, 93−100.

Azadivar, F., Tompkins, G., 1999. Simulation optimization with qualitative variables and structural model changes: a genetic algorithm approach. Eur. J. Oper. Res. 113, 169−182.

Baugh, J.W., Caldwell, S.C., Brill, E.D., 1997. A mathematical programming approach for generating alternatives in discrete structural optimization. Eng. Optimiz. 28 (1), 1−31.

Brill, E.D., Chang, S.Y., Hopkins, L.D., 1982. Modelling to generate alternatives: the HSJ approach and an illustration using a problem in land use planning. Manag. Sci. 28 (3), 221−235.

Brugnach, M., Tagg, A., Keil, F., De Lange, W.J., 2007. Uncertainty matters: computer models at the science−policy interface. Water Resour. Manag. 21, 1075−1090.

Cagnina, L.C., Esquivel, C.A., Coello, C.A., 2008. Solving engineering optimization problems with the simple constrained particle swarm optimizer. Informatica. 32, 319−326.

Fu, M.C., 2002. Optimization for simulation: theory vs. practice. INFORMS J. Comput. 14 (3), 192−215.

Gandomi, A.H., Yang, X.S., Alavi, A.H., 2011. Mixed variable structural optimization using firefly algorithm. Comput. Struct. 89 (23−24), 2325−2336.

Imanirad, R., Yang, X.S., Yeomans, J.S., 2012a. A computationally efficient, biologically-inspired modelling-to-generate-alternatives method. J. Comput. 2 (2), 43−47.

Imanirad, R., Yang, X.S., Yeomans, J.S., 2012b. A co-evolutionary, nature-inspired algorithm for the concurrent generation of alternatives. J. Comput. 2 (3), 101−106.

Janssen, J.A.E.B., Krol, M.S., Schielen, R.M.J., Hoekstra, A.Y., 2010. The effect of modelling quantified expert knowledge and uncertainty information on model based decision making. Environ. Sci. Policy. 13 (3), 229−238.

Kelly, P., 2002. Simulation optimization is evolving. INFORMS J. Comput. 14 (3), 223−225.

Linton, J.D., Yeomans, J.S., Yoogalingam, R., 2002. Policy planning using genetic algorithms combined with simulation: the case of municipal solid waste. Environ. Plann. B: Plann. Des. 29 (5), 757−778.

Loughlin, D.H., Ranjithan, S.R., Brill, E.D., Baugh, J.W., 2001. Genetic algorithm approaches for addressing unmodeled objectives in optimization problems. Eng. Optimiz. 33 (5), 549−569.

Matthies, M., Giupponi, C., Ostendorf, B., 2007. Environmental decision support systems: Current issues, methods and tools. Environ. Model. Softw. 22 (2), 123−127.

Pierreval, H., Tautou, L., 1997. Using evolutionary algorithms and simulation for the optimization of manufacturing systems. IIE Trans. 29 (3), 181−189.

Walker, W.E., Harremoes, P., Rotmans, J., Van der Sluis, J.P., Van Asselt, M.B.A., Janssen, P., Krayer von Krauss, M.P., 2003. Defining uncertainty—a conceptual basis for uncertainty management in model-based decision support. Integr. Assess. 4 (1), 5−17.

Yang, X.S., 2009. Firefly algorithms for multimodal optimization. Lect. Notes Comput. Sci. 5792, 169−178.

Yang, X.S., 2010. Nature-Inspired Metaheuristic Algorithms. second ed. Luniver Press, Frome, UK.

Yeomans, J.S., 2007. Solid waste policy planning under uncertainty using evolutionary simulation−optimization. Socio-Econ. Plan. Sci. 41 (1), 38−60.

Yeomans, J.S., 2008. Applications of simulation−optimization methods in environmental policy planning under uncertainty. J. Environ. Inform. 12 (2), 174−186.

Yeomans, J.S., 2012. Waste management facility expansion planning using simulation−optimization with grey programming and penalty functions. Inter. J. Environ. Waste Manage. 10 (2/3), 269−283.

Yeomans, J.S., Gunalay, Y., 2011. Simulation−optimization techniques for modelling to generate alternatives in waste management planning. J. Appl. Oper. Res. 3 (1), 23−35.

Zechman, E.M., Ranjithan, S.R., 2004. An evolutionary algorithm to generate alternatives (EAGA) for engineering optimization problems. Eng. Optimiz. 36 (5), 539−553.

15 Structural Optimization Using Krill Herd Algorithm

Amir Hossein Gandomi[1], Amir Hossein Alavi[2] and Siamak Talatahari[3]

[1]Department of Civil Engineering, University of Akron, Akron, OH, USA; [2]Department of Civil and Environmental Engineering, Engineering Building, Michigan State University, East Lansing, MI, USA; [3]Marand Faculty of Engineering, University of Tabriz, Tabriz, Iran

15.1 Introduction

Structural optimization is a new variant of engineering optimization that deals with structural criteria used to evaluate the merit of a design. The design objectives in the structural optimization are commonly minimum construction cost, minimum life cycle cost, minimum weight, and maximum stiffness (Sahab et al., 2013), and they are usually nonlinear problems (Gandomi et al., 2013a). Consequently, only global optimization algorithms can be used to obtain optimal solutions. Metaheuristic algorithms can be defined as upper level general methodologies. They can be used as guiding strategies in designing underlying heuristics to handle structural optimization problems (Gandomi et al., 2013a,b; Talbi, 2009). The main characteristics of metaheuristics are (i) intensification and (ii) diversification (Yang, 2009). Intensification searches around the current best solutions and selects the best candidates or solutions. Diversification guarantees that the algorithm can explore the search space more efficiently (Yang and Gandomi, 2012).

The main goals of developing modern metaheuristic methods are to solve problems faster, to solve large problems, and to obtain robust algorithms (Talbi, 2009). The efficiency of metaheuristic algorithms is related to the fact that they imitate the best features in nature. The most typical types of metaheuristics are genetic algorithms (GA) and particle swarm optimization (PSO). However, some more effective metaheuristics have been proposed and used for engineering optimization such as ant colony optimization, firefly algorithm, cuckoo search, and bat algorithm (Yang, 2010).

Swarm Intelligence and Bio-Inspired Computation. DOI: http://dx.doi.org/10.1016/B978-0-12-405163-8.00015-6

Krill herd (KH) algorithm is a new metaheuristic search algorithm. This algorithm is based on simulating the herding behavior of krill individuals using a Lagrangian model and genetic operators. This algorithm was developed by Gandomi and Alavi (2012), and the preliminary studies showed that it is very promising and could outperform existing algorithms. In this chapter, the KH algorithm is further validated against various engineering optimization problems. The introduced search strategy is compared with other popular optimization algorithms. Finally, the unique features of KH are discussed and topics for further studies are proposed.

15.2   Krill Herd Algorithm

15.2.1   Lagrangian Model of Krill Herding

Predation has three main effects: (i) it removes individuals, (ii) it results in reduction of the average krill density, and (iii) it distances the krill swarm from the food location. It is considered as an initialization phase in the KH algorithm. In the natural system, the fitness of each individual is supposed to be a combination of the distance from the food and from the highest density of the krill swarm.

The time-dependent position of an individual krill is governed by the following actions (Hofmann et al., 2004):

- movement induced by other krill individuals,
- foraging activity,
- random diffusion.

For n-dimensional space, the following Lagrangian model is generalized to a decision space:

$$\frac{dX_i}{dt} = N_i + F_i + D_i \tag{15.1}$$

where N_i, F_i, and D_i are motions induced by other krill individuals, foraging motion, and the physical diffusion of the ith krill individual, respectively.

15.2.1.1   Motion Induced by Other Krill Individuals

For a krill individual, this movement is formulated as

$$N_i^{new} = N^{max}\alpha_i + \omega_n N_i^{old} \tag{15.2}$$

and

$$\alpha_i = \alpha_i^{local} + \alpha_i^{target} \tag{15.3}$$

where N is the maximum induced speed which is equal to 0.01 (m/s), α_i is the direction of motion induced, ω_n is the inertia weight of the motion induced, N_i^{old} is the last motion induced, α_i^{local} is the local effect provided by the neighbors, and α_i^{target} is the target direction effect provided by the best krill individual.

The effect of the neighbors in a krill movement individual can be formulated as

$$\alpha_i^{local} = \sum_{j=1}^{NN} \hat{K}_{i,j} \hat{X}_{i,j} \tag{15.4}$$

$$\hat{X}_{i,j} = \frac{x_j - x_i}{\|x_j - x_i\| + \varepsilon} \tag{15.5}$$

$$\hat{K}_{i,j} = \frac{K_i - K_j}{K^{worst} - K^{best}} \tag{15.6}$$

where K^{worst} and K^{best} are, respectively, the worst and the best fitness values of the krill individuals up to now; K_i represents the fitness value of the ith krill individual; K_j is the fitness of jth neighbor; X represents the related positions; and NN is the number of the neighbors.

For choosing the neighbor, a sensing distance (d_s) is determined using

$$d_{s,i} = \frac{1}{5N} \sum_{j=1}^{N} \|X_i - X_j\| \tag{15.7}$$

where $d_{s,i}$ is the sensing distance for the ith krill individual and N is the number of the krill individuals. Based on this equation, if the distance of two krill individuals is less than d_s, they are neighbors.

The effect of the individual krill with the best fitness on the ith individual krill is formulated as

$$\alpha_i^{target} = C^{best} \hat{K}_{i,best} \hat{X}_{i,best} \tag{15.8}$$

where C^{best} is the effective coefficient defined as

$$C^{best} = 2 \left(rand + \frac{I}{I_{max}} \right) \tag{15.9}$$

where rand is a random value in the range [0,1], I is the actual iteration number, and I_{max} is the maximum number of iterations.

15.2.1.2   Foraging Motion

The foraging motion has two main terms, the food location and the previous experience. This motion can be expressed for the ith krill individual as follows:

$$F_i = V_f \beta_i + \omega_f F_i^{old} \tag{15.10}$$

and

$$\beta_i = \beta_i^{food} + \beta_i^{best} \tag{15.11}$$

where V_f is the foraging speed which is taken as 0.02 (m/s) based on Price (1989), ω_f is the inertia weight of the foraging motion, F_i^{old} is the last foraging motion, β_i^{food} is the food attractive, and β_i^{best} is the effect of the best fitness of the ith krill up to now.

For an iteration, the center of food can be defined as

$$X^{food} = \frac{\sum_{i=1}^{N}(1/K_i)X_i}{\sum_{i=1}^{N}(1/K_i)} \tag{15.12}$$

and the food attraction for the can be defined as follows:

$$\beta_i^{food} = C^{food} \hat{K}_{i,food} \hat{X}_{i,food} \tag{15.13}$$

where C is determined as

$$C^{food} = 2\left(1 - \frac{I}{I_{max}}\right) \tag{15.14}$$

The effect of the best fitness of the ith krill individual during it history is formulated as

$$\beta_i^{best} = \hat{K}_{i,ibest} \hat{X}_{i,ibest} \tag{15.15}$$

where K_{ibest} is the best previously visited position.

15.2.1.3   Physical Diffusion

The physical diffusion is a random process which can be formulated as follows:

$$D_i = D^{max}\left(1 - \frac{I}{I_{max}}\right)\delta \tag{15.16}$$

where $D^{\max} \in [0.002, 0.010]$ (m/s), based on (Morin et al., 1988), and it is the maximum diffusion speed, and δ is the random directional vector and its arrays are random values in the range $[-1, 1]$.

15.2.1.4 Motion Process of the KH Algorithm

Using different motions, the position vector of a krill individual during the interval t to $t + \Delta t$ is formulated as

$$X_i(t + \Delta t) = X_i(t) + \Delta t \frac{dX_i}{dt} \tag{15.17}$$

where Δt can be obtained from

$$\Delta t = C_t \sum_{j=1}^{NV} (UB_j - LB_j) \tag{15.18}$$

where NV is the total number of variables, LB_j and UB_j are respectively the lower and upper bounds of the jth variables, and C_t is a constant number which is considered as 0.5 in this study.

15.2.1.5 Crossover

As it is evaluated in the first KH paper, crossover is effective in the algorithm. By generating a vector with uniformly distributed random values in the range $[0, 1]$, the mth component of X_i, $x_{i,m}$, is manipulated as

$$x_{i,m} = \begin{cases} x_{r,m} & \text{rand}_{i,m} < Cr_i \\ x_{i,m} & \text{else} \end{cases} \tag{15.19}$$

$$Cr_i = 0.2\, \hat{K}_{i,\text{best}} \tag{15.20}$$

where Cr_i is crossover probability of the ith krill individual.

15.3 Implementation and Numerical Experiments

Structural optimization problems are commonly nonlinear and complex, and the optimal solutions of interest do not exist. In order to see how the KH algorithm performs, three structural engineering problems are solved, including structural design of a pin-jointed plane frame, reinforced concrete beam design, and 25-bar space truss design.

15.3.1   Case I: Structural Design of a Pin-Jointed Plane Frame

The first case is design of a pin-jointed plane frame with a fixed base for minimum weight utilizing KH. This case study is originally presented by Majid (1974). Figure 15.1A shows the frame. The vertical deflections at joints 1 and 2 are limited to 5 mm. All members of the frame have the same cross-sectional area (A) equal to 100 mm^2; the vertical forces P_1 and P_2 are respectively 100 and 50 kN, and the length of the base (l) is 1000 mm. The frame is symmetric and therefore, just half of the frame is considered, as illustrated in Figure 15.1B. Thus, member 3 has half the cross-sectional area of the other members. Joints 1 and 2 move vertically, and the joint displacement vector is $\Delta = (\Delta_1, \Delta_2)^T$. As shown in Figure 15.1B, the angles of members 1 and 2 (θ_1 and θ_2) specify the design and define the structure of this frame (Gandomi et al., 2013b).

Then the lengths of the members can be calculated using the following equations:

$$l_1 = \frac{l}{2\cos(\theta_1)} \tag{15.21}$$

$$l_2 = \frac{l}{2\cos(\theta_2)} \tag{15.22}$$

$$l_3 = \frac{l}{2\cos(\theta_1)\cos(\theta_2)} \sqrt{\cos^2(\theta_1) + \cos^2(\theta_2) - 2\cos(\theta_1)\cos(\theta_2)\cos(\theta_1 - \theta_2)} \tag{15.23}$$

The materials and cross-sectional areas of all the members are assumed to be the same. Hence, the weight of the frame is a linear function of the total length of the members. Thus, the objective function of the problem for the three-member frame (NM is the number of members) will be as follows (Gandomi et al., 2013b):

$$\text{minimize } f(\theta_1, \theta_2) = \sum_{i=1}^{NM} l_i \tag{15.24}$$

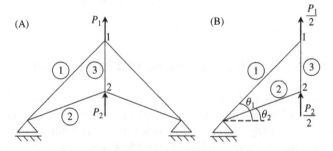

Figure 15.1 Pin-jointed plane frame example.

subject to displacements less than 5:

$$|\Delta_1(\theta_1, \theta_2)| \leq 5 \tag{15.25}$$

$$|\Delta_2(\theta_1, \theta_2)| \leq 5 \tag{15.26}$$

where $-B/3 \leq \theta_1$, $\theta_2 \leq B/3$, and the displacements $\Delta = (\Delta_1, \Delta_2)^T$ can be derived as

$$K\Delta = F \text{ or } F = K^{-1}F \text{ and } K = B^T k B$$

where

$$k = \begin{bmatrix} \dfrac{EA}{l_1} & 0 & 0 \\ 0 & \dfrac{EA}{l_2} & 0 \\ 0 & 0 & \dfrac{EA}{l_3} \end{bmatrix} \tag{15.27}$$

and

$$B = \begin{bmatrix} \sin(\theta_1) & 0 \\ 0 & \sin(\theta_2) \\ 1 & -1 \end{bmatrix} \tag{15.28}$$

Therefore, the displacements Δ for the problem are given by $K\Delta = F$, which is

$$EA \begin{bmatrix} \dfrac{\sin^2(\theta_1)}{l_1} + \dfrac{1}{2l_3} & -\dfrac{1}{2l_3} \\ -\dfrac{1}{2l_3} & \dfrac{\sin^2(\theta_2)}{l_2} + \dfrac{1}{2l_3} \end{bmatrix} \begin{bmatrix} \Delta_1 \\ \Delta_2 \end{bmatrix} = \begin{bmatrix} \dfrac{P_1}{2} \\ \dfrac{P_2}{2} \end{bmatrix} \tag{15.29}$$

The assumption is that two frames are remarkably different if their shapes are significantly different. This criterion is characterized by the angles of the members. Thus, the distance between two frames can be specified using the Euclidean distance between them in design space.

The KH algorithm was run to find the global optima of this design problem. The results of this study and the best results reported by Li et al. (2007a) are presented in Table 15.1 and the frame shapes are shown in Figure 15.2. Note that $\theta_1 = \theta_2$ for both global solutions. This is to be expected because the weight (total length) is selected as the objective function. Before KH was used to solve this problem, its objective function was thought to be multimodal with two global solutions.

Table 15.1 Statistical Results of the Pin-Jointed Plane Frame Example

Method	Shape (A)			Shape (B)		
	θ_1 (rad)	θ_2 (rad)	F_{min}	θ_1 (rad)	θ_2 (rad)	F_{min}
GA	0.475784	0.472764	1125.98	−0.478625	−0.479701	1127.59
KH	0.477384	0.477384	1125.87	−0.477384	−0.477385	1125.87

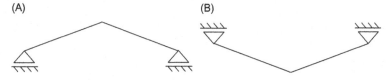

Figure 15.2 Optimal frame shapes.

The results indicate that the KH algorithm has successfully obtained two global solutions as expected. As it can be seen from Table 15.1, the KH results are better than the solutions obtained by Li et al. (2007b) using GA.

15.3.2   Case II: A Reinforced Concrete Beam Design

A simplified optimization of the total cost of a reinforced concrete beam, shown in Figure 15.3, was presented by Amir and Hasegawa (1989). The beam is assumed to be simply supported with a span of 30 ft and subjected to a live load of 2.0 klbf and a dead load of 1.0 klbf including the weight of the beam. The concrete compressive strength (Φ_c) is 5 ksi, the yield stress of the reinforcing steel (Φ_y) is 50 ksi. The cost of concrete is $0.02/in²/linear ft and the cost of steel is $1.0/in²/linear ft. It is required to determine the area of the reinforcement (A_s), the width of the beam (b), and the depth of the beam (h) such that the total cost of structure is minimized. Here, the cross-sectional area of the reinforcing bar (A_s) is taken as a discrete type variable that must be chosen from the standard bar dimensions as listed by Amir and Hasegawa (1989). The width of concrete beam (b) is assumed to be an integer variable. The variable h denoting the depth of the beam is a continuous variable. The effective depth of the RC beam is assumed to be $0.8h$.

The structure should be proportioned to have a required strength based on the ACI 318-77 (1977) as follows:

$$M_u = 0.9 A_s \sigma_y (0.8h)\left(1.0 - 0.59\frac{A_s \sigma_y}{0.8bh\sigma_c}\right) \geq 1.4 M_d + 1.7 M_l \qquad (15.30)$$

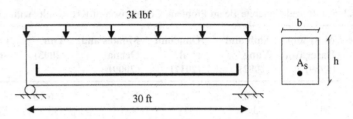

Figure 15.3 Illustration of reinforced concrete beam.

Table 15.2 Statistical Results of the KH Algorithm for the Reinforced Concrete Beam Problem

Best	Mean	Median	Worst	SD
359.2076	360.42077	359.2124	362.6364	1.5569

where M_u, M_d, and M_l are respectively the flexural strength, dead load, and live load moments of the beam. In this case, $M_d = 1350$ in.kip and $M_l = 2700$ in.kip. The depth to width ratio of the beam is restricted to be less than or equal to 4. The optimization problem can be expressed as

$$\text{minimize } f(A_s, b, h) = 2.9A_s + 0.6bh \tag{15.31}$$

subject to

$$g_1 = \frac{h}{b} - 4 \leq 0 \tag{15.32}$$

$$g_2 = 180 + 7.375\frac{A_s^2}{b} - A_s h \leq 0 \tag{15.33}$$

The variable bounds are A_s: {6.0,6.16,6.32,6.6,7.0,7.11,7.2,7.8,7.9,8.0,8.4} in.², b: {28,29,30,31,...,38,39,40} in., and $5 \leq h \leq 10$ in. The constrained functions of g_1 and g_2 are derived by Liebman et al. (1981). They are later used by Amir and Hasegawa (1989) and also in this study.

Statistical results of the KH optimization runs executed for the reinforced concrete beam problem are presented in Table 15.2. From this table, the ratio between the optimized costs corresponding to worst and best designs is 1.01, which seems very interesting.

Table 15.3 presents the optimum designs of this problem and the parameters used. One can see that the performance of the KH method is the best solution, as compared with the other results reported in the literature.

Table 15.3 Reinforced Concrete Beam Problem: Comparison of KH Results with Literature

Reference	Amir and Hasegawa (1989)	Shih and Yang (2002)	Gandomi et al. (2011)	Montes and Ocana (2009)	Yun (2005)	Present Study
A_s	7.8	6.6	6.32	N.A.	6.16	6.32
b	31	33	34	N.A.	35	34
h	7.79	8.495227	8.5000	N.A.	8.7500	8.49998
g_1	−4.2012	[a]0.0159	−0.2241	N.A.	−3.6173	−0.2240
g_2	−0.0205	−0.1155	0	N.A.	0	0.0000
f_{min}	374.2	362.2455	359.2080	376.2977	364.8541	359.2076

[a]Violated set.

15.3.3   Case III: 25-Bar Space Truss Design

This problem is a benchmark truss optimization problem (Gandomi and Yang, 2011). For optimum design of structures, the objective function can be expressed as

$$\text{minimize } W(A) = \sum_{i=1}^{NM} \gamma A_i L_i \tag{15.34}$$

where $W(A)$ *is* the weight of the structure; NM is the number of members which is equal to 25; γ represents the material density of the members, which is same for all members, and it is 0.1 lb/in.^{3} (2767.990 kg/m^3); L_i is the length of member i; and A_i is the cross-sectional area of member i chosen between 0.01 and 3.4 in.^{2} (or 0.6452 and 21.94 cm^2).

The topology and nodal numbers of this transient truss structure are shown in Figure 15.4. The modulus of elasticity is taken as 10,000 ksi (68,950 MPa). The truss members are categorized into eight groups: (i) A_1, (ii) A_{2-5}, (iii) A_{6-9}, (iv) A_{10-11}, (v) A_{12-13}, (vi) A_{14-17}, (vii) A_{18-21}, and (viii) A_{22-25}.

This 25-bar truss is subjected to two different loading conditions as presented in Table 15.4. Displacement constraints of ±0.35 in. (±8.89 mm) are imposed on every node in every direction. Maximum axial stress limitations vary for each group as given in Table 15.5 (Gandomi et al., 2012).

The statistical values of the best solutions obtained by proposed algorithm are presented in Table 15.6. The convergence characteristic of the KH is analyzed by plotting the fitness function versus the number of iterations (see Figure 15.5), which shows that KH is a fast converged algorithm.

Table 15.7 illustrates the optimum results obtained by the KH and those reported in the literature. The same problem has also been solved by other algorithms such as BB-BC (Kaveh and Talatahari, 2009), TA (Zhu, 1986), OC (Zhou and Rozvany,

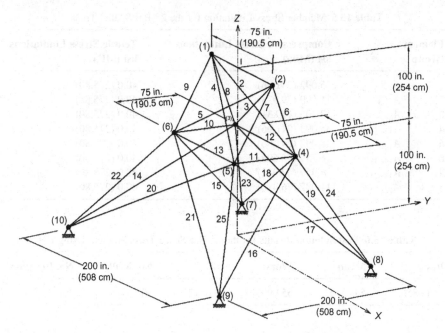

Figure 15.4 25-bar space truss.

Table 15.4 Two Different Loading Conditions for the 25-Bar Space Truss

Node	Case 1			Case 2		
	P_X kips (kN)	P_Y kips (kN)	P_Z kips (kN)	P_X kips (kN)	P_Y kips (kN)	P_Z kips (kN)
1	0.0	20.0 (89)	−5.0 (22.25)	1.0 (4.45)	10.0 (44.5)	−5.0 (22.25)
2	0.0	−20.0 (89)	−5.0 (22.25)	0.0	10.0 (44.5)	−5.0 (22.25)
3	0.0	0.0	0.0	0.5 (2.22)	0.0	0.0
6	0.0	0.0	0.0	0.5 (2.22)	0.0	0.0

1993), CSS (Kaveh and Talatahari, 2010), CP (Farshi and Alinia-ziazi, 2010), GP (Adeli and Kamal, 1986), SA (Lamberti, 2008), PSO (Schutte and Groenwold, 2003), ABC (Sonmez, 2011), and GA (Rajeev and Krishnamoorthy, 1992). The best weight obtained by the KH is 545.085 lb, and this shows that the KH approach has better performance than the results by all other popular algorithms.

Table 15.5 Member Stress Limitation for the 25-Bar Spatial Truss

Element Group		Compressive Stress Limitations ksi (MPa)	Tensile Stress Limitations ksi (MPa)
1	A_1	35.092 (241.96)	40.0 (275.80)
2	A_{2-5}	11.590 (79.913)	40.0 (275.80)
3	A_{6-9}	17.305 (119.31)	40.0 (275.80)
4	A_{10-11}	35.092 (241.96)	40.0 (275.80)
5	A_{12-13}	35.092 (241.96)	40.0 (275.80)
6	A_{14-17}	6.759 (46.603)	40.0 (275.80)
7	A_{18-21}	6.959 (47.982)	40.0 (275.80)
8	A_{22-25}	11.082 (76.410)	40.0 (275.80)

Table 15.6 Best Solution Results for the 25-Bar Space Truss Problem Using KH

Best	Mean	Worst	SD	No. Krill	No. Iteration
545.0850	548.155	554.993	3.0112	50	400

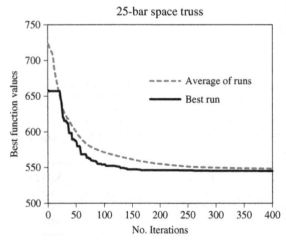

Figure 15.5 Convergence plot of the 25-bar space truss.

15.4 Conclusions and Future Research

The new KH algorithm is utilized to structural optimization. The results indicate that the KH algorithm is very efficient for solving structural engineering problems. Furthermore, the current results show that KH can perform superior to different existing algorithms. This powerful optimization method can be modified and extended to study multiobjective optimization applications with various constraints.

Table 15.7 Performance Comparison of Different Methods for the 25-Bar Spatial Truss

	BB-BC	TA	OC	CSS	CP	GP	SA	PSO	ABC	GA	KH
A_1	0.01	0.1	0.01	0.01	0.01	0.01	0.01	0.01	0.011	0.1	0.01025
A_{2-5}	1.993	1.9	1.987	2.003	1.998	1.986	1.987	2.121	1.979	1.8	2.02437
A_{6-9}	3.056	2.6	2.994	3.007	2.983	2.961	2.994	2.893	3.003	2.3	3.04154
A_{10-11}	0.01	0.01	0.01	0.01	0.01	0.01	0.01	0.01	0.01	0.2	0.01029
A_{12-13}	0.01	0.01	0.01	0.01	0.01	0.01	0.01	0.01	0.01	0.1	0.01081
A_{14-17}	0.665	0.8	0.684	0.687	0.684	0.806	0.684	0.671	0.69	0.8	0.6895
A_{18-21}	1.642	2.1	1.677	1.655	1.675	1.68	1.677	1.611	1.679	1.8	1.62002
A_{22-25}	2.679	2.6	2.662	2.66	2.667	2.53	2.662	2.717	2.652	3	2.65501
Weight (lb)	545.16	562.93	545.16	545.1	545.37	545.66	545.23	545.21	545.193	546	545.085

BB-BC, Big Bang—Big Crush; TA, Templeman's algorithm; OC, optimality criteria; CSS, charged system search; CP, center points; GP, geometrical programming; SA, simulated annealing; PSO, particle swarm optimization; ABC, artificial bee colony; GA, genetic algorithms; KH, krill herd.

References

ACI 318-77, 1977. Building code requirements for reinforced concrete. American Concrete Institute, Detroit, Mich.

Adeli, H., Kamal, O., 1986. Efficient optimization of space trusses. Comput. Struct. 24, 501−511.

Amir, H.M., Hasegawa, T., 1989. Nonlinear mixed-discrete structural optimization. J. Struct. Eng. 115 (3), 626−645.

Farshi, B., Alinia-ziazi, A., 2010. Sizing optimization of truss structures by method of centers and force formulation. Int. J. Solids Struct. 47, 2508−2524.

Gandomi, A.H., Alavi, A.H., 2012. Krill herd: a new bio-inspired optimization algorithm. Commun. Nonlinear Sci. Numer. Simul. 17 (12), 4831−4845.

Gandomi, A.H., Yang, X.S., 2011. Benchmark problems in structural optimization. In: Koziel, S., Yang, X.S. (Eds.), Computational Optimization, Methods and Algorithms. Springer-Verlag, Berlin, pp. 267−291.

Gandomi, A.H., Yang, X.S., Alavi, A.H., 2011. Mixed variable structural optimization using firefly algorithm. Comput. Struct. 89 (23−24), 2325−2336.

Gandomi, A.H., Talatahari, S., Yang, X.S., Deb, S., 2012. Design optimization of truss structures using cuckoo search algorithm. Struct. Des. Tall Spec. Buildings. 10.1002/tal.1033.

Gandomi, A.H., Yang, X.-S., Talatahari, S., Alavi, A.H., 2013a. Metaheuristic Applications in Structures and Infrastructures. Elsevier, Waltham, MA.

Gandomi, A.H., Yang, X.S., Alavi, A.H., 2013b. Cuckoo search algorithm: a metaheuristic approach to solve structural optimization problems. Eng. Comput. 29 (1), 17−35.

Hofmann, E.E., Haskell, A.G.E., Klinck, J.M., Lascara, C.M., 2004. Lagrangian modelling studies of Antarctic krill (Euphasia superba) swarm formation. ICES J. Mar. Sci. 61, 617−631.

Kaveh, A., Talatahari, S., 2009. Size optimization of space trusses using Big Bang−Big Crunch algorithm. Comput. Struct. 87 (17−18), 1129−1140.

Kaveh, A., Talatahari, S., 2010. Optimal design of skeletal structures via the charged system search algorithm. Struct. Multidisc. Optim. 41, 893−911.

Lamberti, L., 2008. An efficient simulated annealing algorithm for design optimization of truss structures. Comput. Struct. 86, 1936−1953.

Li, J.L., Huang, Z.B., Liu, F., Wu, Q.H., 2007a. A heuristic particle swarm optimizer for optimization of pin connected structures. Comput. Struct. 85, 340−349.

Li, J.-P., Balazs, M.E., Parks, G.T., 2007b. Engineering design optimization using species-conserving genetic algorithms. Eng. Optmiz. 39 (2), 147−161.

Liebman, J.S., Khachaturian, N., Chanaratna, V., 1981. Discrete structural optimization. J. Struct. Div. 107 (ST11), 2177−2197.

Majid, K.I., 1974. Optimum Design of Structures. Newnes-Butterworth, London.

Mezura-Montes, E., Hernández-Ocaña, B., 2009. Modified bacterial foraging optimization for engineering design. In: Dagli, C.H., Bryden, K.M., Corns, S.M., Gen, M., Tumer, K., Süer, G. (Eds.), Proceedings of the Artificial Neural Networks in Engineering Conference (ANNIE'2009). ASME Press Series, Intelligent Engineering Systems Through Artificial Neural Networks, vol. 19, pp. 357 − 364.

Morin, A., Okubo, A., Kawasaki, K., 1988. Acoustic data analysis and models of krill spatial distribution. Scientific Committee for the Conservation of Antarctic Marine Living Resources, Selected Scientific Papers, Part I. pp. 311−29.

Price, H.J., 1989. Swimming behavior of krill in response to algal patches: a mesocosm study. Limnol. Oceanogr. 34, 649–659.

Rajeev, S., Krishnamoorthy, C.S., 1992. Discrete optimization of structures using genetic algorithms. J. Struct. Eng. 118 (5), 1233–1250.

Sahab, M.G., Toropov, V.V., Gandomi, A.H., 2013. A review on traditional and modern structural optimization: problems and techniques (Chapter 2). In: Gandomi, A.H., Yang, X.S., Talatahari, S., Alavi, A.H. (Eds.), Metaheuristic Applications in Structures and Infrastructures. Elsevier, Waltham, MA.

Schutte, J.J., Groenwold, A.A., 2003. Sizing design of truss structures using particle swarms. Struct. Multidisc. Optim. 25, 261–269.

Shih, C.J., Yang, Y.C., 2002. Generalized Hopfield network based structural optimization using sequential unconstrained minimization technique with additional penalty strategy. Adv. Eng. Soft. 33, 721–729.

Sonmez, M., 2011. Artificial bee colony algorithm for optimization of truss structures. Appl. Soft. Comput. 11 (2), 2406–2418.

Talbi, E., 2009. Metaheuristics: From Design to Implementation. John Wiley & Sons, Hoboken, NJ.

Yang, X.-S., 2009. Harmony search as a metaheuristic algorithm. In: Geem, Z.W. (Ed.), Music-Inspired Harmony Search: Theory and Applications. Springer, Berlin, pp. 1–14.

Yang, X.-S., 2010. Engineering Optimization: An Introduction with Metaheuristic Applications. John Wiley & Sons, Hoboken, NJ.

Yang, X.S., Gandomi, A.H., 2012. Bat algorithm: a novel approach for global engineering optimization. Eng. Comput. 29 (5), 464–483.

Yun, Y.S., 2005. Study on Adaptive Hybrid Genetic Algorithm and Its Applications to Engineering Design Problems, MSc thesis. Waseda University.

Zhou, M., Rozvany, G.I.N., 1993. DCOC: an optimality criteria method for large systems. Part II: algorithm. Struct. Optim. 6, 250–262.

Zhu, D.M., 1986. An improved Templeman's algorithm for optimum design of trusses with discrete member size. Eng. Optim. 9, 303–312.

16 Artificial Plant Optimization Algorithm

Zhihua Cui and Xingjuan Cai

Complex System and Computational Intelligence Laboratory,
Taiyuan University of Science and Technology, Shanxi, China

16.1 Introduction

With the developments of industry and economics, many new problems are brought up with nondifferential, multimodal, and high-dimensional characters. To solve these problems efficiently and accurately, scientists propose stochastic optimization methods. Up to now, many optimization algorithms have been developed, such as genetic algorithm, firefly algorithm (Yang, 2010), group search optimizer (He, 2010), Krill herd (Gandomi and Alavi, 2012), seeker optimization algorithm (Dai et al., 2009), artificial physics optimization (Xie et al., 2010) and social emotional optimization algorithm (Cui and Cai, 2011). Among them, particle swarm optimization (PSO) (Eberhart and Kennedy, 1995; Kennedy and Eberhart, 1995) and ant colony optimization (ACO) (Dorigo et al., 2006) drew much attention due to their simple concept and high efficiency by simulating animal social behaviors. For instance, the individual of PSO is called particle. Unlike the common evolutionary computation, each particle possesses its information of both position and velocity. They communicate with each other and update their own positions according to their decisions.

Recently, a novel evolutionary methodology proposed by Cui et al. (2012a,b,c) was denominated as artificial plant optimization algorithm (APOA) which was inspired by natural plant growing process. In APOA, each individual represents one potential branch and several operators are adopted during the growing period. Photosynthesis operator is dedicated to producing the energy created by sunlight and other materials while phototropism operator guides the growing direction according to different conditions. In addition, apical dominance operator is essential to make minor adjustment for the growing directions.

The rest of this chapter is organized as follows: Section 16.2 illustrates a primary framework of APOA and the standard version is presented in Section 16.3. Finally, the conclusion is provided.

Swarm Intelligence and Bio-Inspired Computation. DOI: http://dx.doi.org/10.1016/B978-0-12-405163-8.00016-8

16.2   Primary APOA

16.2.1   Main Method

To simulate the plant growing phenomenon, it is important to provide a connection between growing process and optimization problem. In principle, the search space should be mapping into the whole plant growing environment, and each individual denotes a virtual branch. Moreover, the provisions should be supplied. For example, water, carbon dioxide and other materials are supposed to be inexhaustible except the sunlight. Since the light intensity is varying for different branches, it could be considered as the fitness value for each branch. More details can be found in Table 16.1.

Furthermore, the pseudo code of the primary APOA is listed as follows (Algorithm 16.1).

The procedure Initialization is used to sample m branches randomly from the problem search space, which is an n-dimensional hypercube. Each coordinate of a point is assumed to be uniformly distributed between the corresponding upper and lower bounds. The procedure Calc () means the computation of the fitness values for all branches.

16.2.2   Photosynthesis Operator

Photosynthesis is aiming at producing the energy for the branch growing. In wikipedia, photosynthesis is defined as follows (http://en.wikipedia.org/wiki/Photosynthesis):

> *Photosynthesis occurs in plants, algae, and many species of bacteria, but not in archaea. Photosynthetic organisms are called photoautotrophs, since they can*

Table 16.1 Similarity Between Plant Growing Process and Optimization Problem

Problem Search Space	Plant Growing Environment
Iteration	Growing period
Global optimum	Highest light intensity
Fitness value	Light intensity
Point	Branch
Position update	Branch growth

Algorithm 16.1 PAPOA ()

1: Initialization ()
2: Iteration←1
3: while iteration<MAXITER do
4: Calc ()
5: Photosynthesis ()
6: Phototropism ()
7: Iteration←iteration+1
8: end while

create their own food. In plants, algae, and cyanobacteria, photosynthesis uses carbon dioxide and water, releasing oxygen as a waste product. Photosynthesis is vital for all aerobic life on Earth.

Photosynthetic rate plays an important role to measure how much energy produced. In botany, light response curve is used to measure the photosynthetic rate, and many models have been proposed in the past research, such as rectangular hyperbolic model, nonrectangular hyperbolic model, updated rectangular hyperbolic model, parabola model, straight line model and exponential curve models (Piao and Qiang, 2007). In this chapter, rectangular hyperbolic model is employed to measure the quality of the obtained energy:

$$p_i(t) = \frac{\alpha Uf_i(t)P_{max}}{\alpha Uf_i(t) + P_{max}} - R_d \tag{16.1}$$

where $p_i(t)$ is the photosynthetic rate of branch i at time t, α is the initial quantum efficiency, P_{max} is the maximum net photosynthesis rate, and R_d is the dark respiratory rate. α, P_{max}, and R_d are three parameters to control the size of photosynthetic rate. According to the corresponding references (Piao and Qiang, 2007), they are set as 0.055, 30.2, and 1.44, respectively. $Uf_i(t)$ denotes the light intensity and is defined as follows:

$$Uf_i(f) = \frac{f_{worst}(t) - f_i(t)}{f_{worst}(t) - f_{best}(t)} \tag{16.2}$$

where $f_{worst}(t)$ and $f_{best}(t)$ are the worst and best light intensities at time t, respectively, $f_i(t)$ means the light intensity of branch i.

The steps of photosynthesis operator are listed as follows (Algorithm 16.2).

16.2.3 Phototropism Operator

In wikipedia, phototropism is defined as follows (http://en.wikipedia.org/wiki/Phototropism):

Phototropism is directional growth in which the direction of growth is determined by the direction of the light source. In other words, it is the growth and response to a light stimulus. Phototropism is most often observed in plants, but can also occur in other organisms such as fungi.

Photosynthesis ()   **Algorithm 16.2** Photosynthesis ()

1: for i=1 to m do

2: Computing the light intensity $Uf(x_i)$;

3: Computing the photosynthetic rate p_i;

4: end do

In APOA, branches favor those positions with high light intensities so that they can produce more energy. In other words, each branch will be attracted by these positions. Therefore, branch i takes the following growing:

$$x_i(t+1) = x_i(t) + \text{Gp } F_i(t) \cdot \text{rand}() \tag{16.3}$$

where Gp is a parameter reflecting the energy conversion rate and used to control the growing size per unit time. $F_i(t)$ denotes the growing force guided by photosynthetic rate, rand() represents a random number sampled with uniformly distribution.

For each branch i, $F_i(t)$ is computed by:

$$F_i(t) = \frac{F_i^{\text{total}}}{||x_i(t) - x_p(t)||} \cdot (x_i(t) - x_p(t)) \tag{16.4}$$

where $||\cdot||$ means the Euclidean distance, F_i^{total} is computed as follows:

$$F_i^{\text{total}}(t) = \sum_{i \neq p} \text{coe} \cdot e^{-\dim P_i(t)} - e^{-\dim P_p(t)} \tag{16.5}$$

Symbol dim represents the problem dimensionality, coe is a parameter used to control the direction:

$$\text{coe} = \begin{cases} 1 & \text{if} & p_i(t) > p_p(t) \\ -1 & \text{if} & p_i(t) < p_p(t) \\ 0 & \text{otherwise} \end{cases} \tag{16.6}$$

Furthermore, a small probability p_m is introduced to reflect some random events influences:

$$x_i(t+1) = x_{\min} + (x_{\max} - x_{\min}) \cdot \text{rand}_1(), \quad \text{if } (\text{rand}_2() < p_m) \tag{16.7}$$

where $\text{rand}_1()$ and $\text{rand}_2()$ are two random numbers with uniformly distribution, respectively.

As a primary APOA only photosynthesis and phototropism mechanisms are simulated and noted as PAPOA briefly. The steps of phototropism operator are listed as follows (Algorithm 16.3).

16.2.4 Applications to Artificial Neural Network Training

Artificial neural network (ANN) is an implied model of the biological neuron to make decisions and conclusions by simulating human brain's work (Bryant and Frigaard, 2006). Every neuron model is composed of a processing

Phototropism ()   **Algorithm 16.3** Phototropism ()

1: for i=1 to n do

2: if $rand_2() < pm$

3: $x_i(t+1) \leftarrow x_i(t)$ with Eq. (7)

4: else

5: calculating coe ;

6: calculating $F_i(t)$

7: $x_i(t+1) \leftarrow x_i(t)$ with Eq. (3)

8: end if

9: end do

element with synaptic input connections and a single output. The neuron can be defined as:

$$y = f(W \times X + \theta_j) = f\left(\sum_{i=1}^{n} \omega_{ij}x_i - \theta_j \right)$$

where x is input signals, ω_{ij} is synaptic weights of neuron, f is the activation function, and y is the output signal of neuron.

The error signal for the pth neurons of output layer is $e_{kp}(n) = d_{kp}(n) - y_{kp}(n)$, and the energy errors of the pth are $(1/2)e_{kp}^2(n)$, then sum of the energy errors for all neural network output layers are:

$$E(n) = \frac{1}{2} \sum_{p=1}^{P} e_{kp}^2(n)$$

This least-squared error function is employed as the fitness function. To verify the algorithm, we here adopt PAPOA to optimize the connection weights and bias terms of the ANN, which can be called the trained ANN as PAPOAANN.

In order to evaluate the performance of PAPOA, PAPOAANN was applied to two real-world problems (Cui et al., 2012a). We first use one well-studied benchmark function from the UCI machine learning repository, Cleveland heart disease classification data. There are missing attribute values in the data sets of the Cleveland heart disease classification problem. In addition, we also solve one forecasting problem, the sum sport number forecasting problem. The sunspot forecasting problem is a chaotic time series. Therefore, they represent some of the most challenging problems in the ANN and the machine learning field (Yao and Liu, 1999).

To show the validity of PAPOAANN, we also implemented a modified backpropagation training algorithm: gradient descent with momentum and adaptive learning rate (BPANN); and three training algorithm based on evolutionary algorithms: (i) simple genetic algorithm (SGA); (ii) evolutionary programming (EP); (iii) PSO.

16.2.4.1 The Cleveland Heart Disease Data Set

This data set comes from the Cleveland Clinic Foundation and was supplied by Robert Detrano of the V.A. Medical Center, Long Beach, CA. The goal of this data set is to predict the presence of heart disease in the patient. This database contains 76 attributes, but all published experiments refer to using a subset of 14 of them. And one of these attributes has demonstrated patient's condition, it is integer valued from 0 (no presence) to 4. Experiments with the Cleveland database have concentrated on simply attempting to distinguish presence (values 1, 2, 3, and 4) from absence (value 0). The database originally contained 303 instances but 6 of them had missed some values and 27 of the remains were still in case of dispute. Since handling the missing attribute values is out of the scope of this chapter, we remove the instances with missing attribute values in the data set, leaving a final total of 270 which includes 120 instances with heart disease and 150 instances without heart disease. According the guidelines of Prechelt (1994), in the Cleveland heart disease classification problem, each set of data was divided into three sets: 50% of the patterns were used for learning, 25% of them for validation and the remaining 25% for testing the generalization of the trained ANN. So the 270 instances were partitioned into the training set of 134 instances, the validation set of 68 instances, and the testing set of the final 68 instances. To carry on the training well to the neural network, the ratio of the instances with heart disease to the instances without heart disease in each set is the same as 4:5.

Table 16.2 compares PAPOAANN's result against those ANNs trained by other algorithms (EPANN, GAANN, PSOANN, and BPANN are coming from He (2010)). We may find that PAPOAANN generated the best average result in terms of testing error rate.

16.2.4.2 Sunspot Forecasting Problem

The sunspot is the most basic and obvious kind of solar activities which occur on the photosphere layer of the sun. Generally speaking, the sunspot is actually the

Table 16.2 Error Rate of ANNs of the Cleveland Heart Disease Data Set

Algorithm		PAPOAANN	EPANN	GAANN	PSOANN	BPANN
Training set	Mean	7.91	12.54	12.53	10.03	29.23
	STD	4.00	3.28	2.35	1.23	9.96
	Best	2.24	9.72	8.89	8.46	11.19
	Worst	15.67	20.89	18.21	14.73	51.75
Validation set	Mean	6.93	17.86	17.88	13.65	30.56
	STD	3.04	7.37	4.21	1.18	10.02
	Best	3.96	11.97	12.04	11.55	11.76
	Worst	14.36	46.33	34.07	16.40	54.70
Test set	Mean	12.50	21.37	20.88	16.08	43.28
	STD	3.48	8.43	5.04	3.30	17.64
	Best	5.88	13.24	14.71	11.76	13.24
	Worst	16.18	45.58	33.82	25.00	77.94

huge maelstrom of intensely hot gas on the solar surface, its temperature is about 4500°C. Because this temperature is 1000–2000°C lower than the temperature of solar photosphere layer's surface (the temperature of solar photosphere layer's surface is about 6000°C), so the sunspot looks like some spots of deep dark colors. The sunspot is seldom moving alone, it is usually in groups to appear. The sunspot activity is cyclical and its cycle is for about 11 years. When the sunspot activity is active, it would impact on magnetic field, cause the climate coldly, and bring damage to each kind of electron product and electric appliances. Therefore, it becomes more and more important to predict the sunspot especially in our modern world.

The data set used in our experiment recorded the sunspot activity over the last 300 years. The sunspot cycles from 1700 to 2010 are shown in (He, 2010). To compare fairly with other methods, we used the first 180 years (1700–2010) as the training set to train the proposed PAPOAANN, the inputs x_i of the APPMANN consists of three past data points (Leung et al., 2003): $x_1 = y(t - 1)$, $x_2 = y(t - 2)$, and $x_3 = y(t - 3)$, where t denotes the year and $y(t)$ denotes the sunspot number at the year t. The output is the prediction of the sunspot number at year t:$z(t)$. The performance (forecasting error rate) of the trained APPMANN can be calculated from:

$$\text{err} = \sum_{t=1885}^{1980} \left(\left| \frac{z(t) - y(t)}{96} \right| \right)$$

We tabulated the results of training errors and forecasting errors in Table 16.3. We can see that PAPOAANN generated the best mean forecasting error. Simulation results show the prediction with PAPOAANN is very close to the actual data.

16.3   Standard APOA

16.3.1   Drawbacks of PAPOA

Although the primary APOA trains the ANN successfully, some drawbacks still exist, for example,

1. For phototropism operator, the computational complexity is too time-consuming since each branch needs calculate all the influences from others.
2. In phototropism operator, all branches are updated with the same manner, which is contradictory to the natural phenomenon. In fact, the geotropism may be distinct for different branches. For instance, long branches may be attracted by gravity significantly while this effect could be ignored safely for short one. Therefore, the performance should be improved if we introduce this phenomenon into the methodology of APOA.
3. So far, only two phenomena are employed. However, there are many important phenomena missed during the tree growing process, such as apical dominance, artificial pruning.

In this section, we propose an updated version of APOA. Phototropism operator is redesigned, and apical dominance and artificial pruning are employed to enhance the performance. To avoid confusion, we call it the standard version (SAPOA, in brief) because it is more suitable for high-dimensional multimodal problems than PAPOA. The pseudo code is listed as follows (Algorithm 16.4).

16.3.2 Phototropism Operator

In phototropism operator of PAPOA, the gravity is omitted, and all branches are updated with the same manner. However, the growing direction of each branch should be changed dynamically due to the gravity. To account for this phenomenon, the phototropism operator is redesigned in the standard version by employing the influence of gravity to adjust the growing direction. In nature, the gravity plays a significant role on the growing direction if the branch is long enough. Therefore, in the standard version, the population is divided into two species: growing-motion branch and maturing-motion branch.

If branch i belongs to the growing-motion branch, it grows as follows:

$$x_i^k(t+1) = x_i^k(t) + (x_{best}^k(t) - x_i^k(t)) \cdot growth \cdot r \tag{16.8}$$

where growth is one parameter, r is one random number sampled with uniformly distribution, and $x_{best}^k(t)$ receives the highest light intensity.

Algorithm 16.4 APOA ()

1: Initialization ()
2: Iteration←1
3: while iteration<MAXITER do
4: Calc ()
5: Photosynthesis ()
6: Phototropism ()
7: Apical ()
8: Iteration←iteration+1
8: end while

Table 16.3 Error Rate of ANNs of the Sunspot Forecasting Problem

Algorithm		PAPOAANN	EPANN	GAANN	PSOANN	BPANN
Training set	Mean	10.60	13.22	13.41	11.88	13.36
	STD	0.45	0.49	0.91	0.23	1.17
	Best	10.07	12.53	11.89	11.53	11.79
	Worst	11.42	14.52	15.17	12.44	16.22
Test set	Mean	13.32	14.77	16.68	13.55	14.40
	STD	0.71	1.73	7.46	0.75	0.90
	Best	12.39	12.05	11.83	12.22	12.79
	Worst	14.59	22.60	43.76	15.59	16.17

On the other hand, if branch i is located in the maturing-motion branch, the growing motion is defined by:

$$x_i^k(t+1) = x_i^k(t) + \text{growth} \cdot r \cdot D_i^k \tag{16.9}$$

where $D_i^k(\text{angle}_i^k) = (d_i^1, d_i^2, \ldots, d_i^n)$ is the bending degree that translates Cartesian coordinate into polar coordinate as follows:

$$d_i^1 = \prod_{p=1}^{n-1} \cos(\text{angle}_i^p)$$

$$d_i^k = \sin(\text{angle}_i^k) \prod_{p=1}^{n-1} \cos(\text{angle}_i^p)$$

$$d_i^n = \sin(\text{angle}_i^{n-1})$$

At each time, one branch maintains one parameter $\text{angle}_i(t) = (\text{angle}_i^1(t), \text{angle}_i^2(t), \ldots, \text{angle}_i^n(t))$ (n denotes the dimensionality) to reflect the gravity influence, and is updated with:

$$\text{angle}_i^k(t+1) = \text{angle}_i^k(t) + \theta_i^k$$

where

$$\theta_i^k = K_{0i}^k \sqrt{|\cos(\text{beta} + \text{angle}_i^k) - \cos(w + \text{angle}_i^k)|}$$

The beta is a constant between interval $[\pi/40, \pi/2]$, and w is in $[\pi/20, \pi/2]$, K_{0i}^k is calculated by:

$$K_{0i}^k = 2\sqrt{\frac{|P_i^k|}{0.25\pi R_e}}$$

The pseudo code is listed as follows (Algorithm 16.5).

Photosynthesis ()
1: for i=1 to m do
2: Sorting the fitness values of all branches, the better half of the best populations are taken as growing-motion branches, as well as other branches are maturing-motion branches
3: Updating the position with Eq. (8) for growing-motion branch
4: Updating the position with Eq. (9) for maturing-motion branch
5: end do

Algorithm 16.5 Photosynthesis ()

16.3.3 Apical Dominance Operator

Apical dominance is also an important phenomenon. In wikipedia, apical dominance is defined by (http://en.wikipedia.org/wiki/Apical_dominance):

Apical dominance is the phenomenon whereby the main central stem of the plant is dominant over (i.e., grows more strongly than) other side stems; on a branch the main stem of the branch is further dominant over its own side branchlets.

In apical dominance phenomenon, all buds are divided into two parts: apical bud and lateral bud. For each branch, the growing buds may affect the branch growing direction significantly. Therefore, if we want to change the growing direction for some branches, we may make manual pruning process to remove the apical bud, this may enhance the exploration capability to escape from local optimum. On the contrary, if we still let apical bud to survive, then the exploitation may focus on the neighbors of this bud.

In SAPOA, the best position of all branches can be viewed as the apical bud because its fitness value (light intensity) is better than other buds. Furthermore, if there are at least two branches with the same light intensities, only one branch would be selected with uniformly distribution eventually.

Suppose $x_{\text{best}}(t) = (x_{\text{best}}^1(t), x_{\text{best}}^2(t), \ldots, x_{\text{best}}^n(t))$ is the best position in the current population, apical dominance operator is then performed on $x_{\text{best}}(t)$ because it achieves the best performance. Suppose rand(1) and rand(2) are two random numbers with uniformly distribution, then one of the following manners will be performed according to difference conditions (rate is a parameter):

If rand(1) < rate

$$x_{\text{best}}^k(t + 1) = x_{\text{best}}^k(t) + (x_{\text{best}}^k(t) - x_{\text{worst}}^k(t)) \cdot \text{growth} \cdot r \tag{16.10}$$

Else if rand(2) < 1/n

$$x_{\text{best}}^k(t + 1) = x_{\text{max}} + (x_{\text{max}} - x_{\text{min}}) \cdot r \tag{16.11}$$

Else

$$x_{\text{best}}^k(t + 1) = x_{\text{best}}^k(t) \tag{16.12}$$

16.3.4 Application to Toy Model of Protein Folding

Although a protein is formed by a combination of 20 possible standard amino acids, Toy model is only comprised of two "amino acids" (Dill, 1985). For simplicity, "A" and "B" represent hydrophobic amino acids and hydrophilic amino acids, respectively. They are linked together by rigid unit length (distance = 1) bonds to form linear unoriented polymers that reside in two dimensions. Any protein structure composed of N-monomers could be simplified as AB model, N-2 bend angles will be needed. These angles are defined in the range $-\pi \leq \theta_i \leq \pi$.

The energy function for a protein structure with N-monomers (N-mers) is given by:

$$\phi = \sum_{i=2}^{N-1} V_1(\theta_i) + \sum_{i=1}^{N-2} \sum_{j=i+2}^{N} V_2(d_{ij}, \xi_i, \xi_j)$$

This energy function can be divided into two parts: backbones bend potentials (V_1) and nonbonded interactions (V_2). The former is independent of the A, B sequence, while the latter is varying with the sequence and dependent on other neighbors. The backbone potential (V_1) has a simple trigonometric form:

$$V_1(\theta_i) = 1/4 \cdot (1 - \cos \theta_i)$$

The residue pair interactions (V_2) which only operate between unlinked residues possess a species-dependent Lennard-Jones form:

$$V_2(d_{ij}, \xi_i, \xi_j) = 4 \cdot (d_{ij}^{-12} - C(\xi_i, \xi_j) \cdot d_{ij}^{-6})$$
$$C(\xi_i, \xi_j) = 1/8 \cdot (1 + \xi_i + \xi_j + 5 \cdot \xi_i \, \xi_j)$$

where d_{ij} is the distance between residues i and j, and the discrete variables ξ_i denote residue species:

$$d_{ij} = \left\{ \left[1 + \sum_{k=i+1}^{j-1} \cos \sum_{l=i+1}^{k} \theta_l \right]^2 + \left[\sum_{k=i+1}^{j-1} \sin \sum_{l=i+1}^{k} \theta_l \right]^2 \right\}^{\frac{1}{2}}$$

$$\xi_i(A) = +1, \quad \xi_i(B) = -1$$

where the coefficient $C(\xi_i, \xi_j)$ is $+1$ for an AA pair, $+1/2$ for a BB pair, and $-1/2$ for an AB pair. Apparently, the interactions between homo-species particles are attractive while repulsive force is revealed between hetero-species particles. This diversity mimics in a simple way that of real amino-acid residues, which vary in size, polarity, and degree of hydrophobicity.

Here, we use some artificial sequence to demonstrate the performance of SAPOA. First, some short sequences (Stillinger, 1993) are calculated and the results are tabulated in Table 16.4. Clearly, our method can generate the identical equilibrium state as Stillinger's.

The Fibonacci sequence is also widely used in the protein folding experiment. We optimize two Fibonacci sequences whose length is 13 and 34. Results are depicted in Figure 16.1, and the obtained best solutions are listed as follows:

S13: 1.4914; 1.5000; -0.8687; 1.4796; 1.5191; -1.4658; 1.9532; -1.4487; 1.5165; 1.4827; -1.0415

S34: 0.2266; 0.4312; 1.8654; 0.7870; -0.0496; -1.8094; 1.9356; -0.1943; 1.4288; 1.3829; -1.8439; 0.8788; 1.3739; -1.5179; 1.9411; -0.0340; -0.2539; 0.4633; -0.6113; 1.9571; -1.7060; -0.1293; 0.9454; 1.8076; 0.3205; 0.3784; -1.3029; 0.0365; 0.7215; -0.1987; 0.5119; -0.3637

Finally, we conduct our method on real protein sequences. When sequence becomes long, the determination of the objective function value is extremely time-consuming. So only two real protein sequences: 1BXP and 1EDP are discussed here.

Table 16.4 SAPOA Results for Short Sequences

Sequence	APOA	Sequence	APOA
AAA	−0.65821	AAAAA	−2.84828
AAB	0.03223	AAAAB	−1.58944
ABA	−0.65821	AAABA	−2.44493
ABB	0.03223	AAABB	−0.54688
BAB	−0.03027	AABAA	−2.53170
BBB	−0.03027	AABAB	−1.34774
		AABBA	−0.92662
AAAA	−1.67633	AABBB	0.04017
AAAB	−0.58527	ABAAB	−1.37647
AABA	−1.45098	ABABA	−2.22020
AABB	0.06720	ABABB	−0.61680
ABAB	−0.64938	ABBAB	−0.00565
ABBA	−0.03617	ABBBA	−0.39804
ABBB	0.00470	ABBBB	−0.06596
BAAB	0.06172	BAAAB	−0.52108
BABB	−0.00078	BAABB	0.09621
BBBB	−0.13974	BABAB	−0.64803
		BABBB	−0.18266
		BBABB	−0.24020
		BBBBB	−0.45266
AABABB	−1.361979	AAABAA	−3.697501

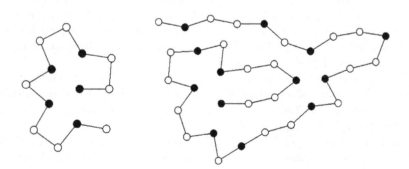

Figure 16.1 Predicted structures of Fibonacci sequences.

The obtained structures are displayed in Figure 16.2 and the obtained best solutions are listed as follows:

1BXP: −1.9281; 0.3913; −1.5180; −1.4950; 0.5099; 0.8061; −0.8181; −1.7897; −0.6548; 0.4825; 0.1258; 0.8396; 0.8442; 1.7371; 0.1294

1EDP: −1.9282; 0.3913; −1.5181; −1.4951; 0.5099; 0.8062; −0.8181; −1.7897; −0.6548; 0.4825; 0.1258; 0.8397; 0.8443; 1.7371; 0.1294

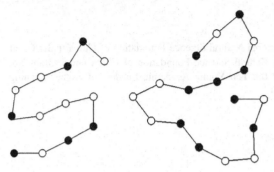

Figure 16.2 Predicted structures of real sequences.

16.4 Conclusion

In general, most bio-inspired computation was focused on physical/chemical laws and animal social behaviors, and little attention was paid on plant growing process (some results can be found in (Li et al., 2005; Murase, 2009)). Unlike animals, plants need broader incidence of growth, which reveals that the growing process of plant may provide a different path to solve optimization problems due to its self-organization and self-learning.

In this chapter, a new algorithm inspired by plant growth process is proposed. Photosynthesis operator, phototropism operator, and apical dominance operator are designed. Photosynthesis is a process used by plants to convert the light energy into chemical energy. During this process, energies generated by different branches may be distinct, yielding various growing speeds. On the other hand, phototropism is directional growth in which the growing speed is determined by the light source. Inspired by these two phenomena, the methodology of primary APOA is developed. Each branch represents a potential solution and updates with the corresponding equations. Photosynthesis operator is dedicated to obtaining the energies while phototropism operator guides the growing directions. The quality of this algorithm is verified by training the ANN. Numerical results are perfectly matched to the predictions from existing literatures.

This PAPOA is limited to the high-dimensional problems since some important factors are ignored. Therefore, a new phototropism operator is designed in which branches are divided into two types: growing-motion branch and maturing-motion branch. Different growing process is generated based on the type of branches. Furthermore, apical dominance mechanism is also incorporated into the methodology. To avoid the confusion, we designate this new algorithm as standard APOA (SAPOA). To verify the performance, SAPOA is adopted to solve toy model of protein folding (Stillinger and Gordon, 1995). Simulation results are consistent with reported numerical data, indicating that the new optimization approach is valid and exhibits its potentially broad applications in other fields.

Acknowledgment

This paper was supported by the National Natural Science Foundation of China under Grant No. 61003053, the Shanxi Province Natural Science Foundation of China under Grant No. 2011011012-1, and the Program for the Top Young Academic Leaders of Higher Leaning Institutions of Shanxi.

References

Bryant, D.A., Frigaard, N.U., 2006. Prokaryotic photosynthesis and phototrophy illuminate. Trends Microbiol. 14 (11), 488−496.

Cui, Z.H., Cai, X.J., 2011. Optimal coverage configuration with social emotional optimisation algorithm in wireless sensor networks. Inter. J. Wireless Mobile Comput. 5 (1), 43−47.

Cui, Z.H., Yang, C.X., Sanyal, S., 2012a. Training artificial neural networks using APPM. Inter. J. Wireless Mobile Comput. 5 (2), 168−174.

Cui, Z.H., Cai, X.J., Zeng, J.C., 2012b. A new stochastic algorithm to direct orbits of chaotic systems. Inter. J. Comput. Appl. Technol. 43 (4), 366−371.

Cui, Z.H., Liu, D.M., Zeng, J.C, Shi, Z.Z., 2012c. Using splitting artificial plant optimization algorithm to solve toy model of protein folding. J. Comput. Theor. Nanosci. 9 (12), 2255−2259.

Dai, C.H., Chen, W.R., Zhu, Y.F., Zhang, X.X., 2009. Seeker optimization algorithm for optimal reactive power dispatch. IEEE Trans. Power Syst. 24 (3), 1218−1231.

Dill, K.A., 1985. Theory for the folding and stability of globular proteins. Biochemistry. 24 (6), 1501−1509.

Dorigo, M., Birattari, M., Stutzle, T., 2006. Ant colony optimization—artificial ants as a computational intelligence technique. IEEE Comput. Intell. Mag. 1 (4), 28−39.

Eberhart, R., Kennedy, J., 1995. New optimizer using particle swarm theory. Proceedings of the Sixth International Symposium on Micro Machine and Human Science. IEEE CS Press, Nagoya, Japan, pp. 39−43.

Gandomi, A.H., Alavi, A.H., 2012. Krill herd: a new bio-inspired optimization algorithm. Commun. Nonlinear Sci. Numer. Simul. 17 (12), 4831−4845.

He, S., 2010. Training artificial neural networks using Lévy group search optimizer. J. Mult. Valued Logic Soft Comput. 6 (6), 527−545.

Kennedy, J., Eberhart, R., 1995. Particle swarm optimization. In: Proceedings of IEEE International Conference on Neural Networks. IEEE CS Press, Perth, WA, Australia, pp. 1942−1948.

Leung, F.H.F., Lam, H.K., Ling, S.H., Tam, P.K.S., 2003. Tuning of the structure and parameters of a neural network using an improved genetic algorithm. IEEE Trans. Neural Netw. 14 (1), 79−88.

Li, T., Wang, C.F., Wang, W.B., Su, W.L., 2005. A global optimization bionics algorithm for solving integer programming—plant growth simulation algorithm. Syst. Eng. Theory Appl. 1 (1), 76−85 (in Chinese).

Murase, H., 2009. Finite element inverse analysis using a photosynthetic algorithm. Comput. Electron. Agric. 29 (1−2), 115−123.

Piao, Y.Z., Qiang, Y., 2007. Comparison of a new model of light response of photosynthesis with traditional models. J. Shenyang Agric. Univ. 38 (6), 771−775 (in Chinese).

Prechelt, L., 1994. Problem1 — A Set of Neural Network Benchmark Problems and Benchmarking Rules. Technical Report 21, Fakultat fur Informatik Universitat Karlsruhe, 76128 Karlsruhe, Germany.

Stillinger, F.H., Gordon, T.H., Hirshfeld, C.L., 1993. Toy model for protein folding. Phys. Rev. E. 48, 1469–1477.

Stillinger, F.H., Gordon, T.H., 1995. Collective aspects of protein folding illustrated by a toy model. Phys. Rev. E. 52 (3), 2872–2877.

Xie, L.P., Tan, Y., Zeng, J.C., Cui, Z.H., 2010. Artificial physics optimisation: a brief survey. Inter. J. Bio-Inspired Comput. 2 (5), 291–302.

Yang, X.S., 2010. Firefly algorithm, stochastic test functions and design optimization. Inter. J. Bio-Inspired Comput. 2 (2), 78–84.

Yao, X., Liu, Y., 1999. A new evolutionary system for evolving artificial neural networks. IEEE Trans. Neural Netw. 8 (3), 694–713.

17 Genetic Algorithm for the Dynamic Berth Allocation Problem in Real Time

Carlos Arango, Pablo Cortés, Alejandro Escudero and Luis Onieva

Ingeniería de Organización, Engineering School of Seville, University of Seville, Camino de los Descubrimientos s/n 41092, Seville, Spain

17.1 Introduction

Ports are important nodes in intermodal transport networks. According to the International Maritime Organization more than 90% of world trade is transported by sea and almost 80% is transported in containers. For that reason all operations of a container terminal (CT) must be optimized (Ambrosino et al., 2004). Some of the main operations are defined by the following problems: container premarshalling problem, landside transport, stowage planning problem, and yard allocation problem. All of them have been tackled in surveys, such as Voß and Stahlbock (2004) and Steenken and Voß (2008), which are probably the most complete existing reviews. Figure 17.1 shows a classification of the main port operations. This flowchart represents the normal containers flow inside the CT; the operations are grouped according to the handling resources and process. We consider three principal groups with eight operations in total.

Several authors, such as Notteboom (2007), affirm that is not possible to solve all the operations in a global way due to the high complexity of the global problem. In fact, the literature provides lots of works, each of them addressing a specific operation due to the large number of variables and parameters involved in each of the problems (all of them NP-hard problems).

This work focuses on the first operation during the ship planning process, which is called the "berth allocation problem" (BAP), but we will consider general aspects of two more operations that are directly related. They are the quay crane scheduling problem (QCSP) and the yard allocation one.

When a ship arrives to the CT, the planners take into account its basic characteristics such as size, number of containers to be unloaded and loaded, and the

Swarm Intelligence and Bio-Inspired Computation. DOI: http://dx.doi.org/10.1016/B978-0-12-405163-8.00017-X

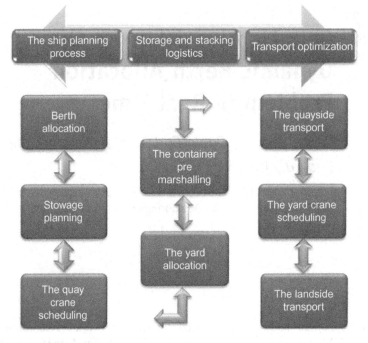

Figure 17.1 Operations of a CT.

locations of these containers in the storage area (SA), in order to decide the best berth allocation. This information is used in advance to plan the berth allocation and considers:

- Containers export (load) localization in the SA. This must be as close as possible to the berth allocation, and also the reservation of space in the SA for those containers to be unloaded.
- Planning time to be used for each dock segment according to the ships arrived.

The objective of the BAP problem is to minimize the total service time, which includes waiting time of the ship to come in port and loading and unloading time (operation time).

The optimization, management, and control of CT operations are very complex tasks (Polo and Diaz, 2006). This complexity is inherent to the nature of terminal related processes and in the need to ensure high receptivity levels. In such context, the capability of CTs resources and facilities to support different sizes of ships, the optimal dock design and the ability to improve decision-making are crucial aspects. Regarding the ship size, important advances have been made and the load capacity of ships has increased considerably. In fact, now the capacity of the largest containerships in the world is up to 12,000 twenty-foot equivalent units (TEUs) with lengths greater than 350 m and service speed up to 25 knots allowing a travel time of 4 days between China and the US west coast.

Moreover, the small vessels which make short trips cannot be neglected; this type of transportation is well known as Short Sea Shipping (SSS) and is supported by many governments and international institutions promoting the reduction of environmental impacts. Several research works dealing with SSS can be found in the literature, that is, Paixao and Marlow (2002) present the main strengths and weaknesses of SSS whereas Martinez and Olivella (2005) discuss specific opportunities for SSS. As mentioned above, to ensure high levels of receptivity and manage vessels of variable size optimally, an excellent dock design is required.

In this work, we propose an optimization model to solve a dynamic berth allocation problem (DBAP) that considers as optimality criterion the minimization of the operating time of each ship in a specific time period. A Spanish port is used as simulation scenario to carry out the validation of the models. We develop a genetic algorithm to solve the mixed integer model under three different situations. In the following section we summarize the main works relations to the BAP (Section 17.2) and then we explain the optimization models detailing the mathematical formulation (Section 17.3). Section 17.4 depicts the characteristics of the implemented genetic algorithm. Simulation results are detailed in Section 17.5. Finally, the main conclusions and future work are addressed.

17.2 Literature Review

The DBAP approach is a problem arising in hub CTs due to the management of vessels of variable size. Imai et al. (2005a,b) define two dock design strategies: one is based on a discrete location with fixed points for berths while the other is based on a continuous location with no fixed points for berths. The continuous location strategy ensures higher flexibility and allows different kinds of ships being allocated to docks, so the authors have decided to adopt it in this research work.

Several authors have approached the BAP problem. For example, Imai et al. (2001), and Nishimura et al. (2001) determine the BAP as a DBAP, which is a generalization of the static berth allocation problem (SBAP). They propose a genetic algorithm in public berth systems which can be adapted to real-world application. Cordeau et al. (2005) addressed a DBAP with time windows for both discrete and continuous cases based upon data from a terminal in the port of Gioia Tauro. The problem was formulated as a multiple depot vehicle routing problem with time windows (MDVRPTW), and solved by a tabu search heuristic.

Park and Kim (2003), Liu et al. (2006), and Lim (1998) consider BAP and QCSP as a single problem making berth scheduling dependent on the crane number that is assigned to the ship. Arango et al. (2011) consider de BAP with first-come-first-served (FCFS) allocation strategy. Imai et al. (2008) approach BAP in a multiuser container terminal (MUT). They solve the BAP by genetic algorithms at a port with indented berths, where megacontainerships and feeder ships are served for higher berth productivity.

Imai et al. (2003, 2007a,b) consider the relations between the ports and shipping lines. In the first work they addressed the case of vessel operators that claim high priority services; the authors have named this problem as a BAP with service priority. Lee and Wang (2010) integrated discrete berth allocation and QCSP, and formulated the problem as a mixed integer programming model. A genetic algorithm is proposed to obtain solutions which were compared with lower bounds. Giallombardo et al. (2010) combined tabu search and mathematical programming to solve a new model of berth allocation and quay crane assignment problem. Barros et al. (2011) developed and analyzed a berth allocation model with tidal time windows, where ships can only be served by berths during those time windows. Buhrkal et al. (2011) studied several mathematical programming formulations of the DBAP, and compared their performance via computational experiments.

17.3   Optimization Model

In this section we explain the proposed model to solve the DBAP. The models are adapted to a hub CT. Figure 17.2 shows the layout for the case of study depicting the most important areas.

a. Trains area: This area is composed of the railway coming to the CT and therefore allows trains to achieve the operations of loading and unloading containers.

b. Trucks area: This area is the gateway for land transport.

c. Storage area: The main objective is to store containers waiting to be loaded and dispatched by sea or land transport.

d. Ships operation area: This corresponds to the docks where ships berth at the CT.

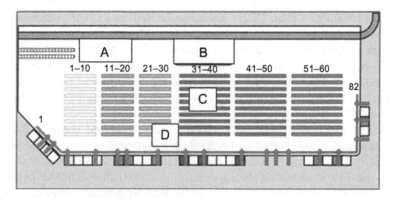

Figure 17.2 Layout of the CT.

The scenario under study is a real system and corresponds to the Algeciras CT, which is one of the most important ports of Europe. This terminal is located in the Juan Carlos I Quay and its main characteristics are:

- Covers area: 686,132 m²
- Container capacity: 10,476 TEUs (20-foot containers)
- Beth line: 1941 m with 14−16 m draughts.
- Portainer cranes: 20 (10 of them post-Panamax, 4×70 tm, 4×65 tm, 6×50 tm, 6×40 tm)
- Transtainer—RTG: 46 (19×61 tm, 19×40 tm, 8×32 tm).

This information, along with all the data for the optimization model development, (resources, facilities and traffic data like arrival dates, departure dates, unload containers numbers, load containers numbers, etc.) have been taken from the annual report of the Port Authority of Algeciras 2010. Table 17.1 shows an abstract on freight traffic (159 ships came to the port in October). The 159 containerships transported 214,065 TEUs and 88.7% of this freight traffic was transit traffic toward other ports; therefore, the Algeciras terminal container is considered a singular hub CT due to its characteristics and relevance in maritime transport.

Every time that a ship arrives to the system, the model searches the best possible berth allocation for loading and unloading its containers, and determines the amount of quay cranes to be assigned to it. It takes into account the location of the containers load and unloads in the storage area and the availability of resources. The model takes into account the following assumptions:

- The dock is divided into 82 segments of 24 m each.
- Three types of ships are considered, small vessels; whose length does not exceed 8 segments, medium-sized ship with a length between 8 and 14 segments, and large ships with a length between 15 and 17 segments.
- As quay cranes move on the same railway, possible interferences between displacements are considered.
- Only 40 ft standards containers size is considered.
- The maximum number of working sections per ship is three.
- The staking plan is known
- One free segment between two ships in operation at minimum is considered.
- The model will decide on which container block in the storage area will be unloaded the containers. The precise location (microsimulation) is not considered in this work.

Table 17.1 Freight Traffic

Traffic	Total 2010	October 2010	Represent (%)
Total TEUs	2,810,242	214,065	7.62
Transit TEUs	2,493,872	195,852	7.85
Import TEUs	81,323	8829	10.86
Export TEUs	86,439	9384	10.86
Containerships	2308	159	6.89

Given the previous considerations, the DBAP may be formulated as follows:

17.3.1 Sets

B	Number of ships where $b \in B$
M	Segments of docks
T	Time horizon where $t \in T$
S	Storage sections in the ship where $s \in S$
G	Number of quay crane where $j \in G$
C	Number of container blocks in the storage area where $c \in C$
I,E	Index by import and export container

17.3.2 Parameters

h_b	Quay crane time needs for the ship b
L_b	Length of ship b
A_{bs}	Vector with a length equal to s for each ship b. It shows integer figures if ship section has containers for loading/unloading and zero otherwise. The integer number is the same that the section number.
m_b	Maximum limit of available quay crane for ship b. Limit is equal to work sections in the ship b.
g_{jt}	Position of the quay crane j in the time t.
CI_{bs}	Containers to be imported in the section s of the ship b.
CE_{bs}	Containers to be exported in the section s of the ship b.
d_{mc}	Distance between the container block c and the dock segment m.
PE_{bc}	Binary vector with a length equal to c for each ship b. It takes a value equal to 1 to show the block c where are being stored containers to be exported in ship b.
K_c	Available space for containers in the block c.

17.3.3 Decision Variables

X_b	Dock segment assigned to ship b, the ship tip is located in this segment
T_b	Initial time for handling operations in ship b.
B_{bmt}	Binary variable. It takes a value equal to 1 if the ship b is located in segment m in the time t and 0 otherwise.
G_{bsjt}	Binary variable. It takes a value equal to 1 if the section s of the ship b is operated with the quay crane j in the time t and 0 otherwise.
PI_{bc}	Binary variable. It takes a value equal to 1 if the containers of ship b are located in the block c and 0 otherwise.

Minimize

$$\sum_{b=1}^{B}\sum_{m=1}^{M}\sum_{t=1}^{T}\sum_{s=1}^{S}\sum_{c=1}^{C}(B_{bmt}^{*}CE_{bs}^{*}d_{mc}^{*}PE_{bc}) + (B_{bmt}^{*}CI_{bs}^{*}d_{mc}^{*}PI_{bc})$$
$$+ (G_{bsjt}^{*}|g_{jt} - [X_b + (A_{bs} - 1)]|)$$

(17.1)

Subject to:

$$\sum_{b=1}^{B} B_{bmt} \leq 1 \quad \forall m = 1 \ldots M, \, \forall t = 1 \ldots T \tag{17.2}$$

$$\sum_{m=1}^{M} B_{bmt} = L_b \quad \forall b = 1 \ldots B, \, \forall t = 1 \ldots T \tag{17.3}$$

$$B_{bmt} \leq B_{b(m+1)t} \quad \forall m = 1 \ldots (X_b + L_b - 1), \, \forall t = 1 \ldots T, \, \forall b = 1, \ldots, B \tag{17.4}$$

$$\sum_{b=1}^{B} \sum_{s=1}^{S} \sum_{j=1}^{G} G_{bsjt} \leq G \quad \forall t = 1 \ldots T \tag{17.5}$$

$$X_b + l_b \leq M \quad \forall b = 1 \ldots B \tag{17.6}$$

$$K_c \geq \left(\sum_{S=1}^{3} \mathrm{CI}_{bS} \right) * PI_{bc} - \left(\sum_{S=1}^{3} \mathrm{CE}_{bS} \right) * PE_{bc} \quad \forall b = 1 \ldots B, \, \forall c = 1 \ldots C \tag{17.7}$$

$$\sum_{j=1}^{G} \sum_{s=1}^{S} G_{bsjt} \geq 1 \quad \forall b = 1 \ldots B, \, \forall t = 1 \ldots T \tag{17.8}$$

$$\sum_{j=1}^{G} \sum_{s=1}^{S} G_{bsjt} \leq m_b \quad \forall b = 1 \ldots B, \, \forall t = 1 \ldots T \tag{17.9}$$

$$\sum_{j=1}^{G} \sum_{t=0}^{T} G_{bit}^* 1/W \geq h_b \quad \forall b = 1 \ldots B \tag{17.10}$$

$$G_{bsjt} - G_{bs(j+1)t} \leq M(G_{bs(j+1)t} - G_{bs(j+2)t}) \quad \forall b = 1 \ldots B, \, \forall j = 1 \ldots G, \\ \forall s = 1 \ldots S, \, \forall t = 1 \ldots T \tag{17.11}$$

$$B_{bmt} = \{0, 1\} \quad \forall\, b = 1\ldots B,\ \forall\, m = 1\ldots M,\ \forall\, t = 1\ldots T \tag{17.12}$$

$$PI_{bc} = \{0, 1\} \quad \forall\, b = 1\ldots B,\ \forall\, c = 1\ldots C \tag{17.13}$$

$$PE_{bc} = (0, 1) \quad \forall\, b = 1\ldots B,\ \forall\, c = 1\ldots C \tag{17.14}$$

$$X_b \geq 0 \text{ integer } \forall\, b = 1\ldots B \tag{17.15}$$

$$G_{bsjt} = \{0, 1\}\, \forall\, b = 1\ldots B,\ \forall\, s = 1\ldots S,\ \forall\, j = 1\ldots G,\ \forall\, t = 1\ldots T \tag{17.16}$$

$$K_c \geq 0 \text{ integer } \forall\, c = 1\ldots C \tag{17.17}$$

$$T_b \geq 0 \text{ integer } \forall\, b = 1\ldots B \tag{17.18}$$

The objective function (Eq. 17.1) minimizes the distances traveled by the fork-lifts and the quay cranes for the container loading and unloading operations. These distances are directly linked to the times due to the handling operations carried out in each ship arriving at the CT. Therefore, it minimizes three aspects: (i) traveled distances between the dock segments and the container blocks carrying the export containers, (ii) traveled distances between the container blocks and the dock segments carrying the import containers, and (iii) traveled distances by quay crane displacements in the work sections.

Constraint (17.2) ensures that each segment m can only be assigned to a ship b in the time t. Constraint (17.3) guarantees that the number of segments used by each ship is equal to its length during the operation time. Constraint (17.4) forces that the segments assigned to the each ship will be consecutive.

Constraint (17.5) ensures that the sum of assigned quay cranes depends on the maximum amount of available quay cranes in the port. Constraint (17.6) guarantees the amount of docks segments allocated to each ship with respect to maximum limit. Constraint (17.7) guarantees that the available capacity in block c that has been assigned for storing the containers of ship b has to be greater than the number of containers to be stored in this block.

Constraints (17.8) and (17.9) ensure the minimum and maximum limits with respect to the amount of allocated quay cranes for each ship. Constraint (17.10) guarantees that the quay cranes assigned to each ship complete its workload. Constraint (17.11) forces that the quay cranes assigned to the each ship will be consecutive. Finally, Eqs. (17.12)–(17.18) determine the specifications for integer variables.

17.4 Solution Procedure by Genetic Algorithm

To solve the proposed mixed integer lineal programming model, we propose a genetic algorithm. A genetic algorithm is a search heuristic that reproduces the process of natural evolution. This heuristic is routinely used to generate feasible solutions to optimization and search problems. This bio-inspired approach is similar to the biologically inspired algorithm used by Gandomi and Alavi (2012), and Gandomi et al. (2013). Genetic algorithms belong to the larger class of evolutionary algorithm, which generate solutions to optimization problems using techniques bio-inspired by natural evolution, such as inheritance, mutation, selection, and crossover.

The genetic algorithm is run every time that a containership arrives to the CT. Each obtained solution applies to the ship that has just arrived and the rest of ships waiting in queue for free segments of dock, so reallocation are possible. Therefore, we use the genetic algorithm with a dynamic approach.

17.4.1 Representation

Instead of using the traditional binary bit representation, chromosomes are represented as charter strings. Figure 17.3 shows a generic chromosome representation for berth allocation. The chromosome used for the berths programming is composed of 60 bits, which are grouped into 6 representing a gene (ship in the port). The bit 1 of each group represents the location of the dock where the ship initial section was located, bit 2 shows the number of assigned cranes which is complemented by bits 3, 4, and 5 stating which specific cranes are assigned. Finally, bit 6 determines the block number in the storage area where the unloaded containers are stored. The population is conformed for 60 chromosomes.

17.4.2 Fitness

The fitness of every individual is calculated as the sum of the operation times by each ship waiting in queue for free segments of dock. The total time corresponds to: (i) times due to the required transport between the container blocks and the dock segments carrying the export containers, (ii) times due to the required transport between the container blocks and the dock segments carrying the import containers, and (iii) times due to required travels by quay cranes displacements in the work sections. The objective function of the optimization model represents the

Figure 17.3 Chromosome representation.

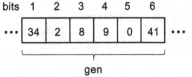

fitness function. The GA is resolved 100 times before organizing individuals based on their fitness.

The DBAP is a minimization problem; thus, lower fitness values lead to lower objective function values. To deal with this fact, the fitness function is defined as the reciprocal of the objective function following the Kim and Kim (1996) suggestion.

17.4.3 Selection of Parents and Genetic Operators

The selection criterion to choose the parents in the population was based on the fitness of the individuals. Those fitter individuals have a higher priority to be selected with a discrete probability. This mechanism leads to a faster convergence of the GA.

Genetic operators implemented were crossover and mutation. Tests were carried out with different probabilities for crossover and mutation operators. In case of mutation, it was found that varying the probability from 50% to 100% had little effect on performance. With a value of 80–90% being marginally optimal for tests carried out. A value of 90% is used in the main replications. For crossover, values between 10% and 20% were seen to be giving better results than typically smaller values. A value of 10% is used in the main replications in order to enrich the genetic variety of the population.

17.4.4 Mutation

The reproduced chromosomes constitute a new population and mutation is performed to introduce new chromosomes. The process is divided into two steps: step 1 takes a single individual from the population making a random selection. Then its information is stored in the array *offspring*; step 2 changes the information in bits 1, 2, and 6 (location of the dock, quay cranes, and block, respectively). Settings remain subject to various relevant constraints of the model that are conditioned by bits 1, 2, and 6. Figure 17.4 shows the mutation operation.

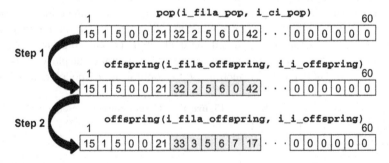

Figure 17.4 Mutation operation.

17.4.5 Crossover

The chromosome representation states six bits (a gen stating the ship in the port). So, the crossover operation can be undertaken only over those individuals with at least two genes different from zero, in other words when there are at least two containerships in the waiting queue. Figure 17.5 shows an example of crossover operator.

The optimization model is solved as many times as a ship arrives at the port. Finally, the algorithm provides as the better solution, that one that has reached a better fitness value within the population.

17.5 Results and Analysis

As it has been previously introduced, computational experiments have been carried out in one of the most relevant Spanish ports (the Algeciras port and its CT). To do so, we have introduced two specifics constraints (17.19) and (17.20) in the general model presented in Section 17.2 (such constraints model specific morphologies of the Algeciras CT). These constraints are the following:

$$B_{b8t} + B_{b9t} = 1 \quad \forall\, b = 1 \ldots B, \quad \forall\, t = 1 \ldots T \tag{17.19}$$

$$B_{b70t} + B_{b71t} = 1 \quad \forall\, b = 1 \ldots B, \quad \forall\, t = 1 \ldots T \tag{17.20}$$

These constraints are complementing to constraints (17.3) and (17.4). The aim is guarantee that the segments 8−9 and 70−71 cannot be consecutive allocated, due to these segment are in a corner.

We produced three different scenarios to verify and validate the optimization model proposal. The initial scenario takes the input data from historical recorded by the Algeciras terminal arrivals in October 2010 (which is available at the Algeciras port web site, www.apba.es). The information includes the arrival times and lengths of ships. The remaining information such as the number of sections of

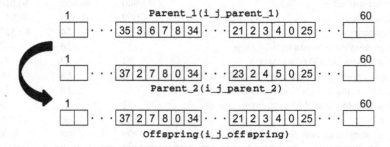

Figure 17.5 Crossover operation.

work and container to load and unload are calculated according to the real freight traffic.

For the second scenario, the parameters that determine the arrival times by ship are constant with respect to the initial scenario, but increasing the number of containers carried by each ship. For the third scenario, the parameters that determine the number of containers and sections by ship are constant with respect to the initial scenario, but it increases in 20 the number of ship arrivals to CT, which represents an increase of 12.5%. The time of arrival of these vessels has been randomly taken within the time frame set at 1 month, as well as its length.

We undertook three model replications for each considered scenario, resulting in a total of nine replications. In this section we report the results obtained for the first replication obtained in each scenario.

Table 17.2 summarizes the freight traffic for each scenario. The considered horizon is 30 days, and we can see that the increase of containers moved in scenario 2 with respect to 1 is almost 21% that is near to the increase in scenario 3 (20%). Scenario 3 considers increases of ship arrivals at a rate of 12.5%.

Figures 17.6−17.8 show the total hours of operation by dock segment, the sections with a higher number of hours worked are grouped into the center of the docks. This is due to the special morphology of the Algeciras port that is shown in Figure 17.1.

In the three previous figures we can see that certain sections present the highest workload because these sections are located very close to the ways between the container blocks in the storage area. These ways are used by all the vehicles for transporting the containers within the CT.

The Quay cranes workload has been analyzed also, in fact it is very important to schedule this resource properly for maintenance activities. Figure 17.9 shows the containers handled for each crane and it is possible to notice that cranes number 1 and 2 have the lowest workload owing to their localization in the initial dock line.

Table 17.2 Ships and Containers by Scenario

Counters	Scenario 1	Scenario 2	Scenario 3
Container unload	33,940	40,855	40,610
Container load	34,049	41,309	40,917
Total containers	67,989	82,164	81,527
Average number of containers by ship	427	516	513
Ships with less of 300 containers	24	27	37
Ships with containers between 300 and 500	88	68	90
Ships with containers between 500 and 700	16	18	15
Ships with more than 700 containers	32	47	38
Ship arrivals	160	160	180
Average number of containers handled by quay crane	3399	4108	4076

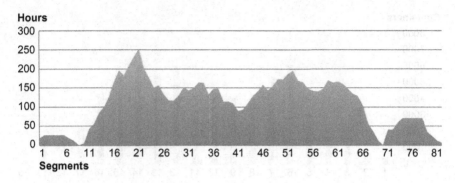

Figure 17.6 Workload by each segment in hours for scenario 1.

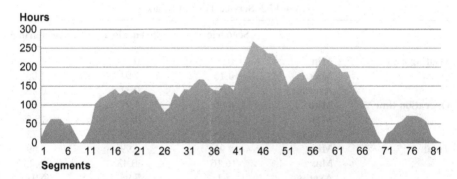

Figure 17.7 Workload by each segment in hours for scenario 2.

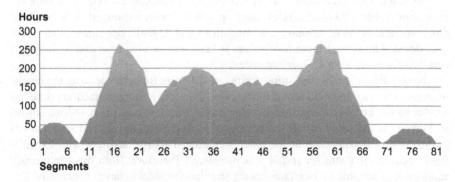

Figure 17.8 Workload by each segment in hours for scenario 3.

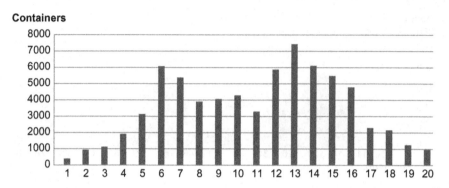

Figure 17.9 Quay cranes workload.

Table 17.3 Service Time in Hours

		Scenario 1	Scenario 2	Scenario 3
Waiting time	**Min**	0	0	0
	Max	4.15	7.91	4.05
	Average	0.25	0.31	0.25
Operation time	**Min**	4.96	4.99	4.69
	Max	15.96	19.24	15.8
	Average	6.85	7.65	6.72
Total	**Min**	4.96	4.99	4.69
	Max	16.16	20.43	16.33
	Average	7.1	7.98	6.97

The objective of the optimization model is to minimize the operation time for each ship. Table 17.3 summarizes ships operations times expressed in hours; handling operations time, resources waiting time and logistic operations time were considered. The sum of these time values is known as service time and is an important data for evaluating CT performances.

The containers' traffic and ships' traffic are different for each scenario; the results in terms of service time are also different. However, the minimum handling time has similar values because the probability that a ship with few containers to load/unload will arrive, is the same for all the scenarios. Furthermore, the second scenario has the worst results compared to the other scenarios. This is consistent with expectations because the container traffic was increased. Therefore, from this preliminary analysis, it is possible to ascertain that the simulation model behaves coherently.

The results show that although container traffic was increased in scenarios 2 and 3 by 21%, the average operation time was reduced by 8% for the third scenario.

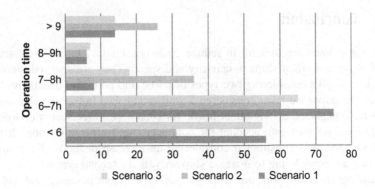

Figure 17.10 Ships according the service time.

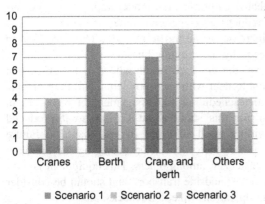

Figure 17.11 Main bottlenecks.

This reduction was due to the allocation of such new container traffic in 20 new ships arriving to the CT.

To complement the service time table, Figure 17.10 shows the number of ships classified in seven time ranges according to the service time. The first range is for those with less than 6 h and the second range is for those with 6−7 h. It can be appreciated that these two ranges represent more than 70% of arrivals to the CT.

The main causes of waiting time were studied. As reported in Figure 17.11, the main bottleneck in the Algeciras CT is the berth and its bottleneck effect increases when the traffic increases. Lastly, the bottleneck called "Others" represents other resources less important for this study, such as Tugboats, Trucks, Forklifts, etc.

The numerical experimentations were performed on a personal computer equipped with 3 GB of RAM and 2.1 GHz Intel dual core processor. The average run time for each scenario was 17 min and 57 s. The simulation includes the ship arrivals between 160 and 180; therefore, the genetic algorithm was used the same time. The average run time for the algorithm was approximately 2.07 s, with a maximum of 4.12 s and a minimum of 1.17 s.

17.6 Conclusion

The shipping lines are looking to reduce costs constantly. One of their actuation lines is to improve their ships in capacity and speed. They are also redesigning the transport networks considering two types of ports; hub ports and destination/source ports. In our paper we have considered a well-established hub port: Algeciras port and we have analyzed the container traffic for such port. Three scenarios were considered. First, we took into account the container ship traffic in October 2010; the second scenario was constructed considering an increase in the traffic containers; finally, we are considering to increase ship arrivals for second scenario.

Analyzing such hub port, our work focuses on efficient planning and use of the docks to increase its competitiveness and status for the port. An optimization model supporting berth allocation has been constructed and presented, and allows improving internal organization and operations management.

The results allow us to affirm that our optimization model improves the performance of the port in its CT. The reduction of operation times at berths has been valued in an 8% according to an increase of the traffic by 21%. This reduction in the operation time is perceived directly by the shipping lines.

From a computational perspective, the obtained results allow us to affirm that genetic algorithms are valuable tools to deal with such problems, and they include great potential of application for the scheduling and assignment of resources in ports in general and in particular for this study about CTs. Also it produced suitable computational effort providing good solutions in less than 3 s. Future works make necessary to offer proposals also focused on managing the handling equipment such as forklifts and reachstacker, among others. This equipment is used mainly by the quayside transport and the landside transport, and should be consider in order to minimize costs, handling operations time, bottlenecks, etc.

References

Ambrosino, D., Scimachen, A., Tanfani, E., 2004. A decomposition heuristics for the container ship stowage problem. J. Heuristics. 12, 211–233.

Arango, C., Cortés, P., Muñuzuri, J., Onieva, L., 2011. Berth allocation planning in Seville inland port by simulation and optimization. Adv. Eng. Inform. 25, 452–461.

Barros, V.H., Costa, T.S., Oliveira, A.C.M., Lorena, L.A.N., 2011. Model and heuristic for berth allocation in tidal bulk ports with stock level constraints. Comput. Ind. Eng. 60 (4), 606–613.

Buhrkal, K., Zuglian, S., Ropke, S., Larsen, J., Lusby, R., 2011. Models for the discrete berth allocation problem: a computational comparison. Trans. Res. Part E. 47 (4), 461–473.

Cordeau, J.F., Laporte, G., Legato, P., Moccia, L., 2005. Models and tabu search heuristics for the berth-allocation problem. Trans. Sci. 39 (4), 526–538.

Gandomi, A.H., Alavi, A.H., 2012. Krill herd: a new bio-inspired optimization algorithm. Commun. Nonlin. Sci. Numer. Simul. 17 (12), 4831–4845.

Gandomi, A.H., Yang, X.S., Talatahari, S., Alavi, A.H., 2013. Metaheuristics in modeling and optimization. In: Gandomi, A.H., Yang, X.S., Talatahari, S., Alavi, A.H. (Eds.), Metaheuristic Applications in Structures and Infrastructures. Elsevier, Waltham, MA, doi: 10.1016/B978-0-12-398364-0.00001-2, (Chapter 1).

Giallombardo, G., Moccia, L., Salani, M., Vacca, I., 2010. Modeling and solving the tactical berth allocation problem. Trans. Res. Part B. 44 (1), 232−245.

Imai, A., Nishimura, E., Papadimitriou, S., 2001. The dynamic berth allocation problem for a container port. Trans. Res. Part B. 35, 401−417.

Imai, A., Nishimura, E., Papadimitriou, S., 2003. Berth allocation with service priority. Trans. Res. Part B. 37 (5), 437−457.

Imai, A., Sun, X., Nishimura, E., Papadimitriou, S., 2005a. Berth allocation in a container port: using a continuous location space approach. Trans. Res. Part B. 39, 199−221.

Imai, A., Sun, X., Nishimura, E., Papadimitriou, S., 2005b. Berth allocation in a container port: using a continuous location space approach. Trans. Res. Part B. 39 (3), 199−221.

Imai, A., Nishimura, E., Hattori, M., Papadimitriou, S., 2007a. Berth allocation at indented berths for mega-containerships. Eur. J. Oper. Res. 179 (2), 579−593.

Imai, A., Zhang, J.T., Nishimura, E., Papadimitriou, S., 2007b. The berth allocation problem with service time and delay time objectives. Marit. Econ. Logistics. 9 (4), 269−290.

Imai, A., Nishimura, E., Papadimitriou, S., 2008. Berthing ships at a multi-user container terminal with a limited quay capacity. Trans. Res. Part E. 44 (1), 136−151.

Kim, J.-U., Kim, Y.-D., 1996. Simulated annealing and genetic algortihms for scheduling products with multi-level product structure. Comput. Oper. Res. 23, 857−868.

Lee, D.H., Wang, H.Q., 2010. Integrated discrete berth allocation and quay crane scheduling in port container terminals. Eng. Optim. 42 (8), 747−761.

Lim, A., 1998. The berth planning problem. Oper. Res. Lett. 22, 105−110.

Liu, J., Wan, Y.-w., Wang, L., 2006. Quay crane scheduling at container terminals to minimize the maximum relative tardiness of vessel departures. Naval Res. Logistics. 53, 60−74.

Martinez, F., Olivella, J., 2005. Short sea shipping opportunities for the pyrenean cargo flows. J. Marit. Res. 11 (2), 66−80.

Nishimura, E., Imai, A., Papadimitriou, S., 2001. Berth allocation planning in the public berth system by genetic algorithms. Eur. J. Oper. Res. 131, 282−292.

Notteboom, T., 2007. Strategic challenges to container ports in a changing market environment. Res. Trans. Econ. 17, 29−52.

Paixao, A., Marlow, P., 2002. Strengths and weaknesses of short sea shipping. Mar. Policy. 26, 167−178.

Park, Y.-M., Kim, K.H., 2003. A scheduling method for berth and quay cranes. OR Spectr. 25, 1−23.

Polo, G., Díaz, D., 2006. A new generation of containerships: cause or effect of the economic development? J. Marit. Res. 3, 3−18.

Steenken, D., Voß, S., 2008. Operations research at container terminals: a literature update. OR Spectr. 30, 1−52.

Voß, S., Stahlbock, R., 2004. Container terminal operations and operations research: a classification and literature review. OR Spectr. 26, 3−49.

18 Opportunities and Challenges of Integrating Bio-Inspired Optimization and Data Mining Algorithms

Simon Fong

Department of Computer and Information Science, University of Macau, Macau SAR, China

18.1 Introduction

Data mining, which is a multidisciplinary analytical technique comprising statistics, computer science, mathematics, and database technology, has become popular in many applications. In general, data mining is deployed at application situations where some underlying insights are needed to be discovered from a huge amount of data. Such underlying patterns that are subtle and elusive could be revealed only by using some specially designed algorithms, which search and track down the patterns through a very large computational search space. For the example of prediction/classification in data mining, a target class is to be mapped from a combination of attributes with specific values or conditions. The multiple attributes can be complex and many, so are their values. There exists a large search space aka a set of possibilities for mapping the appropriate attribute values to the target class. It is an art of science in finding the relation between the input attribute values and the output target class, through usually some heuristic mathematical computation.

From the past several decades, data mining algorithms have ever improved and innovated with new features in the heuristics or other supporting mechanisms. The new features are aimed at shortening the model construction process for better efficiency and/or enhancing the model accuracy for more accurate predictions. Many of such new features were designed to overcome the limitations of some precedent versions. Active research activities have been going on, especially since the launches of the pioneer IEEE International Conference of Data Mining (ICDM) in 2011 and ACM Special Interest Group on Knowledge Discovery and Data Mining (ACM SIGKDD) Conference (KDD) in 1994. The two flagship conferences expanded in scope and participants. The research endeavor for improving data

Swarm Intelligence and Bio-Inspired Computation. DOI: http://dx.doi.org/10.1016/B978-0-12-405163-8.00018-1

mining algorithms has ever been progressing. There have been plenty of rooms for research innovation in continually improving the data mining techniques.

However, data mining algorithms which are positioned under the banner of "machine learning" and bio-inspired optimization techniques that belong to a branch of "metaheuristics" are usually placed at separate sessions in the conference programs. Although they are grouped as two individual mainstream scientific research areas, we often see papers contributed to the fusions of the two. Not to be exhaustive, but several important contributions worth mentioning as follows.

García del Amo et al. (2005) applied Scatter Search on data mining, and it has been proven useful for the main paradigms of data mining such as clustering, classification, and feature selection. Scatter search is a population-based metaheuristic that constructs solutions by combining others in an evolving set of solutions, called reference set. The method joins solutions of the reference set and runs a local search procedure to find a local optimum that would be used to update the reference set depending on the results of the improvements.

Olafsson et al. (2008) pointed out the potential of applying metaheuristics as a general form of operation research and optimization in almost every step of data mining process, from data visualization and preprocessing, to inductive learning, and selecting the best model after learning. In their paper, they highlighted the intersections of data mining and metaheuristics, and advocated that it was only the beginning in this exciting convergence of the two areas; one will find a research niche as long as one can how optimization methods can help to identify constraints and reduce the search space in data mining tasks. For instance, Freitas (2002) published a booked on about applying evolutionary algorithms to data mining. He claimed that evolutionary algorithms are robust search methods which perform a global search in the space of candidate solutions. In contrast, most rule induction methods in data mining perform a local, greedy search in the space of candidate rules. He advocated that, though only intuitively, the global search of evolutionary algorithms can discover interesting rules and patterns that would be missed by the greedy search performed by most rule induction methods. He illustrated several cases by using Genetic Algorithms in optimizing data mining tasks.

In the pursuit of applying evolutionary algorithms into data mining, other researchers contributed a share of their knowledge and efforts as the following highlights follow. Ant Colony Optimization has been hybridized to a new form of data miner called Ant-miner for better discovering of unordered rule sets (Smaldon and Freitas, 2006). Tabu Search was used in improving feature selection by weighing the features by using K-nearest neighbor classifier (Tahir et al., 2007). A similar attempt for feature selection by using Simulated Annealing was done by Debuse and Rayward-Smith (1997). In the context of swarm intelligence where the optimization methods have cooperative and intercommunication abilities, Particle Swarm Optimization (PSO) has been exploited with its heuristic advantages in optimizing a set of features in feature selection by researchers Wang et al. (2007) and Correa et al. (2006). Likewise, Neural Network which is another classical optimization tool has been widely applied in data mining; several books have been published in reviewing the potential of modern metaheuristics in DM (Abbass et al., 2002; De la Iglesia et al., 1996; Rayward-Smith, 2005).

All these above-mentioned works serve as both impetus and springboard for fellow researchers to continue the research endeavor in combing the two types of techniques, because they do give better results than any one of them being used alone.

The author in this chapter essentially wants to explore the potential in incorporating bio-inspired optimization into data mining algorithms. The possibility is discussed in first revealing the underlying working mechanisms which are in common between both of them, and more importantly how these optimization algorithms can improve the shortcomings of the classical data mining algorithms. Then the discussion would be supported by the results of some empirical experiments which were conducted in the hope of verifying and measuring the potential improvement. A new angle is offered in showing the technical possibility of fusing the two scientific disciplines.

18.2 Challenges in Data Mining

Seeking for better versions of data mining algorithms can be dated back to October 2005. An epitome is the effort of soliciting top 10 challenging issues in data mining research, during ICDM 2005, by consulting some of experts in data mining and machine learning for their outlooks on what are considered critical and worthy topics for future research in data mining (Yang and Wu, 2006). Out of the ten challenges, two particular ones are related to the problems of searching in a very large computational space. Namely these two challenges are: (i) Scaling Up for High-Dimensional Data and High-Speed Data Streams and (ii) Mining Sequence Data and Time Series Data, not in order.

18.2.1 Curse of Dimensionality

When considering difficulties in optimization and dynamic programming, Richard E. Bellman (Haas, 1954) coined the phenomenon called the curse of dimensionality. The gravity of this phenomenon states that when the dimensionality expands for a set of data, the volume of the space increases disproportionally fast that inhabits most of the search algorithms. Central to this problem is the effect of combinatorial explosion. In data mining often one would characterize an instance as a row or vector of data that hold values for a number of attributes. A decision model is then to be constructed from such data, generally known as training data. Each variable pertaining to each attribute can take on one of the categorical or nominal values that could cover a finite range of possibilities. When all these variables (factors) are considered together, a huge number of combinations of values are to be processed through. The number of possible combinations which is exponential in the dimensionality is $O(m^d)$ where m is the range of values in the variables and d is the dimension or the number of variables. Generally, adding each dimension would double the effort to try all combinations.

The effect of dimensionality is known to have adverse effect on data mining. One of the objectives in data mining is to learn a model that is generalized and representative enough for describing an overall "character" from a given set of data samples in multidimensional feature space with each feature containing a number of possible values. According to Hughes (1968) with his well-known theory of the Hughes effect the predictive power of a data mining model declines as the dimensionality increases with a limit amount of training samples. For each additional dimension, an enormous amount of corresponding training data are needed to ensure that there are sufficient samples with each combination of values for that new feature. Hughes effect especially has an impact in classification algorithms such as decision trees in data mining. Decision trees are sensitive to noise that induces redundant attributes and widens the range of attribute values. For training data sets that have a very large number of features (like hundreds or thousands), correspondingly a very huge amount of training instances are needed for ensuring a stable decision model.

Clustering which is another prominent family of algorithms in data mining, suffers however from the curse of dimensionality. Clustering works by measuring the distance between pairs of data objects in order to group similar data objects into certain clusters. Typically Euclidean distance is used as the measure that is defined using many coordinates that represent multidimensions. When the dimensions become too huge, the search space increases exponentially and there is little significant difference in the distance between different pairs of data objects. This impacted and impaired both the computation time required and the accuracy of the clustering.

A common approach to demonstrate the vastness of high-dimensional Euclidean space is to compare the proportion of a hypersphere with radius r and dimension d, to that of a hypercube with slides of length $2r$, and equivalent dimension. The volume of the hypersphere is $2r^d \pi^{d/2}/d\Gamma(d/2)$. The volume of the cube would be $(2r)d$. As the dimension d of the space rises up, the hypersphere becomes an insignificant volume relative to that of the hypercube. This can clearly be seen by comparing the proportions as the dimension d goes to infinity,

$$\frac{\pi^{d/2}}{d2^{d-1}\Gamma(d/2)} \to 0, \text{ as } d \to \infty$$

Therefore in some sense, nearly all of the high-dimensional space becomes far away from the center. Putting it in another way, the high-dimensional unit space can be said to consist almost entirely of the corners of the hypercube, with almost no middle within. Given a single data distribution, the minimum and the maximum occurring distances become indiscernible as the difference between the minimum and maximum value compared to the minimum value converges to 0, $\lim_{n\to\infty}$ dist$_{max}$ − dist$_{min}$/dist$_{min}$→0. This illustration is often cited as distance functions losing their usefulness in high dimensionality. Such problem in data mining, especially for clustering, translates to producing poor quality clusters where randomness is high and both interdissimilarity and intrasimilarity suffer.

18.2.2 Data Streaming

Another important problem is data mining is the training data come in the form of a stream. A stream of data can potentially be infinite, continuous and probably ever changing in the number of attributes and the underlying semantic patterns. Consequently, data mining algorithms which are designed to handle data streams are usually online process, continuously learns from the input data, rather than an occasional one-shot batch training process.

One particular instance is from high-speed network traffic where one hopes to mine information for various purposes, including identifying anomalous events possibly indicating attacks of one kind or another. A technical problem is how to compute models over streaming data, which accommodate changing environments from which the data are drawn. This is the problem of "concept drift" or "environment drift." This problem is particularly hard in the context of large streaming data. How may one compute models that are accurate and useful very efficiently?

Besides a great deal of computing power and resources to store a lot of data, computationally it could be a difficult task because the data stream may consist of variable and many attributes over time, and the inevitable fact that distributed data like those streaming data are prone to noise. Inherently, the data mining model will be deterred with the drop of accuracy, by the curse of dimensionality, as discussed above. Worse still the problem of the combinational explosion will be more severe because the number of attributes and the variation of the attribute values could be widened in moving data. In terms of search space, since the data volume is not fixed prior to training, it makes the search more difficult as multiple scans of the past data may not be possible. This sort of problems implies that deterministic optimization is likewise not possible because there is no fixed data to work with as required by most deterministic algorithms at the initial start-up.

The good news perhaps is stochastic optimization algorithms are available; but the search will be confronted with ever-changing local optima as the data stream continue to flow, and obtaining an absolute global optimum would be almost impossible when there is no end in the input data. Given the dynamic data streams, new optimization algorithms are required to adapt to the arrival of the new data. Incrementally the algorithms would help shape the data mining models to its near optimum or optimum at the best effort.

To sum up, the two inherent problems in data mining are: (i) high dimensionality in the features leads to vast search space; (ii) data streams are vulnerable to noise hence missing and/or corrupted data resided in the training data set, and the unbounded incoming data makes model construction difficult. Some difficulties include but are not limited to, finding the optimal parameters in building the model, training the decision model in batch model, and the ever-changing undiscovered patterns/concepts that laid within the data without confirming their end.

18.3   Bio-Inspired Optimization Metaheuristics

Bio-inspired computing and metaheuristics (BiCam) is gaining popularity in computational intelligence, data mining, and optimization applications. Borrowed from the wonders of nature, BiCam algorithms computationally optimize complex search problems, and they show an edge in performance and search efficiency, compared to earlier optimization techniques. Some contemporary BiCam algorithms are introduced below, without going into depth of details. Readers, who are interested in their mathematical formulations, are recommended to follow the references cited in the text.

Firefly algorithm (FA) is a metaheuristic algorithm, inspired by the flashing behavior of fireflies (Yang, 2009). The primary purpose for a firefly's flash is to act as a signal system to attract other fireflies. Xin-She Yang formulated this firefly algorithm by assuming: (i) All fireflies are unisex, so that one firefly will be attracted to all other fireflies; (ii) Attractiveness is proportional to their brightness, and for any two fireflies, the less brighter one will attract and thus move to the brighter one; however, the brightness can decrease as their distance increases; (iii) If there are no fireflies brighter than a given firefly, it will move randomly. The brightness should be associated with the objective function. Recent studies show that FA is particularly suitable for nonlinear multimodal problems.

Cuckoo Search (CS) is an optimization algorithm developed by Yang and Deb (2009). It was inspired by the obligate brood parasitism of some cuckoo species by laying their eggs in the nests of other host birds (of other species). Some host birds can engage in direct conflict with the intruding cuckoos. For example, if a host bird discovers the eggs are not their own, it will either throw these alien eggs away or simply abandon its nest and build a new nest elsewhere. Some cuckoo species have evolved in such a way that female parasitic cuckoos are often very specialized in the mimicry in colors and pattern of the eggs of a few chosen host species. CS idealized such breeding behavior, and thus can be applied for various optimization problems. CS uses the following representations: Each egg in a nest represents a solution, and a cuckoo egg represents a new solution. The aim is to use the new and potentially better solutions (cuckoos) to replace a not-so-good solution in the nests. In the simplest form, each nest has one egg. In many applications, cuckoo search can outperform other algorithms such as PSO and ant colony optimization. The algorithm can be extended to more complicated cases in which each nest has multiple eggs representing a set of solutions.

Their invention "Novel 'Cuckoo Search Algorithm' Beats Particle Swarm Optimization" was recently reported at ScientificComputing.com (http://www.scientificcomputing.com/news-DA-Novel-Cuckoo-Search-Algorithm-Beats-Particle-Swarm-Optimization-060110.aspx)

Accelerated Particle Swarm Optimization: The recently developed Accelerated PSO is combined with a nonlinear support vector machine to form a framework for solving business optimization problems. The proposed APSO-SVM is applied to production optimization, and then it is used for income prediction and project scheduling. It shows advantages over Tabu search, PSO, Genetic algorithms, and variants of GA (Yang et al., 2011).

Bat Algorithms: Bat-inspired algorithm is a metaheuristic search optimization developed by Yang (2010). This bat algorithm is based on the echolocation behavior of microbats with varying pulse emission and loudness. The idealization of echolocation can be summarized as follows: Each virtual bat flies randomly with a velocity v_i at position (solution) x_i with a varying frequency or wavelength and loudness A_i. As it searches and finds its prey, it changes frequency, loudness, and pulse emission rate r. Search is intensified by a local random walk. Selection of the best continues until certain stop criteria are met. Recently the Bat algorithm was applied in optimizing topology in microelectronic applications (Yang et al., 2012), satisfactory results are obtained in the optimization.

Wolf Search Algorithm (WSA) is one of the most recent metaheuristic algorithms (Tang et al., 2012a), developed by Simon Fong. It is inspired by the hunting behavior of wolves that move as a pack; each individual searching agent hunts for a prey individually, silently (without any communication) and they merge by moving their current positions to their peers' positions if the new terrains are better than the old ones. Wolves have certain visual range and move in levy flight in the food-searching mode. A random hunter is implemented from which a wolf will jump out of its current visual range to a random position upon encounter. This random escape enables the wolves to stay out of a local subspace. WSA was shown to be more superior to the existing bio-inspired algorithms in Tang et al. (2012a).

18.4 The Convergence

Modern metaheuristic algorithms such as bee algorithms, PSO, and those mentioned above start to demonstrate their power in dealing with tough optimization problems and even NP-hard problems. The study of metaheuristic or BiCam algorithms in general has a history of contributions[1] in computer science, applications of business and engineering optimization. The research momentum is picking up recently as optimal solutions for combinatorial optimization are possible to be sought by Metaheuristics. The research about finding new BiCam algorithms as well as improving from some existing ones is of great importance, for applying in data mining applications so as to produce optimal solutions in the most efficient way.

The benefits offered by BiCam algorithms complement very well the limitation of data mining because data mining models usually face multidimensional combinatorial problems which are typically NP-hard, with very large search space including about finding global optima and overcoming local optima. Data mining models are well known to be prone to suffer from the curse of dimensionality as discussed earlier, which also makes them infeasible for exhaustive search or analytical methods. The other problem is the user-defined constants that need to be set manually

---

[1] http://en.wikipedia.org/wiki/Metaheuristic#Main_contributions

as parameters in data mining model. Quite often such variables should be updated in run-time when the statistical distributions of the input data change, in order to obtain global optima, most traditional algorithms cannot cope with such complexity, nonlinearity, and variability. The other shortcoming stemmed from stream mining such as the lack of the luxury of processing the full data set, could be sought from the stochastic nature of BiCam. Instead of producing a deterministic and absolutely best solution at final, BiCam runs iteratively and evolutionarily for improving the currently best solution on hand till a stopping criterion is met. Because their natures in common are the stochastic operation, a welcoming possibility exists in integrating the stochastic optimization into the incremental data stream mining process. Overall BiCam is a promising solution to these problems, like fitting a glove into a hand.

Two case studies are given below, for demonstrating the possible integration of BiCam algorithms into some classical data mining algorithms—namely clustering and feature selection in classification.

18.4.1   Integrating BiCam Algorithms into Clustering

K-Means clustering algorithm (Tang et al., 2012b) is based on partitioning approach that keeps relocating data points to the nearest centroids and fine-tuning the shapes of the clusters. Its performance however depends very much on the initial values of the seed starting centroids that are randomly generated each time it is run. It is known that K-Means can easily fall into local optimum which is not the best clustering result. Achieving a globally optimum clustering result requires exhaustively trying for all the possibilities of partitioning which is computationally prohibited. A heuristic approach is to search for the global optima in each step of iterative computation with an aid of some optimization algorithm.

On the other hand, bio-inspired optimization methods work by intimating group swarm behaviors. Each individual data point move (search) in its own way but they communicate and they are guided toward a common optimization goal. Here we attempt to test out hybrids of such bionic algorithms with existing data mining algorithms, such as K-means.

Supposedly bionic optimization algorithms should solve the limitations of K-Means clustering algorithms with regards to finding globally optimum clusters. An experiment is setup to verify this possibility by testing out four different bionic optimization methods which are to be integrated into K-Means Clustering algorithm. This integration is significant because it will serve as a pioneer successful example for breeding future hybrid bionic data mining algorithms. The details of the K-Means clustering and the bionic optimization methods are not repeated here. Readers can refer to the references for the details of the algorithms.

The proposed new hybrid clustering algorithms are tested by using six data sets which are downloaded from UCI machine learning repository (http://archive.ics. uci.edu/ml). The results of C-Firefly, C-Cuckoo, C-Bat, and C-Ant are compared with traditional K-means clustering algorithm as a benchmarking reference. The experiment environment was implemented in MatLab program and executed on a

MacBook Pro computer with the configuration of (CPU 2.3 GHz, RAM 4 GB). In each run of the experiment, each data set is processed repeatedly 10 times for measuring the average of the CPU time taken, and to find the average of the best objective function values/best fitness values. The data sets contain Iris, Wine, Libras Movement, Synthetic Control Chart Time Series, Haberman's Survival and a simple artificially generated clustering data set. The number of attributes and the classes are shown in Table 18.1.

A snapshot of the experiment run of Iris data set is shown in Figure 18.1. The original data points are on top and the data points by the new clustering algorithms are below.

The experimental results are shown in Tables 18.2–18.6. One can easily observe that the C-Cuckoo and C-Bat algorithms achieve much better objective values when compare to C-Ant and C-Firefly. In general all the bionic hybrid clustering algorithms perform faster and achieve in more accurate clustering than the original K-Means. This supports our hypothesis that the nature-inspired algorithm indeed accelerates the process of finding centriods in clustering, and potentially all types of partitioning clustering methods can be integrated with nature-inspired algorithms for accelerating search and for avoiding local optima. Specifically in this experiment, two new clustering algorithms namely C-Cuckoo and C-Bat which have never been tested by other researchers, demonstrate more efficient and accurate performance than C-Ant and C-Firefly. This contribution is significant for the advance of knowledge because it sheds light and hopes that further sophisticated bionic optimization can potentially be integrated with existing clustering algorithms.

K-Means clustering which is a classical algorithm is known to have the disadvantage of falling into local optima. On the other hand, bio-inspired optimization algorithms which have recently become a hot research topic are designed to work with disparate data points and to converge them toward global optima. Given the shortcoming of K-means and the merits of bio-inspired optimization algorithms, naturally it may be suitable for integrating them to function together. In this experiment, four new types of clustering algorithms, evolved from empowering K-means with bionic optimization algorithms are proposed and evaluated. The results from the experiments demonstrate advantage in performance especially by C-Cuckoo and C-Bat which have never been reported in other literature. The success of the integration of the algorithms and the advantage in performance gain laid an optimistic endeavor for further inventing sophisticated optimization-mining algorithms.

Table 18.1 Data Set Information

Data Set	Instances	Attributes	Clusters
Iris	150	4	3
Wine	178	13	3
Libras	360	91	15
Haberman's	306	3	4
Synthetic	600	60	6

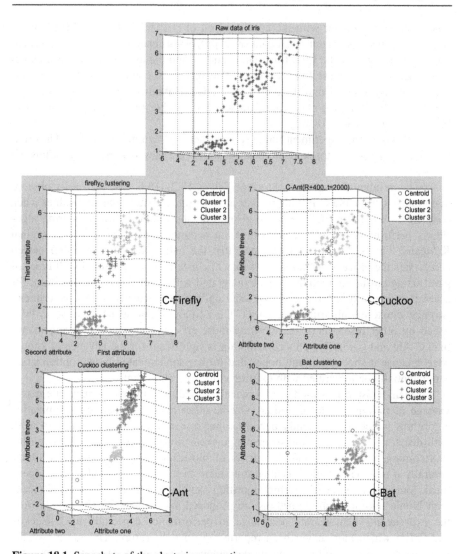

Figure 18.1 Snapshots of the clustering operations.

18.4.2   Integrating BiCam Algorithms into Feature Selection

Feature Selection (FS) in data mining is a preprocessing step that selects a significant subset of attributions whose values describe the instances in the training set, and they usually contribute to improving the accuracy of classification. Choosing the right attributes (and hence their values) to be included during model induction is crucial for optimal accuracy; it is as well as a tricky task especially when a high dimensionality is being dealt within the training data.

Table 18.2 Experimental Result for Iris

	Best	Worst	Average
Objective Function Value			
K-means	78.9451	152.3687	127.8941
C-Ant	139.3081	150.9815	144.79
C-Firefly	78.9408	109.4036	89.88241
C-Cuckoo	78.9408	78.9408	78.9408
C-Bat	78.9408	81.2655	79.46626
CPU Time(s)			
K-means	51.291414	51.673431	51.444755
C-Ant	440.7980	443.9105	443.0668
C-Firefly	142.899517	177.743484	167.2426438
C-Cuckoo	15.499098	15.798136	15.7319299
C-Bat	8.6212	8.8354	8.75495

Table 18.3 Experimental Result for Wine

	Best	Worst	Average
Objective Function Value			
K-means	2.3707e + 006	2.3707e + 006	2.3707e + 006
C-Ant	2.3707e + 006	2.3707e + 006	2.3707e + 006
C-Firefly	2.3707e + 006	2.3707e + 006	2.3707e + 006
C-Cuckoo	2.3707e + 006	2.3707e + 006	2.3707e + 006
C-Bat	2.3707e + 006	2.3707e + 006	2.3707e + 006
CPU Time(s)			
K-means	73.793875	77.226464	75.7386
C-Ant	623.3123	695.2312	653.2154
C-Firefly	260.725002	278.206271	267.8236183
C-Cuckoo	18.582329	19.137426	18.7511367
C-Bat	10.3032	10.8225	10.42148

So far there is no golden rule of thumb in picking neither the so-called right attributes nor deciding the exact number of attributes. This remains as an important challenge in data mining, though generally and intuitively it is known that we should acquire those attributes that are somehow related to the prediction target. Some standard algorithms exist and they are widely adopted, such as correlation analysis, information gain, and techniques that minimize the redundancy and maximize the relevance. Different results are yielded however, when different FS techniques are

Table 18.4 Experimental Result for Libras

	Best	Worst	Average
Objective Function Value			
K-means	822.8381	899.2441	842.3452
C-Ant	1.1361e + 003	1.6345e + 003	1.3981e + 003
C-Firefly	743.3432	892.0506	777.1993
C-Cuckoo	707.5916	819.1392	763.1102
C-Bat	745.8008	918.2488	841.71931
CPU Time(s)			
K-means	1332.059811	1392.3113	1362.0344
C-Ant	1.0142e + 004	1.3245e + 004	1.1195e + 004
C-Firefly	260.725002	278.206271	267.8236183
C-Cuckoo	168.502947	169.849548	169.17942
C-Bat	10.3032	10.8225	10.42148

Table 18.5 Experimental Result for Haberman

	Best	Worst	Average
Objective Function Value			
K-means	1.537e + 004	1.9070e + 004	1.6612e + 004
C-Ant	n/a	n/a	n/a
C-Firefly	1.5367e + 004	2.2216e + 004	1.8356e + 004
C-Cuckoo	1.5367e + 004	1.5617e + 004	1.54222e + 004
C-Bat	1.5367e + 004	1.9216e + 004	1.66877e + 004
CPU Time(s)			
K-means	254.880109	264.579686	258.243
C-Ant	n/a	n/a	n/a
C-Firefly	4395.7579	4920.4362	4545.4661
C-Cuckoo	43.228828	50.847262	47.4073
C-Bat	22.4197	22.7304	22.59871

applied in different situations. So can we know which combinations of attributes should be used without using brute-force approach to them all, exhaustively?

FS is heuristic in nature for it does not test out the enumeration of attributes throughout all the possibilities. It is more like a scoring function that tests the relation between the target class and each individual attribute variable. As aforementioned, FS does not guarantee best results always, due to the highly nonlinear relations between pairs of target-attribute and the inclusions of certain attributes.

Table 18.6 Experimental Result for Synthetic

	Best	Worst	Average
Objective Function Value			
K-means	9.88221e + 005	1.0451e + 006	9.9632e + 005
C-Ant	n/a	n/a	n/a
C-Firefly	9.4509e + 005	9.8221e + 005	9.6622e + 005
C-Cuckoo	9.4499e + 005	9.7800e + 005	9.5721e + 005
C-Bat	9.5232e + 005	9.8525e + 005	9.6150e + 005
CPU Time(s)			
K-means	1579.2311	1663.2234	1617.305490
C-Ant	n/a	n/a	n/a
C-Firefly	51,092.57336	51,404.66323	51,232.55324
C-Cuckoo	138.204069	151.547294	141.9006882
C-Bat	77.8049	80.8928	79.63274

It is feasible to integrate BiCam algorithms into FS for optimizing the process of searching for the subset of useful features which are aka attributes without brute force. Instead of scoring the attributes by evaluating their importance pertaining to the paired relation with the target class, heuristically BiCam algorithms search through such huge combinations for finding the ideal attribute subset. The objective function in this case would be the model induction, and the accuracy of the model represents the fitness. Without any *a priori* knowledge of how highest the accuracy will raise, the optimization shuffles in the inclusion of the attributes until no further improvement could be made.

An example is shown as follows for finding the just right candidates of attributes from a case of biosignal classification. Basically biosignal is a time series of collected data (e.g., voltage) that measures the condition of a vital organism like heart beats or brain waves, etc. In order to classify them, analytically, into groups that belong to normal or otherwise, essential features are to be extracted from a bound univariate data set. The upcoming question is how this time series should be characterized by feature attributes such that different groups of biosignals can become mostly distinctive by a compact set of attribute values. Numerous transformation methods exist including those that convert the time series into values of frequency domain and those that discrete the analog data into some representative coefficients. Recently a paper (Fong et al., 2013) is published on combing the features from both frequency domain and time domain of the biosignal time series. The hybrid method is capable of generating the highest possible classification accuracy, but it suffers from producing too many attributes that may slow down the real-time classification process and/or exceed the stringent run-time memory requirement. Details of the feature extraction can be found from the mentioned paper. Figure 18.2 is an illustration of feature extraction where a time series is segmented and the corresponding statistics from each segment are obtained. Essentially the

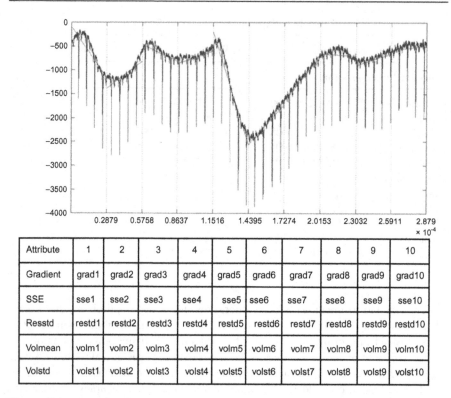

Attribute	1	2	3	4	5	6	7	8	9	10
Gradient	grad1	grad2	grad3	grad4	grad5	grad6	grad7	grad8	grad9	grad10
SSE	sse1	sse2	sse3	sse4	sse5	sse6	sse7	sse8	sse9	sse10
Resstd	restd1	restd2	restd3	restd4	restd5	restd6	restd7	restd8	restd9	restd10
Volmean	volm1	volm2	volm3	volm4	volm5	volm6	volm7	volm8	volm9	volm10
Volstd	volst1	volst2	volst3	volst4	volst5	volst6	volst7	volst8	volst9	volst10

Figure 18.2 A snapshot that shows a time series is partitioned into segments and the corresponding statistics are extracted out of them.

case of biosignal classification is used here because a very large potential number of attributes can be produced during feature extraction. It can well represent some extreme case of high dimensionality that gives rise to a large search space in which many local optima exist.

As a comparison of efficacy of using some popular FS algorithms and applying BiCam algorithm for obtaining the best possible classification accuracy, the following experiment is conducted. We test a set of electromyography (EMG) biosignals that are in the format of two-dimensional time series with an amplitude value in voltage that varies over time. The data were initially acquired for evaluating the electrical activity produced by skeletal muscles from two groups of subjects who were exhibiting aggressive and normal behaviors. The data are recorded and then donated by Theo Theodoridis,[2] University of Essex, UK. Three volunteers of age between 25 and 30, one woman and three men were asked to conduct in turn of aggressive and moderate activities in turn of 10 trials for each type, in a 22 m^2 confined arena. Aggressive activities were expressed by kickboxing a sandbag; the

[2] sites.google.com/site/ttheod

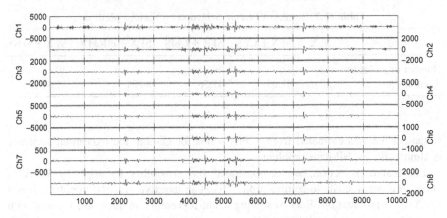

Figure 18.3 Visualization of EMG data set that belongs to the "Normal" group.

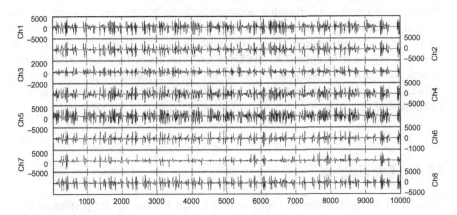

Figure 18.4 Visualization of EMG data set that belongs to the "Abnormal" group.

other type of activities involved just standing and sitting, almost still, with some relatively gentle hand gestures like waving and handshaking. Eight electrodes were placed on the subject's biceps and triceps as well as thighs and hamstrings, at the skin-surface level. A total of 10,000 biosignal samples were collected for each subject, over eight channels; the data contain about 15 actions per trial.

Our experiment was performed by a popular classification algorithm, Bayesian Network (with the default parameters applied) over the three sets of above-mentioned biosignal data using the preprocessing method called SFX (Statistical Feature Extraction) as described in the paper (Fong et al., 2013). Visually the difference between the two EMG biosignals can be seen from Figures 18.3 and 18.4 that differ by both amplitudes and frequencies. However, when it comes to automatic classification by means of machine learning, choosing from a large pool of

Table 18.7 Results of Feature Selection by Various Methods

	SFX	SFX + CFS	SFX + ChiS	SFX + mRMR	SFX + WSA
Number of attributes	124	8	20	20	20
Accuracy %	80.63	81.25	81.56	80.31	82.81

statistical features extracted from a long series for gaining the maximum accuracy is almost like an NP-hard problem.

For feature selection, we demonstrated the possibility by applying WSA to choose the ideal attribute combination. This is an iterative process; therefore, it is a stochastic optimization. Each searching agent represents an attribute. It starts with a single attribute, tries through different ones, and scales up the number of attributes according to the algorithm. Readers who want to find the details are referred to the paper (Tang et al., 2012a). The optimization ceases when there is no further improvement on the classification accuracy and the current set of attributes are deemed as the ideal feature set. Table 18.7 shows a comparison of applying WSA versus other standard feature selection algorithms, such as Correlation (CFS), Chi-Square (ChiS), and Minimum Redundancy and Maximum Relevance (mRMR). It is observed that by using WSA as a BiCam algorithm, improved accuracy (82.81%) is achieved while choosing only 20 attributes compared to the total of 124 attributes.

18.5 Conclusion

A thrust of research effort has been investing into improving the performance of data mining algorithms. In particular, data mining algorithms suffer from two major drawbacks. One of them is the prohibitedly huge search space induced by the increase of data features. The vastness of multidimensional space degraded the accuracy of a learned model as well as elongating the time required for fully learning of a model. The challenges called for numerous researchers to attempt modifying the data mining algorithms for betterment. On the other hand, bio-inspired metaheuristics recently gained attention in research communities for their effectiveness and wide applicability across many application domains. The good news is that data mining and bio-inspired computing both have some similarities: their stochastic executions and they were designed to handle data of multidimensional hyperspaces. In this chapter we advocate that the two should be combined, and bio-inspired computation could actually help improve and relieve the above-mentioned shortcomings of data mining algorithms. For instance, the hybrid version of data mining coupled with optimization methods could work incrementally for finding good solutions; and the stochastic search often save a considerable amount of time for the learning to converge in data mining. It could even help avoid fall into local optima in some cases. We showed these advantages by using two examples; one is integrating bio-inspired optimization in the classical K-means clustering algorithm. The other example is to use bio-inspired optimization techniques to guide feature selection in data mining over a nonlinear time series. Although only two representative examples are illustrated, it is technically possible to extend the hybrid versions of data mining algorithms with optimization functions to other disciplines such as association rules and outlier detection. The hybrid algorithms would work, though yet to be proven, as long as there exists a large search space and the full data sets are unavailable. The successful examples hopefully will serve as a research springboard for fellow researchers to continue the momentum in these two exciting research fields. The numbers from our experiments tell a positive story, but more importantly, this has tested that the integration is technically possible and effectively the fusion is capable of producing better results than data mining alone.

References

Abbass, H., Sarker, R., Newton, C., 2002. Data mining: A heuristic approach. Idea Group Inc (IGI), Janauary 1, 2002.

Correa, E.S., Freitas, S.A., Johnson, C.G., 2006. A New Discrete Particle Swarm Algorithm Applied to Attribute Selection in a Bioinformatic Data Set. GECCO '06: Proceedings of the 8th Annual Conference on Genetic and Evolutionary Computation, pp. 35−42

de la Iglesia, B., Debuse, J.C.W., Rayward-Smith, V.J., 1996. Discovering knowledge in commercial databases using modern heuristic techniques. Proceedings of the Second International Conference on Knowledge Discovery and Data Mining. AAAI Press, pp. 44−49.

Debuse, J.C.W., Rayward-Smith, V.J., 1997. Feature subset selection within a simulated annealing data mining algorithm. J. Intell. Inf. Syst. 9 (1), 57−81.

Freitas, A., 2002. Data Mining and Knowledge Discovery with Evolutionary Algorithms. Springer.

Fong, S., Lan, K., Sun, P., Mohammed, S., Fiaidhi, J., 2013. A time-series pre-processing methodology for biosignal classification using statistical feature extraction. Proceedings of the IASTED International Conference, Biomedical Engineering (BioMed 2013), February 13−15, Innsbruck, Austria, pp. 207−214.

García del Amo, I.J., García Torres, M., Batista, B.M., Pérez, J.A.M., Vega, J.M.M., Martín, R.R., 2005. Data mining with scatter search. In: EUROCAST'05 Proceedings of the Tenth International Conference on Computer Aided Systems Theory, pp. 199−204.

Haas, F., 1954. Review: stability theory of differential equations, by R. Bellman. Bull. Am. Math. Soc. 60 (4), 400−401.

Hughes, G.F., 1968. On the mean accuracy of statistical pattern recognizers. IEEE Trans. Inf. Theory. 14 (1), 55−63. 10.1109/TIT.1968.1054102.

Rayward-Smith, V.J., 2005. Metaheuristics for clustering in KDD. Congr. Evol. Comput. 2380−2387.

Smaldon, J., Freitas, A., 2006. A new version of the ant-miner algorithm discovering unordered rule sets. Proceedings of GECCO '06, pp. 43−50.

Tahir, M.A., Bouridane, A., Kurugollu, F., 2007. Simultaneous feature selection and feature weighting using Hybrid Tabu Search/K-nearest neighbor classifier. Pattern Recognit. Lett. 28, 438−446.

Tang, R., Fong, S., Yang, X.-S., Deb, S., 2012a. Wolf search algorithm with ephemeral memory. In: IEEE Seventh International Conference on Digital Information Management (ICDIM 2012). August 2012, pp. 165−172.

Tang, R., Fong, S., Yang X.-S. Deb S., 2012b. Integrating nature-inspired optimization algorithms to K-means clustering. In: IEEE Seventh International Conference on Digital Information Management (ICDIM 2012). August 2012, pp. 116−172.

Olafsson, S., Li, X., Wu, S., 2008. Operations research and data mining. Eur. J. Oper. Res. 187 (3), 1429−1448.

Wang, X.Y., Yang, J., Teng, X.L., Xia, W.J., Jensen, R., 2007. Feature selection based on rough sets and particle swarm optimization. Pattern Recognit. Lett. 28, 459−471.

Yang, Q., Wu, X.D., 2006. 10 challenging problems in data mining research. Inter. J. Inf. Technol. Decis. Making. 5 (4), 597−604 (World Scientific).

Yang, X.-S., 2009. Firefly algorithms for multimodal optimization. Stochastic Algorithms: Foundations and Applications, SAGA 2009. Lecture Notes in Computer Sciences. 5792. pp. 169−178.

Yang, X.-S., Deb, S., 2009. Cuckoo search via Levy flights. World Congress on Nature & Biologically Inspired Computing (NaBIC 2009). IEEE Publication, USA, pp. 210−214.

Yang, X.-S., 2010. A new metaheuristic bat-inspired algorithm. In: Gonzalez, J.R., Pelta, D.A., Cruz, C., Terrazas, G., Krasnogor, N. (Eds.), Nature Inspired Cooperative Strategies for Optimization (NISCO 2010), vol. 284. Springer, Berlin, pp. 65−74 (Studies in Computational Intelligence).

Yang, X.-S., Deb, S., Fong, S., 2011. Accelerated particle swarm optimization and support vector machine for business optimization and applications. The Third International Conference on Networked Digital Technologies (NDT 2011). Springer CCIS 136. July 11−13, 2011. Macau, China. pp. 53−66.

Yang, X.-S., Karamanoglu, M., Fong, S., 2012. Bat algorithm for topology optimization in microelectronic applications. International Conference on Future Generation Communication Technology (FGCT 2012). British Computer Society, London, UK.

19 Improvement of PSO Algorithm by Memory-Based Gradient Search—Application in Inventory Management

Tamás Varga, András Király and János Abonyi

Department of Process Engineering, University of Pannonia, Veszprém, Hungary

19.1 Introduction

In the last decades, optimization was featured in almost all aspects of human civilization, thus it has truly become an indispensable method. In some aspects, even a local optima can highly improve the efficiency or reduce the expenses, however, most companies want to keep their operational costs as low as possible, i.e., on global minimum. Problems where solutions must satisfy a set of constraints are known as constrained optimization problems. In inventory control theory, one of the most important and most strict constraints is the service level, i.e., the portion of satisfied demands from all customer needs (Schwartz et al., 2006). Stochastic nature of the supply and demand variations in complex supply chains require effective and robust nonlinear optimization for advanced inventory management.

There are two popular swarm-inspired methods in computational intelligence areas: Ant Colony Optimization (ACO) and Particle Swarm Optimization (PSO). ACO was inspired by the behaviors of ants and has many successful applications in discrete optimization problems. The particle swarm concept originated as a simulation of simplified social system. Next to these two there can be found many other swarm intelligence-based method in literature to solve optimization problems, such as Firefly Algorithm (FA), Bat Algorithm (BA), and Krill Herd Algorithm (KHA). FAs are recently developed methods to optimize nonlinear design problems based on the idealized behavior of the flashing characteristics of fireflies (Yang, 2010a). BA is very similar to the PSO; however, it is based on the hunting method of bats using their echolocation ability (Yang, 2010b). One of the latest algorithms is the KHA wherein the benefits of swarm intelligence and the genetic algorithms are

Swarm Intelligence and Bio-Inspired Computation. DOI: http://dx.doi.org/10.1016/B978-0-12-405163-8.00019-3

integrated which results a reliable optimization technique with good conversion rate (Gandomi and Alavi, 2012).

Particle swarm model can be used to solve stochastic and constrained optimization problems (Hu and Eberhart, 2002; Kennedy and Eberhart, 1995). The particle swarm concept originated as a simulation of simplified social system. In PSO, the potential solutions, called particles, fly through the problem space by following the current optimum particles. All of particles have fitness values which are evaluated by the fitness function to be optimized and have velocities in the direction based on their inertia, best fitness value, and the best solution found by the population. PSO is getting more and more widespread tool in solving complex engineering problems since it is easily interpretable and implementable optimization algorithm, and it can be effectively applied to find the extremum of nonlinear optimization problems with many independent parameters. The PSO algorithm has been successfully applied to a wide set of complex problems, like data mining (Sousaa et al., 2004), software testing (Windisch et al., 2007), nonlinear mapping (Edwards et al., 2005), function minimization (Kennedy and Eberhart, 1995), or neural network training (Engelbrecht et al., 1999), and in the last decade, constrained optimization using PSO got a bigger attention (Hu and Eberhart, 2002; Parsopoulos and Vrahatis, 2002; Wimalajeewa and Jayaweera, 2008).

There exist some well-known conditions under which the basic PSO algorithm exhibits poor convergence characteristics (Bergh, 2002). However, only a few studies have considered the hybridization of PSO, especially making use of gradient information directly within PSO. Notable ones are Hybrid Gradient Descent PSO (HGPSO) (Noel and Jannett, 2004) and Guo Tao PSO (GTPSO) (Zhang et al., 2009), which use the gradient-descent algorithm, and PSO, which applies the Flecher–Reeves method (Borowska and Nadolski, 2009). As it will be demonstrated in the following sections, combining these two methods appropriately, the efficiency of the optimization using PSO can be considerably improved.

Classical gradient calculation cannot be applied to stochastic and uncertain systems. In these situations stochastic techniques like Monte-Carlo (MC) simulation can be applied to determine the gradient. These techniques require additional function evaluations. We developed a more economic, memory-based algorithm where instead of generating and evaluating new simulated samples the stored and shared former function evaluations of the particles are sampled to estimate the gradients by local weighted least squares regression. The performance of the resulted fully informed, regional gradient-based PSO is verified by several benchmark problems.

The algorithm has been applied to find the optimal reorder points of a supply chain. The stochastic objective function is based on the linear combination of holding cost in the warehouses, the order cost and the unit price. The inequality constraints are defined based on the minimal service level values. The determination of safety stock in an inventory model is one of the key tasks of supply chain management. Miranda and Garrido (2004) include safety stock in the inventory model. Graves and Willems (2008) give a model for positioning safety stock in a supply chain subject to nonstationary demand and show how to extend their former model to find the optimal placement safety stocks under constant service time (CST) policy. Prékopa (2006) gives an improved model for the so-called Hungarian inventory control model to find the minimal safety stock level that ensures the continuous production, without disruption. The bullwhip effect is an important phenomenon in supply chains. Makajic-Nikolic et al. (2004) show how a supply chain can be modeled and analyzed by colored petri nets (CPN) and CPN tools and they evaluate the bullwhip effect, the surplus of inventory goods, etc., using the beer game as demonstration. More recent research can be found in Caloieroa et al. (2008), which shows that an order policy applied to a serial single-product supply chain with four echelons can reduce or amplify the bullwhip effect and inventory oscillation. Miranda and Garrido investigate the modeling of a two echelon supply chain system and optimization in two steps (2009), while a massive multiechelon inventory model is presented by Seo (2006), where an order risk policy for general multiechelon system is given, which minimizes the system operation cost. A really complex system is examined in Srinivasan and Moon (1999), where it is necessary to apply some clustering for similar items, because detailed analysis could become impossible considering each item individually. The stability of the supply chain is also an intensively studied area. Nagatania and Helbing (2004) show that a linear supply chain can be stabilized by the anticipation of the own future inventory and by taking into account the inventories of other suppliers, and Vaughan (2006) presents a linear order point/lot size model that with its robustness can contribute to business process modeling.

We developed a Monte-Carlo simulator which uses probability distributions based on material usage data posted in the logistic module of an enterprise resource planning (ERP) system. The main objective of this development was to build a simulator that can use simple building blocks to construct models of complex supply chain networks. With the synergistic combination of this tool and the proposed PSO algorithm we minimized the inventory holding cost by changing the parameters of our operational space while keeping the service level at the required value. The results illustrate the benefits of the incorporation of the regional gradients into the PSO algorithm.

19.2 The Improved PSO Algorithm

19.2.1 Classical PSO Algorithm

The original intent was to graphically simulate the choreography of bird of a bird block or fish school. However, it was found that particle swarm model can be used as an optimizer. Suppose the following scenario: a group of birds are randomly searching food in an area. There is only one piece of food in the area being searched. All the birds do not know where the food is. But they know how far the food is in each iteration. So what is the best strategy to find the food? The effective one is to follow the bird which is nearest to the food. PSO is based on this scheme. This stochastic optimization technique has been developed by Kennedy and Eberhart (1995). In PSO, the potential solutions, called particles, fly through the problem space by following the current optimum particles. All of particles have fitness values which are evaluated by the fitness function to be optimized, and have velocities which direct to the flying of the particles.

PSO is initialized with a group of random particles (solutions) and then searches for optima by updating generations. In every iteration, each particle is updated by following two "best" values. The first one is the best solution (fitness) it has achieved so far. (The fitness value is also stored.) This value is called pbest. Another "best" value that is tracked by the particle swarm optimizer is the best value, obtained so far by any particle in the population. This best value is a global best and called gbest. When a particle takes part of the population as its topological neighbors, the best value is a local best and is called lbest.

$$\mathbf{v}_j(k+1) = w \times \mathbf{v}_j(k) + c_1 \times \text{rand}() \times (\mathbf{x}_{\text{pbest},j} - \mathbf{x}_j(k)) + c_2 \times \text{rand}() \times (\mathbf{x}_{\text{gbest}} - \mathbf{x}_j(k))$$
$$(19.1)$$

$$\mathbf{x}_j(k+1) = \mathbf{x}_j(k) + \mathbf{v}_j(k+1) \cdot dt \qquad (19.2)$$

where $j = 1, ..., \lambda$ represents the index of the jth swarm, $\mathbf{v}$ is the particle velocity, rand() is a random number between $[0,1]$, c_1, c_2 are learning factors. Code 19.1 shows the pseudocode of the classical PSO algorithm.

The role of the, w, inertia weight in Eq. (19.1), is considered critical for the convergence behavior of PSO. The inertia weight is employed to control the impact of the previous history of velocities on the current one. Accordingly, the parameter regulates the trade-off between the global and local exploration abilities of the swarm. A large inertia weight facilitates global exploration (searching new areas) while a small one tends to facilitate local exploration, i.e., fine-tuning the current search area.

PSO shares many similarities with evolutionary computation techniques, e.g., with evolutionary algorithms (EAs). Both algorithms start with a group of a randomly generated population, both have fitness values to evaluate the population. Both update the population and search for the optimum with random techniques. Both systems do not guarantee success. The main difference between these algorithms is that PSO does not have genetic operators like crossover and mutation. Particles update themselves with the internal velocity. They also have memory, which is important to the algorithm.

Code 19.1 The pseudocode of the PSO algorithm.

```
procedure PSO; {
       Initialize particles;
       while (not terminate) do {
              for each particle {
                     Calculate fitness value;
                     if fitness <pBest than  pBest = fitness;
              }
              Choose the best particle as the gBest;
              for each particle {
                     Calculate particle velocity;
                     Update particle position;
              }
       }
}
```

Compared with evolutionary algorithms, the information sharing mechanism in PSO is significantly different. In EAs, chromosomes share information with each other. So the whole population moves like a one group toward an optimal area. In PSO, only gBest (or lBest) gives out the information to others. It is a one-way information sharing mechanism, the evolution only looks for the best solution. Compared with EAs, all the particles tend to converge to the best solution quickly even in the local version in most cases. Compared to EA, the advantages of PSO are that PSO is easy to implement and there are few parameters to adjust. Hence, PSO has been successfully applied in many areas: function optimization, artificial neural network training (Engelbrecht et al., 1999), control (Victoirea and Jeyakumar, 2004), scheduling (Wimalajeewa and Jayaweera, 2008), and other areas where GA can be applied.

The basic PSO algorithm exhibits poor convergence characteristics under some specific conditions. We gave a small overview also about the previous gradient-based methods, and in this section we will demonstrate a novel way, how the PSO technique can be improved with the calculation of the gradient of the applied objective function. There are some well-documented algorithms in the literature to boost the convergence of the basic PSO algorithm. Victoirea et al. developed a hybrid PSO to solve the economic dispatch program (Victoirea and Jeyakumar, 2004). They combined PSO with Sequential Quadratic Programming to search for the gradient of the objective function. A very similar algorithm is introduced by Noel and Jannett (2004), in which quasi-Newton−Raphson (QNR) algorithm is applied to calculate the gradient. The QNR algorithm optimizes by locally fitting a quadratic surface and finding the minimum of that quadratic surface.

19.2.2 Improved PSO Algorithm

Our aim is to develop a novel PSO algorithm which is able to consider linear and non-linear constraints and it calculates the gradient of the objective function to improve the affectivity. PSO is initialized with a group of random particles (solutions) and then searches for optima by updating generations. In every generation, each particle is updated by following two "best" values. The first one is the best solution (fitness) it has achieved so far. This value is called pbest. Another "best" value that is tracked by the particle swarm optimizer is the best value, obtained so far by any particle in the population. This best value is a global best and called gbest. When a particle takes part of the population as its topological neighbors, the best value is a local best and is called lbest. Our vision is to apply the gradient of the objective function in every generation to control the movements of the particles. Therefore, the equation which is applied to calculate the velocity of the particles is modified:

$$
\begin{aligned}
v_j(k+1) = w \times v_j(k) + c_1 \times \text{rand}() \times (x_{\text{pbest},j} - x_j(k)) + c_2 \times \text{rand}() \\
\times (x_{\text{gbest}} - x_j(k)) + c_3 \times g_j(f(\mathbf{x}(k)))
\end{aligned}
\tag{19.3}
$$

where $g_j(f(\mathbf{x}(k))) = \partial f(\mathbf{x}(k))/\partial x_j(k)$ represents the partial derivatives of the objective function, and c_3 is the weight for the gradient term.

It should be noted that this concept can be interpreted as inserting a gradient-descent update step into the iterations of classical PSO, $\mathbf{x}(k + 1) = \mathbf{x}(k) - \eta \nabla f(\mathbf{x}(k))$, where the learning rate is equal to $\eta = c_3 dt$.

The above algorithm can be applied only to continuously differentiable objective functions $\nabla f(\mathbf{x}(k))$. The simples approach to calculate the gradient is HGPSO (Noel and Jannett, 2004) is the numerical approximation of the gradient.

$$\frac{\partial}{\partial x_i}(\mathbf{x}(k)) = \frac{f(\mathbf{x}(k) + E_i \varepsilon) - f(\mathbf{x}(k))}{\varepsilon} \tag{19.4}$$

The main drawback of this approach is that the ε step size is difficult to design and the whole approach is selective to noise and uncertainties. It is interesting to note that PSO itself can also be interpreted as a gradient-based search algorithm where point differences are used as approximation of the regional gradient. The normalized gradient evaluated as the point-difference method is:

$$\mathbf{e} = \frac{f(\mathbf{x}_j) - f(\mathbf{x}_i)}{||(\mathbf{x}_j - \mathbf{x}_i)||} \tag{19.5}$$

This point-difference estimate can be considered as regional gradient for the local region of $\mathbf{x}_i$ and $\mathbf{x}_j$. Hence, the velocity of PSO can be interpreted as a weighted combination of a point difference estimated global regional gradient $(x_{\text{gbest}} - x_j(k))$ and a point difference estimated finer regional gradient $(x_{\text{pbest}} - x_j(k))$.

Our aim is to further improve the optimization by providing robust yet accurate estimation of gradients. To obtain a robust estimate a so-called regional gradient should be calculated. When the function is differentiable the gradient for a region S it is calculated as:

$$\nabla f(\mathbf{x})^* = \frac{1}{\text{volume}(S)} \int_{x \in S} \nabla f(\mathbf{x}) d\mathbf{x} \tag{19.6}$$

where S represents the local region where the gradient is calculated.

However, when heuristic optimization algorithm should be applied the objective function is mostly not continuously differentiable or not explicitly given due to limited knowledge. Therefore the gradient is calculated as

$$\nabla f(\mathbf{x})^* = \frac{\int_{x \in S} f(\mathbf{x}) d\mathbf{x}}{\int_{x \in S} d\mathbf{x}} \tag{19.7}$$

An interesting example for this approach is how regional gradient is calculated in the Evolutionary Gradient-Search (EGS) procedure proposed by Salomon and Arnold (2009). In EGS at each iteration generates λ test candidates by applying random "mutations" of $\mathbf{x}(k)$.

$$\mathbf{v}_i = \mathbf{x}(k) + \mathbf{z}_i \tag{19.8}$$

where z_i is a Gaussian distributed variable with zero mean and standard deviation $\sigma/\sqrt{n}$. For $n \gg 1$ these test points will be distributed on a hypersphere with radius σ. By using information given by all candidates the procedure calculates the gradient and a unit vector $e(k)$ that points into the direction of the estimated gradient:

$$g(k) = \sum_{i=1}^{\lambda} f(\mathbf{v}_i) - f(\mathbf{x}(k))(\mathbf{v}_i - \mathbf{x}(k)) \tag{19.9}$$

$$e(k) = \frac{g(k)}{\|g(k)\|} \tag{19.10}$$

These techniques require additional function evaluations. It is important to note that this concept discards all information related to the evaluation of $\mathbf{v}_i$.

We developed a more economic, memory-based algorithm where instead of generating and evaluating new simulated samples the stored and shared former function evaluations of the particles are sampled to estimate the gradients by local weighted least squares regression.

This idea is partly similar to the concept of the fully informed particle swarm (FIPS) algorithm proposed by Mendes et al. (2004). FIPS that can be also considered as a hybrid method for estimating the gradient by a point difference of the weighted regional gradient estimate $(P_j - \mathbf{x}(k))$ based on the lbest solutions and adding an additional gradient related term to the velocity adaptation:

$$v_j(k + 1) = \ldots + c_3(v_j(k - 1) + \varphi(P_j(k) - \mathbf{x}(k))) \tag{19.11}$$

$$P_j(k) = \frac{\sum_{k \in S} \varphi_k \mathbf{x}_{\text{lbest},i}(k)}{\sum_{k \in S} \varphi_k} \tag{19.12}$$

where ϕ_k is drawn independently from the uniform distribution.

FIPS utilizes only the current $\mathbf{x}_{\text{lbest},i}(k)$ values so it does not have a memory.

The main concept of our work is the effective utilization of the previous function evaluations. So instead of generating new and new samples and loosing information from previous generations the whole trajectories of the particles are utilized.

The weighted regression problem that gives a robust estimates of the gradients is formulated by arranging these former function evaluations $\{\mathbf{x}(k), f(\mathbf{x}(k))\}$ into indexed data pairs $\{\mathbf{v}_i, f(\mathbf{v}_i)\}$ and calculating the following differences $\Delta f_i(k) = f(\mathbf{v}_i) - f(\mathbf{x}(k))$, $\Delta x_i(k) = \mathbf{v}_i - \mathbf{x}(k)$

$$\Delta f(k) = \begin{bmatrix} \Delta f_1(1) \\ \Delta f_\lambda(1) \\ \Delta f_1(k - 1) \\ \Delta f_\lambda(k - 1) \end{bmatrix}, \ \Delta X(k) = \begin{bmatrix} \Delta \mathbf{x}_1(1) \\ \Delta \mathbf{x}_\lambda(1) \\ \Delta \mathbf{x}_1(k - 1) \\ \Delta \mathbf{x}_\lambda(k - 1) \end{bmatrix}$$

where λ represents the number of particles.

The weighted least squares estimate is calculated as:

$$\mathbf{g}_j(k) = (\Delta \mathbf{X}^T(k)\mathbf{W}_j(k)\Delta \mathbf{X}(k))^{-1}\Delta \mathbf{X}^T(k)\mathbf{W}_j^T(k)\Delta \mathbf{f}(k)) \tag{19.13}$$

where the $\mathbf{W}_j(k)$ weighting matrix is a diagonal matrix representing the region of the jth particle. Similarly to EGS a Gaussian distributed weighting is used:

$$\beta_{j,i}(k) = \frac{1}{(2\pi)^{n/2}||^{1/2}}\exp\left(\frac{1}{2}(\mathbf{v}_i - \mathbf{x}(k))^T\Sigma^{-1}(\mathbf{v}_i - \mathbf{x}(k))\right) \tag{19.14}$$

where $\mathbf{v}_i$ the ith row of the $\Delta \mathbf{X}$ matrix, j represents the jth particle, $w_{j,i}(k) = \beta_{j,i}(k)/\sum_{i=1}\beta_{j,i}(k)$ is the normalized probability of the sample, $\sum = I\sigma$ is a diagonal matrix where σ parameter represents the size of the region used to calculate the gradients. By using the information given by all previous states of the particles it is possible to calculate a unit vector that points into the direction of the estimated (global) gradient. The resulted algorithm is given in Code 19.2.

19.2.3 Results

We tested the novel algorithm using several functions, including deterministic and stochastic ones as well. Figure 19.1 presents four of them and Table 19.1 contains the mathematical representation of the analyzed functions.

```
procedure improved PSO; {
        Initialize particles;
        while (not terminate) do {
                for each particle {
                        Calculate fitness value;
                        if fitness <pBest than  pBest = fitness;
                }
                Choose the best particle as the gBest;
                for each particle {
                        Calculate local gradient {
                                Calculate normalized distance base
                                weights of previous function evaluations particles by Eq. 14;
                                Calculate regional gradients by Eq. 13;
                        }
                        Calculate particle velocity by Eq. 3;
                        Update particle position by Eq. 2;
                        Store particle position and related cost function in a database, {v_i, f(v_i)}
                }
        }
}
```

Code 19.2 The pseudocode of the improved PSO algorithm.

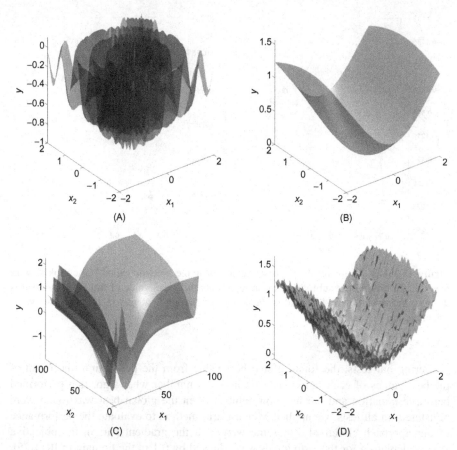

Figure 19.1 Surface of the fitness function called "dropwave" (A) the "Griewank's" function (B), the stochastic function we used (C), and a stochastic version of "Griewank" (D).

Table 19.1 Mathematical Equations of the Analyzed Functions

Function	Equation
Dropwave	$f(x, y) = -\frac{1 + \cos\left(12\sqrt{x^2 + y^2}\right)}{\frac{1}{2}(x^2 + y^2) + 2}$
Griewank's	$f(x) = \frac{1}{4000}\sum_{i=1}^{n} x_i^2 - \prod_{i=1}^{n}\cos\left(\frac{x_i}{\sqrt{i}}\right) + 1$
Griewank's with noise	$f(x) = \frac{1}{4000}\sum_{i=1}^{n} x_i^2 - \prod_{i=1}^{n}\cos\left(\frac{x_i}{\sqrt{i}}\right) + 1 + \text{rand}()$
Stochastic function	$f(x, y) = \sin(120/x) + \cos(60/y)$

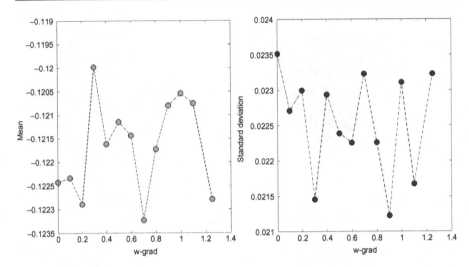

Figure 19.2 Histograms for the "g_best" values using the function called "Griewank's" with noise. In the title of the subfigures, mean represents the mean value of the histogram, std is the standard deviation and w-grad is the weight of the gradient part in the objective value calculation of the individuals.

During our tests, the found global best value from the population, the mean of the best values of each individual, the iteration number what algorithm performed before termination and the iteration number when the global best was found were registered. In all tests, we applied Monte-Carlo method to evaluate the performance of our approach effectively, thus the weight of the gradient part in the objective value calculation for the individuals was adjusted by 0.1 in the domain of [0, 1.25], and for each gradient weight, 500 MC simulations were performed. The result of our tests for the g_best values is presented in Figure 19.2. It can be deducted from the figure that the best global optima was found using 0.7 as the weight of the gradient part (since it is a minimization task), while the standard deviation is slightly smaller than in the classic PSO which is presented by the first data point in Figure 19.2, where the weight is equal to 0 (w-grad = 0). To prove the effectiveness of our method, we present the details of our tests in Table 19.2. The table presents our tests including two different deterministic functions (dropwave and Griewank's) and two stochastic (Griewank's with noise and another stochastic function), highlighting the best results in each cases.

Using our method, PSO finds better solution, i.e., the objective value of the best individual and the mean of all objective values in the population is decreased while the number of iterations until the final solution found is decreased also. It yields stronger convergence during the iterations of the algorithm, thus the novel method increases the efficiency of PSO. Obviously the proper setup for the parameters of the PSO and the weight of the gradient is highly problem-dependent, however, during our tests, we found 0.7 as a generally applicable weight for the gradient, and

Table 19.2 Test Results Performing 500 MC Simulation Modifying the Weight for the Gradient Part

Functions	Weights for the Gradient												
	0	0.1	0.2	0.3	0.4	0.5	0.6	0.7	0.8	0.9	1.0	1.1	1.25
Mean of g_best values													
Dropwave ($\times 10^{-1}$)	−9.98	−9.99	−9.99	−9.99	−9.98	−9.96	−9.94	−9.92	−9.87	−9.77	−9.65	−9.50	−9.40
Griewank's ($\times 10^{-7}$)	3.81	3.17	2.26	1.91	1.41	1.33	1.14	1.02	1.04	1.31	1.99	3.11	5.04
Griewank's with noise ($\times 10^{-1}$)	−1.22	−1.22	−1.22	−1.19	−1.21	−1.21	−1.21	−1.23	−1.21	−1.20	−1.20	−1.20	−1.22
Stochastic function	−9.56	−9.58	−9.58	−9.590	−9.596	−9.591	−9.586	−9.582	−9.56	−9.55	−9.54	−9.52	−9.47
Mean of the mean of best values of each individual													
Dropwave ($\times 10^{-1}$)	−8.45	−9.04	−8.73	−7.95	−6.82	−5.81	−5.49	−5.42	−5.47	−5.68	−6.24	−7.34	−7.72
Griewank's ($\times 10^{-4}$)	226	134	71.6	40.5	19.9	10.5	5.66	3.23	1.78	1.24	1.28	1.87	2.81
Griewank's with noise ($\times 10^{-2}$)	−4.72	−6.90	−7.43	−8.38	−9.13	−9.59	−10.0	−10.40	−10.47	−10.48	−10.49	−10.42	−10.40
Stochastic function	−6.22	−7.00	−7.47	−7.90	−8.03	−8.15	−8.20	−8.15	−8.09	−7.95	−7.76	−7.52	12.73
Mean of iteration numbers what algorithm performed before termination													
Dropwave	125	136	138	144	135	112	102	100	98	90	83	71	60
Griewank's	81	79	79	78	78	79	80	80	83	85	88	92	94
Griewank's with noise	88	92	89	89	89	88	90	90	91	90	88	89	92
Stochastic function	97	95	93	94	89	88	84	82	77	75	70	67	62
Mean of iteration numbers when the g_best were found													
Dropwave	109	93	94	98	89	65	54	51	49	41	34	22	11
Griewank's ($\times 10^{-1}$)	63	62	61	61	61	60	60	61	60	60	57	55	54
Griewank's with noise	40	43	40	40	40	39	41	41	42	42	39	40	44
Stochastic function	141	140	139	140	136	134	132	130	124	123	118	115	110

Best results are highlighted in each row for the objective values.

10% of the domain for σ, which setting in most cases improves the efficiency of PSO. We propose a simple fine-tuning technique in the following to set up the parameters of the algorithm.

1. Set all parameters to zero, i.e., $c_0 = c_1 = c_2 = c_3$.
2. Tune c_3 according to the learning method of classic gradient methods, i.e., increase c_3 gradually, if oscillation occurs, divide it by 10. Find a stable setting.
3. Set the momentum, i.e., c_0, which is typically 0.1 or 0.2 in the literature. Increase it gradually, until some improvement is achieved. Find a stable setting.
4. Tune c_1, i.e., increase it gradually until some improvement is achieved.
5. Finally, set $c_2 = 1.25 - c_3$

These technique propose a reliable method for tuning the parameters, however, our tests showed clearly that $c_3 = 0.7$ is a generally good choice, and with $c_1 = 0.5$ and $c_0 = 0.6$ the algorithm operates stable.

19.3   Stochastic Optimization of Multiechelon Supply Chain Model

Most of the multiechelon supply chain optimization and analysis are mainly based on analytical approach. Simulation however provides a very good alternative, because it can model real-life situations with accuracy, more flexible in terms of input parameters and therefore it is more easy to use in decision support. The simulation results can be analyzed with various statistical methods and numerical optimization algorithms. To analyze complex, especially multiechelon systems, multilevel simulation models can be used, where the results of optimized high-level model feeds into the lower level more detailed models.

The simulation-based approach was published only in the last decade. Junga et al. (2004) make a Monte-Carlo-based sampling from real data, and apply a simulation-optimization framework while looking for managing uncertainty. They use a gradient-based search algorithm, while Köchel and Nieländer (2005) discuss how to use simulation to describe a five-level inventory system, and optimize this model by genetic algorithm. Schwartz et al. (2006) demonstrate the internal model control (IMC) and model predictive control (MPC) algorithms to manage inventory in uncertain production inventory and multiechelon supply/demand networks. A complex instance of inventory model can be found in Hayyaa et al. (2008), where orders cross in time considering various distributions for the lead time. Sakaguchi (2009) investigates the dynamic inventory model in which demands are discrete and varying period by period.

The aim of our research is to create a Monte-Carlo simulator which uses probability distributions based on material usage data posted in the logistic module of an ERP system. The main objective of this development was to build a simulator that can use simple building blocks to construct models of complex supply chain networks. Supply chains processes can be simulated using these modular models, where parameters of Key Performance Indicators (KPI) are analyzed by sensitivity analysis. The developed SIMWARE simulator can be used as a verification tool to analyze and evaluate inventory control strategies (Király et al., 2011, 2012). The simulation of "actual" inventory controlling strategies provides the most important KPIs of these strategies. On the other hand, this simulator can be used for optimization to determine the optimal values of the key inventory control parameters.

The proposed SIMWARE software provides a framework to analyze the cost structure and optimize inventory control parameters based on cost objectives. With this tool we have minimized the inventory holding cost by changing the parameters of the reordering strategy while keeping the service level at the required value. The simulation of "actual" inventory controlling strategies provides the most important KPIs of these strategies. On the other hand, we can use the simulator as part of optimization and determine the optimal values of the key inventory control parameters. We have minimized the inventory holding cost by changing the parameters of our operational space while keeping the service level at the required value.

19.3.1 Inventory Model of a Single Warehouse

The modular model of the supply chain is based on the following classic model of inventory control. This session gives a summary of the most important parameters of this model. In Figure 19.3, Q is the theoretical demand over cycle time T and this is the *Order Quantity*; R is the *Reorder point*, which is the maximum demand can be satisfied during the replenishment lead time (L). The *Cycle time* (T) is the time between two purchase orders. The *Order Quantity* is Q, where $Q = \bar{d} \cdot T$. This is the ordered quantity in a purchase order, and Q is equal to the *Expected demand* and the *Maximum stock level*. *Maximum stock level* is the stock level necessary to cover the *Expected demand* in period T; therefore, it has to be the quantity we order. *Lead time* (L) is the time between the Purchase order and the goods receipt. $\bar{d}_L$ denotes the average demand during the replenishment lead time. $\bar{d}_L = \bar{d} \cdot L$, where $\bar{d}$ is the daily average demand. Using the same logic, $\bar{d}_L$ is a special case; it yields consumption if the service level is 100%. We will use $\bar{d}_L$ to denote the consumption during the paper. *Reorder point* is the stock level when the next purchase order has to be issued. It is used for materials where the inventory control is based on actual stock levels.

S is the *Safety stock*; this is needed if the demand is higher than the expected (line d). In an ideal case R equals to total of safety stock and average demand over

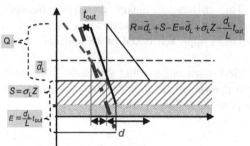

$$R = \bar{d}_L + S - E = \bar{d}_L + \sigma_L Z - \frac{d_L}{L} t_{out}$$

Figure 19.3 The classic model of inventory control.

lead time: $R = \overline{d}_L + S$, where S is the *Safety stock* which is defined to cover the stochastic demand changes. For a given *Service Level* this is the maximum demand can be satisfied over the Lead time.

Assuming constant demand pattern over the cycle time, Average Stock (K) can be calculated as a weighted average of stock levels over the cycle time:

$$K = \frac{Q}{2} + S \tag{19.15}$$

Service Level (SL) is the ratio of the satisfied and the total demand (in general this is the mean of a probability distribution), or in other words it is the difference between the 100% and the ration of unsatisfied demand:

$$\text{SL} = 100 - 100 \frac{(d_L - R)}{Q} \tag{19.16}$$

We assume that all demand is satisfied from stock until stock exists. When we reach stock level R the demand over the lead time ($\overline{d}_L$) will be satisfied up to R. Consequently if $\overline{d}_L < R$, we are getting a stock out situation and there will be unsatisfied demand therefore the service level will be lower than 100%. $\overline{d}_L$ is not known and it is a random variable. The probability of a certain demand level is $P(\overline{d}_L)$. Based on this, the service level is formed as shown in the next equation:

$$\text{SL} = 100 - 100 \frac{\int_{d_L}^{d_{\max}} P(d_L)(d_L - R)d_L}{Q} \tag{19.17}$$

where $\overline{d}_L$ is continuous random variable, and $\overline{d}_{\max}$ is the maximum demand over Lead time. Calculation of SL in practice is simple since probabilities are calculated as frequencies of discrete events and integral is replaced by simple summation of the differences of satisfied and unsatisfied demands.

Based on our experience in analyzing actual supply chain systems we discovered that the probability functions of material flow and demand are different from the theoretical functions (see Figure 19.4 that shows the distribution function of an actual material consumption compared to the normal distribution used in most of the analytical methodologies). This difference makes difference between the theoretical (calculated) and the actual inventory movements, therefore it makes sense using a stochastic simulation approach based on "empirical" distribution functions.

Inventory movements can be modeled much better using stochastic differential equations than modeling based on the theoretical assumption that movements are following normal distribution. We propose the following model:

$$x_{L_{i+1}} = x_{L_i} - W_i + u(x, R, t_u) \tag{19.18}$$

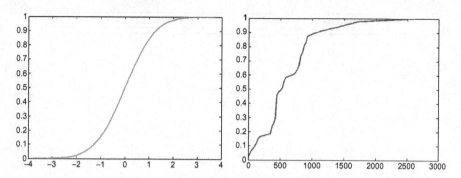

Figure 19.4 The theoretical cumulative distribution function (on the left) and the actual cumulative distribution function for a raw material based on its consumption data (on the right).

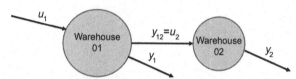

Figure 19.5 The analyzed two-level system.

Where x_i is stock level on the ith week, W_i is a stochastic process to represent consumption. This stochastic process is based on the empirical cumulative distribution function we described in the previous section. u is the quantity of material received on week i, based on purchase orders. Purchase orders are calculated based on the actual inventory level (x), and the replenishment lead time (t_u).

19.3.2 Inventory Model of a Supply Chain

The main objective of this work is to develop the classical PSO algorithm applying the gradients of the objective function as it was shown in Chapter 2. Figure 19.5 shows the supply chain, i.e., the structure of the analyzed two-level system. The investigated case study is a two-level inventory system in which there is a central warehouse from only one local warehouse can order (y_{12}). Only one product is stored in these warehouses. The customers can buy from the local (y_1) and also directly to the central warehouses (y_2). To simulate the customers purchase behavior two normal distribution functions are applied as y_1 and y_2. The mean value is 60 and 50 in the applied distribution functions, while the variance is 15 and 10, respectively. The mean value represents that 60 units of products are averagely consumed in 1 week from the central warehouse. The variance represents the uncertainty of the mean value, in 1 week there can be more customers than the mean value, in the other can be less as in real life.

The analyzed time period is 50 weeks ($n_{week} = 50$). MC simulations are performed to simulate the stochastic behavior of the analyzed warehouses. After the

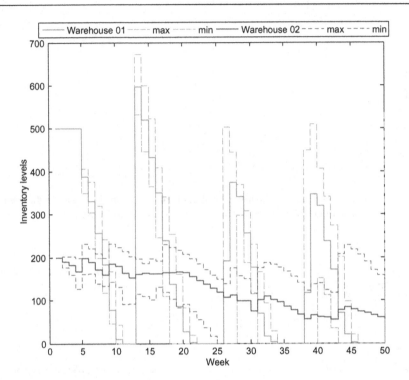

Figure 19.6 Average inventory levels before optimization (reorder points 500 and 200, respectively).

simulations the average properties of the warehouses are calculated. The service levels of both warehouses are determined, they are 0.98 and 0.95. The main objective in the chosen case study is to find the optimal reorder points for both warehouses when the applied objective cost function is at the lowest:

$$f(\text{reorder points}) = \sum_{i=1}^{n_{\text{week}}} \left[\frac{\sum_{j=1}^{n_{\text{MC}}} (x_{j,i,1})}{n_{\text{MC}}} \text{HC}_1 + \frac{\sum_{j=1}^{n_{\text{MC}}} (x_{j,i,2})}{n_{\text{MC}}} \text{HC}_2 \right] \qquad (18.19)$$

where i represents the actual week, j is the actual MC simulation, $x_{j,i,1}$ means the inventory level in the central warehouse at ith week in the jth MC simulation, and HC_1 represents the holding cost in the central warehouse. The fluctuations in the average inventory levels after ten MC simulations ($n_{\text{MC}} = 10$) are shown in Figure 19.6 when the reorder points are 500 and 200, respectively. It can be seen that before optimization the average inventory of the Warehouse 01 is depleted many times and the minimal stock in Warehouse 02 also reaches zero at the 25th week. At the initial reorder points the actual service levels are below the desired values in both of the warehouses (0.60 and 0.89).

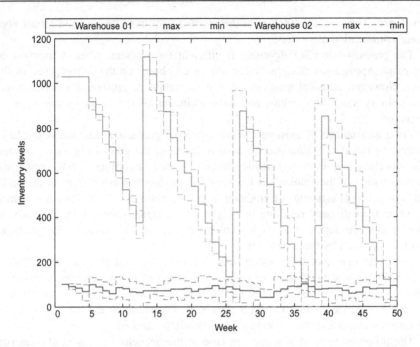

Figure 19.7 Average inventory levels after optimization (reorder points 1031 and 100, respectively).

19.3.3 Optimization Results

The improved PSO algorithm is applied to modify the reorder points due to the value of the objective function and finally to find the global optima. Since the value of the objective function is very high the chosen weight of the gradient for the search is 10^{-3}. After the optimization process the reorder points is changed to 1031 and 100. Due to this modification the service levels are much better than at the initial state (0.99 and 0.91) and the value of the objective function is 3.42×10^5. The improved PSO finishes the search after 127 generations because in the last 50 generations there was no significant improvement in the value of the objective function. The average inventory levels after optimization can be seen in Figure 19.7. Due to the optimization the inventory in the central warehouse is not empty in the crucial periods and the minimal stock in the Warehouse 02 is at zero fewer weeks than before the optimization.

19.4 Conclusion

Since supply chain performance impacts the financial performance companies, it is important to optimize and analyze their performances. To support Monte Carlo analysis of complex supply chains an interactive simulator, SIMWARE has been developed. The stochastic nature of the problem requires effective and robust non-linear optimization algorithm.

The gradient-free PSO algorithm is efficient for problems when derivatives do not exist. Application of estimated gradients can boost up the convergence of the PSO. However, classical gradient calculation cannot be applied to stochastic and uncertain systems; only robust and local estimates of the gradients can improve converge.

The disadvantage of existing methods of local gradient estimation is the large number of function evaluations required to calculate the gradient of each particles. We developed a more economic, memory-based algorithm where numerical approximation of the gradients is based on former function evaluations of the particles. To get local estimates of gradients stored trajectories of particles are weighted based on their distance resulting in weighted least squares regressions. The advantage of this approach is that the size of the region used to calculate the gradients can be controlled by the σ parameter.

The performance of the resulted fully informed, regional gradient-based PSO is verified by several benchmark problems. The effect of the parameters of the algorithms has been analyzed. The results illustrate the benefits of the incorporation of the regional gradients into the PSO algorithm. Drawback of the method is that it requires careful attention in tuning its parameters (c_3 and σ).

The proposed method is applied in case of multiechelon system built from two warehouses. We validated our solution by simulating four stochastic input variables. The results illustrate that the developed tool is flexible enough to handle complex situations and straightforward and simple enough to be used for decision support.

Acknowledgment

The financial support of the GOP-1.1.1-11-2011-0045 and TAMOP-4.2.2.A-11/1/KONV-2012-0071 projects are gratefully acknowledged.

References

Bergh, F.V.D., 2002. An Analysis of Particle Swarm Optimizers. PhD thesis, University of Pretoria, South Africa.

Borowska, B., Nadolski, S., 2009. Particle swarm optimization: the gradient correction. J. Appl. Comput. Sci. 17 (2), 7−15.

Caloieroa, G., Strozzia, F., Comenges, J.-M.Z., 2008. A supply chain as a series of filters or amplifiers of the bullwhip effect. Inter. J. Prod. Econ. 114 (2), 631−645.

Edwards, A.I., Engelbrecht, A.P., Franken, N., 2005. Nonlinear mapping using particle swarm optimization. In: The 2005 IEEE Congress on Evolutionary Computation, vol. 1. IEEE, pp. 306−313.

Engelbrecht, A.P., Engelbrecht, A., Ismail, A., 1999. Training product unit neural networks.

Gandomi, A.H., Alavi, A.H., 2012. Krill herd: a new bio-inspired optimization algorithm. Commun. Nonlinear Sci. Numer. Simulat. 17, 4831−4845.

Graves, S.C., Willems, S.P., 2008. Strategic inventory placement in supply chains: nonstationary demand. Manuf. Serv. Oper. Manage. 10 (2), 278−287.

Hayyaa, J.C., Bagchib, U., Kimc, J.G., Sun, D., 2008. On static stochastic order crossover. Inter. J. Prod. Econ. 114 (1), 404−413.

Hu, X., Eberhart, R., 2002. Solving constrained nonlinear optimization problems with particle swarm optimization. In: Proceedings of the Sixth World Multiconference on Systemics, Cybernetics and Informatics, vol. 5. Citeseer, pp. 203−206.

Junga, J.Y., Blaua, G., Peknya, J.F., Reklaitisa, G.V., Eversdyk, D., 2004. A simulation based optimization approach to supply chain management under demand uncertainty. Comput. Chem. Eng. 28 (10), 2087−2106.

Kennedy, J., Eberhart, R., 1995. Particle swarm optimization. In: Proceedings, IEEE International Conference on Neural Networks, 1995, vol. 4. IEEE, pp. 1942−1948.

Király, A., Belvárdi, G., Abonyi, J., 2011. Determining optimal stock level in multi-echelon supply chains. Hung. J. Ind. Chem. 39 (1), 107−112.

Király, A., Varga, T., Belvárdi, G., Gyozsán, Z., Abonyi, J., 2012. Monte Carlo simulation based sensitivity analysis of multi-echelon supply chains. In: Factory Automation. Veszprém, Hungary.

Köchel, P., Nieländer, U., 2005. Simulation-based optimisation of multi-echelon inventory systems. Inter. J. Prod. Econ. 93, 505−513.

Makajic-Nikolic, D., Panic, B., Vujoševic, M., 2004. Bullwhip effect and supply chain modelling and analysis using CPN tools. In: Fifth Workshop and Tutorial on Practical Use of Colored Petri Nets and the CPN Tools.

Mendes, R., Kennedy, J., Neves, J., 2004. The fully informed particle swarm: simpler, maybe better. Evol. Comput., IEEE Trans. 8 (3), 204−210.

Miranda, P.A., Garrido, R.A., 2004. Incorporating inventory control decisions into a strategic distribution network design model with stochastic demand. Trans. Res. Part E: Logistics Trans. Rev. 40 (3), 183−207.

Miranda, P.A., Garrido, R.A., 2009. Inventory service-level optimization within distribution network design problem. Inter. J. Prod. Econ. 122 (1), 276−285.

Nagatania, T., Helbing, D., 2004. Stability analysis and stabilization strategies for linear supply chains. Physica A: Stat. Mech. Appl. 335 (3), 644−660.

Noel, M.M., Jannett, T.C., 2004. Simulation of a new hybrid particle swarm optimization algorithm. In:Proceedings of the 36th Southeastern Symposium on System Theory, 2004. IEEE, pp. 150−153.

Parsopoulos, K.E., Vrahatis, M.N., 2002. Particle swarm optimization method for constrained optimization problems. Intell. Technol. Theory Appl. New Trends Intell. Technol. 76, 214−220.

Prékopa, A., 2006. On the Hungarian inventory control model. Eur. J. Oper. Res. 171 (3), 894−914.

Sakaguchi, M., 2009. Inventory model for an inventory system with time-varying demand rate. Inter. J. Prod. Econ. 122 (1), 269−275.

Salomon, R., Arnold, D., 2009. The evolutionary-gradient-search procedure in theory and practice, In: Chiong, R., (Ed.), Nature-Inspired Algorithms for Optimisation, vol. 193 of Studies in Computational Intelligence, pp. 77−101.

Schwartz, J.D., Wang, W., Rivera, D.E., 2006. Simulation-based optimization of process control policies for inventory management in supply chains. Automatica. 42 (8), 1311−1320.

Seo, Y., 2006. Controlling general multi-echelon distribution supply chains with improved reorder decision policy utilizing real-time shared stock information. Comput. Ind. Eng. 51 (2), 229−246.

Sousaa, T., Silvaa, A., Neves, A., 2004. Particle swarm based data mining algorithms for classification tasks. Parallel Comput. 30 (5), 767−783.

Srinivasan, M., Moon, Y.B., 1999. A comprehensive clustering algorithm for strategic analysis of supply chain networks. Comput. Ind. Eng. 36 (3), 615−633.

Vaughan, T.S., 2006. Lot size effects on process lead time, lead time demand, and safety stock. Inter. J. Prod. Econ. 100 (1), 1−9.

Victoirea, T.A., Jeyakumar, A., 2004. Hybrid PSO−SQP for economic dispatch with valve-point effect. Electric Power Syst. Res. 71 (1), 51−59.

Wimalajeewa, T., Jayaweera, S.K., 2008. Optimal power scheduling for correlated data fusion in wireless sensor networks via constrained PSO. Wireless Commun. IEEE Trans. 7 (9), 3608−3618.

Windisch, A., Wappler, S., Wegener, J., 2007. Applying particle swarm optimization to software testing. Proceedings of the Ninth Annual Conference on Genetic and Evolutionary Computation. ACM, pp. 1121−1128.

Yang, X.-S., 2010a. Firefly algorithm, stochastic test functions and design optimisation. Inter. J. Bio-Inspired Comput. 2 (2), 78−84.

Yang, X.-S., 2010b. A new metaheuristic bat-inspired algorithm. In: Studies in Computational Intelligence, 2010. In: Proceedings of Nature Inspired Cooperative Strategies for Optimization (NISCO 2010), vol. 4, pp. 1942−1948.

Zhang, R., Zhang, W., Zhang, X., 2009. A new hybrid gradient-based particle swarm optimization algorithm and its applications to control of polarization mode dispersion compensation in optical fiber communication systems. In: International Joint Conference on Computational Sciences and Optimization, vol. 2. IEEE, pp. 1031−1033.

Printed in the United States
By Bookmasters